MEMORY

This best-selling textbook presents a comprehensive and accessible overview of the study of memory. Written by three of the world's leading researchers in the field, it contains everything the student needs to know about the scientific approach to memory and its applications.

Each chapter of the book is written by one of the three authors, an approach which takes full advantage of their individual expertise and style, creating a more personal and accessible text. This enhances students' enjoyment of the book, allowing them to share the authors' own fascination with human memory. The book also draws on a wealth of real-world examples throughout, showing students exactly how they can relate science to their everyday experiences of memory.

Key features of this edition:

- thoroughly revised throughout to include the latest research and updated coverage of key ideas and models;
- a brand new chapter on "Memory and the Brain," designed to give students a solid understanding of methods being used to study the relationship between memory and the brain, as well as the neurobiological basis of memory;
- additional pedagogical features to help students engage with the material, including many "try this" demonstrations, points for discussion, and bullet-pointed chapter summaries.

The book is supported by a Companion Website featuring extensive online resources for students and lecturers.

Alan Baddeley is Professor of Psychology at York University, UK.

Michael W. Eysenck is Professor of Psychology at Royal Holloway, University of London, UK.

Michael C. Anderson is Senior Scientist and Programme Leader at the MRC Cognition and Brain Sciences Unit in Cambridge, UK.

"For Hilary" — Alan Baddeley

"To Christine with love" — Michael W. Eysenck

"In memory of my father, Albin F. Anderson, a model of creativity and vision" — Michael C. Anderson

MEMORY

SECOND EDITION

ALAN BADDELEY,

MICHAEL W. EYSENCK,

AND MICHAEL C. ANDERSON

Ψ Psychology Press
Taylor & Francis Group

LONDON AND NEW YORK

Second edition published 2015
by Psychology Press
27 Church Road, Hove, East Sussex BN3 2FA

and by Psychology Press
711 Third Avenue, New York, NY 10017

Psychology Press is an imprint of the Taylor & Francis Group, an informa business

First edition published by Psychology Press 2009

British Library Cataloguing in Publication Data
A catalogue record for this book is available from the British Library

Library of Congress Cataloging in Publication Data
Baddeley, Alan D., 1934-
Memory / Alan Baddeley, Michael W. Eysenck, and Michael Anderson. — 2nd ed.
pages cm
Includes bibliographical references and index.
1. Memory. I. Eysenck, Michael W. II. Anderson, Michael C. (Michael Christopher)
III. Title.
[DNLM: 1. Memory.]
BF371.B227 2015
153.1'2—dc23
2014016167

ISBN: 978-1-84872-183-8 (hbk)
ISBN: 978-1-84872-184-5 (pbk)
ISBN: 978-1-315-74986-0 (ebk)

Typeset in Sabon and Gill Sans
by Book Now Ltd, London

CONTENTS

About the authors ix
Preface to the First edition xi
Preface to the Second edition xiii

1. What is memory? 3
Why do we need memory? 3
One memory or many? 4
Theories, maps, and models 4
How can we study memory? 5
How many kinds of memory? 8
Sensory memory 10
Short-term and working memory 12
Long-term memory 13
Memory: Beyond the laboratory 15
Summary 17
Points for discussion 18
Further reading 18
References 19

2. Memory and the brain 23
Neuropsychological approaches 23
Observing the brain 26
Observing the working brain 27
Blood flow based measures 31
The cellular basis of memory 32

Genetic approaches 34
Summary 35
Points for discussion 38
Further reading 38
References 38

3. Short-term memory 41
Short-term and working memory:
    What's the difference? 41
Memory span 42
Models of verbal short-term memory 43
Competing theories of verbal short-term
    memory 48
Free recall 49
Visuo-spatial short-term memory 51
Summary 60
Points for discussion 61
Further reading 61
References 61

4. Working memory 67
The modal model 67
The multicomponent model 69
Imagery and the visuo-spatial
    sketchpad 76

The central executive   78
The episodic buffer   81
Individual differences in working
    memory   84
Theories of working memory   84
Educational applications   89
The neuroscience of working memory   92
Summary   98
Points for discussion   99
Further reading   99
References   100

5. Learning   107
Rate of learning   108
Distributed practice   110
Expanding retrieval   112
The importance of testing   113
The importance of feedback   114
Motivation to learn   114
Repetition and learning   115
Implicit learning   117
Learning and consciousness   126
The neurobiological basis of learning   129
Summary   131
Points for discussion   132
Further reading   132
References   132

6. Episodic memory: Organizing
and remembering   137
The Bartlett approach   138
Meaning and memory   141
Memory and predictability   143
Levels of processing   144
The limits of levels   145
Transfer-appropriate processing   145
Why is deeper coding better?   146

Organization and memory   148
Becoming an expert   150
Seriation   152
Episodic memory and the brain   155
Summary   159
Points for discussion   160
Further reading   160
References   160

7. Semantic memory and stored
knowledge   165
Introduction   165
Semantic memory vs. episodic
    memory   166
Organization of concepts:
    Traditional views   168
Using concepts   176
Concepts and the brain   179
Schemas   182
Summary   188
Points for discussion   189
Further reading   190
References   190

8. Retrieval   195
The experience of retrieval failure   195
The retrieval process: General
    principles   198
Factors determining retrieval success   202
Context cues   207
Retrieval tasks   208
The importance of incidental context
    in episodic memory retrieval   211
Recognition memory   217
Source monitoring   223
Concluding remarks   223
Summary   224

Points for discussion   225

Further reading   226

References   226

9. Incidental forgetting   231

A remarkable memory   232

The fundamental fact of forgetting   233

On the nature of forgetting   235

Factors that discourage forgetting   236

Factors that encourage incidental
   forgetting   238

A functional view of incidental
   forgetting   258

Summary   258

Points for discussion   260

Further reading   260

References   260

10. Motivated forgetting   265

Life is good, or memory makes it so   266

Terminology in research on
   motivated forgetting   267

Factors that predict motivated
   forgetting   268

Factors that predict memory recovery   281

Recovered memories of trauma:
   Instances of motivated forgetting?   287

Summary   292

Points for discussion   293

Further reading   294

References   294

11. Autobiographical memory   299

Why do we need autobiographical
   memory?   299

Methods of study   300

Theories of autobiographical memory   306

Psychogenic amnesia   318

Organically based deficits   320

Summary   322

Points for discussion   322

Further reading   322

References   323

12. Eyewitness testimony   329

Introduction   329

Major factors influencing eyewitness
   accuracy   330

Anxiety and violence   338

Age and eyewitness accuracy   340

Remembering faces   341

Police procedures with eyewitnesses   346

From laboratory to courtroom   349

Summary   352

Points for discussion   354

Further reading   354

References   354

13. Prospective memory   361

Introduction   361

Prospective memory in everyday life   365

Types of prospective memory   369

Theoretical perspectives   371

Improving prospective memory   373

Summary   375

Points for discussion   375

Further reading   376

References   376

14. Memory in childhood   381

Introduction   381

Memory in infants   383

Developmental changes in memory
   during childhood   387

Implicit memory   392
Autobiographical memory and
     infantile amnesia   394
Children as witnesses   398
Summary   404
Points for discussion   405
Further reading   405
References   406

15. Memory and aging   411
Approaches to the study of aging   411
Working memory and aging   414
Aging and long-term memory   416
Theories of aging   424
The aging brain   426
Summary   428
Points for discussion   428
Further reading   429
References   429

16. When memory systems
fail   435
Amnesia: The patient and the
     psychologist   435
Episodic memory impairment   438
Traumatic brain injury   448
Alzheimer's disease   450
Rehabilitation of patients with
     memory problems   456

Conclusion   460
Summary   460
Points for discussion   461
Further reading   461
References   462

17. Improving your
memory   469
Introduction   469
Distinctive processing   470
Techniques to improve memory:
     Visual imagery   472
Techniques to improve memory:
     Verbal mnemonics   476
Why are mnemonic techniques
     effective?   477
Working memory training   478
Memory experts   479
Preparing for examinations   483
Learning verbatim   488
Summary   489
Points for discussion   490
Further reading   491
References   491

Glossary   495
Photo credits   503
Author index   505
Subject index   519

Having graduated in Psychology from University College London, Alan Baddeley spent the following year at Princeton, the first of five such stays in the US. He returned to a post at the Medical Research Council Applied Psychology Unit (APU) in Cambridge, completing a Ph.D. concerned with the design of postal codes. He continued to combine applied research, for example on deep-sea diving, with theoretical issues such as the distinction between long- and short-term memory. After moving to the University of Sussex, he and Graham Hitch proposed a multicomponent model of working memory. He also began working with amnesic patients, continuing both these lines of research when he moved, first to a chair at the University of Stirling, then returning to the APU in Cambridge. After 20 years as its Director, he moved first to the University of Bristol, then to his current position in York where he has resumed his collaboration with Graham Hitch. He was awarded a CBE for his contributions to the study of memory, is a Fellow of the Royal Society, of the British Academy and of the Academy of Medical Sciences.

Michael W. Eysenck graduated from University College London. He then moved immediately to Birkbeck University of London as a lecturer, where he completed his Ph.D. on the von Restorff and "release" memory effects. His research for several years focused on various topics within memory research (e.g. levels of processing; distinctiveness). However, for many years his research has focused mainly on anxiety and cognition (including memory). Most of this research has involved healthy populations but some has dealt with cognitive biases (including

memory ones) in anxious patients. This research has been carried out at Birkbeck University of London and at Royal Holloway University of London, where he has been Professor of Psychology since 1987 (Head of Department, 1987–2005). However, it was started during his time as Visiting Professor at the University of South Florida. He has published 40 books in psychology (many relating to human memory), including two research monographs on anxiety and cognition. He has been in 'Who's Who' since 1989.

Michael C. Anderson received his Ph.D. in Cognitive Psychology from the University of California, Los Angeles in 1994. After completing a post-doctoral fellowship in cognitive neuroscience at the University of California, Berkeley, he joined the psychology faculty at the University of Oregon, where he was director of the Memory Control Laboratory through 2007. Anderson is now Senior Scientist and Programme Leader at the MRC Cognition and Brain Sciences Unit in Cambridge England. His research investigates the roles of inhibitory processes as a cause of forgetting in long-term memory. Anderson's recent work has focused on executive control as a model of motivated forgetting, and has established the existence of cognitive and neurobiological mechanisms by which we can willfully forget past experiences. This work begins to specify the mechanisms by which people adapt the functioning of their memories in the aftermath of traumatic experience.

PREFACE TO THE FIRST EDITION

Some years ago, one of us (ADB) accepted an invitation to write a memory book for the general public. The result, *Your Memory: A User's Guide*, took the basic structure of an introductory memory course, but illustrated its points from personal observation and research on everyday memory. Although not designed as a text book, it began to be used, in both its initial and in a somewhat modified form, for introductory memory courses, proving popular with students who liked its more relaxed approach. There have, however, been substantial developments in the study of memory since it was first written. This has included a much more extensive body of research on everyday memory, leading to the suggestion of producing a new book that attempts to keep the virtues of the original, while presenting an updated and extended account of human memory, explicitly designed as a memory text. The three of us jointly agreed to take on this task. In order to keep the personal tone, we agreed that each of us would undertake a number of chapters according with our interests, rather than attempt a more corporate style. Each chapter is therefore identified with one of the three authors.

One issue in writing a memory book is the question of how it should be structured. After a good deal of thought we have opted for the standard approach of following information through the memory system, beginning with sensory memory going on to discuss short-term and working memory, followed by episodic memory which in turn leads to semantic memory and the accumulation of knowledge. There is, of course, substantial work that depends upon this basic framework but goes beyond it, with topics such as auto-biographical memory, prospective memory, memory development and aging, amnesia; and applied issues such as eyewitness testimony and improving your memory. We have chosen to treat such topics separately, while at the same time referring back to earlier chapters. This means that a given topic may be described more than once, often by more than one author. We regard this as a form of distributed practice and hence an advantage rather than a drawback.

A more serious problem is presented by the limitations of the simple information flow structure. First of all, it has become increasingly clear that information flows in both directions, with memory reflecting an alliance of *interactive* systems. For example, working memory plays an important role in long-term learning, but is itself influenced by existing knowledge. We try to make this clear without unduly complicating the picture.

A second problem concerns the different levels of development of research and theory in different areas. In tackling a given area, we tend to approach it from a historical viewpoint, both because of the importance of the early work for subsequent development, and also because earlier work is usually conceptually simpler, providing a clear route into subsequent more complex theory. However, while this might work well *within* chapters, it does not always work for the between-chapter structure. The chapters on short-term and working memory for instance, describe an area that has developed hugely since the 1960s, in the depth and complexity of theoretical development, in the degree of involvement of neuropsychology and neuroimaging, and in breadth of application. Other areas of equal importance are easier to understand. The role of organization in long-term learning for instance is a topic where the basic phenomena and ground rules had been established by the 1970s, with little further development necessary. Many newer applications such as the study of autobiographical memory and prospective memory are still at a relatively early stage of theoretical development, and as a result probably present less of a challenge to the student than some of the earlier chapters. We have therefore tried to structure the book in such a way as to allow the user to pick a different route through the book, if preferred.

In the twenty-first century, no memory book can be complete without taking into account the implications of recent exciting developments in neuroscience. Two of us (MCA and ADB) are currently involved in neuroimaging studies, and two of us (MWE and ADB) in studies involving patients with neuropsychological or emotional difficulties. However, while taking such advances into account where appropriate, our focus is on the *psychology* of human memory, which we believe will provide a sound foundation for developments in the neuroscience of memory, as well as continuing to offer a solid basis for applying knowledge gained in the laboratory to the many problems of memory in everyday life.

This project has depended crucially on the patience, help and support of our colleagues at Psychology Press including Lucy Kennedy who played an important role in planning the book, and Rebekah Edmondson, Veronica Lyons, and Tara Stebnicky who ensured that the plans became a reality. We are also grateful to Michael Forster who proposed the book and provided sustained enthusiasm for it through its long gestation. ADB's contribution owes a great deal to Lindsey Bowes, who not only typed his rambling dictations, but also provided invaluable help with finding references and overcoming the many IT glitches experienced by those of us whose semantic memory comes principally from a pre-computer age. Finally, I am grateful to my wife Hilary, for her support and tolerance of my excuses for not doing the manly chores expected of a husband, initially because I was writing a book on working memory, duly followed by my embarking on the present book. Ah well, back to the chores!

MCA is very grateful to Justin Hulbert, who made useful comments on his chapters; preparing all figures and their captions, key terms, supplementary PowerPoints, and biographies with dizzying efficiency.

MWE is also extremely grateful to his wife, Christine, for her unflagging support. She has become used to the fact that I have been involved almost continuously in book writing for the past 25 years or so. I don't have anyone to thank for typing up my chapters because (ill-advisedly or not) I have always done my own word processing!

Alan Baddeley

PREFACE TO THE SECOND EDITION

We were happy with the reception of the first edition of *Memory*, and given that the basic foundations of our understanding of memory have not changed dramatically in the last five years, have retained most of the original structure and content. The major change has been in the growing impact of neuroscience on the study of memory, something that is reflected throughout the book. Given its importance, we have added a further chapter describing the range of methods used to study memory and the brain with the aim that this will both provide an introductory overview, and a point of reference for the repeated use of such methods in studies throughout the rest of the book. In terms of general content, the degree of change varies across chapters depending on our view of the extent to which interesting and important new developments have taken place. In my own case for example, while the short-term and working memory chapters reflect several new developments, resulting in a degree of restructuring, others such as the introductory chapter and the chapter on organization and memory have fewer changes. There is also some reordering of the later chapters to form what we think is a more logical structure, together with a substantial rewrite of the chapter on amnesia using a more patient-centered approach, and discussing what happens "when memory systems fail."

Michael Forster, the publisher whose enthusiasm led to the first edition, tells me that second editions of textbooks are usually the best. While we would not like to discount the possibility of even better editions in the future we ourselves trust, following the helpful comments of our reviewers, that our efforts have been worthwhile.

Once again we are grateful for the efficiency and good humour of the staff at Psychology Press, and in particular to Mandy Collison and Ceri Griffiths, and to Richard Cook at Book Now who oversaw the production stage to a very tight schedule. My own contribution has again depended crucially on the skills of Lindsey Bowes in coping with my rambling dictation, helping locate references and coping with the many IT glitches that seem to conspire against me. Finally, I am again very grateful to my wife Hilary for her support and encouragement during what has proved to be a surprisingly extensive revision. I shall now have to find another reason avoiding domestic chores!

I (Michael Eysenck) would like to echo my two co-authors by expressing my heartfelt thanks to the staff at Psychology Press for their cheerful and efficient approach to the production of this book. I agree that special thanks are due to Mandy Collison, Ceri Griffiths, and Richard Book for their outstanding efforts. I am indebted to my wife Christine in every way for her continued support for my time-consuming book-writing efforts. When I have finished the book on which I am currently working for Psychology Press, I look forward to having more time available to spend with our delightful grandchildren Sebastian and Clementine.

MCA would like to express his gratitude to his partner, Nami, for her support and patience in the process of preparing this revised edition. She is very pleased that the new edition is now complete, and especially that nowhere in the text are there any stories of embarrassing memory failures involving her (but plenty involving me, about which she feels knowingly bemused).

Alan Baddeley
York, 2014

Contents

Why do we need memory? 3

One memory or many? 4

Theories, maps, and models 4

How can we study memory? 5

How many kinds of memory? 8

Sensory memory 10

Short-term and working memory 12

Long-term memory 13

Memory: Beyond the laboratory 15

Summary 17

Points for discussion 18

Further reading 18

References 19

CHAPTER 1

WHAT IS MEMORY?

Alan Baddeley

emory is something we complain about. Why? Why are we quite happy to claim "I have a terrible memory!" but not to assert that "I am amazingly stupid"? Of course, we do forget; we do sometimes forget appointments and fail to recognize people we have met in the past, and rather more frequently we forget their names. We do not, however, often forget important events; if the bridegroom failed to turn up for his wedding he would not be believed if he claimed to have forgotten. Consequently, failing to recognize an old acquaintance suggests that the person was perhaps not of great importance to us. The obvious excuse is to blame one's terrible memory.

In the chapters that follow, we will try to convince you that your memory is in fact remarkably good, although fallible. We agree with Schacter (2001) who, having described what he refers to as the seven sins of memory, accepts that the sins are in fact the necessary consequences of the virtues that make our memories so rich and flexible. Our memories might be less reliable than those of the average computer but they are just as capacious, much more flexible, and a good deal more user friendly. Let us begin by considering the case of Clive Wearing who has the misfortune to have had much of his memory capacity destroyed by disease (Wilson, Baddeley, & Kapur, 1995).

WHY DO WE NEED MEMORY?

Clive is an extremely talented musician, an expert on early music who was master of a major London choir. He himself sang and was asked to perform before the Pope during a papal visit to London. In 1985, he had the misfortune to suffer a brain infection from the herpes simplex virus, a virus that exists in a large proportion of the population, typically leading to nothing worse than cold sores but very occasionally breaking through the blood–brain barrier to cause encephalitis, an inflammation of the brain that can prove fatal. In recent years, treatment has improved, with the result that patients are more likely to survive, although often having suffered from extensive brain damage, typically in areas responsible for memory.

When he eventually recovered consciousness, Clive was densely amnesic and appeared to be unable to store information for periods longer than seconds. His interpretation of his plight was to assume that he had just recovered consciousness, something that he would announce to any visitor, and something that he repeatedly recorded in a notebook, each time crossing out the previous line and writing "I have now recovered consciousness" or "consciousness has now finally been recovered," an activity that continued for many, many years.

Clive knew who he was and could talk about the broad outlines of his early life, although the detail was very sparse. He knew he had spent 4 years at Cambridge University, but could not recognize a photograph of his college. He could remember, although somewhat vaguely, important events in his life such as directing and conducting the first modern performance of Handel's *Messiah* using original instruments in an appropriate period setting, and could talk intelligently about the historical development of the role of the musical conductor. However, even this selected knowledge was sketchy; he had written a book on the early composer Lassus, but could not recall any of the content. Asked who had written *Romeo and Juliet*, Clive did not know. He had remarried, but could not remember this. However, he did greet his new wife with enormous enthusiasm every time she appeared, even though she might only have been out of the room for a few minutes; every time he declared that he had just recovered consciousness.

Clive was totally incapacitated by his amnesia. He could not read a book or follow a television program because he immediately forgot what had gone before. If he left his hospital room, he was immediately lost. He was locked into a permanent present, something he described as "hell on earth." "It's like being dead—all the bloody time!"

However, there was one aspect of Clive's memory that appeared to be unimpaired, that part concerned with music. When his choir visited him, he found that he could conduct them just as before. He was able to read the score of a song and accompany himself on the keyboard while singing it. For a brief moment he appeared to return to his old self, only to feel wretched when he stopped playing. Over 20 years later, Clive is still just as densely amnesic but now appears to have come to terms with his terrible affliction and is calmer and less distressed.

ONE MEMORY OR MANY?

Although Clive's case makes the point that memory is crucial for daily life, it does not tell us much about the nature of memory. Clive was unfortunate in having damage to a range of brain areas, with the result that he has problems that extend beyond his amnesia. Furthermore, the fact that Clive's musical memory and skills are unimpaired suggests that memory is not a single simple system. Other studies have shown that densely amnesic patients can repeat back a telephone number, suggesting preserved immediate memory, and that they can learn motor skills at a normal rate. As we will see later, amnesic patients are capable of a number of types of learning, demonstrating this by improved performance, even though they do not remember the learning experience and typically deny having encountered the situation before. The evidence suggests, therefore, that rather than having a single global memory system, the picture is more complex. The first few chapters of this book will try to unpack some of this complexity, providing a basis for later chapters that are concerned with the way in which these systems influence our lives, how memory changes as we move through childhood to adulthood and old age, and what happens when our memory systems break down.

In giving our account of memory, we are of course presenting a range of psychological theories. Theories develop and change, and different people will hold different theories to explain the same data. As a glance at any current memory journal will indicate, this is certainly the case for the study of memory. Fortunately, there is a great deal of general agreement between different groups studying the psychology of memory, even though they tend to use somewhat different terminology. At this point, it might be useful to say a little bit about the concept of theory that underpins our own approach.

THEORIES, MAPS, AND MODELS

What should a psychological theory look like? In the 1950s, many people thought they should look like theories from physics. Clark Hull studied the learning behavior of white rats and attempted to use his results to build a rather grand general theory of learning in which the learning behavior of both rats and people was predicted using a series of postulates and equations that were explicitly modeled on the example set by Isaac Newton (Hull, 1943).

By contrast, Hull's great rival, Edward Tolman (1948), thought of rats as forming "cognitive maps," internal representations of their environment that were acquired as a result of active exploration. The controversy rumbled on from the 1930s to the 1950s, and then was abandoned quite suddenly. Both sides found that they had to assume some kind of representation that went beyond the simple association between stimuli impinging on the rat and its learned behavior, but neither seemed to have a solution to the problem of how these could be investigated.

The broad view of theory that we shall take is that theories are essentially like maps. They summarize our knowledge in a simple and structured way that helps us to understand what is known. A good theory will help us to ask new questions and that in turn will help us find out more about the topic we are mapping. The nature of the theory will depend on the questions we want to answer, just as in the case of maps of a city. The map that will help you travel by underground around London or New York looks very different from the sort of map that you would need if you wanted to walk, with neither being a direct representation of what you would see if you stood at a given location. That does not of course mean that they are bad maps, quite the opposite, because each map is designed to serve a different purpose.

In the case of psychological theories, different theories will operate at different levels of explanation and focus on different issues. An argument between a shopkeeper and customer, for example, would be explained in very different ways by a sociologist, who might emphasize the economic and social pressures, a social psychologist interested in interpersonal relationships, a cognitive psychologist interested in language and a physiological psychologist who might be interested in the emotional responses of the two disputants and how these are reflected in the brain. All of these explanations are relevant and in principle should be relatable to each other, but none is the single "correct" interpretation.

This is a view that contrasts with what is sometimes called reductionism. This assumes that the aim of science is to reduce each explanation to the level below: Social psychology to cognitive psychology, which in turn should be explained physiologically, with the physiology then being interpreted biochemically and ultimately in terms of physics. Although it is clearly valuable to be able to explain phenomena at different but related levels, this is ultimately no more sensible than for a physicist to demand that we should attempt to design bridges on the basis of subatomic particle physics, rather than Newtonian mechanics.

The aim of the present book is to outline what we know of the *psychology* of memory. We believe that an account at the psychological level will prove valuable in throwing light on accounts of human behavior at the interpersonal and social level, and will play an important role in our capacity to understand the neurobiological factors that underpin the various types of memory. We suggest that the psychology of memory is sufficiently understood to begin to interface very fruitfully with questions at both of these levels, and hope to illustrate this over the subsequent chapters.

HOW CAN WE STUDY MEMORY?

The case of Clive Wearing demonstrates how important memory is, and how complex, but leaves open the question of how it can best be studied. The attempt to understand human memory extends at least as far back as Aristotle, and forms one of the classic questions within the philosophy of mind, although without reaching any firm conclusions. This was vividly illustrated by a lecture on memory by the eminent philosopher

KEY TERM

Reductionism: The view that all scientific explanations should aim to be based on a lower level of analysis: psychology in terms of physiology, physiology in terms of chemistry, and chemistry in terms of physics.

A. J. Ayer that I attended as a student. He began, rather unpromisingly, by declaring that memory was not a very interesting philosophical question. He seems to have demonstrated this pretty effectively as I can remember none of the lecture, apart from his statement that his memory was totally devoid of imagery, prompting a skeptical questioner to ask "If I tell you that the band of the grenadier guards is marching past the end of the street, banners flying and trumpets sounding, do you not hear or see anything?" "No" replied the philosopher; "I don't believe you!" said the questioner and sat down crossly.

This point illustrates a limitation of a purely philosophical approach to the understanding of memory in particular, and to mind in general, namely its reliance on introspection, the capacity to reflect and report our on-going thoughts. These are not unimportant, but are not a reliable indication of the way our minds work for two principal reasons. The first of these, as our example shows, is that, people differ in what they appear to experience in a given situation; does memory depend on visual imagery, and if not, why do some of us experience it? Second, and even more importantly, we are only consciously aware of a relatively small proportion of the mechanisms underpinning our mental life, and as we will see, the tip of the mental iceberg that is available to conscious awareness is not necessarily a good guide to what lies beneath.

While there are still important issues addressed by the philosophy of mind, it is now generally acknowledged these can best be pursued in collaboration with a scientific approach based on empirical evidence. To return to the question of imagery, as I suspect Ayer knew, in the late nineteenth century, Sir Francis Galton had asked a number of "eminent men" to reflect on their breakfast table from that morning and describe the vividness of the resulting memory, finding a huge range of responses. What was not known by Galton is that these huge differences are not reflected in how accurate our memories are, suggesting that accuracy depends on some nonconscious process. Could it be that different people have the same experience but just describe it differently? Or do they have different memory systems? Or perhaps they have the same basic system but have a different strategy for using it? Hence, although they are interesting, subjective reports do not provide a very solid basis for understanding how our memory works.

So how can we move beyond introspection?

An answer to this started to develop in Germany in the latter half of the nineteenth century. It was concerned initially with the discipline of *psychophysics*, an attempt to systematically map the relationship between physical stimuli such as brightness and loudness onto their perceived magnitude. Despite success in linking physical stimuli to the psychological experience of participants, capacities such as learning and memory were initially regarded as unsuitable for experimental study. This view was dramatically overturned by a German philosopher, Herman Ebbinghaus, who conducted an intensive series of experiments on himself over a 2-year period, showing that it was indeed possible to plot systematic relationships between the conditions of learning and the amount learned. Having published this, the first classic book on the science of memory (Ebbinghaus, 1885), he moved on to

Ebbinghaus (1850–1909) was the first person to demonstrate that it was possible to study memory experimentally.

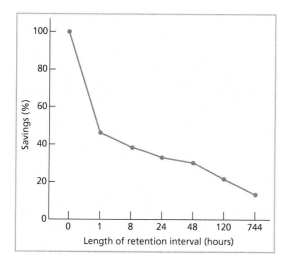

Figure 1.1 Forgetting over time as indexed by reduced savings during relearning. Data from Ebbinghaus (1885/1913).

study color vision, intelligence and a range of other questions in the newly developing field of experimental psychology.

So what did Ebbinghaus do? He began by simplifying the experimental situation, attempting to develop material that was devoid of meaning but was verbally learnable and reportable, inventing what has become known as the nonsense syllable, consonant–vowel–consonant items such as *zug*, *pij*, and *tev*. He served as his own subject, always holding constant the room in which he learned, the time of day and the rate of presentation, which was rapid, so as to avoid any temptation to attempt to find meaning in the stimuli. Ebbinghaus established some of the basic principles of learning that will discussed in Chapter 5 and the classic forgetting curve shown in Figure 1.1 that forms the basis of all subsequent work in this area (see Chapter 9).

The Ebbinghaus tradition was subsequently most strongly developed in the US, focusing particularly on the factors and conditions surrounding the important question of how new learning interacted with what was already known. Results were interpreted in terms of associations that were assumed to be formed between stimuli and responses, using a limited range of methods that typically involved remembering lists of nonsense syllables or words (McGeoch & Irion, 1952). This is often referred to as the verbal learning approach. It developed from the 1930s to the 1960s, particularly in mid-Western laboratories, and emphasized the careful mapping of phenomena rather than the ambitious building of grand theories such as that proposed by Clark Hull. When the grand theories appeared to collapse, however, the more staid approach that had previously been disparagingly discounted by its critics as "dust bowl empiricism" began to attract a broader range of investigators interested in studying learning and memory. This led to the founding of a new journal *The Journal of Verbal Learning and Verbal Behavior*, which, when the term "verbal learning" later became unfashionable, became *The Journal of Memory and Language*.

A second development that occurred at this point had its roots in both Europe and North America. In the 1930s, a German approach known as Gestalt psychology began attempting to apply ideas developed in the study of perception to the understanding of human memory. Unlike the behaviorist approaches, *Gestalt* psychologists tended to emphasize the importance of internal representations rather than observable stimuli and responses, and to stress the active role of the remberer. Gestalt psychology suffered badly from Nazi persecution, but enough Gestalt psychologists moved to North America to sow the seeds of an alternative approach to verbal learning; an approach that placed much more emphasis on the activity of the learner in organizing material. This approach was typified by two investigators who had grown up in Europe but had then emigrated and been trained in North America: George Mandler and Endel Tulving.

KEY TERM

Verbal learning: A term applied to an approach to memory that relies principally on the learning of lists of words and nonsense syllables.

Gestalt psychology: An approach to psychology that was strong in Germany in the 1930s and that attempted to use perceptual principles to understand memory and reasoning.

In Britain, a third approach to memory developed, based on Frederick Bartlett's (1932) book *Remembering*. Bartlett explicitly rejected the learning of meaningless material as an appropriate way to study memory, using instead complex material such as folk tales from other cultures, reflecting his interest in social psychology and stressing the importance of the remember's "effort after meaning." This approach emphasized the study of the memory errors that people made, explaining them in terms of the participants' cultural assumptions about the world. Bartlett proposed that these depended on internal representations that he referred to as schemas. His approach differed radically from the Ebbinghaus tradition, relying on quite complex tasks but, as was the case with the later followers of Tolman and Hull, Bartlett was left with the problem of how to study these elusive inner representations of the world.

A possible answer to this problem evolved gradually during the Second World War with the development of computers. Mathematicians such as Weiner (1950) in the US, and physiologists such as Gray Walter (1953) in the UK described machines that were able to demonstrate a degree of control that resembled purposive behavior. During the 1940s, a Scottish psychologist, Kenneth Craik (1943), working with Bartlett in Cambridge produced a brief but influential book entitled *The Nature of Explanation*. Here he proposed the idea of representing theories as models, and using the computer to develop such models. He carried out what were probably the first psychological experiments based on this idea, using analog computers (digital computers were still being invented) and applying his computer-based theoretical model to the practical problem of gun-aiming in tanks.

Tragically, in 1945 he was killed in a traffic accident while still a young man.

Fortunately, the new approach to psychology, based on the computer metaphor, was being taken up by a range of young investigators, and in the years following the war, this information-processing approach to psychology became increasingly influential. Two books were particularly important. Donald Broadbent's *Perception and Communication* (1958) developed and applied Craik's seminal ideas to a range of work carried out at the Medical Research Council Applied Psychology Unit in Cambridge, England, much of it stimulated by practical problems originating during the war. Some 9 years later, this growing field was then brilliantly synthesized and summarized by Ulric Neisser (1967) in a book whose title provided a name for this burgeoning field: *Cognitive Psychology*.

Using the digital computer as an analogy, human memory could be regarded as comprising one or more storage systems. Any memory system—whether physical, electronic, or human—requires three things, the capacity to *encode*, or enter information into the system, the capacity to *store* it, and—subsequently—the capacity to find and *retrieve* it. However, although these three stages serve different functions, they interact: The method of registering material or encoding determines what and how the information is stored, which in turn will limit what can subsequently be retrieved. Consider a simple physical memory device, a shopping list. If it is to work, you need to write legibly in a language the recipient shopper understands. If it were to get wet, the ink would blur (impaired storage) making it less distinct and harder to read (retrieval). Retrieval would be harder if your handwriting was poor (an encoding–retrieval interaction), and if the writing was smudged (a storage–retrieval interaction). The situation is further complicated by the discovery that our memories comprise not one, but several interrelated memory systems.

HOW MANY KINDS OF MEMORY?

As the influence of the cognitive approach to psychology grew, the balance of opinion moved

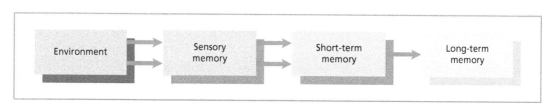

Figure 1.2 An information-processing approach to memory. Information flows from the environment through sensory storage and short-term storage to long-term memory.

from the assumption of a single memory system based on stimulus–response associations towards the idea that two, three or perhaps more memory systems were involved. Figure 1.2 shows the broad view that came to be widely accepted during the 1960s. It assumed that information comes in from the environment and is first processed by a series of sensory memory systems, which could be best regarded as providing an interface between perception and memory. Information is then assumed to be passed on to a temporary short-term memory system, before being registered in long-term memory (LTM). A particularly influential version of this model was proposed by Atkinson and Shiffrin (1968). It was dubbed the modal model because it was representative of many similar models of the operation of human memory that were proposed at the time. As we shall see, a number of the assumptions underlying this model were subsequently questioned, causing it to be further elaborated.

The question of how many kinds of memory remains controversial, some theorists object to the very concept of a memory *store* as too static, arguing instead that we should concerned with *processes* (e.g. Nairne, 1990, 2002; Neath & Surprenant, 2003). They point to similarities across a range of very different memory tasks and suggest that these imply common processes, and hence a unitary memory system. Our own view is that we need to think in terms of both structures such as stores and the processes that operate on them, just as an analysis of the brain requires the contribution of both static anatomical features and a more dynamic concern with physiology. We should certainly look for similarities across domains in the way that these systems perform, but the presence of common features should not encourage us to ignore the differences.

Fortunately, regardless of the question of whether one emphasizes similarities or differences, the broad picture remains the same. In what follows, we ourselves use the distinctions between types of memory as a way of organizing and structuring our knowledge of human memory. As discussed below, we assume separate sensory, short-term and long-term memory systems, each of which can be subdivided into separate components. We do not, however, assume the simple flow of information from the environment into long-term memory that is suggested in Figure 1.2, as there is abundant evidence that information flows in both directions. For example, our knowledge of the world, stored in long-term memory, can influence our focus of attention, which will then determine what is fed into the sensory memory systems, how it is processed and whether it is subsequently remembered. Thus a keen football fan watching a game will see and remember particular plays that her less enthusiastic companion will miss.

We begin with a brief account of sensory memory. This was an area of considerable activity during the 1960s and provides a good illustration of the general principles of encoding, storage, and retrieval. However, given that it relates more to perception than memory, it will not be covered in the remainder of the book. Our outline continues with introductory accounts of short-term and working memory, before moving to a brief preliminary survey of long-term memory.

SENSORY MEMORY

If you wave your hand while holding a sparkler in a dark room, it leaves a trail, which rapidly fades. The fact that the image persists long enough to draw an apparent line suggests that it is being stored in some way, and the fact that the line rapidly fades implies some simple form of forgetting. This phenomenon forms the basis for movies; a sequence of static images is presented rapidly, with blank intervals in between, but is perceived as a continuous moving image. This occurs because the perceptual system stores the visual information long enough to bridge the gap between the static images, integrating each one with the next, very slightly different, image.

Neisser (1967) referred to this brief visual memory system as iconic memory, referring to its auditory counterpart as "echoic memory." In the early 1960s, a number of investigators at Bell Laboratories in the US used the new information-processing approach to analyze this fleeting visual memory system (Sperling, 1960, 1963; Averbach & Sperling, 1961).Sperling (1960) briefly presented a visual array of twelve letters in three rows of four, and then asked for recall (Figure 1.3). People could typically remember four or five items correctly. If you try this task, however, you will have the sensation that you have seen more than four or five, but that they have gone before you can report them. One way of avoiding the problem of forgetting during reporting is to present the same array and reduce the number of items to be reported, but not tell the participant in advance which ones will be selected for recall. Sperling therefore required only one of the three lines to be reported, signaling the line to be recalled by presenting a tone; a high tone for the top line, a medium tone for line two, and a low tone for line three. As he did not tell the participant in advance which line would be cued, the report could be treated as representative of the whole array; multiplying the score by three will thus give an estimate of the total number of letters stored. However, as shown in Figure 1.4, this depends on when the recall tone is presented.

When recall is tested immediately, it should provide an estimate of the total capacity of the memory store, with the fall-off in performance as the tone is delayed representing the loss of information. Note that Figure 1.4 shows two curves, one with a bright field before and after the letters, and the other with the letters preceded and followed by a dark visual field. A subsequent experiment (Sperling, 1963) found that the brighter the light during the interval, the poorer the performance, suggesting that the light is interfering with the memory trace in some way, a process known as masking.

Later work by Michael Turvey (1973) investigated two separate types of masking operating at different stages. The first of these involves *brightness masking*, with the degree of masking increasing when the mask becomes brighter, or is presented closer in time to the stimulus. This effect only occurs if the mask and the stimulus are presented to the same eye, suggesting that it is operating at a peripheral retinal level. If you were a subject in such an experiment, this type of masking would give rise to experiencing a composite of target and mask, with the brighter the mask the less distinct the target. This is distinct from *pattern masking*, the second type studied, which occurs when targets are followed by a mask comprising broadly similar features to the target, for example jumbled fragments of letters. This type of mask operates even when the target is presented to one eye and the mask to the other. This suggests that it influences a later stage of visual processing that occurs

---

KEY TERM

Sensory memory: A term applied to the brief storage of information within a specific modality.

Iconic memory: A term applied to the brief storage of visual information.

Masking: A process by which the perception and/or storage of a stimulus is influenced by events occurring immediately before presentation (forward masking) or more commonly after (backward masking).

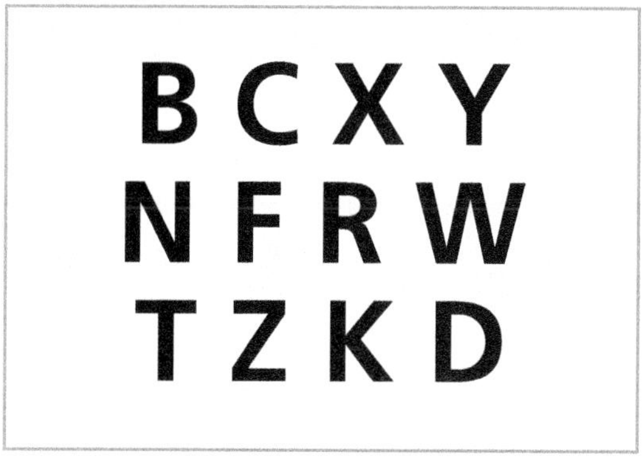

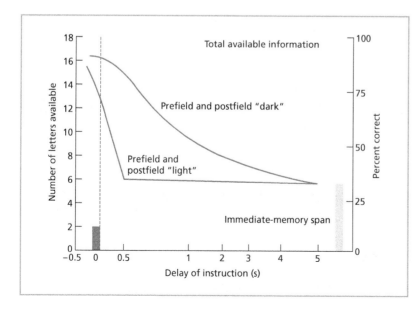

B C X Y
N F R W
T Z K D

Figure 1.3 Stimulus array used by Sperling. Although twelve letters were presented, participants only had to recall one row, that cued by a high, medium, or low tone.

after information from the two eyes has been combined into a single percept. It is relatively insensitive to brightness and subjectively feels as if a clear image has been disrupted before the information could adequately be read off from it.

What function does iconic memory serve other that of keeping psychologists busy, or as Haber concluded in desperation, reading at night in a thunderstorm? The answer is that its function is probably indirect, forming part of the process of perceiving the world. As we scan the visual world, stimuli of huge complexity will

fall on our retina, comprising far more information than it is useful for us to process and store. It seems likely that iconic memory represents two early stages of a process whereby information is read off from the retina, and some of it then fed through to a more durable short-term visual store. It is this that allows us to build up a coherent representation of the visual world and that allows a movie to be perceived, not as a series of static frames with gaps in between, but as a continuous and realistic visual experience. The early stages of iconic memory are probably best regarded as aspects of perception; the subsequent more stable stage will be discussed in the chapter on short-term memory.

The auditory system also involves a brief sensory memory component that Neisser named echoic memory. If you are asked to remember a long telephone number, then your pattern of errors will differ depending on whether the number is heard or read. With visual presentation, the likelihood of an error increases systematically from the beginning to the end of the sequence, whereas, as shown

KEY TERM

Echoic memory: A term sometimes applied to auditory sensory memory.

Figure 1.4 Estimated number of letters available using the partial report method, as a function of recall delay. From Sperling (1963). Copyright © 1963 by The Human Factors Society and Ergonomics Society Inc. Reprinted by permission of Sage Publications.

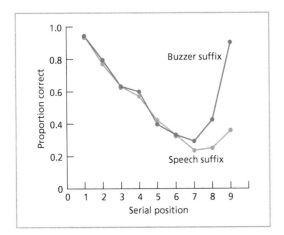

Figure 1.5 Serial recall of a nine-item list when an additional item, the suffix, is either the spoken word *zero* or a sound made by a buzzer. From Crowder (1972). Copyright © 1972 Massachusetts Institute of Technology, by permission of the MIT Press.

in Figure 1.5, with auditory presentation the last one or two items are much more likely to be correct than are items in the middle of the list (Murdock, 1967). This recency advantage can be removed by interposing another spoken item between presentation and recall, even when this item itself does not need to be processed, and is always the same, for example, the instruction "recall." In an extensive series of experiments, Crowder and Morton (1969; Crowder & Raeburn, 1970; Crowder, 1971) showed that the nature of this suffix is critical. A visual or nonspeech-like auditory suffix, such as a buzzer, does not disrupt performance, whereas a spoken suffix does, regardless of its meaning.

Crowder and Morton postulated what they term a precategorical acoustic store as the basis for the auditory recency effect. However, the question of whether the process responsible for the enhanced auditory recency effect is better regarded as a form of memory or an aspect of perception remains controversial (Jones, Hughes, & Macken, 2006; but see also Baddeley & Larsen, 2007). Regardless of its interpretation, the auditory recency component is sufficiently large and robust to play a potentially significant role in studies of verbal short-term memory, and has even been proposed as an alternative to

more conventional views of performance on short-term verbal memory tasks (Jones et al., 2006). We will return to this issue when discussing short-term memory. In the meantime, it seems likely that an adequate explanation of echoic memory will need to be fully integrated with a broader theory of speech perception.

SHORT-TERM AND WORKING MEMORY

As this topic, and that of long-term memory, forms a major part of the book, for present purposes we will limit ourselves to a very brief outline. We use the term short-term memory (STM) in a theory-neutral way to refer to the temporary storage of small amounts of material over brief delays. This leaves open the question of how this storage is achieved. In most, if not all situations, there is likely to be a contribution to performance from long-term memory that will need to be taken into account in evaluating the role of any more temporary storage systems. Much of the work in this area has used verbal material, and there is no doubt that even when the stimuli are not verbal, people will often use verbal rehearsal to help maintain their level of performance over a brief delay (see Chapter 3). It is important to bear in mind, however, that STM is not limited to verbal material, and has been studied extensively for visual and spatial information, though much less extensively for smell and touch.

The concept of working memory is based on the assumption that a system exists for the temporary maintenance and manipulation of information, and that this is helpful in

> **KEY TERM**
>
> **Short-term memory (STM):** A term applied to the retention of small amounts of material over periods of a few seconds.
>
> **Working memory:** A memory system that underpins our capacity to "keep things in mind" when performing complex tasks.

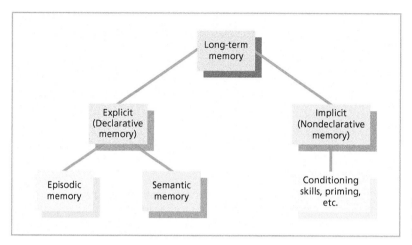

Figure 1.6 Components of long-term memory as proposed by Squire (1992).

performing many complex tasks. A number of different models of working memory have been proposed, with the nature and emphasis of each model tending to depend on the particular area of interest of the theorist, and their theoretical style. However, most assume that working memory acts as a form of mental workspace, providing a basis for thought. It is usually assumed to be linked to attention, and to be able to draw on other resources within short-term and long-term memory (Miyake & Shah, 1999). By no means all approaches, however, emphasize the role of memory rather than attention. One approach that does so is the multicomponent model proposed originally by Baddeley and Hitch in 1974 as a means of linking research on the psychology and neuropsychology of STM to its functional role in performing important cognitive activities such as reasoning, comprehension and learning. This approach has continued to prove productive for over 40 years (Baddeley, 2007) and is the principal focus of Chapter 4, on working memory.

LONG-TERM MEMORY

We shall use the classification of long-term memory proposed by Squire (1992). As shown in Figure 1.6, this classification makes a broad distinction between explicit or declarative memory and implicit or nondeclarative memory. Explicit memory refers to situations that we would generally think of as involving memory, both for specific *events*, such as meeting a friend unexpectedly on holiday last year, and remembering *facts* or information about the world, for example the meaning of the word *testify* or the color of a ripe banana. Implicit memory refers to situations in which some form of learning has occurred, but which is reflected in *performance* rather than through overt remembering, riding a bicycle for example or reading a friend's handwriting more easily because we have encountered it frequently in the past. We will briefly discuss these in turn, leaving a full exploration to subsequent chapters.

KEY TERM

Long-term memory: A system or systems assumed to underpin the capacity to store information over long periods of time.

Explicit/declarative memory: Memory that is open to intentional retrieval, whether based on recollecting personal events (episodic memory) or facts (semantic memory).

Implicit/nondeclarative memory: Retrieval of information from long-term memory through performance rather than explicit conscious recall or recognition.

Explicit memory

As Figure 1.6 shows, this can be divided into two categories, semantic and episodic memory. During the 1960s, computer scientists attempting to achieve automatic language processing discovered that their computer programs needed to have built into them some kind of knowledge of the world, which could represent the meaning of the words being processed. This led psychologists to attempt to study the way in which humans store such semantic information. At a conference convened to discuss these new developments, a Canadian psychologist, Endel Tulving (1972), proposed a distinction that was immediately adopted and has been used extensively ever since, that between *semantic* and *episodic* memory. Semantic memory refers to knowledge of the world. It goes beyond simply knowing the meaning of words and extends to sensory attributes such as the color of a lemon or the taste of an apple. It also includes general knowledge of how society works, what to do when you enter a restaurant or how to book a theatre seat. It is inherently general in nature, although it can in principle be acquired on a single occasion. If you heard that an old friend had died, this would be likely to become part of your general knowledge of that person, hence part of your semantic memory, although you might well forget where or when you had heard this.

If you subsequently recall the particular occasion when and where you had learned this sad news, then this would be an instance of *episodic memory*, which underpins the capacity to remember specific single episodes or events. Hence, a given event can be registered in both types of memory. Tulving himself (2002) now limits the use of the term "episodic memory" to situations in which you actually re-experience some aspect of the original episode, for example remembering how surprised you were that your informant knew your old friend. Tulving refers to this capacity as mental time travel and emphasizes its value, both in allowing us to recollect and "relive" individual events, and to use that information for planning a future action, for example sending a letter of condolence. It is this capacity to acquire and retrieve memories for particular events that tends to be most severely disrupted in amnesic patients, and it is this deficit that has made Clive Wearing's life so unbearably difficult.

How are semantic and episodic memory related? One possibility is that semantic memory is simply the residue of many episodes. For example, I know that Madrid is the capital of Spain, not only because I was told it at school but also because I have encountered this fact in countless news-reels and had it reinforced by visiting Madrid. Consistent with this assumed role of episodic memory in forming semantic memory is the fact that most amnesic patients have difficulty in building up new semantic knowledge. They typically would not know

Semantic memory goes beyond the meaning of words, and extends to sensory attributes such as taste and color; and to general knowledge of how society works, such as how to behave in a supermarket.

KEY TERM

Semantic memory: A system that is assumed to store accumulative knowledge of the world.

Episodic memory: A system that is assumed to underpin the capacity to remember specific events.

Mental time travel: A term coined by Tulving to emphasize the way in which episodic memory allows us to relive the past and use this information to imagine the future.

the name of the current President of the United States of America, or what year it is, or which teams were doing well in their favorite sport. This suggests that although semantic and episodic memory might possibly involve separate systems, they clearly interact (Tulving, 2002).

Implicit memory

Amnesic patients thus tend to show not only grossly disturbed episodic memory, but also a greatly impaired capacity to add to their store of knowledge of the world. There are, however, a number of situations in which they do appear to learn at a normal rate, and the study of these preserved capacities has had an important influence on the development of the concept of implicit or nondeclarative memory.

One preserved form of learning is simple classical conditioning. If a tone is followed by a brief puff of air to the eye, amnesic patients will learn to blink in anticipation (Weiskrantz & Warrington, 1979). Despite learning at a normal rate, they do not remember the experience and cannot explain the function of the nozzle that delivers the air puff to their eye. Amnesic patients can also learn motor skills, such as improving with practice the capacity to keep a stylus in contact with a moving spot of light (Brooks & Baddeley, 1976). Warrington and Weiskrantz (1968) demonstrated that word learning was also preserved in densely amnesic patients under certain conditions. They presented their patients with a list of unrelated words and then tested for retention in a number of different ways. When asked to recall the words or recognize which of the subsequent sequence of words had already been presented, the patients performed very poorly. However, when the nature of the test was changed to one in which the task was to "guess" a word when given the first few letters, both patients and normal participants were likely to "guess" a word that had been seen earlier. For example, a patient who had been shown the word "bring" and was later given the letters "BR– – –" would be just as likely as control participants to guess "bring" rather than "bread," but would not remember having just seen that word.. Patients could take full advantage of their prior experience, despite failing to remember that they had even

been shown any words earlier, indicating that *something* had been stored. As we shall see, this phenomenon, known as priming, is found in a range of perceptual tasks, both visual and auditory, and can also be found in the progressive improvement in more complex activities such as reading mirror writing (Cohen & Squire, 1980) or assembling a jigsaw puzzle (Brooks & Baddeley, 1976).

Given that these are all examples of implicit learning and memory, do they all reflect a single memory system? While attempts continue to be made to account for them all in terms of a single system (see Neath & Surprenant, 2003), our own view is that although they have features in common, they represent a range of different learning systems using different parts of the brain that have evolved for different purposes. They seem to represent a tendency for evolution to develop similar ways of addressing problems across different systems.

MEMORY: BEYOND THE LABORATORY

We have so far discussed the question of how to develop a theoretical understanding of human memory: how it encodes, stores, and retrieves information. However, if our theory is to be useful as well as informative, then it needs to be applicable beyond the confines of the laboratory, to tell about how our memories will work in the world. It must aim to extend beyond the student population, on which much of the research is based, and tell

---

KEY TERM

Classical conditioning: A learning procedure whereby a neutral stimulus (e.g. a bell) that is paired repeatedly with a response-evoking stimulus (e.g. meat powder), will come to evoke that response (salivation).

Priming: The process whereby presentation of an item influences the processing of a subsequent item, either making it easier to process (positive priming) or more difficult (negative priming).

us about how memory functions in children and the elderly, across different cultures and in health and disease.

It is of course much more difficult to run tightly controlled experiments outside the laboratory, with the result that most of the theoretically focused studies that inform the initial chapters are laboratory based. Some investigators argue that we should confine our research to the laboratory, extending it only when we have a thorough understanding of memory. Others have followed Bartlett in suggesting that this is likely to lead to the neglect of important aspects of memory. In response to this rather conservative view, a group of psychologists in South Wales enthusiastically convened an international conference concerned with practical aspects of memory. It was a great success, with people coming from all over the world to talk about their research on topics ranging from memory for medical information to sex differences in facial memory, and from expert calculators to brain-damaged patients (Gruneberg, Morris, & Sykes, 1978).

Ulric Neisser was invited to give the opening address. In it, he lamented the laboratory-based tradition declaring that "If X is an interesting or socially significant aspect of memory, then psychologists have hardly ever studied X!" (Neisser, 1978, p. 4). He was in fact preaching to an enthusiastic audience of the converted, whose work presented over the next few days was already refuting his claim. However, his address was less well received in other quarters, resulting in a paper complaining of "the bankruptcy of everyday memory" (Banaji & Crowder, 1989). This led to a lively, although rather unfruitful, controversy, given that it was based on the false assumption that psychologists should limit their research to *either* the laboratory *or* the world beyond. Both approaches are valuable. It is certainly easier to develop and test our theories under controlled laboratory conditions, but if they tell us little or nothing about the way in which memory works in the world outside, they are of distinctly limited value.

In general, attempts to generalize our theories have worked well, and have in turn enriched theory. One important application of theory is to the memory performance of particular groups such as children, the elderly, and

In Medieval times, accurate and precise articulation of the words of the church liturgy was more important than the sound of the music, with errors taken very seriously. The demon Titivillus was believed to take time off from his other task of inducing errors in written manuscripts to collect such omissions and slips of the tongue. Each day a thousand bags of such lapses would be conveyed to his master Satan, written in a book of errors and used against the unfortunate cleric on the Day of Judgement. It appears that in due course the level of accuracy improved to a point at which Titivillus was driven to filling his sack with idle gossip from the congregation, a rather menial task for a respectable demon (Zieman, 2008).

patients with memory problems. As we will see, these not only demonstrate the robustness and usefulness of cognitive theory, but have also provided ways of testing and enriching theory. A good case in point is the study of patients with a very dense but pure amnesia, which has told us about the everyday importance of episodic memory, has helped develop tests and rehabilitation techniques for clinical neuropsychologists, and has, at the same time, had a major impact on our theories of memory.

A second major benefit from moving beyond the laboratory comes from a realization that certain very important aspects of memory were not being directly covered by existing theories. Some of these have led to important new theoretical developments. This is the case with the study of semantic memory, which, as mentioned earlier, was initially prompted by the attempt of computer scientists to develop programs that could understand language (Collins & Quillian, 1969). Another area of very active research that was driven by a practical need is that of eyewitness testimony, where it became clear that the failures of the judiciary to understand the limitations of human memory were often leading to potentially very serious miscarriages of justice (Loftus, 1979). Other areas have developed as a result of identifying practical problems that have failed to be addressed by theory. A good example of this is prospective memory, remembering to do things. This use of memory is of great practical importance, but for many years was neglected because it reflects a complex interaction between attention and memory. These broader topics are covered in the latter part of the book, which will illustrate the now widely accepted view that theoretical and practical approaches to memory are allies and not rivals.

The contribution of neuroscience

Both the Ebbinghaus and Bartlett approaches to the study of memory were based on the psychological study of memory performance in normal individuals. In recent years, however, this approach has increasingly been enriched by data from neuroscience, looking at the contribution of the brain to our capacity to learn and remember. Throughout this book, you will come across cases in which the study of memory disorders in patients has thrown light on the normal functioning of human memory. In particular, the problems faced by patients with memory problems can often tell us about the function that our memories serve, and how they can be further investigated. Recent years have seen a rapid development of methods that allow the neuroscientist to observe and record the operation of the brain in healthy people both at rest and while performing complex activities, including those involved in learning and remembering. These will be discussed in the next chapter

SUMMARY

- Although we complain about our memories, they are remarkably efficient and flexible in storing the information we need and discarding what is less important.
- Many of our memory lapses result from this important need to forget nonessentials, if we are to remember efficiently.
- The study of memory began with Ebbinghaus, who greatly simplified the experimental situation, creating a carefully constrained approach that continued in North America into the twentieth century.
- Alternative traditions developed in Germany, where the study of perception influenced the way in which Gestalt psychologists thought about memory, and in Britain, where Bartlett used a richer and more open approach to memory.

(Continued)

(Continued)

- During the 1950s and 1960s, these ideas, influenced further by the development of the computer, resulted in an approach that became known as cognitive psychology.
- In the case of memory, this emphasized the need to distinguish between encoding or input into memory, memory storage, and memory retrieval, and to the proposal to divide memory into three broad types, sensory memory, short-term memory, and long-term memory.
- The information-processing model is very well illustrated in Sperling's model of visual sensory memory, in which the various stages were ingeniously separated and analyzed.
- These were assumed to lead into a temporary *short-term* or *working memory*. This was initially thought to be largely verbal in nature but other modalities were subsequently shown to be capable of temporary storage.
- The short-term memory system was assumed to feed information into and out of long-term memory.
- Long-term memory was further subdivided into *explicit* or declarative memory, and *implicit* or nondeclarative memory.
- Explicit memory was further divided into two types: The capacity to recollect individual experiences, allowing "mental time travel," became known as *episodic memory*, whereas our stored knowledge of the world was termed *semantic memory*.
- A range of implicit or nondeclarative learning and memory systems were identified, including classical conditioning, the acquisition of motor skills, and various types of priming
- An important development in recent years has been the increased interest in extending theory beyond the laboratory. Although this has led to controversy; it is clear that we need the laboratory to refine and develop our theories, but that we also need to move outside the laboratory to investigate their generality and practical importance.

POINTS FOR DISCUSSION

- What are the strengths and weaknesses of the approach to memory taken by Ebbinghaus and Bartlett?
- How did the cognitive approach to memory build on these foundations?
- Do we need to assume more than one kind of memory? If so, why?

FURTHER READING

Banaji, M. R., & Crowder, R. G. (1989). The bankruptcy of everyday memory. *American Psychologist, 44,* 1185–1193. A reply to Niesser's challenge.

Craik, K. J. W. (1943). *The nature of explanation.* London: Cambridge University Press. A short but seminal book in cognitive psychology presenting the case for using models to embody theories, an approach that underpins the subsequent cognitive revolution.

Gruneberg, M. M., Morris, P. E., & Sykes, R. N. (1978). *Practical aspects of memory*. London: Academic Press. The proceedings of a classic conference that can be said to have launched the everyday memory moment.

Neisser, U. (1978). Memory: What are the important questions? In M. M. Gruneberg, P. E. Morris, & R. N. Sykes (Eds.), *Practical aspects of memory*. London: Academic Press. An influential paper in the movement to study everyday memory.

Rabbitt, P. (2008). *Inside psychology: A science over 50 years*. New York: Oxford University Press. A series of personal views of the recent history of psychology from individuals who have been involved in a wide range of areas, including memory.

Roediger, H. L., Dudai, Y., & Fitzpatrick, S. M. (2007). *Science of memory: Concepts*. Oxford: Oxford University Press. The proceedings of a conference at which leading figures in learning and memory were invited to summarize their interpretation of the basic concepts underlying the field, and to present their own views. Because available space was limited, this provides a very economical way of accessing current expert views concerning both the psychology and neuroscience of learning and memory.

Sperling, G. (1963). A model for visual memory tasks. *Human Factors*, 5, 19–31. A very good example of the application of the information-processing approach to the study of sensory memory.

REFERENCES

Atkinson, R. C., & Shiffrin, R. M. (1968). Human memory: A proposed system and its control processes. In K. W. Spence & J. T. Spence (Eds.), *The psychology of learning and motivation: Advances in research and theory* (Vol. 2, pp. 89–195). New York: Academic Press.

Averbach, E., & Sperling, G. (1961). Short-term storage of information in vision. In C. Cherry (Ed.), *Information theory* (pp. 196–211). London: Butterworth.

Baddeley, A. D. (2007). *Working memory, thought and action*. Oxford: Oxford University Press.

Baddeley, A. D., & Larsen, J. D. (2007). The phonological loop unmasked? A comment on the evidence for a "perceptual-gestural" alternative. *Quarterly Journal of Experimental Psychology*, 60, 497–504.

Banaji, M. R., & Crowder, R. G. (1989). The bankruptcy of everyday memory. *American Psychologist*, 44, 1185–1193.

Bartlett, F. C. (1932). *Remembering*. Cambridge: Cambridge University Press.

Broadbent, D. E. (1958). *Perception and communication*. London: Pergamon Press.

Brooks, D. N., & Baddeley, A. D. (1976). What can amnesic patients learn? *Neuropsychologia*, 14, 111–122.

Cohen, N. J., & Squire, L. R. (1980). Preserved learning and retention of pattern-analyzing skill in amnesia: Dissociation of knowing how and knowing that. *Science*, 210, 207–210.

Collins, A. M., & Quillian, M. R. (1969). Retrieval time from semantic memory. *Journal of Verbal Learning and Verbal Behavior*, 8, 432–438.

Craik, K. J. W. (1943). *The nature of explanation*. London: Cambridge University Press.

Crowder, R. G. (1971). Waiting for the stimulus suffix: Decay, delay, rhythm, and readout in immediate memory. *Quarterly Journal of Experimental Psychology*, 23, 324–340.

Crowder, R. G., & Morton, J. (1969). Precategorical acoustic storage (PAS). *Perception and Psychophysics*, 5, 365–373.

Crowder, R. G., & Raeburn, V. P. (1970). The suffix effect with reversed speech. *Journal of Verbal Learning and Verbal Behavior*, 9, 342–345.

Ebbinghaus, H. (1885). *Über das Gedächtnis*. Leipzig: Dunker.

Gruneberg, M. M., Morris, P. E., & Sykes, R. N. (1978). *Practical aspects of memory*. London: Academic Press.

Hull, C. L. (1943). *The principles of behaviour*. New York: Appleton-Century.

Jones, D., Hughes, R. W., & Macken, W. J. (2006). Perceptual organization masquerading as phonological storage: Further support for a perceptual-gestural view of short-term memory. *Journal of Memory and Language, 54*, 265–281.

Loftus, E. F. (1979). *Eyewitness testimony*. Cambridge, MA: Harvard University Press.

McGeoch, J. A., & Irion, A. L. (1952). *The psychology of human learning*. New York: Longmans.

Miyake, A., & Shah, P. (Eds.). (1999). *Models of working memory: Mechanisms of active maintenance and executive control*. New York: Cambridge University Press.

Murdock Jr., B. B. (1967). Auditory and visual stores in short-term memory. *Acta Psychologica, 27*, 316–324.

Nairne, J. S. (1990). A feature model of immediate memory. *Memory and Cognition, 18*, 251–269.

Nairne, J. S. (2002). Remembering over the short-term: The case against the standard model. *Annual Review of Psychology, 53*, 53–81.

Neath, I., & Surprenant, A. (2003). *Human memory: An introduction to research, data and theory* (2nd edn.). Belmont, CA: Wadsworth.

Neisser, U. (1967). *Cognitive psychology*. New York: Appleton-Century Crofts.

Neisser, U. (1978). Memory: What are the important questions? In M. M. Gruneberg, P. E. Morris, & R. N. Sykes (Eds.), *Practical aspects of memory*. London: Academic Press.

Schacter, D. L. (2001). *The seven sins of memory: How the mind forgets and remembers*. New York: Houghton-Mifflin.

Sperling, G. (1960). The information available in brief visual presentations. *Psychological Monographs: General and Applied, 74*, 1–29.

Sperling, G. (1963). A model for visual memory tasks. *Human Factors, 5*, 19–31.

Squire, L. R. (1992). Declarative and nondeclarative memory: Multiple brain systems supporting learning and memory. *Journal of Cognitive Neuroscience, 4*, 232–243.

Tolman, E. C. (1948). Cognitive maps in rats and men. *Psychological Review, 55*, 189–208.

Tulving, E. (1972). Episodic and semantic memory. In E. Tulving & W. Donaldson (Eds.), *Organization of memory* (pp. 381–403). New York: Academic Press.

Tulving, E. (2002). Episodic memory: From mind to brain. *Annual Review of Psychology, 53*, 1–25.

Turvey, M. T. (1973). On peripheral and central processes in vision: Inferences from an information processing analysis of masking with patterned stimuli. *Psychological Review, 80*, 1–52.

Walter, W. G. (1953). *The living brain*. London: Norton.

Warrington, E. K., & Weiskrantz, L. (1968). New method of testing long-term retention with special reference to amnesic patients. *Nature, 217*, 972–974.

Weiner, N. (1950). *The human use of human beings*. Boston, MA: Houghton Mifflin.

Weiskrantz, L., & Warrington, E. K. (1979). Conditioning in amnesic patients. *Neuropsychologia, 8*, 281–288.

Wilson, B. A., Baddeley, A. D., & Kapur, N. (1995). Dense amnesia in a professional musician following Herpes Simplex Virus Encephalitis. *Journal of Clinical and Experimental Neuropsychology, 17*, 668–681.

Zieman, K. (2008). *Singing the new song: Literacy and liturgy in Late Medieval England*. Philadelphia, PA: University of Pennsylvania Press.

Contents

Neuropsychological approaches   23

Observing the brain   26

Observing the working brain   27

Blood flow based measures   31

The cellular basis of memory   32

Genetic approaches   34

Summary   35

Points for discussion   38

Further reading   38

References   38

CHAPTER 2

MEMORY AND THE BRAIN

Alan Baddeley

While our main focus will be on the psychology of memory, as knowledge of the field develops, it becomes increasingly possible to link psychological concepts, methods and findings to efforts towards understanding the biological basis of memory (see Box 2.1). Note that this is not a case of simple reductionism; knowing that a particular area of the brain is involved with a given memory function for example, does not constitute an explanation, but does provide an additional source of evidence that may be useful in further developing a psychological explanation, in addition of course to the separate but related issue of understanding how the brain works. We will be referring to such evidence throughout the following chapters, and for that reason it is important to understand something of the methods that are currently used to study the relationship between memory and the brain. We will begin with one of the most established methods, neuropsychology, going on to discuss the rapidly developing field of brain imaging, concluding with a brief account of the more basic biological approaches that go beyond systems neuroscience to study the neurobiological basis of memory, and its potential genetic control, areas that have so far had relatively little impact at the psychological level, but which may in the future prove to be of considerable importance.

NEUROPSYCHOLOGICAL APPROACHES

Patients who suffer brain damage often have memory problems, with the nature of the problem often being associated to a greater or lesser degree with the cause and anatomical location of the damage (see Chapter 16).

Group studies

This approach involves selecting patients whose damage is broadly associated with a specific disease or cause, for example the traumatic brain injury (TBI) that might result from a blow on the head in a traffic accident. This approach is clinically important in providing an overview of the condition necessary for treating patients and in prognosis for recovery, but may be difficult to interpret theoretically. Typically the more severe the accident,

---

KEY TERM

Traumatic brain injury (TBI): Caused by a blow or jolt to the head, or by a penetrating head injury. Normal brain function is disrupted. Severity ranges from "mild" (brief change in mental status or consciousness) to "severe" (extended period of unconsciousness or amnesia after the injury).

Box 2.1 The biological basis of memory

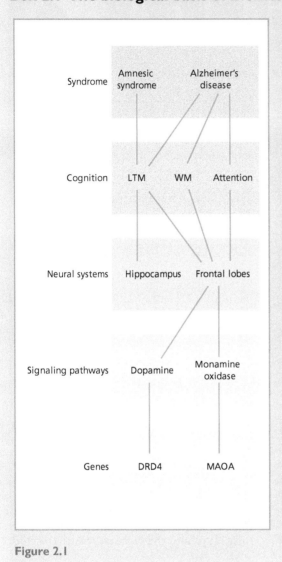

Figure 2.1

The psychology of memory and its dysfunction can be studied at a range of levels. These include its reflection in memory disorders which can then be mapped onto cognitive psychology. This in turn can be analyzed in terms of the neural systems underpinning cognition, together with their representation in different areas of the brain. Such systems themselves depend on neurochemically modulated signaling pathways that transmit information between the systems in ways that are themselves dependent on activity at the gene level. Adjacent levels of explanation tend to interact. Our own focus is at the cognitive level, but evidence from both syndromes and neural systems will be used in developing and evaluating both theory and practice.

Based on Poldrack R. A., Kittur A., Kalar D., Miller E., Seppa C., Gil Y., et al. (2011).

the longer the period of unconsciousness or coma, the greater memory disturbance and the poorer the chance of good recovery. However, in addition to memory deficits such patients will typically have other problems, particularly attentional, making it difficult to separate the memory deficits from other factors. Hence, although TBI is an area of considerable practical importance, it does not lead to clear theoretical conclusions about the nature of memory.

More informative are diseases such as alcoholic Korsakoff syndrome, a result of drinking too much and eating too little, in which memory deficits are particularly prominent, while other cognitive functions can be relatively preserved. Even here, however, most patients will show other deficits including subtle deficits of attentional control, again making clear theoretical interpretation difficult; does the patient have a problem of memory, or attention, or both? Most informative are the rare cases in which the brain damage appears to disrupt a single isolated function such as episodic memory, while intelligence, attention, perception and language capacities are all preserved. The classic case of amnesia is that of Henry Molaison, known by his initials HM (see Box 2.2).

Box 2.2 HM

The most theoretically influential neuropsychological case ever, was that of HM, a young man with temporal lobe epilepsy. In a successful attempt to reduce his seizures, areas of his brain associated with the left and right hippocampus were surgically removed. Unfortunately, HM then became densely amnesic. His capacity to acquire new information was severely limited, as was the case with Clive Wearing discussed earlier. Unlike Clive, however, HM's deficits were principally limited to episodic long-term memory. His digit span was normal, his intelligence was unimpaired, as was his language capacity but his LTM was grossly disrupted. He was unable to remember experiences for more than a few minutes, performed very badly on standard visual and verbal memory tests, failed to learn the names or faces of new people or indeed new presidents and to learn where things were kept when he moved to a new home.

HM's case had a major influence on two aspects of memory. Neurosurgically he demonstrated the practical importance of anatomical location, stimulating extensive later work on brain–behavior relationship. Psychologically his case supported a separation of functions, between memory and intelligence and between long and short-term memory.

When Henry died in 2008 at the age of 82, his importance was recognized worldwide by extensive obituaries, together with a book length account of his life and its contributions to the science of memory (Corkin, 2013).

Henry Molaison, who as a patient (HM) made a major contribution to our understanding of memory.

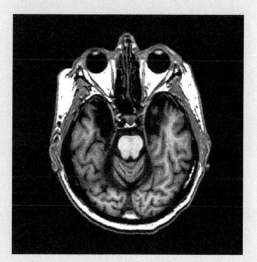

MRI images taken in 1992 of HM's brain. The light grey areas represents preserved brain structure and the dark areas an absence of brain tissue.

HM's case was important in demonstrating that episodic LTM is separable from other cognitive capacities, including STM (Corkin, 2013). Such separation is known as a *dissociation* since the specified deficit is separate or dissociated from deficits in other cognitive functions. As such it is considerably more theoretically powerful than a simple correlation whereby a deficit may just be a general consequence of degree of brain damage. Such rare single cases are informative, but need subsequently to be supported by other similar cases, and by coherence with what we already know of normal memory, before strong theoretical conclusions can be drawn. Such support rapidly accumulated in the case for HM (e.g. Baddeley & Warrington, 1970), but even so there is always a nagging fear that perhaps those tests that are impaired are simply harder or more open to disruption than those preserved. Perhaps preserved tasks such as digit span, involving hearing and repeating back a sequence of numbers, are simply easier than learning word lists?

To guard against this it is valuable to have a second type of patient showing exactly the opposite pattern, providing what is known as a double dissociation. In the case of the amnesic syndrome, this was provided by the discovery of a class of patient who had apparently normal LTM together with grossly disrupted STM (Shallice & Warrington, 1970). Such patients did not appear to be amnesic and could learn lists of words, but had a memory span of two rather than seven digits. This pattern could not easily be explained in terms of the greater difficulty or vulnerability of one of the types of task. Even a double dissociation is not a perfect design, however, since it is possible that more than two systems are involved.

As we shall see, such single cases have been extremely important in developing memory theory. They are, however, a very limited resource, for two reasons. First, because they are rare; most brain damage affects more than one system producing complex and variable deficits. The second problem concerns the increasing complexity of the models of memory that have emerged as study has advanced. While a double dissociation between two systems is desirable and possible, a three-component explanation would logically require a triple dissociation, and a four-component explanation requiring a quadruple dissociation becomes quite impracticable. At this point it is necessary to rely on a method known as *converging operations*. This involves carrying out a whole series of experiments using different methods and different participant groups, all focused on the same theoretical question. The hope is that although each single experiment is likely to be open to interpretation in more than one way, only one explanation will be able to explain all the results. This is the approach taken to a subsystem such as the phonological loop in working memory discussed in Chapter 4.

Neuropsychology has a further limitation. It requires access to patients, by no means easily achieved in the UK at least. It then needs the skills of a neuropsychologist with a keen eye for theoretically interesting patients, together with access to the experimental and conceptual tools necessary to bring out the significance of the findings. The substantial growth in the number of studies on memory and the brain in recent years has therefore not come principally from the study of such rare patients, but from the development of methods of studying the intact brains of healthy people.

OBSERVING THE BRAIN

Structural imaging

For many centuries, our knowledge of the structure of the brain was based on post mortem evidence. It became possible to observe the structure of living patients with the development of the X-ray-based technique known as

---

KEY TERM

Double dissociation: A term particularly used in neuropsychology when two patient groups show opposite patterns of deficit, e.g. normal STM and impaired LTM, versus normal LTM and impaired STM.

computerized tomography (CT). This involves rotating an X-ray tube around the patient's head, providing multiple viewpoints of the brain which are then fed into a computer that creates a three-dimensional representation of the person's brain. This method is still used clinically, but for research purposes it has largely been replaced by magnetic resonance imaging (MRI).

MRI involves placing the person's head in a strong magnetic field. The scanner emits radio waves in a series of brief pulses of different frequency. These are absorbed by the brain, which, when the field is turned off, releases the absorbed energy. The absorption characteristics of the brain's grey matter (neuronal cell bodies) differ from those of the white matter (axons linking different brain areas) and the cerebrospinal fluid (which fills the ventricles, hollow chambers in the brain, carries away waste metabolites and also provides protective cushioning for the brain). MRI allows a three-dimensional image to be created that differentiates these aspects of brain structure. The spatial resolution of the resulting image depends upon the strength of the magnet. A typical clinical scanner would have a field strength of 1.5 Tesla, giving a resolution of about 1mm. Many research scanners have field strengths of 3 Tesla, and some much higher.

MRI has the advantage over CT in that it does not involve radiation, and gives much more precise images. By varying the frequency of the radio pulse, MRI can be used to emphasize different aspects of brain structure, for example grey matter versus white matter. An example of its value is shown in Figure 2.2.

An increasingly important aspect of MRI is the technique known as *diffusion tensor imaging* (DTI). This takes advantage of the fact that the myelin sheaths that surround the white matter fiber tracts connecting different areas of the brain are relatively fatty, causing

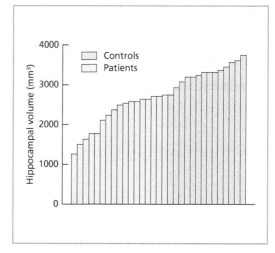

Figure 2.2 Variation in the volume of the hippocampus across 17 patients with a relatively pure episodic memory deficit and 14 controls. Note that volume varies, not only in the patient group but also in the controls, allowing a correlation to be calculated between volume and memory performance across the whole sample. Size of hippocampus had little effect on the capacity to recognize that a word had occurred, but a clear relationship was found between volume and the capacity to associate words to a background against which they were learned. Reprinted from Horner et al. (2012). Further discussion of this study occurs in Chapter 16 (p. 443). Copyright © 2012, with permission from Elsevier.

the water within to flow along that fiber. This approach, sometimes known at *tractography*, allows the mapping of the important white matter bundles that transfer information from one area of the brain to another, allowing the different areas to coordinate functions across the brain.

OBSERVING THE WORKING BRAIN

Functional imaging

While imaging the structure of the brain is obviously important and helpful, from the viewpoint of a psychologist it is much more valuable to be able to observe the brain in action and to relate this to the ongoing

---

KEY TERM

Magnetic resonance imaging (MRI): A method of brain imaging that relies on detecting changes induced by a powerful magnetic field.

Visualization of a DTI (diffusion tensor imaging) measurement of a human brain. Depicted are reconstructed fiber tracts that run through the mid-sagittal plane.

mental activity of the participant. Some of the earlier developments here resulted from implanting electrodes in the brains of animals, a method that is clearly of limited application to humans. Exceptions do occur, however; for example, when patients are undergoing brain surgery to treat intractable epilepsy. The brain itself does not contain pain receptors, and so the patient can remain conscious and report their experiences when different areas are stimulated. Of particular relevance to memory are studies involving the hippocampus. Early reports that this occasionally evoked specific and verifiable episodic memories have proved difficult to replicate; however, recent work suggests that such stimulation may evoke a feeling of déjà vu, a sense of familiarity when confronted with a quite novel stimulus, something that could have been interpreted by the patient as a genuine memory (Gloor, 1990; Vignal, Maillard, McGonigal, & Chauvel, 2007).

In addition to stimulation, implanted electrodes can be used to *record* from single cells, a procedure that is proving promising (Rutishauser, Schuman, & Mamelak., 2008).

Although recording from implanted electrodes is giving exciting new data, its use is of course limited by the fact that it can only ethically be used in a very limited number of patients and is confined to brain areas that are directly relevant to treatment.

Transcranial Magnetic Stimulation (TMS)

A much less invasive method of influencing the brain is offered by this method, in which a current is passed through a set of coils held close to the participant's head. This results in a magnetic field which can polarize or depolarize the underlying brain tissue, causing a temporary, hence reversible, "lesion" that can then provide evidence for the importance of that area of the brain in the observed cognitive activities. TMS can be delivered either as a single pulse at a precise point in processing, for example before stimulus presentation, or used repeatedly, leading to a disruption of that brain area that can last for many minutes. It has the advantage that it allows the experimenter to control the situation, comparing performance with and without stimulation, in contrast to the brain observation studies we will discuss next. In such cases, unlike TMS, the investigator may observe that a particular area of the brain is activated during a specific task, but that does mean that it is *essential* for that task. TMS like neuropsychological lesion studies is able to go beyond this and demonstrate that without this brain area, the task cannot be performed.

Limitations of TMS are that currently it tends to affect a relatively large area with its influence typically limited to areas near the surface of the brain. Furthermore, while in general safe, it can result in discomfort, and occasionally even seizure in susceptible patients. Nevertheless, as methods develop it is likely to continue to play an important role in cognitive neuroscience.

Electroencephalography (EEG)

This much more widely applicable method involves recording the ongoing electrical

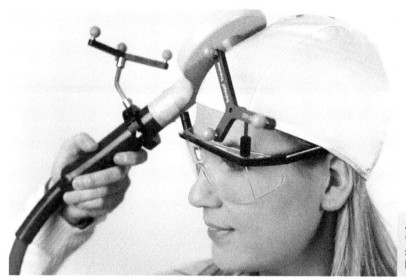

A woman undergoing transcranial magnetic stimulation (TMS) of the brain.

activity of the human brain (see the photo below), it is noninvasive and involves picking up the electrical activity of the person's brain through an array of electrodes on the scalp. This process records fluctuating voltages across the brain, ranging in frequency from a few cycles to 70 cycles per second or more. An electroencephalogram (EEG) is used clinically to detect epileptic foci that may result in seizures; it also plays an important role in studying sleep, with the various stages of sleep being identified with different frequency bands. Electroencephalography has been widely used to study cognitive function, for example showing a different pattern of activation when participants in a memory experiment are actively remembering or recollecting an experience as opposed to merely finding it familiar (see Chapter 8). However, EEG reflects a complex pattern of activation across the whole brain, and it may be hard to identify the contribution to this overall pattern that is associated with the performance of particular processes.

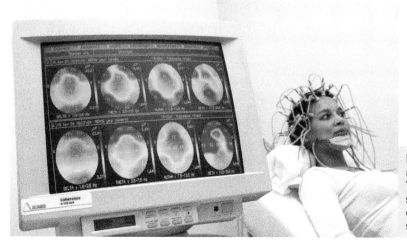

Electrophysiological recording of brain activity. The images on the screen show the distribution of brain activity across successive time periods.

A more precise way of evaluating the brain's response to specific cognitive activities is through event-related potentials (ERPs). These are obtained by time-linking an event to a specific component of the EEG. This involves precise timing, allowing each stage of performance of a task to be linked to the EEG activation at that specific moment. This can allow the effects of cognitive processing to be monitored over a period of milliseconds, hence providing a picture of the way in which the brain reacts to that specific event. Such ERP signals tend, however, to be weaker than the background EEG within which they are embedded, but nevertheless can be extracted by averaging over many repetitions of the same cognitive activity. While the location of evoked response signals is typically not precise, it is possible to identify broad regions of particular activity which may change over time, presumably reflecting the role of different brain areas in the successive processes involved in that particular task.

Magnetoencephalography (MEG)

While EEG and ERP signals reflect the variation in electrical voltage on the surface of the brain, such activity can also be detected by associated changes in *magnetic* activity using a technique known as magnetoencephalography (MEG). This also uses a range of detectors around the head. It differs from ERP in being most sensitive to activity in the *sulci*, the valleys within the folds of the brain, whereas ERP is more sensitive to the peaks or *gyri*. MEG signals are less subject to distortion from passing through the skull and the electrodes than is the case with ERP. It gives a less complex pattern than ERP, and potentially offers a more precise localization of its origin within the brain. Although substantially more expensive than ERP, these advantages are resulting in the increasingly wide use of MEG (see Figure 2.3).

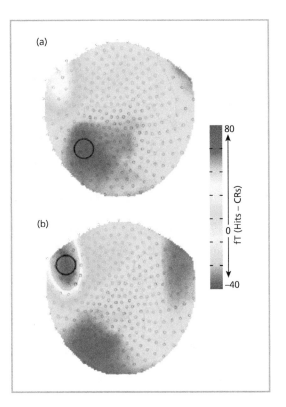

Figure 2.3 MEG reflects the rapidly changing activity of the brain across time. Level of activity is typically mapped by color, with brighter colors reflecting greater activity. The example shown is taken from a study by Horner et al. (2012). The brain activity linked to recognizing that a word had previously been presented is compared to that associated with the capacity to tell whether the given word had been presented together with that particular background. Activity peaked at two separate points. The early pattern shown in A peaks at 330 ms and is linked to recognizing words. The lower pattern, peaking about 60 ms later reflects the capacity to link the word to its specific contextual scene. This second component was not found in patients with hippocampal damage. Reprinted from Horner et al. (2012), Copyright © 2012, with permission from Elsevier.

BLOOD FLOW BASED MEASURES

Both ERP and MEG measures have good temporal resolution; they allow the tracking of brain activity over periods ranging from milliseconds to seconds, but have poor spatial resolution; it is unclear where the activity originates within the brain. Much more precise localization is possible by using methods that rely on the assumption that when a particular area of the brain is active, this is reflected in its metabolism, usually measured in terms of the amount of oxygen being used by that area.

Positron emission topography (PET)

The first of these methods to be developed was positron emission tomography (PET). This involves injecting a radioactive tracer substance into the blood stream; it is conveyed to the brain, with areas of greater activity demanding greater blood flow leading to more radiation. An array of detectors around the head is then able to pick up such radiation, hence localizing areas of maximum activity. PET was very important during the early years of functional imaging. It has much poorer temporal resolution than ERP and MEG, but is much more spatially specific. A major drawback, however, is the need for radioactive reagents, potentially dangerous if the same participant is to be scanned repeatedly, and costly, as preparation requires a cyclotron, preferably on site.

Functional magnetic resonance imaging (fMRI)

Because of this, PET has largely been replaced as a research tool by *functional magnetic resonance imaging (fMRI)*, which also depends on measuring the flow of oxygen within different areas of the brain, and on the assumption that an active area of the brain will utilize more oxygen. The oxygen is carried by hemoglobin. As the oxygen is depleted, the hemoglobin changes its magnetic resonance signal. This can then be picked up by a series of detectors arrayed around the brain, with the pattern of receptor activation being used to locate the various areas in which oxygen is being depleted. This method has the advantage that it is noninvasive since it relies on activities that are already happening within the brain being *externally* detected. Activation can be relatively precisely localized, providing better spatial resolution than PET, especially with more recent equipment containing more powerful magnets. It does, however, provide relatively poor temporal resolution. The typical response to a stimulus will start 1 or 2 seconds after stimulus presentation, peak at 5 to 6 seconds, and return to baseline 10 to 20 seconds later; very much slower than EEG or MEG.

As we shall see, fMRI has already begun to play an important part in the study of human memory, though like all methods it has its limitations. Although less expensive than PET, it is still sufficiently expensive and time-consuming in terms of analysis to make exact replication of studies relatively rare, with investigators tending to move on to the next question rather than checking the robustness of each study, resulting in problems of the reliability

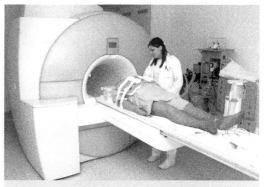

Functional magnetic resonance imaging (fMRI) scans have become an important source of data in psychology. The patient is about to be slid into the machine that will create the magnetic field.

KEY TERM

Positron emission tomography (PET): A method whereby radioactively labeled substances are introduced into the bloodstream and subsequently monitored to measure physiological activation.

of observed results. The pattern of brain areas activated can be relatively large, resembling a mountain range of activation, although this is often simplified to show only the "peaks" (see Figure 2.4). Unfortunately, identifying such peaks will depend on a number of factors. First of all, on the comparison condition. A typical design will involve presenting a task, for example seeing and remembering a sequence of digits, together with a baseline control, for example seeing the digits but not attempting to remember them. The next step is to look at the difference between the patterns of activation across these two, typically using a *subtraction method* where what is shown is the *difference* in activation between trials when memory is required, and those when it is not. Finding an appropriate baseline condition to subtract is crucial and can be tricky, particularly with complex cognitive activities.

Having subtracted the baseline condition, we are left with a set of adjusted activation levels across the brain. Deciding which of these many differences is reliable and important presents a challenging statistical task whose outcome will depend on setting an appropriate significance level. Having achieved this statistically significant difference pattern, it must then be interpreted. In the case of a cognitive study, this will involve attempting to link the pattern to underlying psychological theory, not always an easy task, or one about which different investigators agree.

Multi-voxel pattern analysis (MVPA)

This and related problems has recently led to the development of a more automatic procedure known as *multi-voxel pattern analysis* (MVPA). A scan will result in a visual representation of the brain that can be divided into an array of tiny spatial areas known as voxels. In standard fMRI, each of these is treated as independent from the rest, hence losing information about any overall pattern resulting from the systematic co-occurrence of different areas of stimulation across the brain. MVPA uses powerful machine-learning techniques to look for cross-voxel regularities that occur in the brain, when the same event is presented repeatedly. Significance levels can be set in advance and the problem of possible experimenter bias reduced. Using this approach, the computer can be used as a pattern classifier, gradually building up a model of the brain's response to a particular type of stimulus, for example a human face or a house. Having acquired this statistical representation, the computer can then analyze new scans in which it can reliably detect whether houses or faces are presented (see Tong & Pratte, 2012 for a recent review).

Quite dramatic results have been obtained using the method which is sometimes referred to as "mind reading" since it appears to allow the scientist to know just what the participant is thinking. Commercial companies are already being set up claiming to use the method for lie detection (see Box 2.3). It is important to note, however, that it is not lying *per se* that is being detected, but the cognitive and emotional processes that are associated with lying. An attempt to use this method in an actual court case concluded that the method had not gained widespread acceptance among scientists, that its validity and accuracy had yet to be assessed in real world settings, and hence it should not be accepted as evidence (Shen & Jones, 2011).

THE CELLULAR BASIS OF MEMORY

This is a huge and highly active field, but one that has so far had relatively little impact on the analysis of memory at a cognitive level. Classic work by the Nobel Prize Laureate Eric Kandel used a very simple animal *aplysia*, a sea slug, to analyze two basic types of learning, *habituation* and *sensitization*. Habituation was studied by repeatedly touching the

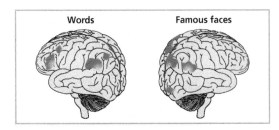

Figure 2.4 Brain regions associated with the remembering of words and famous faces by healthy controls. Reprinted from Simons et al. (2008), Copyright © 2008, with permission from Elsevier.

Box 2.3   Neuroimaging and lie detection

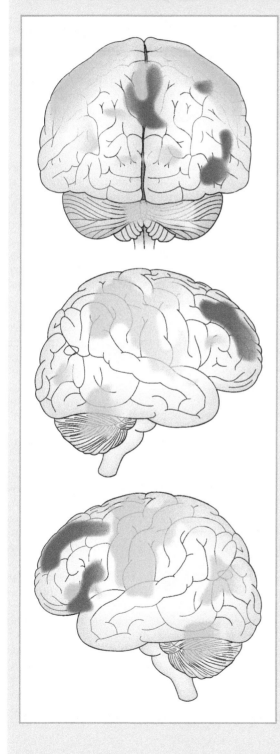

If "mind reading" is possible, could it not be used to tell whether a suspect is lying or not? A number of studies have explored this. In one study (Davatzikos et al., 2005), participants were given an envelope containing two cards, the five of clubs and the seven of spades, followed by a sequence of cards containing both other cards and examples of both. The task was to consistently tell the truth about possession of one of the cards and lie about the other. Brain activation was then recorded and a computer-based pattern analyzer used to identify those areas of the brain consistently accompanying truth and falsehood. The results are shown in Figure 2.5. Using the pattern analyzer, the experimenters were able to detect the instances of lying with over 80% accuracy.

It is important to bear in mind, however, that it is not lying per se that is being detected, but the activation of the certain areas of the brain which reflect a range of cognitive and emotional processes associated with lying. Such processes are likely to occur in other situations, particularly under stress, and in a legal situation may well be evoked in innocent people, emotionally disturbed by the threatening situation even when telling the truth. It is also not clear whether criminals, particularly those with psychopathy will be equally emotionally aroused while lying. Furthermore, the guilty may be able to subvert the process by covertly engaging in other cognitive activities (Ganis, Rosenfeld, Meixner, Kievit, & Schendan, 2011).

Despite this, private companies are being set up claiming to detect lies using neuroimaging. In 2010, a hearing was held in Tennessee to decide whether fMRI lie detection could be accepted as valid scientific evidence. The CEO of one such private company presented evidence of scans which he claimed indicated the innocence of a defendant on a charge of fraud. A neuroscientist and a statis-

Figure 2.5   Different 3D views of regions showing relatively higher activity during truth telling (green) or lying (red). Reprinted from Davatzikos et al. (2005), Copyright © 2005, with permission from Elsevier.

(Continued)

tician were asked to comment on the technology, leading the judge to conclude that despite some support by peer-review publications the method was not widely accepted among scientists, had not yet been validated in real-world settings, and that a well-standardized protocol was not currently available, hence ruling out such evidence (Shen & Jones, 2011). A similar note of caution was reached in the UK by a recent committee of the Royal Society concerned with neuroscience and the law. They also noted that if reliable lie detection should become possible, there would be considerable ethical issues as to if and when such measures should be used (Mackintosh, 2011).

animal's syphon; this resulted in withdrawal of its gill, a response that decreased systematically over repeated stimulation. The opposite effect, sensitization, occurred when touch was linked to the delivery of shock to the animal's tail, a basic form of classical conditioning as originally demonstrated by Pavlov with dogs. Repeated presentation of the touch–shock pairing can be shown to lead to gene expression, new protein synthesis and the development of new synaptic connections, all of which are associated with the long-term retention of the enhanced response to touch.

Further research in this area has identified two potential mechanisms of learning, long-term potentiation (LTP) and *long-term depression* (LTD), and these have been extensively studied at the molecular level, implicating neurotransmitter systems and genes. While this level of biological analysis is likely in the future to have clear implications for the understanding of memory at the cognitive level, and vice versa, it does not yet feature strongly in the chapters that follow.

GENETIC APPROACHES

Sir Francis Galton, a cousin of Charles Darwin, was probably the first to focus attention on the field that has become known as behavioral genetics. He noted that talent in particular areas tended to run in families, the Bach family in music for example, while in the UK a small number of academic families who included the Darwins, the Wedgewoods and Hodgkins appear to have produced a surprisingly large number of talented scientists. Galton was aware of course that the members of such families had much more in common than genes, notably an environment and social position that was likely to foster their talent and facilitate its further development within society. He noted, however, that "twins have a special claim upon our attention; it is, that their history affords means of distinguishing between the effects of tendencies received at birth, and those that were imposed by the special circumstances of their after lives" (Galton, 1869).

The basis of twin studies is the comparison between identical twins, who share 100% of their genes, and fraternal twins who on average share only 50%, the same as is likely for any nonidentical sibling. Of course twins are typically brought up together which means that their environment is also likely to be common. An exception, however, is when twins are separated at birth and brought up within different families; the difference between the performance of fraternal and identical twins on any given function is then used to assess just how much is attributable to genetic and how much to environmental influences.

The whole area of genetic factors has been bedeviled by its association with the eugenics movement, originally driven by the fear in Victorian times that poorer and less intelligent people would have larger families, leading to a gradual degradation of the nation's intelligence. This has proved not to be the case; on the contrary, systematic measures of intelligence across a wide range of tests and countries shows a steady increase extending over many generations, called the Flynn effect after its discoverer (Flynn, 1987). A particular pernicious version of eugenics was developed by the Nazis in Germany who attempted to "purify" the population by encouraging the breeding of those who most resembled an invented racial type, the blonde Aryans, coupled with the mass slaughter of those with "undesirable" genes such as Jews, gypsies and the mentally handicapped. A milder echo of this issue arose in the US during the twentieth century in connection with average differences in performance on standard intelligence tests between different races, who do of course tend to grow up in radically different physical and social environments (see Neisser et al., 1996 for an extensive discussion).

Interest in genetics has grown substantially following the discovery some 50 years ago by Crick and Watson of the structure of the human genome, a structure that contains the genes that determine the way in which all organisms develop. This led to a huge effort focused on reading the genome, together with a growing interest in studies concerning the genetic basis of many aspects of life, including behavior. It had been known for many years that some diseases are genetically based. In some cases such as Huntington's disease this was obvious because of the way in which it afflicted certain families, functioning as would be predicted by what was already known from earlier genetic studies. Other cases such as Down syndrome also proved to be *genetic* in the sense that they reflect chromosomal damage but *sporadic* in the sense that there is no evidence that it runs in families. Other diseases such as Alzheimer's disease are typically sporadic and probably not genetically determined, but can occasionally be found in a genetic form in which half the members of the family possess a gene leading them to succumb to the disease at an early age (see Chapter 16, p. 455).

However, although family and twin studies continue to provide valuable insights, much of the work on behavioral genetics comes from large population studies, typically measuring a range of psychological and behavioral measures and attempting to relate them to specific genes. This has tended to cause excitement in the press when a study appears to reveal "the gene for X," where X can be anything from intelligence to homosexuality. It is, however, proving increasingly clear that most complex behavior is dependent on many genes, each of which interacts with the environment, which may cause the relevant gene to be "switched on" only in specific circumstances. The study of gene–environment interaction, *epigenetics* is clearly an area of great future importance, but one that is likely to require further methodological development before its full promise is realized.

SUMMARY

- A range of methods are increasingly able to link the psychological study of memory with the brain systems that underpin it (see Table 2.1).
- Among the earliest approaches are those based on the study of patients with memory deficits resulting from brain damage.
- Rare single cases with a very specific deficit are particularly informative theoretically, but group studies are of considerable practical importance.
- Patient-based approaches are supplemented by a range of methods of observing the structure of the healthy brain.

(Continued)

(Continued)

- Approaches began with computerized tomography (CT) relying on X-rays.
- This was followed by magnetic resonance imaging (MRI) which relies on the fact that different structures within the brain differ in their response to the energy produced by a surrounding magnetic field.
- In an extension of MRI, diffusion tensor imaging (DTI) is able to image the white matter tracts that connect different areas of the brain.
- A range of methods allow us to observe the working brain in real time. They include:

  - Stimulation by *implanted electrodes,* and transcranial magnetic stimulation (TMS). Both allow specific brain functions to be experimentally and temporarily disrupted.
  - Electroencephalography (EEG) reflects the ongoing electrical activity of the brain and its response to specific stimuli, through event-related potentials (ERPs).
  - A more recent electrophysiological development is that of magneto encephalography (MEG) which relies on the magnetic activity of the brain.

- A number of measures have been developed for studying the activity of the brain through blood flow. These include:

  - Positron emission topography (PET) which depends on injecting and then detecting a radioactive tracer within the blood. The need for intravenous radioactive tracers is a problem, resulting in the development of noninvasive research methods.
  - Functional magnetic resonance imaging (fMRI) also depends on imaging blood flow in areas of the brain assumed to be activated by psychological processes, but is noninvasive, relying on picking up the tiny magnetic forces generated in the brain.
  - Multi-voxel pattern analysis (MVPA) uses a powerful statistical technique to identify patterns of activity associated with specific cognitive activities.

- Studies at the cellular level although of crucial basic importance have so far not connected strongly with the psychology of memory.
- Genetic studies are also promising but not yet influential in the memory field.

TABLE 2.1 Main sources of evidence regarding psychology of memory and the brain

Technique	Main advantages	Main disadvantages
Patient studies	Occur naturally. Can potentially strongly implicate a particular brain area.	Usually complex and varied in extent and location. Do not identify specific networks or temporal resolution. Patients may be rare and effects may change during recovery.
Transcranial magnetic stimulation (TMS)	Can implicate specific brain regions. Is reversible. Relatively inexpensive. Some temporal specificity.	Spatial resolution limited. Confined to surface of the cortex. Discomfort and some safety concerns.
Electroencephalography (EEG)	Rapid and inexpensive. Good temporal resolution. Noninvasive.	Poor spatial resolution. Not clearly specific to cognitive function.
Event-related potentials (ERPs)	Fast and inexpensive. High temporal resolution. Noninvasive.	Poor spatial resolution. May be hard to separate influence of different components. Correlational; may be present but not essential to a task.
Magnetoencephalography (MEG)	High temporal resolution. Noninvasive. Better localization than ERP.	Limited spatial localization. Relatively expensive. Susceptible to interfering noise. Correlational.
Positron emission tomography (PET)	Good spatial resolution. Can identify network of regions.	Very poor temporal resolution. Invasive, need radioactive injection. Expensive, needs cyclotron. Indirect, relies on assumptions about blood flow. Correlational.
Functioning magnetic resonance imaging (fMRI)	Good spatial resolution. Reasonably good temporal resolution. Can identify networks. Noninvasive but relatively expensive.	Temporal resolution fairly low (seconds). Depends on indirect measure of blood flow. Correlational.

What are the advantages and disadvantages of the study of brain damaged patients as compared to the neuroimaging of healthy participants?

Neuroimaging studies often focus on brain localization; what are the strengths and weaknesses of this for a theoretical understanding of memory?

Suppose we developed a perfect method of "mind reading" using neuroimaging; what ethical issues would this raise?

FURTHER READING

Gluck, M. A., Mercado, E., & Myers, C. E. (2014). *Learning and memory: From brain to behavior* (2nd edn.). New York: Worth. Complements our own approach to memory by providing a brain-based analysis.

Kolb, B., & Wishaw, I. Q. (2014). *An introduction to brain and behavior* (4th edn.). New York: Worth. Again takes a brain-based approach, with a somewhat greater emphasis on evidence from patients.

Ward, J. (2010). *The student's guide to cognitive neuroscience* (2nd edn.). Hove: Psychology Press. Provides a broad and readable account of the ways in which cognition can be investigated using the rapidly developing methods of neuroscience.

REFERENCES

Baddeley, A. D., & Warrington, E. K. (1970). Amnesia and the distinction between long- and short-term memory. *Journal of Verbal Learning and Verbal Behavior, 9*, 176–189.

Corkin, S. (2013). *Permanent present tense: The man with no memory and what he taught the world*. New York: Basic Books.

Davatzikos, C., Ruparel, K., Fan, Y., Shen, D. G., Acharyya, M., et al. (2005). Classifying spatial patterns of brain activity with machine learning methods: Application to lie detection. *NeuroImage, 28*, 663–668.

Flynn, J. R. (1987). Massive IQ gains in 14 nations: What IQ tests really measure. *Psychological Bulletin, 101*, 171–191.

Galton, F. (1869). *Hereditary genius*. London: Macmillan.

Ganis, G., Rosenfeld, J. P., Meixner, J., Kievit, R. A., & Schendan, H. E. (2011). Lying in the scanner: Covert countermeasures disrupt deception detection by functional magnetic resonance imaging. *NeuroImage, 55*, 312–319.

Gloor, P. (1990). Experiential phenomena of temporal lobe epilepsy: Facts and hypotheses. *Brain, 113*, 1673–1694.

Horner, A. J., Gadian, D. G., Fuentemilla, L., Jentschke, S., Vargha-Khadem, F., & Duzel, E. (2012). A rapid, hippocampus-dependent, item-memory signal that initiates context memory in humans. *Current Biology, 22*, 2369–2374.

Mackintosh, N. (2011). *Brain Waves 4: Neuroscience and the law*. London: The Royal Society.

Neisser, U., Boodoo, G., Bouchard, T. J., Boykin, A. W., Brody, N., Ceci, S. J., et al. (1996). Intelligence: Knowns and unknowns. *American Psychologist 51*, 77. doi: 10.1037/0003-066X.51.2.77

Poldrack R .A., Kittur A., Kalar D., Miller E., Seppa C., Gil Y., Parker, D. S., Sabb, F. W., & Bilder, R.M. (2011). The cognitive atlas: Toward a knowledge foundation for cognitive neuroscience. *Frontiers in Neuroinformatics, 5*, 17.

Rutishauser, U., Schuman, E. M., & Mamelak, A. N. (2008). Activity of human hippocampal and amygdala neurons during retrieval of declarative memories *Proceedings of the National Academy of Sciences of the USA, 105*, 329–334.

Shallice, T., & Warrington, E. K. (1970). Independent functioning of verbal memory stores: A neuropsychological study. *Quarterly Journal of Experimental Psychology, 22*, 261–273.

Shen, F. X., & Jones, O. D. (2011). Brain scans as evidence: Truths, proofs, lies, and lessons. *Mercer Law Review, 62*, 861.

Tong, F., & Pratte, M. S. (2012). Decoding patterns of human brain activity. *Annual Review of Psychology, 63*, 483–509.

Vignal, J. P., Maillard, L., McGonigal, A., & Chauvel, P. (2007). The dreamy state: Hallucinations of autobiographic memory evoked by temporal lobe stimulations and seizures. *Brain, 130*, 88–99.

Contents

Short-term and working memory: What's the difference?   41

Memory span   42

Models of verbal short-term memory   43

Competing theories of verbal short-term memory   48

Free recall   49

Visuo-spatial short-term memory   51

Summary   60

Points for discussion   61

Further reading   61

References   61

CHAPTER 3

SHORT-TERM MEMORY

Alan Baddeley

I n 1887, John Jacobs, a schoolmaster in London, wanted to assess the abilities of his students. He devised an apparently simple test in which the student heard a sequence of digits, like a telephone number and repeated them back. The measure used was digit span, the longest sequence that could be repeated back without error (Jacobs, 1887). Digit span is still included in the most widely used intelligence test, the Wechsler Adult Intelligence Scale (WAIS). In this basic version, span does not correlate very highly with general intelligence but, as we will see, a somewhat more complex version, working memory span, does an excellent job of predicting a wide range of cognitive skills, including performance on the reasoning tasks often used to assess intelligence.

The digit span test is typically referred to as reflecting *short-term memory* (STM), and the more complex task as *working memory span*. The terms short-term memory (STM) and working memory (WM) seem often to be used interchangeably, so is there a difference?

KEY TERM

Digit span: Maximum number of sequentially presented digits that can reliably be recalled in the correct order.

Working memory span: Term applied to a range of complex memory span tasks in which simultaneous storage and processing is required.

SHORT-TERM AND WORKING MEMORY: WHAT'S THE DIFFERENCE?

The term "short-term memory" is a rather slippery one. To the general public, it refers to remembering things over a few hours or days, the sort of capacity that becomes poorer as we get older and is dramatically impaired in patients with Alzheimer's disease. To psychologists, however, these are long-term memory (LTM) problems. Remembering over a few minutes, hours or a few years all seem to depend on the same long-term memory system.

We will use the term *short-term memory* (STM) to refer to performance on a particular type of task, one involving the simple retention of small amounts of information, tested either immediately or after a short delay. The memory system or systems responsible for STM form part of the *working memory* system. "Working memory" is the term we will use for a system that not only temporarily stores information but also manipulates it so as to allow people to perform such complex activities as reasoning, learning, and comprehension. Before going on to discuss working memory in the next chapter, we will examine the simpler concept of STM, the capacity to store small amounts of information over brief intervals, beginning with the digit-span task devised by Jacobs.

In contrast to our use of STM simply to describe an experimental situation, the term *working memory* is based on a theoretical assumption, namely that tasks such as reasoning and learning depend on a system that is capable of temporarily holding and manipulating information, a system that has evolved as a mental workspace. A number of different theoretical approaches to working memory have developed, some influenced strongly by the study of attention (e.g. Cowan, 2001), some on studies of individual differences in performance on complex tasks (e.g. Miyake, Friedman, Emerson, Witzki, Howerter, & Wager, 2000; Engle & Kane, 2004), and others driven by neurophysiological considerations (Goldman-Rakic, 1996). All, however, assume that WM provides a temporary workspace that is necessary for performing complex cognitive activities.

The approach used in the next two chapters reflects a multicomponent account of WM (Baddeley & Hitch, 1974) that was strongly influenced by the experimental and neuropsychological studies of human memory that form the core of the present book. It has proved durable and widely applicable, but should be seen as complementary to a range of other approaches rather than as *the* theory of working memory (Miyake & Shah, 1999).

MEMORY SPAN

Before proceeding, test yourself using Box 3.1.

If your digit span is rather lower than you might hope, don't worry; in this simple form, as we shall see later, it depends on a small but useful aspect of our memory system, not on general intelligence. It is limited to about six or seven digits for most people, although some people can manage up to ten or more, whereas others have difficulty recalling more than four or five. What sets this limit and why does it vary between one person and the next?

Memory span measures require two things: (1) remembering what the *items* are; and (2) remembering the *order* in which they were presented. In the case of the digits one to nine, we already know the items very well, so the test becomes principally one of memory for order. If, however, I were to present you with sequence of digits in an unfamiliar language,

---

Box 3.1 Digit span test

Read each sequence as if it were a telephone number, then close your eyes and try to repeat it back. Start with the four digit numbers and continue until you fail on both sequences at a given length. Your span is one digit less than this.

9 7 5 4
3 8 2 5
6 5 1 4
9 4 3 1 8
6 8 2 5 9
3 8 1 4 7
9 1 3 8 2 5
6 4 8 3 7 1
5 9 6 3 8 2
7 9 5 8 4 2 3
5 3 1 6 8 4 2
7 9 1 8 5 4 6
8 6 9 5 1 3 7 2
5 1 7 3 9 8 2 6
5 1 3 9 8 2 4 7
7 1 9 3 8 4 2 6 1
1 6 3 8 7 4 9 5 2
6 2 5 9 4 3 8 2 6
9 1 5 2 4 3 8 1 6 2
7 1 5 4 8 5 6 1 9 3
1 5 2 8 4 6 7 3 1 8

Finnish for example, your span would be very much less. You would of course have much more to remember, as you would need to recall the order of the sounds comprising the Finnish digits, as well the order of the digits.

Suppose I were to use words, but not digits, would that matter? Provided I used the same words repeatedly, you would soon become familiar with the set, and would do reasonably well. However, if I were to use a different set of words on each trial it would become somewhat harder as you would again need to remember both what the items were and their order, although this would be easier than for the unfamiliar Finnish digits.

Suppose we move from numbers to letters; test yourself on the next sequence by reading each letter out loud, then close your eyes and try to repeat the letters in the order they are written.

C T A I I L T C S F R O

Very hard? Now try the next sequence.

F R A C T O L I S T I C

I assume you found the second sequence easier, even though it used exactly the same letters as the first. The reason is that the order of the letters in the second sequence allowed you to break it up into pronounceable word-like subgroups or *chunks*. In a classic paper, George Miller (1956) suggested that memory capacity is limited not by the number of *items* to be recalled, but by the number of *chunks*. The first sequence comprised twelve apparently unrelated letters, making it hard to reduce the number of chunks much below twelve, whereas the second could be pronounced as a string of four pronounceable syllables that, together, made a sequence that, although meaningless, could plausibly be an English word.

Chunking in this case depends on letter sequences that are consistent with long-term language habits, making the important point that LTM can influence STM. Grouping can also be induced by the rhythm with which a sequence of items is presented. Suppose I were to read out nine digits. If I interposed a slightly longer pause between items three and four and items six and seven, recall would be significantly improved. Hence 791–684–352 is easier than 791684352. Pauses in other locations can also be helpful, but grouping in threes seems to be best (Wickelgren, 1964; Ryan, 1969). It seems likely that chunking is taking

---

KEY TERM

Chunking: The process of combining a number of items into a single chunk typically on the basis of long-term memory.

---

advantage of cues from prosody, the natural rhythms that occur in speech and that make its meaning clearer by separating into coherent phrases the continuous sequence of sounds that make up the normal speech stream.

Although remembering strings of numbers was probably of little interest to Mr. Jacobs' students, it has in recent years become much more critical because of the increasing use in our culture of digit and letter sequences, initially as telephone numbers, then as postal codes and subsequently as PINs and passwords. In the early 1960s, Dr. R. Conrad was asked by the British Post and Telecommunications Service to investigate the relative advantages and disadvantages of codes based on letters and numbers. One of his experiments involved visually presenting strings of consonants for immediate recall. He noticed an interesting pattern in his results, namely that, despite being presented visually, errors were likely to be similar in *sound* to the item they replaced, hence *P* was more likely to be misremembered as *V* than the more visually similar letter *R* (Conrad, 1964). Conrad and Hull (1964) went on to investigate this effect further, demonstrating that memory for sequences of consonants is substantially poorer when they are similar in sound (*C V D P G T* versus *K R X L Y F*). Conrad interpreted his results in terms of a short-term memory store that relies on an acoustic code, which fades rapidly, resulting in forgetting. This was assumed to be particularly disruptive of recall of the acoustically similar letters as they had fewer distinguishing features, making each item more likely to be confused with adjacent items, resulting in errors in order of recall (e.g. *P T C V B* recalled as *P T V C B*).

MODELS OF VERBAL SHORT-TERM MEMORY

By the late 1960s, the evidence seemed to be swinging firmly in the direction of abandoning the attempt to explain STM in terms of a unitary system, in favor of an explanation involving a number of interacting systems, one of which was closely identified with the extensive evidence accumulated from verbal STM. I will use one out of a range of models of verbal STM, the concept of a *phonological loop*, to tie together the rich body of research that continues to develop in this area, before going on to give a brief account of alternative theories.

The phonological loop

The concept of a phonological loop forms part of the multicomponent working memory model proposed by Baddeley and Hitch (1974). The phonological loop is assumed to have two subcomponents, a short-term store and an articulatory rehearsal process. The store is assumed to be limited in capacity, with items registered as memory traces, which decay within a few seconds. However, the traces can be refreshed by subvocal rehearsal, saying the items to yourself, which depends on a vocal or subvocal articulatory process.

Consider the case of digit span. Why is it limited to six or seven items? If there are few digits in the sequence, then you can say them all in less time than it takes for the first digit to fade away. As the number of items increases, total time to rehearse them all will be greater, and hence the chance of items fading before they are refreshed will increase, hence setting a limit to memory span. The loop model is able to account for the following prominent features of verbal STM:

The phonological similarity effect
A major signature of the store is the phonological similarity effect, Conrad's (1964) demonstration that letter span is reduced for similar sounding items.

KEY TERM

Phonological loop: Term applied by Baddeley and Hitch to the component of their model responsible for the temporary storage of speech-like information.

Phonological similarity effect: A tendency for immediate serial recall of verbal material to be reduced, when the items are similar in sound.

Is Conrad's discovery based on letters also true for words or does meaning change the pattern of results? Try it for yourself: Read out this sequence of words at a rapid rate, close your eyes and try to recall it, then move on to the next sequence.

pit, day, cow, pen, top

Close your eyes and recall. How well did you do? Try the next:

mad, can, man, mat, cap

Close your eyes and recall. I assume you found this set somewhat harder. That suggests that similarity of sound creates problems and is consistent with Conrad's suggestion that STM uses an "acoustic" code. But perhaps any kind of similarity would cause similar confusion? Try the next one. Ready?

big, wide, large, high, tall

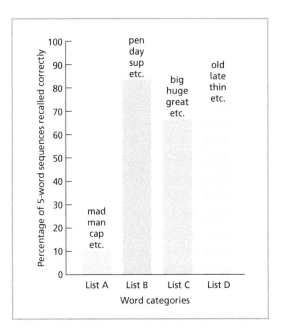

Figure 3.1 The effect of phonological and semantic similarity on immediate serial recall of five-word sequences. Phonological similarity leads to poor immediate recall whereas similarity of meaning has little effect. From Baddeley (1966a). Copyright © Psychology Press.

Close your eyes and recall. How did you do? Rather easier than the *mad, can, man* set I assume, since that is what we found with our subjects as shown in Figure 3.1.

One final point to this story is that the phonological similarity effect disappears if the lists are increased in length and participants are allowed several learning trials. Under these circumstances, similarity of meaning becomes much more important (Baddeley, 1966b). This does not mean that phonological coding is limited to STM, as without phonological LTM we could never learn to pronounce new words. It is, however, the case that LTM typically gains more from relying on meaning than on sound. We return to this point in Chapters 5 and 6.

The phonological similarity effect is assumed to occur at retrieval, when information is read out from the short-term memory trace; similar items have fewer distinguishing features, and hence are likely to be confused. Auditory speech is assumed to feed directly into the phonological store. Visually presented items can also be fed into the store if they are nameable, such as digits, letters, or nameable objects, through a process of vocal or subvocal articulation, whereby you say the items to yourself.

The subvocal rehearsal system can be blocked if you are required to repeatedly say something unrelated such as the word "the," an activity known as articulatory suppression. Saying "the" means that you are not able to refresh the memory trace by subvocally pronouncing the remembered material. It also prevents you from subvocally naming visually presented items, such as letters, which prevents them from being registered in the phonological store. For that reason, it does not matter whether items are phonologically similar or not, when they are presented visually and accompanied by articulatory suppression. Both similar and dissimilar items will be retained, but at a lower and equivalent level.

KEY TERM

Articulatory suppression: A technique for disrupting verbal rehearsal by requiring participants to continuously repeat a spoken item.

However, it is important to note that even when suppressing, people can still remember up to four or five visually presented digits. This suggests that, although the phonological loop typically plays an important role in digit span, it is not the only basis of span. We will return to this point later. With *auditory* presentation, the words gain direct access to the phonological store despite articulatory suppression, and hence a similarity effect still occurs.

The word length effect

Before moving on we should try just one more small experiment using exactly the same procedure. Remember, read rapidly close your eyes and then recall. Ready?

pot, lark, stick, nut, flow

Close eyes and recall. How did you do? Pretty well, I suspect. Now try the next set of five words:

opportunity, refrigerator, tuberculosis, university, hippopotamus

Close eyes and recall. Did you find the long words harder? As Figure 3.2 shows, people can remember sequences of five dissimilar one-syllable words relatively easily. As word length increases, performance drops from around 90% for five monosyllables to about 50% for lists of five-syllable words. As word length is increased, the time taken to speak the words also increases (Figure 3.2). This relation between recall and the rate of articulation can be summarized by the statement that people can remember about as many words as they can say in 2 seconds (Baddeley, Thomson, & Buchanan, 1975).

We explained our findings as follows: Rehearsal takes place in real time, as does trace decay, with the result that longer words, taking longer to say, allow more decay to occur. We thus attributed the word length effect to forgetting during subvocal rehearsal. However, Cowan, Day, Saults, Keller, Johnson, and Flores (1992) demonstrated that word length also caused forgetting during the recall phase due to the fact that longer words take longer to recall, allowing more forgetting to occur. Baddeley,

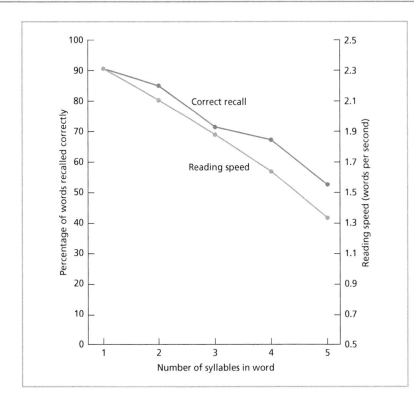

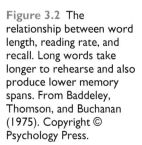

Figure 3.2 The relationship between word length, reading rate, and recall. Long words take longer to rehearse and also produce lower memory spans. From Baddeley, Thomson, and Buchanan (1975). Copyright © Psychology Press.

Chincotta, Stafford, and Turk (2002), showed that word length effects occur during *both* rehearsal and recall. Both of these results are consistent with the assumption that the word length effect reflects a time-based rehearsal process. If rehearsal is prevented, then the word length effect should be lost. This can be tested using *articulatory suppression*, requiring participants to repeat an irrelevant sound such as the word "the" while performing the memory task. As predicted, this abolishes the word length effect (Baddeley et al., 1975).

The word length effect is extremely robust but its interpretation remains controversial. An alternative to the Baddeley et al. (1975)

KEY TERM

Word length effect: A tendency for verbal memory span to decrease when longer words are used.

time-based trace decay interpretation, is the proposal that longer words are more complex and this leads to more interference (e.g. Caplan, Rochon, & Waters, 1992). A third interpretation suggests that long words, having more components to be remembered, are more vulnerable to fragmentation and forgetting (e.g. Neath & Nairne, 1995), although this interpretation has now been abandoned by its earlier proponents (Hulme, Neath, Stuart, Shostak, Suprenant, & Brown, 2006), in favor of the SIMPLE model described in the section on "Free recall."

Irrelevant sound effects

Students often claim that they work better to a background of their favorite music or radio program. Are they right? In 1976, Colle and Welsh showed that STM for sequences of visually presented digits was impaired when participants were required to ignore speech even though it was in an unfamiliar foreign language, and hence devoid of meaning. However, digit recall was not impaired when irrelevant foreign speech was replaced by unpatterned noise.

Both Salame and Baddeley (1982) and Colle (1980) suggested that the irrelevant speech effect might be seen as the memory equivalent to the masking of auditory speech perception by irrelevant sound. Perhaps the irrelevant spoken item gains access to the phonological store, and adds noise to the memory trace? However, white noise disrupts perception, but does not impair recall, whereas irrelevant speech does. Furthermore, in contrast to auditory masking, STM performance is not influenced by the intensity of the irrelevant sound (Colle, 1980). Even more problematic for the auditory masking analogy is the fact that the degree of disruption of STM is unrelated to the phonological similarity between the irrelevant sound and the items remembered. Irrelevant words that are similar in sound to the remembered items are no more disrupting than are dissimilar words (Jones & Macken, 1995; Le Compte & Shaibe, 1997).

But what about music? Salame and Baddeley (1989) found that music interfered with digit recall, finding that vocal music was more disruptive than instrumental. Jones and Macken (1993) observed that even pure tones will disrupt performance, provided they fluctuate in pitch. They proposed what they termed the *Changing State hypothesis*. This assumes that retention of serial order, whether in verbal or visual memory, can be disrupted by irrelevant stimuli providing that these fluctuate over time (Jones, Macken, & Murray, 1993). Jones (1993) relates the irrelevant sound effect to theories of auditory perception, presenting as an alternative to the phonological loop hypothesis their *Object-Oriented Episodic Record (O-OER) hypothesis*. Regardless of whether one accepts the O-OER hypothesis, there is strong evidence that the irrelevant sound effect is based on disruption of memory for serial order.

The problem of serial order

It was clear by this time that the purely verbally specified phonological loop model had two major shortcomings. First, it had no adequate explanation of how serial order is stored. Given that the classic digit-span task principally involves retaining serial order, this is clearly a major limitation. Second, the model has no clear specification of the crucial processes involved in *retrieval* from the phonological store. Both of these limitations demand a more detailed model, preferably computationally or mathematically simulated so that clear predictions can be made and tested. Fortunately, it has proved possible to convince several groups with the appropriate skills that this is a worthwhile enterprise.

A number of models based on the phonological loop have been developed, handling the question of serial order in somewhat different ways, agreeing on which issues are important but differing on how best to tackle them (see Box 3.2). The various models tend to agree in assuming both a phonological store and a separate mechanism for serial order, with similarity influencing retrieval from the store. Most phonological-loop-related models reject a chaining interpretation of serial order, proposing instead that order information is carried either by some form of ongoing context (Burgess & Hitch, 1999, 2006), by links to the first item as in the *Primacy model* of Page and Norris (1998) or links to both the first and last items (Henson, 1998). Rehearsal is assumed to involve the retrieval of items from the phonological store and their subsequent re-entry as rehearsed stimuli.

Only one of these models appears so far to have explicitly addressed the irrelevant sound effect, attributing it to the serial order mechanism rather than to the phonological store, the component responsible for the effects of phonological similarity (Box 3.2). This provides an explanation of why similarity between the remembered and the irrelevant items has no effect; they influence different parts of the system and hence do not interact.

KEY TERM

Irrelevant sound effect: A tendency for verbal STM to be disrupted by concurrent fluctuating sounds, including both speech and music.

Box 3.2 Methods of storing serial order

1 Chaining

A → B → C → D

Each item is associated with the next. Recall begins with the first item (A), which evokes the second (B).

2 Context

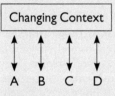

Each item is linked to a changing context, which may be time-based. The context then acts as recall cue.

3 Primacy

Each item presented receives activation. The first receives the most, the next a little less, and so forth. Items are recalled in order of strength. Once recalled, that item is suppressed and the next strongest chosen.

Strength ↑   A I   B I   C I   D I

COMPETING THEORIES OF VERBAL SHORT-TERM MEMORY

We have so far focused our discussion mainly on the explanation of short-term verbal memory offered by the phonological loop hypothesis. This approach has two advantages: it provides a coherent account of a range of very robust STM phenomena, and it does so in a way that explicitly links them to those other aspects of working memory that will be discussed in the next chapter. It is important to bear in mind, however, that other ways of explaining these data have been proposed.

Some of these will be described briefly before moving on to a broader discussion of working memory, and the question of why we need a working memory.

One approach to STM is that proposed by Dylan Jones and colleagues (Jones, 1993; Jones & Macken, 1993, 1995) as the Object-Oriented Episodic Record (O-OER) theory of STM. This was developed to account for the influence on STM of irrelevant sound. It is influenced by research on auditory perception and proposes that sequences of items are represented as points on a multimodal surface; however, it assumes that both auditory and visual serial recall involve the same system operating on a common representation. Recall involves retrieving the trajectory of the points representing the sequence, rather like reading off points on a graph. Irrelevant sounds might create competing trajectories, disrupting subsequent recall (Jones, 1993).

The assumption that verbal STM and visual STM involve the same system has not been supported by subsequent experiments (Meiser & Klauer, 1999) and is inconsistent with evidence from neuropsychological studies in which some patients are found with impaired verbal STM and preserved visual STM (Shallice & Warrington, 1970; Vallar & Papagno, 2002) whereas other patients show the opposite pattern (Della Sala & Logie, 2002). Furthermore, its account of memory for serial order would appear to depend on chaining, an approach that is not well supported.

Another model that has been applied to verbal STM is James Nairne's *Feature model* (Nairne, 1988, 1990), which replaces the proposed separation between LTM and STM by proposing a single memory system in which each memory item is assumed to be represented by a set of features, which are of two basic types: *modality dependent* and *modality independent*. If you read the word *hat*, it will have both visually dependent features, such as the case in which it is printed, and visually independent features, such as its meaning. When you hear *hat*, rather than read it, the independent features such as meaning will be the same but the dependent features will be acoustic rather than visual.

Forgetting is assumed to depend on interference, with new items disrupting the features set up by earlier items, resulting in errors in recall.

The Feature model is represented by a computer program that can be used to make predictions as to the outcome of different experimental manipulations. By making various assumptions, it is possible to use the model to account for many of the results that have been used to support the phonological loop hypothesis. The phonological similarity effect is explained on the grounds that similar items have more common features, leading to a greater likelihood that a similar but incorrect item will be retrieved. Irrelevant sound is assumed to add noise to the memory trace of each individual item. Articulatory suppression is also assumed to add noise, and in addition to be attention demanding (Nairne, 1990). By making detailed assumptions about the exact proportion of modality-dependent and modality-independent features and the relative effect on these of articulatory suppression and irrelevant sound, the Feature model is able to simulate a wide range of results (Neath & Surprenant, 2003), although very little justification is given for the very specific assumptions required by the various simulations.

The Feature model does have difficulty in accounting for a number of findings. It predicts that irrelevant sound will impair recall only when it occurs at the same time as the memory items are encoded. However, it disrupts recall even when it occurs *after* presentation of the memory items, even when rehearsal is prevented by suppression (Norris, Baddeley, & Page, 2004). The Feature model also has a problem explaining why the word length effect disappears in mixed lists of long and short words. This has led to its abandonment by some of its proponents in favor of the next model to be described: the SIMPLE model (Hulme et al., 2006; Brown, Neath, & Chater, 2007).

Brown et al. (2007) propose a very broad-ranging memory model that they call the SIMPLE (Scale Invariant Memory, Perception, and Learning) model, which they apply to both STM and LTM. It is basically a model of forgetting based on retrieval, with more distinctive items being more readily retrievable. It places emphasis on temporal discriminability but goes beyond earlier attempts to use this mechanism to explain recency effects in free recall by developing a detailed mathematical model. It is probably too early to evaluate SIMPLE, which appears to handle free recall well but appears to be less well suited to explaining serial recall (Lewandowski, Brown, Wright, & Nimmo, 2006; Nimmo & Lewandowski, 2006). As in the case of the Feature model, SIMPLE does not currently attempt to cover the executive aspects of working memory.

A further way of modeling serial order is to assume that order is maintained by a context signal. As mentioned earlier, one of these approaches assumes a time-based context incorporating trace decay (Burgess & Hitch, 1999, 2006). This assumption is rejected by Farrell and Lewandowski (2002, 2003), who propose—in their SOB (Serial-Order-in-a-Box) model—that order is maintained using an event-based context signal, with forgetting based on interference between events.

It might seem strange that the apparently simple task of recalling a sequence of digits in the right order should prove so difficult to explain. However, as mentioned earlier, the problem of how a system like the brain that processes events in parallel can preserve serial order has challenged theorists since it was first raised by Karl Lashley (1951), over 50 years ago.

FREE RECALL

Most of the work on verbal STM described so far has involved limited sets of digits, letters or words used repeatedly, with the emphasis on recalling serial order. The use of such constrained sets is of course intentional, so as to emphasize the demands of serial order recall and minimize that of remembering the specific items. If, for example, new words are used on every trial, then aspects of verbal LTM would become more important, such as the meaningfulness of the words to be recalled (Walker & Hume 1999). With short lists, people often begin by trying to recall in serial order, but then find this is not a good strategy with longer lists (Murdock, 1962).

Try it for yourself: Read out the following list of 16 words at a steady rate, then close your eyes and write down as many as you can remember in any order you like. Ready? Read and remember

barricade, children, diet, gourd, polio,
meter, journey, mohair, phoenix, crossbow,
alligator, doorbell, muffler, menu,
archer, carpet

Now close your eyes, look away, and write down what you can remember.

How well did you do? That would depend on how long you took and what you did with the words as you were reading them, but if you kept up a brisk pace you are likely to remember rather less than half of them. Now go back and check where your correct recalls came from within the list. Results from a single trial are inevitably rather unreliable, particularly in free recall where people are often still settling

on a strategy, but the pattern of recall usually found is shown in Figure 3.3.

The most striking feature of this typical serial position effect is the tendency for excellent recall on the last few items, the so called recency effect. There is also a tendency for the first few items to be relatively well recalled, the primacy effect, although this is usually much less pronounced than recency, unlike the case of serial recall, when primacy dominates. Note also the red line; this is the level of performance that can be expected if recall is delayed by the requirement to perform a brief attentional demanding task such as counting backwards in threes for 10 seconds (Postman & Phillips, 1965).

How could we explain this pattern of results? A highly influential interpretation was offered by Glanzer and Cunitz (1966) who proposed that the earlier items were held in LTM, while recency reflected a separate component based on STM; a brief filled delay is sufficient to eliminate the STM contribution while leaving those items in LTM relatively unaffected. Evidence in favor of this interpretation came from a wide range of sources, finding that variables that are known to influence LTM impact upon the earlier items but not on the recency effect. LTM variables studied include:

1 Presentation rate: slower is better;
2 Word frequency: familiar words are easier;
3 Imageability of the words: words that are visualizable are better;
4 Age of the participant: young adults remember more than children or the elderly;
5 Physiological state: drugs such as marijuana and alcohol impair performance.

While all of these were found to influence the earlier part of the serial position curve none

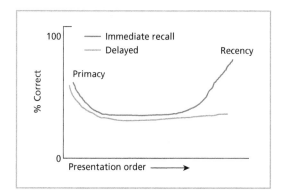

Figure 3.3 A typical serial position curve for free recall: when participants recall a list of unrelated words in any order they wish, there is a clear advantage to the last few items, the *recency effect*, which vanishes when recall is briefly delayed.

KEY TERM

Recency effect: A tendency for the last few items in a list to be well recalled.

Primacy effect: A tendency for the first few items in a sequence to be better recalled than most of the following items.

impacted on recency (Glanzer, 1972). What of the primacy effect? This probably reflects a tendency to rehearse the first few items as they come in, while sometimes continuing to rehearse these items throughout the list (Rundus, 1971; Tam & Ward, 2000). The assumption that recency simply reflects the output of a short-term store was, however, subsequently challenged by the demonstration that recency effects can occur under conditions in which the short-term trace ought to have been disrupted. In one study, Bjork and Whitten (1974) required their subjects to recall sequences of words presented under three conditions. The baseline condition involved presenting a list of words for immediate free recall. As expected, this resulted in a clear recency effect. In a second condition, the gap between presentation and recall was filled by a 20-second backward counting task, which—as expected—removed the recency effect. In a third, crucial condition, 20 seconds of backward counting was interposed between each of the words presented, as well as between the end of the list and recall. Under these conditions, a recency effect re-emerged.

Recency effects have also been demonstrated over much longer intervals. In one study, for example, Baddeley and Hitch (1977) tested the capacity of rugby players to recall which teams they had played that season; their recall showed a clear recency effect. As not all the players had played in all the games, it proved possible to assess whether forgetting was more reflective of the amount of time elapsed, or of the number of intervening games. Number of games proved to be the better predictor, suggesting that a simple time-based decay hypothesis would not provide a good account of these findings. Similar long-term recency effects have been found in remembering parking location (Pinto, da Costa, & Baddeley, 1991), although—sadly—I can report that as I get older, even recency does not always prevent

the need for an embarrassed wander around the supermarket parking lot.

The fact that recency effects are found across such a wide range of situations, with some cases being disrupted by a few seconds of unrelated activity such as counting whereas others persist over months, suggests that the recency effect is not limited to any single type of memory system but instead reflects a specific retrieval strategy that takes advantage of the fact that the most recent events are the most readily available to recall.

When was the last party you attended? Which was the party before that? And the one before? I suspect recalling your most recent party was the easiest, although it was perhaps not the best party.

The greater accessibility of the most recent experience of a given type could serve the highly important role of orienting yourself in space and time. When traveling and staying in a new place, how do you know where you are when you wake up? And if staying in a hotel, how do you remember your current room number and don't recall instead the number from last night or the night before that?

The most plausible interpretation of recency seems to be in terms of retrieval. Crowder (1976) likens the task of retrieving items from a free-recall list to that of discriminating telephone posts located at regular intervals along a railway track. The nearest post will be readily distinguishable from the next, while as the posts recede into the distance, the problem of separating one from the other becomes increasingly hard. This process can be seen in terms of a discrimination ratio, based on the temporal distance between the item being retrieved and its principal competitor, the one immediately before it. On immediate recall, the most recent item has a considerable advantage, but with increasing delay, discriminating an item from the one before becomes less and less easy (Baddeley & Hitch, 1977; Brown et al., 2007; Glenberg et al., 1980).

VISUO-SPATIAL SHORT-TERM MEMORY

Imagine you are in a well lighted room that is suddenly plunged into darkness. Would you

---

KEY TERM

Long-term recency: A tendency for the last few items to be well recalled under conditions of long-term memory.

Crowder's (1976) analogy likened the task of retrieval from a free-recall list to that of discriminating between a string of telephone posts; the further away the post is from the observer, the more difficult it becomes to distinguish it from its neighbor.

be able to find the door? There was a box of matches on the desk in front of you, would you remember that it was there? These two questions concern two related but separable aspects of visual working memory, one concerned with spatial memory (*where?*) and the other with memory for objects (*what?*). The evidence suggests that you would be able to maintain a general heading towards the door for about 30 seconds (Thomson, 1983). Your memory for precise location within reach declines rather more rapidly (Elliot & Madelena, 1987).

But has nature endowed us with visual STM simply to prepare us for the occasional power cut? And even if this were the case, would LTM not suffice? A brief consideration of the processes underlying visual perception suggests a rather more convincing interpretation of our need for visual STM. As we look around, we perceive objects within a complex environment. However, despite our experience of smoothly scanning a visual scene, the underlying process is not continuous, but rather is based on a series of discreet eye movements to different parts of the scenes (see Box 3.3). These can be quite rapid. In reading for example they can occur at a rate of about two per second, with each fixation creating a separate image of the world. In the case of scanning a scene, where the eye may move from the foreground to the distance and from one object to another, these aspects may be very different. If the eye functioned like a camera, superimposing these images, the result would be visual chaos. Nature's solution to this problem is to combine these brief glimpses into a coherent representation, namely visual STM.

If it is to work effectively in maintaining a representation of a world that is constantly changing as we move around, visual STM needs to hold its representation of the world over time, but to allow for a constant updating as we move around, and when the focus of attention switches from where you are to what you want to do, perhaps searching for and picking up a stone and aiming at a wolf that might be taking a little too much interest in you. To achieve this, the visual system needs to be able to bind together the perceptual features that constitute an object, the stone or the wolf, together with its spatial framework, and to hold these together long enough for action to be planned and the plan carried out. We will consider these in turn, beginning with object-based STM, going on to discuss spatial aspects before considering in the next chapter the more complex issue of the role of memory in thinking and planning.

Object memory

As is typical of many areas of experimental psychology, the study of visual STM has largely relied on simple easily specified stimuli, such as colored shapes or letters, rather than stones or wolves. The reason is that such stimuli are much easier to create, control, and

Box 3.3 Eye movement

A scene used by Vogt and Magnussen (2007). The central picture shows a normal eye-movement scanning pattern and that on the right the scanning pattern of a typical artist.

When we look at scene such as that below, we experience it as continuous and static. This experience is, however, built up from a series of brief rapid eye movements; typically each will be focused on a separate aspect of the scene with the result that simply superimposing them would cause visual confusion. Instead, each is fed into a coherent framework based on visual STM. As the two examples show, the pattern of scanning is far from random, tending to focus on points likely to give most information, a factor that will reflect the aims and expertise of the perceiver. People typically focus on recognizable objects and on human figures, whereas trained artists tend to scan more widely. The central picture shows a normal scanning pattern and the right that of a typical artist. From Vogt and Magnussen (2007).

specify, and this means that others can repeat your findings; such replication is an essential and basic feature of all science. However carefully a study is designed and carried out, it may be subject to chance factors such as an atypical participant group, or sample of stimulus material, as I myself can testify. Replication with different participants and a different sample of material avoids such problems.

Having developed principles and theories using simple and well-controlled material such as colored shapes, the next stage is to take such findings beyond the laboratory, demonstrating in due course what is termed their "ecological validity," their applicability to the "real world." A detailed analysis of visual STM has only developed relatively recently, hence most of the work to be described does use relatively simple stimuli, although there is a growing interest in extending visual memory beyond such simple paradigms and applying it, for example, to complex real world scenes (see Henderson, 2008; Hollingworth, 2008).

Visual STM and LTM: How do they differ?

Using a method known as *change detection*, Phillips (1974) presented participants with a series of checkerboard patterns varying in complexity from 4 × 4 to 8 × 8, with half the cells black and half white in each case. After delays ranging from 0 to 9 seconds, a test stimulus followed, being either identical or having one cell changed. On immediate test, performance was virtually perfect, but declined over time with more complex patterns showing poorer performance (see Figure 3.4) suggesting that visual STM has a limited capacity.

In a later very influential paper Luck and Vogel (1997) developed a variant of the change detection task that has over recent years been extremely fruitful in probing the nature of visual STM. In a typical study, participants might view an array of squares differing in color, followed after varying delays by a pattern that is identical, or has the color of one square changed (see Figure 3.5A).

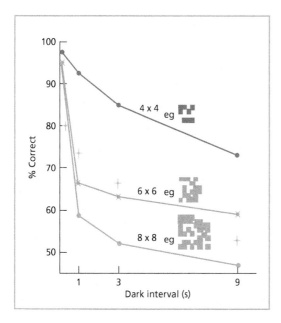

Figure 3.4 Recognition memory for random patterns as a function of complexity. Examples of the three types of pattern are shown. Each pattern was followed by a test item comprising either an identical pattern or one which had a single square changed. From Phillips (1974). Reprinted by permission of the Psychonomics Society, Inc.

Unlike the complex matrix patterns used by Phillips, colored squares can be verbalized and hence remembered nonvisually. To

prevent this, participants are usually required to occupy the verbal rehearsal system by continually repeating a simple sequence such as *one, two, three* (see p. 45). Luck and Vogel varied the number of colored squares from one to twelve, finding like Phillips that performance declined steeply as number of squares increased, but also showing that capacity was limited to three of four items (see Figure 3.5B).

This differs dramatically from LTM, where capacity appears to be extremely large. In a classic study Standing, Conezio and Haber (1970) presented 2560 color slides for 10 seconds each, subsequently testing memory several days later by presenting two items one of which had been shown before, categorized as "old," while the other had not, "new." Despite the number and the delay, participants scored 90% correct. This has been replicated and extended in recent years in a series of studies showing that people can detect often quite subtle changes, such as left–right reversal or a full versus half-full glass of orange juice (see Brady, Konkle, & Alvarez, 2011 for a review). This does not necessarily mean that every detail of such pictures has been retained, but does suggest that people can remember more than the broad semantic gist of a very large number of stimuli, in contrast to the four-item capacity of visual STM.

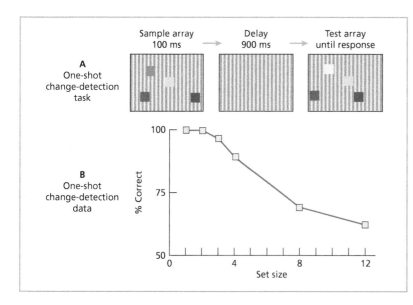

Figure 3.5 (A) The change detection task used by Luck and Vogel (1997). In this example, the green square has been changed to yellow. (B) The probability of detecting a change declines with the number of squares to be remembered. Adapted from Luck and Vogel (2008), reprinted by permission of Oxford University Press.

Another difference between visual STM and LTM is their capacity to store complex stimuli. As the Phillips's (1974) study showed, as the matrices became more complex, performance declined, whereas visual LTM can store a huge amount of complexity. Consider for example what you can recall of the contents of your own kitchen, the faces of your parents, or the colors of fruit and animals. Our visual LTM clearly holds a vast amount of information about the world around us.

Another difference between visual STM and LTM is in encoding speed. This is quite rapid for visual STM. Figure 3.6 shows the results of a study by Vogel, Woodman and Luck (2006) who presented arrays of one to four colored squares, interrupting the display with a mask, after delays ranging from 100 to 350 ms. As Figure 3.6 shows, participants were able to register individual objects at a rate of approximately 50 ms per stimulus, leveling off in this study at around a capacity of 2.5 squares. In contrast, visual LTM tends to benefit from longer exposure, in line with the total time hypothesis (see p. 108), with the Standing (Standing et al., 1970) study presenting stimuli for 10 seconds each, and the later studies described by Brady et al. (2011) typically using 3 to 5 seconds per picture.

Active rehearsal in visual STM

Visual STM appears to benefit from an active attempt to maintain an item in the focus of attention. McCollough, Machizawa and Vogel (2007) have used event-related potentials (ERPs) to study this by measuring brain activity during the delay between presentation and test in a visual STM study. They asked participants to remember items presented on one side of the visual field, observing electrophysiological activity starting some 200 ms later which persisted until the test item was presented (see Figure 3.7). They found that the amount of activation increased with number of items up to a maximum of around four and that unsuccessful trials tended to be associated with a lower level of activation. A study by Vogel, McCollough and Machizawa (2005) provided further evidence for their suggestion that such activity reflected the operation of short-term visual memory. They studied a range of participants who varied in their capacity to perform the visual STM task, showing a direct association between their neurophysiological measure and their participants' memory performance.

What is stored in visual STM?

Most of the studies described so far involve relatively simple stimuli, typically colored

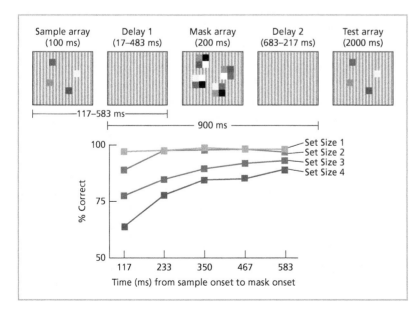

Figure 3.6 Rate of uptake of information varies with number of items in the stimulus set, with performance reaching a ceiling of around 600 milliseconds. From Vogel, Woodman and Luck (2006). Copyright © American Psychological Association. Reproduced with permission.

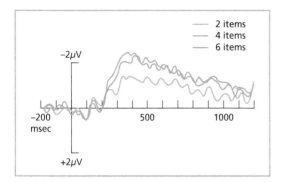

Figure 3.7 The effect of memory load on brain activity. Event-related potentials (ERPs) began some 200ms following presentation of a visual stimulus array and persisted until the test item. Level of activation increased with stimulus load up to four items, assumed to be the limit of capacity. Data from McCollough et al. (2007). Copyright © 2007, with permission from Elsevier.

squares. What happens when stimuli are allowed to vary on more than one dimension? This was studied by Vogel, Woodman and Luck (2001) who used the stimuli that varied on a range of dimensions such as orientation, color, width, and texture.

Vogel et al. found that people were able to combine several features into a single object, with little apparent cost. This may not apply for more complex stimuli such as objects made up from two or more components. If this were not the case, there would be no complexity effects and people would be able to remember 8 × 8 matrices as well as 4 × 4, which Phillips (1974) showed was not the case. But what constitutes an object?

As noted earlier, the visual system processes the world through a range of separate sensory channels, with shape, color, and movement, for example, all being detected by different neural systems. The fact that we experience an object such as a red square means that the *separate* features of color and shape that are present in the stimulus, must *then* have been recombined, a process known as "binding." The fact that binding has occurred can be shown as follows: Suppose we have a range of different shapes (e.g. square, circle, triangle) and a range of different colors (e.g. red, green, blue) that are combined and presented as colored shapes.

People can be asked to remember only the colors in an array, or just the shapes, or both bound together as a single object such as a red triangle. Suppose we present a red triangle, a blue square and a green circle and then test retention of color by presenting a red patch. Participants should say "yes" it has occurred, whereas a yellow patch should evoke a "no" response. Similarly with a shape only condition, a square should evoke "yes," a diamond "no." Participants might, however, be asked to remember the binding or combination of shape and color, in this case a red triangle should evoke "yes" but a red circle "no," since although red and circle have both been presented, they have not been bound together into a red circle. When participants perform these three tasks, the binding condition is often no worse than the harder of the two single-feature conditions, suggesting that the additional process of binding shape and color may operate automatically, although this conclusion was questioned by the results of Wheeler and Treisman (2002) using a different variant of the change detection task.

Allen, Baddeley and Hitch (2006) took a different approach to the question of whether attentional resources are needed to form such bindings, proposing that if this were the case, then giving people an attentionally demanding task to perform at the same time should interfere more with the binding condition than with the conditions where only separate features needed to be maintained. Our results are shown in Figure 3.8. As is often the case, colors appear to be easiest to remember, shapes somewhat harder, and bound features nonsignificantly harder again. In each case, a concurrent attentional task interfered with performance, but crucially, the impairment was no greater in the binding condition than it was in the single-feature cases. The act of binding appears to be relatively automatic, although remembering is clearly not, as all conditions suffer from the additional task. We were somewhat surprised at this result, but found it to replicate, and moved on to more demanding binding tasks, for example separating the color and shape spatially, a patch of color next to a shape, requiring participants to combine them in to a bound shape in their "mind's eye," or presenting the shape visually

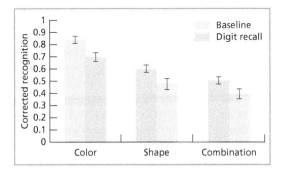

Figure 3.8 Effect of a demanding concurrent task on retention of colors, shapes, and colored shapes. The attentional disruption did not differ across conditions, suggesting that the process of binding shape and color is automatic. From Allen et al. (2006). Copyright © American Psychological Association. Reproduced with permission.

and the color auditorily. Despite this, we still found that the binding process did not depend on general executive resources (Karlson, Allen, Baddeley, & Hitch, 2010).

Does this mean that visual STM is totally divorced from attention? We think not. Chun and Johnson (2011) draw a distinction between two types of attention: one type is concerned with our capacity to direct and control the flow of *sensory* information from the world around us, perhaps best seen as an aspect of perception; a second type concerns the internally oriented aspects of attentional control. These are discussed in the next chapter through the concept of the *central executive* component of working memory. Our results suggest that this system does play a role in overall memory performance, which is impaired when an

executive load such as concurrent counting is required; the fact that the extra load does not disrupt binding, however, suggests that such binding is relatively automatic.

The visual–spatial distinction

We have made a distinction between spatial STM—remembering *where*—and object memory—remembering *what*. In practice, these two systems work together but tasks have been developed that particularly emphasize one or other of these two forms of visuo-spatial memory. A classic *spatial* task is the block tapping test in which the participant is faced with an array of nine blocks (Figure 3.9). The experimenter taps a number of blocks in sequence and the participant attempts to imitate this, with the length of sequence increasing until performance breaks down. This is known as *Corsi span*, after the Canadian neuropsychologist who invented it, and is typically around five blocks, usually about two items below digit span.

Visual span can be measured using a series of matrix patterns of the type used by Phillips (1974) in which half the cells are filled and half left blank. The participant is shown a pattern and asked to reproduce it by marking the filled cells in an empty matrix. Testing starts with a simple 2 × 2 pattern, the number of cells in the matrix is gradually increased to a point at which performance breaks down, usually around the point at which the matrix reaches around 16 cells.

Evidence for the distinction between these two measures of spatial and visual span comes from studies in which a potentially interfering activity is inserted between presentation and

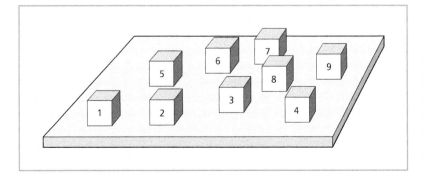

Figure 3.9 The Corsi test of visuo-spatial memory span. The experimenter taps a sequence of blocks and the participant seated opposite attempts to imitate. The numbers are there to help the experimenter.

test. When this involves spatial processing, such as sequentially tapping a series of keys, Corsi span is reduced; pattern span is more disrupted by a visual processing task such as viewing shapes (Della Sala, Gray, Baddeley, Allamano, & Wilson, 1999).

Visual STM is not of course limited to remembering patterns, but also involves shapes and colors. This is shown particularly clearly in a series of studies by Klauer and Zhao (2004) in which they contrast a spatial task that involves remembering the location of a white dot on a black background, and a visual task involving memory for Chinese ideographs. In each case,

the stimulus is presented and followed by a 10-second retention interval, after which participants must choose which of eight test items has just been presented. During the 10-second delay, participants perform either a spatial or a visual task. In the spatial task, 12 asterisks are presented, with 11 moving randomly and the twelfth stationary; the task is to identify the stationary item. The visual interfering task involves processing a series of colors, seven of which are variants of one color, perhaps red, whereas one, the target, is in the blue range. As shown in Figure 3.10, the spatial location of dots was disrupted by movement but not color, whereas ideographs showed the opposite effect.

Neuropsychological approaches to the study of short-term memory

In 1966, Brenda Milner reported the case of the young man, HM, who you may recall had had the misfortune to suffer from intractable epilepsy (see Chapter 2, p. 25).

Deficits in verbal short-term memory

The study of a relatively small number of patients with a very pure deficit in verbal STM has played a major role in theoretical development of the field. It began with a study by Tim Shallice and Elizabeth Warrington (1970) of patient KF who had a digit span of only two items, and showed little recency in free recall. Other patients were subsequently identified who showed an equivalent pattern (Vallar & Shallice, 1990). Shallice and Warrington's patient proved not to have a general deficit in STM, but rather a specific phonological STM deficit. Consequently, his performance was much better when his digit span was tested using visual presentation, consistent with his preserved visual memory as tested on the Corsi block tapping test. A similar pattern was

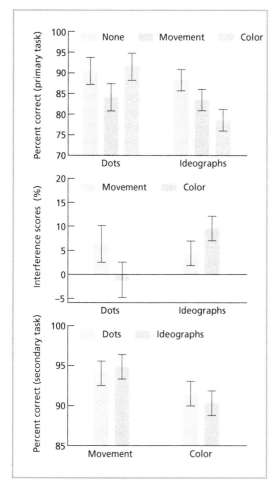

Figure 3.10 Memory for dot location and for Chinese ideographs. Spatial memory is disrupted by movement and pattern memory by color. Data from Klauer and Zhao (2004).

KEY TERM

Corsi block tapping: Visuo-spatial counterpart to digit span involving an array of blocks that the tester taps in a sequence and the patient attempts to copy.

shown by patient PV (Basso, Spinnler, Vallar, & Zanobia, 1982; Vallar & Baddeley, 1987), who developed a very pure and specific deficit in phonological STM following a stroke. Her intellect and language were otherwise unimpaired, but she had a digit span of two and failed to show either a phonological similarity or word length effect in verbal STM.

As is characteristic of such patients, PV showed a grossly reduced recency effect in immediate verbal free recall. She did, however, show normal long-term recency. This was tested using a task involving the solution of a series of anagram puzzles, followed by an unexpected request for recall (Vallar, Papagno, & Baddeley, 1991). Both PV and control patients showed a clear recency effect with better recall of later solutions, even though

recall was unexpected and had been followed by the need to tackle later anagrams. This pattern suggests that it is not PV's capacity to use a recency strategy that is impaired, but rather her capacity to use this to boost immediate verbal memory, which presumably relies on a phonological or verbal/lexical code.

Deficits in visuo-spatial short-term memory

Whereas some patients such as KF and PV have a deficit that is limited to verbal STM, other patients show the opposite pattern with normal verbal STM and impaired performance on either visual or spatial STM measures. One such patient, LH, had suffered a head injury

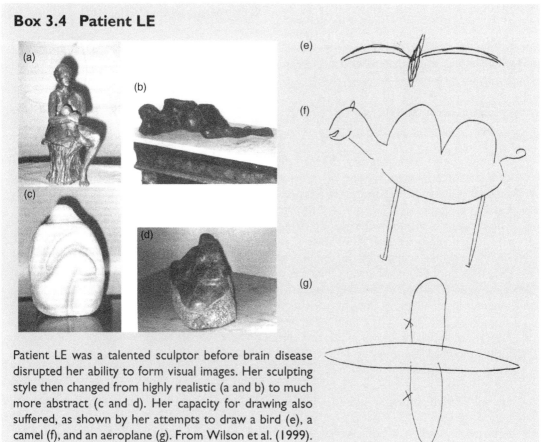

Box 3.4 Patient LE

(a)

(b)

(c)

(d)

(e)

(f)

(g)

Patient LE was a talented sculptor before brain disease disrupted her ability to form visual images. Her sculpting style then changed from highly realistic (a and b) to much more abstract (c and d). Her capacity for drawing also suffered, as shown by her attempts to draw a bird (e), a camel (f), and an aeroplane (g). From Wilson et al. (1999). Copyright © Psychology Press.

in a traffic accident and was grossly impaired in his capacity to remember colors or shapes. However, he had excellent memory for spatial information such as locations and routes (Farah, Hammond, Levine, & Calvanio, 1988). Another patient, LE, suffered brain damage as a result of lupus erythematosus. She also had excellent spatial memory and was well able to drive an unfamiliar route between her home and the laboratory where her cognitive skills were tested. However, she did have impaired visual memory, coupled with a grossly impaired capacity to draw from memory (Wilson, Baddeley, & Young, 1999). She was a talented sculptor, who found that she had lost her capacity to visualize. She could not remember what her earlier sculptures looked like and dramatically changed her style (Box 3.4).

Other cases occur whose visual STM is preserved, but who have impaired spatial memory. Carlesimo, Perri, Turriziani, Tomaiuolo, and Caltagirone (2001) describe patient MV, who suffered damage to the right frontal lobe following a stroke, whose visual memory performance was normal, but who was very impaired on the Corsi block tapping span and on a task requiring STM for imaging a path through a matrix. Luzzatti, Vecchi, Agazzi, Cesa-Bianchi, and Vergani (1998) report a similar case in which progressive deterioration of the right hemisphere led to spatial memory deficits on tasks such as describing the location of landmarks in her home town, while having a good memory for colors and shapes.

You might have noticed that the deficits shown by patients with visuo-spatial STM problems tend to go beyond the simple storage of visual and spatial stimuli, involving more complex tasks such as creating and manipulating mental images and using these in complex tasks, such as sculpting and spatial orientation. They have, in other words, led to deficits in both STM and working memory, the topic of the next chapter.

KEY TERM

Visuo-spatial STM: Retention of visual and/or spatial information over brief periods of time.

SUMMARY

- The term short-term memory (STM) refers to the temporary storage of relatively small amounts of information, whereas working memory (WM) is a complex system that is capable of both storing and manipulating information.
- Early approaches to STM involved the digit span and related sequential verbal tasks.
- The concept of a phonological loop explains verbal STM by assuming a temporary store and an articulatory rehearsal process.
- It gives a simple account of the phonological similarity effect, the word length effect, and the effect on these of subvocal rehearsal.
- It is assumed to help in learning new words and also in controlling actions.
- Inherent in the memory span task is the problem of serial order and how it is maintained, a problem that has led to a number of detailed models.
- Free recall typically shows a marked recency effect, which has resulted in a number of influential models applied to both STM and LTM.
- Most current studies of visual STM focus on simple stimuli such as colors and shapes and the question of how these are bound into unified colored shapes.
- Spatial STM is separable from its visual equivalent and depends on somewhat different neural systems.
- Laboratory studies of both verbal and visual STM have been extended and enriched by studies of patients with STM deficits.

The concept of a phonological loop attempts to explain a range of major findings in verbal STM. What are they and what are the weaknesses of the basic model.

How can a parallel system like the brain remember serial order?

What is the evidence for separate storage of visual and spatial information?

FURTHER READING

Logie, R. H. (1995). *Visuo-spatial working memory*. Hove, UK: Lawrence Erlbaum Associates. An account of visual STM from a multicomponent working memory perspective.

Luck, S. J., & Vogel, E. K. (1997). The capacity of visual working memory for features and conjunctions. *Nature, 390,* 279–281. An important paper that forms a link between the study of visual attention and visual STM.

Melton, A. W. (1963). Implications of short-term memory for a general theory of memory. *Journal of Verbal Learning and Verbal Behavior, 2,* 1–21. A classic paper presenting an interpretation of STM in terms of stimulus–response interference theory.

Vallar, G. (2006). Memory systems: The case of phonological short-term memory. A festschrift for *Cognitive Neuropsychology*. *Cognitive Neuropsychology, 23,* 135–155. An explanation and account of phonological loop from the viewpoint of neuropsychology.

Waugh, N. C., & Norman, D. A. (1965). Primary memory. *Psychological Review, 72,* 89–104. Another classic paper presenting an information-processing alternative to interference theory.

REFERENCES

Allen, R., Baddeley, A. D., & Hitch, G. J. (2006). Is the binding of visual features in working memory resource-demanding? *Journal of Experimental Psychology: General, 135,* 298–313.

Baddeley, A. D. (1966a) Short-term memory for word sequences as a function of acoustic, semantic and formal similarity. *Quarterly Journal of Experimental Psychology, 18,* 362–365.

Baddeley, A. D. (1966b). The influence of acoustic and semantic similarity on long-term memory for word sequences. *Quarterly Journal of Experimental Psychology, 18,* 302–309.

Baddeley, A. D., & Hitch, G. J. (1974). Working memory. In G. A. Bower (Ed.), *The psychology of learning and motivation: Advances in research and theory.* (Vol. 8, pp. 47–89). New York: Academic Press.

Baddeley, A. D., & Hitch, G. (1977). Recency re-examined. In S. Dornic (Ed.), *Attention and performance* (Vol. VI, pp. 647–667). Hillsdale, NJ: Lawrence Erlbaum Associates.

Baddeley, A. D., Chincotta, D., Stafford, L., & Turk, D. (2002). Is the word length effect in STM entirely attributable to output delay? Evidence from serial recognition. *Quarterly Journal of Experimental Psychology, 55A,* 353–369.

Baddeley, A. D., Thomson, N., & Buchanan, M. (1975). Word length and the structure of short-term memory. *Journal of Verbal Learning and Verbal Behavior, 14,* 575–589.

Basso, A. H., Spinnler, G., Vallar, G., & Zanobia, E. (1982). Left hemisphere damage and selective impairment of auditory verbal short-term memory: A case study. *Neuropsychologica, 20,* 263–274.

Bjork, R. A., & Whitten, W. B. (1974). Recency-sensitive retrieval processes. *Cognitive Psychology, 6,* 173–189.

Brady, T. F., Konkle, T., & Alvarez, G. A. (2011). A review of visual memory capacity: Beyond individual items and toward structured representations. *Journal of Vision 11*, 1–4.

Brown, G. D. A., Neath, I., & Chater, N. (2007). A temporal ratio model of memory. *Psychological Review, 114*, 539–576.

Burgess, N., & Hitch, G. J. (1999). Memory for serial order: A network model of the phonological loop and its timing. *Psychological Review, 106*, 551–581.

Burgess, N., & Hitch, G. J. (2006). A revised model of short-term memory and long-term learning of verbal sequences. *Journal of Memory and Language, 55*, 627–652.

Caplan, D., Rochon, E., & Waters, G. S. (1992). Articulatory and phonological determinants of word-length effects in span tasks. *Quarterly Journal of Experimental Psychology, 45A*, 177–192.

Carlesimo G.A., Perri R., Turriziani P., Tomaiuolo F., & Caltagirone, C. (2001). Remembering what but not where: Independence of spatial and visual working memory in the human brain. *Cortex, 37*, 519–534.

Chun, M. M., & Johnson, M. K. (2011). Memory: Enduring traces of perceptual and reflective attention. *Neuron, 72*, 520–535.

Colle, H. A. (1980). Auditory encoding in visual short-term recall: Effects of noise intensity and spatial location. *Journal of Verbal Learning and Verbal Behavior, 19*, 722–735.

Colle, H. A., & Welsh, A. (1976). Acoustic masking in primary memory. *Journal of Verbal Learning and Verbal Behavior, 15*, 17–32.

Conrad, R. (1964). Acoustic confusion in immediate memory. *British Journal of Psychology, 55*, 75–84.

Conrad, R., & Hull, A. J. (1964). Information, acoustic confusion and memory span. *British Journal of Psychology, 55*, 429–432.

Cowan, N. (2001). The magical number 4 in short-term memory: A reconsideration of mental storage capacity. *Behavioral and Brain Sciences, 24*, 87–114; discussion 114–185.

Cowan, N., Day, L., Saults, J. S., Keller, T. A., Johnson, T., & Flores, L. (1992). The role of verbal output time and the effects of word-length on immediate memory. *Journal of Memory and Language, 31*, 1–17.

Crowder, R. G. (1976). *Principles of learning and memory*. Hillsdale, NJ: Lawrence Erlbaum Associates.

Della Sala, S., & Logie, R. H. (2002). Neuropsychological impairments of visual and spatial working memory. In A. D. Baddeley, M. D. Kopelman, & B. A. Wilson (Eds.), *Handbook of memory disorders*. (2nd edn., pp. 271–292). Chichester: Wiley.

Della Sala, S., Gray, C., Baddeley, A., Allamano, N., & Wilson, L. (1999). Pattern span: A tool for unwelding visuo-spatial memory. *Neuropsychologia, 37*, 1189–1199.

Elliot, D., & Madalena, J. (1987). The influence of premovement visual information on manual aiming. *Quarterly Journal of Experimental Psychology, 39A*, 542–559.

Engle, R. W., & Kane, M. J. (2004). Executive attention, working memory capacity and two-factor theory of cognitive control. In B. Ross (Ed.), *The psychology of learning and motivation.* (pp. 145–199). New York: Elsevier.

Farah, M. J., Hammond, K. M., Levine, D. N., & Calvanio, R. (1988). Visual and spatial mental imagery: Dissociable systems of representation. *Cognitive Psychology, 20*(4), 439–462.

Farrell, S., & Lewandowsky, S. (2002). An endogenous model of ordering in serial recall. *Psychonomic Bulletin and Review, 9*, 59–60.

Farrell, S., & Lewandowsky, S. (2003). Dissimilar items benefit from phonological similarity in serial recall. *Journal of Experimental Psychology: Learning, Memory and Cognition, 29*, 838–849.

Glanzer, M. (1972). Storage mechanisms in recall. In G. H. Bower (Ed.), *The psychology of learning and motivation: Advances in research and theory* (Vol. 5). New York: Academic Press.

Glanzer, M., & Cunitz, A. R. (1966). Two storage mechanisms in free recall. *Journal of Verbal Learning and Verbal Behavior, 5*, 351–360.

Glenberg, A. M., Bradley, M. M., Stevenson, J. A., Kraus, T. A., Tkachuk, M. J., Gretz, A. L., et al. (1980). A two-process account of long-term serial position effects. *Journal of Experimental Psychology: Human Learning and Memory, 6*, 355–369.

Goldman-Rakic, P. S. (1996). The prefrontal landscape: Implications of functional architecture for understanding human mentation and the central executive. *Philosophical Transactions of the Royal Society (Biological Sciences), 351*, 1445–1453.

Henderson, J. M. (2008). Eye movements in scene memory. In S. J. Luck & A. Hollingworth (Eds.), *Visual Memory* (pp. 87–123). Oxford: Oxford University Press.

Henson, R. N. A. (1998). Short-term memory for serial order. The Start-End Model. *Cognitive Psychology, 36*, 73–137.

Hollingworth, A. (2008). Visual memory for natural scenes. In S. J. Luck & A. Hollingworth (Eds.), *Visual Memory* (pp. 123–163). Oxford: Oxford University Press.

Hulme, C., Neath, I., Stuart, G., Shostak, L., Suprenant, A. M., & Brown, G. D. A. (2006). The distinctiveness of the word-length. *Journal of Experimental Psychology: Learning, Memory and Cognition, 32,* 586–594.

Jacobs, J. (1887). Experiments in "prehension". *Mind, 12,* 75–79.

Jones, D. M. (1993). Objects, streams and threads of auditory attention. In A. D. Baddeley & L. Weiskrantz (Eds.), *Attention: Selection, awareness and control* (pp. 87–104). Oxford: Clarendon Press.

Jones, D. M., & Macken, W. J. (1993). Irrelevant tones produce an irrelevant speech effect: Implications for phonological coding in working memory. *Journal of Experimental Psychology: Learning, Memory and Cognition, 19,* 369–381.

Jones, D. M., & Macken, W. J. (1995). Phonological similarity in the irrelevant sound effect: Within- or between-stream similarity. *Journal of Experimental Psychology: Learning, Memory, and Cognition, 21,* 103–115.

Jones, D. M., Macken, W. J., & Murray, A. C. (1993). Disruption of visual short-term memory by changing-state auditory stimuli: The role of segmentation. *Memory and Cognition, 21*(3), 318–366.

Karlson, P., Allen, R. J., Baddeley, A. D., & Hitch, G. J. (2010). Binding across space and time in visual working memory. *Memory and Cognition, 38,* 292–303.

Klauer, K. C., & Zhao, Z. (2004). Double dissociations in visual and spatial short-term memory. *Journal of Experimental Psychology: General, 133,* 355–381.

Lashley, K. S. (1951). The problem of serial order in behavior. In L. A. Jeffress (Ed.), *Cerebral mechanisms in behavior: The Hixon symposium.* New York: John Wiley.

Le Compte, D. C., & Shaibe, D. M. (1997). On the irrelevance of phonological similarity to the irrelevant speech effect. *Quarterly Journal of Experimental Psychology, 50A,* 100–118.

Lewandowsky, S., Brown, G. D. A., Wright, T., & Nimmo, L. M. (2006). Timeless memory: Evidence against temporal distinctiveness models of short-term memory for serial order. *Journal of Memory and Language, 54,* 20–38.

Luck, S. J., & Vogel, E. K. (1997). The capacity of visual working memory for features and conjunctions. *Nature, 390,* 279–281.

Luzzatti, C., Vecchi, T., Agazzi, D., Cesa-Bianchi, M., & Vergani, C. (1998). A neurological dissociation between preserved visual and impaired spatial processing in mental imagery. *Cortex, 34,* 461–469.

McCollough, A. W., Machizawa, M. G., & Vogel, E. K. (2007). Electrophysiological measures of maintaining representations in visual working memory. *Cortex, 43,* 77–94.

Meiser, T., & Klauer, K. C. (1999). Working memory and changing-state hypothesis. *Journal of Experimental Psychology: Learning, Memory and Cognition, 25*(5), 1272–1299.

Miller, G. A. (1956). The magical number seven, plus or minus two: Some limits on our capacity for processing information. *Psychological Review, 63,* 81–97.

Milner, B. (1966). Amnesia following operation on the temporal lobes. In C. W. M. Whitty, & O. L. Zangwill (Eds.), *Amnesia* (pp. 109–133). London: Butterworths.

Miyake, A., & Shah, P. (Eds.). (1999). *Models of working memory: Mechanisms of active maintenance and executive control.* New York: Cambridge University Press.

Miyake, A., Friedman, N. P., Emerson, M. J., Witzki, A. H., Howerter, A., & Wager, T. D. (2000). The unity and diversity of executive functions and their contributions to complex "frontal lobe" tasks: A latent variable analysis. *Cognitive Psychology, 41,* 49–100.

Murdock, B. B., Jr. (1962). The serial position effect in serial recall. *Journal of Experimental Psychology, 64,* 482–488.

Nairne, J. S. (1988). A framework for interpreting recency effects in immediate serial recall. *Memory and Cognition, 16,* 343–352.

Nairne, J. S. (1990). A feature model of immediate memory. *Memory and Cognition, 18,* 251–269.

Neath, I., & Nairne, J. S. (1995). Word-length effects in immediate memory: Overwriting trace-decay theory. *Psychonomic Bulletin and Review, 2,* 429–441.

Neath, I., & Surprenant, A. (2003). *Human memory: An introduction to research, data and theory.* (2nd edn.). Belmont, CA: Wadsworth.

Nimmo, L. M., & Lewandowsky, S. (2006). Distinctiveness revisited: Unpredictable temporal isolation does benefit short-term serial recall of heard or seen events. *Memory and Cognition, 34,* 1368–1375.

Norris, D., Baddeley, A. D., & Page, M. P. A. (2004). Retrospective effects of irrelevant speech on serial recall from short-term memory. *Journal of Experimental Psychology, 30,* 1093–1105.

Page, M. P. A., & Norris, D. (1998). The primacy model: A new model of immediate serial recall. *Psychological Review, 105,* 761–781.

Page, M. P. A., & Norris, D. (2003). The irrelevant sound effect: What needs modeling, and a tentative model. *Quarterly Journal of Experimental Psychology, 56A,* 1289–1300.

Phillips, W. A. (1974). On the distinction between sensory storage and short-term visual memory. *Perception and Psychophysics, 16*, 283–290.

Pinto, A., da Costa, & Baddeley, A. D. (1991). Where did you park your car? Analysis of a naturalistic long-term recency effect. *European Journal of Cognitive Psychology, 3*, 297–313.

Postman, L., & Phillips, L. W. (1965). Short-term temporal changes in free recall. *Quarterly Journal of Experimental Psychology, 17*, 132–138.

Rundus, D. (1971). Analysis of rehearsal process in free recall. *Journal of Experimental Psychology, 89*, 63–77.

Ryan, J. (1969). Temporal grouping, rehearsal and short-term memory. *Quarterly Journal of Experimental Psychology, 21*, 148–155.

Salame, P., & Baddeley, A. D. (1982). Disruption of short-term memory by unattended speech: Implications for the structure of working memory. *Journal of Verbal Learning and Verbal Behavior, 21*, 150–164.

Shallice, T., & Warrington, E. K. (1970). Independent functioning of verbal memory stores: A neuropsychological study. *Quarterly Journal of Experimental Psychology, 22*, 261–273.

Standing, L., Conezio, J., & Haber, R. N. (1970). Perception and memory for pictures: Single-trial learning of 2500 visual stimuli. *Psychonomic Science, 19*, 73–74.

Tam, L., & Ward, G. (2000). A recency-based account of the primacy effect in free recall. *Journal of Experimental Psychology: Learning, Memory, and Cognition, 26*, 1589–1625.

Thomson, J. A. (1983). Is continuous visual monitoring necessary in visually-guided locomotion? *Journal of Experimental Psychology, 9*, 427–433.

Vallar, G., & Baddeley, A. D. (1987). Phonological short-term store and sentence processing. *Cognitive Neuropsychology, 4*, 417–438.

Vallar, G., & Papagno, C. (2002). Neuropsychological impairments of verbal short-term memory. In A. D. Baddeley, M. D. Kopelman, & B. A. Wilson (Eds.), *Handbook of memory disorders.* (2nd edn., pp. 249–270). Chichester: Wiley.

Vallar, G., & Shallice, T. (1990). *Neuropsychological impairments of short-term memory*. Cambridge: Cambridge University Press.

Vallar, G., Papagno, C., & Baddeley, A. D. (1991). Long-term recency effects and phonological short-term memory: A neuropsychological case study. *Cortex, 27*, 323–326.

Vogel, E. K., McCollough, A. W., & Machizawa, M. G. (2005). Neural measures reveal individual differences in controlling access to working memory. *Nature 438*, 500–503.

Vogel, E. K., Woodman, G. F., & Luck, S. J. (2001). Storage of features, conjunctions, and objects in visual working memory. *Journal of Experimental Psychology: Human Perception and Performance, 27*(1), 92–114.

Vogel, E. K., Woodman, G. F., & Luck, S. J. (2006). The time course of consolidation in visual working memory. *Journal of Experimental Psychology: Human Perception and Performance, 32*, 1436–1451.

Vogt, S., & Magnussen, D. (2007). Expertise in pictorial perception: Eye-movement patterns and visual memory in artists and laymen. *Perception, 36*, 91–100.

Walker, I., & Hulme, C. (1999). Concrete words are easier to recall than abstract words: Evidence for a semantic contribution to short-term serial recall. *Journal of Experimental Psychology: Learning, Memory and Cognition, 25*, 1256–1271.

Wheeler, M. E., & Treisman, A. M. (2002). Binding in short-term visual memory. *Journal of Experimental Psychology: General, 131*, 48–64.

Wickelgren, W. A. (1964). Size of rehearsal group and short-term memory. *Journal of Experimental Psychology, 68*, 413–419.

Wilson, B. A., Baddeley, A. D., & Young, A. W. (1999). LE, a person who lost her "mind's eye". *Neurocase, 5*, 119–127.

Contents

The modal model   67

The multicomponent model   69

Imagery and the visuo-spatial sketchpad   76

The central executive   78

The episodic buffer   81

Individual differences in working memory   84

Theories of working memory   84

Educational applications   89

The neuroscience of working memory   92

Summary   98

Points for discussion   99

Further reading   99

References   100

CHAPTER 4

WORKING MEMORY

Alan Baddeley

How are you at mental arithmetic? Could you multiply 27 × 3? Try it. Different people use different methods; in my own case, I multiplied the 7 by 3 resulting in 21, then held the 1 in mind and carried the 2, before then going on to multiply 2 × 3, and so forth, interleaving the retrieval of numerical facts, with holding and manipulating the temporary totals. I had, in short, to use working memory, simultaneously holding and processing information. This active use of memory is the focus of the present chapter.

The idea that short-term memory (STM) serves as a working memory was proposed by Atkinson and Shiffrin (1968), who devised the model briefly described in Chapter 1. Because it had a great deal in common with many similar models that were popular at the time, it became known as the *modal model*.

THE MODAL MODEL

As Figure 4.1 illustrates, the modal model assumes that information comes in from the environment and is processed first by a parallel series of brief temporary sensory memory systems, including the iconic and echoic memory processes discussed in Chapter 1. From here, information flows into the *short-term store*, which forms a crucial part of the system, not only feeding information into and out of the *long-term store*, but also acting as a *working memory*, responsible for selecting and operating strategies, for rehearsal,

and generally serving as a global workspace. Atkinson and Shiffrin (1968) created a mathematical simulation of their model, concentrating on the processes involved in the rote rehearsal of verbal items and on the role of rehearsal in the transfer of information from the short-term to the long-term store. For a while, the modal model seemed to offer a neat solution to the question of how information is manipulated and stored. Before long, however, problems began to appear.

One problem concerned the assumption that simply holding items in the short-term store for long enough would guarantee learning. This view was challenged by Craik and Lockhart (1972), who proposed instead the principle of levels of processing, which maintains that learning depends on the way in which material is processed, rather than time in short-term storage. This important theory is discussed in Chapter 6.

The Atkinson and Shiffrin model also had difficulty in accounting for some of the neuropsychological evidence. You may recall that Shallice and Warrington (1970) described a patient who appeared to have a grossly defective short-term store, a digit span of two and

KEY TERM

Levels of processing: The theory proposed by Craik and Lockhart that asserts that items that are more deeply processed will be better remembered.

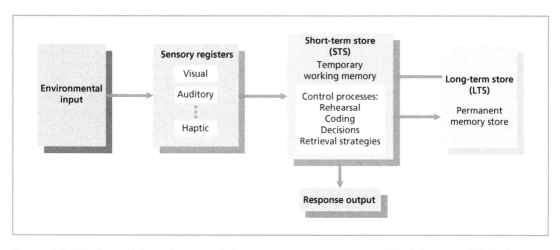

Figure 4.1 The flow of information through the memory systems as conceived by Atkinson and Shiffrin's modal model. Copyright © 1971 Scientific American. Reproduced with permission.

no recency effect. According to the modal model, the short-term store plays a crucial role in transferring information into and out of long-term memory (LTM). This STM deficit should therefore lead to greatly impaired long-term learning in such patients. Furthermore, if the short-term store acts as a general working memory, these patients should suffer severe disruption of such complex cognitive activities as reasoning and comprehension. This was not the case: one patient with grossly impaired STM was a very efficient secretary, another ran a shop and raised a family, and a third was a taxi driver (Vallar & Shallice, 1990). In short, they showed no signs of suffering from a general working memory deficit.

Within a very few years, the concept of STM had moved from simplicity to complexity. A wide range of new experimental techniques had been invented, but none of them mapped in a simple straightforward way onto any of the original theories proposed to account for the wide range of studies of STM. At this point, many investigators abandoned the field in favor of the study of LTM, opting instead to work on the exciting new developments in the study of levels of processing and of semantic memory.

At just the point that problems with modal model were becoming evident, Graham Hitch and I were beginning our first research grant in which we had undertaken to look at the relationship between STM and LTM. Rather than attempt to find a way through the thicket of experimental techniques and theories that characterized both fields, we opted to ask a very simple question, namely, if the system or systems underpinning STM have a function, what might it be? If, as was generally assumed, it acted as a working memory, then blocking it should interfere with both long-term learning and complex cognitive activities such as reasoning and comprehending. Not having access to patients with this specific STM deficit, we attempted to simulate such patients using our undergraduate students, a process that happily did not require physical removal of the relevant part of their brain, but did involve keeping it busy while at the same time requiring participants to reason, comprehend, and learn (Baddeley & Hitch, 1974).

Virtually all theories agreed that if verbal STM was characterized by any single task, that task was digit span, with longer sequences of digits occupying more of the capacity of the underlying short-term storage system. We therefore combined digit span with the simultaneous performance of a range of other tasks such as reasoning, learning, and comprehension, which were assumed to depend on this limited-capacity system. Participants were given a sequence of digits that they were continually required to rehearse out loud at the same time as they were performing other cognitive tasks.

Box 4.1 Examples from the grammatical reasoning test used by Baddeley and Hitch (1974)

		True	False
A follows B	B → A		
B precedes A	A → B		
B is followed by A	B → A		
A is preceded by B	B → A		
A is not preceded by B	A → B		
B does not follow A	A → B		

Answers: T, F, T, T, T, F.

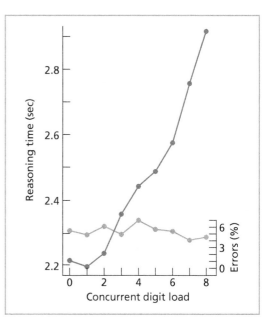

Figure 4.2 Speed and accuracy of grammatical reasoning as a function of concurrent digit load. From Baddeley (1986). Copyright © Oxford University Press. Reproduced with permission.

By varying the number of digits being held, it should be possible to vary the demand on this limited-capacity system. If it did indeed reflect a working memory responsible for reasoning and other tasks, then the longer the sequence, the greater the digit load and the greater the interference should be.

One experiment involved presenting a simple reasoning task in which students had to verify a statement about the order of two letters, a test that correlates with verbal intelligence (Baddeley, 1968). The task is shown in Box 4.1. Try it yourself.

Somewhat to our surprise, people were able to do this, even when holding simultaneously and repeating sequences of up to eight digits, beyond memory span for many of those tested. As Figure 4.2 shows, average time to verify the sentences increased systematically with digit load, but not overwhelmingly so. The total time taken with eight digits was about 50% more than baseline. Perhaps more remarkably, the error rate remained constant at around 5%, regardless of concurrent digit load.

What are the implications of these results for the view that the short-term store serves as a working memory? The error rate suggests that performance can go ahead quite effectively regardless of concurrent digit load, whereas the processing time data suggest that there is *some* involvement, although not one of overwhelming magnitude. Results from studies of learning and comprehension gave broadly equivalent results (Baddeley & Hitch, 1974), supporting some kind of working memory hypothesis, but not one that depended entirely on the memory system underpinning digit span.

We therefore proposed a somewhat more complex model which we called *working memory*, a term invented but not further elaborated by Miller, Galanter, and Pribram (1960). The emphasis on "working" aimed to dissociate it from earlier models of STM, which were primarily concerned with storage, and to emphasize its functional role as a system that underpins complex cognitive activities, a system that supports our capacity for mental work and coherent thought.

THE MULTICOMPONENT MODEL

The model we proposed had three components (Figure 4.3); one of these, the *phonological loop*, is assumed to be specialized for holding

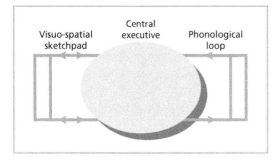

Figure 4.3 The initial Baddeley and Hitch working memory model. The double arrows are intended to represent parallel transfer of information to and from the sketchpad, and the single arrows the serial rehearsal process within the phonological loop.

sequences of acoustic or speech-based items. A second subsystem, the visuo-spatial sketchpad performs a similar function for visually and/or spatially encoded items and arrays. The whole system is controlled by the *central executive*, an attentionally limited system that selects and manipulates material in the subsystems, serving as a controller that runs the whole show. One way of gaining a feeling for the concept is to try the following: Think of your current house or apartment, and work out how many windows it has. Then move on to the next paragraph.

How many windows? How did you reach that number? You probably formed some sort of visual image of your house; this relies on the sketchpad. You presumably then counted the windows verbally using the phonological loop. Finally, throughout this process there was a need for your central executive to select and run the strategy. These three components of working memory will be considered in turn, beginning with the phonological loop, which—as mentioned previously—could be regarded

as a model of verbal STM embedded within a more general theory of working memory.

The phonological loop

As we saw in Chapter 3, the phonological loop is basically a model of verbal STM. It accounts for a wide and rich range of findings using a simple model that assumes a temporary store and a verbal rehearsal process. It is not free of critics, but has proved fruitful for over 30 years without—so far—being replaced by a widely accepted better model. But how does it fit into the broader context of working memory? What is it for?

What use is the phonological loop?

On the evidence presented, the phonological loop simply increases span by two or three items on the rather artificial task of repeating back numbers. So what, if any, is its evolutionary significance? Has evolution thoughtfully prepared us for the invention of the telephone? And if not, is the loop anything more than "A pimple on the anatomy of cognitive psychology," as suggested by one critic?

In an attempt to answer this question, two Italian colleagues, Giuseppe Vallar and Costanza Papagno, and I began to study a patient—PV—who had a very pure phonological loop deficit. Her digit span was two items but her intelligence, LTM, and short-term visual memory were excellent. She spoke fluently and her general language skills seemed normal. PV ran a shop, successfully raised a family, and seemed to have few problems in her everyday life. Did she have any areas of major difficulty? If she did, this would give us a clue as to what function was served by her defective phonological loop.

Functions of the phonological loop

We began with the hypothesis that the loop might have evolved to assist language comprehension (Vallar & Baddeley, 1987). PV did have some problems, but only with a particular type of long sentence, where it is necessary to hold on to the first few words until the end of the sentence in order to understand it. This was not enough to create problems for PV in everyday life, and it is hard to see evolution favoring the development of a special subsystem to support the use of long-winded sentences.

A second hypothesis was that the phonological loop system has evolved to help us learn language. People who have acquired a phonological loop deficit when adult, as is the case for PV, would experience few difficulties because they would already have mastered their native language. However, if they were required to learn a new language, they might have problems. We investigated this by requiring PV to learn to associate each of eight Russian words with their equivalent in Italian, PV's native language (Baddeley, Papagno, & Vallar, 1988). With spoken presentation, after ten trials, all of the control participants had learned all eight Russian words, whereas PV had not learned one (Figure 4.4). Could it simply be that she was amnesic? This was not the case, as when the task involved learning to associate two unrelated native language words such as *castle-bread*, a task that typically relies on semantic coding (Baddeley & Dale, 1966), she was quite unimpaired. Our results thus lent support to the possibility that the phonological loop is involved in language acquisition.

However, while a single case can be extremely informative, it is possible that the individual might be highly atypical, and hence ultimately misleading. Given that STM-deficit patients are rare, we opted to test our hypothesis further by disrupting the phonological loop in normal participants who were attempting to learn foreign language vocabulary. We predicted that disrupting the loop would cause particular problems in learning foreign vocabulary, just as in the case of PV. In one study, articulatory suppression was used (Papagno,

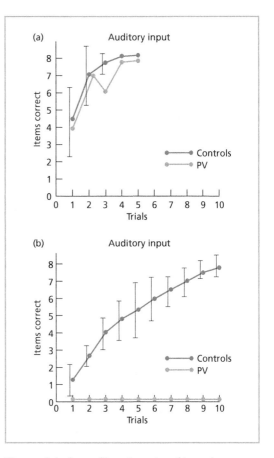

Figure 4.4 Rate of learning pairs of items by patient PV and controls. Her capacity to learn pairs of meaningful words was unimpaired (panel a), but she was not able to learn foreign language vocabulary (panel b). From Baddeley, Papagno, and Vallar (1988). Copyright © Elsevier. Reproduced with permission.

Valentine, & Baddeley, 1991). When participants were required continually to repeat an irrelevant sound during learning, this proved to disrupt foreign language learning, assumed to rely on the phonological loop, but had little effect on learning pairs of native language words. In another study, Papagno and Vallar (1992) varied either the phonological similarity or the length of the foreign words to be learnt, manipulating two factors known to influence the phonological loop. When the responses were foreign words, then similarity and length impaired performance to a much more substantial extent than occurred when both words were in the native language of the participants. The conclusions drawn from PV of the importance of the loop for learning new word forms therefore appeared to be supported. However, they still were confined to adults acquiring a second language. The system would clearly be more important if it also influenced the acquisition by children of their native tongue.

Susan Gathercole and I investigated this question by testing a group of children with a specific language impairment (Gathercole & Baddeley, 1990). These children were 8 years old, had normal nonverbal intelligence, but had the language development of 6-year-olds. Could this reflect a phonological loop deficit? When given a battery of memory tests, they proved to be particularly impaired in their capacity to repeat back unfamiliar pseudo words. Note that this task not only requires participants to hear the nonwords, but also to hold them in memory for long enough to repeat them. On the basis of this, we developed the nonword repetition test in which pseudo words of increasing length are heard and must be repeated (e.g. *ballop*, *woogalamic*, *versatrational*). We tested language-impaired children, other children of the same age with normal language development, and a group of 6-year-olds who were matched for level of language development with the language-impaired group but who, being younger, had a lower level of nonverbal performance. The results are shown in Figure 4.5, from which it is clear that the language-disordered 8-year-old children performed more poorly even than the 6-year-olds. In fact, they were equivalent to 4-year-olds in their nonword repetition capacity. Could their poor nonword repetition performance be related to their delayed language development? Is level of vocabulary related to nonword repetition performance in normal children too?

In an attempt to investigate this, a cohort of children between the ages of 4 and 5 years

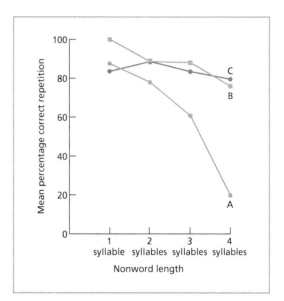

Figure 4.5 Percent correct repetition of nonwords by children with a specific language impairment (A), children of the same age (B), and children matched for language level (C). Adapted from Gathercole and Baddeley (1990).

who were just starting school in Cambridge, England, were tested using the nonword repetition test, together with a test of nonverbal intelligence and a measure of vocabulary. This involved presenting four pictures and pronouncing the name of one of them; the child's task was to point to the appropriate picture. As the test proceeded, the words became less and less common. Testing ended when performance broke down because the child no longer knew the words. Performance on these three tests was then correlated to see to what extent vocabulary was related to intelligence and to nonword repetition. The results are shown in Table 4.1, from which it is clear there was a substantial correlation between the capacity to hear and echo back a word and level of vocabulary development.

Of course, correlation does not mean causation. It is just as plausible to assume that having a good vocabulary will help you repeat back unfamiliar sounds, as it is to assume that capacity for repeating unfamiliar sounds will help you acquire new vocabulary. A study of the development of vocabulary in 5- to 6-year-old children (Gathercole & Baddeley, 1989) suggested that phonological memory was

KEY TERM

Nonword repetition test: A test whereby participants hear and attempt to repeat back nonwords that gradually increase in length.

TABLE 4.1 Relation between vocabulary scores at age 4 and other variables. There is a strong relationship with nonword repetition performance. From Gathercole and Baddeley (1989).

Measures	Correlation coefficient	Simple regression (% variance)	Stepwise regression (% variance)
Chronological age	0.218	5[a]	5[a]
Nonverbal intelligence	0.388	15[b]	13[b]
Nonword repetition	0.525	27[b]	15[b]
Sound mimicry	0.295	9[b]	0
Total	0.578	33[b]	—

[a] $P < 0.05$; [b] $P < 0.01$.

indeed the crucial factor at this stage. However, as children become older they are increasingly able to use existing vocabulary to help learn new words (Baddeley, Gathercole, & Papagno, 1998). This is reflected in the fact that new words that contain letter sequences that resemble fragments of existing vocabulary (e.g. *tramponist*) are easier to repeat back than words that have a more unfamiliar letter structure (e.g. *skiticult*). However, the capacity to further increase vocabulary is better predicted by performance on these unusual words. This is presumably because such words gain less support from existing vocabulary and hence continue to rely on the phonological loop (Gathercole, 1995).

Most of the evidence linking the phonological loop to both native and second language learning has been based on the task of nonword repetition, which has itself been shown to depend not only on verbal STM, but is also correlated with a number of other capacities, such as speech perception, attentional capacity and also *phonological awareness*, the ability to reflect on spoken stimuli, to report on aspects such as rhyme, and to manipulate the incoming items. There are several approaches to testing phonological awareness ranging from rhyme judgments to the more complex task of switching the initial sounds of two words such as *dear–queen* to produce *queer–dean*. This capacity correlates highly with the development of reading skills (Wagner & Torgesen, 1987). A task of this latter complexity is, of course, likely to depend on both the phonological and executive components of working memory, making

it difficult to entangle a causal path, given that native language skills are likely to depend heavily on family background and parental influence. This has led to studies of children learning a second language at school, under more controlled conditions. Service (1992) studied the learning of English by Finnish school children, finding that phonological STM was indeed a good predictor of success.

A more recent attempt to tease apart the factors contributing to second language vocabulary studied the acquisition of English vocabulary by French-speaking school children over a 3-year immersion class in which they were taught all subjects in English, rather than their native French (Nicolay & Poncelet, 2013). A range of measures correlated with English vocabulary acquisition, with phonological STM emerging as the best predictor, particularly over the initial phase. Broadly similar conclusions were reached by Engel de Abreu and Gathercole (2012) in a study of second language learning in bi- and tri-lingual Luxemburgish children.

Whereas the link with vocabulary acquisition is probably the clearest evolutionary application of the phonological loop, it is likely that the loop also facilitates the acquisition of grammar, and probably also of reading (Baddeley et al., 1998; Service, 1992). Indeed, the nonword repetition test is used widely in the diagnosis of dyslexia, although reduced phonological loop capacity is likely to represent only one of a range of variables that can impact on the complex skill of learning to read, with phonological awareness also being important in allowing the child to analyze and break down words, their sounds and their spelling (Wagner & Torgersen, 1987).

The phonological loop and action control

We have so far discussed the loop as a rather limited storage system that plays a relatively passive role in cognition. Miyake and Shah (1999) suggested that this might well under-estimate its importance, and this is proving to be the case. In one study, for example (Baddeley, Chincotta, & Adlam, 2001), we were interested in the capacity to switch attention between two tasks. We used the simple task of adding or subtracting one from a series of digits, thus, given 8, the response should be 9 in one case and 7 in the other. Participants were given a column of additions, a column of subtractions or were required to alternate, adding to the first, subtracting from the second, adding to

---

Box 4.2 Task switching

A simple task: For Column 1, add 1 to each of the ten digits. For Column 2, subtract 1. For Column 3, alternate adding for the first, subtracting for the second, etc. You'll probably find Column 3 slower.

1. Add 1 to each	2. Subtract 1 from each	3. Alternate + − + −
7	6	3
1	8	8
4	2	2
6	3	4
2	4	7
8	7	5
5	5	6
4	9	8
7	4	2
3	8	5

Now repeat the exercise below this time continuously saying the word "rabbit".

1. Add	2. Subtract	3. Alternate
4	2	7
8	9	4
1	6	2
6	8	9
8	3	6
5	9	3
2	4	7
7	2	5
4	5	8
7	3	2

Most people find that suppressing speech by saying an irrelevant word has little effect on Columns 1 and 2, but makes alternation harder. Why do you think this is the case?

Box 4.3 Alexander Luria

The Russian psychologist Alexander Romanovitch Luria developed an ingenious method for studying the influence of language on the control of action. In one experiment, he asked children of different ages to squeeze a bulb when a red light came on, but not to squeeze for a blue light. Before the age of three, children typically press in response to both lights, even though they can report the instruction correctly, and can perform it correctly if given the instruction "press" when the red light comes on but no instruction with the blue light. A few months later, they are themselves able to make the appropriate verbal responses, but still do not perform the action. By age five, they are able both to speak and act appropriately, only later managing to act without giving themselves a verbal cue. Luria also demonstrated that patients with frontal lobe damage could have difficulty with this task, and could be helped through verbal self-cueing.

The influential Russian neuropsychologist Alexander Luria (1902–1977).

the third etc (e.g. 5 →6: 8 →7: 3 →4, etc.). Go to Box 4.2 and try it yourself.

Alternation markedly slows down performance, particularly when participants have to suppress articulation while performing the switching condition, suggesting that they have been relying on a subvocal set of instructions to keep their place. Similar effects have been observed and investigated further by Emerson and Miyake (2003) and by Saeki and Saito (2004), and more recently we have shown that subvocalized self-instruction appears to help in more long-term task switching where it appears to help people resist disruption from earlier habits (Saeki, Baddeley, Hitch, & Saito, 2013).

It is notable that participants in psychological experiments very frequently appear to rely on verbal coding to help them perform the task. This was investigated by two Russian psychologists—Lev Vygotsky (1962) and Alexander Luria (1959)—who emphasized the use of verbal *self-instruction* to control behavior, studying its application to the rehabilitation of brain-damaged patients and to its development in children (Box 4.3). Sadly, Vygotsky and Luria have so far had little direct influence on recent developments in mainstream cognitive psychology. One can only hope that further investigation of the role of speech in the control of action will remedy this.

We have described the development of the phonological loop model in some detail. This is not because it is the only, or indeed the most important, component of working memory; it certainly is not, but it is the component that has been investigated most extensively and, as such, provides an example of how relatively simple experimental tasks can be used to study complex cognitive processes and their practical implications.

We move on now to the visuo-spatial sketchpad, which has been rather less extensively investigated. The sketchpad involves

How would you describe the Taj Mahal? Would vivid, visual imagery be the basis of your description?

visual and spatial STM as described in the previous chapter, but it goes beyond simple storage to include the manipulation of visual and spatial information, often relying heavily on executive resources. The most active area of investigation has been concerned with the topic of visuo-spatial imagery.

IMAGERY AND THE VISUO-SPATIAL SKETCHPAD

Suppose you were asked to describe a famous building such as the Taj Mahal or the White House. How would you do it? Close your eyes and try.

You probably based your description on some form of visuo-spatial representation, a visual image perhaps? An observer might also have seen you using your hands as a spatial supplement to your verbal account. People vary hugely in the extent to which they report having visual imagery. In the late nineteenth century, Sir Francis Galton, a Victorian gentleman, contacted his friends and asked them to remember their breakfast table from that morning, and then describe the experience. Some reported imagery that was almost as vivid as vision, whereas others denied having any visual imagery whatsoever. Such differences in reported vividness appear to have surprisingly little relationship to how well people perform on tasks that would be expected to make heavy demands on visual imagery, such as visual recall (Di Vesta, Ingersoll, & Sunshine, 1971). Those studies that have found any difference tend, somewhat surprisingly, to observe *poorer* performance on visual memory tasks by participants reporting strong visual imagery (Heuer, Fischman, & Reisberg, 1986; Reisberg, Clayton, Heuer, & Fischman, 1986). The reason for this unexpected finding appears to be that people with vivid imagery do not have better *memories*, but use vividness as a sign of the accuracy of their recall and are more likely to misjudge a vivid but erroneous memory to be correct. This raises the question of whether different people have genuinely different subjective experiences, or simply describe their experience differently. Another possibility is that differences in retrieval strategy underpin the different reports. This could represent either differences in stored information, or alternative ways of accessing a common memory, a situation resembling that of a computer that can display the same information numerically, or graphically.

Image manipulation

Figure 4.6 shows a task studied by Shepard and Feng (1972). If the shapes depicted were made out of paper, both could be folded to create a solid, with the shaded area being the base. Your task is to imagine folding the shapes (shown on the left-hand side of Figure 4.6) and decide whether the arrows will meet head on. Try it.

Shepard and Feng found that the time it took participants to come to a solution was systematically related to the number of folds that would have been required.

Tasks like this are often used to select people for jobs that are likely to involve visual or spatial thinking, such as architect and engineer. They also tend to be somewhat better performed by men than by women, who are likely to use a less spatial and more analytic and piecemeal approach (Linn & Petersen, 1985).

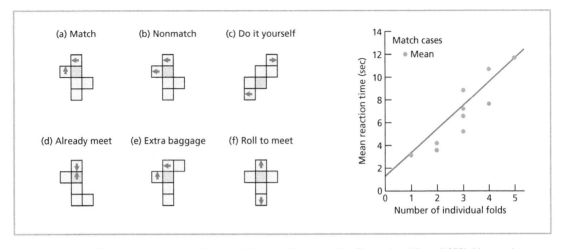

Figure 4.6 Left: Examples of six types of paper folding problems used by Shepard and Feng (1972). Your task is to decide what would happen if the shapes were folded and made into a cube. Would the arrows meet? Right: Average time to decide whether the arrows on the cubes would match as a function of number of imaginary folds necessary to reach that decision. The circles represent each of ten different types of problem. Data from Shepard and Feng (1972).

A study by Hsi, Linn, and Bell (1997) found that female University of California Berkeley engineering students were less good at performing a spatial manipulation test and were also likely to do less well on a difficult graphics course for which 25% of female students obtained either a D or failed grade. Hsi et al. spoke to experienced engineers about the strategies of spatial manipulation they used and, on the basis of this, produced a 1-day intensive course on spatial manipulation strategies. This was highly successful in improving performance to a point at which the gender differences disappeared and virtually no failures occurred.

A number of studies have tried to study spatial manipulation within the laboratory. Finke and Slayton (1988) developed the following task:

First, form an image of the capital letter J. Then imagine capital D. Now rotate the D through 90 degrees to the left and place it on top of the J. What does it look like?

The answer is an umbrella. Pearson, Logie, and Gilhooly (1999) tried to analyze in more detail the processes involved. They gave their participants four, six, or eight symbols (e.g. square, triangle, circle, etc.), requiring them to use them to create an object that they should then name, and afterwards draw. If they had failed to produce an object after 2 minutes, participants were required simply to recall the memorized symbols. The roles of the visuospatial sketchpad and the phonological loop in the task were studied by means of concurrent tasks, using either articulatory suppression to disrupt the loop, or tapping a series of spatial locations to disrupt the sketchpad. Pearson et al. found that spatial tapping disrupted the capacity to create novel objects, suggesting that this aspect depends on the sketchpad, but had no effect on the capacity to remember what shapes were involved. However, the latter was disrupted by articulatory suppression, suggesting that the names of the shapes to be manipulated were held in the phonological loop.

The study by Pearson et al. is a good example of the way in which the visuo-spatial sketchpad and phonological loop can work together to enhance performance. A very striking example of this comes from a study using a group of Japanese experts in mental calculation who are very skilled at using the traditional calculating aid, the abacus, which involves manipulating beads within a framework. Hatano and Osawa (1983a, 1983b) studied calculators who were able to dispense with the actual abacus, relying instead on imagining the abacus. Experts can mentally add and subtract up to 15 numbers, each comprising from 5 to 9 digits. They also have extremely high digit spans, around 16 for forward and 14 for backward recall. However, their enhanced span was limited to digits. Their span for other verbal material, such as consonants, for which the abacus imagery could not be used, was no better than that of a control group. As would be expected if the experts were relying on visuo-spatial imagery, their digit span was markedly disrupted by a concurrent spatial task, unlike control participants, whose performance was more disrupted by articulatory suppression.

Just as spatial activity can disrupt imagery, so imagery can interfere with spatial processing. A striking example of this occurred when I was visiting the US. I was listening to an American football game between UCLA and Stanford and forming a clear image of the game while driving along the San Diego freeway. I suddenly realized that the car was weaving from lane to lane. I switched to music and survived, and on returning to Britain decided to study the effect under slightly less risky conditions. We did indeed find that a spatial task involving keep a stylus in contact with a moving spot of light disrupted STM based on spatial imagery (Baddeley, Grant, Wight, & Thomson, 1973). The interference proved to be spatial in nature rather than visual, since performance was disrupted by the task of tracking the *location* of an *auditory* sound source while blindfolded, but not by making a *visual* but nonspatial brightness judgment (Baddeley & Lieberman, 1980).

Whereas this particular task appears to depend on spatial imagery, more purely visual imagery can also help in verbal recall. A powerful way of learning to associate pairs of words is to combine them into an interactive image; for example, to associate *violin* and *banana*, one might imagine a concert violinist using a large banana as a bow. Such object-based imagery tends to be disrupted by presentation of irrelevant pictures or colors which participants are instructed to ignore (Logie, 1995). Indeed, under appropriate conditions, even a flickering dot pattern can disrupt the use of visual imagery (Quinn & McConnell, 1996a, 1996b).

THE CENTRAL EXECUTIVE

Working memory is assumed to be directed by the central executive, an attentional controller rather than a memory system. Its main mode of operation is assumed to be that proposed by Norman and Shallice (1986), who assumed two modes of control, one of which is automatic and based on existing habits whereas the other depends on an attentionally limited executive. Driving a car would be an example of the first type of semi-automatic control. The activities involved can be relatively complex, so that potential conflicts can occur, for example between continuing to drive and slowing down in response to a traffic signal, or another driver entering the road. There are assumed to be well-learned procedures for resolving such conflicts automatically. Because such behavior is based largely on well-learned habits, it requires little attention. Have you ever had the somewhat worrying experience of arriving at your driving destination with no recollection of how you got there? Were you conscious during the trip? You almost certainly were, but thinking about other matters and leaving the routine decisions to your conflict-resolution system.

However, when automatic conflict resolution is not possible, or when a novel situation arises, for example, a road is closed for repairs, then a second system is called into action, the supervisory attentional system (SAS). This is able to intervene, either in favor of one or other of the competing options or else to activate strategies for seeking alternative solutions. It is the SAS component that is assumed to be crucial to the central executive.

Donald Norman and Tim Shallice had somewhat different purposes in jointly producing their model. On the one hand, Norman was interested in slips of action, whereby a

KEY TERM

Supervisory attentional system (SAS): A component of the model proposed by Norman and Shallice to account for the attentional control of action.

lapse of attention produces unforeseen consequences. These are sometimes trivial, as when you set off on a Saturday morning to drive to the supermarket and find yourself taking your regular route to work instead. On other occasions, such slips of attention can have tragic consequences, as when pilot error can lead to a plane crash. Both of these reflect situations in which the SAS fails to operate when it should.

Shallice, on the other hand, was principally interested in patients with frontal-lobe damage, who appear to have problems of *attentional control*. This is sometimes reflected in perseveration, repetitively performing the same act or making the same mistake repeatedly. Patient RR, for example (Baddeley & Wilson, 1988), was asked during an occupational therapy session to measure and cut a series of lengths of tape. He persistently grasped the tape at the wrong point, leaving very short tape lengths. When this was pointed out, he crossly responded "I know I'm getting it wrong!", but was unable to break out of the incorrect action sequence.

On other occasions, the same patient might continually fail to *focus* attention, simply responding to whatever environmental cues are present. This sometimes leads to what is known as *utilization behavior*, in which the patient uninhibitedly makes use of whatever is around, drinking the tester's cup of tea for example, or on one occasion picking up a hypodermic syringe and attempting to inject the examining doctor! In the absence of control from the SAS, the patient simply reverts to habit-based control, responding automatically to any cues or opportunities afforded by the environment. The frontal lobes are assumed to be the part of the brain necessary for adequate operation of the SAS, with damage potentially leading to failures in the attentional control of action, particularly when the damage is extensive and extends to both the right and left frontal lobes.

Another function of the frontal lobes is to *monitor* behavior, checking that it is appropriate. Failure to do this can lead to bizarre behavior or confabulation. Patient RR, for example, woke up in bed on one occasion and demanded from his wife, "Why do you keep telling people we are married?", At that time, it was very unusual to live together if

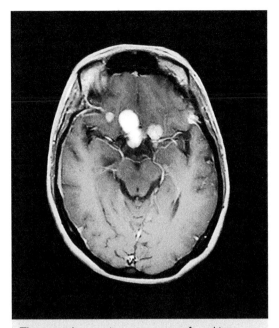

The central executive component of working memory is assumed to depend heavily on the frontal lobes. Much of the earlier evidence came from patients with frontal lobe damage such as the patient illustrated, whose MRI indicates a frontal lobe tumor.

not married. "But we are" she said, "we have three kids," going on to produce the wedding photographs. "That chap looks like me but it's not because I am not married," the patient replied. An hour or so later he appeared to have forgotten the incident and strongly denied it (Baddeley & Wilson, 1986).

A major function of the central executive is that of attentional focus, the capacity to direct attention to the task in hand. Consider a complex task like playing chess. What is the role of working memory? One approach is to use concurrent tasks to disrupt each of the subcomponents of working memory. Holding (1989) showed that counting backwards disrupted the capacity of players to remember

KEY TERM

Confabulation: Recollection of something that did not happen.

a chess position, concluding that verbal coding was important. However, counting backwards also demands executive processing. We addressed this by comparing the effects on the recall of chess positions of articulatory suppression (to disrupt the loop), spatial tapping (to disrupt the sketchpad), and an attentionally demanding task known as random generation, in which participants try to produce a stream of numbers, making the sequence as random as possible (Robbins et al., 1996). We tested both highly expert and relatively inexperienced players. The two groups differed greatly in overall performance, but all showed the same interference pattern. Articulatory suppression had no influence, suggesting that the phonological loop was not involved, whereas the visuo-spatial task did impair performance but not as much as random generation. We found the same result when the task was changed from remembering the chess positions to choosing the best next move, indicating an important role for both the sketchpad and central executive in planning as well as remembering a chess position.

Another attentional capacity that is attributed to the central executive is that of dividing attention between two or more tasks, for example chatting to a passenger while driving. On the whole, this seems to proceed reasonably safely. If the traffic situation becomes complex, the driver can cease speaking and the passenger is likely to see

According to Robbins et al. (1996), selecting good chess moves requires use of the central executive and the visuo-spatial sketchpad but not of the phonological loop.

why, and postpone the conversation. This is not the case with a mobile phone conversation, however, during which there might also be a much more serious attempt to convey complex information or discuss an important business matter. As we saw in the section on the sketchpad, if spatial information is involved, this is likely to interfere with steering control. Even more important, however, is the effect of concurrent telephoning on the capacity to make sensible driving decisions. In an early study, Brown, Tickner, and Simmonds (1969) had their participants drive a route marked out on an airfield that involved going through gaps of varying width between polystyrene blocks. A concurrent verbal reasoning task did not impair the drivers' skill in steering through such gaps, but it seriously disrupted their judgment with the result that they tended to attempt gaps that were narrower than the car. The danger in telephoning while driving does not principally result from what the driver's hands are doing but from what the brain is neglecting to do (Box 4.4).

Studies of patients with Alzheimer's disease suggest that they find dividing their attention across tasks particularly hard. One study (Baddeley, Bressi, Della Sala, Logie, & Spinnler, 1991) compared the capacity to combine activities across three groups: Alzheimer patients were compared with elderly and young control participants. Two tasks were used, a visuo-spatial tracking task that involved keeping a stylus in contact with a moving spot of light and a verbal task based on digit span. The experiment began by ensuring that the three groups were performing at the same level. This involved establishing digit span and tracking skill for each participant, and resulted in the use of somewhat shorter digit sequences and slower target speeds in the patients and elderly controls. At this point, we required all groups to perform both tasks at the same time. We found that the normal elderly and young groups showed a similar modest drop in performance under combined conditions, whereas the Alzheimer patients showed a marked deficit. Subsequent research showed that this was not the result of simply increasing the cognitive load as our patients showed a clear dual-task deficit even when the two tasks were made very simple.

Box 4.4 Inattention when driving causes accidents

A naturalistic study that videoed drivers and the road ahead for a total of 2 million miles of driving time recorded 82 crashes, with 80% implicating driver inattention during the previous 3 seconds (National Highway Safety Administration, 2006). Cell (mobile) phone use is a potent source of such inattention, with accidents being four times more frequent when a cell phone is in use, regardless of whether or not it is hand held (Redelmeier & Tibshirani, 1997).

A laboratory study by Strayer and Johnston (2001) showed that drivers who were using cell phones were substantially more likely to miss a red light and were significantly slower at applying the brakes, regardless of whether or not the phone was hand held.

Furthermore, this differential deficit did not occur with single tasks—even when they were made more difficult, patients and controls responded in a very similar way (Logie, Cocchini, Della Sala, & Baddeley, 2004). A practical implication of this finding is that such patients might be able to follow a conversation with one person quite well, but lose track when more people take part (Alberoni, Baddeley, Della Sala, Logie, & Spinnler, 1992).

It has been suggested that the central executive is required if attention has to be switched between two or more tasks (Baddeley, 1996). However, the idea that switching might always be the function of a single attentional system appears to be an oversimplification, with some aspects of switching being relatively automatic whereas others are almost certainly attentionally demanding (Allport, Styles, & Hsieh, 1994; Monsell, 2005).

THE EPISODIC BUFFER

A major problem with the three-component model of working memory was that of explaining how it was linked to LTM. Memory span for words in a sentence is about 15 compared to a span of 5 or 6 for unrelated words (Brener, 1940). However, it is not clear how this can be accounted for within the three-component model. Fifteen words are substantially more than the capacity of the phonological loop, and enhanced recall of sentences is not limited to those that can readily be turned into visual imagery. At a broader level, it is of course unsurprising that this is the case. The order of words within a sentence is constrained by the rules of grammar and by the overall meaning of the sentence, both allowing the chunking process described in Chapter 3 to increase span, and in both cases depending on LTM. However, this then raises the question of exactly how working memory is able to take advantage of long-term knowledge: How do working memory and LTM interact?

This was by no means the only problem for the three-component model. Digit span itself presents a challenge. Given that we can typically remember seven or more digits, and two or three of these come from the loop, where are the other items stored? If in visual STM, how is this combined with phonological STM? In a study on the role of working memory in imagery, Baddeley and Andrade (2000) noted that images based on LTM, such as a familiar market scene, or the sound of Margaret Thatcher's voice, do not appear to depend at all heavily on the visuo-spatial and phonological subsystems. So where is the information for such complex images held while the judgment of vividness is made? In an attempt to provide an answer to these questions, I proposed a fourth component, the episodic buffer (Baddeley, 2000).

The episodic buffer is assumed to be a storage system that can hold about four chunks of information in a multidimensional code. It is assumed to be able to hold episodes or chunks based on a range of different dimensions, including visual, verbal and semantic, which may come from a range of sources in addition to working memory, notably including both perception and long-term memory. Each of these information sources uses a different code, but these can be combined within the multidimensional buffer.

I also proposed that information was retrieved from the episodic buffer through conscious awareness. This linked the working memory model with an influential view as to the function of consciousness. Baars (1997, 2002) suggests that conscious awareness serves the function of pulling together separate streams of information from the various senses and binding them into perceived objects and scenes. He links this to the proposal that consciousness serves as a mental workspace that assists in performing complex cognitive activities, in short, a working memory. He uses the metaphor of a theater, in which consciousness is represented by the stage on which an ongoing play is played by actors, who are seen as analogous to the various interactive cognitive processes.

In its initial form (Baddeley, 2000), the episodic buffer was assumed to be an active system, entirely controlled by the central exec-utive. It was assumed to be capable of binding together previously unrelated concepts, to create new combinations, for example, the concepts of ice hockey and elephants to imagine an ice-hockey-playing elephant. This novel representation can be manipulated in working memory, allowing one to answer questions such as what position the elephant should play. It could, for instance, do some crunching tackles, but might it be even more useful in goal?

At a more routine level, it was suggested that executive processes were necessary to bind the words in a sentence into meaningful chunks, or indeed to bind perceptual features such as shapes and colors into perceived objects. If this were the case, then you would expect that disrupting the executive with a demanding concurrent task would interfere with binding. In recent years, my colleagues and I have tested this hypothesis extensively. Demanding concurrent tasks impair overall performance, but do not have any greater impact on the binding of color and shape into colored objects than they have on storing the individual features (Allen, Baddeley, & Hitch, 2006). Similarly, the process of binding words into chunks when sentences are recalled also appears automatic and resistant to the effect of an attentional load (Baddeley, Hitch, & Allen, 2009). In short, the episodic buffer seems to be less like Baars' stage, the center of the action, and to be more like a passive screen, with the action originating and being controlled from elsewhere. Furthermore, since binding still occurs regardless of disruption of the central executive, it seems likely that binding may depend on different systems for different materials; binding shape to color is probably based on visual-attentional systems, while binding in sentence processing seems to depend on long-term language processing (Baddeley, 2007, 2012).

The concept of an episodic buffer is still at a relatively early stage of development, but has already proved useful in a number of ways. At a theoretical level, it bridges the gap between the multicomponent Baddeley and Hitch (1974) model with its emphasis on storage, and the more attentionally

KEY TERM

Episodic buffer: A component of the Baddeley and Hitch model of working memory model that assumes a multidimensional code, allowing the various subcomponents of working memory to interact with long-term memory.

Binding: Term used to refer to the linking of features into objects (e.g. color red, shape square, into a red square), or of events into coherent episodes.

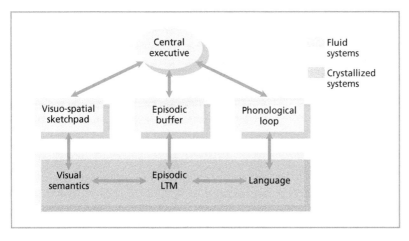

Figure 4.7 The Baddeley (2000) version of the multicomponent working memory. Links to long-term memory have been specified and a new component, the episodic buffer, added.

focused model of Cowan (1999, 2005). In doing so, it has emphasized the important question of how working memory and LTM interact, and more specifically has stimulated research on the issue of how different sources of information are bound together. This has led to further links between the multicomponent model and studies concerned with visual attention and memory (Luck & Vogel, 1997; Vogel, Woodman, & Luck, 2001), and with the classic issues of language comprehension (Daneman & Carpenter, 1980; Kintsch & van Dyck, 1977).

The current model of working memory is shown in Figures 4.7 and 4.9 (on page 85). These involve two major changes. One of these reflects the assumed link to LTM from the phonological and visuo-spatial subsystems, one allowing the acquisition of language, and the other performing a similar function for visual and spatial information. This is much less investigated than is the language link, but is assumed to be involved in acquiring visual and spatial knowledge of the world, for example, learning the shape and color of a banana, or the layout of a city.

The second major change (Figure 4.8) is the inclusion of the episodic buffer. In the original (Baddeley, 2000) version, the buffer was accessed only through the central executive. However, the evidence just described on binding visual and verbal information into chunks suggests that information can access the buffer directly from the visuo-spatial and phonological subsystems and from LTM (Figure 4.8, arrows d and e). You will notice two additional arrows accessing the episodic buffer, dotted rather than solid, to emphasize their tentative status. They reflect the speculation that smell and taste may gain access

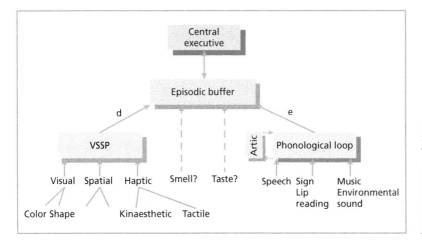

Figure 4.8 A speculative view of the flow of information from perception to working memory. VSSP, visuo-spatial sketchpad. From Baddeley (2012), reproduced with permission. Copyright © *Annual Reviews*.

to the buffer and that the experience might potentially be attentionally maintained.

Finally, the model reflects a recent attempt to account for the way in which emotion influences working memory, a process which also assigns a major role to the episodic buffer (Baddeley, 2007, 2012, 2013; Baddeley, Banse, Huang, & Page, 2012).

INDIVIDUAL DIFFERENCES IN WORKING MEMORY

Virtually all the evidence described up to this point has been based on the experimental method of contrasting two or more groups or conditions. An alternative is the correlational approach, which takes advantage of differences between individuals to explore the structure of the underlying system. The previously reported link between verbal span and second language learning (Service, 1992) is an example of this approach. This approach has played a central role in the study of working memory, following an influential study by Daneman and Carpenter (1980), who were interested in the possible role of working memory in language comprehension. They took as the defining feature of working memory, the need for the simultaneous storage and processing of information, and then set out to develop a task that would measure this. They proved remarkably successful. The task they produced appears to be a very simple one. Participants are required to read a series of sentences out loud and subsequently recall the last word of each. Try it for yourself:

A sailor returned from a long voyage having acquired a parrot as a pet.

It was a terribly cold winter with many violent storms.

The play was an enormous success and ran for many years.

What were the three last words?
They were *pet, storms, years.* Span is typically between two and four sentences.

Daneman and Carpenter (1980) showed that their working memory span task was able to predict the prose comprehension capacity of their student participants, a result that has been replicated many times. Daneman and Merikle (1996) review 74 studies showing broadly similar results. A total of 38 studies looked at working memory span and global comprehension, finding an average correlation of .41; another 36 studies correlated performance with more specific language processing measures and found an average correlation of .52. In both cases, correlations were higher than those obtained for standard verbal STM tasks (.28 and .40, respectively).

Working memory span has also proved able to predict a wide range of other capacities. High span participants are better at prose composition (Benton, Kraft, Glover, & Plake, 1984), obeying complex instructions (Engle, Carullo, & Collins, 1991), and taking notes (Kiewra & Benton, 1988). The capacity to predict performance extends beyond language tests to performance on a course concerning logic gates (Kyllonen & Stephens, 1990), and on a 40-hour long course on the PASCAL programming language (Shute, 1991). A study by Kyllonen and Christal (1990) compared performance on a series of working memory tasks with a battery of reasoning ability measures taken from standard IQ tests, finding a very high correlation. The principal difference was that the IQ tests appeared to depend somewhat more on prior experience, and the working memory measures somewhat more on speed. Engle, Tuholski, Laughlin, and Conway (1999) obtained a similar result finding a high correlation between working memory and fluid intelligence.

THEORIES OF WORKING MEMORY

Given the predictive power of complex span measures, there is great interest in understanding why they are successful. If we could identify the crucial component, this might provide a deeper understanding of both working memory and intelligence. Attempts to develop a theory of working memory based on individual differences typically involve breaking working memory performance down into a number of more basic components, devising tasks that aim to tap these components, and then examining the extent to which each of these is able to predict performance on tests of reasoning, intelligence, or academic performance. Part of this process of analysis involves studying the extent to which particular tasks are related to each other, in ways that might suggest the nature of the underlying structure of the memory and processing systems involved.

Happily, there tends to be broad agreement, with most analyses stressing the importance of an attentionally based control system, analogous to the central executive within the multicomponent working memory model. This tends to be strongly involved in complex tasks, with a smaller contribution from two or more components that appear to be responsible for the simple storage of verbal and visuo-spatial material, respectively (Engle et al., 1999; Miyake, Friedman, Rettinger, Shah, & Hegarty, 2001; Gathercole, Pickering, Ambridge, & Wearing, 2004a). Again, this broadly resembles the structure proposed by the Baddeley and Hitch model. Most theories of working memory focus on the executive component, often simply attributing the STM functions to relatively unspecified "activation of LTM," although the use of active verbal rehearsal is typically accepted as a source of temporary storage.

Although most theories derived from the study of individual differences have proved to be broadly compatible with the multicomponent model, this resemblance is not always obvious. Nelson Cowan's influential approach to working memory is a good example of a conflict that is more apparent than real (Baddeley, 2007, 2012; Cowan, 2001, 2005).

Alternative approaches to working memory

A major feature of the multicomponent model of working memory is that its approach is 'bottom-up', beginning with the study of verbal span and only later being prepared to address the difficult questions of attentional control. Most alternative approaches have on the contrary, taken a 'top-down' approach, starting with the hard questions and being less concerned with the links to STM. A good example of this is Nelson Cowan's influential model.

Cowan's embedded processes model

Cowan described working memory as "cognitive processes that retain information in an unusually accessible state" (Cowan, 1999, p. 62). For Cowan, working memory depends on activation that takes place within LTM, and is controlled by attentional processes (Figure 4.9). Activation is temporary and decays unless maintained either through active verbal rehearsal or continued attention.

Activated memory is multidimensional, as in my own concept of an episodic buffer, the main difference being that I assume that information is downloaded from LTM

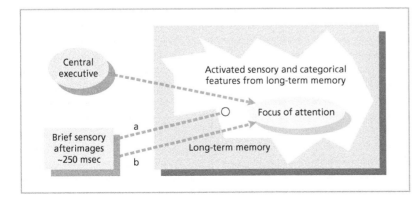

Figure 4.9 Cowan's embedded-processes model of working memory. A central executive controls focus of attention, which acts on recently activated features from long-term memory. The focus can hold approximately four objects in mind at the same time. Adapted from Cowan (1988).

and represented within the episodic buffer, whereas Cowan suggests that only the "addresses to locations in LTM are held." It is not clear at this point how one would distinguish between these two views. The main consequence is a differential emphasis, with Cowan being particularly concerned with working memory *capacity* where he argues strongly for a capacity of about four chunks (Cowan, 2005), rather than the seven originally proposed by Miller (1956). Cowan's model reflects his interest in attention, and his research on the development of memory during childhood rather than in the more peripheral aspects of working memory and the neuropsychological evidence that influenced my own approach. The importance of a verbal subsystem is certainly not denied by Cowan, who has in fact done important work on phonological STM (e.g. Cowan, 1992; Cowan, Day, Saults, Keller, Johnson, & Flores, 1992), but his principal concern is with the attentional focus and control of working memory, which in my own model would be represented by the interface between the central executive and the episodic buffer.

Both Cowan and I have principally used an approach based on the experimental method. However, a great deal of research on working memory, particularly in North America, has used a more correlational approach, strongly influenced by methods based on individual differences between normal participants.

Engle's inhibitory control model

One of the most active and innovative groups using the individual differences approach to working memory is that associated with Randy Engle and colleagues. Whereas much of the early work using the working memory span measure has been limited to observing correlations between span and various cognitive capacities, Engle has consistently focused on the theoretical issue of understanding what capacities and processes underpin such associations, and has used a fruitful combination of experimental and correlational methods.

Turner and Engle (1989), for example, demonstrated that the predictive capacity of complex span was not limited to measures based on sentence processing. They developed the *operation span* measure in which each to-be-remembered word is followed by an arithmetic operation; for example, *Apple*, 7 + 2 − 1 = ? *House*, 5 − 1 + 6 = ? and so on; after which the words must be recalled. This measure correlates highly with the initial-sentence span task and is also a good predictor of a broad range of cognitive performance measures.

Engle (1996) proposes that performance on a complex span task is made difficult by the need to protect the memory of the presented items from *proactive interference (PI)*, the tendency for earlier items to compete at retrieval with the items to be recalled. Evidence for this comes from a range of sources and is typically based on a procedure whereby a complex span task is given to a large group of students, with those performing particularly well or particularly badly then being chosen for further investigation. Then, rather than looking for an overall correlation across participants, Engle uses an experimental design testing for differences between these two extreme high and low span groups in their capacity to perform various other tasks.

In one study (Kane & Engle, 2000) participants were required to remember three successive free recall lists, each based on words from a set of ten semantic categories, for example, one animal list, one color list and one list of country names. If the same category is used for several successive lists, this leads to poorer recall of later lists, even though different words are used in each list, an example of proactive interference (see Chapter 9, pp. 245–6). As predicted, this interference effect proved to be reliably greater in low working memory span participants. Performance on the first list did not differ, suggesting that resistance to interference from earlier lists rather than learning capacity was the crucial factor.

Engle suggests that the capacity to resist interference is not limited to memory. In one study Conway, Cowan, and Bunting (2001) required participants to repeat a stream of digits presented to one ear and ignore messages presented to other. Unexpectedly, the person's name was included in the unintended stream. When subsequently questioned, the low span participants were much more likely to have detected their names, even though instructed to ignore that source, presumably because they were less able to shut out the irrelevant material, as predicted by the inhibition theory (Conway et al., 2001).

These and other studies do indeed suggest that there is a genuine and important link between complex span and capacity to resist interference, although it is entirely plausible to assume that both reflect some kind of more general executive capacity that plays an equally important role in other cognitive functions (see Box 4.4). However, the nature of inhibition is itself open to question. A study by Friedman and Miyake (2004) found evidence for two types of inhibition, one reflecting a capacity to resist interference within memory, as previously described, together with a separate ability to inhibit a powerful response tendency, such as moving your eyes to fixate a visual target that has just popped up. Both were modestly related to the Daneman and Carpenter reading span measure: for response inhibition the correlation was .23, whereas resistance to inhibition in memory correlated .33. Further evidence for the importance of working memory in resistance to interference is shown in Box 4.5.

More recently, Unsworth and Engle (2007) have developed a model that interprets individual differences in working memory in terms of two components which they

Box 4.5   High WM capacity helps resistance to distractors in visual WM

Fukuda and Vogel (2009) used measures of evoked response potential (ERP see p. 30) to study resistance to distracting stimuli in participants varying in working memory capacity as measured by the number of visual targets they could successfully hold over a brief delay. When distractors are similar to targets, higher working memory capacity is needed to resist capture. When there are no distractors or dissimilar distractors, there is no effect of working memory capacity.

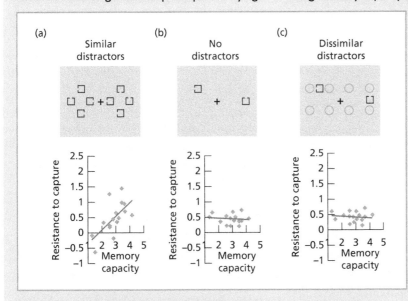

Figure 4.10   From Fukuda and Vogel, 2009, reproduced with permission. Copyright © Society for Neuroscience.

refer to as *primary* and *secondary* memory. The primary component involves a dynamic attentional capacity for the temporary maintenance of items and is reflected in the recency effect in free recall of word lists. The secondary component involves the capacity for cue-dependent search in LTM. As the terminology suggests this approach has much in common with views regarding working memory as a mode of operation of LTM. While Unsworth and Engle (2007) apply their model to a wide range of existing data on individual differences, it is not yet clear how productive it will be in a broader context.

The time-based resource-sharing model

Whereas Engle and colleagues focus on the importance of interference with the remembered words, an alternative possibility is that complex span reflects the capacity to prevent the decay of the memory trace through rehearsal. This does not necessarily mean subvocal rehearsal, but simply "keeping in mind" the items, perhaps by intermittently focusing attention on the fading trace. Evidence for such rehearsal comes from the observation that the capacity to retain a small memory load such as three consonants is disrupted by a demanding backward counting task, but not when simple articulatory suppression is required (Baddeley, Lewis, & Vallar, 1984a). This suggests that participants can maintain the items in some way without needing to continue to verbalize them, but that such activation is disrupted by a competing attentional activity.

The resource-sharing hypothesis has been further developed by a French group led by Pierre Barrouillet and Valerie Camos, who replaced the arithmetic task used in Turner and Engle's (1989) operation span task with a simple letter-reading task that was, however, strictly paced. Thus, participants were required to remember words while concurrently processing letters coming rapidly one after the other. This apparently simple task correlated even more highly with measures of reading and arithmetic than did conventional complex span measures (Lépine, Barrouillet, & Camos, 2005). Barrouillet, Bernardine, and Camos (2004) explained this, and other related findings, by arguing that most complex span tasks allow brief gaps in which attention-based rehearsal might occur, whereas their more rigidly controlled simple task minimizes such rehearsal.

A related theory is the task-switching hypothesis proposed by Towse and Hitch (1995; Towse, Hitch, & Hutton, 2000), who also assume a trace decay interpretation with participants switching attention between maintaining the trace and performing the secondary task.

A similar concept of an attentional focus capable of maintaining about four items features in a recent very ambitious model by Oberauer and Hein (2012), who make the further assumption that only a single item can be held in focus at any one time. Oberauer and Hein provide a much more detailed model than those discussed previously, which includes an interesting distinction between *declarative* WM, those aspects of which we are aware (the episodic buffer perhaps?), and *procedural* WM, the underlying processes (the loop and sketchpad perhaps?). They are, however, much more specific in the detailed mechanisms that underpin their model than is the case more generally.

It will be clear by this point that the top-down approach to working memory is currently a "hot" area. While type and level of detail varies greatly, all, including the multicomponent model, seem to agree on the need for some kind of active maintenance of the remembered material within an attentionally limited focus.

EDUCATIONAL APPLICATIONS

Variants of the working span task are already being applied to practical problems. They form an important component of a battery of tests developed by Susan Gathercole and Susan Pickering based on the multicomponent working memory model, which they have applied to detecting and predicting learning problems in school-age children (Gathercole & Pickering, 2000a). Their test battery has separate measures of phonological loop and sketchpad performance based on tasks involving verbal or visuo-spatial STM, together with complex span tasks— involving visual and verbal processing. As in the Daneman and Carpenter task, these demand simultaneously storing and manipulating information and hence are assumed to tap the central executive.

Analysis of the performance of school-age children is broadly consistent with predictions from the multicomponent model, allowing the separate components of working memory to be estimated and related to academic performance. Children who have been identified as having special educational needs perform poorly overall on the working memory battery (Gathercole, Pickering, Knight, & Stegmann, 2004b). Scores on specific subtests are also informative, with delayed reading and arithmetic being associated with poor performance on both phonological STM and complex span tasks in 7- to 8-year-old children (Gathercole & Pickering, 2000b), while complex span continues to predict maths and science scores at the age of 14 (Gathercole, Lamont, & Alloway, 2006).

What are children with poor working memory performance like? Gathercole's group decided to sit in on classes and observe how these children differed from their classmates. Children with low working memory scores were typically described by their teachers as "dreamy" or inattentive; not disruptive, but failing to follow instructions and to do the right thing at the right time. Gathercole et al. noted, however, that the instructions were often quite complex, for example "Put your reading cards back in the envelope, your pencils back in the box, and then sit on the carpet in the corner." The child would begin the task

Gathercole et al. found that children with low working memory scores were typically described by their teachers as "dreamy" or inattentive; however ADHD may well be responsible as it is linked to working memory performance.

and then apparently lose track. The children themselves reported that they forgot. However, this memory problem was not something that the teacher typically realized.

It later became clear that a good number of these children had been diagnosed with ADHD (attention deficit hyperactivity disorder), which, as its name suggests, has two potentially separable components of which one—attention deficit—might well be linked to working memory performance (Holmes, Gathercole, Place, Dunning, Hilton, & Elliott, 2010). This is being investigated by Gathercole's group, which has developed a program to enable teachers to identify children with problems based on working memory limitations and to modify their teaching accordingly (Gathercole & Alloway, 2008).

Can working memory be trained?

While views differ on the theoretical interpretation of working memory, there is general agreement that it plays an important role in life, and that a working memory deficit can be a major handicap. Could it be remedied, perhaps by training? This question was addressed by Torkel Klingberg, a Swedish neurologist who developed a training program he named Cogmed™. This was presented in a format resembling a computer game, with participants encouraged to strive to improve their performance in regular sessions extending over many hours. Not only did performance improve but, importantly, it generalized to tests other than those used for training. If, as Holmes et al. (2010) suggested, attention deficit hyperactivity syndrome reflects poor working memory, than it might be possible to help children with this disorder by training their working memory. In one study, for example, Klingberg et al. (2005) administered their training program to groups of ADHD children and matched controls on the full program, in each case also testing a control group using a less demanding regime that was not expected to be effective. These groups were included to ensure that any advantage that might be gained is not simply the result of receiving more attention. Groups were then tested on a range of new and different working memory-related tests, together with Raven's Matrices, a widely used test of nonverbal intelligence. In order to avoid bias, a double-blind procedure was used. Assignment to the groups was random, while people giving the final test of the effectiveness of training were unaware as to which group each participant had come from. Klingberg et al. (2005) observed a clear improvement in performance in the Cogmed trained group over the control group that extended to both the novel working memory tests and to Raven's Matrices.

There is as yet relatively little targeted research on what underpins the WM training effect. However, Klingberg's group has begun to investigate the neurobiological bases of their training program. A study by McNab and Klingberg (2008) reported a correlation between WM performance and activity in the prefrontal cortex and basal ganglia, while an fMRI study by Olesen, Westerberg and Klingberg (2004) found that five weeks of practice on Cogmed led to increased activation in the frontal and parietal cortex, areas that are generally accepted as being associated with WM. McNab et al. (2009) reported changes in the dopamine system, finding an increase in D1 dopamine receptor plasticity in prefrontal and parietal cortical areas. The relationship between WM and the complexities of the dopamine system are, however, only just beginning to be understood.

Despite considerable skepticism, Klingberg's work evoked widespread interest. ADHD is a common and disruptive problem, typically treated using drugs, an approach that is not without its critics. Furthermore, if Cogmed worked for ADHD children, there might perhaps be other areas of childhood disability that might profit from WM training; indeed, perhaps all children could benefit from such a training regime? Klingberg's program became commercially available but, given its complexity, was not cheap. Hence, people began to explore other possible training regimes, often with apparent success. The commercial potential of setting up such schemes rapidly became obvious, and a range of variants has become widely available.

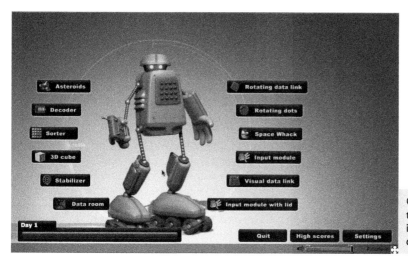

Cogmed is a memory training program presented in a format resembling a computer game.

However, it is much easier to set up a training regime than to conduct adequate trials that demonstrate that it really achieves something of practical value, and many such products tend to be poorly supported by experimental evidence.

So how good is the evidence? Melby-Lervåg and Hulme (2013) conducted a meta-analysis, combining the results of all the available studies that were at all adequately designed, and hence that at least included an appropriate control group. They found 30 such studies, concluding that there was good evidence for short-term gains that generalize to tasks other than those studied. However, those studies that had followed up and retested after a delay of weeks or months gave less encouraging results, with no evidence for improved verbal WM, some evidence for a continuing advantage in visual WM, but very little evidence for generalization to nonlaboratory tasks. Reviewing the data from a more theoretical perspective, Shipstead, Redick and Engle (2012) identify methodological problems with many of the studies, and in the case of the studies that were adequately designed they question the extent to which they generalize beyond the laboratory. Finally, Shipstead et al. comment that, where training appears to succeed, it is by no means clear that working memory is the crucial factor.

In a paper entitled "Let's be realistic about intervention research," Gathercole, Dunning and Holmes (2012) suggest that the reviews by Melby-Lervåg and Hulme (2013) and by Shipstead et al. (2012) might by unduly pessimistic. If programs can be developed that genuinely increase WM capacity, this could be of great practical value. Such programs are, however, likely to be expensive both financially and in the time and effort demanded by both students and tutors. Before being widely used therefore, they should pass stringent tests. Gathercole et al. point out, however, that it is in the nature of applied research, that the process of moving from a broad proof of concept to final application is likely to involve many stages. They suggest that an adequate evaluation should include the following:

1   A design involving three groups, a treatment group, an untreated group and a third group who actively participate in a program that is not expected to influence WM, to act as a placebo* condition.
2   Participants to be randomly allocated to conditions.
3   Valid outcome measures based on more than a single test.
4   A test of the degree of generalization, for example to school work.
5   Enough participants to have good statistical power.

Such a study is likely to be expensive both in time and money and likely to be financially supported only if smaller and simpler studies can be shown to have considerable promise.

Gathercole et al. describe their own involvement in this area, beginning with their existing involvement in the educational application of cognitive psychology, and more specifically, the link between WM and ADHD. They initially decided to carry out a small study attempting to replicate the Cogmed findings on ADHD by Klingberg et al. (2005), attaching it to larger already funded project. The results of this preliminary study were positive (Holmes et al., 2010), encouraging them to move on to study non-ADHD children with low WM performance. Here they included a further control group of children who also took the Cogmed training program but instead of being pushed constantly to improve their performance, were left to continue to perform at span level. While the group given the standard approach of steadily increasing demand again showed a clear benefit, the low demand group did not show improvement or generalization (Holmes, Gathercole, & Dunning 2009). On the basis of their results, they received a grant to conduct a larger and more rigorous study which "after a gruelling three years" has been completed and submitted for publication.

Their conclusions are broadly in line with the overall reviews, namely that there is good evidence for an effect of training, with generalization to other WM tasks, but little evidence

---

* A placebo is a condition that reassembles treatment but is not expected to be directly effective, for example, a sugar pill in a trial of antidepressants. It is an important control as simply believing you are being treated can have a powerful effect.

that it automatically generalizes to real-world environments. This is a familiar problem in a range of areas of psychological and medical rehabilitation; a patient who is able to climb stairs in the rehabilitation centre may often not do so at home and a patient whose phobic response may have been treated in the clinic, may not be free of fear once outside. Generalization can occur, but it needs the therapist or trainer to build a bridge between the clinic and the world outside.

So can we train working memory? Generalization to other laboratory tasks seems to be reasonably well established, although the durability of improvement is open to question. Finally, however, evidence for the practical transfer to scholastic topics such as reading and arithmetic is at present extremely weak. My own current assessment is that what is being trained is not WM as a whole, but probably one or more of its executive components, perhaps the capacity to focus attention and inhibit distraction. If this is so, then it might be possible to achieve generalization, but it may need specific training. This is an area that is certainly worth further investigation, but I would not buy shares in it just yet!

THE NEUROSCIENCE OF WORKING MEMORY

This chapter has focused on the psychology of working memory based almost entirely on behavioral methods of study. However, a great deal of work has been concerned with investigating the anatomical and neurophysiological basis of working memory. Initially, this approach relied principally on patient-based neuropsychological evidence; more recently, two further methods have become prominent, single-cell recording in monkeys, and neuroimaging studies based on healthy human participants.

Single-cell recording approaches to working memory

Single-cell recording involves placing electrodes in individual cells within the brain, typically of an awake monkey and then recording the cell's activity as a function of a range of presented stimuli. The method was pioneered by Hubel and Weisel (1979; see Hubel, 1982 for a review), who were awarded the Nobel Prize for their work on the analysis of visual processing using single-cell recording. This method was applied to the study of memory by Fuster (1954) and by Patricia Goldman-Rakic (1988), who carried out a series of classic studies in which monkeys were taught to fixate a central point on a screen, maintaining their gaze while a peripheral light stimulus was presented in one of several locations. If they maintained fixation until a recall signal, and then moved their eyes to the appropriate location, they received a reward. Funahashi, Bruce, and Goldman-Rakic (1989) detected cells within the frontal lobe of the monkey that were active during the period between presentation and test. If such activity continued until the recall signal, a correct response was typically made, whereas discontinued activity was followed by forgetting. This led some commentators to identify the particular area in the frontal lobe as *the* source of working memory. However, later work has identified cells behaving in a similar way in other parts of the brain (Goldman-Rakic, 1996), suggesting that the frontal areas were part of more general system, with the frontal lobes being concerned with control of WM while storage depends on the parietal lobes (Rowe, Toni, Josephs, Frackowiak, & Passingham, 2000), analogous perhaps to the central executive and sketchpad components of the multicomponent model.

A behavioral version of this task has been developed for use with human participants, with schizophrenic patients being found to be impaired (Park & Holzman, 1992). This has caused some excitement, because of the potential link between an important disease and a very specific neurophysiologically related measure. However, although this certainly does indicate a deficit in working memory in schizophrenic patients, the WM effect is not particularly dramatic and other deficits, such as those in episodic LTM, are probably more important from a practical viewpoint (see McKenna, Ornstein, & Baddeley, 2002 for a review). However, it seems likely that single-unit recording methods of studying memory will continue to provide an important link between psychological and neurobiological approaches to memory.

Neuroimaging working memory

A closer and more extensive link between psychological and neurobiological approaches to memory is provided by a rapidly growing body of work applying the various techniques of brain imaging described in Chapter 2 to the study of working memory. The initial studies used positron emission topography (PET), which you might recall involves introducing a radioactive substance into the bloodstream and using this to monitor the amount of activity occurring in different brain regions (see Chapter 2, p. 31). Two research groups were initially particularly active in applying this method to the study of working memory. In London, Paulesu, Frith, and Frackowiak (1993) carried out a study that was based on the phonological loop hypothesis. They identified two separate regions, one in the area between the parietal and temporal lobes of the left hemisphere, which appeared to be responsible for phonological storage, and a second more frontally based region known as Broca's area, known to be involved in speech production, that appeared to be linked to subvocal rehearsal (Figure 4.11).

The second group, led by Jon Jonides and Edward Smith at the University of Michigan, was active in further extending the use of neuroimaging to investigate working memory, carrying out a sustained series of carefully designed and theoretically targeted experiments (Smith & Jonides, 1997). The first

direct comparison of visual and verbal working memory was provided by Smith, Jonides, and Koeppe (1996). In their verbal memory task, participants were shown four letters, followed by a probe letter. Participants had to decide whether the probe letter had been contained in the previous set of four. A baseline control involved presenting both the stimulus and the probe simultaneously: everything was the same except for the need to remember. If the amount of brain activation in this baseline condition is subtracted from the activation involved when memory is also required, then the difference in blood flow should reflect the additional demand made by the need to remember, over and above that involved in perceiving and processing the experimental stimuli. Like Paulesu et al., Smith and colleagues found that verbal STM activated two separate areas in the left hemisphere.

In the case of visuo-spatial memory, participants were shown an array of three dots, followed after a delay by a circle (Figure 4.12). They had to decide whether this coincided

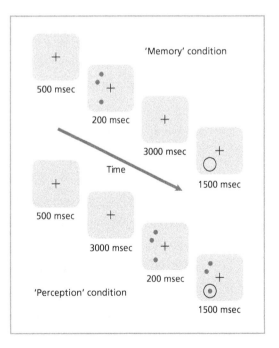

Figure 4.12 Schematic drawing of the events on each trial of the spatial memory and spatial perception tasks used by Smith et al. (1996). Copyright © Oxford University Press. Reproduced with permission.

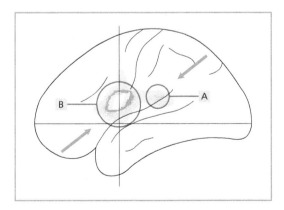

Figure 4.11 Neuroimaging the phonological loop. An early study using positron emission tomography identified area A with phonological storage and B with the articulatory rehearsal process. Redrawn from Paulesu et al. (1993).

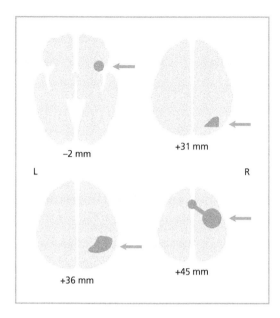

-2 mm

+31 mm

L

R

+36 mm

+45 mm

Figure 4.13 Illustration depicting PET images of the four areas activated in the visuo-spatial working memory study. Based on Smith et al. (1996).

with the location of one of the dots. Again, a baseline was established in which the dots and circle were presented at the same time. As indicated in Figure 4.13, visual memory resulted in activation in a series of areas mainly in the right hemisphere (Smith et al., 1996).

Further studies (reviewed by Smith & Jonides, 1997) observed a distinction between spatial working memory, as described above, and memory for an *object or pattern*, such as an abstract shape. Spatial memory activates more dorsal or upper regions of the brain whereas object memory tends to be more concentrated on lower or ventral areas (Figure 4.14). It is notable that research on visual processing in nonhuman primates (Mishkin,

Ungerleider, & Macko, 1983) has identified two separable visual processing streams, with the dorsal stream being concerned with spatial location (*where*), and the ventral processing stream with shape and object coding (*what*).

There is broad agreement that attentional control, as reflected in the central executive, is linked to the frontal lobes. The term attention is of course a rather broad one. An influential approach to a study of attention is that of Posner who distinguishes three types, each associated with a separate brain network. The first of these is concerned with alerting, the second with orienting attention, and the third with executive control (Posner & Rothbart, 2007). Working memory is principally concerned with this third system. Chun, Golomb and Turk-Browne (2011) make a distinction between two broad aspects of the control of attention, one essentially perceptual in nature that takes in information from the world, while the other is internally focused and concerned with such factors as the selection of strategies and the control and manipulation of cognitive operations. Both of these draw on a common limited pool of attentional capacity; hence when we are "lost in thought" (or engaged in a mobile phone conversation?), we may not notice our neighbor who is wondering why we are being so standoffish. The neuromodulator dopamine appears to be associated with the executive control system and to involve the anterior cingulate area. Effortful attention and executive control tends to be associated with the anterior cingulate (Bush, Luu, & Posner, 2000), which also appears to be associated with difficulties in resolving conflicts in cognitive tasks and with children who have difficulty in controlling their emotions and behavior (Rothbart & Rueda, 2005).

However, although there is no doubt that the frontal lobes play a crucial role in executive processing, there is much less agreement on the extent to which specific executive capacities are located in particular frontal areas. Shallice (2002; Shallice & Cooper, 2011) takes this approach, drawing evidence from studies ranging from single case neuropsychological studies through group lesion studies to studies using neuroimaging, then attempting to account for this array of evidence using a computer-based model. Shallice and Cooper (2011) review

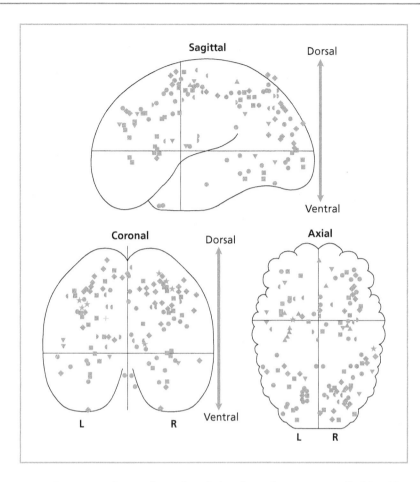

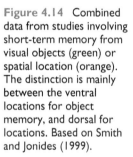

Figure 4.14 Combined data from studies involving short-term memory from visual objects (green) or spatial location (orange). The distinction is mainly between the ventral locations for object memory, and dorsal for locations. Based on Smith and Jonides (1999).

extensive research on the role of the frontal lobes in different aspects of attentional control; we will describe just two studies. The first is an fMRI study that examines the role of selection in healthy adults, comparing relatively difficult discriminations with rather easier ones (Thompson-Schill, D'Esposito, Aguirre, & Farah, 1997). The difficult discriminations involved potential conflict.; for example, asking for two items of similar color from the set *tooth, tongue, bone*, where the incorrect response *tongue* is more closely associated in location than the correct one. This was compared to an easier judgment such as which is the more similar to *flea: tick, well* or *shoe*. Increased difficulty was associated with an increase in activation in a specific location within the frontal lobes, the left inferior frontal gyrus.

A very different but crucial role of the central executive and of the frontal lobes is to energize and drive behavior. This capacity was studied by Alexander, Stuss, Shallice, Picton and Gillingham (2005) in a large sample of patients with frontal-lobe lesions, divided into groups on the basis of the localization of their lesions (Figure 4.15). The task was a simple one. A series of five lights were each associated with a key. The task was to press the relevant key when a light came on. After a brief 200 ms delay, the next light came on, continuing for a total of 500 responses. Despite this demanding schedule, most of the frontal-lobe-lesioned patients tended to maintain their speed throughout the session. Only one group was consistently slower than controls, those who had their damage in the superior medial area of the frontal lobes, an area that contains the anterior cingulate gyrus, regarded by Posner and DiGirolamo (1998) as facilitating the supervisory aspect of attention and shown to be involved in the Stroop task which requires participants to override dominant habits.

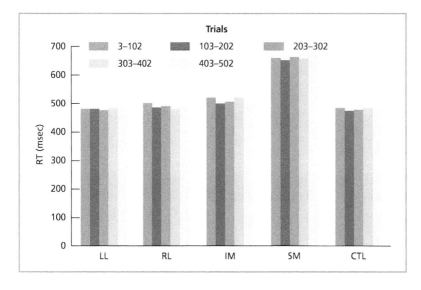

Figure 4.15 Performance of a control group (CTL) and four groups of patients with differing areas of frontal lobe damage on a five choice serial reaction time task. Only patients with damage to the superior medial frontal lobes were impaired. Reproduced from Shallice and Cooper (2011) with permission from Oxford University Press.

In contrast to Shallice's attempt to identify specific processes within frontal regions, Duncan and Owen (2000) took a more general approach, pointing to the lack of consistency across a range of studies of the frontal lobes at anything other than the broadest level. They performed a meta-analysis of a wide range of functional imaging studies covering task novelty, working memory load, response competition, delay and perceptual difficulty, finding that all of them appear to load on the anterior cingulate area, arguing for a common process which they link to Spearman's concept of general intelligence, *g*. A compromise position is suggested by Posner (2013) who suggests that a good deal of neural computation operates within relatively localized networks, but accepts that "it is certainly possible and perhaps even likely that more complex reasoning and memory retrieval processes involve less specific localization," while cautioning that "these differences may be more due to our weakness in correctly specifying the operations involved than they are to problems with localization" (Posner, 2013, p. 245)

Is working memory simply activated LTM?

A number of investigators using fMRI have detected activity in areas associated with both sensory processing and/or LTM (e.g. Ruchkin, Grafman, Cameron, & Berndt, 2003). Such findings are sometimes interpreted as supportive of a view that working memory is simply activated LTM, together with activation in the relevant sensory processing areas. As an explanation, of course, this is no more satisfactory than stating that language is just activated LTM; LTM is certainly involved in both cases, but an explanation requires specifying just when and how. The necessary further complexity is increasingly recognized. An example is the "sensory recruitment model" of Serences, Ester, Vogel and Awh (2009), which regards WM as resulting from interaction between top-down control and the neural representations of perceptual, conceptual, linguistic, affective, and other stimuli. Within the multicomponent model, this would seem to be a reasonable description of the role of the episodic buffer, and as such does not necessarily constitute a "contrast with the concept of transfer to one or more dedicated storage buffers," as suggested by Rissman and Wagner (2012, p. 108). The multicomponent model assumes *both* emergent interaction *and* specialized buffers. The crucial issue concerns how such interaction is achieved.

This is an important question and one in which progress is being made, with some very interesting recent results based on multi-voxel pattern analysis (MVPA). As you may recall from Chapter 2 (p. 32) this is a method whereby the overall brain activation associated with a particular stimulus is averaged over many presentations, allowing a pattern categorizer to detect regularities. The categorizer is then directed at the participant's ongoing brain activity, and often proves capable of detecting whether the participant is viewing, for example, a face or a house. In an ingenious study, Harrison and Tong (2009) carried out a very simple STM experiment in which participants were presented with either red or green circles filled with lines of two different orientations. They were required to attend to color on some trials and orientation on others. The brain activation associated with each was recorded and fed into a pattern categorizer. The second, STM stage involved viewing stimuli which they were then required to retain for 15 seconds during which they were told whether color or orientation would be tested. As Figure 4.16 shows, this instruction evoked a pattern of activation similar to that produced by viewing the color or the orientation, suggesting that they may have been maintaining the relevant dimension at a quite peripheral level of the visual system.

Within the multicomponent model, I would interpret this as a demonstration of the process of "refreshing" the stimulus representation, a term developed by Marcia Johnson (Chun & Johnson, 2011) to reflect the continued maintenance of a representation by focused attention, a method of rehearsal that appears to be common to many sensory systems which lack a specialized rehearsal system such as the phonological loop.

MPVA has also been used to investigate the role of working memory in retrieval from LTM. Lewis-Peacock and Postle (2008) first familiarized their participants with a series of faces, locations, and common objects by asking them to make pleasantness judgments. During this phase, a pattern categorizer learned the pattern of activity associated with each of the stimuli. A series of six pairs were then selected at random and participants were trained to remember the second item of each pair when presented with the first. In a final stage, each stimulus was presented for 1 second followed by an 11 second delay, after which either the appropriate or an inappropriate item was presented and the participant

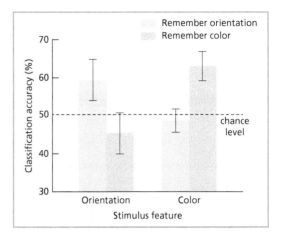

Figure 4.16 When participants are asked to view a figure and concentrate on either its color or the orientation of stripes within it, different brain areas are activated. A similar pattern is observed when they are required to hold each of the two types of feature in memory, prior to a test. As a result it is possible in each case, to tell from the brain activation which of the two features the participant is "holding in mind". From Serences et al. (2009). Copyright © American Psychological Association. Reproduced with permission.

responded "yes" or "no" for a match or mismatch. If the correct response was, for example, a face, then the face pattern was typically activated during the delay, as if the participant was holding the appropriate response "in mind." The pattern recognizer seemed to tell us what the participant was "thinking about" during this delay. If so, what is this telling us about memory? It is, however, not clear that the activation picked up by the analyzer is causally linked to retention, rather than being an incidental reflection of another deeper process. Logie, Pernet, Buonocore and Della Sala (2011) compared mental rotation in people who report vivid visual imagery and those who do not. The pattern of cortical activation was very different between those reporting vivid visual imagery and those who did not, but level of performance was the same. This suggested that information may be stored at a different level, based on a common memory representation which is then "displayed" to conscious awareness in different forms. Hence I would regard Lewis-Peacock and Postle's (2008) work as directly relevant to the concept of an episodic buffer but less directly relevant to a basic understanding of working memory more generally.

So *is* WM simply activated LTM? This is the issue that is sometimes seen as critically separating my own views from those of Nelson Cowan. In fact neither of us believes that this is the case. The crucial word in the question is *simply*. There is no doubt that working memory depends heavily on LTM; consider the simple example of digit span: It is greater in one's native language than in an unfamiliar language such as Finnish, because digits are already represented in LTM whereas Finnish digits would have to be held as a long sequence of meaningless speech sounds. Likewise, the fact that memory span for sentences is better than that for scrambled words again relies on LTM through the impact of syntax and meaning, which both depend on LTM.

My good friend and long-term collaborator Robert Logie and I used to disagree on the role of LTM in visual WM. He argued that all information goes through LTM *before* entering WM. That seemed too extreme to me; surely STM for the brightness of a light would not involve LTM? Logie's argument boiled down to the view that when, for example, we survey a scene, we do not perceive it as a meaningless array of brightness, colors and shapes, but as objects, and that this implies the involvement of LTM. I realized that my disagreement was with the suggestion that all visual information had to pass through LTM *before* entering WM. My own view is that the interface between WM, perception and LTM is complex, flexible and interactive rather than

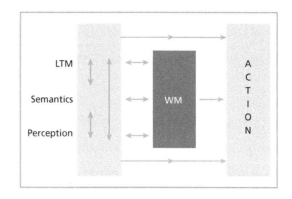

Figure 4.17 My current view of the complex and multiple links between working memory (WM) and long-term memory (LTM).

purely sequential. We eventually compromised on Figure 4.17, which is intended to indicate that working memory is a crucial link between cognition and action. It can take in information at a range of levels from sensory through perception to long-term memory. The precise way in which these links occur will depend on the information to be processed and the resultant action. Note also that not everything needs to go through working memory; threat stimuli can activate an avoidance response even before the stimulus is registered in conscious awareness (LeDoux, 1996; Öhman & Soares, 1994). In conclusion, like Nelson Cowan, I am sure that working memory certainly involves activated LTM. We do not, however, regard this as an explanation, but rather as a challenge to explore the ways in which this complex, multilevel interaction is achieved. We will return to this question in later chapters.

SUMMARY

- Working memory is a system that combines temporary storage and executive processing in order to help perform a range of complex cognitive activities.
- The multicomponent model of Baddeley and Hitch tries to combine storage and processing.
- It has four components; the phonological loop; the visuo-spatial sketchpad; the central executive and the episodic buffer.
- The phonological loop provides temporary storage for verbal/acoustic material.
- The visuo-spatial sketchpad stores information from visual and spatial coding.
- The central executive is an attentionally limited system that provides overall control.

- The episodic buffer involves a passive multidimensional store that is accessible to conscious awareness.
- An alternative approach is that proposed by Cowan, who sees working memory as reflecting a limited attentional capacity focused on activated representations in LTM.
- While this is often seen as incompatible with the multicomponent model, the differences can be seen as those of emphasis and focus, rather than fundamental.
- Much of the work on the executive control of working memory has used correlational measures based on individual differences, sometimes in combination with experimental methods.
- Influential in the area is the work of Engle and colleagues who emphasize the role of working memory in inhibiting potentially distracting material and facilitating retrieval from LTM.
- Other approaches such as that of Barrouillet and Camos emphasize the role of attentional maintenance in WM.
- Most agree with Cowan that the capacity of WM is about four chunks.
- Educational applications of WM explore the implications of WM deficits and raise the question as to whether WM can be trained.
- Neuroscience approaches to WM extend from single-cell recording in monkey to neuroimaging.
- Studies using fMRI suggest the joint activation of areas responsible for perception, LTM, and executive control when performing WM tasks.
- The question of whether these are all essential to WM, or simply reflect the high degree of connectivity in the brain, remains an open one.

POINTS FOR DISCUSSION

Why do we need models of working memory? Will models of attention and LTM not suffice?
What has neuroscience contributed to our knowledge of working memory?
What might be the practical applications of a good model of working memory?

FURTHER READING

Andrade, J. (2001). *Working memory in perspective*. Hove, UK: Psychology Press. A discussion of the strengths and limitations of the Baddeley and Hitch multicomponent model of working memory by a group of younger investigators working in the area.

Atkinson, R. C., & Shiffrin, R. M. (1971). The control of short-term memory. *Scientific American, 225*, 82–90. A good summary of the modal model for the general scientific reader.

(Continued)

(Continued)

Cowan, N. (2005). *Working memory capacity*. Hove, UK: Psychology Press. A recent overview of Cowan's approach to working memory. It proposes that the capacity of working memory is four chunks, rather than Miller's magic number seven.

Engle, R. W., Cantor, J., & Carullo, J. J. (1992). Individual differences in working memory and comprehension: A test of four hypotheses. *Journal of Experimental Psychology: Learning, Memory, and Cognition, 18*, 972–992. Discusses a range of hypotheses about working memory and the methods for evaluating them.

Fletcher, P. C., & Henson, R. N. A. (2001). Frontal lobes and human memory: Insights from functional neuroimaging. *Brain, 124*, 849–881. Discussion of the role played by the frontal lobes in memory from a neurological and psychological viewpoint.

Logie, R. H. (2003). Spatial and visual working memory: A mental workspace. *Psychology of Learning and Motivation, 42*, 37–78. An overview of the visuo-spatial aspects of working memory by one of the leading investigators in the field.

REFERENCES

Alberoni, M., Baddeley, A. D., Della Sala, S., Logie, R. H., & Spinnler, H. (1992). Keeping track of conversation: Impairments in Alzheimer's disease. *International Journal of Geriatric Psychiatry, 7*, 639–646.

Alexander, M. P., Stuss, D. T., Shallice, T., Picton, T. W., Gillingham, S. (2005). Impaired concentration due to frontal lobe damage from two distinct lesion sites. *Neurology, 65*, 572–579.

Allen, R., Baddeley, A. D., & Hitch, G. J. (2006). Is the binding of visual features in working memory resource-demanding? *Journal of Experimental Psychology: General, 135*, 298–313.

Allport, A., Styles, E. A., & Hsieh, S. (1994). Shifting attentional set: Exploring the dynamic control of tasks. In C. Umilta & M. Moscovitch (Eds.), *Attention and performance XV.* (pp. 421–462). Cambridge, MA: MIT Press.

Atkinson, R. C., & Shiffrin, R. M. (1968). Human memory: A proposed system and its control processes. In K. W. Spence & J. T. Spence (Eds.), *The psychology of learning and motivation: Advances in research and theory.* (Vol. 2, pp. 89–195). New York: Academic Press.

Baars, B. J. (1997). *In the theater of consciousness*. New York: University Press.

Baars, B. J. (2002). The conscious access hypothesis: Origins and recent evidence. *Trends in Cognitive Sciences, 6*(1), 47–52.

Baddeley, A. D. (1968). A 3-min reasoning test based on grammatical transformation. *Psychonomic Science, 10*, 341–342.

Baddeley, A. D. (1996). Exploring the central executive. *Quarterly Journal of Experimental Psychology, 49A*(1), 5–28.

Baddeley, A. D. (2000). The episodic buffer: A new component of working memory? *Trends in Cognitive Sciences, 4*(11), 417–423.

Baddeley, A. D. (2007). *Working memory, thought and action*. Oxford: Oxford University Press.

Baddeley, A. (2012). Working memory, theories models and controversy. *The Annual Review of Psychology, 63*, 12.11–12.29.

Baddeley, A. (2013). Working memory and emotion: Ruminations on a theory of depression. *Review of General Psychology, 17*, 20–27. doi:10.1037/a0030029

Baddeley, A. D., & Andrade, J. (2000). Working memory and the vividness of imagery. *Journal of Experimental Psychology: General, 129*, 126–145. doi: 10.1037//0096-3445.129.1.126

Baddeley, A. D., & Dale, H. C. A. (1966). The effect of semantic similarity on retroactive interference in long- and short-term memory. *Journal of Verbal Learning and Verbal Behavior, 5*, 417–420.

Baddeley, A. D., & Hitch, G. J. (1974). Working memory. In G. A. Bower (Ed.), *The psychology of learning and motivation: Advances in research and theory.* (Vol. 8, pp. 47–89). New York: Academic Press.

Baddeley, A. D., & Lieberman, K. (1980). Spatial working memory. *Attention and Performance, VIII,* 521–539.

Baddeley, A. D., & Wilson, B. (1986). Amnesia, autobiographical memory and confabulation. In D. Rubin (Ed.), *Autobiographical memory* (pp. 225–252). Cambridge: Cambridge University Press.

Baddeley, A. D., & Wilson, B. (1988). Frontal amnesia and the dysexecutive syndrome. *Brain and Cognition, 7*(2), 212–230.

Baddeley, A. D., Banse, R., Huang, Y.-M., & Page, M. (2012). Working memory and emotion: Detecting the hedonic detector. *Journal of Cognitive Psychology, 24,* 6–16.

Baddeley, A. D., Bressi, S., Della Sala, S., Logie, R., & Spinnler, H. (1991). The decline of working memory in Alzheimer's Disease: A longitudinal study. *Brain, 114,* 2521–2542.

Baddeley, A. D., Chincotta, D., & Adlam, A. (2001). Working memory and the control of action: Evidence from task switching. *Journal of Experimental Psychology: General, 130,* 641–657.

Baddeley, A. D., Gathercole, S., & Papagno, C. (1998). The phonological loop as a language learning device. *Psychological Review, 105,* 158–173.

Baddeley, A. D., Grant, S., Wight, E., & Thomson, N. (1973). Imagery and visual working memory. In P. M. A. Rabbitt & S. Dornic (Eds.), *Attention and Performance V* (pp. 205–217). London: Academic Press.

Baddeley, A. D., Hitch, G. J., & Allen, R. J. (2009). Working memory and binding in sentence recall. *Journal of Memory and Language, 61,* 438–456.

Baddeley, A. D., Lewis, V. J., & Vallar, G. (1984). Exploring the articulatory loop. *Quarterly Journal of Experimental Psychology, 36,* 233–252.

Baddeley, A. D., Papagno, C., & Vallar, G. (1988). When long-term learning depends on short-term storage. *Journal of Memory and Language, 27,* 586–595.

Barrouillet, P., Bernardin, S., & Camos, V. (2004). Time constraints and resource sharing in adults' working memory spans. *Journal of Experimental Psychology: General, 133,* 83–100.

Benton, S. L., Kraft, R. G., Glover, J. A., & Plake, B. S. (1984). Cognitive capacity differences among writers. *Journal of Educational Psychology, 76*(5), 820–834.

Brener, R. (1940). An experimental investigation of memory span. *Journal of Experimental Psychology, 26,* 467–483.

Brown, I. D., Tickner, A. H., & Simmonds, D. C. V. (1969). Interference between concurrent tasks of driving and telephoning. *Journal of Applied Psychology, 53,* 419–424. doi: http://dx.doi.org/10.1037/h0028103

Bush, G., Luu, P., & Posner, M. I. (2000). Cognitive and emotional influences in anterior cingulate cortex. *Trends in Cognitive Sciences, 4,* 215–222.

Chun, M. M., & Johnson, M. K. (2011). Memory: Enduring traces of perceptual and reflective attention. *Neuron, 72,* 520–535.

Chun, M. M., Golomb, J. D., & Turk-Browne, N. B. (2011). A taxonomy of external and internal attention. *Annual Review of Psychology, 62,* 73–101.

Conway, A. R. A., Cowan, N., & Bunting, M. F. (2001). The cocktail party phenomenon revisited: The importance of working memory capacity. *Psychonomic Bulletin and Review, 8*(2), 331–335.

Cowan, N. (1988). Evolving conceptions of memory storage, selective attention, and their mutual constraints within the human information-processing system. *Psychological Bulletin, 104*(2), 163–191.

Cowan, N. (1992). Verbal memory span and the timing of spoken recall. *Journal of Memory and Language, 31*(5), 668–684.

Cowan, N. (1999). An embedded-processes model of working memory. In A. M. P. Shah (Ed.), *Models of working memory* (pp. 62–101). Cambridge, UK: Cambridge University Press.

Cowan, N. (2001). The magical number 4 in short-term memory: A reconsideration of mental storage capacity. *Behavioral and Brain Sciences, 24,* 87–114; discussion 114–185.

Cowan, N. (2005). *Working memory capacity.* Hove, UK: Psychology Press.

Cowan, N., Day, L., Saults, J. S., Keller, T. A., Johnson, T., & Flores, L. (1992). The role of verbal output time and the effects of word-length on immediate memory. *Journal of Memory and Language, 31,* 1–17.

Craik, F. I. M., & Lockhart, R. S. (1972). Levels of processing. A framework for memory research. *Journal of Verbal Learning and Verbal Behavior, 11,* 671–684.

Daneman, M., & Carpenter, P. A. (1980). Individual differences in working memory and reading. *Journal of Verbal Learning and Verbal Behavior, 19,* 450–466.

Daneman, M., & Merikle, P. M. (1996). Working memory and language comprehension: A meta-analysis. *Psychonomic Bulletin and Review, 3,* 422–433.

Di Vesta, F. J., Ingersoll, G., & Sunshine, P. (1971). A factor analysis of imagery tests. *Journal of Verbal Learning and Verbal Behavior, 10,* 471–479.

Duncan, J., & Owen, A. M. (2000). Common regions of the human frontal lobe recruited by diverse cognitive demands. *Trends in Neurosciences, 23,* 475–483.

Emerson, M. J., & Miyake, A. (2003). The role of inner speech in task switching: A dual-task investigation. *Journal of Memory and Language, 48,* 148–168.

Engle, R. W. (1996). Working memory and retrieval: An inhibition-resource approach. In J. T. E. Richardson, R. W. Engle, L. Hasher, R. H. Logie, E. R. Stoltfus, & R. T. Zacks (Eds.), *Working memory and human cognition* (pp. 89–119). New York: Oxford University Press.

Engle, R. W., Carullo, J. W., & Collins, K. W. (1991). Individual differences in working memory for comprehension and following directions. *Journal of Educational Research, 84,* 253–262.

Engle, R. W., Tuholski, S. W., Laughlin, J. E., & Conway, A. R. A. (1999). Working memory, short-term memory, and general fluid intelligence: A latent-variable approach. *Journal of Experimental Psychology: General, 128,* 309–331.

Engel de Abreu, P. M. J., & Gathercole, S. E. (2012). Executive and phonological processes in second language acquisition. *Journal of Educational Psychology, 104,* 976–986.

Finke, R. A., & Slayton, K. (1988). Explorations of creative visual synthesis in mental imagery. *Memory and Cognition, 16,* 252–257.

Friedman, N. P., & Miyake, A. (2004). The relations among inhibition and interference control functions: A latent variable analysis. *Journal of Experimental Psychology: General, 133,* 101–135.

Fukuda, K., & Vogel, E. K. (2009). Human variation in overriding attentional capture. *The Journal of Neuroscience, 29,* 8726–8733.

Funahashi, S., Bruce, C. J., & Goldman-Rakic, P. S. (1989). Mnemonic coding of visual space in the monkey's dorsolateral prefrontal cortex. *Journal of Neurophysiology, 61,* 331–349.

Fuster, J. M. (1954). *Memory in the cerebral cortex.* Cambridge, MA: MIT Press.

Gathercole, S. E. (1995). Is nonword repetition a test of phonological memory or long-term knowledge? It all depends on the nonwords. *Memory and Cognition, 23,* 83–94.

Gathercole, S. E., & Alloway, T. P. (2008). *Working memory & learning: A practical guide.* London: Sage Press.

Gathercole, S. E., & Baddeley, A. D. (1989). Evaluation of the role of phonological STM in the development of vocabulary in children: A longitudinal study. *Journal of Memory and Language, 28,* 200–213.

Gathercole, S. E., & Baddeley, A. D. (1990). Phonological memory deficits in language-disordered children: Is there a causal connection? *Journal of Memory & Language, 29,* 336–360.

Gathercole, S. E., & Pickering, S. J. (2000a). Assessment of working memory in six- and seven-year-old children. *Journal of Educational Psychology, 92,* 377–390.

Gathercole, S. E., & Pickering, S. J. (2000b). Working memory deficits in children with low achievements in the national curriculum at seven years of age. *British Journal of Educational Psychology, 70,* 177–194.

Gathercole, S. E., Dunning, D.L., & Holmes, J. (2012). Cogmed training: Let's be realistic about intervention research. *Journal of Applied Research in Memory and Cognition, 1,* 201–203.

Gathercole, S. E., Lamont, E., & Alloway, T. P. (2006). Working memory in the classroom. In S. Pickering (Ed.), *Working memory and education* (pp. 220–241). London: Elsevier Press.

Gathercole, S. E., Pickering, S. J., Ambridge, B., & Wearing, H. (2004a). The structure of working memory from 4 to 15 years of age. *Developmental Psychology, 40,* 177–190.

Gathercole, S. E., Pickering, S. J., Knight, C., & Stegmann, Z. (2004b). Working memory skills and educational attainment: Evidence from National Curriculum assessments at 7 and 14 years of age. *Applied Cognitive Psychology, 40,* 1–16.

Goldman-Rakic, P. S. (1988). Topography of cognition: Parallel distributed networks in primate association cortex. *Annual Review of Neuroscience, 11,* 137–156.

Goldman-Rakic, P. S. (1996). The prefrontal landscape: Implications of functional architecture for understanding human mentation and the central executive. *Philosophical Transactions of the Royal Society (Biological Sciences), 351,* 1445–1453.

Harrison, S. A., & Tong, F. (2009). Decoding reveals the contents of visual working memory in early visual areas *Nature, 458,* 632–635. doi: 10.1038/nature07832

Hatano, G., & Osawa, K. (1983a). Digit memory of grand experts in abacus-derived mental calculation. *Cognition, 15,* 95–110.

Hatano, G., & Osawa, K. (1983b). Japanese abacus experts' memory for numbers is disrupted by mechanism of action. *Journal of Clinical Psychology, 58(1),* 61–75.

Heuer, F., Fischman, D., & Reisberg, D. (1986). Why does vivid imagery hurt colour memory? *Canadian Journal of Psychology, 40,* 161–175.

Holding, D. H. (1989). Counting backward during chess move choice. *Bulletin of Psychonomic Society, 27,* 421–424.

Holmes, J., Gathercole, S. E., & Dunning, D. L. (2009). Adaptive training leads to sustained enhancement of poor working memory in children. *Developmental Science*. doi: 10.1111/j.1467-7687.2009.00848

Holmes, J., Gathercole, S. E., Place, M., Dunning, D. L. Hilton, K. A., & Elliott, J. G. (2010). Working memory deficits can be overcome: Impacts of training and medication on working memory in children with ADHD. *Applied Cognitive Psychology, A24*, 827–836. doi: 10.1002/acp.1589

Hsi, S., Linn, M. C., & Bell, J. A. (1997). The role of spatial reasoning in engineering and the design of spatial instruction. *Journal of Engineering Education, 86*, 151–158.

Hubel, D. H. (1982). Exploration of the primary visual cortex, 1955–78. *Nature, 299*, 515–524.

Hubel, D. H., & Weisel, T. N. (1979). Brain mechanisms of vision. *Scientific American, 24*, 150–162.

Kane, M. J., & Engle, R. W. (2000). Working-memory capacity, proactive interference, and divided attention: Limits on long-term memory retrieval. *Journal of Experimental Psychology: Learning, Memory and Cognition, 26*(2), 336–358.

Kiewra, K. A., & Benton, S. L. (1988). The relationship between information-processing ability and note taking. *Contemporary Educational Psychology, 13*, 33–44.

Kintsch, W., & van Dyck, T. (1977). Toward a model of text comprehension and production. *Psychological Review, 85*, 63–94.

Klingberg, T., Fernell, E., Olesen, P. J., Johnson, M., Gustafsson, P., Dahlström, K., et al. (2005). Computerized training of working memory in children with ADHD— a randomized, controlled trial. *Journal of the American Academy of Child and Adolescent Psychiatry, 44*, 177–186.

Kyllonen, P. C., & Christal, R. E. (1990). Reasoning ability is (little more than) working memory capacity. *Intelligence, 14*, 389–433.

Kyllonen, P. C., & Stephens, D. L. (1990). Cognitive abilities as the determinants of success in acquiring logic skills. *Learning and Individual Differences, 2*, 129–160.

LeDoux, J. E. (1996). *The emotional brain*. New York: Simon & Schuster.

Lépine, R., Barrouillet, P., & Camos, V. (2005). What makes working memory spans so predictive of high-level cognition? *Psychonomic Bulletin and Review, 12*, 165–170.

Lewis-Peacock, J., & Postle, B. R. (2008). Temporary activation of long-term memory supports working memory. *The Journal of Neuroscience, 28*, 8765–8771.

Linn, M. C., & Petersen, A. C. (1985). Emergence and characterization of sex differences in spatial ability: A meta-analysis. *Child Development, 56*, 1479–1498.

Logie, R. H. (1995). *Visuo-spatial working memory*. Hove, UK: Erlbaum.

Logie, R. H., Cocchini, G., Della Sala, S., & Baddeley, A. (2004). Is there a specific capacity for dual task co-ordination? Evidence from Alzheimer's Disease. *Neuropsychology, 18*(3), 504–513.

Logie, R. H., Pernet, C. R., Buonocore, A., & Della Sala, S. (2011). Low and high imagers activate networks differentially in mental rotation *Neuropsychologia, 49*, 3071–3077.

Luck, S. J., & Vogel, E. K. (1997). The capacity of visual working memory for features and conjunctions. *Nature, 390*, 279–281.

Luria, A. R. (1959). The directive function of speech in development and dissolution, Part I. *Word, 15*, 341–352.

McNab, F., & Klingberg, T. (2008). Prefrontal cortex and basal ganglia control access to working memory. *Nature Neuroscience, 11*, 103–107. doi: 10.1038/nn2024

McNab, F., Varrone, A., Farde, L., Jucaite, A., Bystritsky P., Forssberg, H., Klingberg, T. (2009). Changes in cortical dopamine D1 receptor binding associated with cognitive training. *Science, 323*, 800–802.

McKenna, P., Ornstein, T., & Baddeley, A. (2002). Schizophrenia. In A. D. Baddeley, M. D. Kopelman, & B. A. Wilson (Eds.), *The handbook of memory disorders* (2nd edn., pp. 413–436). Chichester: Wiley.

Melby-Lervåg, M., & Hulme, C. (2013). Is working memory training effective? A meta-analytic review. *Developmental Psychology, 49*, 270–291.

Miller, G. A. (1956). The magical number seven, plus or minus two: Some limits on our capacity for processing information. *Psychological Review, 63*, 81–97.

Miller, G. A., Galanter, E., & Pribram, K. H. (1960). *Plans and the structure of behavior*. New York: Holt, Rinehart & Winston.

Mishkin, M., Ungerleider, L. G., & Macko, K. A. (1983). Object vision and spatial vision: Two cortical pathways. *Trends in Neurosciences, 6*, 414–417.

Miyake, A., & Shah, P. (1999). Toward unified theories of working memory: Emerging general consensus, unresolved theoretical issues and future directions. In A. Miyake & P. Shah (Eds.), *Models of working memory: Mechanisms of active maintenance and executive control* (pp. 28–61): Cambridge University Press.

Miyake, A., Friedman, N. P., Rettinger, D. A., Shah, P., & Hegarty, P. (2001). How are visuospatial working memory, executive functioning, and spatial abilities related? A latent-variable analysis. *Journal of Experimental Psychology: General, 130*(4), 621–640.

Monsell, S. (2005). The chronometrics of task-set control. In J. Duncan, L. Phillips, & P. McLeod (Eds.), *Measuring the mind: Speed, control, and age.* (pp. 161–190). Oxford: Oxford University Press.

National Highway Safety Administration (2006). *The impact of driver inattention on near crash/crash risk: an analysis using the 100-car naturalistic driving study data (DOTHS810-594).* Washington, DC: US Department of Transportation.

Nicolay, A., & Poncelet, M. (2013). Cognitive abilities underlying second-language vocabulary acquisition in an early second-language immersion education context: A longitudinal study. *Journal of Experimental Child Psychology, 115,* 655–671.

Norman, D. A., & Shallice, T. (1986). Attention to action: Willed and automatic control of behaviour. In R. J. Davidson, G. E. Schwartz, & D. Shapiro (Eds.), *Consciousness and self-regulation. Advances in research and theory* (Vol. 4, pp. 1–18). New York: Plenum Press.

Oberauer, K., & Hein, L. (2012). Attention to information in working memory. *Current Directions in Psychological Science, 21,* 164–169.

Öhman, A., & Soares, J. J. F. (1994). "Unconscious anxiety": Phobic responses to masked stimuli. *Journal of Abnormal Psychology, 103,* 231–240.

Olesen, P., Westerberg, H., & Klingberg, T. (2004). Increased prefrontal and parietal brain activity after training of working memory. *Nature Neuroscience, 7,* 75–79.

Papagno, C., & Vallar, G. (1992). Phonological short-term memory and the learning of novel words: The effect of phonological similarity and item length. *Quarterly Journal of Experimental Psychology, 44A,* 47–67.

Papagno, C., Valentine, T., & Baddeley, A. D. (1991). Phonological short-term memory and foreign language vocabulary learning. *Journal of Memory and Language, 30,* 331–347.

Park, S., & Holzman, P. (1992). Schizophrenics show spatial working memory deficits. *Archives of General Psychiatry, 49,* 975–982.

Paulesu, E., Frith, C. D., & Frackowiak, R. S. J. (1993). The neural correlates of the verbal component of working memory. *Nature, 362,* 342–345.

Pearson, D. G., Logie, R. H., & Gilhooly, K. J. (1999). Verbal representations and spatial manipulation during mental synthesis. *European Journal of Cognitive Psychology, 11*(3), 295–314.

Posner, M. I. (2013). The expert brain. Expertise and skill acquisition. In J. J. Staszewski (Ed.), *Expertise and skill acquisition: The impact of William G. Chase* (pp. 243–260). New York: Psychology Press.

Posner, M. I., & DiGirolamo, G. J. (1998). Executive attention: Conflict, target detection, and cognitive control. In R. Parasuraman (Ed.), *The attentive brain* (pp. 401–423). Cambridge, MA: MIT Press.

Posner, M. I., & Rothbart, M. K. (2007). Research on attention networks as a model for the integration of psychological science. *Annual Review of Psychology, 58,* 1–23.

Quinn, G., & McConnell, J. (1996a). Irrelevant pictures in visual working memory. *Quarterly Journal of Experimental Psychology, 49A*(1), 200–215.

Quinn, G., & McConnell, J. (1996b). Exploring the passive visual store. *Psychologische Beitrage, 38*(314), 355–367.

Redelmeier, D. A., & Tibshirani, R. J. (1997). Association between cellular-telephone calls and motor vehicular collisions. *New England Journal of Medicine, 336,* 453–458.

Reisberg, D., Clayton, C. L., Heuer, F., & Fischman, D. (1986). Visual memory: When imagery vividness makes a difference. *Journal of Mental Imagery, 10,* 51–74.

Rissman, J., & Wagner, A. D. (2012). Distributed representations in memory: Insights from functional brain imaging. *Annual Review of Psychology, 63,* 101–128.

Robbins, T., Anderson, E., Barker, D., Bradley, A., Fearneyhough, C., Henson, R., et al. (1996). Working memory in chess. *Memory and Cognition, 24*(1), 83–93.

Rothbart, M. K., & Rueda, M. R. (2005). The development of effortful control. In U. Mayr, E. Awh, & S. Keele (Eds.), *Developing individuality in the human brain: A tribute to Michael I. Posner* (pp. 167–188). Washington, DC: American Psychological Association.

Rowe, J. B., Toni, I., Josephs, O., Frackowiak, R. S., & Passingham, R. E. (2000). The prefrontal cortex: Response selection or maintenance within working memory? *Science, 288,* 1656–1660.

Ruchkin, D. S., Grafman, J., Cameron, K., & Berndt, R. S. (2003). Working memory retention systems: A state of activated long-term memory. *Behavioral and Brain Sciences, 26,* 709–777.

Saeki, E., & Saito, S. (2004). The role of the phonological loop in task switching performance: The effect of articulatory suppression in the alternating runs paradigm. *Psychologica, 47,* 35–43.

Saeki, E., Baddeley, A. D., Hitch G. J., & Saito, S. (2013). Breaking a habit: The role of the phonological loop in action control. *Memory and Cognition, 41,* 1065–1078. doi:10.3758/s13421-013-0320-y

Serences, J., Ester, E., Vogel, E.K., & Awh, E. (2009). Stimulus-specific delay activity in human primary visual cortex. *Psychological Science, 20*, 207–214.

Service, E. (1992). Phonology, working memory and foreign-language learning. *Quarterly Journal of Experimental Psychology, 45A*(1), 21–50.

Shallice, T. (2002). Fractionation of the supervisory system. In D. T. Stuss & R. T. Knight (Eds.), *Principles of frontal lobe function.* (pp. 261–277). New York: Oxford University Press.

Shallice, T., & Cooper, R. P. (2011). *The organisation of mind.* Oxford: Oxford University Press.

Shallice, T., & Warrington, E. K. (1970). Independent functioning of verbal memory stores: A neuropsychological study. *Quarterly Journal of Experimental Psychology, 22*, 261–273.

Shepard, R. N., & Feng, C. (1972). A chronometric study of mental paper-folding. *Cognitive Psychology, 3*, 228–243.

Shipstead, Z., Redick, T. S., & Engle, R. W. (2012). Is working memory training effective? *Psychological Bulletin.* doi: 10.1037/a0027473

Shute, R. (1991). *Psychology in vision care.* Oxford: Butterworth Heinemann.

Smith, E., & Jonides, J. (1997). Working memory: A view from neuroimaging. *Cognitive Psychology, 33*, 5–42.

Smith, E., Jonides, J., & Koeppe, R. A. (1996). Dissociating verbal and spatial working memory using PET. *Cerebral Cortex, 6*, 11–20.

Strayer, D. L., & Johnston, W. A. (2001). Driving to distraction: Dual-task studies of simulated driving and conversing on a cellular telephone. *Psychological Science, 12*, 462–466.

Thompson-Schill, S. L., D'Esposito, M., Aguirre, G. K., & Farah, M. J. (1997). Role of left prefrontal cortex in retrieval of semantic knowledge: A re-evaluation. *Proceedings of the National Academy of Sciences of the USA, 94*, 14792–14797.

Towse, J. N., & Hitch, G. J. (1995). Is there a relationship between task demand and storage space in tests of working memory capacity? *Quarterly Journal of Experimental Psychology, 48A*(1), 108–124.

Towse, J. N., Hitch, G. J., & Hutton, U. (2000). On the interpretation of working memory span in adults. *Memory & Cognition, 28*(3), 341–348.

Turner, M. L., & Engle, R. W. (1989). Is working memory capacity task-dependent? *Journal of Memory and Language, 28*, 127–154.

Unsworth, N., & Engle, R. W. (2007). The nature of individual differences in working memory capacity: Active maintenance in primary memory and controlled search from secondary memory. *Psychological Review, 114*, 104–132.

Vallar, G., & Baddeley, A. D. (1987). Phonological short-term store and sentence processing. *Cognitive Neuropsychology, 4*, 417–438.

Vallar, G., & Shallice, T. (1990). *Neuropsychological impairments of short-term memory.* Cambridge: Cambridge University Press.

Vogel, E. K., Woodman, G. F., & Luck, S. J. (2001). Storage of features, conjunctions, and objects in visual working memory. *Journal of Experimental Psychology: Human Perception and Performance, 27*(1), 92–114.

Vygotsky, L. S. (1962). *Thought and language* (E. Hanfmann & G. Vakar, Trans.). Cambridge, MA: MIT Press.

Wagner, R. K., & Torgesen, J. K. (1987). The nature of phonological processing and its causal role in the acquisition of reading skills. *psychological Bulletin, 101*, 192–212.

Contents

Rate of learning   108

Distributed practice   110

Expanding retrieval   112

The importance of testing   113

The importance of feedback   114

Motivation to learn   114

Repetition and learning   115

Implicit learning   117

Learning and consciousness   126

The neurobiological basis of learning   129

Summary   131

Points for discussion   132

Further reading   132

References   132

CHAPTER (5)

LEARNING

Alan Baddeley

Why are you reading this chapter? I assume that at one level or another you hope to learn something, although perhaps only enough to get through your next test! If you are a student, then you have probably spent a large part of your life learning. Such a lengthy period of learning is not evolution's usual solution to survival in a complex world. Many very successful species, such as ants, crocodiles, viruses and butterflies, come into the world preprogrammed with the equipment to survive. Humans, however, are a species that can only survive by learning. Without it, we would have no language, no complex tools, no transport systems, and little in the way of society. So what do we know about learning?

As the next few chapters will illustrate, we know a good deal; we know there are different kinds of learning leading to different kinds of memory. We know that forgetting reflects the capacity to retrieve what we have learned. And we know that this in turn depends on how we learned it. In short, the various stages of learning and memory are interrelated and, ideally, should be discussed together. However, that would result in a single, huge, and complex chapter. Instead, we have opted for a series of interlinked chapters moving from learning, through episodic memory to retrieval and forgetting, attempting to remind you of the important links by cross-chapter references.

Philosophers have considered the nature of learning and remembering for over 2000 years, without coming to an agreed understanding, so when in the 1880s, a young German philosopher,

Herman Ebbinghaus, proposed an experimental study of memory, he was being extremely bold. Ebbinghaus devoted 2 or 3 years to this ambitious enterprise before moving on to study other topics such as intelligence and color vision. However, in that brief period he laid the foundations of a new science of learning and memory, a science that is particularly relevant to rapidly changing societies like our own, in which people need to learn far more than did earlier generations.

Ebbinghaus decided that the only way to tackle the complex subject of human memory was to simplify the problem. He tested only one person—himself—and as he wished to study the learning of new information and to minimize any effects of previous knowledge, he invented some entirely new material to be learned. This material consisted of nonsense syllables: word-like consonant–vowel–consonant sequences, such as *wux*, *caz*, *bij*, and *zol*, which could be pronounced but had no meaning. He taught himself sequences of such words by reciting them aloud at a rapid rate, and carefully scored the number of recitations required to learn each list, or to relearn it after a delay had caused him to

KEY TERM

Nonsense syllables: Pronounceable but meaningless consonant-vowel-consonant items designed to study learning without the complicating factor of meaning.

forget it. During his learning, he carefully avoided using any associations with real words, and he always tested himself at the same time of day under carefully controlled conditions, discontinuing the tests whenever "too great changes in the outer or inner life occurred." Despite, or perhaps because of, his use of this rather unpromising material, Ebbinghaus was able to demonstrate to the world that memory can be investigated scientifically, and in the short period of 2 years, he was able to show some of the fundamental characteristics of human memory.

If you want to assess any system for storing information, three basic questions must be answered: How rapidly can information be fed into the system? How much information can be stored? How rapidly is information lost? In the case of human memory, the storage capacity is clearly enormous, so Ebbinghaus concentrated on assessing the rate of input and, as we shall see later, of forgetting.

RATE OF LEARNING

Consider the rate at which information can be registered in memory. If you spend twice as much time learning, do you remember twice as much information? Or is there perhaps a law of diminishing returns, with each additional learning episode putting a little less information into storage? Or perhaps the relationship is the other way round: The more information you have acquired, the easier and quicker it is to add new information, rather like a rolling snowball picking up more snow with each successive revolution? Ebbinghaus investigated this problem very simply, by creating a number of lists each containing 16 meaningless syllables. On a given day, he would select a fresh list (one he had not learned before) and recite it at a rate of 2.5 syllables per second for 8, 16, 24, 32, 42, 53, or 64 repetitions. Twenty-four hours later, he would find out how much of the list he had remembered by seeing how many additional trials he needed to relearn the list by heart. To get some idea of what his experiment was like, try reading the following list of nonsense syllables as rapidly as you can for two successive trials:

jih, baz, fub, yox, suj, xir, dax, leq,
vum, paq, kel, wab, tuv, zof, gek, hiw

The results of this very tedious exercise are shown in Figure 5.1. The relationship between the number of learning trials on day 1 and the amount retained on day 2 proved to be a straight line, signifying that the process of learning shows neither diminishing returns nor the snowball effect, but obeys the simple rule that the amount learned depends on time spent learning: If you double the learning time, you double the amount of information stored. In short, as far as learning is concerned, you get what you pay for. This simple relationship has been explored extensively in the 100 years since it was discovered by Ebbinghaus and is known as the total time hypothesis.

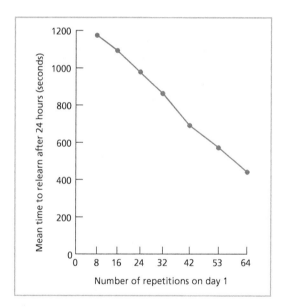

Figure 5.1 Influence of number of learning trials on retention after a 24-hour delay. From Ebbinghaus (1885).

KEY TERM

Total time hypothesis: The proposal that amount learned is a simple function of the amount of time spent on the learning task.

It would, of course, be unwise to base such a sweeping conclusion on a single study, even by someone as august as Herman Ebbinghaus, but there is ample further evidence. For example, do you want to become a more skilled writer? If so, the answer is to practice. A study by Astin (1993) found that the best predictor of self-reported skill in writing was number of writing skills classes taken, with amount of feedback provided by the instructor being the second best predictor. One might reasonably argue that this result is based on self-assessment, which is likely to be an unreliable measure. However, a similar conclusion was obtained by Johnstone, Ashbaugh, and Warfield (2002), who observed a steady increase in writing skill over a sequence of courses as assessed by others. This is further illustrated in the case of professional writers such as Norman Mailer (2003), who reports that he learnt to write by writing, estimating that he must have written more than half a million words before he came to his famous novel *The Naked and the Dead*.

Ericsson, Krampe, and Tesch-Römer (1993) emphasized the importance of practice across a number of skills, including chess, typing, and music. In relation to the last, they suggest that the very best violinists have accumulated more than 10,000 hours of solitary practice compared to 7500 for lesser experts, 5000 for the least accomplished experts, and around 1500 hours for the committed amateur.

This theme has been picked up by popular science writer, Malcolm Gladwell, who in a recent book (Gladwell, 2008) asserted that "The emerging pictures from such studies is that 10,000 hours of practice is required to achieve the level of mastery associated with being a world-class expert—in anything. In study after study of composers, baseball players, fiction writers, ice skaters, concert pianists, chess players, common master criminals and what have you, this number comes up again and again" (Gladwell, 2008, p. 44). Could we all become Mozart or major league football stars if only we practiced enough? Ericsson (2013) objects to the concept of a "10,000 hours rule." He points out that although the average for a violinist was 10,000 hours, half were less than 5000, while winners of piano competitions continuing beyond their 20s can

often clock up over 25,000 hours of practice, while in less heavily populated fields such as digit sequence memorizers, 500 to 1000 hours are typical.

At a more theoretical level, he points out that his views differ from those of his mentor, Herbert Simon, whose theory implied that simple repeated experience is enough to develop expertise, arguing that performing a given skill repeatedly will lead to a performance plateau. To move beyond, deliberate practice is required, developing new skills and targeting weakness. A study by Young and Salmela (2010) of national versus regional middle-distance runners, for example, found that the number of hours of training did not differ greatly, but the national runners devoted more of their time to weight and technical training (see Figure 5.2). Ericsson's current view (Ericsson, 2013) is that extensive practice will indeed enhance performance, as in the case of speaking our native language, but that this eventually levels out; if you want to be a professional novelist or an accomplished poet, you need to continue to strive to focus on your weaknesses and develop your strengths.

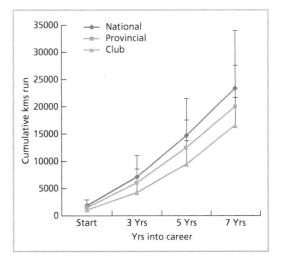

Figure 5.2 Young and Salmela (2010) found that the number of hours of training done by national and regional middle-distance runners was the same, but that national runners devoted more of their time to weight and technical training. From Young and Salmela (2010). Reprinted with permission of *International Journal of Sport Psychology*.

Such a commitment of time and energy is likely to demand a high degree of motivation which in turn will depend on social factors and access to opportunities, as well as genetic influences, both temperamental and physical. Regardless of amount of practice, major league basketball players are no more likely to make winning jockeys than the reverse. Ericsson (2013) now accepts such complexities, asserting that in the past in emphasizing the importance of practice, he had simply pointed out that there was no convincing *evidence* for other variables such as genetic factors, in contrast to the powerful and widespread evidence for the effects of many hours of training. It is of course, very hard to derive unequivocal evidence. In the case of genetic factors, as described in Chapter 2, although there are many instances of talents such as music (the Bach family) or an aptitude for science (Darwins and Huxleys) to run in families, it is hard to separate out the genetic from the environmental influences. If you were born into a family with several generations of successful professional musicians like the Bach family, you would be expected to learn an instrument, and practice from an early age. Furthermore, it seems likely that someone who has a particular talent will enjoy exercising that talent, and hence will accumulate far more practice than someone who performs badly. Ericsson has shown practice is certainly important but his evidence is at base correlational; the detailed causal pathways underlying genius are likely to prove difficult to untangle.

Happily, the area is now moving on from simply collecting further evidence of the relationship between practice and the specific skills needed to become an expert in specific areas, for example becoming a successful soccer professional (Williams, Ward, Bell-Walker, & Ford, 2012). Studies are also beginning to emerge relating the development of expertise to changes in brain structure. In the area of sport, Wei, Zhang, Jiang, and Luo (2011) have reported increases in cortical thickness associated with degree of practice in high divers, while Hu et al. (2011) have studied children extensively trained in calculation and music, finding an increase in myelination, the process of development of the white matter that is assumed to enhance neuronal function.

The generalization that "you get what you pay for" is therefore a reasonable rule of thumb for learning, but to move beyond competence to true excellence is likely to need much more than simple repetitive practice. Furthermore, despite the general relationship between practice and the amount retained, there are ways in which one can get better value for time spent. The rest of this chapter is concerned with ways of beating the total time hypothesis.

DISTRIBUTED PRACTICE

If you examine the Ebbinghaus learning graph closely, bearing in mind the amount of time spent in practice on day 1, you will notice that total time for learning is not in fact constant, as time spent on day 1 gives a disproportionate saving on relearning the next day. For example, 64 of Ebbinghaus's rapid trials on day 1 took about 7.5 minutes; a similar time was needed to learn the list completely on day 2, making a total of 15 minutes. However, if only eight trials are given on day 1 (about 1 minute), then it takes nearly 20 minutes to learn the list on day 2. Dividing practice fairly evenly over the 2 days, therefore, results in more efficient learning than cramming most of the practice into the second day. This is an instance of a very widespread phenomenon, known as the distributed practice effect. What this means is that it is better to distribute your learning trials sparsely across a period of time than to mass them together in a single block of learning. As far as learning is concerned, "little and often" is an excellent precept.

A good example of this arose a few years ago when my colleagues and I were asked to advise the British Post Office on a program that aimed to teach a very large number of postal workers to type. Postal coding was

> **KEY TERM**
>
> Distributed practice: Breaking practice up into a number of shorter sessions; in contrast to massed practice, which comprises fewer, long, learning sessions.

being introduced and this required the mail sorters to type the postal code using a keyboard resembling that of a typewriter. The Post Office had the option of either taking postmen (they were all men) off their regular jobs and giving them intensive keyboard training, or of combining the training with their regular jobs by giving them a little practice each day. There were four feasible schedules: an intensive schedule of two 2-hour sessions per day; intermediate schedules involving either one 2-hour or two 1-hour sessions per day; or a more gradual approach involving a single 1-hour session of typing per day. We therefore assigned postmen at random to one of the four groups and began the training.

Figure 5.3 shows the rate at which the four groups acquired typing skill. The time it took to learn the keyboard (the point at which each learning curve starts) and the subsequent rate of improvement were both strongly affected by the particular training schedule used. The postmen who trained for only 1 hour a day learned the keyboard in fewer hours of training and improved their performance more rapidly than those who trained for 2 hours a day; and they in turn learned more rapidly than those who trained for 4 hours per day. Indeed, the 1-hour-per-day group learned as much in 55 hours as the 4-hours-per-day group learned in 80. They also appeared to continue to improve at a faster rate and, when tested after several months without further practice, they proved to have retained their skill better than the 4-hours-per-day group (Baddeley & Longman, 1978).

This result did not stem from fatigue or discontent on the part of the 4-hours-per-day group. Indeed, when questioned afterwards, the 1-hour-per-day postmen were the least contented with their training schedule because, when measured in terms of the number of days required to acquire typing skill, they appeared to be progressing less rapidly than their 4-hours-per-day colleagues. In drawing practical conclusions, of course, this should be borne in mind; 4 hours per day might be a relatively inefficient way of learning to type when measured on an hourly basis, but it did mean that the group reached in 4 weeks the standard it took the 1-hour-a-day group 11 weeks to achieve. Distributed practice is more efficient, but it might not always be practical or convenient.

In recent years there has been a good deal of interest in a method originally proposed by Tom Landauer and Robert Bjork (1978) that involves what might be called the microdistribution of practice. Suppose you are trying to learn French vocabulary and have the following list of words to master:

- stable = *l'écurie*
- horse = *le cheval*
- grass = *l'herbe*
- church = *l'église*
- castle = *le château*
- cat = *le chat*
- table = *la table*
- bird = *l'oiseau*

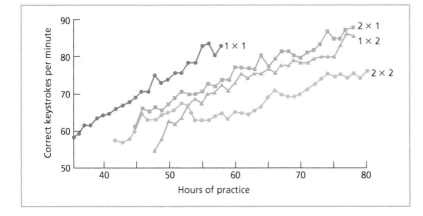

Figure 5.3 Rate of learning a typing skill for a range of training schedules: 1 × 1 equals one session of 1 hour per day, 2 × 1 equals two such sessions, 1 × 2 is one session of 2 hours and 2 × 2 two 2-hour sessions. From Baddeley and Longman (1978). Copyright © 1978 Taylor & Francis. Reproduced by permission (http://www.tandf.co.uk/journals).

If you are presented with a single item on two occasions, do you remember it better if it is presented and tested in rapid succession, or is recall better if the two presentation and test are spaced further apart? Fortunately, the answer is clear; spaced presentation enhances memory. On that basis alone, one should go through the whole vocabulary list before testing by re-presenting the first item, as that will maximize the space between two successive presentations. Unfortunately, however, life is not so simple, as it is also the case that if you succeed in remembering an item for yourself, this strengthens the memory more than if you have the item provided for you; this is known as the *generation effect*. The implications of this are exactly the opposite to the distribution of practice effect. The sooner an item is tested, the greater the probability that you will be able to successfully retrieve it, and hence the greater the probability that learning will be strengthened.

EXPANDING RETRIEVAL

The solution to this dilemma is to use a flexible strategy in which a new item is tested initially after a short delay, ensuring that it is still recallable. Then, as the item becomes better learned, the practice–test interval is gradually extended, the aim being to test each item at the longest interval at which it can reliably be recalled. Hence, a learning sequence for the list of French words just given might be as shown in Table 5.1. If the learner fails an item in the vocabulary list, it should be presented after a shorter delay; whenever the learner is correct, the delay should be increased.

In creating their new mnemonic method, known as expanding retrieval, Landauer and Bjork (1978) combined two basic principles derived from the laboratory study of verbal memory. The first is the distribution of practice

TABLE 5.1 Expanding retrieval—an example based on learning French vocabulary.

Teacher	Learner
stable = l'écurie	
stable?	l'écurie
horse = le cheval	
horse?	le cheval
stable?	l'écurie
horse?	le cheval
grass = l'herbe	
grass?	l'herbe
stable?	l'écurie
horse?	le cheval
grass?	l'herbe
church = l'église	
church?	l'église
grass?	l'herbe
church?	l'église
stable?	l'écurie
grass?	l'herbe
horse?	le cheval

effect and the second is the generation effect; items that you yourself have generated successfully are remembered best. In recent years, a number of studies have explored these underlying principles in more detail, part of a very welcome current concern to apply the results of the memory laboratory to learning in the classroom. Pashler, Rohrer, Cepeda, and Carpenter (2007) studied the spacing effect across a range of different materials, including the acquisition of foreign language vocabulary, learning to solve mathematical problems, acquiring obscure facts, learning the definition of uncommon words, and learning from maps. They found that spacing is beneficial for all of these materials.

How far apart should spacings be? This proves to depend on the length of the delay

KEY TERM

Expanding retrieval: A learning schedule whereby items are initially tested after a short delay, with pretest delay gradually increasing across subsequent trials.

between learning and testing, with the optimum interval between learning episodes being between 10 and 20% of test delay. Hence, for testing after 10 days there should be a delay of 1 or 2 days between trials, whereas for a 6-month test delay, a 20-day interval between learning trials is best. In general, longer inter-trial delays are preferable to short. It should be noted, however, that it is important for participants to receive feedback as to the correct answers, having made their response, although it proves not to be crucial whether the feedback is immediate or somewhat delayed (Pashler et al., 2007).

As in the case of the postmen learning to type, later studies have confirmed that spaced practice leads to less forgetting. In one study, Pashler et al. (2007) gave their students one sequence of ten mathematical problems, or two sets of five, presented 2 weeks apart. When tested after 1 week, the two groups were equivalent, but after 4 weeks there was a clear advantage to spaced learning.

THE IMPORTANCE OF TESTING

A second crucial feature of the Landauer and Bjork method is the importance of testing one's

memory. Pashler et al. found that giving a test trial with feedback was more effective than giving an extra learning trial. The importance of retrieval for learning was shown particularly clearly in an elegant study by Karpicke and Roediger (2008). They studied foreign language vocabulary learning across four conditions. The first involved the standard procedure of repeatedly presenting and testing a list of 40 Swahili–English word pairs (e.g. *mashua–boat*). A second adopted the procedure of dropping a pair, once it had been learned, a procedure often recommended in study guides as it allows the learner to concentrate on the unlearned items. A third condition ceased testing learned pairs but continued to present them. The final condition did the opposite: learned pairs were not presented but continued to be tested. Recall was then tested a week later. Which conditions do you think led to best recall?

The results are shown in Figure 5.4. We should first note that the rate of learning in week 1 was identical across conditions. Retention was not. The two conditions that had continued *testing* learned pairs both recalled 80%; the two conditions in which testing was abandoned when pairs were learned were equally poor, at around 30% recall. Repeated presentation without test had had no effect at

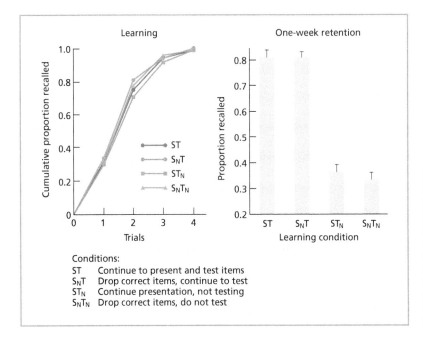

Figure 5.4 The importance of testing for later remembering. The pattern of learning and test trials had no effect on rate of learning, but the presence of tests had a major effect on what was remembered 1 week later. From Karpicke and Roediger (2008). Copyright © 1980 AAAS. Reprinted with permission.

all. Remember this next time you are revising for a test!

The importance of the generation effect—producing the answer from memory rather than being given it—was also stressed by Metcalf and Kornell (2007), who tested foreign language vocabulary learning, for example learning that the French word for *house* is *maison*. At test, they found that even a brief delay between testing with the English item (*house*) and being given the answer (*maison*) was enough to induce an attempt at retrieval that was much more helpful to long-term learning than presenting the English and foreign words at the same time.

Does it matter how knowledge is tested? Marsh, Roediger, Bjork, and Bjork (2007) found that a multiple-choice test enhanced subsequent long-term recall. However, McDaniel, Roediger, and McDermott (2007) observed that short-answer tests were more effective than multiple-choice in enhancing subsequent recall.

THE IMPORTANCE OF FEEDBACK

One danger of encouraging learners to generate answers is that they can produce errors, which, in the absence of explicit feedback, might then persist. Kay (1955) required his students to learn a prose passage and then recall it once a week for several weeks. He found that although the passage was repeated every week, errors made at the beginning tended to persist. Fortunately, this does not appear to be the case if direct feedback is given. In one study, Pashler et al. (2007) encouraged various levels of guessing on a multiple-choice task involving obscure facts such as:

The weight of what land animal is equal to the weight of a blue whale's tongue?

  a. Bengal tiger

  b. Grizzly bear

  c. Wolverine

  d. African elephant

  (The answer is d.)

Pashler et al. found no difference between groups instructed not to guess, those required to guess but given immediate feedback, and those for whom the feedback was delayed. It is, however, perhaps worth noting at this point that an encouragement to guess is not helpful for amnesic patients, presumably because they are not able to remember the feedback (Baddeley & Wilson, 1994). Unlike healthy young participants, they benefit more from learning procedures that try to avoid errors (see Chapter 16, p. 459).

Expanding retrieval is a rare example of a completely new learning technique resulting from verbal learning research. It prompted Ulrich Neisser, normally rather skeptical about the achievements of modern memory research, to produce the following limerick:

You can get a good deal from rehearsal
If it just has the proper dispersal.
You would just be an ass,
To do it en masse:
Your remembering would turn out much worsal.

MOTIVATION TO LEARN

An important factor that has not been mentioned so far is motivation. This might seem strange in the light of most studies of animal learning, in which motivation is regarded as of paramount importance. This is probably because rewarding or punishing the animal is the only way the experimenter can be sure that the animal will attend to the experimental conditions and exhibit what it has learned. Fortunately, experimental human subjects are in general rather more cooperative. Most subjects in memory experiments want to do well, to please the experimenter or to convince themselves that they have good memories, or perhaps because it is simply more interesting to attempt to do well than to display a complete lack of interest. Provided participants give their full attention to a task, level of motivation is not usually an important factor.

A Swedish professor, Lars-Göran Nilsson (1987), found his students very reluctant to accept this view, so he set up the following experiment to prove his point. He had groups of students learn lists of words under various conditions. In one condition no pressure was put on the students to do well; they were simply told that they were taking part in an experiment on memory. In a second condition, the students were not given motivating instructions during learning, but at the time of recall were told that a substantial cash prize would be given to the person who recalled the greatest number of words. Students in a third group were told about the cash prize before they began learning. The learning performance of the three groups did not differ. A subsequent experiment included social competition as a means of increasing motivation and produced exactly the same result: no effect of motivation level on learning.

Does this mean that motivation is quite irrelevant to learning? As any schoolteacher will tell you, this is certainly not the case. The effect of motivation is indirect, however: It will determine both the amount of time and the degree of attention devoted to the material to be learned, and this in turn will affect the amount of learning. Hence, if I were to ask you to learn a list of words comprising ten animal names and ten flower names, and I were to offer you a coin for each animal name recalled and a banknote for each flower, there is little doubt that you would remember more flowers than animals. The reason would be that you would simply spend more time on the flowers, producing a result that would be equivalent to my presenting the flowers for a longer time. In a classroom situation, motivation is likely to affect learning because it affects the amount of attention children give to the material they are being taught. If they are interested, they will pay attention; if they are bored, they are likely to think about other things. This is not, of course, limited to the classroom; as described in connection with Ericsson's theory of expertise, reaching the highest levels of performance is likely to demand focusing on any weaknesses and the determination to tackle them, rather than the easier task of continuing to practice areas of strength. In addition, peak performance, for example in an Olympic athletic final, is likely to demand the capacity to bring to bear the maximum motivation at the optimal time.

REPETITION AND LEARNING

However, although repetition may not be the whole story, it is surely important? Such a view would probably have appealed to Ebbinghaus and to Victorian educators, with their emphasis on learning by heart. However, a number of experiments have recently suggested that simple repetition, with no attempt by the learner to organize the material, might not lead to learning. Think of a penny in your pocket. Can you remember exactly what is on each side? Try it! Figure 5.5 shows the results of a study by Rubin and Kontis (1983), who asked their

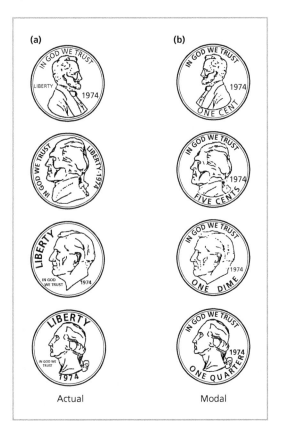

Figure 5.5 The results of a study by Rubin and Kontis (1983) recording the features that most US students thought appeared on each of four coins. Column (a) shows the actual features and column (b) the most frequent responses. From Rubin and Kontis (1983). Copyright © The Psychonomic Society. Reproduced with permission.

participants to recall the features of four American coins. The coins are shown on the left of the figure, and the most commonly recalled version of each coin is shown on the right.

A colleague, Debra Bekerian, and I were able to explore the importance of repetition in connection with a major advertising campaign (Bekerian & Baddeley, 1980). A number of years ago, a new international agreement among European radio stations made it necessary for the BBC to reassign some of the British wavelengths. To acquaint the public with this fact, and to familiarize them with the changes, the BBC embarked on an extensive advertising campaign. Over a period of 2 months, radio programs were regularly interrupted by detailed information about the new wavelengths, supplemented by slogans and complex jingles.

We decided to test the effectiveness of the campaign by questioning about 50 members of our panel of people who volunteered to come along to the Applied Psychology Unit in Cambridge to take part in experiments on functions such as memory, visual perception, and hearing. In this instance, most of our volunteers were Cambridge housewives. At that time, it was common for mothers to stay at home when their children were young. We asked them how much time they spent listening to each radio channel and, on the basis of this and information provided by the BBC about the frequency of announcements, we estimated that most of them had heard the announcements about the new wavelengths well over a thousand times. We asked them to recall the new wavelengths both by writing down the numerical frequencies and by marking a visual display resembling a radio dial.

How much had our subjects learned? The BBC had been successful in conveying the fact that the change was about to occur, as virtually every participant was aware of it. There was also considerable knowledge about the exact date of the change, with 84% reporting it correctly. However, memory for details of the new wavelengths was appalling. Only 25%, on average, even attempted to give the numerical frequencies, and although more people were prepared to attempt to represent them by marking the dial display, most of these attempts were little better than would be expected on the basis of pure guessing. Furthermore, knowledge of the old frequencies was little

better. People probably relied on visual cues on the radio dial to tune in to their favorite programs. So why was the date of changeover so well remembered? Presumably because our participants *did* regularly use dates.

Fortunately, in addition to the radio advertising campaign, the BBC also circulated every household by mail with information about the new wavelengths, and included adhesive stickers with the letters. When we conducted a follow-up survey shortly after the changeover, we found that it was these stickers that had saved the day for most people. Seventy percent of our follow-up group had indeed had difficulty learning the new wavelengths, but for the most part they coped successfully by waiting until the changeover had taken place, then hunting for the new wavelengths and marking them with the stickers that the BBC had sensibly provided.

What conclusions can we draw from this? One is that such saturation advertising is not particularly suitable for conveying complex information. If one simply wants people to remember "Botto washes whitest," telling them so a thousand times will cause the message to be retained, although not necessarily believed. In the case of complex information that does not map onto one's existing way of thinking, however, the total effect appears to be minimal learning and maximum frustration.

Change blindness

Although it might be somewhat surprising that so little was learned about pennies and radio wavelengths despite so many presentations, one could argue that this is because we were testing fine detail of no real interest to the learner. You don't need to check your pennies to make sure they are genuine, and our radio listeners simply did not use wavelength information. Somewhat more surprising, perhaps, are instances of what is become known as change blindness, whereby some prominent feature of the visual

---

KEY TERM

Change blindness: The failure to detect that a visual object has moved, changed, or been replaced by another object.

environment is dramatically changed, without the perceiver apparently noticing.

In one study, for example, the experimenter stopped a passer-by and asked for directions. During the conversation, it was arranged that a pair of men carrying a board passed between the two conversants, allowing the experimenter to be surreptitiously replaced by another quite different experimenter. People rarely appeared to detect this (Rensink, O'Regan, & Clark, 1997; Simons & Levin, 1998).

Could this perhaps reflect a failure to take notice of the appearance of the questioner, or of the fragility of visual STM? These possibilities were ruled out in a study by Rosiell and Scaggs (2008), who asked students to identify what was wrong with a picture of a familiar location on college campus. These were quite dramatic, for example removing the library from the scene (Figure 5.6). Ninety-seven percent of participants rated the scene as familiar, but only 20% detected the change. Despite frequent experiences, our LTM for complex scenes appears to be much less detailed than one might imagine.

IMPLICIT LEARNING

You might recall that in Chapter 1 we distinguished between *declarative* memory, in

Original scene   **Altered scene**

Figure 5.6 Change blindness: the original scenes are on the left; the images on the right are the altered versions that participants were required to judge. From Rosiell and Scaggs (2008). Copyright © Psychology Press.

which we explicitly remember the information retrieved, and *nondeclarative* or implicit memory, in which the evidence of learning comes from a change in behavior. When riding a bicycle, for example, we do not need explicitly to remember what to do; we simply get on the bike and pedal away. The learning of motor skills is just one of a wide range of tasks that can be acquired implicitly. They can be divided into three broad categories: classical conditioning; priming in which an existing representation such as a word is activated; and procedural learning, of which motor skills are one example. These will be described in turn.

Classical conditioning

In 1902, a young American psychologist, E. B. Twitmyer, reported work on the knee-jerk reflex in which a bell sounded after which a lead hammer struck the subject's knee causing an involuntary twitch. He noted that on one occasion the bell rang but the hammer was not delivered; nevertheless the reflex occurred, something that the participant reported as involuntary. Twitmyer (1902) pursued this line of research and reported it at a meeting of the American Psychological Association some 2 years later. However, his enthusiasm for the topic was not shared by the chairman of his session, Professor William James of Harvard, who cut short the discussion to avoid delaying lunch.

At about the same time, an eminent Russian physiologist, Professor I. P. Pavlov, who was shortly to receive the Nobel Prize for his work on digestion, made a similar observation. He was working on the salivatory reflex using dogs and noted that the dogs began to salivate when they heard the experimenter arrive. He pursued this insight and became even more famous than he already was (Pavlov, 1927).

As every basic textbook describes, Pavlov found that when a bell was presented at the same time as meat powder, after a few presentations, the bell alone would evoke salivation, reflecting the basic feature of classical conditioning—that pairing a neutral stimulus, the bell, with a reflex response, salivation, leads to learning.* Pavlov also noted that if the bell was sounded repeatedly without food powder, salivation would reduce and gradually cease, he termed this the *extinction* of the conditioned response.

What would one expect if the bell followed the meat powder? Would backward conditioning occur? Although some evidence of backward or trace conditioning has been reported, the effect is very weak.

Given that sounding the bell alone leads to extinction of the conditioned response, what is

---

* I can happily confirm that Professor Pavlov's observations are not limited to Russian dogs. On mention of the word "treat," our West Highland Terrier immediately starts licking his lips.

Russian psychologist Ivan Pavlov, a dog, and his staff, photographed circa 1925–1926.

the effect of sounding the bell alone for many times *before* introducing the association with food powder? This impairs the capacity to condition the salivating response; a phenomenon known as latent inhibition. Presenting the bell alone, whether before or after the food, breaks the clear link between bell and food.

One area that has taken advantage of classical conditioning is advertising, in which it is common practice to attempt to improve the public's evaluation of a product by associating it with a pleasant and attractive surround experience. Although there is little research on advertising in the memory literature, a relevant study was carried out a few years ago by Stewart, Shimp, and Engle (1987), who presented participants with a slide picture of a "new" brand of toothpaste in a green and yellow tube, labeled "Brand L Toothpaste." The toothpaste was presented with three other fictitious commodities, "Brand R Cola," "Brand M Laundry Detergent," and "Brand J Soap," which were paired with neutral pictures, whereas the toothpaste was always followed by one of four particularly pleasant slides, sunset over an island, for example, or sky and clouds seen through the masts of a yacht. Different groups experienced the items from 1 to 20 times, and were then asked which products they would probably buy. As the graph in Figure 5.7 shows, the toothpaste was rated as more likely to be bought than the other three items, with likelihood of purchase increasing as the number of exposures increased.

The investigators went on to test two more detailed predictions from the conditioning laboratory. The first of these was that presenting the toothpaste for many trials under neutral conditions would reduce the effect of pairing it with the pleasant slides later, the latent inhibition effect. This is indeed what happened. A third study presented the pleasant slides immediately *before* the toothpaste, setting the scene for backward conditioning, which is known to be much weaker than forward conditioning. As predicted, the level of acquired pleasantness was much less, suggesting that conditioning might indeed provide a suitable model for this aspect of advertising.

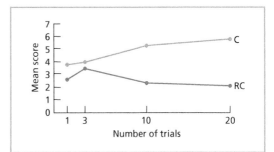

Figure 5.7 Conditioned attitude to a novel brand of toothpaste as a function of the number of conditioning trials. Participants rated the likelihood that they would choose the positively conditioned brand over the randomly associated control brand. C, conditioning; RC, random control. Data from Stewart et al. (1987).

Whereas Stewart et al. (1987) explicitly tried to associate a product with a positive feeling, another conditioning phenomenon suggests that even this is not strictly necessary. Simply increasing our exposure to a novel stimulus will increase its rated pleasantness, the mere exposure effect (see Bornstein, 1989, for a review). The effect occurs even with such unpromising materials as irregular polygons presented so briefly that participants are not aware, and resulting in no subsequent recognition (Kunst-Wilson & Zajonc, 1980). Perfect and Askew (1994) investigated the mere exposure effect is an advertising context. They presented their participants with 25, full-page, color magazine advertisements. Half the participants were instructed to remember the adverts and half were not. They were then shown the 25 together with 25 new adverts and asked to rate them on the extent to which each was eye-catching,

KEY TERM

Latent inhibition: Classical conditioning phenomenon whereby multiple prior presentations of a neutral stimulus will interfere with its involvement in subsequent conditioning.

Mere exposure effect: A tendency for a neutral stimulus to acquire positive value with repeated exposure.

distinctive, appealing, and memorable, after which they were asked to judge which they had seen before. Participants instructed to remember recognized around 60% of the adverts they had seen compared to only 11% for the noninstructed incidental group. However, both groups rated the advertisements they had seen as more appealing and memorable, an effect that was equivalent for the two groups. It seems to be the case, therefore, that although simple repetition is not a very good way of learning about detail, it does—perhaps unfortunately—influence our emotional evaluation.

One of the reasons for rejecting the idea that all types of implicit learning and memory reflect a single system is the evidence that different neural structures are involved in different types of learning. This is shown particularly clearly in the case of classical conditioning. Studies based on animals suggested an important role for the amygdala, an almond-shaped structure within the brain that has repeatedly been found to be involved in emotion and fear conditioning (LeDoux, 1998). Evidence for the importance of the amygdala in human conditioning comes from a study by Bechara, Tranel, Damasio, Adolphs, Rockland, and Damasio (1995), who describe a conditioning study involving a healthy control group and three very different patients. One had bilateral damage to the amygdala; a second had bilateral damage to the hippocampus, which is known to be important for episodic memory; and a third had bilateral damage to both structures. In one study, a series of different-colored slides were presented, with one color—blue—being followed by a blast from a loud horn. This aversive stimulus leads to an increase in skin conductance, a measure of anxiety that became conditioned as a response to the blue slide but not to slides of other colors in the controls.

After the experiment, each of the three patients and the control group were asked what colored slides they had seen, and whether one was associated with the loud horn.

The results are shown in Figure 5.8. The patient with bilateral amygdala damage (SM) failed to condition, but was able to remember the colors and identify the blue slide as associated with the horn. In short, he had explicit episodic memory but did not condition. The second patient, a classic amnesic case with hippocampal damage but intact amygdala (WC), showed clear evidence of conditioning but was unable to describe the slides (see Chapter 1, p. 15 for further discussion). The third patient with damage to both the hippocampus and the amygdala (RH) showed no conditioning and no evidence of recollection. The control participants showed both conditioning and episodic memory for the slides.

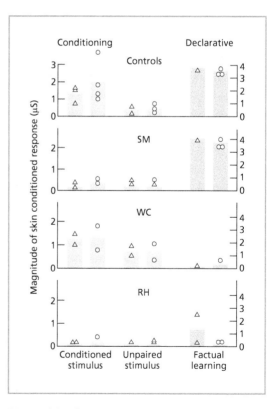

Figure 5.8 Control data and performance of three contrasted patients (SM, WC and RH) studied by Bechara et al. (1995). Copyright © 1995 AAAS. Reprinted with permission.

KEY TERM

Amygdala: An area of the brain close to the hippocampus that is involved in emotional processing.

Hippocampus: Brain structure in the medial temporal lobe that is important for long-term memory formation..

Further evidence for the crucial role of the amygdala comes from a range of neuroimaging studies (see Chapter 2). In one study, Büchel, Morris, Dolan, and Friston (1998) used faces as stimuli, associating one with a loud aversive tone. They observed conditioning in a system involving the amygdala, the cingulate cortex and in motor-related regions that they identify with a "readiness to escape" response. A further study by Morris, Öhman, and Dolan (1998) demonstrated that conditioning was possible even when faces were masked to a point at which participants failed to report them. Interestingly, activation was principally in the right amygdala when the stimulus was masked, whereas it was principally in the left in the unmasked condition.

Priming

Priming is said to occur if presenting an item influences its subsequent perception or processing. For example, you might be required to read out a list of words and then, in an apparently separate experiment, to report words presented very briefly. Those words that you had read would be more likely to be detected than new words, even though you might not be able to remember the old words. Priming occurs across the whole range of senses, leading Schacter (1992) to categorize perceptual priming as forming a coherent memory system, on the grounds that similar principles apply to all modalities.

Priming is also found in verbal memory, and offers one way in which even densely amnesic patients can demonstrate apparently normal memory (see Chapter 16, p. 459). This was discovered by Warrington and Weiskrantz (1968), who presented amnesic patients and controls with a list of words, which were then tested. When the standard recognition procedure was used, with participants required to identify those words that they had seen previously, amnesic patients performed very badly. However, they performed normally when tested using a priming procedure. This involved visually degraded versions of each word, with the instruction to "guess" what the word might be.

Related methods of using priming to demonstrate implicit memory for words include stem completion and word fragment completion. Stem completion tests implicit memory by presenting the first few letters and inviting the patient to "provide" a word that would fit (e.g. present *stamp* and test with *st– – –*). Note that if the patient is asked to "guess" an appropriate word, this is an implicit task, whereas given exactly the same situation and asked to "remember" the word makes it an explicit test. Graf, Squire, and Mandler (1984) tested amnesic and control participants by presenting a list of words and testing retention by free recall, cued recall in which they were asked to remember the word, and by stem completion. Their patients did very badly on free recall, were clearly impaired on cued recall but showed no deficit when tested by stem completion.

A crucial feature of priming is that it is often, although not always, dependent on reinstating the physical conditions under which encoding occurred. Graf and Mandler (1984) visually presented a list of words, such as *stamp*, instructing subjects to process them either semantically, or in terms of their visual appearance. Retention was then tested either by stem completion or by means of an associated semantic cue (e.g. *letter*). There was a major advantage to semantic coding under the explicit cued recall condition, as would be expected, as semantic coding is, in general, a good method of explicit learning, as we will see in Chapter 6. However, no semantic advantage was found when performance was tested implicitly using the word fragment completion test (Figure 5.9).

A related measure of implicit memory is known as fragment completion. In this task, a previously presented word such as *elephant* is tested by giving the word with half the letters omitted e.g. *– l – p – a – t* and asking what

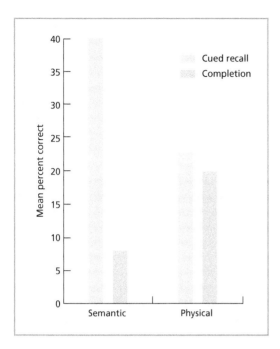

Figure 5.9 Influence of encoding semantically or physically on explicit cued recall versus implicit stem completion. Based on Graf and Mandler (1984) Experiment 3.

word would fit that fragment. Both of these methods show preserved learning in amnesic patients (see Chapter 16). Using the fragment completion task with normal subjects, Tulving, Schacter, and Stark (1982) studied the durability of explicit and implicit verbal learning. When tested after only an hour, the request to recall the words led to better performance than fragment completion; but, after a week's delay, the pattern reversed with little decrement in fragment completion but substantial forgetting for recall.

The neural basis of priming was studied by Schott et al. (2005) who used fMRI to investigate the implicit and explicit components of the stem completion task. They began by presenting participants with 160 words, with the instruction to count the number of syllables in each. Participants were then tested by being presented with 240 stems comprising the initial letters of each of the 160 old words, together with 80 new words. In the first experiment, participants were given an explicit memory instruction to try to remember the

words, but that if they could not recall, then to produce the first words that came to mind. A second study was equivalent except that no mention of memory was made, participants were simply asked to produce the first word that came to mind. Explicit memory in the first condition was associated with *increased* blood flow in both left and right parietal and temporal lobes and in the left frontal region. By contrast, priming in the absence of memory was associated with *decreases* in blood flow in the left fusiform gyrus and in both frontal and occipital regions. This reduction in blood flow presumably reflected the easier processing of the primed words.

We have so far limited discussion of priming to verbal memory. However, as Warrington and Weiskrantz (1970) showed, priming also operates for the retention of line drawings of objects. When memory is tested by recognition, amnesic patients are severely impaired, but when the task is to identify a fragmented version of the original drawing, they show normal implicit memory. Schacter, Cooper, and Delaney (1990) showed a similar effect for two-dimensional drawings of three-dimensional objects, an effect that was absent when the drawings had represented "impossible objects" that in fact could not be represented in three dimensions, and hence that presumably did not result in a coherent and primeable representation in the brain.

Finally, whereas most priming studies have operated at a perceptual level, equivalent effects can be obtained at a deeper level. Srinivas and Roediger (1990) required participants to process lists of words that included animal names such as *rat* and *hyena*. This was followed by an apparently unrelated task involving generating as many words as possible in 60 seconds from a series of semantic categories. Items that had been encountered earlier such as *rat* and *hyena* were more likely to be generated.

Procedural learning

Some years ago, I took a course on learning to sail. It began with theory, explaining the relationship between the direction of the wind, the set of the sails, and the control of the rudder. Trying to bear these three factors in mind while handling the small boat as it keeled over in one direction or another proved far from simple, and after a while I just gave up worrying and did what seemed to work. The boat mysteriously began to behave, as did other boats on subsequent occasions. Somehow, the brain seemed to be solving problems that were beyond the reach of the conscious mind. This, of course, is not uncommon in the performance of skills. When a fielder runs to catch a cricket ball or a baseball, it is necessary to solve some complex equations to ensure that the ball and the hands reach the same place at the same time, equations that the fielder almost certainly could not solve consciously. That is not to say that performance cannot sometimes be improved by conscious strategy; for example, by giving advice as to what height to attempt to intercept the falling ball. Such strategies can, however, be limited in their value, and can on occasion be counterproductive.

This was demonstrated in an intriguing experiment by Masters (1992), who was interested in the response to stress known as "choking," in which a skilled sportsman such as a golfer appears to lose their skill under pressure, going into the last round of a tournament several shots ahead, having played brilliantly, only to make a series of simple putting mistakes and lose the tournament. Masters studied this by devising a simple putting task in which participants had to knock a golf ball into a hole. A total of 400 training trials were given. Half the participants performed a demanding attentional task during learning and half did not. The crucial test occurred over the last 100 trials, which operated normally or under a stress condition. Stress was induced by telling participants that they were about to be judged by a golf professional of considerable distinction. He would decide whether participants received an increased prize or lost virtually all the money they had so far earned. The so-called professional (in fact a stooge) was clad in a golf sweater and coughed occasionally, before disappearing behind a screen. Unbeknown to the subject he actually left the room, leaving behind a tape recording of occasional coughs to convince the participants they were being watched. The results of this study are shown in Figure 5.10. It is clear that whereas learning is somewhat impaired by the demanding concurrent task, this condition

was much more resistant to stress. When questioned afterwards, it proved to be case that the group given the concurrent task during learning were much less likely to have evolved explicit conscious strategies (less than one per person) than the control group (typically more than three).

Of the many forms of procedural learning, one that has been studied extensively is the serial reaction time task. In a typical version, participants would have four keys, each associated with a light, and would be required to press the relevant key as rapidly as possible when the lights came on. This would then activate the next light and so on. The sequence would initially be random, but would then switch to a sequence containing regularities such that some sequential patterns were more frequent than others. With practice, performance on these sequences improves. The sequence is then switched back to random, whereupon participants who have shown a learning effect slow down, as their learning is no longer relevant. Learning on this task also occurs in amnesic patients. The implicit nature

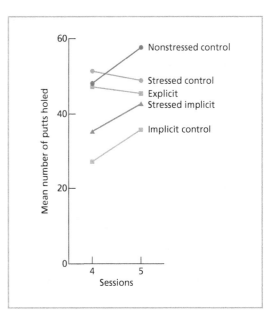

Figure 5.10 Mean number of putting shots holed as a function of skill acquisition phase (sessions 1–4) and a test phase (session 5) in the study by Masters (1992). Implicit learning led to lower performance but was more resistant to the effects of stress at test.

of learning is also shown by the fact that when normal participants are simultaneously performing a demanding task that is sufficient to make them unaware of the regularities, learning still occurs (Nissen & Bullemer, 1987; Nissen, Knopman, & Schacter, 1987).

Hazeltine, Grafton, and Ivry (1997) carried out a neuroimaging study using this task, in which the implicit condition involved a demanding concurrent tone-counting task. This was then repeated with eight random and eight quasi-random blocks under single-task conditions. Neuroimaging data indicated that when learning was implicit because of dual-task conditions, learning-related changes were found in the *left* motor and supplementary motor cortex, whereas a shift to the *right* hemisphere occurred under the single-task conditions, with the right prefrontal cortex, premotor cortex, and the right temporal lobe involved, as in a previous study (Grafton, Hazeltine, & Ivry, 1995).

Learning artificial grammars

One important form of learning that appears to be acquired implicitly is the grammar of our native language, which, as linguists have pointed out, tends to be lawful but complex, and appears to be acquired by native speakers with no formal grammatical instruction. A feature of grammars is that they are *generative*, that is that the items of the language can be combined and recombined in a virtually infinite

number of ways, without producing ungrammatical sequences. The study of this phenomenon led to the development of a number of so-called artificial grammars, involving sequences of letters that allow certain combinations to occur while others are illegal. Figure 5.11 shows one such grammar in which each node represents a letter and each arrow leads to a permissible subsequent letter, including the possibility of repetition for some, but not all letters. Reber (1967) showed that people were able to learn such grammars, as shown by a capacity to decide at a better-than-chance level whether a completely new letter sequence was "grammatically" correct (e.g. TTVRX) or was not (e.g. TTXRV). However, successful learners were unable to say how they performed this task. Even more surprisingly, Reber (1967) showed that, having learned one grammar, participants could transfer their skill to a second grammar in which the grammatical structure was equivalent but the letters different, suggesting that they had learned rules rather than letters.

It remains open to question, however, just what is being learned in this situation. Perruchet and Pacteau (1990) point out that, given that performance on such grammar-learning tasks is typically far from perfect, much of it could be based on learning to recognize particular pairs or triplets of letters as familiar, and hence potentially grammatically acceptable. Whereas the fact that learning could transfer to other letters might seem to rule this

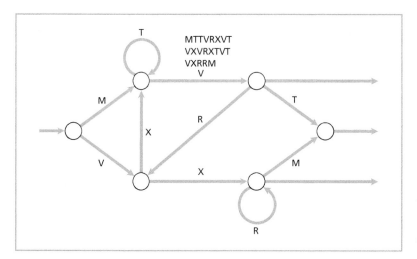

MTTVRXVT
VXVRXTVT
VXRRM

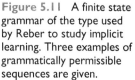

Figure 5.11 A finite state grammar of the type used by Reber to study implicit learning. Three examples of grammatically permissible sequences are given.

out, Brooks and Vokey (1991) point out that similarity might operate at a number of levels other than that of the specific letters. For example, given the sequence "ABBBXA and YXXXKY," similarities exist in three ways, the existence of a triple letter, its location in the sequence and the fact that the sequence begins and ends with the same letter.

It is, of course, questionable as to whether one can generalize from simple artificial grammars to natural grammars and, if so, whether it is better to learn the grammar of a foreign language by explicitly learning grammatical rules—as is usually the case—or more implicitly by the immersion method of attempting to learn in a context in which only the second language is spoken.

It is difficult to run controlled experiments on the immersion method, but studies have been performed on teaching grammar by rule or example. Ellis (1993, 1994) compared three methods of teaching Welsh grammar. One simply involved presenting instances of the relevant grammatical forms in a random sequence, with each instance followed by its English translation. Participants rapidly learned to provide the relevant English translation for each instance, but showed no capacity to generalize to other material, either by stating rules or judging grammaticality. A second group was taught the relevant rules. Members of this group showed good explicit grammatical knowledge but again had difficulty in generalizing to other material. A third group was given explicit rules and then required to apply them to a range of material. Although slow, this group *was* successful in coping when novel items were introduced.

These results, and others (Scott, 1989; 1990), might seem to suggest that learning a language by the immersion method is not possible. However, this is clearly not the case, as this is how we learn our native language. The conditions of learning are, however,

KEY TERM

Immersion method: A strategy for foreign language teaching whereby the learner is placed in an environment where only the foreign language is used.

very different, both in the number of hours of exposure and in the age at which we acquire the language.

Complex system control

As the world becomes more complex, jobs that used to depend on basic manual and perceptual skills are increasingly being replaced by automatic processes. However, these processes themselves might need control, possibly involving situations in which automation is not yet adequate, as for example in the case of the job of an air traffic controller. There has therefore been considerably interest in understanding how such complex control tasks are learned. Berry and Broadbent (1984) developed a computer game that involved controlling a simulated sugar factory, with the need to maintain efficiency by optimizing input of raw material, its storage, and processing and controlling product output, all simultaneously. After 60 trials, participants had achieved a level of up to 80% of optimal performance. However, as in the case of sailing or grammar learning, most subjects were not clear quite what they did or why, and there was no correlation between the amount of explicit knowledge reported and level of performance.

Of course, one possibility is that the apparent lack of explicit knowledge might simply reflect the difficulty of reporting in words a strategy that was not itself verbal. A number of attempts to tackle this issue have used a method known as "teach back," in which the learner is asked to instruct a naïve participant how to perform the task. Stanley, Mathews, Buss, and Kotler-Cope (1989) used this method in a study extending to 570 trials, and found some evidence for the capacity to transmit information, but only after many, many learning trials.

We have discussed implicit and explicit memory as though they were two separate but broadly equivalent classes of learning. This view has led to a number of attempts to come up with a coherent explanation of this dichotomy (Roediger & McDermott, 1993; Neath & Surprenant, 2003). Such attempts, however, assume that the various types of learning, described as implicit, form a coherent category. An alternative, and I myself think more plausible, view is that what these various demonstrations of implicit learning have in common is the *absence* of the involvement of episodic learning and remembering, a system that allows us to "travel back in time" and "relive" specific experiences and events. As we shall see in Chapter 6, this involves a specific system that is geared to "gluing together" events that we experience at the same time, so as to locate the particular experience in time and place, something that is not necessary for implicit learning and memory.

Implicit memory is in short, a category defined by exclusion. The fact that a number of instances *lack* a given feature is not a very solid basis for seeking a common explanation for them. Insects, birds, reptiles, and crustaceans all have in common the fact that they are not mammals; this does mean that we would expect them to be similar in any fundamental way. Perceptual priming, classical conditioning, motor skill learning, and grammar acquisition can all be characterized as *not* requiring episodic memory. However, the fact that they involve widely different perceptual processing and learning systems, and tend to depend on different areas of the brain, suggests that it is unlikely that they will form a coherent group reflecting a single common learning mechanism.

LEARNING AND CONSCIOUSNESS

There is no doubt that a great deal of our learning is implicit, in the sense that we can learn skills without being able to reflect and report on precisely what we know. That does not, of course, mean that consciousness is not necessary for learning. Addressing this issue requires consideration of a definition of consciousness. For present purposes, I suggest we use as our basis what Damasio (1994) refers to as *core consciousness*. By core consciousness, Damasio means the dimension that ranges from being fully awake and alert, to deep sleep and indeed coma. Learning clearly tends to be better when one is awake

than asleep, or indeed half asleep, but is any learning possible in the absence of normal consciousness?

An issue of considerable recent concern stems from cases of patients undergoing surgery under general anesthesia who subsequently report that they were conscious during the operation. This is both possible and alarming. A general anesthetic typically contains three components: an analgesic to dull the pain; an anesthetic to cause loss of consciousness; and a muscle relaxant, which, although helpful to the surgeon, means that even if you *can* experience the surgery, you are not able to indicate that fact.

In an attempt to assess the frequency of conscious awareness under anesthesia, Sebel et al. (2004) interviewed patients on several occasions following anesthesia, detecting a faint memory of the operation in about 1 in every 600 operations for adults, while Davidson et al. (2005) found a rate of about 1 in a 100 for children, who for safety reasons would typically be given a lower dose of anesthetics. These rates may seem rather low, but given the huge number of anesthetics given per year (about 2.9 million in the UK alone), there are enough to be a concern.

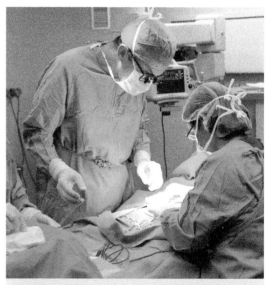

Anesthetists need to bear in mind that their patients just might be able to hear what they are saying!

As mentioned above, one problem with the clinical situation is that because of the muscle relaxant, patients cannot respond. One way around this is to put a tourniquet around the arm which then prevents the relaxant from entering the arm and hence allows that hand to respond. Using this technique it is possible to demonstrate that patients are sufficiently conscious and communicative to respond, at levels showing no subsequent explicit recall (Andrade, 1996). By combining the isolated forearm technique, together with electrophysiological measures, it is possible to be reasonably sure that the patient is not conscious. Even then, however, it is possible to demonstrate *implicit* memory for spoken words. For example the patient might be better able to detect those words when presented in noise, or to complete a word stem, for example present *metal* and test *me– – –* (Andrade & Deeprose, 2006). But if the learning is not consciously available, does it matter? There are reports of negative effects of the implicit memory in which patients develop anxiety. On the other hand (Wang, 2010), there are claims that positive effects can be obtained presenting positive messages during anesthesia such as "you'll make a good recovery" (Lebovits, Twersky, & McEwan, 1999), although the evidence for this is not strong, and of course there is the possibility that the effects represent periods of consciousness during the anesthetic procedure. Perhaps the message here is for anesthetists to bear in mind that their patients just might be able to hear what they are saying and act accordingly.

Sleep and learning

Wouldn't it be nice if, instead of spending time studying, you could simply go to sleep and wake up next morning having learned your quota for the day? This has been claimed in the past, and there are still advertisements online offering to teach you languages while you sleep. Sadly, attempts to test such claims have found little evidence of learning, and what little is found seems to reflect periods of wakefulness, as detected by EEG (Druchman & Bjork, 1994). However, although there is not much mileage in learning during sleep there is

considerable and growing evidence for the role of sleep in consolidating memory.

The Roman teacher of rhetoric, Quintillian, noted that the interval of a single night would increase the strength of memory, a process he likened to ripening or maturing. The term *consolidation* was proposed by two German psychologists, Müller and Pilzecker (1900), as a process of hardening or making more robust the memory of an association just learned. A classic study by Jenkins and Dallenbach (1924) found, just as Quintillian suggested, that participants who slept after learning remembered more than those who learned and recalled during the same day.

There are of course other possible explanations for such a result. It could be due to *retroactive interference*, the process whereby

Although there have been claims that we can learn during sleep, these claims are not readily substantiated. There is, however, evidence that sleep may indeed help consolidate what we have already learned.

new learning disrupts old (see Chapter 9, p. 242); sleep protects you from further experiences that would otherwise interfere with the earlier learning. There are also problems of interpretation resulting from the 24-hour fluctuations that occur in alertness. People tested in the evening might be more fatigued than those tested next morning, and if both groups are tested at the same time of day, one is likely to have to sleep at an unaccustomed time. Such complexities discouraged research for many years, but more recently with a growing interest in the neuroscience of consolidation, people have increasingly been willing to tackle these complexities, and a coherent and interesting pattern of evidence is beginning to emerge.

Evidence for the importance of sleep in word learning comes from a series of studies by Gaskell and Dumay (2003). They took advantage of the fact that the time to recognize a spoken word takes a little longer if it has a near neighbor, for example detecting the word *catalyst* would be slowed down by *catalogue*, presumably because you need to wait until the middle of the word to be sure which of the two has been spoken. They taught people new words that resembled old, e.g. *cathedruke*, then tested speed of responding to *cathedral*. Despite being able to recall *cathedruke*, it only interfered with *cathedral* after a night's sleep, suggesting that new words need sleep to be fully integrated into the language system.

If sleep is necessary for learning, then one might expect retention of learning to be poorer after sleep deprivation. This was indeed found by Stickgold, James and Hobson (2000) who required people to learn a visual discrimination task. A group given normal sleep showed improvement increasing over several days following training, whereas those deprived of a night's sleep immediately after learning showed no such improvement. There is now growing evidence for the importance of sleep in memory consolidation that is detectable long after the initial learning (Gais et al. (2007).

There is increasing evidence that sleep-dependent memory processes are selective, with material that is salient in some way showing an advantage, as if the brain is sorting through memories from the previous day and favoring those that are most important.

For example Payne, Stickgold, Swanberg and Kensinger (2008) presented a series of negatively valenced objects presented against neutral backgrounds, testing after delays ranging from 30 minutes to 12 hours while awake, and after a 12-hour delay that included sleep. During waking, memory declined for both negative objects and their background at the same rate, whereas during sleep, less forgetting occurred for the negative objects. They suggest that such a pattern might be valuable from an evolutionary viewpoint.

It is also the case that simply instructing participants that one set of items is more important than another, or more likely to be tested, enhances the positive effect of sleep. Fischer and Born (2009) trained participants on two different sequential finger tasks. When training was complete, a monetary reward was offered for one of the two. This was followed by 12 hours including sleep, after which a slightly different instruction was given, namely that the reward would be based on the *average* performance across the two conditions. Nonetheless, the sequence that had been emphasized *before* sleep showed enhanced performance, an effect that was not present in a second group who remained awake during the 12 hours. It appears therefore that sleep had favored the designated task, an effect that showed despite the changed instructions.

Why does sleep enhance learning? Protection from interference may be one factor, but it is not enough to explain the rich range of studies that have recently implicated sleep in the learning process (see Stickgold & Walker, 2013 for a review). The generally accepted current view is that sleep helps the process of consolidation of the memory trace, whereby its representation within the brain becomes more robustly established. But how is this achieved? An early study by Wilson and McNaughton (1994) monitored individual cells within the hippocampus of rats that were becoming familiar with a novel environment. This process leads to the development of *place cells* which fire when the rat approaches a particular part of the learned environment. During the process of deep sleep, the place cells were reactivated as if facilitating some process of transfer

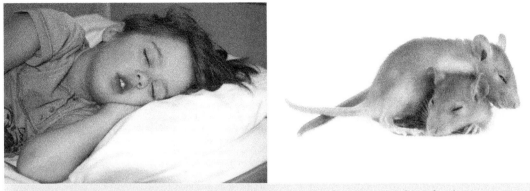

While there is little evidence that we can learn while sleeping, there is growing evidence for the importance of sleep in consolidating memory of what has been learned.

or consolidation. More recently, the neural activity generated by daytime singing in birds has been found also to occur during sleep (Dave & Margoliash, 2000). It is not of course feasible to carry out single unit cell recordings in healthy human participants; however, neuroimaging studies have shown brain activations linked to motor skill learning and spatial navigation that appear to recapitulate those observed during the learning process, and to be associated with sleep spindles within the EEG (see Oudiette & Paller 2013 for a review).

THE NEUROBIOLOGICAL BASIS OF LEARNING

In 1949, the great Canadian psychologist Donald Hebb produced a speculation about the biological basis of learning that continues to be influential. He proposed that long-term learning is based on cell assemblies.

KEY TERM

Cell assembly: A concept proposed by Hebb to account for the physiological basis of long-term learning, which is assumed to involve the establishment of links between the cells forming the assembly.

These occur when two or more nerve cells are excited at the same time. This involves the synapse—the gap between two separate neurons—being repeatedly activated, whereupon the chemistry of the synapse changes, leading to a strengthened connection. This is often summarized by the phrase "neurons that fire together wire together." Hebb (1949) contrasts the long-term development of cell assemblies with a short-term memory process based on temporary electrical activity within existing cell assemblies. Hebb's proposal that long-term learning is based on the development and growth of further synaptic connections, known as "Hebbian learning," has continued to be influential, both through its impact on the search for the neurobiological basis of learning and also for its influence on computer-based simulations of learning.

In the 1960s, a neurophysiological mechanism that appeared to perform in the way Hebb proposed was identified. Bliss and Lomo (1973) found that repeated electrical stimulation of an axonal pathway led to a long-term increase in the size of potentials generated by the neurons beyond the synapse, a process they termed *long-term potentiation (LTP)*. They found that LTP was particularly strongly represented in the hippocampus and surrounding regions, an area that research on animals and on brain-damaged patients suggests is intimately concerned with long-term memory (see Chapter 16).

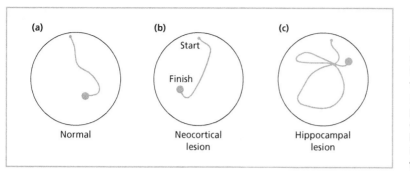

Figure 5.12 Typical swimming paths shown by rats within a Morris water maze. Normal rats (a) rapidly acquire a direct path, as do rats with cortical lesions (b), whereas hippocampal lesions result in a failure to learn (c). Data from Morris et al. (1982).

Evidence for the importance of the hippocampus in learning and in long-term potentiation (LTP) comes from a series of studies using the Morris water maze. This involves a circular tank filled with milky water that obscures the location of a platform located just below the surface. A rat placed in the tank will swim around until it finds the platform and then pull itself up. As shown in Figure 5.12a and b, in later trials the rat can locate the platform much more rapidly. This is not the case for rats with lesions to the hippocampus, which, as Figure 5.12c demonstrates, show little evidence of learning. In a second series of studies, instead of being lesioned the rats were administered a substance known as AP5, which has been shown to block the induction of LTP in the hippocampus. This impaired spatial learning, with the degree of impairment increasing with the size of dose of AP5 (Morris, Garrud, Rawlings, & O'Keefe 1982; Morris, Davis, & Butcher, 1990).

Further evidence for the possible role of LTP came from studies demonstrating that drugs that enhance synaptic transmission also tend to enhance learning (Staubli, Rogers, & Lynch, 1994). LTP is also found in other parts of the brain, including the amygdala, which is closely associated with fear-based learning. Drugs that block LTP have also been shown to reduce such learning (LeDoux, 1998).

A great deal is known about the complex relationship between neurotransmitters and learning, with one form of glutamate, N-methyl-D-aspartate (NMDA) playing an important role in LTP (Abel & Lattal, 2001). In addition to analysis at the neurochemical level, it is now becoming increasingly clear that genetic factors play an important role. (See Kandel, 2006, for a detailed review of this area by one of its pioneers, who has recently become a Nobel laureate.)

However, although it is widely accepted that NMDA receptors are *necessary* for the synaptic change that is assumed to underpin learning, it is less certain that they are *sufficient* to induce learning, or whether other psychological processes, such as attention for example, mediated by other brain mechanisms might also be necessary (Shors & Matzel, 1997; Martin, Ungerleider, & Haxby, 2000).

Underlying much of the work just described is the concept of consolidation, a term that can be used in two ways, one, synaptic consolidation, refers to changes at a molecular level, as discussed here, the other applies to a process at a systems level whereby information in one part of the brain is modulated or transferred to another part. This is covered in Chapter 6. Other evidence comes from attempts to interfere with consolidation using either electrical brain stimulation or a drug, typically resulting in the disruption of learning. However, this does not necessarily mean that the trace has been damaged, simply that it is not retrievable at the time of testing (Miller & Springer, 1974).

KEY TERM

Consolidation: The time-dependent process by which a new trace is gradually woven into the fabric of memory and by which its components and their interconnections are cemented together.

A classic example comes from early studies that taught rats that stepping down from a block led to paw shock, something that animals learn rapidly and refuse to step down. However, when learning is followed by an equivalent of electroconvulsive therapy (ECT) in humans, they appeared to lose the memory, and readily step down. Initially, it was suggested that this demonstrated the failure of the memory trace to consolidate. However, it was subsequently discovered that the memory trace had not in fact been destroyed, as giving the animal a foot shock acted as a "reminder" that effectively reinstated the learning. The trace had not been abolished, simply made more difficult to retrieve (Miller & Matzel, 2000).

A second source of difficulties for the classic concept of consolidation came from the observation by Nader, Schafe, and LeDoux (2000) of a phenomenon they termed "reconsolidation." This reflects the fact that memory traces become vulnerable to disruption whenever they are recalled. This raises the question of why something that is already consolidated should become disruptable. This, and related results, have led to modifications of the original concept of consolidation. Nadel and Moscovitch (1997, 1998), for example, have put forward their *multiple trace theory*, in which each retrieval sets up new traces which can then interfere with older traces (Nadel, 2007).

SUMMARY

- The study of human learning began with Ebbinghaus in 1885, who, using himself as a subject, demonstrated regular and measurable features of memory.
- One result was what has become known as the *total time hypothesis*, a simple relationship between time spent and amount learned.
- This is reflected in the claim that it requires 10,000 hours in any field to become a true expert, a view rejected by Ericsson who data this was based on. He emphasizes the variability across fields and the need for careful targeting of practice to remedy weaknesses.
- Distribution of practice, a little and often, is an important factor as is:
- The generation effect; retrieval has a major impact on learning.
- Motivation *per se* does not ensure learning, but is necessary to focus attention and maintain practice goals.
- Much learning is implicit, reflected in performance rather than directly through memory.
- Varieties of implicit learning include conditioning, perceptual priming, procedural and skill learning, and a series of complex associational tasks such as learning grammar or the control of complex systems.
- Conscious awareness is usually necessary for learning although some degree of implicit learning can occur under anesthesia.
- There is little evidence of learning during sleep, but considerable evidence that memory traces may consolidate while sleeping.
- Two forms of consolidation have been proposed, an initial phase principally involving the hippocampus, and a more gradual process linking the hippocampus to other brain regions.
- At a neuronal level, LTM is assumed to depend on a process of long-term potentiation (LTP), with the neural transmitter glutamate, NMDA, playing an essential role.

A student just starting college believes that learning time and repetition should be the basis of study. How would you advise him to improve on this?

What are the major differences between implicit and explicit learning?

What has the study of sleep told us about the nature of learning?

FURTHER READING

Hartley, J. (1998). *Learning and studying*. London: Routledge. A discussion of the implications of what we know about learning for the way in which we should study.

Hill, W. F. (2002) *Learning* (7th edn.). Boston, MA: Allyn & Bacon. A text providing a broad overview of the psychology of learning.

Kandel, E. R. (2006). *In search of memory: The emergence of a new science of mind*. New York: Norton. A scientific autobiography from the Nobel Prize laureate. It covers the neurobiological basis of memory in a very clear and accessible way.

Schacter, D. L. (1994). Priming and multiple memory systems: Perceptual mechanisms of implicit memory. In D. L. Schacter & E. Tulving (Eds.), *Memory systems 1994* (pp. 233–268). Cambridge, MA: MIT Press. Schacter makes the case for regarding a range of perceptual priming phenomena as components of a coherent system.

Squire, L. R. (1993). The organization of declarative and non-declarative memory. In T. Ono, L. R. Squire, M. E. Raichle, D. I. Perrett, & M. Fukuda (Eds.), *Brain mechanisms of perception and memory: From neuron to behaviour* (pp. 219–227). New York: Oxford University Press. An account of Squire's views on the structure of long-term memory.

REFERENCES

Abel, T., & Lattal, K. M. (2001). Molecular mechanisms of memory acquisition, consolidation and retrieval. *Current Opinion in Neurobiology, 11*, 180–187.

Andrade, J. (1996). Investigations of hypesthesia: Using anesthetics to explore relationships between consciousness, learning and memory. *Conscious and Cognition, 5*, 562–580.

Andrade, J., & Deeprose, C. (2006). A starting point for consciousness research: Reply to Thomas Schmidt. *Conscious and Cognition, 15*, 28–30.

Astin, A. W. (1993). *What matters in college?: Four critical years revisited*. San Francisco, CA: Jossey-Bass.

Baddeley, A. D., & Longman, D. J. A. (1978). The influence of length and frequency of training sessions on the rate of learning to type. *Ergonomics, 21*, 627–635.

Baddeley, A. D., & Wilson, B. A. (1994). When implicit learning fails: Amnesia and the problem of error elimination. *Neuropsychologia, 32*, 53–68.

Bechara, A., Tranel, D., Damasio, H., Adolphs, R., Rockland, C., & Damasio, A. R. (1995). Double dissociation of conditioning and declarative knowledge relative to the amygdala and hippocampus in humans. *Science, 269*, 1115–1118.

Bekerian, D. A., & Baddeley, A. D. (1980). Saturation advertising and the repetition effect. *Journal of Verbal Learning and Verbal Behavior, 19*, 17–25.

Berry, D. C., & Broadbent, D. E. (1984). On the relationship between task performance and associated verbalizable knowledge. *Quarterly Journal of Experimental Psychology, 36A*, 209–231.

Bliss, T. V. P., & Lomo, T. (1973). Long-lasting potentiation of synaptic transmission in the dentate area of the unanaesthestized rabbit following stimulation of the perforant path. *Journal of Physiology, 232*, 331–356.

Bornstein, R. F. (1989). Exposure and affect: Overview and meta-analysis of research, 1968–1987. *Psychological Bulletin, 106*, 265–289.

Brooks, L. R., & Vokey, J. R. (1991). Abstract analogies and abstracted grammars: A comment on Reber, Mathews et al. *Journal of Experimental Psychology: General, 120*, 316–323.

Büchel, C., Morris, J., Dolan, R. J., & Friston, K. J. (1998). Brain systems mediating aversive conditioning: An event-related fMRI study. *Neuron, 20*, 947–957.

Damasio, A. R. (1994). *Descartes' error: Emotion, reason, and the human brain.* New York: Putnam.

Dave, A. S., & Margoliash, D. (2000). Song replay during sleep and computational rules for sensorimotor vocal learning. *Science, 290*, 812–816.

Davidson, A. J., Huang, G. H., Czarnecki, C., Gibson, M. A., Stewart, S. A., Jamsen, K., & Stargatt, R. (2005). Awareness during anesthesia in children: A prospective cohort study. *Anesthesia and Analgesia, 100*, 653–661.

Druchman, D., & Bjork, A. (1994). *Learning, remembering, believing: Enhancing human performance.* Washington, DC: National Academy Press.

Ebbinghaus, H. (1885). *Über das Gedächtnis.* Leipzig: Dunker.

Ellis, N. C. (1993). Rules and instances in foreign language learning: Interactions of explicit and implicit knowledge. *European Journal of Cognitive Psychology, 5*, 289–318.

Ellis, N. C. (1994). Implicit and explicit processes in language acquisition: An introduction. In N. Ellis (Ed.), *Implicit and explicit learning of languages* (pp. 1–32). London: Academic Press.

Ericsson, K. A. (2013). Training history, deliberate practice and elite sports performance: An analysis in response to Tucker and Collins Review— "What makes champions?". *British Journal of Sports Medicine, 47*, 533–535.

Ericsson, K. A., Krampe, R. T., & Tesch-Römer, C. (1993). The role of deliberate practice in the acquisition of expert performance. *Psychological Review, 100*, 363–406.

Fischer, S., & Born, J. (2009). Anticipated reward enhances offline learning during sleep. *Journal of Experimental Psychology: Learning, Memory, and Cognition, 35* 1586–1593. doi: 10.1037/a0017256

Gais, S., Albouy, G., Boly, M., Dang-Vu, T. T., Darsaud, A., Desseilles, M. et al. (2007). Sleep transforms the cerebral trace of declarative memories. *Proceedings of the National Academy of Sciences of the USA, 104*, 18778–18783.

Gaskell, M. G., & Dumay, N. (2003). Lexical competition and the acquisition of novel words. *Cognition, 89*, 105–132.

Gladwell, M. (2008). *Outliers: The story of success.* New York: Little, Brown & Co.

Graf, P., & Mandler, G. (1984). Activation makes words more accessible, but not necessarily more retrievable. *Journal of Verbal Learning and Verbal Behavior, 23*, 553–568.

Graf, P., Squire, L. R., & Mandler, G. (1984). The information that amnesic patients do not forget. *Journal of Experimental Psychology: Learning, Memory and Cognition, 10*, 164–178.

Grafton, S., Hazeltine, E., & Ivry, R. (1995). Functional mapping of sequence learning in normal humans. *Journal of Cognitive Neuroscience, 7*, 497–510.

Hazeltine, E., Grafton, S. T., & Ivry, R. (1997). Attention and stimulus characteristics determine the locus of motor sequence learning: A PET study. *Brain, 120*, 123–140.

Hebb, D. O. (1949). *The organization of behavior.* New York: Wiley.

Hu, Y., Geng, F., Tao, L., Hu, N., Du, F., Fu, K., et al. (2011). Enhanced white matter tracts integrity in children with abacus training. . *Human Brain Mapping, 32*, 10–21.

Jenkins, J. G., & Dallenbach, K. M. (1924). Oblivescence during sleep and waking. *American Journal of Psychology, 35*, 605–612.

Johnstone, K. M., Ashbaugh, H., & Warfield, T. D. (2002). Effects of repeated practice and contextual-writing experiences on college students' writing skills. *Journal of Educational Psychology, 94*, 305–315.

Kandel, E. R. (2006). *In search of memory: The emergence of a new science of mind.* New York: Norton.

Karpicke, J. D., & Roediger III, H. L. (2008). The critical importance of retrieval for learning. *Science, 319*, 966–968.

Kay, H. (1955). Learning and retaining verbal material. *British Journal of Psychology, 46*, 81–100.

Kunst-Wilson, W., & Zajonc, R. (1980). Affective discrimination of stimuli that cannot be recognized. *Science, 207*, 557–558. doi: 10.1126/science.7352271

Landauer, T. K., & Bjork, R. A. (1978). Optimum rehearsal patterns and name learning. In

M. M. Gruneberg, P. E. Morris, & R. N. Sykes (Eds.), *Practical aspects of memory* (pp. 625–632). London: Academic Press.

Lebovits, A. H., Twersky, T., & McEwan, B. (1999). Intraoperative therapeutic suggestions in day-case surgery. *British Journal of Anaesthesia 82*, 861–866.

LeDoux, J. (1998). *The emotional brain*. London: Weidenfeld & Nicolson.

Mailer, N. (2003). *The spooky art: Some thoughts on writing*. New York: Random House.

Marsh, E. J., Roediger III, H. L., Bjork, R. A., & Bjork, E. L. (2007). The memorial consequences of multiple-choice testing. *Psychonomic Bulletin and Review, 14*, 194–199.

Martin, A., Ungerleider, L. G., & Haxby, J. V. (2000). Category specificity and the brain: The sensory/motor model of semantic representations of objects. In M. S. Gazzaniga (Ed.), *The new cognitive neurosciences* (2nd edn., pp. 1023–1036). Cambridge, MA: MIT Press.

Masters, R. S. W. (1992). Knowledge, knerves and know-how: The role of explicit versus implicit knowledge in the breakdown of a complex skill under pressure. *British Journal of Psychology, 83*, 343–358.

McDaniel, M. A., Roediger, H. L., III, & McDermott, K. B. (2007). Generalising test-enhanced learning from the laboratory to the classroom. *Psychonomic Bulletin and Review, 14*, 200–206.

Metcalf, J., & Kornell, N. (2007). Principles of cognitive science in education: The effects of generation, errors, and feedback. *Psychonomic Bulletin and Review, 14*, 225–229.

Miller, R., & Matzel, L. D. (2000). Memory involves far more than 'consolidation'. *Nature Neuroscience Reviews, 1*, 214–216.

Miller, R. R., & Springer, A. D. (1974). Implications of recovery from experimental amnesia. *Psychological Review, 81*, 470–473.

Morris, J. S., Öhman, A., & Dolan, R. J. (1998). Conscious and unconscious emotional learning in the human amygdala. *Nature, 393*, 467–470.

Morris, R. G. M., Davis, S., & Butcher, S. P. (1990). Hippocampal synaptic plasticity and NMDA receptors: A role in information storage?. *Philosophical Transactions of the Royal Society of London B, 329*, 187–204.

Morris, R. G. M., Garrud, P., Rawlings, J. M. P., & O'Keefe, J. (1982). Place navigation impaired in rats with hippocampal lesions. *Nature, 297*, 681–683.

Müller, G. E., & Pilzecker, A. E. (1900). Experimentelle Beiträge zur Lehre vom Gedächtniss (Experimental contributions to the science of memory). *Zeitschrift für Psychologie. Ergänzungsband, 1*, 1–300.

Nadel, L. (2007). Consolidation: The demise of the fixed trace. In H. L. Roediger III, Y. Dudai, & S. M. Fitzpatrick (Eds.), *Science of memory* (pp. 177–182).New York: Oxford University Press.

Nadel, L., & Moscovitch, M. (1997). Memory consolidation, retrograde amnesia and the hippocampal complex. *Current Opinion in Neurobiology, 7*, 217–227.

Nadel, L., & Moscovitch, M. (1998). Hippocampal contributions to cortical plasticity. *Neuropharmacology, 37*, 431–439.

Nader, K., Schafe, G., & LeDoux, J. E. (2000). The labile nature of the consolidation theory. *Nature Neuroscience Reviews, 1*, 216–219.

Neath, I., & Surprenant, A. (2003). *Human memory: An introduction to research, data and theory.* (2nd edn.). Belmont, CA: Wadsworth.

Nilsson, L.-G. (1987). Motivated memory: Dissociation between performance data and subjective reports. *Psychological Research, 49*, 183–188.

Nissen, M. J., & Bullemer, P. (1987). Attentional requirements of learning: Evidence from performance measures. *Cognitive Psychology, 19*, 1–32.

Nissen, M. J., Knopman, D. S., & Schacter, D. L. (1987). Neurochemical dissociations of memory systems. *Neurology, 37*, 789–794.

Oudiette, D., & Paller, K. A. (2013). Upgrading the sleeping brain with targeted memory reactivation. *Trends in Cognitive Sciences, 17*, 142–149. doi: 0.1016/j.tics.2013.01.00

Pashler, H., Rohrer, D., Cepeda, N. J., & Carpenter, S. K. (2007). Enhancing learning and retarding forgetting: Choices and consequences. *Psychonomic Bulletin and Review, 14*, 187–193.

Pavlov, I. P. (1927). *Conditioned reflexes: An investigation of the physiological activity of the cerebral cortex*. London: Oxford University Press.

Payne, J. D., Stickgold, R., Swanberg, K., & Kensinger, E. A. (2008). Sleep preferentially enhances memory for emotional components of scenes. *Psychological Science 19*, 781–788.

Perfect, T. J., & Askew, C. (1994). Print adverts: Not remembered but memorable. *Applied Cognitive Psychology, 8*, 693–703.

Perruchet, P., & Pacteau, C. (1990). Synthetic grammar learning: Implicit rule abstraction or explicit fragmentary knowledge? *Journal of Experimental Psychology: General, 119*, 264–275.

Reber, A. S. (1967). Implicit learning of artificial grammars. *Journal of Verbal Learning and Verbal Behavior, 6*, 855–863.

Rensink, R. A., O'Regan, J. K., & Clark, J. J. (1997). To see or not to see: The need for attention to perceive changes in scenes. *Psychological Science, 8*, 368–373.

Roediger, H. L., & McDermott, K. B. (1993). Encoding specificity in perceptual priming. In A. Garriga-Trillo, P. R. Minon, C. Garcia-Gallego, P. Lubin, J. M. Merino, & A. Villarino (Eds.), *Fechner Day' 93: Proceedings of the Ninth Annual Meeting of the International Society for Psychophysics* (pp. 227–232). Madrid, Spain.

Rosiell, L. J., & Scaggs, W. J. (2008). What if they knocked down the library and nobody noticed? The failure to detect large changes to familiar scenes. *Memory, 16*, 115–124.

Rubin, D. C., & Kontis, T. C. (1983). A schema for common cents. *Memory and Cognition, 11*, 335–341.

Schacter, D. L. (1992). Priming and multiple memory systems: Perceptual mechanisms of implicit memory. *Journal of Cognitive Neuroscience, 4*, 244–256.

Schacter, D. L., Cooper, L. A., & Delaney, S. M. (1990). Implicit memory for unfamiliar objects depends upon access to structural descriptions. *Journal of Experimental Psychology: General, 199*, 5–24.

Schott, B. H., Henson, R. N., Richardson-Klavehn, A., Becker, C., Thoma, V., Heinze, H. J., et al. (2005). Redefining implicit and explicit memory: The functional neuroanatomy of priming, remembering, and control of retrieval. *Proceedings of the National Academy of Sciences of the USA, 102*, 1257–1262.

Scott, V. (1989). An empirical study of explicit and implicit teaching strategies in French. *The Modern Language Journal, 73*, 14–22.

Scott, V. (1990). Explicit and implicit grammar teaching strategies: New empirical data. *The French Review, 63*, 779–789.

Sebel, P. S., Bowdle, T. A., Ghoneim, M. M., Rampil, I. J., Padilla, R. E., Gan, T. J., & Domino, K. B. (2004). The incidence of awareness during anesthesia: A multicenter United States study. *Anesthesia and Analgesia, 99*, :833–839.

Shors, T. J., & Matzel, L. D. (1997). Long-term potentiation: What's learning got to do with it? *Behavioral and Brain Sciences, 20*, 597–655.

Simons, D. J., & Levin, D. T. (1998). Failure to detect changes to people during a real-world interaction. *Psychonomic Bulletin and Review, 5*, 644–649.

Srinivas, K., & Roediger, H. L. (1990). Classifying implicit memory tests: Category association and anagram solution. *Journal of Memory and Language, 29*, 389–412.

Stanley, W. B., Mathews, R. C., Buss, R. R., & Kotler-Cope, S. (1989). Insight without awareness: On the interaction of verbalization, instruction, and practice in a simulated process CDCT. *Quarterly Journal of Experimental Psychology, 41*, 553–577.

Staubli, U., Rogers, G., & Lynch, G. (1994). Facilitation of glutamate receptors enhances memory. *Proceedings of the National Academy of Sciences of the USA, 91*, 777–781.

Stewart, E. W., Shimp, T. A., & Engle, R. W. (1987). Classical conditioning of consumer attitudes: Four experiments in an advertising context. *Journal of Consumer Research, 14*, 334–349.

Stickgold, R., & Walker, M. P. (2013). Sleep-dependent memory triage: Evolving generalization through selective processing. *Nature Neuroscience, 16*, 139–145.

Stickgold, R., James, L., & Hobson, J. A. (2000). Visual discrimination learning requires sleep after training. *Nature Neuroscience, 3*, 1237–1238.

Tulving, E., Schacter, D. L., & Stark, H. A. (1982). Priming effects in word-fragment completion are independent of recognition memory. *Journal of Experimental Psychology: Learning, Memory and Cognition, 8*, 336–342.

Twitmyer, E. B. (1902). *A study of the knee jerk.* Philadelphia, PA: Winston.

Wang, M. (2010). Implicit memory, anesthesia and sedation In G. W. Davies (Ed.), *Current issues in applied memory research* (pp. 165–184). London: Psychology Press.

Warrington, E. K., & Weiskrantz, L. (1968). New method of testing long-term retention with special reference to amnesic patients. *Nature, 217*, 972–974.

Warrington, E. K, & Weiskrantz, L. (1970). Amnesic syndrome: Consolidation or retrieval? *Nature, 226*, 628–630.

Wei, G., Zhang, Y., Jiang T, & Luo, J. (2011). Increased cortical thickness in sports experts: A comparison of diving players with the controls. *PLoS One, 6*, e17112. doi: 10.1371/journal.pone.0017112

Williams, A. M., Ward, P., Bell-Walker, J., & Ford, P. R. (2012). Perceptual-cognitive expertise, practice history profiles and recall performance in soccer. *British Journal of Psychology, 103*, 393–411. doi: 10.1111/j.2044–8295.2011.02081.x

Wilson, M. A., & McNaughton, B. L. (1994). Reactivation of hippocampal ensemble memories during sleep. *Science, 265*, 676–679.

Young, B. W., & Salmela, J. H. (2010). Examination of practice activities related to the acquisition of elite performance in Canadian middle distance running. *International Journal of Sport Psychology, 41*, 73–90.

Contents

The Bartlett approach   138

Meaning and memory   141

Memory and predictability   143

Levels of processing   144

The limits of levels   145

Transfer-appropriate processing   145

Why is deeper coding better?   146

Organization and memory   148

Becoming an expert   150

Seriation   152

Episodic memory and the brain   155

Summary   159

Points for discussion   160

Further reading   160

References   160

CHAPTER 6

EPISODIC MEMORY: ORGANIZING AND REMEMBERING

Alan Baddeley

Where were you at 8.00 p.m. yesterday evening? What is your earliest memory? When did you last see the sea? All these questions demand a special kind of memory, one that allows you to access specific memories located at a particular point in time: they require *episodic memory*. You will recall from Chapter 1 that this term was devised by Endel Tulving to emphasize the difference between the recollection of specific events and *semantic memory*, generalized knowledge of the world. It is episodic memory that allows what Tulving calls "mental time travel," allowing us to travel back and "relive" earlier episodes, and to use this capacity to travel forward and anticipate future events. You might remember meeting a friend yesterday evening and agreeing to play tennis tomorrow afternoon for instance, and will "travel forward in time" to plan your day accordingly.

The crucial feature of episodic memory is the capacity to remember specific events. For this, you need some kind of mental filing system that will allow you to distinguish that event from similar events on other occasions. This in turn needs three things. The first is a system that allows you to encode that particular experience in a way that will distinguish it from others. Second, it requires a method of storing that event in a durable form, and finally it requires a method of searching the system and retrieving that particular memory. The present chapter is concerned with the first of these processes, the way in which organization is used to "catalog" our experiences so

as to make them accessible when we need to remember them.

Although the defining feature of episodic memory is the capacity to recollect specific events, such events might then accumulate and consolidate to form the basis of semantic memory, our knowledge of the world. Although the precise relationship between episodic and semantic memory remains controversial (e.g. Tulving, 2002; Squire, 2004), impaired episodic memory in amnesic patients is generally associated with impaired knowledge acquisition, the capacity to continue to develop knowledge of the world, rather than the capacity to retrieve existing knowledge. Thus a patient might be unable to remember the current US president, but be able to recall the name of the US president and UK prime minister during the Second World War. Healthy people, however, are likely to have both semantic and episodic components of memory for a recent event. Martin Conway and colleagues studied the learning and retention of material from a psychology course. After a short delay, much of the information was recalled as episodes; for example, the experience of being told about rats swimming through milky water in the Morris study of the role of the hippocampus in learning. When tested several months later, however, this information had become separated from recollection of the learning event and had become incorporated into the semantic memory, at least of the more successful students (Conway, Cohen, & Stanhope, 1992). In that sense, the chapter that follows is as much about learning as is the previous chapter.

The psychology of memory has been, and continues to be, influenced by two rather different traditions. The first of these is the Ebbinghaus tradition, whereby the study of human memory is made possible by focusing on clearly specified experiments with tightly constrained goals. The danger of this approach is that it could lead us to focus on narrow problems that tell us little about how memory works in the world outside the laboratory.

THE BARTLETT APPROACH

The second tradition attempts to tackle the study of memory in all its complexity, accepting that our capacity to control any single study will inevitably be limited, but trusting in the belief that multiple studies will allow clear conclusions to be drawn. This more naturalistic approach was pioneered by Frederick Bartlett, a British philosopher turned experimental psychologist who had wide interests in anthropology and social psychology. Bartlett (1932) argued that, in attempting to control the experimental situation, Ebbinghaus had simply thrown out the most important and interesting aspects of human memory. Bartlett deliberately chose to study the recall of complex material, such as drawings and folk tales from unfamiliar cultures. Rather than study the gradual accumulation of information over successive learning trials, he preferred to use the errors that his participants made as a clue to the way in which they were encoding and storing the material. His methods of study were much more informal than those used by Ebbinghaus, often including several recalls by the same participant over periods of days or even longer. In a typical study, Bartlett (1932) would present his Cambridge University students with a North American Indian folk tales such as:

The War of the Ghosts

One night two young men from Egulac went down to the river to hunt seals, and

while they were there it became foggy and calm. Then they hear war-cries, and they thought: "Maybe this is a war-party." They escaped to the shore, and hid behind a log. Now canoes came up, and they heard the noise of paddles, and saw one canoe coming up to them. There were five men in the canoe, and they said: "What do you think? We wish to take you along. We are going up the river to make war on the people."

One of the young men said: "I have no arrows."

"Arrows are in the canoe," they said.

"I will not go along. I might be killed. My relatives do not know where I have gone. But you," he said, turning to the other, "may go with them."

So one of the young men went, but the other returned home. And the warriors went up the river to a town on the other side of Kalama.

The people came down to the water, and they began to fight, and many were killed. But presently the young man heard one of the warriors say: "Quick, let us go home: that Indian has been hit."

Now he thought: "Oh, they are ghosts."

He did not feel sick, but they said he had been shot.

So the canoes went back to Egulac, and the young man went ashore to his house, and made a fire. And he told everybody and said: "Behold I accompanied the ghosts, and we went to fight. Many of our fellows were killed, and many of those who attacked us were killed. They said I was hit, and I did not feel sick."

He told it all, and then he came quiet. When the sun rose he fell down. Something black came out of his mouth. His face became contorted. The people jumped up and cried. He was dead.

Now close the book and try to recall the story as accurately as you can.

What Bartlett (1932) found was that the remembered story was always shorter, more coherent, and tended to fit in more closely with the participant's own viewpoint than the original story. A central feature of Bartlett's approach was to stress the participant's *effort after meaning*; exactly the opposite of Ebbinghaus's explicit attempt to avoid meaning. Rather than being a simple recipient of information, participants were actively striving after meaning, trying to capture the essence of the material presented. Indeed, one of Bartlett's students, Bronislav Gomulicki (1956), observed that the recall protocols provided by people attempting to remember one of Bartlett's stories were indistinguishable by independent judges from the attempts of others to produce summaries, with the story present.

A second feature of Bartlett's theory was his postulation of the concept of a *schema*, a long-term structured representation of knowledge that was used by the rememberer to make sense of new material and subsequently store and recall it. This concept of schema has subsequently proved to be highly influential and will be discussed further in Chapter 7, which is concerned with semantic memory. Bartlett emphasized the role of social and cultural influences on the development of schemas, which in turn determine the way in which material is encoded, stored, and subsequently recalled. These tendencies were especially great with a story like *The War of the Ghosts*, in which several features were incompatible with European expectations (or those of Americans unfamiliar with the North American Indian culture). Hence, the supernatural aspect of the story was often omitted. In addition, features of the story that were puzzling to the readers were rationalized by distorting them to fit their expectations. Hence "something black came out of his mouth" became "foamed at the mouth."

Bartlett (1932) interpreted his findings by arguing that the systematic errors and distortions produced in the participants' recalls were due to the intrusion of their schematic knowledge. However, it is possible to criticize Bartlett's experimental approach. The instructions he gave to his participants were rather vague and he hardly ever carried out any statistical tests on his data! More worryingly, many of the recall distortions he observed were due to deliberate guessing rather than genuine problems in memory. This was demonstrated by Gauld and Stephenson (1967), who found that clear instructions emphasizing the need for accurate recall eliminated almost half of the errors obtained using Bartlett's vague instructions.

There is an important general point here. As you will discover, a good deal of research in the psychology of memory has focused in recent years on errors, as is well-illustrated in Schacter's (2001) excellent *The Seven Sins of Memory*. However, as Neisser (1988) points out, such errors tend to occur when we are encouraged to go beyond the limits of what we can clearly recall. This is common in the legal situation with the attempt to maximize the available evidence, but is much less so in everyday life, where we are more likely to say we just can't remember. So, errors are potentially revealing and can be very important, but as Schacter (2001) points out, occasional errors are the price we sometimes pay for our generally very effective memory systems.

Despite these problems with Bartlett's procedures, there is convincing support for his major findings from well-controlled studies. For example, consider a study by Sulin and Dooling (1974). They set out to test Bartlett's theory, including his assumption that systematic, schema-driven errors will be greater at a long retention interval than after a short delay because schematic information lasts longer in memory than more detailed information in the text. Sulin and Dooling presented some participants with a story about Gerald Martin: "Gerald Martin strove to undermine the existing government to satisfy his political ambitions ... He became a ruthless, uncontrollable dictator. The ultimate effect of his rule was the downfall of his country" (Sulin & Dooling, 1974, p. 256). Other participants were given the same story but the main actor was called Adolf Hitler. Those

In Sulin and Dooling's (1974) study, participants used their schematic knowledge of Hitler to incorrectly organize the information about the story they had been told. The study revealed how schematic organization can lead to errors in long-term memory and recall.

participants told the story was about Adolf Hitler were much more likely than the other participants to believe incorrectly they had read the sentence, "He hated the Jews particularly and so persecuted them." Their schematic knowledge

about Hitler distorted their recollections of what they had read at a long retention interval (1 week) but not at a short one (5 minutes).

A more controlled way of studying memory bias than story recall is by using ambiguous stimuli and providing disambiguating labels. The classic study here is again a very old one. Carmichael, Hogan, and Walter (1932) presented the visual stimuli shown at the centre of Figure 6.1 for subsequent recall. Each item was sufficiently ambiguous as to fit two different verbal labels, for example a beehive or a hat. When participants were later asked to draw the stimuli from memory, their drawings were strongly influenced by the label they had been given. It is tempting to think of this again as a bias in the way in which the material was perceived and stored. However, a subsequent study by Prentice (1954) suggested otherwise. The encoding conditions were the same as for the Carmichael et al. study, but retrieval load was minimized by using recognition rather than recall. The label effect disappeared under these circumstances, suggesting that the bias occurred at retrieval rather than encoding; the appropriate information was stored but the difficult task of recalling by drawing led to an undue influence of the verbal labels. We shall return to the topic of bias and memory in Chapter 14 on eyewitness testimony.

Before moving on from the role of verbal labeling, we should note that it can also be

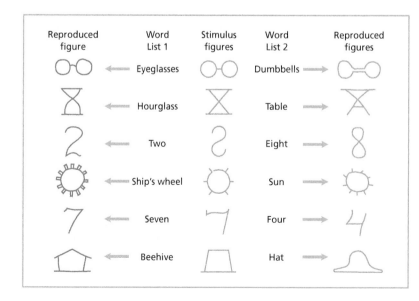

Figure 6.1 Examples of the ambiguous items used by Carmichael et al. (1932). Copyright © American Psychological Association. Reproduced with permission.

helpful. This was shown by Bower, Karlin, and Dueck (1975) in a study in which people were asked to recall apparently meaningless patterns or "droodles" such as shown in Figure 6.2. Free recall of these patterns was very poor. However, recall was greatly improved when each droodle was accompanied by an interpretative label. Bower et al. conclude that "memory is aided whenever contextual cues arouse appropriate schemata."

MEANING AND MEMORY

Bartlett's principal criticism of Ebbinghaus was that his attempt to separate memory from meaning meant that he was studying simple repetition habits, which had very little relevance to the way in which our memories work in everyday life. In fact, by the time Bartlett was making his criticism of Ebbinghaus's approach, it was already clear that, whereas Ebbinghaus himself might have succeeded in

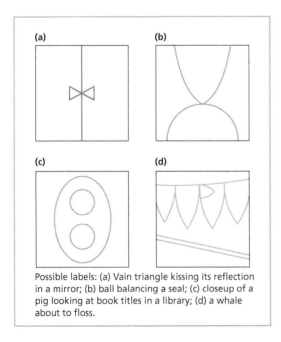

Possible labels: (a) Vain triangle kissing its reflection in a mirror; (b) ball balancing a seal; (c) closeup of a pig looking at book titles in a library; (d) a whale about to floss.

Figure 6.2   A set of droodles of the type used by Bower et al. (1975). Subsequent recall was greatly enhanced when the droodles were accompanied by their titles. What titles would you suggest? Possible answers are given below the figure.

excluding meaning from his learning strategy, this was not the case for the less determined students who subsequently participated in verbal learning experiments. In 1928, Glaze had his students rate the extent to which each possible consonant–vowel–consonant suggested one or more real words; some suggested several words, for example, the syllable *CAS* might suggest *castle*, *cast*, and *casino*, whereas a syllable such as *ZIJ* is far harder to link with meaningful existing words. There is clear evidence that syllables rated as more meaningful are easier to recall (Jung, 1968).

So does that mean that people are explicitly relying on words to remember the syllables? The rate at which Ebbinghaus recited these syllables made that unlikely, and even at the subsequent slower standard rate of 2 seconds per syllable, forming and using associations is very difficult for all except the most meaningful syllables. It seemed more likely that Bartlett's suggestion that this task involves developing "repetition habits" might be closer to the mark, with those syllables that follow most closely the structure of English being the easiest to acquire because they are consistent with well-learned language habits, an effect that we have already noted for immediate memory. This indeed also proved to be the case for long-term learning (Underwood & Schulz, 1960; Baddeley, 1964).

By the 1960s, the use of nonsense syllables in verbal learning studies was dying out and being replaced by studies using word lists, for which meaning was clearly highly important. The dominant tradition in verbal learning was still that of stimulus–response associationism, with interest focusing on the influence of pre-existing associations between words on ease of list learning. Underpinning this approach was the view that memory could be explained purely in terms of associations or links between words. When prior interword associations were strong, such as *bread–butter*, learning would be easier than when they were more remote, such as *castle–tower*, or absent, as in *lobster–symphony*.

Up to this point, investigators into verbal learning had tended to rely largely on such standard tasks as serial recall, in which items are recalled in the order presented, and paired-associate learning, in which participants were required to learn word pairs, (e.g. *dog–bishop*), so that when given the first item the stimulus (*dog*) they must produce the response (*bishop*). By the 1950s, however, experimenters were increasingly using the less constrained task of free recall, in which participants are asked to produce as many words from the list as they can remember, in any order (see also Chapter 3, p. 42). Using this method, Deese (1959) showed that lists of words that were highly associated with each other were easier to recall than lists with few interword associations, and Jenkins and Russell (1952) noted that when a number of associated words, such as *thread*, *needle*, and *mend*, were included in a mixed list, even though they were presented separately, they tended to be recalled as a cluster.

One of the most surprising developments at this time was the recognition of the importance of visual imagery. The verbal learning tradition was firmly against the use of introspection and did not welcome the idea of subjects indulging in anything as nonbehavioral as visual imagery. However, there was overwhelming evidence that ratings of the extent to which a word evoked an image were a very powerful predictor of how well it would be remembered. The person who made this discovery was Allen Paivio, a muscular Canadian of Finnish descent, who had had the further distinction of being Mr. Canada. Paivio placated the more traditionalist verbal learners by pointing out that he was merely predicting one form of behavior, remembering word lists, on the basis of another behavior, the rating responses of his participants. The fact that the rating instruction relied on introspection, the extent to which a given word evoked a subjectively experienced image, could then be conveniently ignored.

I suggest you try a free recall experiment for yourself. Take a sheet of paper and a pen. Then read out the following list of words (List A), at a steady rate of about 2 seconds per word. Then close your eyes and recite the alphabet to get rid of the recency effect before writing down as many words as you can in any order.

List A:

virtue, history, silence, life, hope, value, mathematics, dissent, idea

How many did you remember? Now try the next list (List B) using exactly the same procedure.

List B:

church, beggar, carpet, arm, hat, teapot, dragon, cannon, apple

You probably found the second list easier. As you might have noticed, the second list comprises words that are more concrete and more imageable than the first. Paivio studied the effect of imageability extensively, explaining his findings in terms of the dual-coding hypothesis, whereby words that were imageable, such as the name of concrete objects (e.g. *crocodile*), could be encoded in terms of both their visual appearance and their verbal meaning. For example, a visual image of a crocodile could be generated and linked to one or more other imageable words from the list. If football had also occurred, you might image the crocodile biting a football. Creating interacting images tends to be much harder for abstract words such as *hope* and *theory*. There are therefore two routes to retrieval for imageable words —visual and verbal—so if one route is lost the other might still survive and allow recall (Paivio, 1969, 1971).

Before we move on, try one more list, reading it out and then recalling in just the same way as lists A and B.

List C:

large, grey, elephants, terrified, by, roaring, flames, trampled, tiny, defenseless, rabbits

How many did you get that time. I suspect rather more than for lists A or B for an obvious reason. Unlike A and B, list C comprised a meaningful, if slightly odd sentence.

KEY TERM

Dual-coding hypothesis: Highly imageable words are easy to learn because they can be encoded both visually and verbally.

two passages. The first is from a children's storybook, the second from a classic novel.

The dual-coding hypothesis assumes that concrete and imageable words can be encoding in terms of both their visual appearance and their verbal meaning, whereas abstract words are only encoded verbally. The visual representations can then be combined into a single composite image; for example a crocodile biting a football when one word of the pair is presented, for example *crocodile*, it automatically tends to evoke the football.

MEMORY AND PREDICTABILITY

What is the crucial difference between sentences and unrelated word strings? One obvious difference stems from the fact that strong relationships exist between the words in a sentence but not between the words in a list. Language is redundant in the sense that successive words are not equally probable; adjectives tend to come before nouns and pronouns are generally followed by verbs. The meaning of the topic being written or spoken about also constrains the selection of words. All of these are reflected in the tendency for each word in a sentence to be predictable on the basis of surrounding words. Hence, if I were to ask you to play a guessing game in which I presented parts of sentences and asked you to guess the next word, you would do reasonably well.

Even within meaningful text, quite marked differences occur in the degree of redundancy or predictability. One way of measuring this is the Cloze technique: People are presented with a passage from which every fifth word has been deleted. Their task is to guess the missing words. Try it yourself on the following

The sly young fox — to eat the little — hen for his dinner. — made all sorts of — to catch her. He — many times to — her. But she was — clever little hen. Not — of the sly fox's — worked. He grew quite — trying to catch the — red hen. One day — sly young fox said — his mother, "Today I — catch the little red —. I have made the — plan of all." He — up a bag and — it over his back. "— shall put the little — hen in this bag," — said to his mother.
(**Extract from** *The Sly Fox* by Vera Southgate)

In the first place, — had by that time, — the benefit of his — education: continual hard work, — soon and concluded late, — extinguished any curiosity he — possessed in pursuit of —, and any love for — or learning. His childhood's — of superiority, instilled into — by the favors of — Mr. Earnshaw, was faded —. He struggled long to — up an equality with — in her studies, and — with a poignant though silent —: but he yielded completely; — there was no prevailing — him to take a — in the way of — upward, when he found — must, necessarily, sink beneath — former level.
(**Extract from** *Wuthering Heights* by Emily Brontë)

The missing words from the first passage were *wanted, red, he, plans, tried, catch, a, one, plans, thin, little, the, to, will, hen, best, picked, slung, I, red, he.* From the second passage the words omitted were *he, lost, early, begun, had, once, knowledge, books, sense, him, old, away, keep, Catherine, yielded, regret, and, on, step, moving, he, his.* Most people find the children's text more predictable and fill in considerably more words. Redundancy as measured by the Cloze technique is a reasonably good predictor of both the judged readability of text and of its memorability. The more redundant and predictable a piece of prose, the easier it is to recall (Rubenstein & Aborn, 1958).

LEVELS OF PROCESSING

All the previous examples could be regarded as reflecting the influence of meaning, extending from the richness with which individual items can be encoded through to passages varying in their predictability. But why does meaning facilitate long-term learning?

One possibility is that storage in STM relies on a phonological code, whereas LTM is semantically based. This is an unsatisfactory explanation for two reasons. First, it is clear that we *can* demonstrate long-term learning for phonological information, otherwise how would we ever learn the sound of words in the language? Furthermore, simply saying that LTM uses a semantic code does not explain why a semantic code is helpful.

An answer to this puzzle was offered by Craik and Lockhart (1972) with their *Levels of Processing* hypothesis. This moves away from the idea of memory stores that have particular codes, emphasizing instead that the way in which material is processed determines its durability in LTM. They propose that information is taken in and processed to varying depths. In the case of a printed word for example, they suggest that its visual characteristics would be processed first, followed by the spoken sound of the word, and then its meaning. They suggest that each of these processes will leave a memory record, with deeper processes leaving a more durable trace.

Craik and Tulving (1975) carried out a series of experiments in which words were presented visually and participants asked to make three different types of judgment. One involved shallow visual processing (Is this word in upper or lower case? *TABLE*), one was phonological (Does this word rhyme with dog? *Log*), and the deepest required semantic processing (Does the word *field* fit into this sentence? The horse lived in a —).

Having performed these various operations on the words, participants were unexpectedly confronted with a list of words and asked which ones they had just been shown. Half of the words were new and half had been processed in one of the three ways, involving case, rhyme or semantic judgment. Craik and Tulving found that, the greater the depth of processing had been, the better the subsequent memory. As Figure 6.3 shows, this was a clear effect and was particularly marked for questions to which the answer was "yes."

This demonstration of better recognition following deeper processing was, of course, exactly as predicted by the levels of processing hypothesis, but why were "yes" responses better recalled than "no"? Craik and Tulving suggest that this is because, for positive items, the word to be recalled was integrated more closely with the encoding question, particularly in the semantic condition. If a sentence made sense when linked with the target words, as in "The horse lived in a field," remembering the sentence would help remind you of the target, perhaps an image of a horse in a field. This source of help would not be so readily

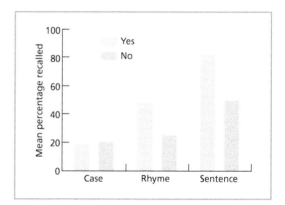

Figure 6.3 Effects of type of encoding task on subsequent word recognition. Based on Craik and Tulving (1975).

KEY TERM

Depth of processing: The proposal by Craik and Lockhart that the more deeply an item is processed, the better will be its retention.

available for a negative item such as "Does the word *fork* fit into 'The horse lived in a —'?"

Could it be the case that semantic judgments lead to better recall simply because they take longer, in line the with total time hypothesis? In their initial experiments, it was certainly the case that deeper processing took longer. In a later experiment, Craik and Tulving slowed down the two more superficial processing tasks by making them more difficult, for example by replacing the decision as to whether the word was in upper or lower case with the requirement to count the number of vowels in the target word. They found no evidence that slower processing led to enhanced recognition.

The general principle that deeper and more elaborate processing leads to better memory has been supported by many other studies. Hyde and Jenkins (1973), for example, carried out an extensive series of experiments studying no fewer than 22 different encoding tasks and finding general support for a major influence of processing level on memory. This levels-of-processing effect is found for both recall and recognition, regardless of whether participants do or do not expect a later memory test. During the 1970s, many similar studies provided substantial support for Craik and Lockhart's proposals. Indeed, as a basic generalization or rule of thumb, the principle that deeper and more elaborate processing leads to better retention is arguably our most useful generalization about human memory. The effect is robust, reliable and, as we will see, very useful for anyone wanting to maximize their learning capacity. It has not, however, escaped criticism, at both a theoretical and practical level.

THE LIMITS OF LEVELS

One problem acknowledged by Craik and Tulving (1975) is that of measuring *depth of processing*. As we saw earlier, simply using processing time as a measure does not work, as a slow but superficial processing task such as counting the number of vowels in a word leads to longer processing but not to better recall. Indeed, the whole concept of processing depth has come under criticism, with increasing evidence suggesting that many different features of a stimulus might be processed at the same time, rather than in the strict serial order assumed, of vision-then-phonology-then-semantics. It is indeed unlikely that when a participant decides whether *dog* rhymes with *log*, he or she is totally unaware of the meaning, although the attention paid to that aspect of the word is likely to be much less than in the semantic processing case. Consequently, in the 30 years following Craik and Lockhart's important paper, levels of processing has come to be seen as an extremely valuable rule of thumb, but has not itself generated great further theoretical development.

TRANSFER-APPROPRIATE PROCESSING

A second set of problems concerns situations in which deeper processing does not always lead to better performance. Students might do poorly on retrieving information during exams not because they fail to study but because they focus on the wrong type of knowledge. Consider this thought experiment. Suppose you don't know how to ride a bicycle. You approach an expert on bicycle riding, who has written a 200-page book detailing all the rules and facts that one needs to know, describing even the minutest adjustments in posture. Being an excellent student, you spend weeks memorizing everything. If you were given a test on the book, you would score 100%. Then you get on the bicycle and what happens? You crash within seconds, unable to keep balanced. You don't really know what is important about riding bicycles. You have excellent factual knowledge, but no skill.

This illustrates a broad principle known as transfer-appropriate processing. This principle states that for a test to reveal prior learning, the processing requirements of the test should

> **KEY TERM**
>
> Transfer-appropriate processing (TAP):
> Proposal that retention is best when the mode of encoding and mode of retrieval are the same.

match the processing conditions at encoding. This principle has been invoked to explain the powerful phenomenon of depth of processing. As mentioned earlier, people are quite poor at later recalling words about which they have made visual or phonological judgments, but are very good at remembering words about which they made a meaning-based judgment. This might partially reflect a bias in the way items are tested. In particular, during recall tests, people might be used to remembering the meanings of words they just encountered, and so the test implicitly places emphasis on meaning. To illustrate this point, Morris, Bransford, and Franks (1977) examined whether retention was determined by what people do while encoding, or was instead determined by how well the processing requirements of the test matched encoding. Morris and colleagues asked participants to make either a phonological or semantic judgment about each item in a word list.

As is commonly the case in experiments on levels of processing, participants were not warned they would have to recall. This feature, known as incidental learning, has the advantage that participants are not tempted to use other learning strategies over and above performing the task requested by the experimenter. The deep condition involved semantic processing, for example "Does the word that follows fit the gap in the sentence, 'The — ran into the lamp-post': *car*"?; whereas the shallow condition involved a judgment of rhyme such as "Does it rhyme with fighter? *Writer.*" Memory was then tested by one of two recognition tests; the first was a standard condition in which the words were presented (e.g. *car*, *writer*), mixed in with an equal number of nonpresented words (e.g. *fish*, *lawyer*). The second type of test involved presenting a series of words and asking if an item had been presented that rhymed with that word (e.g. *bar*, *lighter*).

Morris et al. found that deeper processing led to much better performance under the standard recognition conditions, just as Craik

and Tulving (1975) had shown. However, the opposite occurred with rhyme recognition: The shallower rhyme-based encoding task led to better performance.

A subsequent study by Fisher and Craik (1977) broadly replicated this result, but emphasized that there *was*, overall, a clear advantage to deeper processing. However, both sets of authors agree that it only makes sense to talk about the efficiency of a learning method in the context of the way in which memory is subsequently tested, an issue that will be explored further in Chapter 8 concerned with recognition memory.

WHY IS DEEPER CODING BETTER?

As Fisher and Craik (1977) point out, although it is not always the case, deeper processing does tend to convey an advantage under a wide range of conditions. Why should that be? Craik and Tulving (1975) suggest that semantic coding is advantageous because it allows a richer and more elaborate code, which in turn becomes more readily retrievable. They describe an experiment that supports this view. Their participants are required to judge whether a given word will or will not fit into a sentence. The sentences can be either relatively simple, such as "She dropped her *pen*" or more complex, for example: "The little old man hobbled across the castle courtyard and dropped his *pen* in the well." Memory was then tested by giving the sentence frame, and requiring the target word to be recalled. There was a very clear advantage to words embedded in the semantically richer sentences. This advantage was also found with unprompted free recall, but was much weaker (Craik & Tulving, 1975).

The idea that elaboration helps recall extends back at least to William James (1890), who suggested that of two men with equivalent mental capacity:

The one who THINKS over his experiences most, and weaves them into systematic relations with each other will be the one

with the best memory … All improvement
of the memory lies in the line of elaborating
the associates.
(James, 1890, p. 662)

The idea that deeper processing involves elaboration fits in neatly with a distinction made by Craik and Lockhart (1972) between two kinds of rehearsal. One of these, maintenance rehearsal involves continuing to process an item at the *same* level; the rote rehearsal of a telephone number by saying it to oneself would be a good example of maintenance rehearsal. They contrast maintenance rehearsal with elaborative rehearsal, which involves linking the material being rehearsed to other material in memory, both within the set of items being learned and beyond, just as James proposes. Craik and Lockhart suggest that only elaborative rehearsal enhances delayed long-term learning.

Evidence for this view comes from an ingenious study by Glenberg, Smith, and Green (1977), who presented their participants with numbers that were to be remembered over a delay. During the delay, participants were required to read out words, a task that they were led to believe was used simply to stop them rehearsing the numbers. Some words occurred only once during this delay-filling activity, others many times. Having recalled the numbers, people were then asked unexpectedly to recall as many of the words as they could. A nine-fold increase in number of repetitions led to only 1.5% increase in recall, although it did have a more substantial effect

on recognition, with recognition probability increasing from 0.65 to 0.74. It seems likely that the slight increase in familiarity based on the recent repetition is enough to boost recognition, but that this does not provide a sufficiently powerful cue to allow the original words to be evoked.

So does maintenance rehearsal never help long-term recall? Once again, it depends on the task. Mechanic (1964) required his participants to articulate each of a series of nonsense syllables either once, or as often as possible in the time available. One group was warned of a subsequent recall test, while the second group was told that the purpose of the study was to measure their speed of articulation. Mechanic's results are shown in Figure 6.4. Repeated articulation led to enhanced recall, regardless of whether recall was expected or not, whereas participants from whom a single repetition was required did very poorly in the incidental learning condition. Presumably, knowing that recall would be required encouraged additional processing in the intentional learning group, whereas the requirement to articulate repeatedly rapidly discouraged further processing in either group.

So what is the difference between the results of Glenberg et al. (1977), who found

KEY TERM

Maintenance rehearsal: A process of rehearsal whereby items are "kept in mind" but not processed more deeply.

Elaborative rehearsal: Process whereby items are not simply kept in mind, but are processed either more deeply or more elaborately.

Intentional learning: Learning when the learner knows that there will be a test of retention.

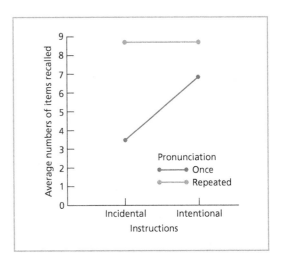

Figure 6.4 Average number of nonsense syllables recalled as a function of learning instruction and number of repetitions. Under these conditions, rote repetition enhances learning. Data from Mechanic (1964).

virtually no advantage to repetition, and those of Mechanic, who found that repetition helped recall? A crucial issue concerns the question of exactly what the participants are learning. In the case of Mechanic's study, the syllables are unfamiliar and do not form natural existing chunks. Repeating them is likely to boost their representation in phonological LTM. In Glenberg's study, there is no need to learn the words, as they are already in the vocabulary of the participants. The memory task in this case is to recall which particular word had just been presented, something that, as we shall see, typically depends on meaningful links *between* the words. This is likely to be helped by the rich array of semantic features that is typical of words but not of nonsense syllables.

ORGANIZATION AND MEMORY

Why does semantic coding help?

One reason why deeper processing is generally good for learning is that it emphasizes the use of a semantic code, which is potentially much richer than a code representing the sound or printed appearance of a word. But why should this help? To answer this question we need to think about the task that faces a participant in a typical levels-of-processing experiment, which is to view or hear a sequence of words and then try to reproduce as many as possible. The words are not, strictly speaking, being learned, as they will already be in the learner's vocabulary. The problem is to make available those words that have been presented, and no others.

One way to do this is to bind the separate words into chunks and to recall the chunks. A study by Tulving (1962) suggests that this is exactly what people do. He repeatedly presented participants with a list of words, changing their order on each trial and asking participants to recall as many as possible. Despite the fact that the order of the words was scrambled every time, Tulving noted that as people gradually learned the list, they tended to produce words in clusters or chunks that came out in the same order trial after trial. Learning consisted of building bigger and bigger chunks, a

process that Tulving referred to as subjective organization.

What sort of factors encourage such chunking? As you might expect, such organization tends to reflect semantic variables. Read through the list below three times and then see how many you can recall.

thread, pin, eye, sewing, sharp, point, prick, thimble, haystack, thorn, hurt, injection, syringe, cloth, knitting

You probably did rather well. Why?

The list was easy to recall because all the items were strongly related. They were, in fact, all *associates* of a single key word, *needle*. We shall return to this effect, which was originally developed by James Deese (1959), in Chapter 8 on retrieval.

Recall is also helped if the items can be chunked in terms of their semantic *categories*. Tulving and Pearlstone (1966) tested recall of lists containing groups of one, two or four words per semantic category for example; try the following:

pink, green, blue, purple, apple, cherry, lemon, plum, lion, zebra, cow, rabbit

How may did you recall? Now try the next set:

cabbage, table, river, shirt, gun, square, iron, dentist, sparrow, mountain, hand, granite

How many that time?

Participants given sets of four items from the same category did better; they tended to recall items in category-based chunks, although sometimes omitting some categories completely. This was not because these items were entirely forgotten, as when participants in either group were then given the category names, new words from omitted categories were then recalled.

A particularly effective way of organizing material is through a hierarchical structure such as that shown in Figure 6.5. Bower, Clark, Lesgold, and Winzenz (1969) presented this material either in the form of a logically structured hierarchy or with the items in scrambled order. Participants given the hierarchical condition averaged 65% correct compared with only 19% when the same words were scrambled. Of course, it is not always possible to organize material in terms of a hierarchy. Fortunately, as Broadbent, Cooper, and Broadbent (1978) demonstrated, considerable benefit can also be obtained by structuring material in a matrix such as that shown in Table 6.1.

The examples we have provided so far rely on material that is artificially designed to fit into generally accepted semantic categories. It is often the case, however, that the material we must remember is not formally organized in this way. Does that mean that organization is not relevant? Certainly not, as we saw from Tulving's (1962) subjective organization study; when asked to learn an apparently meaningless jumble of unrelated words, people will begin to make links that form them into meaningful chunks. Indeed, given the semantic richness of language and the ingenuity of learners,

TABLE 6.1 Data from Broadbent et al. (1978).

	Mammals	Birds
Farmyard	Cow	Chicken
	Sheep	Turkey
	Pig	Duck
	Goat	Goose
Pets	Dog	Budgerigar
	Cat	Canary
	Hamster	Parrot
	Guinea pig	Macaw

it is virtually impossible to produce a string of words that do not suggest at least some possible clusters.

There are, however, some techniques that are more effective than others. One of these is to try to link the various words into a coherent story. This has the advantage that it not only creates chunks, but it also links the chunks together, making it less likely that any will be left out. For example given a list such as:

church, beggar, carpet, arm, hat, teapot, dragon, cannon, apple

A participant might create a story such as the following: "He came out of the *church* and gave an *apple* to a *beggar* sitting on a *carpet*. With his withered *arm* he clutched a *hat* and

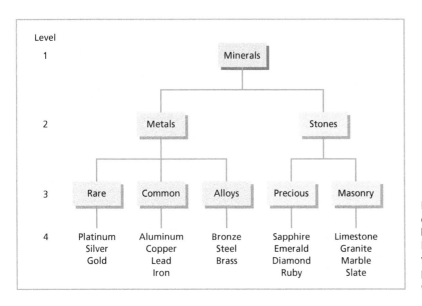

Figure 6.5 The "minerals" conceptual hierarchy used by Bower et al. (1969). Recall is much higher than when the same words were presented in scrambled order.

held his *hand* out for money, which he put in a *teapot* decorated by a *dragon* being shot at by a *cannon*."

Although it might be very effective, creating such stories is quite demanding and it can prove very difficult to form semantic links, particularly with rapid presentation of unrelated words (Campoy & Baddeley, 2008). There is also a danger of recalling words that were included to make a good story but which were not in the original, as in the case of "money," included in the above example to help make a plausible story. A more flexible method is that based on visual imagery, in which items are linked by imagining them interacting in some way. The interaction need not be plausible, so one can, for example, imagine a *swan* riding a *motorbike* if one wished to link those two words. Imagery mnemonics have formed an important part of the craft of memory since classical times. They are discussed in more detail as part of Chapter 17, which is concerned with improving your memory.

Intention to learn

Given that you are attending to material in an active and interested way, does it matter whether or not you are *trying* to learn it? Somewhat surprisingly, the answer appears to be "No." What is important is what you *do* with the material, not what your purpose is. This was demonstrated very neatly in a study by Mandler (1967), which involved memory for a list of relatively unrelated words. Participants were presented with a pack of cards, with a word on each. One group was told to commit the words to memory, a second group was asked to sort the words into categories comprising items that had something in common, while a third group was given this instruction together with a warning that recall would then be required. Finally, a fourth group was simply asked to arrange the words in columns. Subsequent recall showed that the group asked to organize the words on the basis of their meaning, with no mention of later recall, did just as well as participants instructed to learn, or indeed to organize *and* learn. All first three groups remembered more than the fourth incidental learning group, who had simply arranged the words in columns.

As we saw earlier, the levels-of-processing effect does not depend on whether participants *know* that recall will be required, performance depends only on what processing task is performed (Hyde & Jenkins, 1973). These results have clear implications for how you should study. The important thing is not the desire to remember, but the way in which you *process* the material. If you think about its meaning, relate it to what you already know, and consider its wider implications you have a much better chance of learning than if you simply read and note the major points. The importance of organization in memory does, of course, extend well beyond the standard laboratory experiment, a point that is well illustrated by the study of expertise.

BECOMING AN EXPERT

In July 1977, Anders Ericsson, a young Swedish psychologist, joined Carnegie-Mellon University in the US on a two-year fellowship. A major interest in the department was the way in which expertise developed, a topic that played an important role in the theorizing of Herbert Simon, a psychologist who had incidentally won a Nobel Prize for economics (as more recently did Daniel Kahneman). Looking for a project, Ericsson and William Chase decided to see if they could improve digit span by practice. They employed a graduate student, SF, who dutifully came regularly and practiced hearing and repeating back sequences of digits for about an hour a day. Figure 6.6 shows his performance over 200 such sessions— even Ebbinghaus didn't show this devotion to duty!

As you can see, performance steadily improved, but why? It turned out that the long-suffering participant was an enthusiastic runner, who worked out ways of encoding successive digits in terms of running times, for example recording the digits 4 3 8 as 4 minutes 38 seconds, a reasonable time for a mile. Other groups such as 7 9 2 which were not readily encodable in terms of running times were coding in terms of age, 79.2 years. These were then encoded within a hierarchical structure which also involved a degree of spatial coding. Initially, this process was relatively

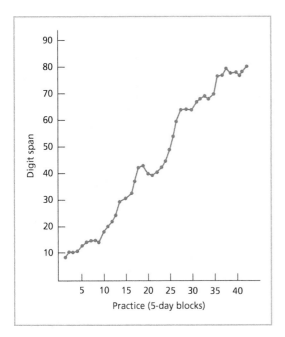

Figure 6.6 Chase and Ericsson's student, SF, regularly practiced hearing and repeating back sequences of digits for about an hour a day—this graph shows his improvement over 200 sessions. From Chase and Ericsson (1981). Copyright © Psychology Press.

slow, but with practice it speeded up. It was, of course, specific to digits, and depended on a remarkably rich and detailed knowledge of times achieved in a range of races, but particularly mile running, for which Chase and Ericsson (1982) report no fewer than 15 subcategories, ranging from the broad "good collegiate time," to specific notable races, for example "Coe versus Ovett." Note that "a good collegiate" time does not give a precise mapping. The model thus requires the further assumption that a more precise memory trace has been bound to the broad location during initial learning.

Ericsson went on to study expert memory more widely, moving on to study many forms of expertise, from a waiter with a remarkable capacity for remembering orders to the training of concert violinists. On the basis of this work, Ericsson and Kintsch (2006) developed the concept of *long-term working memory*. This refers to the development of structures in long-term memory that are then actively used

for temporary storage. An example might be expert calculators in Japan who initially performed their calculations on an abacus, a simple but potentially rapid and effective computational device comprising a frame with beads representing digits. Given sufficient practice, experts are able to discard the abacus and replace it with an imaginary mental representation. This allows them to add and subtract up to 15 numbers, each comprising from five to nine digits. They also have very high digit spans, around 16 for forward and 14 for backward recall. This is, however, limited to digits, with their letter span being normal. The fact that their skill is based on visual imagery was demonstrated by its disruption by a concurrent spatial task, a task that had no influence on control participants, whose coding was verbal and was disrupted by articulatory suppression (Hatano & Osawa, 1983a, 1983b).

How does Ericsson's *concept of long-term working memory* (LTWM) differ from the multicomponent working memory system described in Chapter 4? The most crucial difference is that LTWM is a term to describe a particular *function*, not a single unified cognitive system. It refers to any situation whereby a complex skill has been developed in order to deal with future accessibility to relevant knowledge within a particular domain of expertise. As such it can reflect many different mechanisms based on quite different processes occurring in different parts of the brain. In the examples discussed semantic knowledge of typical times for running a mile is of course very different from the sophisticated visual imagery used by abacus experts. In contrast, the multicomponent WM system referred to by Ericsson and Delaney (1999) as *short-term working memory* assumes that the *same* system is used for many different tasks. The system is of course assumed to comprise more than one component, and not all of these would be used equally, but effectively working memory is regarded as an integral whole and can in principle be mapped onto underlying brain structures. An important characteristic of this latter system is that it has limited capacity, whereas LTWM has no fixed capacity. Ericsson and Delaney (1999) assume that LTWM is the set of knowledge structures that are currently active. These are based on long-term memory structures that are likely to be large in capacity. In short, the concept of LTWM tries to capture a class of situations in which *expert* long-term knowledge is used to help perform specific cognitive tasks. As such it constitutes a different use of the term "working memory," rather than an alternative structural model or theory.

SERIATION

One form of organization that plays an important role in theories of STM, but has not been discussed so far, is that of placing items in serial order. Clearly this can also play an important part in LTM, as with days of the week, months of the year, and of course counting. So can we simply transfer the theoretical models of serial order in STM described in Chapter 3 (p. 47)? If you recall, chaining, whereby each item is associated with the next, did not fair very well in comparison to theories that assumed that individual items were attached to some form of marker involving either the initial item in the case of the primacy model (Page & Norris, 1998), or the temporal context in the case of the proposal by Burgess and Hitch (1999).

But can those models work for LTM? Have you ever had the experience of playing a CD you have not listened to recently, with a number of unrelated songs; when one song finishes, you "know" what is coming next? That would seem to suggest something like chaining—we have learned to associate the end of one song with the start of the next. What about the experience that I have of hearing the first few notes of a piece of music and immediately knowing what comes next? Is that a result of chaining, or can the primacy and positional marker models still explain these apparent effects?

Of course, my intuitions may be quite wrong. A more evidence-based demonstration of chaining-like effects in serial LTM is provided by Oliver and Ericsson (1986) who studied the memory of a small number of actors participating in a visiting Shakespeare festival. They chose expert actors who had mastered at least two substantial parts. They checked first that accurate verbatim recall was shown in the productions, as oppose to the re-creation within a broad narrative framework constrained by rhyme and rhythm, the method

shown by traditional bards in some cultures (Rubin, 1995). The actors did indeed all know their lines; but how well? This was tested by selecting lengthy passages that contained words or phrases that were unique to that passage, and then asking the actors what followed. They used probes of one, two or four words, observing virtually perfect recall for their four-word sequences while even a single word probe yielded 77% correct recall.

Recall typically took a few seconds, so that the actors could not have been using a primacy cue based on the beginning of the play. Nor was it plausible to assume serial markers for every word in the play. So can the models of serial order based on STM be extended to cover LTM? This issue is currently being very actively pursued by a number of STM theorists, including the advocates of both the primacy model (Page & Norris, 2009) and of a contextual marker model (Burgess & Hitch, 1999, 2006). In both cases the approach principally focuses on a phenomenon known as the Hebb effect.

In addition to his major contribution to theory, the great Canadian psychologist Donald Hebb invented an ingenious experimental technique that has continued to generate productive theoretical challenges. The method is simple: participants are presented with a sequence of digits, just beyond their span, for immediate serial recall. What they do not know, however, is that every third sequence will be identical; will performance on this regularly repeated item gradually improve, suggesting a persisting long-term memory component, or will it function as just another short-term sequence? As Figure 6.7 shows, performance on the repeated sequence gradually improves. Perhaps people just spot the repetition and give it enhanced attention? This seems not to be the case, as people who become aware do no better than those who do not notice. Furthermore, the Hebb effect occurs even with very long gaps in between repetitions, making detection unlikely.

The Hebb effect has not featured prominently in memory theory until recently revived by groups interested in modeling serial order in verbal STM, mainly within a broadly phonological loop framework. As you may recall from Chapter 4, Baddeley, Gathercole and Papagno (1998) suggested that the loop may have evolved to facilitate the acquisition of vocabulary. This

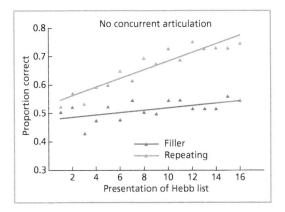

Figure 6.7 The Hebb effect: Mean recall of sequences of eight letters across successive trials. Sequences that were repeated every three trials show a gradual improvement, unlike nonrepeated sequences. From Page et al. (2006). Copyright © American Psychological Association. Reproduced with permission.

of course involves the long-term learning of the sequential *order* of the sounds comprising a new word. We proposed that this could be helped by holding the sequence in the phonological loop, hence providing more time for long-term learning, to occur. Understanding this process presented an important challenge that was taken up by groups who had already developed models of serial order in verbal STM. The scope of such models would increase substantially if they could be shown to be relevant to language learning, an issue of considerable evolutionary significance.

The Hebb effect appeared to offer a way into this problem, with steady progress made both in understanding the Hebb effect and in applying theories of serial order developed initially for the phonological loop. At an empirical level, Hitch, Flude and Burgess (2009) showed that, unlike the verbal STM task on which it was based, the Hebb effect was *not* sensitive to either phonological similarity or articulatory suppression, reinforcing the case for separable long- and short-term components in the serial STM task. Hitch et al. also showed that participants can learn several Hebb sequences at the same time, an important feature if the results are to generalize to vocabulary learning in normal language acquisition. Direct evidence has

now begun to accumulate for a positive link between Hebb performance and vocabulary learning. Mosse and Jarrold (2008) showed that Hebb performance correlates positively with a long-term verbal task involving learning pairs of nonwords. In a study involving nonwords, Szmalek, Page and Duyck (2012) incorporated occasionally repeated sequences in a Hebb paradigm. The repeated nonwords subsequently behaved like words. Both results suggest that Hebb-based nonwords were registering in the long-term language system.

What do we know about neural basis of the Hebb effect? Using multi-voxel pattern analysis (see Chapter 2, p. 32), Kalm, Davis and Norris (2013) compared the pattern of brain activation found across trials in the Hebb effect to the pattern of activation found on nonrepeated sequences. They showed that Hebb-based learning was associated with areas previously known to be related to long-term learning, namely the hippocampus, the temporal lobes and the insula, reinforcing the evidence for a separate long-term learning process.

At a theoretical level, two groups have been particularly active. Hitch, Flude, and Burgess (2013) have attempted to generalize their context-based model to results from the Hebb effect, while Page and Norris (2009) have applied their primacy model to Hebb results. The two groups combined in an important recent study, specifically targeted at a series of questions concerning the plausibility of a link between STM and word learning (Page, Cumming, Norris, McNeil, & Hitch, 2013). They propose that repeated presentation leads to implicitly acquired chunks, each comprising a subsequence, with each chunk being based on the primacy process. In principle, this seems plausible for the acquisition of new words, although the detailed modeling becomes quite complex. But what about our Shakespearian actors? So long as the stimulus word or phrase was unique within that speech, it can presumably act as a cue to the relevant chunk; or can it? I suspect all would agree that it is too soon to rule out chaining in long-term serial recall.

Seriation as a strategy

We have so far focused on situations in which serial order is essential to correct recall. There are, however, situations in which recall of material is not inherently serial, but where performance can be improved by imposing a serial strategy. Earhard (1967), studying the free recall of unrelated words, found, as expected, that those participants who were better at combining words into meaningful chunks recalled more. When required to recall in a fixed order, however, despite the additional demand, the poor chunkers actually improved their performance. Why should an extra demand help? An analogy between retrieval and searching may be appropriate here. Suppose you get back from a walk and find you have lost your wallet. One strategy would be to guess where it might have happened; did you pull something else out of your pocket for example? A more certain strategy, however, would be to retrace the whole walk so as to make sure you look at all the possible locations. Serial recall thus can be a way of making sure you recall everything; free recall is easier but tends to result in missing a few of the items, those you have learned but don't retrieve.

A practical example of the use of serial search occurs in the case of a pilot checking the various instruments in his cockpit before beginning a flight. This then requires the pilot to learn the sequence, typically within the cockpit or a simulator. Given the number of checks, this can result in failing to check everything. Hence, rather than leave this process to the individual, it is generally the case that a fixed order of checks is imposed, so as to ensure everything is covered on every occasion. In order to deal with this, a psychologist working with the Royal Air Force proposed what he called the *cardboard cockpit*. This involved pieces of folded cardboard representing the relevant dials and controls and accurately simulating their location on the plane. This meant that pilots could take the cardboard cockpit home and master this sequence on their own, rather than using up precious simulator time. Was this ingenious and inexpensive invention welcomed? Not by training staff who hated it, deriding it as the KKF (Kellogs Kutout Fighter). Its lack of expensive bells and whistles went directly against the "toys for the boys" approach to equipment that I suspect is not uncommon in the military, or indeed perhaps with "boys" in general!

I wanted to acknowledge my inventive friend but could not remember his name

so without much expectation of success I typed "cardboard cockpit" into Google. To my astonishment large numbers of entries cropped up, some offering to sell me a cardboard cockpit, others simply selling cardboard, while most came from enthusiastic amateur pilots keen on passing their test! So what had happened? At 5.45 am the next morning, the name *John Rolfe* popped into my bleary mind; it seemed that my personal google had been working on the night shift! The final step was to look up John Rolfe on Google. I discovered lots of entries, principally because John Rolfe was the name of the Virginian settler who had married the famous native American princess, Pocahontas. But none were associated with cardboard cockpits, so I still don't know whether my night-shift search got it right.*

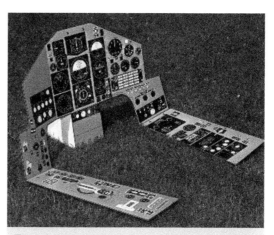

The cardboard cockpit: An inexpensive training device that helps pilots with the important task of learning the sequence of pre-flight instrument checks. It was initially disdained by top brass, but was welcomed by pilots and is now used very widely.

---

*Fortunately I finally tracked John down and learned the full story. The Commander-in-Chief wanted to fly the new fighter himself, and having little time to train, accepted a cardboard cockpit, used it, was very enthusiastic, flew the plane and ordered it to be used in the training program where it proved very popular (Rolfe: personal communication, November 2013).

EPISODIC MEMORY AND THE BRAIN

As mentioned in Chapter 5, a great deal of research has been carried out on the role of the brain in learning, using animals to study the processes involved at both the cellular and the brain systems level. Whereas most of this probably also applies to much human learning, it is less clear as to whether it applies to episodic memory, the capacity to recollect specific events. Indeed, if one uses Tulving's strict definition in terms of the capacity to "re-experience" the past, this assumes a level of conscious awareness that seems unlikely to occur in many of the organisms such as the giant sea snail *Aplysia*, on which much of the work on the neural basis of learning has been developed. However, as Box 6.1 shows, if one uses a more behavioral definition of episodic memory, in terms of the capacity to demonstrate memory for the *what*, *where*, and *when* of an event, then this can certainly be shown in certain types of bird, for example the scrub jay, which collects and hides food for later use, and potentially in a wider range of species.

In the case of episodic memory, however, we are on firmer ground in using evidence from neuropsychological patients. In Chapter 1, I

Box 6.1   Is episodic memory uniquely human?

It all depends. Using Tulving's definition, in terms of the experience of mental time travel it would be very difficult to establish that an animal had this particular experience. Defined behaviorally, however, as the capacity to combine memory for *what*, *where*, and *when*, there is evidence for this ability in scrub jays, birds that hide food (*what*) and subsequently remember *where* it was hidden. An ingenious experiment by Clayton and Dickinson (1999) indicates that the birds also remember the *time* at which the food was hidden. Clayton and Dickinson allowed their birds to hide two types of food—mealworms, which were most preferred but that deteriorate over time, and less attractive but more durable peanuts. Depending on the delay between hiding and the opportunity to retrieve the food, birds prefer mealworms after a short delay, but peanuts when the delay is longer.

In this photo, a female Western scrub jay, Sweetie Pie, is caching meal worms, as part of an experiment showing a capacity to remember *what*, *where*, and *when*; which can be interpreted as a demonstration of episodic memory in birds.

mentioned the classic case of HM who became densely amnesic following surgery to the temporal lobes and hippocampus on both the left and right side (Milner, 1966). There is no doubt that the hippocampus plays an important role in both learning and memory, but the nature of this role and the involvement of other related brain systems remain controversial.

Doubts began to arise in studies of the effects of hippocampal damage in animals. The hippocampus lies deep within the animal's brain, making it difficult to lesion without damaging surrounding areas. However, as surgical techniques have improved this has become possible, leading to the claim that something akin to recognition memory is possible even when the hippocampus is severely damaged, provided that certain areas feeding into the hippocampus, known as the *rhinal* and *perirhinal cortex* are intact. This evidence was reviewed by Aggleton and Brown (1999), who also surveyed the human neuropsychological literature. They identified a number of cases in which otherwise dense amnesia appeared to be accompanied by well-preserved recognition memory. They suggested that although the hippocampus is important, other surrounding areas are equally important, particularly in the case of recognition, a view that is by no means universally accepted (Manns & Squire, 1999; Squire, 2004).

Further support for the Aggleton and Brown position came from the discovery of a new type of amnesic patient by Farenah Vargha-Khadem and colleagues. Vargha-Khadem, Gadian, Watkins, Connelly, Van Paesschen, and Mishkin (1997) report the case of three young people who became amnesic at an early age and who show a highly atypical pattern of amnesia. The clearest of these cases is a young man, Jon, who suffered from anoxia at the time of birth, which resulted in a severe memory problem as he entered childhood. He is now in his 30s and on standard memory tests is clearly amnesic, sufficiently so as to make it challenging, although not impossible, to live independently. Neuroimaging studies indicate that Jon has damage that appears to be limited to the hippocampus, which is abnormal in structure and only half the size that would be expected. Despite this, Jon has developed above-average intelligence and has an excellent semantic memory. This seems to clash with the widely held

assumption that semantic memory depends on episodic memory, which in turn relies on the hippocampus. Jon will be discussed in more detail in Chapter 16 on Amnesia.

Episodic memory and the healthy brain

Brewer, Zhao, Desmond, Glover, and Gabrieli (1998), used event-related fMRI (see Chapter 2, p. 31) to study episodic memory. This involves separate scans for each designated event, allowing the experimenter to study the encoding of each individual item presented. It is then possible to separate out those items that were subsequently remembered from those forgotten, and go back to study the brain activation associated with successful learning. Brewer et al. presented a total of 48 photographs of scenes, which participants were required to categorize as indoor or outdoor. This was subsequently followed by an unexpected memory test in which the previously presented "old" scenes were mixed with new ones and participants required to categorize each as to whether they thought it was old or new. If judged old, the participants were asked whether they could "remember" the experience of observing that scene, a clear example of episodic memory, or if they just felt that they "knew" that they had seen it. Of the studied pictures, 25% were "remembered," 27% were judged as familiar, and 48% forgotten. A number of brain areas were then identified for which activation was higher when that particular picture had been "remembered." As Figure 6.8 illustrates, one of these was in the right frontal lobe and two were in the left and right hippocampal areas. Neither scenes subsequently judged to be familiar but not remembered, nor those forgotten, proved to have activated these brain areas during the encoding phase, suggesting a specific link between the frontal lobes, the hippocampus and the registration of an in episodic memory.

A broadly similar approach was applied to memory for words rather than scenes by Wagner et al. (1998), again using event-related fMRI. A sequence of words was presented, with participants required to make a semantic judgment on each—deciding whether the word was concrete or abstract. The pattern of brain activation evoked by these word presentations was recorded

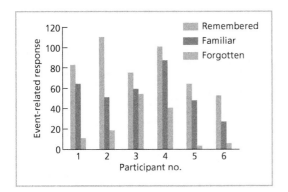

Figure 6.8 Activation in the area of the hippocampus as a function of whether an item was subsequently remembered, judged familiar, or forgotten. High activation is associated with good recall. Data from Brewer et al. (1998).

separately for later analysis. Following this process, participants were presented with a mix of new and old words and were required to respond to each, saying whether they had seen it before or not, together with their level of confidence.

As expected, many areas of the brain were linked with the complex task of seeing and processing words. However, three areas were correlated with a successful remembering of a word with high confidence. These were in the left frontal region and in the areas surrounding the left and right hippocampus, just as in the study by Brewer et al., except that whereas their study, based on visual scenes involved *right* frontal activation the verbal stimuli used by Wagner et al. was linked to *left* frontal activity, reflecting the well-established association between the left hemisphere and language.

We have discussed areas of activation associated with memory, but presumably these must result in actual physical changes that persist over time. There is indeed evidence at a microscopic level for the growth of new connections within the brain (Gao, van Beugen, & DeZeeuw, 2012). Evidence at a more macro level is provided by an ingenious study of London taxi drivers. Before becoming a licensed London cabbie, it is necessary to acquire "the knowledge," which involves detailed mastery of all the London streets and major buildings, with the capacity to go from one to the other by the shortest route. This takes several years to acquire, and presumably is further developed over time spent as a cabbie.

Maguire, Vargha-Khadem, and Mishkin (2001) used structural MRI to map out the physical characteristics of the brain of very experienced taxi drivers. They found that the posterior region of the hippocampus was larger than in novice drivers, whereas other areas of the hippocampus were smaller, suggesting that the years of expert navigation had led to a physical modification of their brain. In a related study, Maguire et al. (2001) used PET to monitor the brain activity of the cabbies while they were performing a task simulating driving through London. When required to use their geographical knowledge, the right hippocampus was activated; this was not the case when they were simply following a sequence of arrows.

Hartley, Maguire, Spiers, and Burgess (2003) compared the activation associated with following a novel path from a map with that of

Maguire et al.'s (2006) study found that London taxi drivers had greater gray matter volume in the mid-posterior area of the hippocampi, and less in the anterior, as compared to bus drivers.

Box 6.2 Mental time travel

Welcome time travelers! You may be pleased to know that you all have your personal time machine, courtesy of episodic memory, with a little help from working memory and of course semantic memory to make sense of what you see. David Ingvar (1985), a Swedish neuroscientist who was a pioneer of neuroimaging, pointed out that an important function of LTM was to use past experience to predict the future; we remember what has happened before and use this to imagine what is going to happen next, and plan accordingly.

Endel Tulving (1985) labeled this process *mental time travel*, emphasizing the importance of episodic memory for this activity. Appropriately, given its originator, neuroimaging has featured prominently in exploring this idea (see Schacter, Addis, & Buckner, 2007 for a review).

In one study Schacter et al. asked their participants to recall a series of specific episodes, one might be *meeting Anna in Harvard Square*, another, *losing your keys at the cinema*. Testing took place under fMRI, and was followed by the request to combine two of these episodes into a future scenario, imagining, for example, losing your keys in Harvard Square. They found the same areas of the hippocampus activated in both the initial recollection and in the subsequent creation of a future scenario, a process which also involved frontal lobe activity, suggesting the need for executive processing, presumably involving working memory, to achieve this recombination. Further evidence for the importance of the hippocampus comes from the observation that amnesic patients have great difficulty in carrying out the future thinking task (Hassabis, Kumaran, Vann, & Maguire, 2007), although not all amnesic patients appear to show this deficit (Squire, van der Horst, McDuff, Frascino, Hopkins, & Mauldin, 2010). This is currently a very active area of research where there is considerable evidence for an involvement of episodic memory and the hippocampus, although given the complexity of the task other memory systems and areas of the brain are almost certainly also involved (Berryhill, Phuong, Picasso, Cabeza, & Olson, 2007; Hassabis & Maguire, 2007).

simply completing a well-worn route, finding that the hippocampus was strongly involved in working out the novel route whereas other areas were active when the route was familiar. One could argue, of course, that London taxi drivers are an atypical group in a number of ways. Theirs is a potentially stressful occupation involving heavy traffic, cramped conditions, and air pollution. To control for this, Maguire, Woollett, and Spiers (2006) studied a group of London bus drivers with similar amounts of London driving experience but always based on specific routes, comparing them with taxi drivers. As predicted, they found that taxi drivers had greater gray matter volume in the mid-posterior area of the hippocampi, and less in the anterior, than the bus drivers. Furthermore, the longer the experience of taxi driving, the greater the difference.

On cognitive testing, the taxi drivers were better at recognizing which of a series of landmarks was from London and which was not, and at judging the distance as the crow flies between selected London landmarks. Both groups were then tested on a task involving new learning. This required first copying a complex figure and then, after a delay, reproducing it from memory. On this new learning task, the cabbies were significantly worse than the bus drivers. It appears, therefore, that the extensive experience of the taxi drivers had built up a very complex and effective spatial representation of London, but that this had come at the expense of a reduction in the capacity for new visuo-spatial learning.

SUMMARY

- Episodic memory refers to our capacity to recollect specific experiences, and to use this for "mental time travel."
- It depends on the capacity to encode and then retrieve specific events, something that is greatly helped if material is meaningful and well organized.
- Bartlett, who was influential in breaking away from the Ebbinghaus rote learning tradition, studied memory for complex material such as folk tales from other cultures.
- He emphasized effort after meaning, and the role of schemas, mental structures that help us organize our world knowledge.
- Research on the role of meaning carried out within the traditional verbal learning tradition concentrated on associations between words.
- Paivio stressed the importance for the "imageability" of words, proposing the dual-coding hypothesis.
- Craik and Lockhart proposed the Levels of Processing hypothesis, whereby deeper processing leads to better memory.
- The need to specify the nature of both encoding and retrieval led to the concept of transfer-appropriate processing.
- Effective methods of organizing material include hierarchies, matrices, and the linking of concepts into coherent stories.
- Intention to learn is not essential, but is helpful if it leads to persistence and to the use of good learning strategies.
- The hippocampus plays an important role in episodic memory, although the relative roles of the hippocampus and surrounding anatomical regions are not fully understood.
- The frontal lobes are important during encoding. The role of the left and right frontal lobes in learning and retrieval depends in part on whether the material learned is verbal or visuo-spatial.
- Evidence is beginning to accumulate for physical changes occurring in the adult brain as a result of learning. This is illustrated by the case of London taxi drivers, whose many years of acquiring spatial knowledge has resulted in a change in their hippocampal structure.

What are the relative strengths and weaknesses of the Ebbinghaus and Bartlett approaches to the study of memory?

To what extent does the impact of organization on memory reflect the concept of levels of processing?

What role do difference parts of the brain play in episodic memory?

FURTHER READING

Hartley, J. (1998). *Learning and studying*. London: Routledge. A discussion of the implications of what we know about learning for the way in which we should study.

Hill, W. F. (2002) *Learning* (7th edn.). Boston, MA: Allyn & Bacon. A text providing a broad overview of the psychology of learning.

Kandel, E. R. (2006). *In search of memory: The emergence of a new science of mind*. New York: Norton. A scientific autobiography from the Nobel Prize laureate. It covers the neurobiological basis of memory in a very clear and accessible way.

Schacter, D. L. (1994). Priming and multiple memory systems: Perceptual mechanisms of implicit memory. In D. L. Schacter & E. Tulving (Eds.), *Memory systems 1994* (pp. 233–268). Cambridge, MA: MIT Press. Schacter makes the case for regarding a range of perceptual priming phenomena as components of a coherent system.

Squire, L. R. (1993). The organization of declarative and non-declarative memory. In T. Ono, L. R. Squire, M. E. Raichle, D. I. Perrett, & M. Fukuda (Eds.), *Brain mechanisms of perception and memory: From neuron to behaviour* (pp. 219–227). New York: Oxford University Press. An account of Squire's views on the structure of long-term memory.

REFERENCES

Aggleton, J. P., & Brown, M. W. (1999). Episodic memory, amnesia, and the hippocampal–anterior thalamic axis. *Behavioral and Brain Sciences, 22,* 425–489.

Baddeley, A. D. (1964). Language habits, S-R compatibility and verbal learning. *American Journal of Psychology, 77,* 463–468.

Baddeley, A. D., Gathercole, S., & Papagno, C. (1998). The phonological loop as a language learning device. *Psychological Review, 105,* 158–173.

Bartlett, F. C. (1932). *Remembering*. Cambridge: Cambridge University Press.

Berryhill, M. E., Phuong, L., Picasso, L., Cabeza, R., & Olson, I. R. (2007). Parietal lobe and episodic memory: Bilateral damage causes impaired free recall of autobiographical memory. *Journal of Neuroscience, 27,* 14415–14423.

Bower, G. H., Clark, M. C., Lesgold, A. M., & Winzenz, D. (1969). Hierarchical retrieval schemes in recall of categorised word lists. *Journal of Verbal Learning and Verbal Behavior, 8,* 323–343.

Bower, G. H., Karlin, M. B., & Dueck, A. (1975). Comprehension and memory for pictures. *Memory and Cognition, 3,* 216–220.

Brewer, J. B., Zhao, Z., Desmond, J. E., Glover, G. H., & Gabrieli, J. D. E. (1998). Making memories: Brain activity that predicts how well visual experience will be remembered. *Science*, *281*, 1185–1187.

Broadbent, D. E., Cooper, P. J., & Broadbent, M. H. (1978). A comparison of hierarchical retrieval schemes in recall. *Journal of Experimental Psychology: Human Learning and Memory*, 4, 486–497.

Burgess, N., & Hitch, G. J. (1999). Memory for serial order: A network model of the phonological loop and its timing. *Psychological Review*, *106*, 551–581.

Burgess, N., & Hitch, G. J. (2006). A revised model of short-term memory and long-term learning of verbal sequences. *Journal of Memory and Language*, *55*, 627–652.

Campoy, G., & Baddeley, A. D. (2008). Phonological and semantic strategies in immediate serial recall. *Memory*, *16*, 329–340.

Carmichael, L., Hogan, H. P., & Walter, A. A. (1932). An experimental study of the effect of language on the reproduction of visually perceived form. *Journal of Experimental Psychology*, *15*, 73–86.

Chase, W. G., & Ericsson, K. A. (1982). Skill in working memory. In G. H. Bower (Ed.), *The psychology of learning and motivation* (Vol. 16). New York: Academic Press.

Clayton, N. S., & Dickinson, A. (1999). Scrub jays remember when as well as where and what food items they cached. *Journal of Comparative Psychology*, *113*, 403–416.

Conway, M. A., Cohen, G., & Stanhope, N. M. (1992). Very long-term memory for knowledge acquired at school and university. *Applied Cognitive Psychology*, *6*, 467–482.

Craik, F. I. M., & Lockhart, R. S. (1972). Levels of processing. A framework for memory research. *Journal of Verbal Learning and Verbal Behavior*, *11*, 671–684.

Craik, F. I. M., & Tulving, E. (1975). Depth of processing and the retention of words in episodic memory. *Journal of Experimental Psychology: General*, *104*(3), 268–294.

Deese, J. (1959). Influence of inter-item associative strength upon immediate free recall. *Psychological Reports*, *5*, 305–312.

Earhard, M. (1967). Subjective organization and list organization as determinants of free-recall and serial-recall memorization. *Journal of Verbal Learning and Verbal Behavior*, *6*, 501–507.

Ericsson, K. A., & Delaney, P. F. (1999). Long-term working memory as an alternative to capacity models of working memory in everyday skilled performance. In A. Miyake & P. Shah (Eds.), *Models of working memory: Mechanisms of active maintenance and executive control* (pp. 257–297). Cambridge: Cambridge University Press.

Ericsson, K. A., & Kintsch, W. (1995). Long-term working memory. *Psychological Review*, *102*(2), 211–245.

Fisher, R. P., & Craik, F. I. M. (1977). Interaction between encoding and retrieval operations in cued recall. *Journal of Experimental Psychology: Learning, Memory and Cognition*, *3*, 701–711.

Gao, Z., van Beugen, B. J., & DeZeeuw, C. I. (2012). Distributed synergistic plasticity and cerebellar learning. *Nature Reviews Neuroscience*, *13*, 619–635.

Gauld, A., & Stephenson, G. M. (1967). Some experiments relating to Bartlett's Theory of Remembering. *British Journal of Psychology*, *58*, 39–49.

Glaze, J. A. (1928). The association value of nonsense syllables. *Journal of Genetic Psychology*, *35*, 255–269.

Glenberg, A. M., Smith, S. M., & Green, C. (1977). Type I rehearsal: Maintenance and more. *Journal of Verbal Learning and Verbal Behavior*, *16*, 339–352.

Gomulicki, B. R. (1956). Recall as an abstractive process. *Acta Psychologica*, *12*, 77–94.

Hartley, T., Maguire, E. A., Spiers, H. J., & Burgess, N. (2003). The well-worn route and the path less travelled: Distinct neural basis of route following and wayfinding in humans. *Neuron*, *37*, 877–888.

Hassabis, D., & Maguire, E. A. (2007). Deconstructing episodic memory with construction. *Trends in Cognitive Sciences*, *11*, 299–306.

Hassabis, D., Kumaran, D., Vann, S. D., & Maguire, E. A. (2007). Patients with hippocampal amnesia cannot imagine new experiences. *Proceedings of National Academy of Sciences of the USA*, *104*, 1726–1731.

Hatano, G., & Osawa, K. (1983a). Digit memory of grand experts in abacus-derived mental calculation. *Cognition*, *15*, 95–110.

Hatano, G., & Osawa, K. (1983b). Japanese abacus experts' memory for numbers is disrupted by mechanism of action. *Journal of Clinical Psychology*, *58*(1), 61–75.

Hitch, G. J., Flude, B., & Burgess, N. (2009). Slave to the rhythm: Experimental tests of a model for verbal short-term memory and long term sequence learning. *Journal of Memory and Language*, *61*, 97–111.

Hyde, T. S., & Jenkins, J. J. (1973). Recall for words as a function of semantic, graphic, and syntactic orienting tasks. *Journal of Verbal Learning and Verbal Behavior*, *12*, 471–480.

Ingvar, D. H. (1985). Memory of the future: An essay on the temporal organization of conscious awareness. *Human Neurobiology, 4,* 127–136.

James, W. (1890). *The principles of psychology.* New York: Holt, Rinehard and Winston.

Jenkins, J. J., & Russell, W. A. (1952). Associative clustering as a function of verbal association strength. *Psychological Reports, 4,* 127–136.

Jung, J. (1968). *Verbal learning.* New York: Holt, Rinehart and Winston.

Kalm, K., Davis, M. H., & Norris, D. (2013)). Individual sequence representations in the medial temporal lobe. *Journal of Cognitive Neuroscience, 25,* 1111–1121.

Maguire, E. A., Vargha-Khadem, F., & Mishkin, M. (2001). The effects of bilateral hippocampal damage on fMRI regional activations and interactions during memory retrieval. *Brain, 124,* 1156–1170.

Maguire, E. A., Woollett, K., & Spiers, H. J. (2006). London taxi drivers and bus drivers: A structural MRI and neuropsychological analysis. *Hippocampus, 16,* 1091–1101.

Mandler, G. (1967). Organization and memory. In K. W. Spence & J. T. Spence (Eds.), *The psychology of learning and motivation: Advances in research and theory.* (Vol. 1, pp. 328–372). New York: Academic Press.

Manns, J. R., & Squire, L. R. (1999). Impaired recognition memory on the Doors and People Test after damage limited to the hippocampal region. *Hippocampus, 9,* 495–499.

Mechanic, A. (1964). The responses involved in the rote learning of verbal materials. *Journal of Verbal Learning and Verbal Behavior, 3,* 30–36.

Milner, B. (1966). Amnesia following operation on the temporal lobes. In C. W. M. Whitty & O. L. Zangwill (Eds.), *Amnesia* (pp. 109–133). London: Butterworths.

Morris, C. D., Bransford, J. D., & Franks, J. J. (1977). Levels of processing versus transfer appropriate processing. *Journal of Verbal Learning and Verbal Behavior, 16,* 519–533.

Mosse, E. K., & Jarrold, C. (2008). Hebb learning, verbal short-term memory, and the acquisition of phonological forms in children. *Quarterly Journal of Experimental Psychology, 61,* 505–514.

Neisser, U. (1988). Time present and time past. In M. M. Gruneberg, P. E. Morris & R. N. Sykes (Eds.), *Practical aspects of memory: Current research and issues* (Vol. 2, pp. 545–560). Chichester, UK: Wiley.

Oliver, W. L., & Ericsson, K. A. (1986). Repertory actors' memory for their parts. *Proceedings of the Eighth Annual Conference of the Cognitive Science Society, Amherst, MA* (pp. 399–406). Hillsdale, NJ: Lawrence Erlbaum.

Page, M. P. A., & Norris, D. (1998). The primacy model: A new model of immediate serial recall. *Psychological Review, 105,* 761–781.

Page, M. P. A., & Norris, E. (2009). A model linking immediate serial recall, the Hebb repetition effect and the learning of phonological word forms. *Philosophical Transactions of the Royal Society: B Biological Science, 364,* 3737–3753.

Page, M. P. A., Cumming, N., Norris, D., McNeil, A. M., & Hitch, G. J. (2013). Repetition-spacing and item-overlap effects in the Hebb repetition task. *Journal of Memory and Language, 69,* 506–526.

Paivio, A. (1969). Mental imagery in associative learning and memory. *Psychological Review, 76,* 241–263.

Paivio, A. (1971). *Imagery and verbal processes.* London: Holt Rinehart and Winston.

Prentice, W. C. H. (1954). Visual recognition of verbally labelled figures. *American Journal of Psychology, 67,* 315–320.

Rubenstein, H., & Aborn, M. (1958). Learning, prediction, and readability. *Journal of Applied Psychology, 42,* 28–32.

Rubin, D. C. (1995). *Memory in oral traditions: The cognitive psychology of epic, ballads, and counting-out rhymes.* New York: Oxford University Press.

Schacter, D. L. (2001). *The seven sins of memory: How the mind forgets and remembers.* New York: Houghton-Mifflin.

Schacter, D. L., Addis, D. R., & Buckner, R. L. (2007). Remembering the past to imagine the future: The prospective brain. *Nature Reviews Neuroscience, 8,* 657–651.

Squire, L. R. (2004). Memory systems of the brain: A brief history and current perspective. *Neurobiology of learning and memory, 82,* 171–177.

Squire, L. R., van der Horst, A. S., McDuff, S. T. R., Frascino, J. C., Hopkins, R. O., & Mauldin, K. N. (2010). The role of the hippocampus in remembering the past and imagining the future. *Proceedings of National Academy of Sciences of the USA, 107,* 19044–19048.

Sulin, R. S., & Dooling, D. J. (1974). Intrusion of a thematic idea in retention of prose. *Journal of Experimental Psychology, 103,* 255–262.

Szmalec, A., Page, M. P. A., & Duyck, W. (2012). The development of long-term lexical representations through Hebb repetition learning. *Journal of Memory and Language, 67,* 342–354.

Tulving, E. (1962). Subjective organisation in free recall of "unrelated" words. *Psychological Review, 69,* 344–354.

Tulving, E. (1985). Memory and consciousness. *Canadian Psychology, 26,* 1–12.

Tulving, E. (2002). Episodic memory: From mind to brain. *Annual Review of Psychology*, *53*, 1–25. doi: org/10.1146/annurev.psych.53.100901.135114

Tulving, E., & Pearlstone, Z. (1966). Availability versus accessibility of information in memory for words. *Journal of Verbal Learning and Verbal Behavior*, *5*, 381–391.

Underwood, B. J., & Schulz, R. W. (1960). *Meaningfulness and verbal learning*. Chicago, IL: Lippincott Company.

Vargha-Khadem, F., Gadian, D. G., Watkins, K. E., Connelly, A., Van Paesschen, W., & Mishkin, M. (1997). Differential effects of early hippocampal pathology on episodic and semantic memory. *Science*, *277*, 376–380.

Wagner, A. D., Schacter, D. L., Rotte, M., Koutstaal, W., Maril, A., Dale, A. M., & et al. (1998). Building memories: Remembering and forgetting of verbal experiences as predicted by brain activity. *Science*, *281*, 1188–1191.

Contents

Introduction   165

Semantic memory vs. episodic memory   166

Organization of concepts: Traditional views   168

Using concepts   176

Concepts and the brain   179

Schemas   182

Summary   188

Points for discussion   189

Further reading   190

References   190

CHAPTER 7

SEMANTIC MEMORY AND STORED KNOWLEDGE

Michael W. Eysenck

INTRODUCTION

What is the capital of France? How many months are there in a year? Who is the current President of the United States? Do rats have wings? What is the chemical formula for water? Is *umplitude* an English word? What does a seismologist do? Is New York south of Washington, DC? What is the typical sequence of events when having a meal in a restaurant?

I am sure you found all the above questions relatively easy to answer and that you answered them rapidly. It would not be hard to fill the whole of this book with such questions—all of us possess an enormous store of general knowledge that we take for granted. The division of memory that stores all this information is generally referred to as *semantic memory*. Binder and Desai (2011, p. 527) provided a more complete definition of semantic memory: "It is an individual's store of knowledge about the world. The content of semantic memory is abstracted from actual experience and is therefore said to be conceptual, that is, generalized and without reference to any specific experience."

If you stopped the first woman you saw and tested her vocabulary, you would probably discover she knew the meaning of anywhere between 20,000 and 100,000 words. She might also know a foreign language. She would certainly know a great deal (in geographical terms) about her own neighborhood and about the wider world. She functions well in her environment because she has learned to drive a car, use a cell or mobile phone, use credit cards, and so on.

She also has a great deal of specialist knowledge acquired in connection with work, hobbies, and pastimes. In addition, she has the usual interesting but nonvital mental baggage (much of it media-related) that most of us carry around in our heads—facts and images to do with politics and sport, movies and music, TV programs and advertising.

There is much overlap in the knowledge each of us has stored in semantic memory (e.g. basic vocabulary; general knowledge of the world). However, it is also obvious there are large individual differences in the contents of semantic memory. As you would expect, we generally have more information in semantic memory than most people in those areas of special interest and importance to us (e.g. work-related knowledge). This is certainly true of expert chess players. Chassy and Gobet (2011) analyzed over 70,000 games played by chess players of varying skill levels. They estimated chess masters have memorized 100,000 opening moves! There was a very strong relationship between chess-playing skill and knowledge of opening moves—average players had memorized far few opening moves than masters.

How important is semantic memory? The devastating effects of lacking semantic memory were vividly described by the Colombian novelist Gabriel Garcia Márques in his novel *One Hundred Years of Solitude*. In this novel, the inhabitants of Macondo are struck by the insomnia plague. This gradually causes them to lose information about the meanings and functions of the objects around them, thereby producing a state of despair.

Here is how the central character (José Arcadio Buerdia) responds to this desperate situation:

The sign that he hung on the neck of the cow was an exemplary proof of the way in which the inhabitants of Macondo were prepared to fight against loss of memory: This is the cow. She must be milked every morning so that she will produce milk, and the milk must be boiled in order to be mixed with coffee to make coffee and milk.

SEMANTIC MEMORY VS. EPISODIC MEMORY

I have discussed briefly some key features of semantic memory. It is important to distinguish between semantic memory (general knowledge about the world) and episodic memory (memory for events occurring at a specific time in a specific place; see Chapter 6). However, there are important similarities between them. Suppose you remember meeting your friend yesterday afternoon at a coffee shop. That clearly involves episodic memory because you are remembering an event at a given time in a given place. However, semantic memory is also involved—some of what you remember involves your general knowledge about coffee shops, what coffee tastes like, and so on.

There are important differences between the subjective experiences associated with episodic and semantic memory. Retrieval of information from episodic memory is typically (but not always) accompanied by a sense of consciously recollecting the past. There is no such sense of conscious recollection when we retrieve general knowledge from semantic memory. In other words, episodic memory involves "self-knowing" whereas semantic memory involves "knowing awareness" (Wheeler, Stuss, & Tulving, 1997).

Other differences between semantic and episodic memory were identified by Tulving (2002, p. 5): "Episodic memory … shares many features with semantic memory, out of which it grew … but also possesses features that semantic memory does not … Episodic memory is a recently evolved, late-developing, and early-deteriorating past-oriented system, more vulnerable than other memory systems to neuronal dysfunction."

Findings: Separate systems

We will start our coverage of research on semantic and episodic memory by considering research suggesting these two forms of long-term memory operate relatively independently of each other. According to Tulving's (2002) views (discussed above) the adverse effects of brain damage on memory should generally be less for semantic memory than episodic memory. That is typically the case with amnesic patients who have suffered brain damage to the hippocampus and related brain areas (see Chapter 16 for detailed coverage of amnesia). Spiers, Maguire, and Burgess (2001) reviewed 147 cases of amnesia. Episodic memory was impaired in all cases, whereas many of the patients had only modest problems with semantic memory. This evidence suggests (but certainly does not prove) the two types of memory are distinctly different from each other.

There is some additional support for the notion of separate episodic and semantic memory systems if we focus on amnesics' memory for information and events acquired *prior* to the onset of amnesia. Forgetting of such information and events is known as retrograde amnesia. The extent of retrograde amnesia for episodic memories in amnesic patients often spans several years (Bayley, Hopkins, & Squire, 2006). In contrast, retrograde amnesia for semantic memories is generally reasonably intact except for knowledge that was acquired shortly before the onset of amnesia (Manns, Hopkins, & Squire, 2003).

So far we have discussed patients whose episodic memory is much more impaired than their semantic memory. Other brain-damaged patients exhibit the opposite pattern of severe problems with semantic memory but relatively intact episodic memory. These patients suffer from semantic dementia, the symptoms of which are remarkably similar to those of the fictional character José Arcadio Buerdia (described earlier; Rascovsky, Growdon, Pardo,

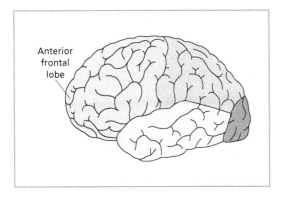

Figure 7.1 Semantic dementia is associated with damage to the anterior frontal temporal lobes.

Grossman, & Miller, 2009). Semantic dementia involves a severe loss of concept knowledge from semantic memory even though their episodic memory and most cognitive functions are reasonably intact at least in the early stages of the condition. Semantic dementia is associated with damage to the anterior frontal temporal lobes (see Figure 7.1), whereas with amnesia patients it is typically the medial temporal lobe that is most damaged.

Patients with semantic dementia find it very hard to access information about most concepts stored in semantic memory (see Mayberry, Sage, & Lambon Ralph, 2011, for a review). In spite of that, their performance is often reasonably good on some tasks involving episodic memory. For example, consider a study by Adlam, Patterson, and Hodges (2009). Patients with semantic dementia were asked to remember what tasks they had performed 24 hours earlier, where those tasks were performed, and when during the sessions they occurred. The patients as a group performed at a comparable level to healthy controls.

Findings: Interdependent systems

Episodic memory and semantic memory often combine in an interdependent fashion in their

functioning (see Greenberg & Verfaellie, 2010, for a review). Relevant evidence comes from cognitive neuroscience. Burianova, McIntosh, and Grady (2010) compared patterns of brain activation during episodic, semantic, and autobiographical memory retrieval. Their key finding was that the *same* neural network including various frontal, temporal, and parietal areas was activated during the retrieval of all these types of memory.

Kan, Alexander, and Verfaellie (2009) obtained evidence that a task apparently involving only episodic memory also involved semantic memory. Amnesic patients and healthy controls were instructed to learn the prices of grocery items. The prices of some items corresponded to participants' prior knowledge (congruent items), whereas others were incongruent.

Healthy controls and amnesic patients with fairly intact semantic memory had better memory performance for congruent grocery prices than incongruent ones. In contrast, amnesic patients with poor semantic memory were unable to use their semantic memory effectively on the memory tasks and so showed no congruency effect.

Finally, we consider patients with semantic dementia having severe problems with semantic memory but apparently relatively intact episodic memory. Irish, Hornberger, Lah, Miller, Pengas, Nestor, et al. (2011) found that there was a nonsignificant difference between such patients and healthy controls in

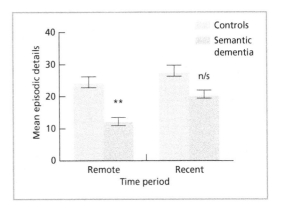

Figure 7.2 Mean recall of autobiographical details from remote and recent time periods by healthy controls and patients with semantic dementia. From Irish and Piguet (2013). Copyright © Muireann Irish and Olivier Piguet, reproduced with permission.

their recall of *recent* autobiographical memories (see Figure 7.2). However, the semantic dementia patients performed considerably worse than the healthy control patients when recalling *remote* autobiographical memories.

What do the above findings mean? According to Irish and Piguet (2013), sensory and perceptual information can be used to recall recent autobiographical memories but not remote ones. Recall of remote memories requires semantic knowledge to provide a framework or scaffolding facilitating the retrieval of episodic information.

Conclusions

The distinction between semantic memory and episodic memory is important. In general terms, retrieval of information from episodic memory is more likely than retrieval from semantic memory to involve conscious recollection. Some of the strongest evidence for the distinction comes from the study of brain-damaged patients. Amnesic patients typically have more severe problems with long-term episodic memory than do patients with semantic dementia, whereas the opposite is the case so far as long-term semantic memory is concerned.

In spite of these differences, note that many long-term memories consist of a mixture of episodic and semantic memory. Of relevance, a rather similar brain network is associated with both forms of long-term memory.

ORGANIZATION OF CONCEPTS: TRADITIONAL VIEWS

What information is stored in semantic memory? Much of it consists of concepts of various kinds, and we will consider how these concepts are stored. Before you read this section, test yourself on the questions in Box 7.1.

Elizabeth Loftus and her colleagues carried out various experiments exploring the task of coming up with particular words, given a category and a first letter as cues. For example,

---

Box 7.1 Organization of concepts

Answer the following questions, noting how long it takes you to answer each one:

Set A

1 Fruit starting with p.
2 Animal starting with d.
3 Metal starting with i.
4 Bird starting with b.
5 Country starting with F.
6 Boy's name starting with H.
7 Girl's name starting with M.
8 Flower starting with s.

Total time taken =

Set B

1. Fruit ending with h.
2. Animal ending with w.
3. Metal ending with r.
4. Bird ending with n.
5. Country ending with y.
6. Boy's name ending with d.
7. Girl's name ending with n.
8. Flower ending with t.

Total time taken =

I imagine you took much less time to complete Set A than Set B. What does this mean? Of course, it means the initial letter is a much more effective cue than the last letter when you are trying to retrieve at the level of basic-level categories. This in turn tells us something about how the names of such categories are stored, as there is no logical reason why the above should be the case. For example, it would be entirely possible to devise a computer program in which words could be retrieved equally rapidly regardless of whether the first, last, second, fourth, or any other letter were provided as a cue.

Loftus and Suppes (1972) found that giving the category first and initial letter afterwards (e.g. *fruit–p*) led to faster responses than giving the initial letter before the category (e.g. *p–fruit*). This suggests it is easier to activate the category *fruit* in preparation for searching for the appropriate initial letter than all words starting with, say, *p*. This is probably because the category *fruit* is reasonably coherent and manageable, whereas words starting with *p* form too large and diffuse a category to be useful.

Evidence supporting the above viewpoint comes from a study in which the category was *type of psychologist* and the initial letter that of the psychologist's surname. Hence a typical question might be, "Give me a developmental psychologist whose name begins with P" (Piaget) versus "Initial letter P–a developmental psychologist." Students just starting to specialize in psychology showed no difference between the two orders of presentation, whereas those who had already specialized were faster when the category was provided first. Presumably they had already developed categories such as "developmental psychologist," whereas the novices simply searched all "psychologists," not having sufficiently developed their categories to operate otherwise.

Hierarchical network model

The first systematic model of semantic memory was put forward by Collins and Quillian (1969). Their key assumption was that semantic memory is organized into a series of hierarchical networks. Part of one such network is shown in Figure 7.3. The major concepts (e.g. *animal*, *bird*, *canary*) are represented as nodes, and properties or features (e.g. *has wings*, *is yellow*) are associated with each concept. You may wonder why the property *can fly* is stored with the *bird* concept rather than with *canary* concept: after all, one characteristic of canaries is that they can fly. According to Collins and Quillian, it would waste space in semantic memory to have information about being able to fly stored with every bird name. If those properties possessed by nearly all birds (e.g. *can fly*, *has wings*) are stored only at the bird node or concept, this satisfies the notion of cognitive economy. The underlying principle is that property information is stored as high up the hierarchy as possible to minimize the amount of information needing to be stored in semantic memory.

Collins and Quillian (1969) tested their model using a task on which participants decided as rapidly as possible whether sentences were true or false. In order to get a feeling for their task, answer the questions in Box 7.2. These are not the specific sentences used by Collins and Quillian. They were devised by Alan Baddeley and Neil Thomson to look at the effects of various stressors on accessing semantic memory. You may not be too surprised to learn that alcohol slowed down the rate at which such sentences can be verified.

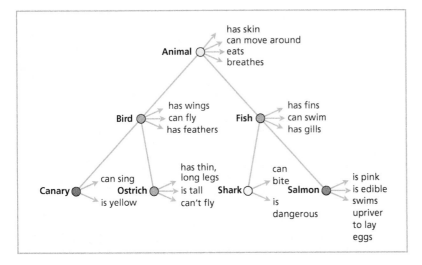

Figure 7.3 Collins and Quillian's (1969) hierarchical network.

Box 7.2 Testing Collins and Quillian's (1969) model

Decide as rapidly as possible whether each sentences is true ("Yes") or false ("No")

	Yes	No

Pork chops can be bought in shops
Jamaica is edible
Oranges drill teeth
California is a state of America
London is a place
Potatoes move around searching for food
Drills are scientists
Aunts are relatives
Spaghetti is a dish
Corporals can be bought in shops
Beer is a liquid
Gin is sold by butchers
Fish and chips are an alcoholic drink
Peas are edible
Antarctica tends the sick
Beefsteaks are people
Chairs are furniture
Priests wear clothes
Flies carry disease
Mayors are elected representatives
Asia has high mountains
Paris is a living creature
Rattlesnakes move around searching for food
Bees treat the mentally ill
Knives are manufactured goods
Trout have fins
Squirrels are fish
Lions are four-legged animals
Sharks have wheels

According to Collins and Quillian's (1969) model, it should be possible to decide very rapidly that the sentence, "A canary is yellow," is true because the concept (i.e. *canary*) and the property (i.e. *is yellow*) are stored together at the same level of the hierarchy. In contrast, the sentence, "A canary can fly," should take longer because the concept and property are separated by one level in the hierarchy. The sentence, "A canary has skin," should take even longer because there are two levels separating the concept and property. As predicted, the time taken to respond to true sentences became progressively slower with increasing separation between the subject of the sentence and the property.

The model is on the right lines in its claim that we often use semantic memory

KEY TERM

Typicality effect: The finding that the time taken to decide a category member belongs to a category is less for typical than atypical members.

successfully by *inferring* the right answer. For example, information that Leonardo da Vinci had knees is not stored directly in our semantic memory. However, we know that Leonardo da Vinci was a human being, and human beings have knees, and so we confidently infer Leonardo da Vinci had knees. This is exactly the kind of inferential process proposed by Collins and Quillian (1969).

Limitations with the model

In spite of its successes, the model suffers from various problems. For example, a sentence such as, "A canary is yellow," differs from, "A canary has skin," not only in the hierarchical distance between the concept and its property, but also in familiarity. Indeed, it is a fair bet you have never encountered the sentence, "A canary has skin," in your life before! Conrad (1972) decided to see whether hierarchical distance or familiarity was more important in determining how long it took to decide whether sentences were true or false. What she found was bad news for Collins and Quillian's model—when familiarity was controlled, hierarchical distance between the subject and the property had little effect on verification time.

There is another limitation with Collins and Quillian's approach. Consider the following statements: "A canary is a bird" and "A penguin is a bird." On their theory, both statements should take the same length of time to verify, because they both involve moving one level in the hierarchy. In fact, however, it takes longer to decide a penguin is a bird than that a canary is a bird. Why is that the case? The members of most categories vary considerably in terms of how typical or representative they are of the category to which they belong. For example, Rosch and Mervis (1975) found that, *oranges*, *apples*, *bananas*, and *peaches* were rated as much more typical fruits than were *olives*, *tomatoes*, *coconuts*, and *dates*. Rips, Shoben, and Smith (1973) found that verification times were faster for more typical or representative members of a category than for relatively atypical members. For obvious reasons, this is known as the typicality effect.

More typical members of a category possess more of the characteristics associated with that category than less typical ones. Rosch (1973) showed this in a study in which she produced a series of sentences containing the word *bird*. Sample sentences were as follows: "Birds eat worms"; "I hear a bird singing"; "I watched a bird fly over the house"; and "The bird was perching on the twig." Now try replacing the word *bird* in each sentence in turn with *robin*, *eagle*, *ostrich*, and *penguin*. *Robin* fits all the sentences, but *eagle*, *ostrich*, and *penguin* fit progressively less well. Thus, penguins and ostriches are less typical birds than eagles, which in turn are less typical than robins.

What does this tell us about the structure of semantic memory? Collins and Quillian (1969) were mistaken in assuming the concepts we use belong to rigidly defined categories. In

The typicality effect determines that it will take longer to decide that a penguin is a bird than that a canary is a bird. A penguin is an example of a relatively atypical member of the category to which it belongs, whereas the canary – being the more representative member – can be verified more quickly.

fact, most categories are loosely determined. This point was made by the philosopher Ludwig Wittgenstein (1958) using the category *games*. What are the defining characteristics of a game? What, for example, do baseball, poker, tennis, and chess have in common? It is very hard (or even impossible!) to think of a single set of features shared by all games. Wittgenstein suggested members of the category *games* (and most other categories) are like members of a family having certain characteristics they tend to share. Some members of the family may share several characteristics, while others may share only one or two, and often not the same one or two.

Convincing evidence that many concepts in semantic memory are fuzzy rather than neat and tidy was reported by McCloskey and Glucksberg (1978). They gave 30 people tricky questions such as, "Is a stroke a disease?" and "Is a pumpkin a fruit?" They found 16 said a stroke is a disease, but 14 said it was not. A pumpkin was regarded as a fruit by 16 participants but not as a fruit by the remainder. When McCloskey and Glucksberg tested the same participants a month later, 11 of them had changed their minds about "stroke" being a disease, and 8 had altered their opinion about "pumpkin" being a fruit!

Verheyen and Storms (2013) identified two reasons why there are individual differences in deciding which items belong to a given category. First, there is *ambiguity*—individuals may use different criteria for categorization (e.g. is strenuous activity a necessary criterion for something to be regarded as a *sport*?). Second, there is *vagueness*—individuals may use different cut-offs to separate members from

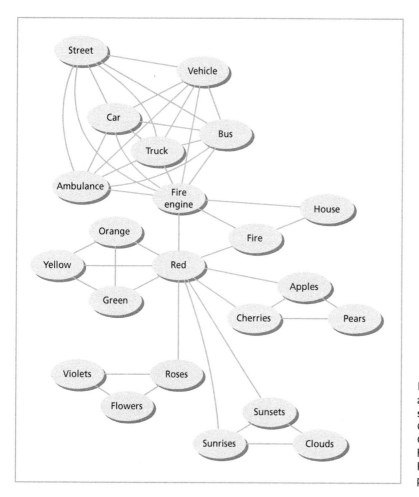

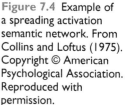

Figure 7.4 Example of a spreading activation semantic network. From Collins and Loftus (1975). Copyright © American Psychological Association. Reproduced with permission.

nonmembers. For example, two individuals may agree that being strenuous is a criterion for an activity being a sport but may disagree about *how* strenuous it must be.

Spreading activation model

Collins and Loftus (1975) put forward a spreading activation theory designed to resolve problems with Collins and Quillian's model. They argued that the notion of logically organized hierarchies was too inflexible. Instead, it is preferable to assume semantic memory is organized on the basis of semantic relatedness or semantic distance. Semantic relatedness can be measured by asking people to decide how closely related pairs of words are. Alternatively, people can list as many members as possible of a particular category. Those members produced most often are regarded as most closely related to the category.

You can see part of the organization of semantic memory assumed by Collins and Loftus (1975) in Figure 7.4. The length of the links between two concepts indicates the degree of semantic relatedness between them. Thus, for example, *red* is more closely related to *orange* than to *sunsets*.

According to spreading activation theory, whenever a person sees, hears, or thinks about a concept, the appropriate node in semantic memory is activated. This activation then spreads most strongly to other concepts that are closely related semantically, and more weakly to those more distant semantically. For example, activation would pass strongly and rapidly from *robin* to *bird* in the sentence, "A robin is a bird," because *robin* and *bird* are closely related semantically. However, it would pass more weakly and slowly from penguin to *bird* in the sentence, "A penguin is a bird." As a result, the model predicts the typicality effect.

Findings

Other predictions of the spreading activation model have been tested experimentally. For example, Meyer and Schvaneveldt (1976) instructed participants to decide rapidly whether a string of letters formed a word. In the key condition, a given target word (e.g. *butter*) was immediately preceded by a semantically related word (e.g. *bread*) or by an unrelated word (e.g. *nurse*). According to the model, activation should have spread from the first word to the second only when they were semantically related and this activation should have made it easier to identify the second word. Thus, *butter* should have been identified as a word faster when preceded by *bread* than by *nurse*. Indeed, there was a facilitation (or semantic priming) effect for semantically related words.

McNamara (1992) used the same basic approach as Meyer and Schvaneveldt (1976). Suppose the first word was *red*. This was sometimes followed by a word one link away (e.g. *roses*), and sometimes by a word two links away (e.g. *flowers*). More activation should spread from the activated word to those one link away than to those two links away, and so the facilitation effect should have been greater in the former case. That is precisely what McNamara (1992) found.

In more recent research, Sanchez-Casas, Ferre, Garcia-Albea, and Guasch (2006) obtained greater semantic priming when the prime and target words were very closely related semantically than when they were somewhat less related. This is as predicted by the theory.

More support for the model comes from an interesting study by Schacter, Reiman, Curran, Yun, Bandy, McDermott, et al. (1996). They used the Deese–Roediger–McDermott paradigm (e.g. Roediger & McDermott, 1995; discussed in Chapter 14). Participants were presented with word lists constructed in a particular way. An initial word (e.g. *doctor*) was selected, and then several words closely associated with it (e.g. *nurse, sick, hospital, patient*) were selected. All these words (with the crucial exception of the initial word) were presented for learning, followed by a test of recognition memory.

What happened when the word not presented on the list (e.g. *doctor*) was presented on the recognition test? According to the model, the missing word should be highly activated because it is so closely related to all the list words. Schacter et al. compared brain activation on the recognition test when participants falsely recognized the missing word and when they correctly recognized words from the list.

The pattern and intensity of brain activation were very similar in both cases, indicating there was substantial activation of the missing word as predicted by the model.

Evaluation

The notion that activation spreads among semantically related concepts has been extremely influential. For example, spreading activation is of central importance in Dell's (1986) theory of speech production. According to this theory, when we plan an utterance, this leads to activation of several of the sounds in the intended sentence before we start to speak. Speech errors occur whenever an incorrect word is more activated than the correct one.

The spreading activation model has generally proved more successful than the hierarchical network model at accounting for the various findings. An important reason is that it is much more flexible. However, flexibility carries with it some disadvantages. It means the model typically does not make very precise predictions, which makes it somewhat difficult to assess its overall adequacy.

Some other limitations with the model will become apparent later in the chapter. Here I will mention two. First, the notion that each concept in semantic memory is represented by a *single* node is oversimplified. As we will see, much of the information about most concepts is distributed in different brain regions rather than all being represented in a node.

Second, the model implies that each concept has a single, fixed representation. In fact, our processing of any given concept is flexible. Consider the following two sentences:

1   Fred greatly enjoyed playing the piano.
2   Fred found it difficult to lift the piano.

I imagine your processing of the word *piano* in the second sentence focused on the heaviness of pianos but this was not the case in the first sentence. Such findings cannot be explained by the spreading activation model.

Naming objects

Suppose you are shown a photograph of a chair and asked to identify the object. On the basis of the relevant information you have stored in semantic memory, you might provide various answers. For example, you might describe it as an *item of furniture*, as a *chair*, or as an *easy chair*. In fact, however, most people would describe the object as a chair rather than an item of furniture or an easy chair.

The above example suggests concepts are organized into hierarchies. Rosch, Mervis, Gray, Johnson, and Boyes-Braem (1976) argued there are three levels within such hierarchies. There are superordinate categories (e.g. *item of furniture*) at the top, basic-level categories (e.g. *chair*) at the intermediate level, and subordinate categories (e.g. *easy chair*) at the bottom.

We do sometimes use superordinate categories (e.g. "That furniture is expensive") or subordinate categories (e.g. "I love my new iPhone"). However, there is generally a strong preference for using basic-level categories. Rosch et al. (1976) asked participants to name pictured objects. Basic-level categories were used 1595 times during the course of the experiment, subordinate names 14 times, and superordinate names only once.

Why do we make such extensive use of basic-level categories? The basic level typically provides the best balance between informativeness and distinctiveness. Informativeness is lacking at the superordinate level (e.g. simply knowing an object is an item of furniture tells you little. Distinctiveness is lacking at the lowest level (e.g. most types of chairs possess very similar attributes or features).

There are other ways basic-level categories have special properties not shared by categories at other levels. First, it is the most general level at which people use similar motor movements for interacting with category members. For example, nearly all chairs can be sat on in approximately the same way, differing markedly from how we interact with tables. Second, the basic level is the one usually acquired first by young children. Bourdais and Pecheux (2009) found categorization was easiest at the basic level for 13- and 16-month infants and hardest at the superordinate level.

Findings

In spite of what has been said so far, some individuals do *not* prefer basic-level categories.

Consider a professional botanist describing the plants in a garden. We would expect him/her to distinguish among the different plants (i.e. use subordinate categories) rather than calling them all plants! This expectation is reasonable given that subordinate categories are much more informative for experts than for nonexperts.

The prediction contained in the previous paragraph was confirmed by Tanaka and Taylor (1991) in a study of birdwatchers and dog experts naming birds and dogs. Both groups used subordinate names in their expert domain much more often than their novice domain. More specifically, bird experts used subordinate names 74% of the time with birds, dog experts used subordinate names 40% of the time with dogs, and both groups used subordinate names only 24% of the time in their novice domain.

Cultural factors are also important. Some research (Coley, Medin, & Atran, 1997; Medin & Atran, 2004) has compared categorization in members of the Itza culture in Guatemala and American undergraduate students. The Itza were more likely than the Americans to categorize plants, animals, and birds at the subordinate level. This probably reflects their closer contact with the natural environment.

Nearly everyone typically uses subordinate categories rather than basic-level ones for one type of object—faces! When you spot a friend's face in a crowd, it is improbable you would say, "Look at that face!" Anaki and Benton (2009) presented participants with a category label at the superordinate, basic, or subordinate level followed by the face of a familiar face (a celebrity). Participants decided whether the face matched the label. Matching occurred faster at the subordinate level than at the basic level.

The findings discussed so far may suggest expertise is necessary for categorization at the subordinate level to occur fastest. Anaki and Bentin (2009) argued that is *not* the case on the basis of a second experiment. Participants were presented with photographs of familiar towers (e.g. Eiffel tower; learning tower of Pisa) preceded by labels at different hierarchical levels. Matching occurred faster at the subordinate than the basic level. Thus, for example, most participants found it easier to decide the Eiffel tower was the Eiffel tower than that it was a tower. Thus, individual familiarity with objects at the subordinate level can produce very fast categorization.

The typical finding that people *prefer* to categorize at the basic level does not necessarily mean they categorize *faster* at that level than any other. Rogers and Patterson (2007) varied how long participants had available to make categorization judgments. Performance accuracy was greater for superordinate categorization than basic-level categorization when fast responding was required.

Macé, Joubert, Nespoulous, and Fabre-Thorpe (2009) obtained similar findings in a study involving categorization of photographs of scenes. Participants were 40–65 milliseconds faster to decide whether a scene contained an animal (superordinate level) than whether it contained a given species of animal (basic level) (see Figure 7.5).

Why is categorization often faster at the superordinate level than the basic level? Close and Pothos (2012) argued that categorization at the basic level is generally more informative than at the superordinate level and so requires more information processing. Rogers and Patterson (2007) obtained support for this viewpoint studying patients with semantic dementia (a condition involving loss of concept knowledge; discussed earlier in the chapter). Patients

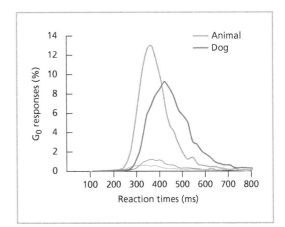

Figure 7.5 Reaction time distributions on correct trials (thick lines) in Macé et al.'s (2009) experiment—participants were faster to decide whether a scene contained an 'animal' than whether it contained a 'dog'. From Macé et al. (2009). doi:10.1371/journal.pone.0005927.g002

with mild semantic dementia had comparably accurate categorization at the basic and superordinate levels. Of more theoretical importance, patients with severe semantic dementia performed better at the superordinate than the basic level because it required less information processing.

Conclusions

Categorization at all three levels within concept hierarchies is of value. Categorization at the superordinate level is often the fastest because it requires less cognitive processing than categorization at the other two levels. Categorization at the basic level is often preferred because it combines informativeness and distinctiveness. Finally, categorization at the subordinate level is often preferred to categorization at the basic level by those possessing relevant expertise. This happens because categorization at the subordinate level is much more informative for experts than for nonexperts.

USING CONCEPTS

As we have seen, numerous concepts are represented in semantic memory. *What* do these representations look like? There has been much theoretical controversy on this issue (Kiefer & Pulvermüller, 2012; Meteyard, Cuadrado, Bahrami, & Vigliocco, 2012). It is often assumed concept representations have the following characteristics:

1   They are *abstract* in nature and are thus detached from input (sensory) and output (motor) processes.
2   They are *stable* in that any given individual uses the same representation of a concept on different occasions.
3   Different people generally have fairly similar representations of any given concept.

In sum, it is assumed within many theories of semantic memory that concept representations, "have the flavor of detached encyclopedia descriptions in a database of categorical knowledge about the world" (Barsalou, 2012, p. 247).

Situated simulation theory

Barsalou (2009, 2012) argued in his situated simulation theory that *all* the above theoretical assumptions are incorrect. In everyday life, we rarely process concepts in *isolation*. Instead, we process them in various different settings, and that processing is influenced by the current context or setting. More generally, the representations of any given concept vary across situations depending on the individual's current goals and the major features of the situation.

Barsalou (2009) illustrated the limitations with many previous theories by considering the concept of a *bicycle*. Traditionally, it was assumed a fairly complete abstract representation of the concept would be activated in all

Figure 7.6 According to Barsalou (2009), those aspects of the bicycle concept activated depend on the individual's current goals.

In Wu and Barsalou's (2009) study participants that were given the word 'watermelon' focused on external properties, whereas when given the words 'half watermelon' they focused more on internal properties such as *pips* and *red*.

situations. This representation would resemble the Chambers Dictionary definition: "vehicle with two wheels one directly in front of the other, driven by pedals."

According to Barsalou (2009), those aspects of the bicycle concept activated depend on the individual's current *goals* (Figure 7.6). For example, information about the tires is especially likely to be activated if you need to repair your bicycle, whereas the height of the saddle is important if you want to ride it.

A final prediction follows from Barsalou's situated simulation theory. The workings of the conceptual system make extensive use of the perceptual system and the motor or action system.

Findings

Evidence that conceptual processing can involve the perceptual system was reported by Wu and Barsalou (2009). Participants wrote down as many properties as possible for nouns or noun phrases. Those given the word *lawn* tended to focus on *external* properties (e.g. *plant, blades*) whereas those given *rolled-up lawn* focused more on *internal* properties (e.g. *dirt, soil*). The same pattern was found with other nouns. For example, *watermelon* generated external properties such as *rind* and *green* whereas *half watermelon* generated internal properties such as *pips* and *red*.

What do the above findings mean? Concept processing can have a perceptual or

imaginal quality about it. Object qualities not visible if you were actually looking at the object itself are harder to think of than those that would be visible.

According to situated simulation theory, concept processing is influenced by the context or setting. Wu and Barsalou (2009) obtained support for that assumption. Participants in their study often wrote down properties referring to the background situation rather than the object itself. Indeed, between 25% and 50% of the total properties produced related to the background situation (e.g. properties of *lawn* can include *picnic* or *you play on it*).

Chaigneau, Barsalou, and Zamani (2009) obtained evidence that situational information is important in object categorization. Observers were shown novel objects in isolation or with situational information. Accurate object categorization was much better when full situational information was provided. These findings support Barsalou's contention that stored conceptual representations of objects include situational information.

There are many objects in the environment to which we generally respond with a particular kind of movement. For example, we poke a doorbell, we hold pliers with an open grasp, and we hold a mug with a closed grasp. When we process such concepts, do we access our knowledge of the relevant movement?

Bub, Masson, and Cree (2008) addressed the above issue. Participants learned to make specific movements to various color cues (e.g. red = poke; blue = open grasp). After that, words referring to objects were presented in these colors. Participants made the *learned* movements to the color.

There were two kinds of trial. On congruent trials, the same movement was relevant to the specified object and the color. For example, when the stimulus was *doorbell* in red, word and color both suggested the poke movement. There were also incongruent trials in which a different movement was relevant to the specified object and the color. For example, when the stimulus was *pliers* in red, the word suggested an open grasp whereas the color suggested a poke movement.

What did Bub et al. (2008) find? Participants took longer to make the appropriate movement to the color on incongruent trials

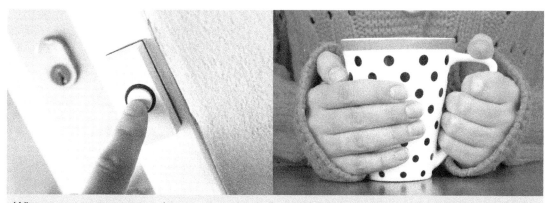

When we process concepts such as pressing a doorbell or holding a mug do we access our knowledge of the relevant movement?

than congruent ones. Thus, words referring to concepts led participants to access relevant movement or gestural knowledge even when it impaired performance.

Connell, Lynott, and Dreyer (2012) found evidence supportive of Barsalou's theory using a more complex task than those used in the studies discussed so far. Participants were presented with pairs of object names and decided which object was larger or which was smaller. Both objects were relatively small (e.g. *coin–Frisbee, almond–pear*) or relatively large (e.g. *car–van, camel–cow*). While performing the object-comparison task, the participants sometimes received tactile stimulation to their hands provided by vibrating cushions.

Connell et al. (2012) argued that a crucial difference between small and large objects is that only the former are easily manipulable by the hands. As a result, tactile information is relevant *only* to small-object concepts. Providing tactile stimulation to the hands should draw attention to this tactile information and thus speed up performance on the object-comparison task with small objects but should have no effect with large objects. That is precisely what Connell et al. found.

So far we have focused on concept processing referring to concrete objects we can see or hear. It is unsurprising that such concepts should have perceptual properties. However, it is less clear that perceptual properties are relevant to the processing of abstract concepts such as *truth, freedom,* and *invention*. However, Barsalou and Wiemer-Hastings (2005)

reported evidence suggesting that is the case. Participants indicated the characteristic properties of various abstract concepts. Many of these properties referred to settings or events associated with the concept (e.g. scientists working in a laboratory for *invention*).

Some abstract concepts (e.g. *peace, hostility*) have a concrete aspect because they have emotional associations. It has been claimed that emotionally positive stimuli automatically elicit *approach* tendencies whereas emotionally negative ones elicit *avoidance* tendencies. There is accumulating evidence that individuals respond faster to positive abstract stimuli with an approach movement but to negative ones with an avoidance movement (Pecher, Boot, & Van Dantzig, 2011).

Evaluation

How we use conceptual knowledge in everyday life often involves the perceptual and motor systems. This helps to explain why concept processing varies across situations depending on the individual's goals. In other words, the precise way we process a concept depends on the situation and the perceptual and motor processes engaged by the current task.

What are the main limitations of Barsalou's theoretical approach? First, he exaggerates the extent to which concept processing *varies* across situations. The traditional view that concepts possess a stable, abstract core has not been disproved by Barsalou (Mazzone & Lalumera, 2010). In reality, both theoretical approaches are partially correct—concepts have a stable core *and* their structures are context-dependent (this is discussed in more detail shortly).

Second, there are several possible interpretations of the finding that concept processing typically involves perceptual and/or motor features. As Barsalou argues, perceptual and motor processes may be of central relevance to understanding the meaning of concepts. Alternatively, these processes may occur only *after* concept meaning has been accessed. The evidence tends to favor the former interpretation but it is mostly somewhat inconclusive (Meteyard et al., 2012).

CONCEPTS AND THE BRAIN

Most research discussed so far has involved behavioral experiments. However, since concepts are stored in the brain, it is of value to identify the brain areas associated with concept processing. Most of the discussion in this section will focus on the influential hub-and-spoke model which describes the complex ways concepts are represented in the brain.

Concepts within the brain

The most obvious assumption is that everything we know about any given object or concept is stored in *one* location in the brain. For example, I know several facts about my cat Lulu—she has gray fur, a small head, is very friendly, chases birds, has a hearty appetite, likes to play, purrs loudly, and so on. It seems reasonable to assume all this information is stored very close together within the brain (perhaps in a 'Lulu node').

In fact, semantic memories are actually stored in more complex ways. As we will see, different kinds of information about a given object are stored in different brain locations. Thus, for example, *visual* information about Lulu may be stored in a different place from *auditory* information (e.g. her loud purr) and from information about what she does (e.g. likes to play). This is a feature-based approach and is consistent with Barsalou's emphasis on the role of perceptual and motor features in concept use.

Much research in this area involves brain-damaged patients. What is the rationale for studying such patients to understand semantic memory in healthy individuals? The major assumption is that the pattern of impairment shown by brain-damaged patients can provide useful information concerning how concept knowledge is organized within the brain.

Suppose a particular patient was very good at identifying pictures of nonliving things (e.g. *table, cake*) but very poor at identifying pictures of living things (e.g. *horse,*

Different kinds of information about a given object are stored in different brain locations. For example, *visual* information about Lulu the cat may be stored in a different place from *auditory* information (e.g. her loud purr) and from information about what she does (e.g. likes to play).

penguin). It would be tempting to conclude that everything we know about living things is stored in one part of the brain and everything we know about nonliving things is stored in a different part. In other words, the patient's pattern of impairment occurs because he/she has suffered brain damage to the brain region in which knowledge about living things is stored. Alas, as we will see, reality is more complex than the above simple example might lead you to expect!

Hub-and-spoke model

We saw earlier that concept processing often involves the perceptual and motor systems. For various reasons, however, it is very unlikely that nothing else is involved in concept processing and use. First, it is hard to see how we could have *coherent* concepts if our processing of any given concept varied considerably across situations. Second, we can detect similarities across concepts differing greatly in perceptual terms. For example, we know *scallops* and *prawns* belong to the same category (i.e. *shellfish*) even though they have different shapes, colors, shell structures, forms of movement, names, and so on (Patterson, Nestor, & Rogers, 2007).

Patterson et al. (2007) proposed a hub-and-spoke model (developed by Pobric, Jefferies, & Lambon Ralph, 2010) that combines and integrates the ideas discussed so far. Key features of the model are shown in Figure 7.7. The spokes in the model consist of several modality-specific brain areas in which sensory

and motor processing occur. The six spokes shown in the figure relate to visual features, verbal descriptors, olfaction (smell), sounds, praxis (motor information), and somatosensory information (sensations from the skin and internal organs).

In addition, each concept has a 'hub'—a modality-independent unified conceptual representation that provides an efficient way of integrating our knowledge of any given concept. It is assumed hubs are located within the anterior temporal lobes. The most convincing evidence for this assumption comes from patients with semantic dementia (discussed earlier in the chapter). These patients have brain damage in the anterior temporal lobes and exhibit a severe loss of information contained within the hubs.

Findings

As we have seen, research on patients with semantic dementia strongly implies that the anterior lateral lobes of the brain are of vital importance with respect to the hubs of the hub-and-spoke model. This is supported by neuroimaging research. Binder, Desai, Graves, and Conant (2009) carried out a meta-analysis of 120 neuroimaging studies in which participants performed tasks involving semantic memory. Among the brain areas consistently activated were the anterior lateral lobes and related regions damaged in semantic dementia. The activated areas were far away from those associated with perceptual and motor processing, suggesting that the activated areas are those involved in 'core' or hub semantic processing.

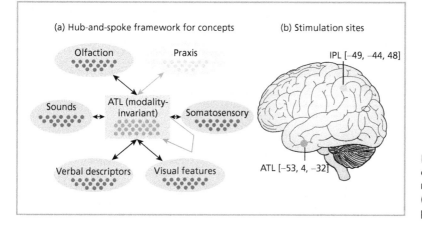

Figure 7.7 Key features of the hub-and-spoke model. From Pobric et al. (2010). Reproduced with permission.

Mayberry et al. (2011) gave patients with semantic dementia the task of deciding whether objects were or were not members of a given category. They argued that semantic dementia involves a progressive loss of core or 'hub' concept information. In other words, semantic dementia causes a *blurring* of the boundary separating members of a category (e.g. birds) from nonmembers. This led them to predict that patients with semantic dementia would have particular problems in making accurate predictions with two kinds of stimuli: (1) atypical category members (e.g. *emu* is an atypical bird); and (2) noncategory members resembling category members (e.g. *butterfly* is like a bird). Both predictions were supported.

We turn now to the 'spokes' of the hub-and-spoke model. Many brain-damaged patients exhibit category-specific deficits, meaning they have problems with specific categories of objects. A very common type of category-specific deficit involves greater difficulty in identifying pictures of living than nonliving things. How can we interpret this finding? Living things have greater contour overlap than nonliving things, are more complex structurally, and are less similar visually (Marques, Raposo, & Almeida, 2013). Patients have problems with identifying living things mainly because of factors such as these, rather than simply because they are living things.

Cree and McRae (2003) identified *seven* different patterns of category-specific deficits following brain damage. Patients exhibiting each pattern differed in the concept features or properties most impaired. Across the seven categories, the most impaired properties included the following: color; taste; smell; visual motion; and function (i.e. object uses). These findings indicate that concepts vary considerably in terms of those properties of most importance.

Some of the most impressive support for the hub-and-spoke model was reported by Pobric et al. (2010). Participants named living things, manipulable objects, and nonmanipulable man-made things. Pobric et al. applied transcranial magnetic stimulation (TMS) to inhibit processing briefly within the anterior temporal lobe or the inferior parietal lobule (assumed to be involved in processing

information relating to actions we can make towards objects) (see Figure 7.7(b)). What was of interest was to assess the slowing down of object naming caused by TMS.

What would we expect to find according to the hub-and-spoke model? First, we consider transcranial magnetic stimulation (TMS) applied to the anterior temporal lobe, which is involved in core or hub semantic concept processing. TMS should increase naming times for all three categories of objects. Second, we consider TMS applied to the inferior parietal lobule. According to the model, this should increase naming times only for manipulable objects and not for nonmanipulable objects or living things. Impressively, the findings were exactly as predicted theoretically.

In sum, the hub-and-spoke model provides a more comprehensive account of semantic memory than previous theoretical approaches. There is considerable support for the notion that concepts are represented in semantic memory by a combination of abstract core (hub) and modality-specific information (spokes). There has been good progress in identifying the brain areas associated with hubs and the various types of spokes.

What are the model's main limitations? First, more remains to be discovered about the information contained within concept hubs. For example, is more information stored in the hubs of very familiar concepts than less familiar ones? Second, how is modality-specific 'spoke' information integrated with

KEY TERM

Meta-analysis: A form of statistical analysis based on combining the findings from numerous studies on a given research topic.

Category-specific deficits: Disorders caused by brain damage in which semantic memory is disrupted for certain semantic categories.

Transcranial magnetic stimulation (TMS): A technique in which magnetic pulses briefly disrupt the functioning of a given brain area; administration of several pulses in rapid succession is known as repetitive transcranial stimulation (rTMS).

modality-independent 'hub' information? Third, there is still no consensus concerning the number and nature of concept 'spokes'.

SCHEMAS

Our discussion so far in this chapter may have created the false impression that nearly all the information in semantic memory is in the form of simple concepts. In fact, much of the knowledge we have stored in semantic memory consists of larger structures of information.

What do these larger knowledge structures look like? An extremely influential early answer to that question was provided by Frederic Bartlett (1932). He argued strongly for the importance of what he called schemata (schemas in American English)—a *schema* is a well-integrated chunk of knowledge about the world, events, people, or actions. Bartlett's key insight was that what we remember is influenced very much by the schematic knowledge we already possess.

The schemas stored in semantic memory include scripts and frames. Scripts deal with knowledge about events and the consequences of event. In contrast, frames are knowledge structures referring to some aspect of the world (e.g. building) containing fixed structural information (e.g. has floors and walls) and slots for variable information (e.g. materials from which the building is constructed).

Bower, Black, and Turner (1979) considered the kinds of information typically found in scripts. For example, they asked people to list 20 actions or events usually occurring during the course of a restaurant meal. In spite of the participants' varied restaurant experiences, there was much agreement on the actions associated with the restaurant script. At least 73% of the participants mentioned

KEY TERM

Scripts: A type of schema relating to the typical sequences of events in various common situations (e.g. having a meal in a restaurant).

Frame: A type of schema in which information about objects and their properties is stored.

sitting down, looking at the menu, ordering, eating, paying the bill, and leaving. In addition, at least 48% included entering the restaurant, giving the reservation name, ordering drinks, discussing the menu, talking, eating a salad or soup, ordering dessert, eating dessert, and leaving a tip.

Schemas vs. concepts

We have assumed there is an important distinction between two major types of information in semantic memory: (1) abstract concepts generally corresponding to individual words; and (2) broader and more flexible organizational structures based on schemas and scripts. If that assumption is correct, we might expect some brain-damaged patients would have greater problems with accessing concept-based information than schema- or script-based information. There should also be others finding it harder to use schema or script information than information about specific concepts. As we will see, there is some support for both predictions.

Which brain-damaged patients have special problems with accessing concept-based information? Many such patients suffer from semantic dementia. This condition (discussed in detail earlier in the chapter) involves severe problems in accessing the meanings of words and objects but with good executive functioning in the early stages of deterioration. Funnell (1996) studied EP, a patient with semantic dementia. Her performance was extremely poor when tested on the meanings of common objects (e.g. *ballpoint pen, needle, scissors*). On one task, each object was presented along with two other objects, one of which was functionally associated with the target object's use (e.g. the *ballpoint pen* was presented together with a *pad of writing paper* and a *small printed book*). She performed at chance level when instructed to select the functionally associated object.

In contrast to her poor ability to remember concept information, EP retained reasonable access to script knowledge. When she was involved in arranging the next research appointment, she went to the kitchen and collected her calendar and a ballpoint pen. EP also used a needle correctly when given a button to sew on a shirt.

Bier, Bottari, Hudon, Jobert, Paquette, and Macoir (2013) studied the script memory of three patients with semantic dementia. They were asked what they would do if they had unknowingly invited two guests to lunch. The required script actions included dressing to go outdoors, going to the grocery store, shopping for food, preparing the meal, having the meal, and clearing up afterwards. One patient described all these script actions accurately in spite of having severe problems with accessing concept information from semantic memory. The other patients needed assistance but remembered script actions relating to dressing and shopping.

Which brain-damaged patients have greater problems with accessing script-related information than concept meanings? Scripts typically have a goal-directed quality (e.g. you use a script to achieve the goal of having an enjoyable restaurant meal). Executive functioning within the prefrontal cortex is of major importance in constructing and implementing goals. As expected, some patients with damage to the prefrontal cortex have particular problems with script memory. Sirigu, Zalla, Pillon, Grafman, Agid, and Dubois (1995) asked patients with prefrontal damage to generate and evaluate various types of scripts (routine events; nonroutine events; novel events). These patients produced as many events as patients with posterior lesions and healthy controls. In addition, they retrieved the relevant actions as rapidly as members of the other two groups.

The above findings suggest the prefrontal patients had as much stored information about actions as other patients and healthy controls. However, the prefrontal patients made many mistakes in *ordering* actions within a script and in deciding which actions were of most importance to the achievement of any given event. In other words, they had particular problems with script-based knowledge when they needed to *assemble* the actions within a script into the optimal sequence.

Cosentino, Chute, Libon, Moore, and Grossman (2006) studied patients with fronto-temporal dementia (involving damage to the prefrontal cortex as well as to the temporal lobes). These patients had attentional deficits and poor executive functioning, as well as impaired semantic memory.

The fronto-temporal patients (as well as those with semantic dementia and healthy controls) were presented with various scripts. Some scripts contained sequencing or script errors (e.g. dropping fish in a bucket *before* casting the fishing line). Other scripts contained semantic or meaning errors (e.g. placing a flower on a hook in a story about fishing).

What did Cosentino et al. (2006) find? Patients with semantic dementia and healthy controls both detected as many sequencing errors as semantic ones. In contrast, the temporo-frontal patients with poor executive functioning failed to detect almost twice as many sequencing errors as semantic ones. Thus, these patients had relatively intact semantic knowledge of concepts combined with fairly severe impairment of script-based knowledge relating to sequencing.

Farag, Troiani, Bonner, Powers, Avants, Gee, et al. (2010) considered script processing in patients with temporo-frontal dementia or semantic dementia (see Figure 7.8 for areas of brain damage). They argued scripts can be broken down into various clusters or subroutines. For example, the script for going

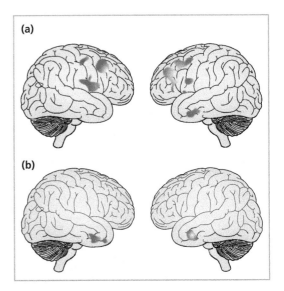

Figure 7.8 Areas of brain damage in the patients studied by Farag et al. (2010). (a) Brain areas damaged in patients with progressive nonfluent aphasia or behavioral variant fronto-temporal degeneration. (b) Brain areas damaged in patients with semantic dementia or mild Alzheimer's disease. From Farag et al. (2010). Reproduced with permission.

fishing contains a cluster relating to worms (open can of worms; place worm on hook) and one relating to use of the fishing line (cast fishing line; reel line back in). The patients (and healthy controls) judged the order of consecutive events from scripts.

What did Farag et al. (2010) find? The healthy controls and patients with semantic dementia had better performance on judging event order *within* clusters than *between* clusters. In contrast, patients with fronto-temporal dementia performed no better on within-cluster events than between-cluster ones. Thus, sensitivity to scripts' organization and structure was present in semantic dementia patients and healthy controls but not in fronto-temporal patients.

In sum, research on brain-damaged patients provides support for the distinction between knowledge of concepts and script knowledge. More specifically, some patients have a greater impairment of conceptual than schematic knowledge, whereas others show the opposite pattern. Areas within the prefrontal cortex are of great relevance on tasks requiring use of script organization. However, they are of much less relevance with respect to concept knowledge.

How useful is schematic knowledge?

We have seen that schematic knowledge in the form of scripts is useful because it allows us to form realistic *expectations*. Schemas (including scripts) make the world more predictable than would otherwise be the case because our expectations are generally confirmed. If our script-based expectations are disconfirmed, we usually take action. For example, if no menu is produced in a restaurant, we try to catch the eye of the waiter or waitress. Sometimes events not matching our schema-based expectations are well remembered because they are distinctive. For example, we generally have excellent memory for unexpected events such as a waiter spilling soup in a customer's lap (Bower et al., 1979) or a lecturer smoking a cigarette (Neuschatz, Lampinen, Preston, Hawkins, and Toglia, 2002).

There are other reasons why schematic knowledge is useful. First, schemas play an important role in reading and listening because they allow us to fill in the gaps in what we are reading or hearing and so enhance our understanding. More specifically, they provide the basis for us to draw *inferences* as we read or listen (see Box 7.3).

Box 7.3 When it is difficult to understand a text (Bransford & Johnson, 1972)

Bransford and Johnson (1972) argued that people would not understand a passage properly if it were written so it was hard to work out the underlying schema or theme. They used a passage, the first part of which is given below. Put yourself in the position of participants in their study, and see whether you can understand it.

The procedure is quite simple. First, you arrange items into different groups. Of course, one pile may be sufficient depending on how much there is to do. If you have to go somewhere else due to lack of facilities that is the next step; otherwise, you are pretty well set. It is important not to overdo things. That is, it is better to do too few things at once than too many. In the short run this may not seem important but complications can easily arise.
(Bransford & Johnson, 1972, p. 722)

Did you work out what the passage was all about? Participants reading the passage in the absence of a title rated it as incomprehensible and recalled an average of only 2.8 different ideas ("idea units") from it. In contrast, those supplied beforehand with the title "Washing clothes" found it easy to understand and recalled 5.8 idea units on average. Relevant schematic knowledge (i.e. the title providing the theme of the passage) had a beneficial effect on recall because it helped comprehension of the passage rather than because the title acted as a useful retrieval cue. We know this because participants receiving the title *after* hearing the passage but *before* recall recalled only 2.6 idea units on average.

Second, schemas help to prevent cognitive overload. For example, consider stereotypes, which are schemas involving simplified generalizations about various groups. When we meet someone for the first time, we often use stereotypical information (e.g. about their sex, age, and ethnicity) to assist us in forming an impression of that person. It is simpler and less demanding (but potentially very misleading) to use such information rather than engage in detailed cognitive processing of his/her behavior (Macrae & Bodenhausen, 2000).

Potential disadvantages of relying on stereotypical information were shown by Reynolds, Garnham, and Oakhill (2006). Read the following passage they used in their study and then answer the question:

A man and his son were away for a trip. They were driving along the highway when they had a terrible accident. The man was killed outright but his son was alive, although badly injured. The son was rushed to the hospital and was to have an emergency operation. On entering the operating theater, the surgeon looked at the boy, and said, "I can't do this operation. This is my son."

How can this be?

If you found the problem difficult, you are in good company. We tend to have a stereotypical view that surgeons are men. However, some surgeons are female and the surgeon in the passage above was the boy's mother. Thus, schemas in the form of stereotypical information can interfere with problem solving.

Third, schematic information can assist us when we perceive visual scenes. Palmer (1975) presented pictures of scenes (e.g. a kitchen) followed by a briefly presented object. Participants were better at identifying the object when it was appropriate to the scene (e.g. loaf) than when no scene was presented initially. Thus, activation of relevant schematic knowledge facilitated visual perception. Yardley, Perlovsky, and Bar (2012) review research showing how we use contextual information to infer what objects are present in a given scene and so reduce processing demands.

Errors and distortions

So far we have seen our schematic knowledge is generally (but not always) very useful. It makes the world a more predictable place, it enhances our understanding of what we read and other people say, and it can facilitate visual perception of the world around us. However, schematic knowledge can cause significant memory costs.

Bartlett (1932) was the first psychologist to focus systematically on the memory costs of schematic memory. He argued that our memory for stories is affected not only by the presented story itself but also by the participant's store of relevant schematic knowledge. He had the ingenious idea of presenting people with stories producing a *conflict* between what was presented to them and their prior knowledge. Suppose people read a story taken from a different culture. Their prior knowledge might produce distortions in the remembered version of the story, making it more conventional and acceptable from their own cultural background.

Bartlett (1932) carried out several studies in which English students read and recalled stories taken from the North American Indian culture. One such story was *The war of the ghosts* (reproduced on pp. 138–9). As he predicted, the participants' schematic knowledge in the form of cultural expectations led to numerous recall errors conforming to that knowledge. Bartlett used the term rationalization for this type of error.

According to Bartlett (1932), memory for the precise information presented is forgotten over time, whereas memory for the underlying schemas is not. Thus, there should be more rationalization errors (which depend on schematic knowledge) at longer retention intervals.

Findings

Bartlett (1932) reported consistent support for his theoretical ideas in his own research. However, that research was flawed. Of particular importance, the instructions to his participants were rather vague. As a result, many recall distortions he observed were due to deliberate guessing rather than being genuinely mistaken memories. Gauld and Stephenson (1967) found that explicit instructions emphasizing the requirement for accurate recall eliminated almost half the errors observed when they used Bartlett's vague instructions. Note, however, that many rationalization errors were made even with explicit instructions.

Brewer and Treyens (1981) argued that much research on Bartlett's schema theory lacked ecological validity (applicability to everyday life). More specifically, most studies prior to 1981 had involved *intentional* learning with participants reading artificially constructed texts knowing their memory for those

The "graduate student's" room used by Brewer and Treyens (1981) in their experiment.

texts would be assessed. Brewer and Treyens argued that much of the information we remember during the course of our everyday lives is acquired incidentally rather than deliberately. Accordingly, they used a naturalistic learning situation. Participants spent about 35 seconds in a room designed to look like a graduate student's office (see photograph). The room contained a mixture of schema-consistent objects you would expect to find in a graduate student's office (e.g. desk, calendar, eraser, pencils) and schema-inconsistent objects (e.g. skull, toy top). Some schema-consistent objects (e.g. books) were omitted.

Schematic knowledge had positive and negative influences on subsequent unexpected recall and recognition. First, objects not present in the room but "recognized" with high confidence were nearly always schema-consistent (e.g. books, filing cabinet). This is clear evidence for schemas leading to errors in memory.

Second, participants recalled more schema-consistent than schema-inconsistent objects for objects that were present *and* those that were not present. In a similar study, Lampinen, Copeland, and Neuschatz (2001) found that far more schema-consistent objects that had not been present were falsely recalled 48 hours after presentation. Thus, the negative impact of schematic knowledge can increase over time.

Steyvers and Hemmer (2012) argued that many studies designed to test schema theories have exaggerated the fallibility of human memory. Consider the study by Brewer and Treyens (1981). Guessing that a graduate student's office contained books is a very reasonable assumption in the real world but led to memory error in the manipulated environment used by Brewer and Treyens. Thus, we might predict that people would be less likely to "recall" objects that had not been present in naturalistic environments than in manipulated ones.

KEY TERM

Ecological validity: The extent to which research findings (especially laboratory ones) can be generalized to everyday life.

Steyvers and Hemmer (2012) tested the above prediction in various experiments using five categories of scene types (kitchen, office, dining room, hotel room, urban scene). In one experiment, participants named objects they would expect to see in each scene (e.g. a television in a hotel scene; a table in a dining room). This provided an assessment of the likelihood of any given object forming part of the relevant schema. Participants were shown naturalistic scenes of the five scene types, with the objects contained in each scene varying in terms of how likely they were to be found in it. As predicted, the false recall rate was much lower for objects having high schema-relevance than those having low schema-relevance (9% vs. 18%, respectively). This happened in part because participants' guesses were more likely to be correct with high-schema-relevance objects.

Steyvers and Hemmer (2012) carried out another experiment using five photographs representing each of the five scene types. The schema-relevance of objects was assessed in terms of a consistency score: objects appearing in all five examples of a given scene type scored 5, those appearing in four examples scored 4, and so on. Participants were presented with photographs of the various scenes and then attempted recall of the objects contained in them.

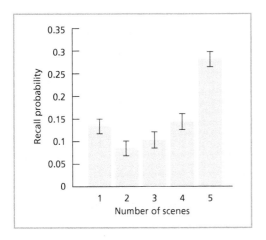

Figure 7.9 In Steyvers and Hemmer's (2012) experiment recall was highest for objects in the most schema-consistent category. Reprinted from Steyvers and Hemmer (2012), Copyright © 2012, with permission from Elsevier.

Recall was easily the highest for objects in the most schema-consistent category (see Figure 7.9). This shows the beneficial effect schematic knowledge can have on long-term memory. Overall, the findings reported by Steyvers and Hemmer (2012) show that schema-consistent information is well remembered and is associated with low levels of false recall in naturalistic environments. Thus, schematic knowledge often has a strong beneficial effect on long-term memory.

The other notable feature of Figure 7.9 is that recall was better for objects that were very schema-inconsistent (consistency score = 1) than for those slightly less schema-inconsistent (consistency score = 2). Why did this happen? It is an example of the von Restorff effect (see Chapter 17) in which information *distinctive* in a given context attracts attention and is well remembered. Evidence for the attention-grabbing nature of unexpected or schema-inconsistent objects was reported by Loftus and Mackworth (1978). Unexpected objects in scenes (e.g. an *octopus* in a farm scene) were fixated earlier, more often, and for longer durations than expected objects.

Evaluation

Schema theories have proved generally successful. As originally argued by Bartlett (1932), learning and memory often involve top-down processes triggered by schematic knowledge. More generally, schemas allow us to form expectations that are often confirmed subsequently. It has also been established that use of schematic knowledge can lead to various memory distortions and to errors in problem solving triggered by stereotypical information.

What are the limitations of schema theories? First, they are rather vague, with the precise scope and nature of schemas remaining unclear. Second, the theories generally de-emphasize the importance of individual differences. For example, Murray and Burke (2003) investigated predictive inferences (e.g. inferring *break* when presented with a sentence such as, "The angry husband threw the fragile vase against the wall"). Only participants with high reading skill drew these inferences rapidly and automatically, indicating some people find it easier than others to access schematic knowledge.

Third, our memory representations are often richer and more complex than implied by schema theories. For example, consider restaurant scripts. It may be true that we have a basic restaurant script. However, we also know that you do not sit down before ordering your food at fast-food restaurants, expensive restaurants are most likely to have wine waiters, you need to book at some restaurants but not others, and so on. Most schema-based theories have not focused on these complexities.

Fourth, schema theories probably exaggerate the number of schema-driven memory errors occurring in everyday life. As Steyvers and Hemmer (2012, p. 140) argued, "In a naturalistic environment, the prior knowledge of the occurrence of objects in a given scene type can lead to effective guesses ... Such guessing with prior [schematic] knowledge can result in high accuracy and a low number of intrusions."

SUMMARY

- There is an important distinction between semantic and episodic memory, with the latter involving more conscious recollection of the past.
- The distinction between semantic and episodic memory is supported by evidence from brain-damaged patients: amnesic patients typically have greater problems with episodic than semantic memory, whereas patients with semantic dementia show the opposite pattern.
- In spite of the differences between semantic and episodic memory, many long-term memories combine episodic and semantic information and there appears to be a common functional brain network associated with both types of long-term memory.
- Information contained within semantic memory is organized in various ways. For example, most people respond much faster when asked to produce a category member starting with a given letter rather than ending with a given letter.
- According to Collins and Quillian's (1969) hierarchical network model, concepts are represented by nodes within hierarchical networks; concept properties or features are stored as far up the hierarchy as possible.
- The hierarchical network model claims that concepts are stored in semantic memory in a much neater and tidier way than is actually the case. The model also fails to acknowledge that concepts can be fuzzy or imprecise.
- According to Collins and Loftus' (1975) spreading activation model, semantic memory is organized on the basis of semantic relatedness or distance. Activation of any given concept causes activation to spread to all other related concepts.
- The spreading activation model assumes that all information about a given concept is stored at a single node, which is a substantial oversimplification.
- Many concepts within semantic memory are organized into hierarchies consisting of a superordinate level (e.g. four-footed animal), a basic level (e.g. dog), and a subordinate level (e.g. collie).
- Most of the time, people prefer the basic level because it combines informativeness and distinctiveness. However, experts often prefer the subordinate level because it is more informative than the basic level.

- Categorization typically occurs faster at the superordinate level than the at basic level because less information is required.
- It has often been argued that the representations of concepts in semantic memory resemble encyclopedic descriptions. In contrast, Barsalou claimed in his situational simulation theory that concept processing (even of abstract concepts) involves the perceptual and motor systems and depends very much on the current context.
- Barsalou's theoretical approach has received much support. However, it de-emphasizes evidence that concepts also have a stable, central core of meaning unaffected by context.
- According to the hub-and-spoke model, concepts consist of hubs (unified abstract representations) and spokes (modality-specific information).
- Evidence from patients with semantic dementia and from neuroimaging studies indicates that hubs are stored in the anterior temporal lobes.
- The existence of patients with category-specific deficits supports the notion of spokes located in several different brain areas.
- It remains to be worked out precisely how information from hubs and spokes is combined and integrated.
- Schemas are well-integrated chunks of knowledge about the world, events, people, and actions. As such, they are broader in scope than concepts.
- There is some support for the distinction between schemas and concepts in research on brain-damaged patients. Patients with semantic dementia generally have greater problems with accessing concepts than schematic information, whereas those with fronto-temporal dementia show the opposite pattern.
- Schemas are useful because they allow us to make predictions about the immediate future and to make inferences while reading.
- However, schemas can cause us to oversimplify reality by, for example, relying excessively on stereotypes.
- Schematic knowledge can also cause distortions in long-term memory when what we read or hear is inconsistent with that knowledge. However, such distortions are relatively infrequent when people are exposed to natural scenes rather than manipulated ones in which objects highly probable in context are deliberately omitted.

POINTS FOR DISCUSSION

Discuss the similarities and differences between semantic and episodic memory.

Describe the spreading activation model and evaluate its contribution to our understanding of semantic memory.

What are basic-level categories? To what extent are they really basic?

Does concept processing generally involve the perceptual and motor systems?

Describe the hub-and-spoke model. To what extent has research on brain-damaged patients supported this model?

Do schema theories provide a satisfactory explanation of memory errors and distortions?

FURTHER READING

Barsalou, L. W. (2012). The human conceptual system. In M. J. Spivey, K. McRae, & M. F. Joanisse (Eds.), *The Cambridge handbook of psycholinguistics* (pp. 239–258). Cambridge: Cambridge University Press. Lawrence Barsalou discusses his influential approach based on the central assumption that there are close links among the perceptual, motor, and conceptual systems.

Greenberg, D. L., & Verfaellie, M. (2010). Interdependence of episodic and semantic memory: Evidence from neuropsychology. *Journal of the International Neuropsychology Society, 16,* 748–753. The authors discuss semantic and episodic memory in terms of research on brain-damaged patients.

Meteyard, L., Cuadrado, S. R., Bahrami, B., & Vigliocco, G. (2012). Coming of age: A review of embodiment and the neuroscience of semantics. *Cortex, 48,* 788–804. Lotte Meteyard and her colleagues provide a comprehensive review of theories of how concepts are represented in semantic memory.

Patterson, K. E., Nestor, P. J., & Rogers, T. T. (2007). Where do you know what you know? The representation of semantic knowledge in the human brain. *Nature Reviews Neuroscience, 8,* 976–987. This article by Karalyn Patterson and her colleagues introduced the influential hub-and-spoke model of semantic memory.

Steyvers, M., & Hemmer, P. (2012). Reconstruction from memory in naturalistic environments. In B. H. Ross (Ed.), *The psychology of learning and motivation, 56,* 126–144. Mark Steyvers and Pernille Hemmer show the importance of testing schema theories in naturalistic settings.

REFERENCES

Adlam, A.-L. R., Patterson, K., & Hodges, J. R. (2009). "I remember it as if it were yesterday": Memory for recent events in patients with semantic dementia. *Neuropsychologia, 47,* 1344–1351.

Anaki, D., & Bentin, S. (2009). Familiarity effects on categorization levels of faces and objects. *Cognition, 111,* 144–149.

Barsalou, L. W. (2009). Simulation, situated conceptualization, and prediction. *Philosophical Transactions of the Royal Society B: Biological Sciences, 364,* 1281–1289.

Barsalou, L. W. (2012). The human conceptual system. In M. J. Spivey, K. McRae, & Joanisse, M. F. (Eds.), *The Cambridge handbook of psycholinguistics* (pp. 239–258). Cambridge: Cambridge University Press.

Barsalou, L.W., & Wiemer-Hastings, K. (2005). Situating abstract concepts. In D. Pecher & R. Zwaan (Eds.), *Grounding cognition: The role of perception and action in memory, language, and thought.* New York, NY: Cambridge University Press.

Bartlett, F. C. (1932). *Remembering.* Cambridge: Cambridge University Press.

Bayley, P. J., Hopkins, R. O., & Squire, L. R. (2006). The fate of old memories after medial temporal lobe damage. *Journal of Neuroscience, 26,* 13311–1331.

Bier, N., Bottari, C., Hudon, C., Jobert, S., Paquette, G., & Macoir, J. L. (2013). The impact of semantic dementia on everyday actions: Evidence from an ecological study. *Journal of the International Neuropsychological Society, 19,* 162–172.

Binder, J. R., & Desai, R .H. (2011). The neurobiology of semantic memory. *Trends in Cognitive Sciences, 15,* 527–536.

Binder, J. R., Desai, R. H., Graves, W. W., & Conant, L .L. (2009). Where is the semantic system? A critical review and meta-analysis of 120 functional neuroimaging studies. *Cerebral Cortex*, *19*, 2767–2796.

Bourdais, C., & Pecheux, M.-G. (2009). Categorizing in 13- and 16-month-old infants: A comparison of two methods. *Année Psychologique*, *109*, 3–27.

Bower, G. H., Black, J. B., & Turner, T. J. (1979). Scripts in memory for text. *Cognitive Psychology*, *11*, 177–220.

Bransford, J. D., & Johnson, M. K. (1972). Contextual prerequisites for understanding. *Journal of Verbal Learning and Verbal Behavior, 11*, 717–726.

Brewer, W. F., & Treyens, J. C. (1981). Role of schemata in memory for places. *Cognitive Psychology*, *13*, 207–230.

Bub, D. N., Masson, M. E. J., & Cree, G. S. (2008). Evocation of functional and volumetric gestural knowledge by objects and words. *Cognition*, *106*, 27–58.

Burianova, H., McIntosh, A.R., & Grady, C.L. (2010). A common functional brain network for autobiographical, episodic, and semantic memory retrieval. *NeuroImage*, *49*, 865–874.

Chaigneau, S. E., Barsalou, L. W., & Zamani, M. (2009). Situational information contributes to object categorization and inference. *Acta Psychologica*, *130*, 81–94.

Chassy, P., & Gobet, F. (2011). Measuring chess experts' single-use sequence knowledge: An archival study of departure from 'theoretical openings'. *PLoS ONE*, *6*(11), e26692.

Close, J., & Pothos, E. M. (2012). "Object categorization: Reversals and explanations of the basic-level advantage" (Rogers & Patterson, 2007): A simplicity account. *Quarterly Journal of Experimental Psychology*, *65*, 1615–1632.

Coley, J. D., Medin, D. L., & Atran, S. (1997). Does rank have its privilege? Inductive inferences within folkbiological taxonomies. *Cognition*, *64*, 73–112.

Collins, A.M., & Loftus, E.F. (1975). A spreading-activation theory of semantic processing. *Psychological Review*, *82*, 407–428.

Collins, A.M., & Quillian, M.R. (1969). Retrieval time from semantic memory. *Journal of Verbal Learning and Verbal Behavior*, *9*, 432–438.

Connell, L., Lynott, D., & Dreyer, F. (2012). A functional role for modality-specific perceptual systems in conceptual representations. *PLoS ONE*, *7*(3), e33321.

Conrad, C. (1972). Cognitive economy in semantic memory. *Journal of Experimental Psychology*, *92*, 149–154.

Cosentino, S., Chute, D., Libon, D., Moore, TP., & Grossman, M. (2006). How does the brain represent scripts? A study of executive processes and semantic knowledge in dementia. *Neuropsychology*, *20*, 307–318.

Cree, G.S, & McRae, K. (2003). Analyzing the factors underlying the structure and computation of the meaning of chipmunk, cherry, chisel, cheese, and cello (and many other such concrete nouns). *Journal of Experimental Psychology: General*, *132*, 163–201.

Dell, G. S. (1986). A spreading-activation theory of retrieval in sentence production. *Psychological Review*, *93*, 283–321.

Farag, C., Troiani, V., Bonner, M., Powers, C., Avants, B., Gee, J., et al. (2010). Hierarchical organization of scripts: Converging evidence from fMRI and fronto-temporal degeneration. *Cerebral Cortex*, *20*, 2453–2463.

Funnell, E. (1996). Response biases in oral reading: An account of the co-occurrence of surface dyslexia and semantic dementia. *Quarterly Journal of Experimental Psychology A*, *49*, 417–446.

Gauld, A., & Stephenson, G. M. (1967). Some experiments relating to Bartlett's Theory of Remembering. *British Journal of Psychology*, *58*, 39–49.

Greenberg, D. L., & Verfaellie, M. (2010). Interdependence of episodic and semantic memory: Evidence from neuropsychology. *Journal of the International Neuropsychological Society*, *16*, 748–753.

Irish, M., & Piguet, O. (2013). The pivotal role of semantic memory in remembering the past and imagining the future. *Frontiers in Behavioral Neuroscience*, *7* (Article 27).

Irish, M., Hornberger, M., Lah, S., Miller, L., Pengas, G., Nestor, P. J., et al. (2011). Profiles of recent autobiographical memory retrieval in semantic dementia, behavioral-variant frontotemporal dementia, and Alzheimer's disease. *Neuropsychologia*, *49*, 2694–2702.

Kan, I. P., Alexander, M. P., & Verfaellie, M. (2009). Contribution of prior semantic knowledge to new episodic learning in amnesia. *Journal of Cognitive Neuroscience*, *21*, 938–944.

Kiefer, M., & Pulvermüller, F. (2012). Conceptual representations in mind and brain: Theoretical developments, current evidence and future directions. *Cortex*, *48*, 805–825.

Lampinen, J. M., Copeland, S .M., & Neuschatz, J. S. (2001). Recollections of things schematic: Room schemas revisited. *Journal of Experimental Psychology: Learning, Memory, and Cognition*, *27*, 1211–1222.

Loftus, E. F., & Suppes, P. (1972). Structural variables that determine the speed of retrieving words from long-term memory. *Journal of Verbal Learning and Verbal Behavior, 11,* 770–777.

Loftus, G. R., & Mackworth, N. H. (1978). Cognitive determinants of fixation location during picture viewing. *Journal of Experimental Psychology: Human Perception and Performance, 4,* 365–372.

Macé, M. J.-M., Joubert, O. R., Nespoulous, J. L., & Fabre-Thorpe, M. (2009). The time-course of visual categorisations: You can spot the animal faster than the bird. *PLoS ONE, 4*(6), e5927.

Macrae, C. N., & Bodenhausen, G. V. (2000). Social cognition: Thinking categorically about others. *Annual Review of Psychology, 51,* 93–120.

Manns, J. R., Hopkins, R. O., & Squire, L. R. (2003). Semantic memory and the human hippocampus. *Neuron, 38,* 127–133.

Marques, J. F., Raposo, A., & Almeida, J. (2013). Structural processing and category-specific deficits. *Cortex, 49,* 266–275.

Mayberry, E. J., Sage, K., & Lambon Ralph, M. A. (2011). At the edge of semantic space: The breakdown of coherent concepts in semantic dementia is constrained by typicality and severity but not modality. *Journal of Cognitive Neuroscience, 23,* 2240–2251.

Mazzone, M., & Lalumera, E. (2010). Concepts: Stored or created? *Minds and Machines, 20,* 47–68.

McCloskey, M.E., & Glucksberg, S. (1978). Natural categories: Well defined or fuzzy sets? *Memory and Cognition, 6,* 462–472.

McNamara, T. P. (1992). Priming and constraints it places on theories of memory and retrieval. *Psychological Review, 99,* 650–662.

Medin, D. L., & Atran, S. (2004). The native mind: Biological categorization and reasoning in development and across cultures. *Psychological Review, 111,* 960–983.

Meteyard, L., Cuadrado, S. R., Bahrami, B., & Vigliocco, G. (2012). Coming of age: A review of embodiment and the neuroscience of semantics. *Cortex, 48,* 788–804.

Meyer, D. E., & Schvaneveldt, R. W. (1976). Meaning, memory structure, and mental processes. *Science, 192,* 27–33.

Murray, J. D., & Burke, K. A. (2003). Activation and encoding of predictive inferences: The role of reading skill. *Discourse Processes, 35,* 81–102.

Neuschatz, J. S., Lampinen, J. M., Preston, E. L., Hawkins, E. R., & Toglia, M. P. (2002). The effect of memory schemata on memory and the phenomenological experience of naturalistic situations. *Applied Cognitive Psychology, 16,* 687–708.

Palmer, S. E. (1975). The effects of contextual scenes on the identification of objects. *Memory and Cognition, 3,* 519–526.

Patterson, K. E., Nestor, P. J., & Rogers, T. T. (2007). Where do you know what you know? The representation of semantic knowledge in the human brain. *Nature Reviews Neuroscience, 8,* 976–987.

Pecher, D., Boot, I., & Van Dantzig, S. (2011). Abstract concepts: Sensory-motor grounding, metaphors, and beyond. In B. Ross (Ed.), *The psychology of learning and motivation,* (Vol. 54, pp. 217–248). Burlington, MA: Academic Press.

Pobric, G., Jefferies, E., & Lambon Ralph, M. A. (2010). Category-specific versus category-general semantic impairment induced by transcranial magnetic stimulation. *Current Biology, 20,* 964–968.

Rascovsky, K., Growdon, M. E., Pardo, I. R., Grossman, S., & Miller, B. L. (2009). The quicksand of forgetfulness: Semantic dementia in *One Hundred Years of Solitude. Brain, 132,* 2609–2616.

Reynolds, D.J., Garnham, A., & Oakhill, J. (2006). Evidence of immediate activation of gender information from a social role name. *Quarterly Journal of Experimental Psychology, 59,* 886–903.

Rips, L. J., Shoben, E. J., & Smith, E. E. (1973). Semantic distance and the verification of semantic relations. *Journal of Verbal Learning and Verbal Behavior, 12,* 1–20.

Roediger, H. L., & McDermott, K. B. (1995). Creating false memories: Remembering words not presented in lists. *Journal of Experimental Psychology: Learning, Memory and Cognition, 21,* 803–814.

Rogers, T. T., & Patterson, K. (2007). Object categorization: Reversals and explanations of the base-level advantage. *Journal of Experimental Psychology: General, 136,* 451–469.

Rosch, E. (1973). Natural categories. *Cognitive Psychology, 4,* 328–350.

Rosch, E., & Mervis, C. B. (1975). Family resemblances: Studies in the internal structure of categories. *Cognitive Psychology, 7,* 573–605.

Rosch, E., Mervis, C. B., Gray, W. D., Johnson, D. M., & Boyes-Braem, P. (1976). Basic objects in natural categories. *Cognitive Psychology, 8,* 382–439.

Sanchez-Casas, R., Ferre, P., Garcia-Albea, J. E., & Guasch, M. (2006). The nature of semantic priming: Effects of the degree of semantic similarity between primes and targets in Spanish. *European Journal of Cognitive Psychology, 18,* 161–184.

Schacter, D. L., Reiman, E., Curran, T., Yun, L. S., Bandy, D., McDermott, K. B., et al. (1996).

Neuroanatomical correlates of veridical and illusory recognition memory: Evidence from positron emission tomography. *Neuron, 17,* 267–274.

Sirigu, A., Zalla, T., Pillon, B., Grafman, J., Agid, Y., & Dubois, B. (1995). Selective impairments in managerial knowledge following prefrontal cortex damage. *Cortex, 31,* 301–316.

Spiers, H. J., Maguire, E. A., & Burgess, N. (2001). Hippocampal amnesia. *Neurocase, 7,* 357–382.

Steyvers, M., & Hemmer, P. (2012). Reconstruction from memory in naturalistic environments. In B. H. Ross (Ed.), *The psychology of learning and motivation* (Vol. 56, pp. 126–144). New York: Academic Press.

Tanaka, J. W., & Taylor, M. E. (1991). Object categories and expertise: Is the basic level in the eye of the beholder? *Cognitive Psychology, 15,* 121–149.

Tulving, E. (2002). Episodic memory: From mind to brain. *Annual Review of Psychology, 53,* 1–25.

Verheyen, S., & Storms, G. (2013). A mixture approach to vagueness and ambiguity. *PLoS ONE, 8*(5), e63507.

Wheeler, M. A., Stuss, D. T., & Tulving, E. (1997). Toward a theory of episodic memory: The frontal lobes and autonoetic consciousness. *Psychological Bulletin, 121,* 331–354.

Wittgenstein, L. (1958). *Philosophical investigations*. New York: Macmillan.

Wu, L. L., & Barsalou, L. W. (2009). Perceptual simulation in conceptual combination: Evidence from property generation. *Acta Psychologica, 132,* 173–189.

Yardley, H., Perlovsky, L., & Bar, M. (2012). Predictions and incongruency in object recognition: A cognitive neuroscience perspective. In D. Weinshall, J. Anemüller, & L. Luc (Eds.), Detection and identification of rare audiovisual cues, *Studies in Computational Intelligence* (Vol. 384). Berlin: Springer.

Contents

The experience of retrieval failure   195

The retrieval process: General principles   198

Factors determining retrieval success   202

Context cues   207

Retrieval tasks   208

The importance of incidental context in episodic memory retrieval   211

Recognition memory   217

Source monitoring   223

Concluding remarks   223

Summary   224

Points for discussion   225

Further reading   226

References   226

CHAPTER 8

RETRIEVAL

Michael C. Anderson

Imagine that it is 10.00 p.m. and you are packing for an international flight early the next morning. You need your passport, but it's nowhere to be found. Deep concern sets in.

It's midnight. Your flight is at 6.00 a.m. You drive to work, dig through drawers, and look on every shelf. *No passport.* Returning to your car, you peer under the floor-mats, rummage through the trunk, and grasp hopefully under the seats, as light rain soaks your back. You are now fully panicked.

Returning home, you march through every room, staring with the full laser beam of consciousness at every inch. You leaf through books, imagining that the passport will drop out gracefully on the floor. At 4.00 a.m., you begin dredging for memories. "When is the last time you had it? I remember putting it in this room that I'm sitting in, but I've already looked there." After concentrating intensely for 20 minutes, memory delivers nothing but fleeting images, and you're left with nothing but a powerful feeling that it's around somewhere. You decide to have one last look.

Then, in a box that you have already inspected numerous times, you lift a paper at the bottom. There it is! It all floods back—the when, how, and why. "Oh yeah ... that's right, I put the passport in this box when I was cleaning my home office in preparation for guests arriving two months ago!" It's 5.00 a.m. You pack madly, race to the airport, and merciful flight attendants allow you on the plane, sleepless, and shoeless because you ran from airport security screening in your two differently colored socks.

This event actually occurred to me and was, to say the least, memorable. The story illustrates a crucial point about memory. Quite often, memories are stored perfectly well but, for whatever reason, we have difficulty retrieving them. Clearly the event of putting the passport in the box was alive and well in my memory; yet, even after 20 minutes of deliberate search, the trace remained vexingly inaccessible. But the instant I saw the passport, the memory returned, in full vividness. Why couldn't I retrieve this information?

Clearly, having good memory is not just about encoding material well. One also has to be able to retrieve information. As any student knows, it is possible to study extensively, and then, on the exam, suddenly be unable to recollect it. In this chapter, we consider the processes of retrieval, and what factors influence retrieval success.

THE EXPERIENCE OF RETRIEVAL FAILURE

Subjectively, perhaps the most convincing evidence that our memory contains information that we cannot access comes from the experience of being asked a question to which we are sure we know the answer, although we cannot produce it at that precise moment; we feel we have it "on the tip of the tongue."

The tip-of-the-tongue state is an extreme form of pause, where the word takes a noticeable time to come out—although the speaker has a distinct feeling that he/she knows exactly what he/she wants to say.

Some years ago two Harvard psychologists, Roger Brown and David McNeil (1966), decided to try and see whether this feeling was based on genuine evidence or was simply an illusion. They set up a tip-of-the-tongue situation by reading out a series of definitions of relatively obscure words to their participants and asking them to name the object being defined. Take, for example, a musical instrument comprising a frame holding a series of tubes struck by hammers. Participants were instructed to indicate if they were in the "tip-of-the-tongue" state (convinced that they knew the word although they were unable to produce it). When this occurred they were asked to guess at the number of syllables in the word and to provide any other information, such as the initial letter. They were consistently much better at providing such information than one would have expected by chance. Other studies

Box 8.1 Tip-of-the-tongue experience

Try recalling the capital cities of each of the countries listed, first by covering up the letters to the right. When you feel you can't recall any more of them, then use the provided letter cues. Did you encounter a tip-of-the-tongue experience? Check your answers at the end of the chapter (Box 8.2).

	Country	First letter of capital city
1	Norway	O
2	Turkey	A
3	Kenya	N
4	Uruguay	M
5	Finland	H
6	Australia	C
7	Saudi Arabia	R
8	Romania	B
9	Portugal	L
10	Bulgaria	S

	Country	First letter of capital city
11	South Korea	S
12	Syria	D
13	Denmark	C
14	Sudan	K
15	Nicaragua	M
16	Ecuador	Q
17	Colombia	B
18	Afghanistan	K
19	Thailand	B
20	Venezuela	C

have shown that giving the participant the initial letter, in this case "x", frequently tends to prompt the correct name, "xylophone."

The task of trying to remember the names of capital cities of countries is a good way of evoking this effect. Read rapidly through the list of countries in Box 8.1, covering up the initial letters of their capital cities. Eliminate those countries that you can immediately produce the answer for and also those for which you feel you do *not* know the answer. Concentrate on the rest. Any luck? If not, see if the letter cues jog your memory. Check your answers at the end of this chapter.

In general, the feeling that you know something is often a good indication that you do—given the right prompting. In a capital city recall test similar to that just described, recall was over 50% when letters were given for the cities people thought they knew, but only 16% for those they thought they didn't. Similarly, my powerful feeling that the passport was located in my home library was, in fact, correct.

Most people find it more than a little vexing to know that they know something, but are unable to recollect it. In the tip-of-the-tongue state, many people struggle mightily to recall the delinquent knowledge. Imagine what your life would be like if you had this sort of experience on a regular basis. Like poor Tantalus, the tortured figure from Greek mythology, you would forever be reaching for your mnemonic fruit, never quite being able to grasp it. In fact, some people do have rather significant difficulties in retrieving their past, even when it can be shown that the sought after experiences are clearly in memory. Thus, these individuals are not amnesic in the sense discussed in Chapter 16 on amnesia, wherein memories are not properly stored and retained; rather, they suffer from disruptions in the retrieval processes necessary to intentionally access their memories. Such difficulties often accompany damage or dysfunction to the prefrontal cortex, a brain structure critically involved in cognitive control more generally.

In one particularly clear example, Jennifer Mangels and her colleagues asked patients with damage to the prefrontal cortex to recall knowledge of events and facts that they learned long before suffering brain damage (Mangels, Gershberg, Shimamura, & Knight, 1996). Testing this type of older, remote memory was a clever approach, because it meant that the authors could be confident that the memories being tested were encoded and stored under normal conditions (i.e. without brain damage), allowing any memory deficits to be clearly attributed to retrieval problems. To assess patients' remote memory, Mangels and colleagues tested memory for salient public events and famous faces that most people alive during a certain era can be expected to know. For example, on the famous faces test, participants received photographs of once famous people and were asked to recall their names. Each of these famous people was chosen carefully to be famous primarily in a particular decade, but not before or after. For instance, Telly Savalis was an actor famous mainly in the 1970s (for the show "Kojak"), but not afterwards. During this test, if, after viewing a photo for a generous amount of time, it was clear that they were having difficulty recalling the name, participants would receive additional hints (e.g. the person is an actor famous in the 1970s, whose name begins with "T"). If even this amount of information was not enough, participants were tested to see if they could recognize the correct name. Famous faces were drawn from each of several decades prior to the experiment. As can be seen in Figure 8.1, patients were uniformly worse at remembering the names of famous people compared to age-matched control participants, regardless of the decade from which the famous face was drawn. This substantial retrieval disadvantage held true even when distinctive cues were given to aid recall, though overall performance clearly did improve. In contrast, patients could easily pick the correct famous names when they were presented to them for recognition (right panel) and were not worse than control participants. Other studies have shown this pattern with events from patients' own lives (Della Salla, Laiacona, Spinnler, & Trivelli, 1993). Thus, damage to the prefrontal cortex hinders recall even for very well learned information from across our lifespans.

We have established, then, that our memory store contains more information than we can access at any given moment. Moreover,

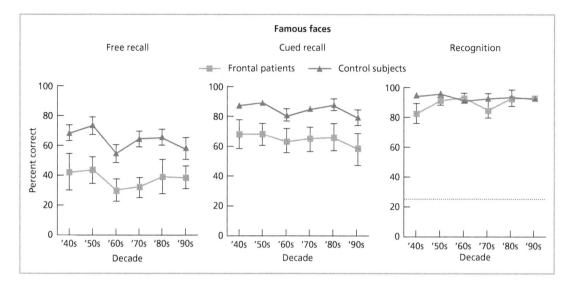

Figure 8.1 The effects of frontal lobe damage on free recall, cued recall and recognition tests of remote memories. Participants were presented with the faces of people who were famous in each decade from 1940 through the 1990s, when the experiment was conducted. In the free recall test, frontal patients and age-matched control subjects were given the face and asked to recall the person's name. In the cued recall test, participants were given additional hints about the person's profession or other characteristics. In the recognition test, participants needed to select the correct name from a group of distractors. Frontal patients exhibit clear deficits in free and cued recall, even though recognition tests reveal that they have the right answers to the questions in memory. From Mangels et al. (1996). Copyright © American Psychological Association. Reproduced with permission.

successful access often relies upon retrieval mechanisms that help to isolate traces in memory, a function strongly reliant on cognitive control processes mediated by the prefrontal cortex, a finding supported by research with fMRI (Badre & Wagner, 2007). What therefore determines the accessibility of this information? To address this question, we need a basic idea of how the retrieval process works.

THE RETRIEVAL PROCESS: GENERAL PRINCIPLES

To describe how retrieval works, it's helpful to introduce some terminology. During retrieval, we are usually seeking a particular memory— either a particular fact, idea, or experience, often called the *target memory* or the *target trace*. Suppose, for example, I asked you to recall what you had for dinner last night. To answer, you would try to recollect the event. In

this case, your memory for having dinner last night would be the target.

When we search for a target in memory, we usually have some idea of what we are looking for. In the dinner example, you knew you were searching for a dinner event that happened yesterday evening. This specification can be likened to the words one might type into the search window of an internet search engine, like Google™. Without such a specification, there is nothing for your memory to work with, and so it would return nothing, just as typing nothing into Google™ would not yield websites. These snippets of information that allow you to access a memory are known as *retrieval cues*, or simply *cues*. In general, retrieval is a

KEY TERM

Retrieval: The process of recovering a target memory based on one or more cues, subsequently bringing that target into awareness.

progression from one or more cues to a target memory, with the aim of making that target available to influence ongoing cognition.

But how do cues help us to retrieve target memories? Traces in memory are believed to be linked up to one another by connections that are usually called *associations* or *links*. Suppose, for example, I ask you to say the first thing that comes to mind for each of the following words: *dog*, *hot*, *up*, or *cow*. Chances are, you probably thought *cat* or *bone* for *dog*, *cold* for *hot*, *down* for *up*, and *milk* for *cow*. These ideas, like dog and cat, are strongly linked in most people's memories—that is, they are associated. Associations are structural linkages between traces that vary in strength. For example, if I asked you to name a *fruit*, you might quickly say *banana*, but a *guava* is also a fruit. The fact that guava does not come to mind so readily reflects its weaker association to *fruit*. Retrieval then, is a progression from one or more cues to a target memory, via associative connections.

Memories can be retrieved from a variety of cues. If instead of asking you, "What did you have for dinner last night," I had asked, "when was the last time you had peas?" you might say, "Oh, I had peas last night for dinner." You would have accessed the same memory but by means of different cues than in the former example. Many things can serve as cues; the smell of peas may remind you of last night; or the song on the radio may be the same one you played while dining on peas. Our memories are remarkably flexible; any aspect of the content of a memory can serve as a reminder that could access the experience, a property known as *content addressable memory*. We essentially have "mental Google™," but we can search with just about any type of information.

The preceding ideas give us basic language for talking about the structures involved in memory, but they do not say much about the process. How do we progress from cues to target memories, via associations? Although there are many theories, one useful and simple idea is that retrieval occurs by a process called spreading activation. According to this idea, each memory has an internal state of its own, reflecting how "excited" or "active" it is, a state referred to as the memory's activation level. Activation has several important properties. The activation level varies, and determines how accessible a trace is in memory, with higher levels of activation reflecting greater accessibility. A trace's activation level increases when something related to it is perceived in the world (e.g. seeing a plate of peas will activate the idea *peas* and probably your dinner of peas), or when attention is focused directly on the trace (when I ask you to think of *peas*). This activation persists for some time, even after attention has been removed.

How does the concept of activation help us to think about retrieval? One idea is that memories automatically spread activation to other memories to which they are associated. This *spreading activation* is like "energy" flowing through connections linking traces. The amount of activation spread from the cue to an associate is larger the stronger the association, and activation is spread in parallel to all associates. If the target accumulates enough activation from the cue, it will be retrieved, even though other associates might be activated as well. So, if you saw the name *Beckham*, attention to this idea would increase its activation, which, in turn, would activate associates, like *football*. As a result, *football*. would be retrieved. The idea that traces have activation that spreads is central to many theories of memory, and provides a useful way of thinking about how cues access memories. To refine our definition of retrieval further then, retrieval is a progression from one or more cues to a target memory, via associative connections linking them together, through a process of spreading activation.

For simplicity, I have described retrieval as a progression from a single cue to a single "target" in memory, as though a memory of your past was a single entity, that simply varied in its activity level. Though this is a helpful simplification, memories are complex, being composed of many different features and details. Whilst eating dinner last night, you may have

KEY TERM

Activation level: The variable internal state of a memory trace that contributes to its accessibility at a given point.

had peas, but you had overcooked peas, while seated at the dinner table with your roomate, with mashed potatoes, and told stories about your day, for example. So, in most instances, it is better to regard a memory as a collection of features that, if activated collectively by cues, would constitute retrieval. Considering this additional complexity then, retrieval involves the reinstatement, via spreading activation, of a *pattern of activation* over *feature units* that represent a memory. Several features of the original experience, provided as cues, will spread activation to other features, completing the missing components of the memory pattern. The process by which spreading activation from a set of cues leads to the reinstatement of a memory's features is often referred to as *pattern completion.*

Our description of the retrieval process so far is general, and fits cases when we are retrieving general semantic knowledge or particular experiences from long-term memory. The above concepts can also apply whether we are spontaneously reminded of a past experience (incidental retrieval), or we are intentionally retrieving a memory. Additional concepts are useful, however, to describe intentional retrieval. During intentional retrieval, we are are targeting a particular trace in memory. As such, cognitive control processes are thought necessary to focus the search process, including processes such as *cue-specification* (i.e. the careful specification of what we are trying to remember, which may also include a retrieval strategy), *cue-maintenance* in working memory, *interference resolution processes* which help to overcome interference from competing memories brought to mind instead of the target (a process addressed in more detail in Chapter 9), and *post-retrieval monitoring* of the products of search, which includes decision processes that evaluate whether what we have retrieved is what we are seeking. For example, while struggling to recall where my passport was, I remember carefully imagining myself storing the passport someplace, hoping that this imagined scenario might call to mind a memory of the passport's location. In imagining this scenario, I was specifying the cue used to search memory (cue-specification). I persisted doggedly with this image, concentrating on it intently (cue-maintenance) to

jar loose relevant memories. Ocassionally, a relevant memory would begin to emerge, and I struggled to call it fully to mind, despite distraction from related passport memories (interference resolution). Finally, when a memory did come to mind, I had to decide whether it was relevant. In one case, I recalled an older memory of storing my passport from when I lived in a different home—which was clearly not relevant. Reflecting on what you retrieve and discerning its relevance is post-retrieval monitoring. Each of these control processes is engaged to some degree whenever you intentionally recall a particular memory, even when you don't struggle as much as I did in this case. One can imagine how intentional recall would be impaired if any of these processes were to break down (Simons & Spiers, 2003). Indeed, damage to the prefrontal cortex disrupts many of these processes, accounting for the retrieval deficits described at the outset of this chapter.

Finally, it is useful to consider *what* it is that is being retrieved, and how this happens in the brain. Although our understanding of the neural basis of memories and retrieval is still evolving, some broad principles are accepted. One central hypothesis that has good support is the idea that retrieval involves the *cortical reinstatement* of the pattern of neural activity that was present at the time that an experience was first encoded into memory. For example, when I reminisce fondly of going to see the first *Austin Powers, International Man of Mystery* movie in the cinema with my friends Chad and Scott in the 1990s, I immediately think of Austin Powers' (i.e. Mike Myers') and Dr. Evil's faces, the ridiculous theme song of the movie, where we sat in the theatre, and Chad's outrageous laugh. When remembering these aspects of the experience, it is likely that I am re-activating the areas of the neocortex that perceptually processed the original stimuli. Indeed, according to the reinstatement hypothesis, I should be reinstating the particular neural patterns associated with perceiving those particular faces (in the brain's face area, or the fusiform face area), the music (in the temporal cortex) and the particular spatial environment (e.g. the parahippocampal place area in the brain). (Surely there must be a dedicated region for Chad's laugh!) I am able to recall these diverse features, represented in widely different areas of the neocortex, presumably because these features are bound together into a memory for the event. Thus, the pattern completion process begins with some of these features, and recreates a brain state in which cortical perceptual processes are recapitulated. As Danker and Anderson put it, we are, in essence experiencing "ghosts of brain states past" (Danker & Anderson, 2010). How we go from cues to this reinstatement, and what the critical neural changes are that enable brain states to be recreated, are fundamental problems in memory.

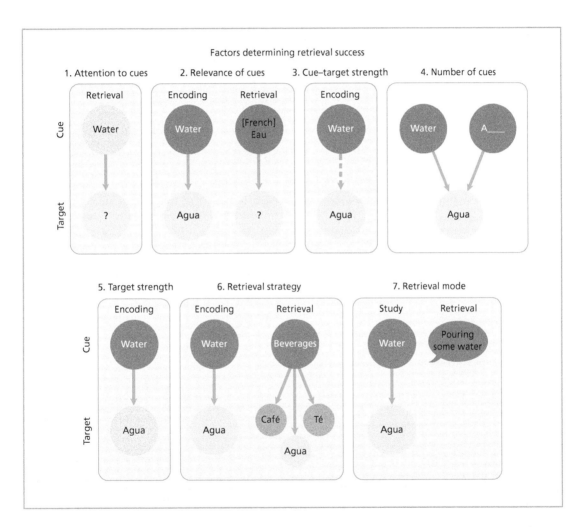

Figure 8.2 Factors determining retrieval success. In this example, assume you are attempting to retrieve the Spanish word for *water*. (1) Failing to take full advantage of the cue (*water*), due to divided attention, renders it a less effective reminder of the target (*agua*). (2) Cues explicitly studied with the target are better than cues that one has not studied with it (e.g. the French word for water, *eau*). (3) If the cue was never strongly associated with the target during encoding, the cue would be less helpful during retrieval. (4) Access to additional relevant cues, such as a letter-stem, facilitates retrieval. (5) Weak items in memory are difficult to retrieve. (6) Adopting an inefficient retrieval strategy (e.g. recalling all sorts of Spanish beverages until you stumble upon the target word) wastes time and generates distracting responses. (7) Encountering a stimulus without the intention to retrieve the target from memory reduces the probability of eliciting the target.

FACTORS DETERMINING RETRIEVAL SUCCESS

Knowing that retrieval is the progression from cues to a target memory did not help when I needed to find my passport. Why does retrieval work sometimes, but not others? We consider several factors here, each demonstrating something important about the nature of retrieval (Figure 8.2).

Attention to cues

Retrieval is less effective if cues are present, but not attended to, or not attended to enough. Suppose for example, that while searching for my passport, I didn't gaze upon the box that contained it. If so, there is no way that the box could have cued memory. In reality, I searched the box many times, and so was clearly looking at it. Even so, I might not have fully attended to the box, distracted by my worries. Many theories assume that the activation given to a concept increases with attention. If so, diminishing attention might make a cue less useful and lead retrieval to fail. This may partially contribute to retrieval deficits observed in patients with damage to the prefrontal cortex.

One way of removing attention from cues is by giving people a secondary task to perform during retrieval. When distracted in this way, people's retrieval usually grows worse, especially if the secondary task requires them to pay attention to related materials (Figure 8.3). This point is made well in several studies by Myra Fernandes and Morris Moscovitch (2000, 2003). They asked people to recall out loud lists of words that had been presented to them auditorally. At the same time, participants made judgments about entirely different items appearing on a computer screen. Compared to a control condition in which people did not do a secondary task, distracting people impaired retrieval by as much as 30–50%, especially when the judgment items were words as well. In contrast, making judgments about numbers or pictures produced far less interference. Such effects of dividing attention are largest when you have to generate items from memory (recall), but are also found when you simply have to recognize whether you have seen something.

Dividing attention can also reduce retrieval even when the secondary task is totally unrelated, although usually not as much. For example, when Craik, Govoni, Naveh-Benjamin, and Anderson (1996) asked people to perform a simple visuo-motor secondary task, it reduced their recall of words presented earlier. The interfering effects of unrelated tasks grow when the task is more demanding (Rohrer & Pashler, 2003). It is worth highlighting, however, that dividing attention at retrieval is less disruptive to how much is

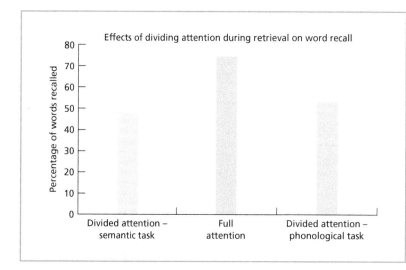

Figure 8.3 Retrieving words under divided attention conditions negatively affects retrieval success, especially with distractor tasks (e.g. semantic or phonological) that are similar to the task of interest (in this case, recalling words). Data from Fernandes and Moscovitch (2000).

recalled than dividing attention at encoding. This asymetry has been taken to indicate that, under such circumstances, retrieval quite often can proceed with less attention, compared to encoding (Baddeley, Lewis, Eldridge, & Thomson, 1984; Craik et al., 1996), especially when the cues guiding search are more specific and complete. For instance, the disruptive effects of dividing attention are larger on recall than on recognition tests, presumably because the latter provide very specific cues for accessing a trace. This pattern parallels the retrieval difficulties observed for patients with prefrontal cortex damage. Thus, though retrieval can in many cases proceed with less attention, full attention is required if more accurate and complete recall is a priority. In Chapter 9 on incidental forgetting, we discuss further an attentional control process—inhibition—that appears to be disrupted by dividing attention.

Relevance of cues

Having retrieval cues does little good if they are unrelated to the target. This might seem too obvious to mention, but we often search memory with inappropriate cues. Consider the

It's tough enough finding your car in a sea of vehicles, but it's even harder to find if you're using the wrong cues. For instance trying to remember where your sports car is wouldn't be very useful if, in fact, you drove the family sedan.

time that I left the grocery store, and stood, trying to remember where I had parked my car. After several minutes of not recollecting anything, I realized that I had driven my neighbor's car. The moment I realized this, up popped the memory. I had essentially asked my memory the wrong question with the wrong cue (*my car*). This type of mistake happens often. Have you ever tried to remember the location of your keys, presuming you must have placed them in one of their usual spots (e.g. a basket on the counter)? If you put your keys in an unusual spot, these retrieval cues will be fruitless.

Sometimes, cues that seem like they ought to be effective turn out not to be effective at all. Consider the time that I intended to return a book to the library. In the morning, standing by the breakfast table, I put the book in my backpack. On the way home later that day, while passing the library, I looked right at the library, but failed to remember to return the book. When I got home, however, and saw the kitchen table, I remembered, "Ahhh, I forget to return the book!" So, why did seeing the library not remind me to return the book? It ought to have been an outstanding cue! And why was the kitchen table such an effective reminder, when kitchen tables have nothing to do with books? Actually, this pattern makes sense, if you consider what was encoded. The thing to be remembered was the intention to return the book, which was encoded in the morning in the kitchen, with the table present. Indeed, the the book was lying on the table, and so was associated to it. By contrast, the library was absent during encoding, and so was not associated with the book. Thus, when the library became available later as a cue, there was no association that could spread activation to the intention to return the book.

The foregoing example illustrates a well-established idea known as the encoding specificity principle. This principle states that for a cue to be useful, it needs to be present at encoding, and encoded with the desired trace. In fact, cues that are specifically encoded with a target are more powerful even if, on the face of it, they might seem less good than other cues that have a pre-existing relationship with the target. In one experiment demonstrating this principle, Tulving and Osler (1968) presented participants with target words for later recall; each target was accompanied by a cue that had a weak association with the word to be retained. An example might be the word *chair* accompanied by the cue word *glue* (e.g. participants might see *glue–chair*). After encoding, participants were asked to recall the targets, either unaided or prompted by the cue with which each was paired. Cue words substantially increased recall of the targets, illustrating the power of cues to facilitate recall. But not all cues should be equally good, accoding to Tulving. For instance, although *table* is a valid associate of *chair*, it will not be as effective a cue as *glue* because *table* was not presented during encoding. Tulving and Thomson (1973) went on to show that this encoding specificity effect is powerful. There are other ways of showing the same effect. For example, if I give you a sentence such as "The man tuned the piano," but give another person the sentence "The man lifted the piano," then the cue *something heavy* is likely to be a very poor retrieval cue for you, but a good one for your colleague (Barclay, Bransford, Franks, McCarrell, & Nitsch, 1974).

Thus we remember what we experience, and we access our memory by using a fragment of that experience as a key to the whole. So, even though the library really seems like it *ought* to be a great cue for remembering to return the book, it is far less effective than the kitchen table because only the latter was encoded with the intention to return the book.

Cue–target associative strength

Retrieval can fail if cues are relevant, but are weak. As discussed previously, associations vary in strength, and it is this strength that determines the rate at which activation spreads between a cue and a target. Hence, if an association between a cue and a target is poor, retrieval failure may occur. Anyone who has ever memorized vocabulary words in a

foreign language knows that associating new words to their native language equivalents can be difficult; it is possible to have stored the foreign word (e.g. be able to recognize it as one that you have seen) and nevertheless be unable to retrieve the right meaning. Similarly, associating a new person's face to their name frequently fails, even when we recognize the person's face, and the name, if it is given to us. Thus, retrieval success depends on how associated the cues are to the target, which depends on the time and attention we spend encoding the association. Perhaps one reason why the box did not remind me of storing the passport is that in hurrying to neaten my home for guests, I did not devote enough attention to the passport's location.

When cue-target associative strength is low, people often can compensate by engaging cognitive control processes to facilitate retrieval. David Badre and Anthony Wagner, for example, have argued that when retrieval cues are too weak to automatically activate a desired memory, a *controlled retrieval process* mediated by the anterior part of the left inferior prefrontal cortex is engaged. In one illustration, Badre and Wagner asked participants to pick which of two words was more associated to cue words like *candle*. Participants showed significantly more activation in the left inferior prefrontal cortex when the correct option was weakly associated to *candle* (*halo*) than when it was strongly related (e.g. *flame*). This pattern is generally observed whenever people have to retrieve weakly associated items from semantic memory, and a similar principle is thought to apply to episodic memory retrieval. Badre and Wagner suggest that the prefrontal cortex acts to sustain attention to cues to bias neural activity in parts of the neocortex that represent the content that needs to be retrieved. In this way, the prefrontal cortex may enhance the pattern completion process and increase the chances of successful retrieval (Badre & Wagner, 2007). Given findings like this, the memory difficulties experienced by people with prefrontal cortex damage are easy to understand.

Number of cues

Retrieval often improves when more relevant cues are added. Consider the exercise you did on the "tip of the tongue." If you had initially tried to recall the meanings of the words and failed, but felt that you knew the right answer, getting the letter as an additional hint probably brought the meaning to mind. Similarly, the cardboard box by itself was insufficient to cue my memory of the passport, but when I saw the passport lying at the bottom of it, I recalled this event instantly. Importantly, the passport, by itself, would not have cued this memory. Suppose that I had been assisted by someone who found the passport while I was in another room. If the other person showed me the passport, I would not have suddenly remembered storing it in the box. I would have said, "Where did you find it?" It was the *combination* of the passport and the box that elicited the memory. It makes sense that adding cues helps. Assuming that the person attends to both cues, both will become activated. This activation will spread to the target; because there are two sources of activation, the target should grow active quickly, and be more easily retrieved.

There is evidence that adding cues does not simply cause additive improvements, however, but may sometimes be superadditive. Research on dual cuing suggests that having two cues is often far more beneficial than you would expect than if you simply added the probability of retrieving the target from each cue separately. Consider an example based on research by Rubin and Wallace (1989), who examined how providing both semantic and rhyme cues affected the likelihood of generating particular responses from memory. If we asked you to name a *mythical being*, you might mention *unicorn* or *boogie monster* or any number of other such creatures. If we asked you to name a word that rhymes with *post*, you might say *host* or *most*, or any of the numerous words that rhyme. But if we instead asked you to name a mythical being that rhymes with *post*, you would be quite likely to say *ghost*. Rubin and Wallace showed that the probability of generating a particular item like *ghost* in response to either cue alone could be quite low (e.g. 14% for a semantic category, 19% for a rhyme cue by itself), but was dramatically higher with the two in combination (97% for both semantic and rhyme cues together). This may be one reason why

it is so useful to encode information elaboratively, as discussed in Chapter 6 on encoding. Elaboration associates the material to many cues that might be used during later retrieval.

Strength of the target memory

If a memory is weakly encoded, even a good cue may be insufficient to trigger retrieval. In the framework described earlier, if the target has low activation, the lower starting point should make it more difficult for a cue to activate that item, even given a relevant cue. For example, words vary greatly in their frequency of usage in a language, with some words being very high frequency, such as *dog* and others being known, but rarely used, such as *helmet*. Higher-frequency words are better recalled. One interpretation is that higher-frequency words are more strongly represented, owing to their repeated exposure. Similarly, how well people will recall a set of singly presented words or pictures varies with the amount of time or elaborative processing given to encode those items, reflecting greater success at encoding.

The strength of a memory depends, in part, on how effectively people engage the hippocampus and other structures within the medial temporal lobes when a memory is encoded. For instance, Anthony Wagner and colleagues (Wagner et al., 1998) scanned people with fMRI as they encoded a long list of words. Afterwards, they tested people's ability to recognize words, and then, for each person, divided the words into ones that they recognized, and ones that they didn't. Wagner and colleagues reasoned that the words that people correctly recognized were likely to have been encoded more effectively than were words that people failed to recognize. If so, then comparing neural activity at encoding for items that were remembered to those that were forgotten, should reveal brain areas whose activity is particularly important to the survival of the memory. Wagner and colleagues found significantly greater activity near the hippocampus for successfully remembered than for subsequently forgotten items. This type of *subsequent memory effect* is often observed in the medial temporal lobes, but is also are found in other brain areas, depending on the content that is being encoded (see Paller &

Wagner, 2002; Spaniol, Davidson, Kim, Han, Moscovitch, & Grady, 2009, for reviews). These effects allow one to measure the neural activity that contributes to the formation of stronger, retrievable traces.

Retrieval strategy

Retrieval can be influenced by the strategy one adopts. For example, after studying a word list, I might (if I were naive) try to recall the words by working through the alphabet and retrieving items associated with each letter. If materials are organized at encoding, going through that organization at retrieval would be an ideal strategy, as discussed in Chapter 6 on organization. In addition, which order to recall a group of items is also a strategy choice; should I start at the beginning, or go in reverse order? In the case of retrieving my passport location, I tried many strategies for retrieving, such as remembering the last time I had the passport, and recalling all my recent trips.

One nice illustration of the impact of retrieval strategy comes from a clever study by Richard Anderson and James Pritchert (1978). Their participants read a story about boys skipping school, hiding out in the home of one of the boys. The story described objects contained in the home, and participants were told, during reading, to adopt the perspective of either a burglar or a homebuyer. On a later test both groups recalled a similar amount, though the items recalled were biased towards things relevant to their respective perspectives. Interestingly, however, participants received a second recall attempt, either adopting the same perspective, or an alternative one. Unsurprisingly, participants adopting the same perspective recalled the same items again; intriguingly, however, those adopting a different perspective (e.g. the perspective of a burglar, after having initially encoded and retrieved as a homebuyer), recalled significantly more items relevant to that new perspective. Thus, retrieval improved because of a mere change in retrieval strategy. This study highlights how we may often—unbeknownst to us—adopt a viewpoint when

recalling the past. This perspective provides a schematic structure that guides retrieval, constraining our recall to things relevant to the schema. To maximize recall, one might try to recall from different perspectives. We return to this idea in our discussion of the cognitive interview method in Chapter 14.

Using a retrieval strategy to increase one's recall relies on cognitive control processes that are believed to demand proper functioning of the prefrontal cortex. In fact, the development and use of a retrieval strategy is simply a more elaborated case of the process of cue-specification, described in our overview of the retrieval process earlier in this chapter. The ability to use retrieval strategies suffers a lot with prefrontal damage. For example, Felicia Gershberg and Art Shimamura found that patients with damage to the prefrontal cortex were significantly less likely to use retrieval strategies when asked to recall lists of words, compared to age-matched controls. Thus, whereas control participants would tend to retrieve items in meaningful clusters or categories, showing an orderly retrieval strategy, patients did so much less. Patients benefited greatly, however, when a strategy was provided for them (Gershberg & Shimamura, 1995). Similar deficits in retrieval strategy use also arise in older adults without brain damage, likely owing to the well-established age-related decline in frontal-lobe volume (see Chapter 13 on memory and aging).

Retrieval mode

During my passport mishap, I looked at the box containing the passport many times. I even searched the box, but it never reminded me of storing the passport. Although the box might have been weakly associated to the passport, another possibiity exists: perhaps I was in the wrong frame of mind when looking at the box. It's true that I focused attention on the box while searching it. But perhaps I was so fixated on searching it that this got in the way of memory. If I had tried to remember that event while looking at the box, it may have proven to be an effective cue.

It is worth considering that many of the stimuli in our daily lives have associations to the past, but we aren't bombarded by memories every waking second. You put on your shoes this morning, but you probably didn't remember when you bought them, even though your shoes are a perfectly good cue for that event, and even though you could probably remember that event if you wanted to. Although we are often spontaneously reminded of experiences without intending to retrieve them, it is perhaps more surprising that we are not always being reminded, given the abundance of cues around us. It seems then, that in some cases, we have to be in the right frame of mind or retrieval mode to recollect our past (Tulving, 1983).

According to research on retrieval mode, for retrieval to be effective, it is necessary to adopt a cognitive set that ensures that stimuli will be processed as probes of episodic memory. A nice illustration was reported by Herron and Wilding (2006), who measured brain electrical activity during retrieval. Participants encoded lists of words that appeared on either the left or right side of a screen. Later, they were presented with these words mixed in with new ones, and were asked to do one of two tasks on each. On episodic trials, they had to judge whether the word was one they had seen earlier, and if so, what side of the screen it had appeared on; on semantic trials, they had to judge whether the word referred to an object capable of moving on it's own (e.g. *buzzard*)—a judgment that did not require recalling what they had just seen. Importantly, each word was preceded for 4 seconds by a cue telling people which judgment they had to perform on the upcoming word. By recording brain activity over the 4 seconds when participants were getting ready to make their judgment, they could see whether there was a distinctive neural pattern linked to getting ready for retrieval. Herron and Wilding found relatively greater positive electrical brain activity over the right frontal cortex—an area involved in attentional control—when people were preparing to retrieve than when they were preparing to make a semantic judgment. Moreover, they found that when people did several episodic judgments consecutively, their judgment accuracy and speed improved with each trial, consistent with the idea that it takes time to "get into the swing" of retrieval. Thus, retrieval benefits from getting into the right mental configuration, a task accomplished by the right prefrontal cortex.

CONTEXT CUES

Although we have been discussing cues generically, it is worth highlighting one variety of cue that is quite important: context cues. Context refers to the cirumstances under which a stimulus has been encoded. For example, you would probably agree that general knowledge of the word *pomegranate* differs from the particular memory of seeing a pomegranate at the local market, or from having seen the word *pomegranate* on this page. The latter cases concern particular occasions or episodic memories, which are distinguishable by the place and time they took place (see Chapter 6 on episodic memory). The spatio-temporal or environmental context of the supermarket event includes the setting of your local market on Tuesday, for example.

Memory retrieval is often influenced by context, sometimes intentionally, other times not. When we intentionally retrieve the past, part of the cue-specification process involves isolating the part of the past we wish to recollect. If your room-mate asks whether you took out the trash, they are not asking you to recollect any event from your past in which you took out the trash. If you did not constrain retrieval to the context of the last day, you might recollect some previous occasion and falsely say you took it out. The result: one annoyed roomate. Thus, one of the cues you must include during retrieval is the spatio-temporal context of the event you are hoping to recollect.

The concept of context is not limited to spatio-temporal context, but also includes other aspects of the circumstances. The mood context of an event refers to the emotional state that a person was in when the event took place, whereas the physiological context refers to the pharmacological/physical state that one was in (e.g. under the influence of a certain drug, or alchohol). One can also distinguish cognitive context, which can mean a particular collection of concepts that one has thought about in the

Have you taken out the trash? The chances are that you have, on many occasions in your lifetime, but it is doubtful that this is what you are being asked! It is vital, therefore, to specify spatio-temporal context if you wish to retrieve a specific event (and avert a wrathful response!).

temporal vicinity of the event. In our later section on context-dependent memory, we will discuss how all of these types of context can constrain what we retrieve of our past, even when we are not aware of it. Context cues also play a role in defining the types of retrieval tasks often used to study memory.

RETRIEVAL TASKS

Each day, life leaves its boot-prints in our mental clay, and these imprints influence us in many ways. Sometimes, we are deliberate users of memory, trying to consciously recollect what happened in times past. Other times, we may not intend to be influenced by memory, but are, without being aware of it. Psychologists have devised numerous methods for testing retrieval that get at these circumstances. These tests reflect various circumstances in daily life, and differences in memory across test types have taught us important lessons about the structures and processes of memory.

Direct memory tests

Tests that ask people to retrieve their past are known as direct tests or explicit memory tests (Schacter, 1987; Richardson-Klavehn & Bjork, 1988). Because they ask people to recall particular experiences, these tests require context as a cue. Direct tests vary in the amount of cues given, the amount to be retrieved, and in the involvement of retrieval strategies. Free recall relies on context the most heavily because people must retrieve an entire set of studied items without overt cues, freely—that is, any order. For example, if you studied 25 words and then tried to recall them in any order, you would be performing free recall. Free recall mimics

KEY TERM

Direct/explicit memory tests: Any of a variety of memory assessments that overtly prompt participants to retrieve past events.

situations in daily life in which we must produce a lot of information in no particular order. Recalling who was at a party last night, recalling the items on a grocery list that you left at home, and even answering the question, "What did you do today?" are all cases of free recall. Free recall also necessitates the use of strategies for generating the answers in some order. Thus, this test is sensitive to one's skills at organizing information at encoding, and selecting strategies at retrieval. As noted earlier, frontal patients have significant difficulties with free recall.

In contrast, cued recall provides additional cues, and very often focuses on particular items in memory. In laboratory studies, this might include providing an associate of a previously studied word or an initial letter as a cue. Cued-recall tests are intended to mimic situations when we are recalling a particular item or experience in response to a cue. Recalling who drove you to the party last night, or which grocery store you went to today, are examples of cued recall. Cued recall requires context as a cue, but context is supplemented with specific information that focuses search. Cued recall is often easier than free recall, and doesn't rely as heavily on retrieval strategies to recall items.

Recognition tests are usually the easiest type of direct test, because they simply require a decision: Did you encounter this stimulus on this occasion? If, after asking you to study a set of 25 pictures or words, I presented you with those 25 items, intermixed with 25 new ones, and asked you to indicate, for each, whether you had seen it in the original list, I would be giving you a recognition test. Recognition tests pop up all the time. One especially critical example that we discuss in Chapter 14 (on eyewitness memory) is when an eyewitness is asked if anyone in a lineup was the person they saw committing a crime. Recognition tests can be accomplished in two ways, one that relies heavily on context, another that relies on it less. We will return to this in depth in a later section on recognition.

Indirect memory tests

In a famous legal case, *Bright Tunes Music v. Harrisongs Music*, George Harrison of the Beatles was sued for borrowing substantial portions of the song *He's So Fine* by the Chiffons and using them in his song *My Sweet Lord*. Harrison lost his case, even though Harrison insisted that he did not consciously copy the song. As a child, Helen Keller was accused of plagiarism due to her story *The Frost King*, which bore remarkable resemblance to Martin Canby's *The Frost Fairies*, a fairy tale that had been read to her when she was very young. Here again, Keller did not have any awareness of what she was doing, and the experience was traumatic for her. There are many apparent cases of such cryptomnesia, in which a person believes they are creating something new, such as a piece of artwork, but is recalling a similar work they have encountered. Can memories influence us unconsciously?

In fact, we are frequently influenced by our experiences, without being aware of it. Suppose, for example, you find an anagram puzzle in your newspaper. As you are trying to solve the anagram for "pomegranate," you might well find that the solution comes very easily if you had just read about pomegranates earlier in the day. Your performance on a task (anagram solving) has benefited from the experience even though you were not trying to recall the past. Many demonstrations show that such influences are possible. These examples illustrate what is known as an *indirect memory test*, which is taken as a measure of *implicit memory* (Schacter, 1987; Richardson-Klavehn & Bjork, 1988).

Indirect tests measure the influence of experience without asking the person to recall the past. These measures have a "sneaky" quality to them, in that they try to eliminate, from the participants' viewpoint, any scent that they are memorizing, or, on the test, retrieving things. In a typical implicit memory experiment, participants might first encode a list of words. For each word, people might make a simple judgment, such as whether the object denoted by the word refers to a living thing—a task chosen to not arouse suspicions that memory might be tested. Afterwards, the participants would perform a task involving some of the old words, mixed with new words. The test usually asks the person to perform some task that can be done without recalling any particular experience. Many indirect tests are possible, and there is usually a "cover story" about why the experimenter is interested in the task. In a lexical decision task, participants would receive words and nonwords (e.g. *glork*) and for each would decide, as quickly as possible, whether the letter string presented was a legal English word. In a perceptual identification task, participants receive briefly presented words (e.g. 30 milliseconds), covered by a visual mask (e.g. a row of Xs) to make it difficult to see. Their task is to simply say the word they saw. On word fragment completion tests (e.g. p–m–gr–n–t–) or word stem completion tests (po——), people would list the first word that comes to mind that fits the letters.

In each of the foregoing tests (Table 8.1), people are better at doing the task for previously viewed words, compared to new words, even when they are unaware of the connection to the prior phase: they make lexical decisions faster, identify difficult-to-see words more accurately, or generate word fragment completions more frequently. Similar tests exist for other stimuli classes, such as for pictures and sounds. Performance consistently shows characteristics that differ from those oberved on explicit tests. For example, the benefit is often sensitive to the perceptual match between encoding and test stimuli. For instance changing perceptual modalities between study and test (from hearing words at encoding, to a visual test) can reduce the benefits observed. Although many of these tests focus on perceptual qualities of the stimulus (i.e.are perceptually driven), some indirect tests measure the influence of experience on conceptual tasks, and are known as conceptually driven indirect tests. For example, if I gave you semantic categories and asked you to generate as many members of each as possible—a measure known as conceptual fluency—you would be more likely to list *buzzard* in the *birds* category than you would be if you had not read this chapter today.

How do indirect and direct tests differ? They do not necessarily differ in the core mechanisms described at the beginning of this chapter. For example, indirect tests provide cues that initiate a retrieval process that accesses a remnant of experience, perhaps through spreading activation. They do differ, however, is that indirect tests do not require recall of the past, and so context is not used intentionally as a cue. Rather, only the directly presented cues, such as the letters of the word, or the fragments of the picture, are used consciously. Despite the absence of contextual cuing, recent experience with the stimulus improves performance, a phenomenon known

TABLE 8.1 Typical types of direct and indirect retrieval tasks used in the laboratory to study explicit and implicit memory

Test category	Test type	Example retrieval instructions
Free recall	Direct/explicit	"Recall studied items in any order."
Cued recall	Direct/explicit	"What word did you study together with *leap?*"
Forced-choice recognition	Direct/explicit	"Which did you study: *ballet* or *monk?*"
Yes/No recognition	Direct/explicit	"Did you study *ballet?*"
Lexical decision	Indirect/implicit	"Is *ballet* a word? Is *mokn* a word?"
Word fragment completion	Indirect/implicit	"Fill in the missing letters to form a word: b–l–e–."
Word stem completion	Indirect/implicit	"Fill in the missing letters with anything that fits: *bal* – – –
Conceptual fluency	Indirect/implicit	"Name all the dance types you can."

as repetition priming (see Ochsner, Chiu, & Schacter, 1998 for a review). Repetition priming is widely accepted as a case in which past experience influences us unconsciously. This implicit influence does not mean that the memory traces accessed by indirect tests are identical to those that underlie episodic memory. In fact, research on the neural correlates of repetition priming indicates that it is mainly a neocortical (as opposed to hippocampal) phenomenon. For instance, stimulus repetitions are typically associated with reduced neural activity in the brain region that responds to the stimulus, a phenomenon known as *repetition suppression* (Grill-Spector, Henson, & Martin, 2006). Repetition suppression is a robust and general phenomenon thought to reflect increased efficiency of neural processing arising from persisting perceptual traces in the sensory cortex. Stimulus repetition-related reductions in neural activity have also been observed at the level of single neurons in the temporal cortex of nonhuman primates (Miller & Desimone, 1994). In contrast, explicit memory is often thought to be supported by additional contextual representations in the hippocampus. Thus, indirect tests differ both in the absence of contextual cuing, and probably in the content and neural locus of the traces which they access.

Of course, it is natural to wonder whether behavioral priming effects on indirect tests are truly unconscious. Perhaps people realize they are being tested on the earlier material, and just recall things intentionally. Indeed, not everyone is fooled. Nevertheless, even when people profess no awareness of the connection, benefits occur. Indeed, amnesic patients, who are unable to recollect much about an experience after just a few moments, show normal performance on indirect tests. This fact—that explicit memory is impaired in amnesia, but implicit memory is intact— led scientists to the view that memory is composed of multiple distinct systems (Squire, 1992; see Gabrieli, 1998 for a review). Indirect tests illustrate how the boot-prints of experience can influence us without our knowing it. All of this ought to leave us more sympathetic to George Harrison and Helen Keller.

THE IMPORTANCE OF INCIDENTAL CONTEXT IN EPISODIC MEMORY RETRIEVAL

When people retrieve the past, they use context to focus retrieval on the desired place and time. But can we be influenced by context unintentionally? Suppose that you experienced an event in one environment or mood, and later wish to retrieve that experience whilst in a different environment or mood. How will memory compare to a situation in which one is in the same location or mood at retrieval that was present at encoding? As it turns out, the match of the current context to the one we are retrieving matters, a phenomenon known as context-dependent memory. Several types of context-dependent memory exist, including environmental, mood, and state-dependent memory.

Environmental context-dependent memory

One evening, I was sitting in my home office, when I decided that I could really go for a cup of tea. After walking downstairs I found myself in the kitchen wondering why I was there. I knew that I had come downstairs for something, and that that something was in the kitchen, but I couldn't remember what it was. So I went upstairs to my home office and it popped into

---

KEY TERM

Repetition priming: Enhanced processing of a stimulus arising from recent encounters with that stimulus, a form of implicit memory.

Context-dependent memory: The finding that memory benefits when the spatio-temporal, mood, physiological, or cognitive context at retrieval matches that present at encoding.

my head: I wanted tea. Why did retrieval fail and then succeed? It seems likely that returning to the original environment reinstates the spatial context in which the event was originally encoded, aiding retrieval.

Context-dependent memory effects do in fact occur. Some years ago Duncan Godden and Alan Baddeley explored this phenomenon in connection with an applied problem, namely that of training deep-sea divers (Godden & Baddeley, 1975). Earlier experiments of Baddeley's on the effect of cold on divers had suggested quite incidentally that the underwater environment might induce strong context dependency. This suggestion was supported by the observations of a friend who was in charge of a team of divers attempting to watch the behavior of fish about to enter, or escape from, trawl nets. Initially he relied on debriefing his divers when they surfaced, only to find that they had apparently forgotten most of the fishy behavior they had seen. Eventually he had to send his divers down with underwater tape recorders so that they could give a running commentary on the fishes' activities. Intrigued by this, Godden and Baddeley set up an experiment in which divers listened to 40 unrelated words either on the beach or under about 10 feet of water. After the 40 words had been heard, the divers were tested either in the same environment or in the alternative one. The results, shown in Figure 8.4, were very clear: material learned underwater was best recalled underwater, and material learned on land was best recalled on land. Similar findings have been observed with a variety of other changes in physical context, including changes in room, and with many types of stimuli, including pictures, words, and faces.

Smith and Vela (2001) reviewed research on context-dependent memory and drew several important conclusions. One broad principle that characterizes when people show sensitivity to environmental context is that people need to pay some attention to the physical environment during encoding. If people have a more inward focus of attention during encoding, it

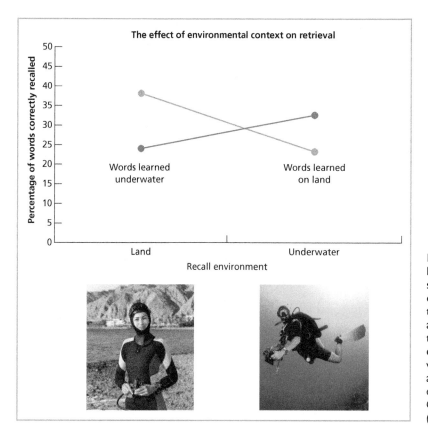

Figure 8.4 Words learned and tested in the same environment (i.e. data points falling within the top half of the graph) are better recalled than those items for which the environmental context varied between study and test (i.e. bottom half of the graph). Data from Godden and Baddeley (1975).

reduces or eliminates incidental context effects. Context-dependent memory effects also grow in size as the delay between encoding and retrieval increases, which may account for why returning to a childhood home one has not visited in a long time creates the feeling of being "flooded" with memories one has not thought about in years. Finally, and, quite usefully, the mere mental reinstatement of context greatly reduces context-dependent memory effects. Hence, if one is trying to retrieve an experience or fact encoded in a vastly different context, it is often beneficial to imagine the elements of the physical environment, such as the objects that were present, layout, and other details.

State-dependent memory

Context-dependent memory effects also occur when the learner's *internal* environment is changed by means of a drug such as alcohol, an effect known as state dependency. Goodwin and colleagues (Goodwin, Powell, Bremer, Hoine, & Stern, 1969) cite clinical evidence of this. Heavy drinkers who hide alcohol or money when drunk are unable to remember where it is hidden once they are sober; when they become drunk again, they remember. Goodwin studied this effect using a whole range of tests and found, in general, that what is learned when drunk is best recalled when drunk. Similar results have been shown with a range of other drugs, for example with nitrous oxide, sometimes used to anesthetize patients, marijuana (Eich, 1980), and even caffeine. In a review, Eich (1980) convincingly showed that state dependency is only observed when memory is tested by recall; it disappears when recognition testing is used. It appears that the participant's internal state helps to access the memory, but that when access is made easy by presenting an item for recognition, search is unnecessary.

State-dependent memory effects also occur from a variety of changes in physiological state that occur naturally. One interesting example comes from a study by Christopher Miles and Elinor Hardman (1998), who examined whether aerobic exercise might produce state-dependent memory. They had participants learn a list of auditorally presented words, either while they were resting comfortably on an exercise bicycle, or while they were pedaling the bike quickly enough to raise their heart rate to 120–150 beats per minute. Then, after rest, they asked their participants to free recall the words while at rest, or while bicycling, as before. Strikingly, people who got to recall the words in the same cardiovascular state—whether at rest both times or exercising both times—recalled the words 20% better than did people who shifted their state between encoding and recall. Thus, aspects of our physiological state get encoded incidentally as part of the episodic experience, and re-creation of that state at retrieval helps memory. Students who read course material while on their stairmaster or exercise bicycle may wish to take note of this, as should athletes who need to remember the lessons about performance learned off the field, while on the field.

Mood-congruent and mood-dependent memory

When depressed people are asked to recall autobiographical memories, they tend to recall unhappy incidents; the more depressed the individual, the more rapidly the unpleasant experience is recalled. Of course, this may simply be because depressives indeed lead less pleasant lives, explaining why they are depressed. One study avoided this problem by selecting patients whose level of depression fluctuated systematically throughout the day, as sometimes occurs in depression (Clark & Teasdale, 1982). During sad times of the day they were consistently less likely to produce happy memories than at other times. Similar results have also been obtained with normal participants, using a procedure known as the Velten technique. A happy or sad mood is induced by encouraging participants to ponder sets of sad or happy statements (Velten, 1968). While sad, participants were slower at evoking positive memories (Teasdale & Fogarty, 1979).

The preceding findings provide evidence of mood-congruent memory (Blaney, 1986).

KEY TERM

Mood-congruent memory: Bias in the recall of memories such that negative mood makes negative memories more readily available than positive, and vice versa. Unlike mood dependency, it does not affect the recall of neutral memories.

This term refers to the greater ease in recalling events that have an emotional tone that matches the current mood of the person. Thus, it is easier to recall happy memories in a happy mood, and sad memories whilst in a sad mood. Indeed, the fact that people in a depressed mood have difficulty retrieving pleasant memories, may be part of the problem of depression. If a person is depressed, he or she will be likely to recall unpleasant incidents from the past, further deepening the depression. Cognitive approaches to the treatment of depression involve helping the person to access less depressing memories and revalue the more positive aspects of their lives. Moreover, given the biases in retrieval evident in mood-congruent memory, one would do well not to make hastey decisions in a powerful mood state. If you are upset with someone, chances are that you will be biased to remember unpleasant experiences about them, even if many positive memories might otherwise be available for retrieval.

Although mood congruent memory is an interesting phenomenon, it is not a demonstration of incidental context-dependent memory, because the main thing determining recall probability is the match of the mood context being retrieved to the current mood. As such, it is not that mood state at encoding is being incidentally attached to otherwise neutral events, and acting as incidental context. To establish

Mood-congruent memory refers to the enhanced ease in recalling events that have an emotional tone similar to our current mood. If we're feeling happy and content, we are more likely to recall pleasant memories; when depressed we are likely to retrieve unpleasant ones.

such mood-dependent memory, one needs to show that the ease with which a memory is recalled depends on the match in mood states between encoding and retrieval, not merely on the congruency of what is recalled with the retrieval mood state. In one demonstration of this, Eric Eich, Dawn Macaulay, and Lee Ryan (1994) found evidence of mood-dependent memory when they asked people to generate events from their past in response to cues (e.g. *ship*, *street*). They induced participants to be in either a pleasant (P) or unpleasant (U) mood at encoding, and then again at retrieval, which took place 2 days later. Mood was induced by having participants listen to either merry or melancholy music, while entertaining elating or depressing thoughts. Once the relevant mood was established (as rated by the participant), encoding or, 2 days later, retrieval commenced. They found that free recall of the events generated 2 days earlier was better when the mood state at test matched that at encoding, irrespective of whether the event recalled was itself positive, neutral, or negative in tone.

Cognitive context-dependent memory

One's internal context also includes the particular ideas, thoughts, and concepts that have occupied our attention during encoding and retrieval. It seems safe to speculate, for example, that during Picasso's Blue Period, that blue was very much on Picasso's mind. Can the general cognitive context in which one encodes an experience influence our ability to retrieve that information later? One example of the influence of cognitive context is the tendency for language context to influence what memories one retrieves most easily.

In a nice illustration by Viorica Marian and Ulric Neisser (2000), a group of Russian–English bilinguals were asked to tell stories about their lives in response to word prompts. The participants were told that that half of the session would be conducted in English, and the other half, in Russian. Within each segment only one of the languages was spoken, and participants received cue words in that same language in response to which they were to generate a memory from any time in their lives. Interestingly, when the interview was conducted in Russian, participants generated Russian memories (i.e. memories they had experienced in a Russian-speaking context) to 64% of the those cues, whereas when the interview was conducted in English, they only generated Russian memories to 35% of the cues. The opposite pattern occurred for English memories.

Marian and Neisser argue that linguistic context acts like other forms of incidental context. They suggest that bilinguals may have two language modes, in which memories took place and were stored. When that mode is re-created by conversing in a given language, their incidental cognitive context favors retrieval of memories acquired in that mode. Other studies have replicated this pattern, and extended it to memory for academic material, and even general semantic knowledge. For example, Marian and Fausey (2006) found that bilinguals were better at remembering information (e.g. about chemistry, history, etc.) when tested in the same language in which the material was studied.

It is fascinating to think that whole segments of your life—both personal memories and general knowledge—may be rendered less accessible by the language you currently speak, a fact, if true, that must affect the sizeable portion of the planet that is bilingual. Given this, students who pursue studies in foreign countries have challenges not faced by their native language colleagues—challenges that extend beyond mastering a new language. The challenges they face provide an illustration of the influence of incidental context on the experiences that lie within our mental grasp.

Reconstructive memory

So far, we have characterized retrieval as bringing to mind an intact memory. Retrieval is sometimes more involved when we are retrieving something on the fringe of accessibility,

however. We may be able to recall aspects of the experience, but be forced to "figure out" other aspects. The term reconstructive memory refers to this active and inferential aspect of retrieval. Some of the flavor of reconstructive memory is given by the following account, which Alan Baddeley produced a few days after the experience had taken place.

November, 1978

On the train platform I notice a familiar face and I decide to see if I can remember who he is. Two associations occur, the name Sebastian and something to do with children. Sebastian seems to me to be a useful cue, but all it calls up is an association with teddy bears through Evelyn Waugh's Brideshead Revisited. I also sense there are some associations with a darkish room with books, but nothing clear enough to suggest any useful further search.

A little later, for no apparent reason, babysitting pops up and I recall that we were both members of a mutual babysitting group, that his name is indeed Sebastian, although I cannot remember his second name, and that he lives in a road whose location I am quite clear about and in a house which I could visualize easily. A clear image of his sitting-room appears, together with the fact that it contains finely printed books, and that he is by profession a printer. I remember noticing that he has a printing press in one room. I have no doubt that I have identified him.

Two days later, it occurs to me that I still have not remembered his surname or the name of the street in which he lives. I have no clues about his name, but know that he lives in either Oxford Road or Windsor Road. I have a colleague who lives in the one that Sebastian does not live in. If I have to guess, I would say that he lives in Oxford Road, and that my colleague lives in Windsor Road. I try again to remember his surname. Sebastian

---

KEY TERM

Reconstructive memory: An active and inferential process of retrieval whereby gaps in memory are filled-in based on prior experience, logic, and goals.

... Nothing. And then for no obvious reason Carter *appears. It feels right, although not overwhelmingly so. Then the association* Penny Carter *appears as his wife's name. I am sure that this is correct, reinforcing my belief that his name is Sebastian Carter.*

I go to the telephone directory. After this effort I had better be right. Carter *is indeed in Oxford Road. I ring and ask him, "Was he on the 14.36 train to Liverpool Street on Tuesday?" He was.*

This experience illustrates several important points. First, there certainly is an automatic retrieval process whereby information "pops up" for no obvious reason. The name *Sebastian* and the association with babysitting were examples. Second, when the appropriate information does not spring to mind, we seem to take the fragments and use them like a detective might use a clue. In the case of the clue *Sebastian*, Alan followed up associations, each of which could be rejected. In contrast, the vague association with children produced *babysitting* and then a clear image of the Carters' house. This in turn produced other information, including the fact that Sebastian Carter is a printer and a visual image of a printing press in his house.

Reconstruction is often driven by background knowledge that suggests plausible inferences. Such inferences may even lead us to believe we are remembering something when we are not. In one nice study, Dooling and Christiaansen (1977) gave participants the following passage to read and study:

Carol Harris's need for professional help
Carol Harris was a problem child from birth. She was wild, stubborn, and violent. By the time Carol turned eight, she was still unmanageable. Her parents were very concerned about her mental health. There was no good institution for her problem in her state. Her parents finally decided to take some action. They hired a private teacher for Carol.

The participants were tested one week later. Just before the test, half of the participants were told that the story about Carol Harris was really about Helen Keller, whereas the other half was told nothing. Interestingly, the participants told

that the story was about Helen Keller were far more likely to claim that they recognized seeing sentences like, "She was deaf, dumb, and blind," when they had not seen them. Presumably, hearing about Helen Keller just before the test activated knowledge they had about her, leading them to believe they remembered something that they did not experience. Here we have a clear example of reconstructive inference influencing what people think they remember. Such errors grow more likely as time goes by, because the original memory grows less accessible (Spiro, 1977).

Although reconstructive processes often lead to errors in recollection, they are in fact quite useful, and often result in us recalling correct information and make plausible inferences about what must have happened. Nevertheless, when veridical recall is essential (e.g. eyewitness memory), reconstructive

Helen Keller c. 1904. In Dooling and Christiaansen's (1977) study participants claimed that they had seen sentences describing Helen Keller as "deaf, dumb, and blind," when in reality they had not. This is an example of reconstructive inference influencing what people think they remember.

errors can have grave consequences. A person who witnesses a fight and later unintentionally misrecollects who started the fight based on stereotype-based reconstructive memory is a serious danger to the accused.

RECOGNITION MEMORY

Thus far, we have focused on free and cued recall as models of retrieval. Very often, however, we use our memories not to generate things, but to make a decision about whether we have encountered a stimulus. We may scan a list of phone numbers in hopes of picking out the one we wish to dial; we may see a person on the street and wonder whether we have met them before; or we may be called upon to identify the perpetrator of a crime in a police lineup. This situation, known as recognition memory, warrants a special discussion because different processes are engaged. Unlike recall, recognition presents the intact stimulus, and hence requires a judgment: did you see this stimulus in a certain context? A number of consequences follow from this that pertain to the measurement of recognition, and to the way that people solve the task.

First, recognition tests fundamentally require a discrimination between stimuli that a person experienced in a particular context, and things that they didn't. Because the person must discriminate "old" from "new," a test is only meaningful if it includes both old *and* new items, forcing the rememberer to show their skill at making good discriminations. These nonstudied items are called distractors, *lures*, or sometimes *foils*, and are akin to the other members of the lineup that the police think are innocent. In laboratory research, distractors are sometimes presented together with the old item, and the person must choose one of the items, which is known as a *forced-choice recognition test*. Other tests present one item at a time, and ask people to make a yes or no decision to each, with old and new items intermixed. This is known as a *yes/no recognition test*. Distractors on such tests provide valuable information about how much a person's recognition judgment can be trusted.

How do we take people's responses to distractors into account? In measuring recogntion for a set of material, a single error does not make someone's retention bad. People with good memory sometimes make mistakes. If so, how do we take the number of mistaken identifications into account? Should somebody with 10% mistaken recognitions be judged as having deficient retention? If so, then is the memory of a person with 10% mistaken recognitions necessarily less good than a person with 5%? What about someone who correctly identifies 85% of the old items, but has 10% mistaken identifications? Is that person's memory worse than someone who recognizes 40% of the old items, but only has 5% mistaken identifications?

To make matters worse, we need to consider people's tendencies for guessing when making a recognition judgment. Sometimes an incorrect judgment of "Yes" to a new item does not reflect a sincere belief in having seen the item (unlike our hypothetical eyewitness), but rather the person's uncertainty together with a need to make a decision. For the same reason, some of the "Yes" responses to old items will reflect guessing. Indeed, in police lineups, the social situation puts pressure on witnesses to identify somebody, leading some people to guess, based on who seems familiar. To see how much influence guessing can have, imagine two participants given a recognition task. Person A is told that there will be both old and new items on the test, but that there will be no penalty for incorrectly circling new items; Person B is told that incorrect responses to new items will be harshly penalized. The latter person will surely be more conservative than the former, greatly reducing their tendency to respond "Yes" to new items, and also their "Yes" responses to old items about which they are somewhat unsure. Clearly, guessing is an issue, and the rate of guessing can vary, depending on people's biases.

This discussion raises a general issue in measuring recognition memory: distinguishing memory from decision making. Some means of estimating the amount of information in memory is essential, and this method must separate out judgment biases. To devise such a method, however, requires a theory of the memory processes that enter in a recognition judgment. We discuss such an approach next.

Signal detection theory as a model of recognition memory

One approach to understanding recognition builds on the concepts developed in signal detection theory, which evolved in research on auditory perception (Green & Swets, 1966). In a typical auditory detection experiment, people listen for a faint tone presented in a background of white noise, and are instructed to press a button if they detect a tone. Depending on how faint the tone is, people will not be perfect, and so four types of event occur. A tone might be presented, and the person might correctly claim that he/she heard it, which is known as a *hit*. Sometimes tones are presented that people do not detect; this is a *miss*. When a tone is not presented, people sometimes mistakenly claim that they heard a tone, which is called a *false alarm*. Finally, people quite often claim not to have heard a tone when the tone was not presented, which is called a *correct rejection*.

A similar situation exists on a yes/no recognition test. On a recognition test, a person must decide whether they sense "familiarity" in the stimulus. Deciding if a stimulus seems familiar enough to classify as "old" is like deciding whether there is enough auditory evidence to claim you heard a tone. As with auditory detection, four outcomes are possible. If the item was studied, and the person correctly classifies it as "old," it's a hit; if it is old, but misclassified as "new," it is a miss. If the item is new, and the person misclassifies it as "old," it is a false alarm, and if they correctly judge it as "new," it is a correct rejection.

Signal detection theory provides a useful way of thinking about recognition that comes with tools necessary to distinguish true memory and guessing. Signal detection theory proposes that memory traces have *strength values* (see the discussion of activation level above, p. 205) that reflect their activation in memory, which dictate how familiar they seem. Traces are thought to vary in their familiarity, depending on how much attention the item received at encoding, or how many times it was repeated. Importantly, the theory assumes that new items will have familiarity as well, though usually less than items that have been studied. Their familiarity might arise if the new items have been seen frequently outside the experiment, or, instead, if they are similar to studied items. In terms of the police lineup example, a person may seem powerfully familiar to a witness because the witness saw them before (just not at the crime), or because they look a lot like the actual perpetrator.

But how do these ideas help? One key idea is that the familiarity of a set of items is normally distributed, and that the studied and new items each have their own distributions. These distributions are likely to vary in the average level of familiarity. In most cases, the average familiarity for studied (old) items will be higher than the average for new items, due to the recent exposure of old items; although, as illustrated in Figure 8.5, these distributions may overlap. This overlap arises because some old items may have been encoded poorly, and so will not have received much of a boost in memory strength, whereas some new items may seem especially familiar. For some participants, these distributions may be very close, with only a minimal difference in average familiarity across the old and new distributions. For others, these distributions might

KEY TERM

Signal detection theory: A model of recognition memory that posits that memory targets (signals) and lures (noise) on a recognition test possess an attribute known as strength or familiarity, which occurs in a graded fashion, with previously encountered items generally possessing more strength that novel items. The process of recognition involves ascertaining a given test item's strength and then deciding whether it exceeds a criterion level of strength, above which items are considered to be previously encountered. Signal detection theory provides analytic tools that separate true memory from judgment biases in recognition.

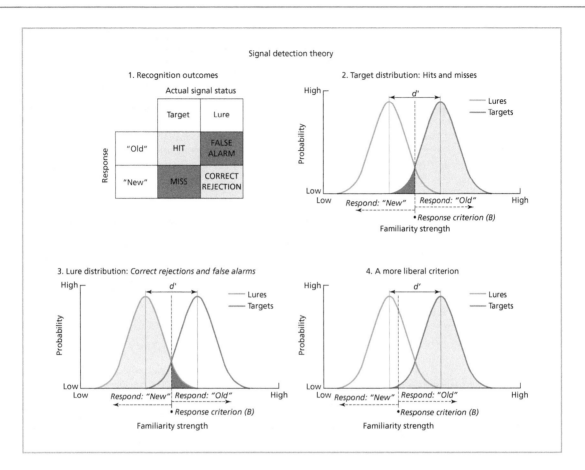

Figure 8.5 Recognition outcomes, jointly based on item (signal) status and the participant's response. (2) Familiarity distributions for targets and lures. Hits are in green; misses in red. (3) Correct rejections (green) and false alarms (red). (4) Shifting the response criterion leftward increases hits and false alarms.

be very far apart, and even nonoverlapping, if they studied the list quite well. Increasing study time, or the number of repetitions of each studied item, would also push the old distribution farther away from new items, increasing overall familiarity.

Importantly, how well a person can discriminate studied from new items depends on the difference in the average familiarity between their old and new distributions. In other words, a participants' ability to discriminate two sets of items can be measured by the distance between the averages of the old and new distributions, as shown in Figure 8.5. In the language of signal detection theory, this distance is known as d′ ("d prime").

But how does a recognition judgment take place? To address this issue, the theory proposes that people choose a *criterion* level of familiarity, above which they will judge a test item as old, and below which they will judge an item as new. The bottom-right panel of Figure 8.5 illustrates one positioning of the criterion on the familiarity continuium. Notice that by placing the criterion in this location, some old items will fall below the criterion for "oldness," and so will be classified as misses. Old items that fall above the criterion, however, will be "hits." Similarly, some new items will have familarity that exceeds the criterion, leading people to classsify them incorrectly as old; these are false alarms. New items falling below the criterion will be classifed as correct rejections. Thus, our four outcomes (hit, miss, false alarm, correct rejection) can be understood, given their familiarity, relative to the criterion and status (old or new).

The idea that people set a criterion for judging "oldness" helps to define what a judgment bias is. To see this, notice what would happen if the criterion is "loosened" by shifting it farther to the left on the familarity continuium, allowing less familiar items to be classified as "old." This would ensure that the vast majority of old items will be hits, and there will be very few misses. Unfortunately, this would also increase the proportion of new items judged as old, and so will increase the false alarm rate. When the criterion is made strict (shifted to the right), a complementary thing happens: People will be unlikely to commit a false alarm, but will suffer increased misses. These two ways of shifting the criterion describe what happens when a person adopts either a liberal or conservative guessing strategy, respectively. By placing the criterion between the means of the two distributions, the person would be unbiased. The familiarity value at which a person places their criterion is referred to as β (beta), and estimates the tendency to guess.

Given this analysis, signal detection theory provides mathematical tools for estimating a person's ability to discriminate old from new items and their guessing strategies. By computing a person's hit rate (proportion of old items judged old) and their false alarm rate (proportion of new items judged old), one can compute d′ and β and so disentangle these factors. More importantly, signal detection theory provides a conceptualization of how recognition judgments take place. The idea that memories lie on a continuium of strength, and that people use this internal "sense" of familiarity to judge their experience with an item has proved to be an extremely useful theory.

Certain phenomena appear challenging, however, for signal detection theory to explain. For example, on free recall tests, words used frequently in a language are better recalled than are words used infrequently. This advantage makes sense considering that high-frequency words, by virtue of repetition, are likely to be represented more strongly in

memory than are low-frequency words, and therefore should be easier to encode (Hall, 1954; Sumby, 1963). If item strength underlies this effect, high-frequency words should also be better recognized according to signal detection theory. In fact, the opposite occurs: low-frequency words are better recognized than high-frequency words, a phenomenon known as the *word frequency effect* in recognition memory (e.g. Gorman, 1961; Kinsbourne & George, 1974; Glanzer & Bowles, 1976). The word frequency effect thus suggests that some factor other than item strength must contribute to recognition memory. For these and other reasons, many theorists believe that another process contributes to recognition—a process that is much more akin to recall. We discuss this view next.

Dual-process accounts of recognition memory

Seeking technical advice one afternoon, I made my way to the Media Services Office, where a pleasant woman greeted me, all smiles. Responding in kind, I extended my hand, introducing myself saying, "Hi, I'm Mike Anderson from the Psychology department, and I was wondering if there was someone here who might help me with my website." She looked at me blankly, paused, and said, "I know who you are." She did look exceedingly familiar, but I wasn't sure where from. She said, "You really don't remember, do you?" I had to admit that I couldn't place her. She explained that we had gone on a date several years earlier—a date lasting *6 hours*. The date took place in an entirely different city (where she used to live) several hours from where we currently were. The moment she revealed this, I remembered the whole context, and recognized her completely, offering embarassed apologies. Good friends now, she will never let me forget this event.

This story illustrates something that has happened to most of us—the experience of *knowing* somebody (or some thing), without having the ability to *remember* where from. The experience illustrates an important point: One can have a very high degree of familiarity for a stimulus, but still feel as though their recognition is incomplete. It seems as though recognition judgments can be made in one of two ways: You can make a judgment based on how familiar a stimulus seems, a process known as familiarity-based recognition; alternatively, you can recognize something by recalling the particulars of the experience, a process known as recollection. According to dual-process theories of recognition, both of these processes contribute to recognition (e.g. Atkinson & Juola, 1974; Mandler, 1980; Jacoby & Dallas, 1981; Aggleton & Brown, 1999; Yonelinas, 1999). The familiarity process is characterized as fast and automatic, yielding, as output, a perception of the memory's strength, without the recall of particulars. It is well characterized by signal detection theory. The recollection process, by contrast, is slow, and more attention demanding, much more like the recall processes emphasized in the earlier part of this chapter—cued recall, to be precise. It involves generating information about the context of experiencing the stimulus.

A number of methods have been developed to isolate the contributions of recollection and familiarity. One method, known as the remember/know procedure (Tulving, 1985), asks people to make judgments on the test about why they feel they recognize the item. In particular, people are asked to report whether they recognize each item on the basis of *remembering* (i.e. consciously recollecting the particulars of the study event), or *knowing* (i.e. judging that the item seems very familiar, in the absence of memory for the details of the event). "Remember" responses are taken to measure recollection, whereas "know" responses are taken to measure familiarity-based recognition (Yonelinas, 2002; see also, Gardiner, Ramponi, & Richardson-Klavehn, 2000). Other methods relying instead on people's ability to prove that they can recollect the details of the conditions under which they encountered an item. For instance, in the process dissociation procedure (Jacoby, 1991), participants might study a visually presented list of words, followed by a second list of auditorally presented items. On the later recognition test, one group of participants is told to say "Yes" for each test item they remember encountering in *either* the seen or

the heard list (the inclusion condition). A different group is asked to say "Yes" *only* to items from the list they heard (i.e. the exclusion condition). In the inclusion condition, people's correct recognition of visually presented items (from the first list) should mix items they recognize based on familiarity, and items they recognize based on recollection. To measure how much of a person's performance is due to the recollection process, we need a way to "subtract out" familiarity. Thus, we need an estimate of familiarity, in the absence of recollection. Cleverly, this can be estimated from people's errors in the exclusion condition. That is, when people are

KEY TERM

Familiarity-based recognition: A fast, automatic recognition process based on the perception of a memory's strength. Proponents of dual process models consider familiarity to be independent of the contextual information characteristic of recollection.

Recollection: The slower, more attention-demanding component of recognition memory in dual process models, which involves retrieval of contextual information about the memory.

Dual-process theories of recognition: A class of recognition models that assumes that recognition memory judgments can be based on two independent forms of retrieval process: recollection and familiarity.

Remember/know procedure: A procedure used on recognition memory tests to separate the influences of familiarity and recollection on recognition performance. For each test item, participants report whether it is recognized because the person can recollect contextual details of seeing the item (classified as a "remember" response) or because the item seems familiar, in the absence of specific recollections (classified as "know" response).

Process dissociation procedure (PDP): A technique for parceling out the contributions of recollection and familiarity within a recognition task.

specifically asked to only say "Yes" to an item if they heard it in the second list, then if they accidentally say "Yes" to an item that had been visually presented, it must imply that the item is familiar, but that people can't remember for sure where the item is from, and so could not be recollecting it. So, recollection can be estimated by simply subtracting these erroneous errors from the overall recognition rate of items from List One in the inclusion condition. These methods can thus be used to isolate the contributions of recollection and familiarity.

In a review of research using these and other methods to measure familiarity and recollection, Andrew Yonelinas (Yonelinas, 2002) identified several generalizations that support the distinction between these processes. First, estimates of whether someone can recollect a stimulus appear to be far more senstive to disruption by distraction. If your attention is divided during an experience, you are less likely later to have the ability to recollect it, but the stimuli involved in the experience may remain familiar. Similarly, distraction during the recognition test itself is consistently more disruptive to recollection than it is to judgments of familiarity. These findings support the claim that recollection is a controlled, attention-demanding process. Consistent with this view, groups with diminished attention such as older adults and patients with damage to the prefrontal cortex, often show deficits in recollection, but an intact sense of familiarity for recently seen stimuli. Information about how familiar a stimulus seems is also retrieved much more quickly than information necessary for recollection, consistent with the view that familarity judgments reflect an automatic process. These findings strongly support the view that two qualitatively distinct retrieval processes underlie recognition.

Familiarity and recollection are supported by distinct structures within the medial temporal lobes. Recalling past experiences, along with their spatial-temporal context relies critically on the hippocampus. The feeling of familiarity, on the other hand, relies on traces in the perirhinal cortex, a brain region adjacent to the hippocampus. You may remember from Chapter 6 (on episodic memory), the case of Jon, a developmental amnesic patient. At birth, Jon had breathing problems and was deprived of oxygen, and, as a result, he suffered remarkably selective damage to his hippocampus. Over two decades later, Jon is now an adult with profound deficits in episodic recollection, showing severely impaired ability to remember particular events. Nevertheless, Jon exhibits above-average intelligence, a normal vocabulary, and he possesses a surprisingly intact sense of familiarity for stimuli to which he has been exposed (we will discuss Jon at greater length in Chapter 16 on amnesia). Interestingly, Jon's perirhinal cortex was largely spared from damage, perhaps accounting for his intact sense of familiarity. A large body of neuroimaging research in neurologically normal participants indicates that familiarity and recollection are dependent on the perirhinal cortex and hippocampus, respectively (Eichenbaum, Yonelinas, & Ranganath, 2007). For example, using the remember /know procedure, Laura Eldridge and colleagues, showed that when people claimed to consciously recollect seeing a word in an earlier study phase (i.e. they gave a "remember" response), they showed significantly greater hippocampal activation than when they claimed to simply "know" that they saw it, without conscious recollection (Eldrige, Knowlton, Furmanski, Bookheimer, & Engel, 2000), a finding well supported in subsequent work (for a review, see Spaniol et al., 2009). Activity in the perirhinal cortex during retrieval, however, is related to the degree of familiarity that one experiences (Montaldi, Spencer, Roberts, & Mayes, 2006).

I have, of course, explained all of the foregoing research to my (now) friend, whom I had forgotten that I had dated. I told her that I simply had a momentary lapse of recollection, perhaps due to failure to engage the hippocampal retrieval processes that support recollection, upon sensing the rhinal cortex activity indicating that she was familiar. This of course only led to more sophisticated jokes at my expense. There can be an upside to not being able to consciously recollect some things, however. Indeed, Faraneh Vargha-Kadem, who studied Jon and other developmental amnesics, has remarked that they consistently exude a pleasant demeanor, never seeming too upset for too long, or holding grudges (unlike my friend). The capacity to forget may indeed be quite useful, which is a topic we will take up again in Chapter 10 (on motivated forgetting).

SOURCE MONITORING

We have talked about retrieval as re-activating a trace based on cues. We often have need, however, to identify the source of what we retrieve. We have already discussed the need to recall the context of an event. Did we take our pills today or yesterday, and did I park here today, or last week? But this is only one case of the broader need to distinguish the sources of one's recollections. Did I hear this story from Susan or Maria? Did I learn this fact from the *National Enquirer* or *Consumer Reports*? Did I *see* the person perform this action, or did somebody *tell* me about it? The processes of examining the origins of what we retrieve and deciding whether it is from a particular source is known as source monitoring (Johnson, Hashtroudi, & Lindsay, 1993). Source monitoring is an example of the post-retrieval monitoring process discussed in our initial characterization of the retrieval process, and requires controlled processes mediated by the prefrontal cortex (see, Mitchell & Johnson, 2009; Spaniol et al. 2009 for reviews).

Unfortunately, people are not always careful in monitoring where their recollections come from, and so make mistakes. Such mistakes sometimes occur when people let their guard down, as in casual conversations, in which it may not seem important to be sure of the source. For example, you may recall that Maria told you something, when Susan did, and get Maria into trouble. Grandparents may misremember which grandchild is interested in which hobby, or whether they have told you their most recent favorite joke, or someone else. When you misattribute the source of your recollections, it is referred to as as a *source misattribution error*.

How do people monitor the sources of their memories? To evaluate source, contextual details need to be recollected so that people can ascertain a memory's origins. According to Marcia Johnson and colleagues, this occurs by exploiting regularities in the information we receive from different sources. For example, if we need to decide whether we learned a fact by hearing it or reading it, we would evaluate the auditory detail and visual detail in the trace. An abundance of auditory detail would allow us to conclude that we heard it, whereas the converse would be true for visual detail. In deciding whether something we have recalled was a real experience or was imagined, the relative prevalance of perceptual detail as opposed to memory for cognitive operations (e.g. as would be involved in generating an image) would guide our decision about the memory's "realness." Of course, people make mistakes. When someone is induced to form a mental image of a word, he/she is more likely to later mistakenly claim he/she saw a picture of the object (Henkel, Franklin, & Johnson, 2000). This reflects an unintended consequence of relying upon the above strategies, with people mistaking imagined details for perceptual experience. Breakdowns in source monitoring may be partially responsible for delusions in which people cannot distinguish their imaginings from true occurrences. We return to a discussion of source misattribution errors in Chapter 10 in our discussion of motivated forgetting, and in Chapter 14, on eyewitness memory.

CONCLUDING REMARKS

As we all know retrieval sometimes fails, even given effective encoding. Retrieval failures of the sort experienced by the author at the outset of this chapter clearly can arise from a variety of sources. It is important to understand the circumstances under which retrieval fails so that we can understand how retrieval works. When retrieval fails, it raises the question of whether information is truly there, or has been forgotten. In the next chapter, we turn to the subject of forgetting.

KEY TERM

Source monitoring: The process of examining the contextual origins of a memory in order to determine whether it was encoded from a particular source.

SUMMARY

- Memory can fail us because retrieval processes fail, even when a memory trace has been successfully stored.
- The "tip-of-the-tongue" state arises when we cannot think of a proper name or a word for a concept, even though we feel we know it.
- Patients with damage to the prefrontal cortex show substantial difficulties in recall, due to the disruption of control processes that support retrieval
- Retrieval can be conceptualized as the effort to activate a target trace, given one or more cues, via a process of spreading activation. Activation spreads via associations in proportion to their strength.
- Memories are likely to be complex constellations of features, the majority of which need to be activated by spreading activation processes for a memory to be retrieved. The retrieval of the remainder of a memory, given a portion of it as cues, is known as pattern completion.
- Intentional retrieval (as opposed to incidental reminding) requires other controlled processes such as cue-specification, cue-maintenance, interference resolution, and post-retrieval monitoring, most of which depend upon the integrity of the prefrontal cortex.
- Retrieving a prior experience is thought to be accomplished, in part, by the reinstatement of the cortical pattern of activity present when an event was first perceived, including the particular sensory cortices that represent the sights, sounds, and spatial locations of the event.
- Retrieval processes can break down when the cues are inappropriate or are only weakly associated to the target, when the target is poorly learned, when we cannot devote adequate attention to retrieval, when we do not have enough cues, or even when we are in the wrong "frame of mind" when retrieving.
- Retrieval success is also influenced, often without our realizing it, by elements of the incidental context at retrieval, and their match to those present at encoding, including environmental, state, mood, and cognitive context.
- Retrieval strategy can influence performance, especially when large amounts of information need to be recalled.
- There are different ways of testing memory retrieval, some of which rely on intentional conscious recall of the past (direct tests), others of which test memory indirectly by measuring its influence on some incidental task (indirect tests).
- Free recall, cued recall, and recognition are direct tests, all of which require the use of a context cue to direct search, although reliance on context cues is thought to be greatest on recall tests, especially free recall. Direct tests generally measure explicit memory.
- Indirect tests do not make reference to memory and thus do not specify contextual cues in the retrieval process, providing a measure of implicit memory.
- Implicit memory phenomena, such as repetition priming, provide evidence of the unconscious influence of memory on behavior and perception, and are largely intact in amnesic patients.
- Repetition priming is thought to rely more on neocortical representations rather than hippocampal representations.
- Repetition suppression is thought to be a neural manifestation of repetition priming, reflecting decreased neural demand to process the same stimulus more than once.

- Explicit memory reflects the contribution of additional brain structures, including the hippocampus, to recall contextual aspects of an experience.
- Memory can also be tested with a recognition test, which requires a judgment about when a stimulus has been encountered before. Recognition is thought to be accomplished by not one, but two psychological processes: familiarity and recollection.
- Signal detection theory has been used to characterize the retrieval processes underlying recognition memory. There is debate about whether signal detection theory can provide an account of all recognition memory, or simply the familiarity component
- Recollection is thought to be a slower, more attention-demanding process, which requires recall of greater contextual detail.
- Many modern theories of the role of the medial temporal lobes in memory distinguish between a contextual recollection process mediated by the hippocampus, and a familiarity process mediated by the rhinal cortex.
- Retrieval is quite often reconstructive in nature, involving not merely the re-activation of traces by spreading activation, but also a process of inference and problem solving. Reconstruction can sometimes lead to memory distortions when general knowledge is used to fill in the gaps of incomplete memories, or to interpret fragmentary recollections.
- People routinely infer the source of what they remember, for example, to ascertain whether a recalled trace is the one they sought, is trustworthy, and, is in fact, a memory or something imagined.
- Attributing a source to a memory involves considering the attributes of the trace recalled, in relation to what would be expected to be stored in memory, given a source.
- Source misattribution errors reflect one way in which retrieval can break down through an error of commission, rather than omission.

POINTS FOR DISCUSSION

Pick three real examples of something that you recently recalled from memory. Drawing on what you learned about the retrieval process, analyze your examples. What were the cues? What type of retrieval situation was it? What type of context cue was present? Try to be thorough in describing the steps and processes involved, using concepts learned throughout the chapter.

Describe what context is, including its different types. Describe when it does and does not come into play in retrieving information from memory.

While walking across campus, you see your Memory professor and approach her to say hello. She nervously admits knowing that you are familiar, but cannot place you. Seeing your golden opportunity, you explain to the professor what type of test they just did, what aspects of memory they just failed at, and what parts of the brain were involved. What would you say to them to ensure that they were impressed?

How is human memory retrieval similar to and different from doing a search in Google? What parallels can you find?

FURTHER READING

Danker, J. F., & Anderson, J. R. (2010). The ghosts of brain states past: Remembering reactivates the brain regions engaged during encoding. *Psychological Bulletin*, *136*(1), 87.

Eichenbaum, H., Yonelinas, A. R., & Ranganath, C. (2007). The medial temporal lobe and recognition memory. *Annual Review of Neuroscience*, *30*, 123.

Mitchell, K. J., & Johnson, M. K. (2009). Source monitoring 15 years later: What have we learned from fMRI about the neural mechanisms of source memory? *Psychological Bulletin*, *135*(4), 638.

Roediger, H. L., & Guynn, M. J. (1996). Retrieval processes. In *Memory* (Vol. 10, pp. 197–236). San Diego, CA: Academic Press.

Rugg, M. D., & Vilberg, K. L. (2012). Brain networks underlying episodic memory retrieval. *Current Opinion in Neurobiology*, *23*, 255–260.

Yonelinas, A. P. (2002). The nature of recollection and familiarity: A review of 30 years of research. *Journal of Memory and Language*, *46*, 441–517.

Box 8.2 Answers to Box 8.1

	Country	Capital city
1	Norway	Oslo
2	Turkey	Ankara
3	Kenya	Nairobi
4	Uruguay	Montevideo
5	Finland	Helsinki
6	Australia	Canberra
7	Saudi Arabia	Riyadh
8	Romania	Bucharest
9	Portugal	Lisbon
10	Bulgaria	Sofia

	Country	Capital city
11	South Korea	Seoul
12	Syria	Damascus
13	Denmark	Copenhagen
14	Sudan	Khartoum
15	Nicaragua	Managua
16	Ecuador	Quito
17	Colombia	Bogota
18	Afghanistan	Kabul
19	Thailand	Bangkok
20	Venezuela	Caracas

REFERENCES

Aggleton, J. P., & Brown, M. W. (1999). Episodic memory, amnesia, and the hippocampal–anterior thalamic axis. *Behavioral and Brain Sciences*, *22*(3), 425–489.

Anderson, R. C., & Pichert, J. W. (1978). Recall of previously unrecallable information following a shift in perspective. *Journal of Verbal Learning and Verbal Behavior, 17*(1), 1–12.

Atkinson, R. C., & Juola, J. F. (1974). Search and decision processes in recognition memory. In D. H. Kroutz, R. C. Atkinson, & P. Suppes (Eds.), *Contemporary developments in mathematical psychology.* San Francisco, CA: Freeman.

Baddeley, A., Lewis, V., Eldridge, M., & Thomson, N. (1984). Attention and retrieval from long-term memory. *Journal of Experimental Psychology: General, 113*(4), 518–540.

Badre, D., & Wagner, A. D. (2007). Left ventrolateral prefrontal cortex and the cognitive control of memory. *Neuropsychologia, 45*(13), 2883–2901.

Barclay, J. R., Bransford, J. D., Franks, J. J., McCarrell, N., & Nitsch, K. (1974). Comprehension and semantic flexibility. *Journal of Verbal Learning and Verbal Behavior, 13,* 471–481.

Blaney, P. H. (1986). Affect and memory: A review. *Psychological Bulletin, 99*(2), 229–246.

Brown, R., & McNeill, D. (1966). The "tip of the tongue" phenomenon. *Journal of Verbal Learning and Verbal Behavior, 5*(4), 325–337.

Clark, D. M., & Teasdale, J. D. (1982). Diurnal variation in clinical depression and accessibility of memories of positive and negative experiences. *Journal of Abnormal Psychology, 91*(2), 87–95.

Craik, F. I., Govoni, R., Naveh-Benjamin, M., & Anderson, N. D. (1996). The effects of divided attention on encoding and retrieval processes in human memory. *Journal of Experimental Psychology: General, 125*(2), 159–180.

Danker, J. F., & Anderson, J. R. (2010). The ghosts of brain states past: Remembering reactivates the brain regions engaged during encoding. *Psychological Bulletin, 136*(1), 87.

Della Salla, S., Laiacona, M., Spinnler, H., & Trivelli, C. (1993). Autobiographical recollection and frontal damage. *Neuropsychologia, 31,* 823–839

Dooling, D. J., & Christiaansen, R. E. (1977). Episodic and semantic aspects of memory for prose. *Journal of Experimental Psychology: Human Learning and Memory, 3,* 428–436.

Eich, E., Macaulay, D., & Ryan, L. (1994). Mood dependent memory for events of the personal past. *Journal of Experimental Psychology: General, 123*(2), 201–215.

Eich, J. E. (1980). The cue-dependent nature of state-dependent retrieval. *Memory and Cognition, 8*(2), 157–173.

Eichenbaum, H., Yonelinas, A. R., & Ranganath, C. (2007). The medial temporal lobe and recognition memory. *Annual Review of Neuroscience, 30,* 123.

Eldridge, L. L., Knowlton, B. J., Furmanski, C. S., Bookheimer, S. Y., & Engel, S. A. (2000). Remembering episodes: A selective role for the hippocampus during retrieval. *Nature neuroscience, 3*(11), 1149–1152.

Fernandes, M. A., & Moscovitch, M. (2000). Divided attention and memory: Evidence of substantial interference effects at retrieval and encoding. *Journal of Experimental Psychology: General, 129*(2), 155–176.

Fernandes, M. A., & Moscovitch, M. (2003). Interference effects from divided attention during retrieval in younger and older adults. *Psychology of Aging, 18*(2), 219–230.

Gabrieli, J. D. (1998). Cognitive neuroscience of human memory. *Annual Reviews in Psychology, 49,* 87–115.

Gardiner, J. M., Ramponi, C., & Richardson-Klavehn, A. (2000). Response deadline and subjective awareness in recognition memory. *Consciousness and Cognition, 8*(4), 484–496.

Gershberg, F. B., & Shimamura, A. P. (1995). Impaired use of organizational strategies in free recall following frontal lobe damage. *Neuropsychologia, 33*(10), 1305–1333.

Glanzer, M., & Bowles, N. (1976). Analysis of the word-frequency effect in recognition memory. *Journal of Experimental Psychology: Human Learning and Memory, 2*(1), 21–31.

Godden, D. R., & Baddeley, A. (1975). Context-dependent memory in two natural environments: On land and underwater. *British Journal of Psychology, 66*(3), 325–331.

Goodwin, D. W., Powell, B., Bremer, D., Hoine, H., & Stern, J. (1969). Alcohol and recall: State-dependent effects in man. *Science, 163*(3873), 1358–1360.

Gorman, A. M. (1961). Recognition memory for nouns as a function of abstractness and frequency. *Journal of Experimental Psychology, 61,* 23–29.

Green, D. M., & Swets, J. A. (1966). *Signal detection theory and psychophysics.* New York: Wiley.

Grill-Spector, K., Henson, R., & Martin, A. (2006). Repetition and the brain: Neural models of stimulus-specific effects. *Trends in cognitive sciences, 10*(1), 14–23.

Hall, J. F. (1954). Learning as a function of word-frequency. *The American Journal of Psychology, 67*(1), 138–140.

Henkel, L. A., Franklin, N., & Johnson, M. K. (2000). Cross-modal source monitoring confusions between perceived and imagined events. *Journal of Experimental Psychology: Learning, Memory and Cognition, 26,* 321–335.

Herron, J. E., & Wilding, E. L. (2006). Neural correlates of control processes engaged before and during recovery of information from episodic memory. *NeuroImage, 30*, 634–644.

Jacoby, L. L. (1991). A process dissociation framework: Separating automatic from intentional uses of memory. *Journal of Memory and Language, 30*(5), 513–541.

Jacoby, L. L., & Dallas, M. (1981). On the relationship between autobiographical memory and perceptual learning. *Journal of Experimental Psychology: General, 110*(3), 306–340.

Johnson, M. K., Hashtroudi, S., & Lindsay, D. S. (1993). Source monitoring. *Psychological Bulletin, 114*(1), 3–28.

Kinsbourne, M., & George, J. (1974). The mechanism of the word-frequency effect on recognition memory. *Journal of Verbal Learning and Verbal Behavior, 13*(1), 63–69.

Mandler, G. (1980). Recognizing: The judgment of previous occurrence. *Psychological Review, 87*, 252–271.

Mangels, J. A., Gershberg, F. B., Shimamura, A. P., & Knight, R. T. (1996). Impaired retrieval from remote memory in patients with frontal lobe damage. *Neuropsychology, 10*(1), 32.

Marian, V., & Fausey, C. M. (2006). Language-dependent memory in bilingual learning. *Applied Cognitive Psychology, 20*(8), 1025–1047.

Marian, V., & Neisser, U. (2000). Language-dependent recall of autobiographical memories. *Journal of Experimental Psychology: General, 129*(3), 361–368.

Miles, C., & Hardman, E. (1998). State-dependent memory produced by aerobic exercise. *Ergonomics, 41*(1), 20–28.

Miller, E. K., & Desimone, R. (1994). Parallel neuronal mechanisms for short-term memory. *Science, 263*(5146), 520–522.

Mitchell, K. J., & Johnson, M. K. (2009). Source monitoring 15 years later: What have we learned from fMRI about the neural mechanisms of source memory? *Psychological bulletin, 135*(4), 638.

Montaldi, D., Spencer, T. J., Roberts, N., & Mayes, A. R. (2006). The neural system that mediates familiarity memory. *Hippocampus, 16*(5), 504–520.

Ochsner, K. N., Chiu, C. Y. P., & Schacter, D. L. (1998). Varieties of priming. *Current Opinion in Neurobiology, 4*, 189–194.

Paller, K. A., & Wagner, A. D. (2002). Observing the transformation of experience into memory. *Trends in Cognitive Sciences, 6*(2), 93–102.

Richardson-Klavehn, A., & Bjork, R. A. (1988). Measures of memory. *Annual Reviews in Psychology, 39*, 475–543.

Rohrer, D., & Pashler, H. E. (2003). Concurrent task effects on memory retrieval. *Psychonomic Bulletin and Review, 10*(1), 96–103.

Rubin, D. C., & Wallace, W. T. (1989). Rhyme and reason: Analyses of dual retrieval cues. *Journal of Experimental Psychology: Learning, Memory, and Cognition, 15*(4), 698–709.

Schacter, D. L. (1987). Implicit memory: History and current status. *Journal of Experimental Psychology: Learning, Memory, and Cognition, 13*(3), 501–518.

Simons, J. S., & Spiers, H. J. (2003). Prefrontal and medial temporal lobe interactions in long-term memory. *Nature Reviews Neuroscience, 4*(8), 637–648.

Smith, S. M., & Vela, E. (2001). Environmental context-dependent memory: A review and meta-analysis. *Psychonomic Bulletin and Review, 8*(2), 203–220.

Spaniol, J., Davidson, P. S., Kim, A. S., Han, H., Moscovitch, M., & Grady, C. L. (2009). Event-related fMRI studies of episodic encoding and retrieval: Meta-analyses using activation likelihood estimation. *Neuropsychologia, 47*(8), 1765–1779.

Spiro, R. J. (1977). Remembering information from text: Theoretical and empirical issues concerning the "state of schema" reconstruction hypothesis. In R. C. Anderson, R. J. Spiro, & W. E. Montague (Eds.), *Schooling and the acquisition of knowledge*. Hillsdale, NJ: Erlbaum.

Squire, L. R. (1992). "Memory and the hippocampus: A synthesis from findings with rats, monkeys, and humans": Correction. *Psychological Review, 99*(3), 582.

Sumby, W. H. (1963). Word frequency and serial position effects. *Journal of Verbal Learning and Verbal Behavior, 1*(6), 443–450.

Teasdale, J. D., & Fogarty, S. J. (1979). Differential effects of induced mood on retrieval of pleasant and unpleasant events from episodic memory. *Journal of Abnormal Psychology, 88*(3), 248–257.

Tulving, E. (1983). *Elements of episodic memory*. Oxford: Oxford University Press.

Tulving, E. (1985). How many memory systems are there? *The American Psychologist, 40*, 385–398.

Tulving, E., & Osler, S. (1968). Effectiveness of retrieval cues in memory for words. *Journal of Experimental Psychology, 77*(4), 593–601.

Tulving, E., & Thomson, D. M. (1973). Encoding specificity and retrieval processes in episodic memory. *Psychological Review, 80*(5), 352–373.

Velten, E. (1968). A laboratory task for induction of mood states. *Behavior Research and Therapy, 6*(4), 473–482.

Wagner, A. D., Schacter, D. L., Rotte, M., Koutstaal, W., Maril, A., Dale, A. M., et al. (1998). Building memories: Remembering and forgetting of verbal experiences as predicted by brain activity. *Science, 281*(5380), 1188–1191.

Yonelinas, A. P. (1999). The contribution of recollection and familiarity to recognition and source–memory judgments: A formal dual-process model and an analysis of receiver operating characteristics. *Journal of Experimental Psychology: Learning, Memory, and Cognition, 25*(6), 1415–1434.

Yonelinas, A. P. (2002). The nature of recollection and familiarity: A review of 30 years of research. *Journal of Memory and Language, 46*, 441–517.

Contents

A remarkable memory   232

The fundamental fact of forgetting   233

On the nature of forgetting   235

Factors that discourage forgetting   236

Factors that encourage incidental forgetting   238

A functional view of incidental forgetting   258

Summary   258

Points for discussion   260

Further reading   260

References   260

CHAPTER 9

INCIDENTAL FORGETTING

Michael C. Anderson

Over the Christmas holiday, my sister asked, "Do you remember when you knocked over the Christmas tree?" I said, "What are you talking about? I never did that!" Puzzled, my sister said, "Yes you did, don't you remember?" My brother added, "Yes, you were hurrying to squeeze behind the tree so you could take a picture of Aunt Dotty and Uncle Jim as they came up the driveway when you knocked the tree over." Indignant, I said, "What … what are you talking about … you must be mixing me up with someone else." My father insisted, "No, you definitely knocked the tree over. It was a big mess, and we made fun of you for it." He added that he remembered me feeling bad about ruining the tree, even though everyone said it was okay. They simply couldn't believe that I had forgotten this.

Reluctantly, I accepted that this event must have happened. I struggled to recall details and couldn't come up with anything. I said, "When did this happen? When I was a kid?" My sister replied, "No, it was about 3 or 4 years ago when we were in New York." I was shocked. I called my other brother and he confirmed every detail and was able to recall the year it had occurred. In fact, I remembered that Christmas in New York and my mother's new camera (which I was using), but I simply could not remember this event. After many months and repeated searching, I still could not bring any trace of the experience to mind.

Before you start wondering whether I'm amnesic, consider how much of *your* life *you* remember. Take a break from reading and try

From life's embarrassing mishaps, to the mundane details of our daily life, many of our memories are forgotten. How and why are certain memories lost while others remain vivid for a lifetime?

an exercise. Get out a sheet of paper and list everything that you did from the time you got up until the time you went to bed yesterday, including details about who you saw, and any conversations or thoughts. Chances are, you did pretty well and came up with a lot of detail. Perhaps you left out one or two minor things that you would recall if reminded. Next, do the same thing for the day that occurred *1 week* earlier. You can probably still recall a lot, but with much more effort, and you most likely feel like you are forgetting more. Finally, try the same thing, but for a day that occurred exactly *1 year* prior to yesterday. Try very hard. Most likely, after significant effort, you probably didn't recall much except perhaps some broad outlines that you are probably only guessing at, and only then after much reconstruction. The same uncomfortable fact is true for the majority of the days in your life, except for truly special events and the recent past.

In fact, consider this: *this very moment* that you are consciously experiencing, will, if your history serves as any guide, join the rest of those lost experiences. One cannot help but wonder how it is possible for something that is the full focus of your consciousness right now can ultimately be so completely lost. Is this the fate of all experience? When you are 80, will you only remember 1% of your life in any detail? Are all of your memories there, and just inaccessible?

The function of memory is never more conspicuous and astonishing than when it fails us. In this chapter, we consider the mechanisms that underlie forgetting. One might wonder why forgetting should be treated in a separate chapter from retrieval, in which we discussed why retrieval fails us. Indeed, retrieval failure *is* a form of forgetting. Forgetting is worthy of being distinguished, however, because of the potential for distinct forgetting processes that contribute to retrieval failure. Moreover, an emphasis on forgetting leads one to focus on changes in retrievability over time. What factors produce those changes? What would life be like if we never forgot?

In addressing these questions, research on memory has focused on both incidental forgetting and motivated forgetting. Incidental forgetting occurs without the intention to forget; motivated forgetting, on the other hand, occurs when people engage processes or behaviors that intentionally diminish accessibility for some purpose. It is likely that to explain the full range of experiences that people have with forgetting, theories of types of

both forgetting are needed. We discuss incidental forgetting here, and motivated forgetting in the next chapter.

A REMARKABLE MEMORY

What would it be like to remember every thing that ever occurred to you? Although no such person has yet been found, there are people with astounding memory. Elizabeth Parker, Larry Cahill, and James McGaugh (2006) reported the fascinating case of Jill Price a 41-year-old woman, who had a breathtaking capacity to remember her past. JP remembers every single day of her life since her teens, in extraordinary detail. Mention any date over several decades, and she finds herself back on that day, reliving events and feelings as though they happened yesterday. She can tell you what day of the week it was, events that took place on all surrounding days, and intricate details about her thoughts, feelings, and public events, all of which an be verified by personal diaries she has kept over 30 years. JP reports that these memories are vivid, like a running movie, and full of emotion. Her remembering feels automatic, and not under conscious control, a claim supported by the fact that her recollections occur immediately, with no struggle.

One might think that having such a remarkable memory would be wonderful. But it's not all good. When unpleasant things happen, JP wishes she could forget, and the constant bombardment by reminders is distracting and sometimes troubling. In JP's words:

My memory has ruled my life ... It is like my sixth sense ... There is no effort to it ... I want to know why I remember everything. I think about the past all the time ... It's like a running movie that never stops. It's like a split screen. I'll be talking to someone and seeing something else ... Like we're sitting here talking and I'm talking to you and in my head I'm thinking about something that happened to me in December 1982, December 17th, 1982, it was a Friday, I started to work at Gs [a store] ... I only have to experience something one time and I can be totally scarred by it ... I can't let go of things because of my memory ... Happy memories hold my head together ... I treasure these memories, good and bad ... I can't let go of things because of my memory, it's part of me ... When I think of these things, it is kind of soothing ... I knew a long time ago, I had an exceptional memory ... I don't think I would never want to have this but it's a burden.

Parker et al. (2006) have termed JP's condition *hyperthymestic syndrome*, from the Greek word *thymesis*, meaning remembering. In short, JP has uncontrollable remembering. Since the initial report by Parker et al., over two dozen cases of hyperthmestic sydrome— also known as highly superior autobiographical memory (abbreviated, HSAM) have been identified worldwide, most with very similar characteristics. They can all remember nearly everyday of their lives, without effort. Strikingly, despite this superior memory for their own personal past, hyperthymestic individuals do not exhibit particularly strong ability to memorize arbitrary information that doesn't have to do with past experiences or events.

Clearly, hyperthymestics' experience of life is very different from ours and illustrates a cost they pay for their perfect memory: they can remember the good times but at the cost of suffering the persistence of bad times. Would you choose JP's memory over your own? Perhaps forgetting is not all bad. Later in this chapter, we will discuss the possiblity that forgetting serves a useful function.

THE FUNDAMENTAL FACT OF FORGETTING

Clearly JP's experience is atypical, as most of us forget the events of our days. How are we to understand forgetting? A good place to begin discussing this phenomenon is to acknowledge a fundamental fact: for most people (and organisms), *forgetting increases as time progresses.* Although this surely comes as no surprise, you may not have considered the nature of the relationship between memory and time. If you had to guess, would you say that people forget at a constant rate? To address this question, one simply needs to measure how likely forgetting is as a memory grows older. Once again, the classic study was conducted by Hermann Ebbinghaus (1913), using himself as the participant and nonsense syllables as the material to be learned. Ebbinghaus learned 169 separate lists of 13 nonsense syllables, then relearned each list after intervals ranging from 21 minutes to 31 days. He always found that some forgetting had occurred and used the amount of time required to learn the list again as a measure of how much had been forgotten. He found a clear relationship between time and retention.

You will recall from Chapter 3 that the relationship between learning and remembering was more or less linear, with the long-term memory store behaving rather like a bath being filled by a tap running at a constant rate. But how about forgetting? Is it simply like pulling the plug out of the bath, causing information to be lost at a constant rate, or is the relationship less straightforward? The results obtained by Ebbinghaus are shown in Figure 9.1. This graph represents a quantitative relationship between memory and time, referred to as a forgetting curve, or sometimes a retention function. As you can see, Ebbinghaus' forgetting was extremely rapid at first, but it gradually

> **KEY TERM**
>
> Forgetting curve/retention function: The logarithmic decline in memory retention as a function of time elapsed, first described by Ebbinghaus.

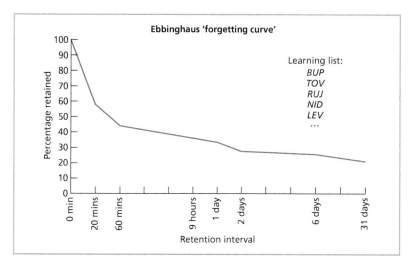

Figure 9.1 The forgetting curve that Ebbinghaus obtained when he plotted the results of one of his forgetting experiments. His finding, that information loss is very rapid at first and then levels off, holds true for many types of learned materials. Data from Ebbinghaus (1913).

slowed down over time; the rate of forgetting he exhibited was more logarithmic than linear. As with Ebbinghaus's other work, this result has stood the test of time and applies across a wide range of learning conditions.

Most studies on the rate of forgetting have, like Ebbinghaus's, concerned themselves with highly constrained materials such as lists of nonsense syllables or unrelated words. Is this representative of what happens to personal memories? What happens when more realistic material is recalled over longer intervals? Answering this presents a major problem. Consider the question posed earlier about what you were doing 1 year ago. If you were to give an answer, how would I know whether you were correct? It is extremely unlikely that the necessary information remains available. One solution is to question respondents about events that were sufficiently noteworthy to attract the attention of most people at the time they happened. This strategy was followed by Meeter, Murre, and Janssen (2005), who selected headlines in both newspapers and television broadcasts for each day over a 4-year period. They amassed over 1000 questions about distinct and dateable events, of which each participant would answer a randomly chosen 40. Cleverly, these investigators used the Internet to attract participants, allowing them to test the memory for over 14,000 participants from widely different age groups from countries across the world. They tested their respondents' memory for these events by both recall and recognition.

The results obtained by Meeter et al. (2005) show that substantial forgetting of public events does occur, with participants' recall for the events dropping from 60 to 30% in just a single year. The forgetting curves showed a steep initial decline, followed by a slowed rate of forgetting at longer delays, especially when recall was tested, much like that observed with nonsense syllables by Ebbinghaus over a century ago. They also found that people performed much more poorly when their recall was tested, recalling only 31% of the answers correctly over the years, compared to 52% correct when they simply had to recognize the right answer from among options. These findings lend confidence to the basic conclusions about forgetting from laboratory studies.

The forgetting curves we have discussed so far have been concerned mainly with memory for distinct events, which are relatively poorly learned. What of information that has been more thoroughly and deliberately learned? Light was thrown on this by an intriguing study by Bahrick, Bahrick, and Wittlinger (1975), who traced 392 American high-school graduates and tested their memory for the names and portraits of classmates. Their study showed that the ability to both *recognize* a face or a name from among a set of unfamiliar faces or names and to match up names with faces, remained remarkably high for over 30 years. In contrast, the ability to *recall* a name in response to a person's picture showed more extensive forgetting, just as was found in the previously discussed study of memory for major news events.

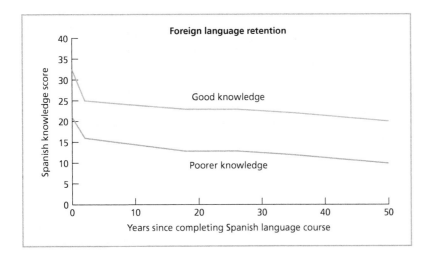

Figure 9.2 People who learned Spanish in college showed rapid forgetting over the first 3 or 4 years, followed by remarkably little forgetting over the next 30 years (Bahrick, 1984). Those who had a good knowledge (upper line, in blue) continued to have a clear advantage, even 50 years later. Data from Bahrick (1984).

Harry Bahrick is a Professor at Ohio Wesleyan University, which in common with many American colleges has an annual reunion for alumni. Bahrick has made ingenious use of this tradition to study the retention by alumni of a range of material: from the geography of the town where the university is located to the vocabulary of foreign languages learned at college. The graph in Figure 9.2 shows the effect of delay on memory for a foreign language (Spanish, in this case). The most striking feature of the graph is the way in which forgetting levels out after about 2 years, with little further loss up to the longest delay, virtually 50 years later. It is as if forgetting occurs only up to a certain point, beyond which memory traces appear frozen. Using an analogy to the permanently frozen ground in Polar regions, known as permafrost, Bahrick (1984) has suggested the term *permastore* for this stable language learning performance. The second point to note is that the overall retention is determined by the level of initial learning, at least as far as learning a foreign language is concerned. Thus, for well-learned materials, it seems, the forgetting curve may flatten out after an initial period of forgetting, and show little additional forgetting over long periods.

ON THE NATURE OF FORGETTING

The discussion of forgetting functions raises an issue concerning what counts as "forgetting." The studies by Meeter et al. and Bahrick found much greater forgetting when recall was tested, compared to recognition. In fact, this is a robust pattern that we touched on in our retrieval chapter: *recognition is generally easier than recall*. A reasonable conclusion to draw from this fact is that recognition tests reveal that more often resides in memory than is measured by recall. If so, is it truly fair to characterize failures to recall information evident in these forgetting functions as actual forgetting, when many of those unrecalled traces reside in memory? Shouldn't we reserve the term *forgetting* to refer to the permanent loss of traces? This issue highlights a distinction aptly named by Endel Tulving—the distinction between a memory's *availability* in the cognitive system (whether it is in storage or not), and its *accessibility* (whether one can access a memory, given that it is stored): the accessibility/availability distinction. Should we count inaccessibility as forgetting, or only unavailability?

Unfortunately, reserving *forgetting* to refer only to memories made unavailable renders it impossible to ever measure forgetting. The reason is that determining whether a memory

> ### KEY TERM
>
> **Accessibility/availability distinction:**
> Accessibility refers to the ease with which a stored memory can be retrieved at a given point in time. Availability refers to the binary distinction indicating whether a trace is or is not stored in memory.

has been permanently lost is quite a bit trickier than one might suspect. What will be our evidence of unavailability? Failed recall? Clearly not, as the foregoing results establish. Failed recognition? Again, recognition can fail, even when it can be proven that a trace is in memory, given the proper reinstatement of context. Although an experience may seem lost forever, perhaps the right cue has just not come along. As discussed in Chapter 8, it took the sight of the passport in the box to pry loose my memory for storing it there. It is thus quite difficult to distinguish inaccessibility from unavailability. Moreover, when memories transition from being recallable to only being recognizable, this may, in principle, be due to weakening of the trace. Permanent loss may not be all or none, but may happen in graded fashion. For these reasons, and because reduced accessibility is a memory failure, inaccessibility is considered forgetting.

FACTORS THAT DISCOURAGE FORGETTING

The studies by Harry Bahrick illustrate how forgetting, though perhaps inevitable for many memories, may be slowed for some types of knowledge. Which factors discourage forgetting? One obvious point is that if you learn something well to begin with, forgetting is less likely, or at least it takes much longer. But are there some ways of strengthening a memory that increase resistance to forgetting more than others? What memories will you have when you are 80?

The apparent flattening out of the forgetting curve over time demonstrates that memories are not equally vulnerable to forgetting at all points in their history. Another way of describing the relationship of time and memory is in terms of *Jost's Law*, named after a nineteenth-century psychologist, which states that if two memories are equally strong at a given time, then the older of the two will be more durable and forgotten less rapidly. It is as if two opposing forces may be at work to determine retention over time; the mechanisms

of forgetting, but also some process that makes surviving memories grow tougher with age. Indeed, it is widely believed that new traces are initially vulnerable to disruption until they are gradually stamped into memory. The time-dependent process by which a new trace is gradually woven into the fabric of memory and by which its components and their interconnections are cemented together is known as *consolidation*. At least two types of consolidation have been proposed. According to research on synaptic consolidation, the imprint of experience takes time to solidify, because it requires structural changes in the synaptic connections between neurons. These modifications rely on biological processes that may take hours to days to complete (Dudai, 2004). Until those structural changes occur, the memory is vulnerable. Research also implicates a process known as *systemic consolidation*, which holds that the hippocampus is initially required for memory storage and retrieval but that its contribution diminishes over time until the cortex is capable of retrieving the memory on its own (Squire, 1992; Dudai, 2004). As will be discussed further in Chapter 11, the hippocampus is thought to accomplish this by recurrently reactivating the brain areas involved in the initial experience (e.g. the areas involved in hearing the sounds, seeing the sights, essentially "replaying" the memory) until these areas are interlinked in a way that could recreate the original memory. Until the memory becomes independent of the hippocampus, it is vulnerable to disruption. Estimates of the duration of systemic consolidation vary, with some evidence suggesting that it may take years in humans. So, it seems that a process may exist that strengthens memories over time, retarding their forgetting, and that this process involves recurring retrieval of some sort.

Over the last decade, neurobiological research has questioned whether memories undergo a single, fixed period of synaptic consolidation. Instead, evidence suggests that each time a trace is reactivated in memory (e.g. by exposing people to a reminder to the event), it is must undergo restabilization once again. A key aspect of this idea is once a memory trace is reactivated, it enters a state of increased vulnerability to disruption. Thus, even consolidated memories, once reactivated, should be disruptable by interventions known to disrupt the normal synaptic consolidation process, such as the administration of consolidation-blocking drugs and electrical stimulation. The idea that memories must restabilize after reactivations is known as *reconsolidation* (Nader, Schafc, & LeDoux, 2000; see Nader & Hardt, 2009 for a review). This line of work does not question the importance of consolidation to creating durable memories, but rather suggests that memories must be restabilized as memories are retrieved. This reconsolidation process, though similar to synaptic consolidation, may be neurobiologically distinct. Functionally, it may allow the memory system flexibility to update representations with new information (Hardt, Einarsson, & Nader, 2010).

Interestingly, behavioral research indicates that intentionally retrieving an experience also has an especially potent effect on the rate at which a memory is forgotten. This fact was illustrated compellingly by Marigold Linton (1975), using herself as a participant. Every day for 5 years, she noted in her diary two events that had occurred. At predetermined intervals she would randomly select events from her diary and judge whether she could recall them. Given the fact that she was sampling in this way any given event could crop up many times. She was therefore able to analyze her results to find out what effect earlier recalls had on the later memorability of the event. Her results are shown in Figure 9.3; the items that were not retested showed dramatic forgetting over a 4-year period (65% forgotten). Even a single test was enough to reduce forgetting, whereas items tested on four other occasions showed an impressively low probability of forgetting after 4 years (only 12% forgotten). So, it seems that personal memories, if retrieved periodically, grow resistant to forgetting, in much the same way, as did the cases of permastore for well-learned material reported by Bahrick and colleagues. Research on the uniquely beneficial effects of retrieval on learning has expanded greatly in recent years, and the educational implications of this finding are significant (Karpicke & Roediger, 2008). Other examples of the memory enhancing power of retrieval are discussed in Chapter 16 on improving your memory.

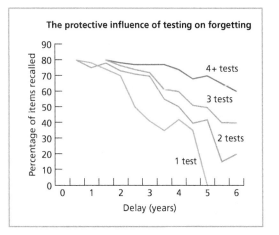

Figure 9.3 The probability of remembering something depends on the number of times it has been retrieved or called to mind. Recalling an event reduces the rate of forgetting. Data from Linton (1975).

Although retrieval enhances retention, we must be cautious about what is being retrieved. People are tempted to assume that if they are recalling something that happened 20 years ago, that they are recalling a 20-year-old memory. This may be true if we have not recalled the memory in the interim. However, if we have retrieved the memory at all, perhaps we are retrieving a memory of what we have retrieved previously. The event of retrieving something is itself a memory, with its own context, and particulars. The more often that we retrieve an experience, the more of these retrieval events will exist in memory. As long as the information retrieved each time is accurate and complete, this process will enhance recall. If recollections are incomplete or inaccurate due to reconstructive inferences, what we remember may not be what originally happened. This is especially true if, during reconsolidation, incorrectly recalled details get integrated with the original memory traces (Hardt et al., 2010). We return to this concern in Chapter 10, in discussing recovered memories of abuse.

It appears then that retrieval may play a very special role in determining which elements of experience will be preserved throughout our lives. Each time that we get together and reminisce with friends or family, we are implicitly selecting which memories to more firmly establish. And for those of us who keep a diary, reviewing the day's events and retrieving them not only provides an objective record of their occurrence, but also may increase the longevity of those memories, especially if they are reviewed from time to time. Retrieval clearly has a special effect on retention. Later on, I will discuss research demonstrating that, ironically, retrieval also plays a powerful and complementary role in determining what we forget.

FACTORS THAT ENCOURAGE INCIDENTAL FORGETTING

Knowing that retrieval retards forgetting is useful, but why does forgetting occur in the first place? What factors contribute to retention loss? Experimental psychologists have traditionally emphasized incidental forgetting, stressing the involvement of passive processes that occur as a by-product of changes in the world or the person. For example, forgetting has been attributed to decay, contextual shifts, and to interference. This passive view fits the general feeling most of us have that we are the unwilling victims of memory loss. This perspective often fits reality: we do forget things unintentionally, even when they are important. Here, we consider several of the most important factors.

Passage of time as a cause of forgetting

The most obvious way of describing the forgetting curve is that memory gets worse as time goes by. Perhaps the cause is that simple: memory traces grow weaker with time. Memories may simply fade, rather like a notice that is exposed to sun and rain gradually fades until it becomes illegible. The idea that memories get weaker over time is known as trace decay. Many investigators favor the view that trace decay partially determines the loss

of information from verbal and visual working memory (e.g. Broadbent, 1958; Baddeley, 1986; Cowan, 1988; Page & Norris, 1998; Towse, Hitch, & Hutton, 2000; Gold, Murray, Sekuler, Bennett, & Sekuler, 2005), although this approach has its critics (Nairne, 2002) and the existence of decay in verbal working memory is actively debated (Berman, Jonides, & Lewis, 2009; Altmann & Schunn, 2012; Oberauer & Lewandowsky, 2013). Decay also plays a role in how theorists think about repetition priming and familiarity, with some proposing that these effects decay quickly (e.g. Eichenbaum, 1994; McKone, 1998; Yonelinas & Levy, 2002). Many proposals about trace decay have in common the idea that activation decays gradually, even if the item remains stored. For example, recent exposure to the word *helmet* may activate a pre-existing concept. Although activation may fade, the concept remains.

There is another sense of decay, however, in which a memory's structural elements degrade, not just activation levels. Thus, associations between features or the features themselves may deteriorate. Does this happen? This issue is related to the age-old question of whether memories are permanently stored, but merely grow inaccessible. On one level, the answer seems obvious: memories are not permanent and decay must exist. We cannot disregard that we are biological beings. Our memories survive in tissue that continually changes, with neurons dying and connections weakening or being modified. We know, for instance, that a time-dependent process degrades the synaptic connections between neurons that support a recently learned behavior in *Aplysia* (a sea slug), with a corresponding degradation in the learned behavior (Bailey & Chen, 1989). It is not far-fetched to believe that a similar degradation occurs in humans, perhaps underlying time-dependent decay. If neurons die, and connections degrade, the survival of memories over long stretches of time in fact seems the greater mystery.

Although many physical changes could underlie decay, an especially promising though counter-intuitive proposal was offered recently by Paul Frankland, Stephan Köhler, and Sheena Josselyn (2013). Rather than conceptualizing decay as necessarily reflecting deterioration of existing tissue that supports a memory, Frankland and colleagues suggest that memory decay may have more to do with the growth of new neurons (i.e. neurogenesis). Over the last two decades, advances in neurobiology have established that new neurons are being generated regularly in the adult brain, especially in the hippocampus. As newborn neurons become integrated into existing circuitry in the hippocampus (a process that can take several weeks), the hippocampus is, bit by bit, structurally remodeled, with its pattern of synaptic connections gradually modified with each generation of interloping neurons. Frankland and colleagues argue that while this new neural tissue may be good for helping us to learn new things effectively (after the neurons are incorporated), it is bad for the retention of existing memories already stored in the hippocampus. In effect, new neurons change the pattern of communication between hippocampal neurons, making the original pattern of firing present during encoding hard to recreate at retrieval, thus impairing retention. These authors present a compelling case that this neurogenesis-induced decay may explain the striking phenomenon of infantile amnesia, to be discussed further in Chapter 12 (Josselyn & Frankland, 2012). Infantile amnesia refers to the difficulty most people have in remembering the first several years of their lives, a period that, strikingly, coincides with high levels of new neurogenesis.

KEY TERM

Infantile amnesia: The tendency for older children and adults to have few autobiographical memories from the early years of life.

Although trace decay seems inevitable, experimental psychologists are rightly skeptical about *behavioral* evidence for it. The reason is that demonstrating decay behaviorally is exceptionally difficult. Proving that decay exists requires a demonstration that forgetting grows over time, in the absence of other activities such as the storage of new experiences or rehearsal. Rehearsal of the memory in question must be controlled because, as discussed earlier, retrieval strengthens memories, which would undercut efforts to see decay. As we will later discuss, storing new experiences after a trace has been encoded must be controlled because new memories introduce interference that may disrupt recall. When these constraints are considered, the person would essentially need to be kept in a mental vacuum, devoid of rehearsal, thoughts, or experiences that might contaminate the state of memory and complicate the interpretation of forgetting. To make matters worse, even if forgetting occurred in the absence of interference, it remains unclear whether the trace has become unavailable, or is merely inaccessible. Thus, it may be impossible to establish evidence for decay behaviorally, even if it does exist.

Correlates of time that cause forgetting

For the foregoing reasons, experimental psychologists have favored the view that time is merely correlated with some other factor that causes forgetting. Two possibilities have been examined. First, as time goes by, the incidental context within which we operate gradually shifts, perhaps impairing retrieval of older memories. Second, over time, people store many new similar experiences that may interfere with retrieving a particular trace. Although these factors do not disprove decay, they provide alternative explanations for the forgetting curve that do not rely upon this process.

Contextual fluctuation

As discussed in Chapter 8, retrieval hinges on the number and quality of cues available during recall. When irrelevant cues are used, retrieval can fail. Retrieval can fail when a cue that was previously relevant changes over time. For instance, family members change in appearance, making them match less well the original cue associated to a memory. Moreover, when incidental context at retrieval does not match the one present at encoding, forgetting is more likely. One explanation of the forgetting curve then, is that as time progresses, changes in context become greater, on average because the world changes and we change. With time, we encounter new stimuli, people, and situations, and we have new thoughts and emotions. As such, one's incidental context will be most similar to the one that we were in a short while ago, and grow less similar over time. The idea that contextual fluctuation contributes to memory has been advocated in numerous models of memory (e.g. Polyn, Norman, & Kahana, 2009).

An interesting example of how contextual change causes forgetting comes from research on mental context. Most of us have, from time to time, found ourselves lost in daydreams, imagining some future or past event. This happens to me whenever I'm on the train or a bus riding some place, and is can be a rather pleasant way to pass the time. When you do this, however, be careful, because you might just make yourself forget something you need to remember. This is particularly true if your imagination takes you to far off places or times that are very different from the present moment. Peter Delaney and his colleagues reported a clever demonstration of this idea (Delaney, Sahakyan, Kelly, & Zimmerman, 2010). Participants studied two lists of 15 unrelated words for a later memory test. Immediately after studying the first list, participants received 90 seconds to perform a simple diverting activity. One group was asked to daydream about a vacation in the last 3 years within the US. A second group was asked to daydream about an international vacation (participants were screened in advance to ensure that they had gone on US or international vacations). A rather less fortunate control group was given 90 seconds to read a passage aloud from a psychology textbook to pass the time. After daydreaming, the participants studied the second list of words, which was followed shortly thereafter by a test of the first list. Participants who daydreamed after studying the first list remembered fewer words from that list, compared to control participants. This effect was especially pronounced for participants who daydreamed about their international holiday, presumably because such daydreams involve large changes to one's mental context, relative to those that might arise from imagining a more ordinary US holiday. Indeed, there was a correlation between the remoteness of the vacation destination (in miles) and how much participants forget the first list! Clearly, changes in mental context can lead to forgetting. We will revisit the context shift process in Chapter 10 on motivated forgetting.

Interference

Over time, experiences accumulate. Like the clutter of papers on your desk, adding new memories affects how easily we find things already stored. When memories are similar, this problem should be even worse, like having many similarly labeled papers on a desk. The idea that storing similar traces impedes retrieval is known as *interference*. Interference is likely to be a serious issue when you consider how people are, by their nature, creatures of habit. People enjoy their routines, be they reading the newspaper in the morning, parking in the same spot each day, or getting their morning coffee at the same time. Sticking to routines, however, makes life less memorable. We remember what we had for dinner last night, but not 2 weeks ago. Such forgetting doesn't simply reflect the passage of time. We can easily remember experiences for a long time if they are unique: having dinner at the neighbors' house a year ago is far more memorable than having dinner at our own house 3 months ago. It is the presence of other traces in memory that compromises retrieval. Because the number of similar traces will increase over time, interference provides a straightforward account of the forgetting curve. The emphasis on interference as a source of forgetting has

---

KEY TERM

Contextual fluctuation: The gradual and persistent drift in incidental context over time, such that distant memories deviate from the current context more so than newer memories, thereby diminishing the former's potency as a retrieval cue for older memories.

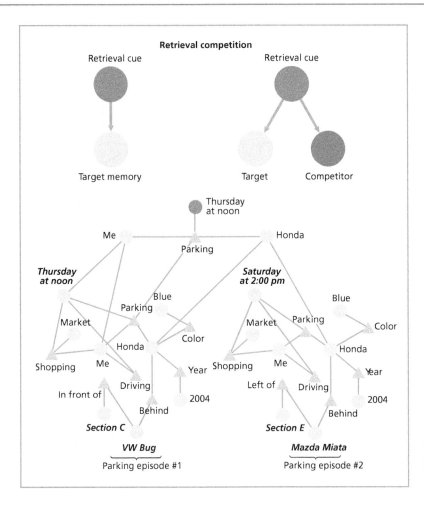

Figure 9.4 Top left: A retrieval cue associated to a single target item. Top right: A retrieval cue becomes associated to a competitor interfering with recall of the target. Bottom: A more complex example of interference, with multiple, shared retrieval cues and complex memories with many features. From Anderson and Neely (1996). Copyright © Elsevier. Reproduced with permission.

a long history (Müller & Pilzecker, 1900) and was a preoccupation of research on memory for nearly three-quarters of a century (see Postman, 1971; Crowder, 1976; Anderson & Neely, 1996, for reviews).

How does adding similar experiences into memory hurt us? To understand this, it is helpful to step back and discuss a fundamental discovery about what likely underlies interference. Early in the history of memory research, investigators identified a central feature in common to most situations associated with interference: Interference arises whenever the cue used to access a target (Figure 9.4, top left) becomes associated to additional memories. The canonical interference situation is illustrated in the top right panel of Figure 9.4 in its most general form, with a single cue linked to many associates. By this view, progressing

from a cue to a target depends not only on how strongly that cue is associated to the target, but also on whether the cue is related to other items. Why does attaching more memories to a cue make retrieving a particular target difficult? Although theories vary about the particulars, most agree that when a cue is linked to multiple items, those items compete with the target for access to awareness, an idea known as the competition assumption

KEY TERM

Competition assumption: The theoretical proposition that the memories associated to a shared retrieval cue automatically impede one another's retrieval when the cue is presented.

(Anderson, Bjork, & Bjork, 1994). Essentially, a cue activates all of its associates to some degree, and they "fight" one another. As such, any associates other than the target memory are called *competitors*. In general, any negative effect on memory arising from having competitors is called interference. Interference increases with the number of competitors a target has. This idea is supported by the tendency for recall to decrease with the number of to-be-remembered items paired with the same cue, a generalization known as the cue-overload principle (see, e.g. Watkins, 1978). In essence, as a cue becomes attached to too many things, its capacity to access any one trace is compromised.

How do these ideas explain why storing similar memories causes interference? Consider an example in which you are recalling where you parked your car in a shopping center you visit frequently. While parking, you will have encoded aspects of your parking experience into a memory. Other parking memories similar to this one will also contain characteristics of the target, including the fact that you drove a car, the type of car you drove (e.g. a 2004 blue Honda) and, perhaps, your goal of shopping. If important elements of the target (e.g. the concepts of yourself, of parking, and of your Honda) serve as the cues to your car's location, other memories sharing those features will be evoked as well. Figure 9.4 (bottom) illustrates this by showing how the situation illustrated with one cue may be scaled up to the many cues available in this example (e.g. "Me," "Parking," and "Honda"). Thus, competition for a shared cue is a useful way of viewing interference between similar traces.

The notion of competition among items that share retrieval cues is very general. For instance, items in memory need not be episodes to compete. Indeed, even retrieving the meaning of a word can involve retrieval interference. To convince yourself of this, try the demonstration in Box 9.1.

For native speakers of English, this task is perplexingly difficult because they instantly retrieve the noun meaning of the word, and must work to get past that dominant association. If this happened to you, you experienced competition from the noun meaning during the retrieval of the verb.

Interference phenomena

A number of qualitatively distinct situations produce interference. For instance, the storage of new experiences can interfere with retrieving older ones, but older memories can also impede retrieval of newer ones. In this section, we review some of the most important interference phenomena and key results that have been discovered. It is important to bear in mind that, although the particulars of these situations vary, the underlying mechanisms that produce forgetting may in fact be similar. In the section to follow, we consider candidate mechanisms.

Retroactive interference

At the beginning of this chapter, we asked you to list all of the things you did yesterday, the same day last week, and the same day last year. If you did this exercise, you undoubtedly confronted the uncomfortable fact that you remember little of what has happened in your life. Why? As we have discussed, the difficulty may be due to several sources, including decay and contextual fluctuation. But there is an excellent chance that a lot of that forgetting comes about due to retroactive interference. Retroactive interference refers to forgetting caused by encoding new traces into memory in between the initial encoding of the target and when it is

---

KEY TERM

Cue-overload principle: The observed tendency for recall success to decrease as the number of to-be-remembered items associated to a cue increases.

Retroactive interference: The tendency for more recently acquired information to impede retrieval of similar older memories.

Box 9.1 Interference effects

Each of the words listed in this table has entirely distinct verb and noun meanings, with the verb meaning being the less common. For each word, try to generate an associate of its verb meaning. For instance, for the word *duck*, you would generate a word like *crouch*, signifying that you thought of the verb meaning. Do this for each word as quickly as possible.

	Cue	Related verb
E.g.	Duck	Crouch
1	Loaf	
2	Post	
3	Court	
4	Root	
5	Sock	
6	Shed	
7	Fence	
8	Lobby	
9	Stump	
10	Fawn	
11	Lodge	
12	Sign	
13	Bark	
14	Pine	
15	Bowl	
16	Prune	
17	Duck	
18	Rail	
19	Sink	
20	Ring	

Adapted from Johnson and Anderson (2004).

tested. Essentially, some process associated with storing newer experiences impairs the ability to recall ones farther back in time. With every new trip to McDonald's, every morning ride on the bus, and every day you spend seated in front of a computer screen at work, previous McDonald's trips, morning rides, and days at work grow farther from your mental grasp.

The methods used to study retroactive interference have tended to focus on simple materials that conform closely to the canonical interference situation described earlier. This phenomenon is often studied using the classic retroactive interference design illustrated in the left half of Figure 9.5. In the *experimental condition*, people study a first list of pairs (upper box), and then a second list. Very often the pairs in the first list (e.g. *dog–sky*) have their cue words repeated in the second list, but are paired with a new response word (e.g. *dog–rock*) that people have to learn in place of the older one. After the second list is learned, people are usually tested by giving them the first word of each pair and asking them to recall the response from the first list (e.g. *dog–?*). In the control condition, people also study a first list, but engage in irrelevant filler activity in the interval, during which people in the experimental condition study the second list. Thus, these two conditions allow us to ask the crucial question: What is the effect of learning new information (i.e. List Two) on the ability to remember information that was previously studied (i.e. List One), relative to a situation in which no additional information was learned at all (i.e. control condition)?

The general findings are that: (1) introducing a highly related second list impairs the ability to recall items from the first list, compared to the control; and (2) increased training on second-list items continues to harm retention of first-list items further, as training progresses. This is especially true when the lists share a common cue word (e.g. *dog*, as in the previous example); in fact, there is often little retroactive interference when the pairs on the two lists are unrelated. Thus, not every type of intervening experience impairs memory—the experience needs to be similar. A typical example of retroactive interference is illustrated in the right half of Figure 9.5, which is taken from a classic study by Barnes and Underwood (1959). Notice that as people were given increasing amounts of training on the second list of pairs, their memory for those pairs gets better, whereas their retention of first-list pairs grows quite a bit worse. We know that this increased forgetting is not due to the mere passage of time, because in the control condition the same amount of time has gone by in between learning the pairs and the final test. Thus, learning something new can impair memory substantially.

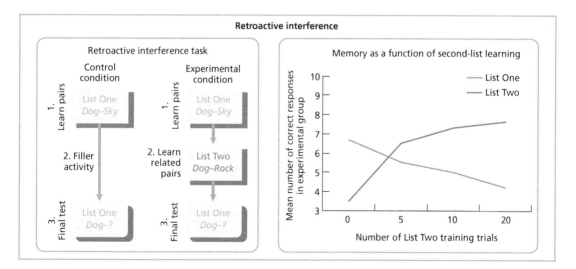

Figure 9.5 Left: A retroactive interference task in which participants learn two lists of word pairs, in series. A control group skips second-list learning. Right: Final cued-recall results (for both lists) by List-Two training trials. Memory for List Two increases with practice, while List One declines with List-Two practice. Data from Barnes and Underwood (1959).

But are the lessons from artificial laboratory materials applicable to memory for personal experiences? It would be helpful if it could be shown that something like retroactive interference occurs with realistic memories. Such studies exist and generally confirm the importance of retroactive interference. In one study by Hitch and Baddeley, rugby players were asked to recall the names of the teams they had played earlier in the season (Baddeley & Hitch, 1977). Figure 9.6 shows the probability of their recalling the name of the last team played, the team before that, and so forth. It proved to be the case that most players had missed some games either due to injury or other commitments, so that for one player the game before last might have taken place a week ago and for another it might have been 2 weeks or even a month before. It was therefore possible to ascertain whether forgetting depended on elapsed time or on the number of intervening games. The result was clear. Time was relatively unimportant, whereas the number of intervening games was critical, indicating that forgetting was due to interference rather than trace decay. Apparently, their memory of having played a whole rugby game could be made less accessible simply because they have played many rugby games since then.

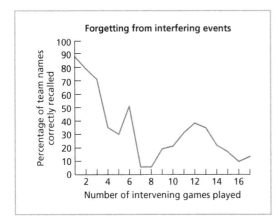

Figure 9.6 This graph, showing rugby players' memory for the names of teams recently played, demonstrates the tendency for recent events to interfere with memory of similar events from the past. Data from Baddeley and Hitch (1977).

Proactive interference

One afternoon, I walked up to the top of an exceptionally steep street outside the psychology department to discover, to my horror, that my car had been stolen. After a moment's reflection, I realized that I had not parked my car there this *afternoon*, but rather this *morning*. This afternoon, I had parked my car on an entirely different, preposterously steep hill one street over. I was the unhappy victim of proactive interference, or the tendency for older memories to interfere with the retrieval of more recent experiences and knowledge. Most of us are acquainted with the irritation of proactive interference. It occurs, for example, when we fail to recall our new password because our old one intrudes during recall, refusing to be ignored or abandoned simply because it is out of date. Or, if we are seriously unlucky, we may call our current partner by our previous partner's name in an absentminded moment. In each case, well-encoded events or facts rear their ugly head and disrupt retrieval of something more recent.

Although we have emphasized how retroactive interference affects long-term retention, proactive interference plays a powerful role in determining the rate of forgetting. This was demonstrated dramatically by Benton Underwood. Underwood (1957) was interested in explaining why participants who had learned a list of nonsense syllables should show so much forgetting after 24 hours. It occurred to Underwood that proactive interference was a real possibility. The reason was that almost all work on human learning at the time was done in a few laboratories, all of which used undergraduate participants. If you happened to be a student in one of these departments, you were likely to be required to participate for many hours in verbal learning studies. Underwood thought that it might be interference from the many *previous* lists of nonsense syllables that caused forgetting. Fortunately it was possible to find out how many previous lists each participant had learned in other experiments and to plot the amount of forgetting in a 24-hour period as a function of this prior experience. In fact, naive students, who had no previous experience remembered 80% of the list items after 24 hours, whereas students with 20 or more prior learning trials on different lists remembered fewer than 20% 24 hours later. Proactive interference had a giant effect on retention, largely determining the rate at which students forgot the material after an extended delay.

Experiments examining proactive interference have often used an experimental design that is highly related to the retroactive interference design described earlier. The proactive interference paradigm (Figure 9.7) resembles the retroactive interference design, except that: (1) it tests people's memory for the List-Two responses rather than the List-One responses; and (2) in the control condition, the rest period (or performance of irrelevant activity) replaces List-One learning rather than List-Two learning. Thus, this design allows us to explore how previously acquired knowledge (i.e. List One) might impair our ability to recollect new information (i.e. List Two), relative to a situation in which the previous knowledge

had not been learned (control, List Two). Studies using the proactive interference procedure have demonstrated that people are more likely to forget items from a list when a prior list has been studied. The amount of proactive interference is greatest when the two lists share a common cue. Proactive interference effects are most severe when recall is tested rather than recognition.

Part-set cuing impairment

Recent exposure to one or more competitors exacerbates the problems we have in retrieving a target memory. For example, most of us have forgotten the name of someone and have been offered assistance by a well-meaning friend who supplies guesses about the name we are seeking. Unless the friend is lucky and guesses correctly, it often feels as though his or her suggestions make matters worse. Sometimes recall fails until a much later point when, unencumbered by the clutter of incorrect guesses, your mind yields the delinquent name. If you have had this happen, you have had firsthand experience with the phenomenon of part-set cuing impairment.

Part-set cuing impairment refers to the tendency for target recall to be impaired by the provision of retrieval cues drawn from the

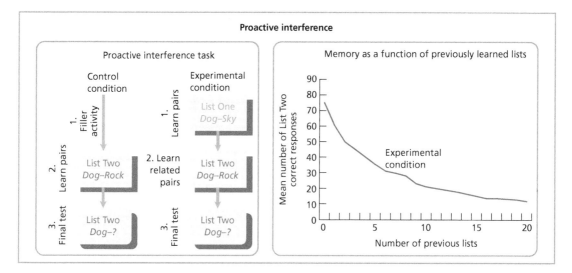

Figure 9.7 A proactive interference task, in which participants learn two lists of word pairs. A control group skips first-list learning. Right: A meta-analysis of final test cued-recall data following a 24-hour delay, given varying numbers of preceding lists. List-Two memory decreases as the number of prior lists increases. Adapted from Underwood (1957).

same set (e.g. category) of items in memory (Mueller & Brown, 1977). The basic finding was discovered by Slamecka (1968), who had people study lists composed of words from several semantic categories (e.g. *trees, birds*). On the final test, some people were given some of the members from each category as cues to help them recall the remainder; others were given no such cues. Of concern was people's recall of the remaining noncue items in the experimental condition relative to recall for those items when no cues were given. Slamecka expected that the cues would help recall for the noncue items. To his surprise, when recall was scored for the noncue items, people receiving cues performed worse than those who received no cues! This has become known as part-set cuing impairment because providing part of the set (in this case, part of the category) as cues impaired recall of the remaining items. Part-set cuing may be one reason why every musical album that we make a "mental note" to purchase the next time we are shopping online for music seems to disappear from our minds the moment we peruse other music on sale.

The idea that supplying hints might impair memory is both surprising and ironic. In retrospect, however, it makes good sense, given the situation of interference described at the outset. Presumably a set of items is defined by some common cue (for example, *fruit* or *birds*), to which many items are associated. If presenting some items from the set strengthens their associations to the cue, perhaps stronger items provide greater competition during the retrieval of noncue items, impairing their recall. The idea that cues *increase competition* is consistent with the finding that as more members of the set are provided as cues, the worse memory becomes for the remainder (see Nickerson, 1984, for a review).

The idea that simply re-presenting cue items strengthens them, causing part-set cuing,

Have you ever walked into a store, only to forget about your intended purchase? Blame part-set cueing, the tendency for the presence of some items as retrieval cues (like a CDs on display in the storefront) to impair one's ability to retrieve other items within the same set (the desired CD).

though appealing, has been questioned by a clever study reported by Karl-Heinz Bauml and Alp Aslan (Bauml & Aslan, 2004). Bauml and Aslan wondered whether merely presenting cues, by itself, was what made people forget the noncue items, or whether forgetting may instead be caused by how people use the cues during memory search. To look into this, they asked participants to study categories (e.g. *fruit*), each with 12 examples. Afterwards, one group was presented with four of the examples and told that the items should be used as cues for retrieving the remaining noncue items. After viewing these cues, the cues disappeared and participants recalled the remaining items from the list, cued with the initial letter for each. In contrast to this *part-set cuing* group, a second *part-set re-study* group saw the same four items, but were asked to study them again before being given the test on noncues. No mention was made of using these items as cues. A final *part-set retrieval* group was instead given a test on the same four items before proceeding to the key test of the noncues; each item's first letter appeared, and participants had to recall it. Interestingly, Bauml and Aslan found that whereas the part-set cuing and part-set retrieval groups showed forgetting of the noncue items, the part-set re-study group did not. A final post-test on the re-exposed items confirmed that re-exposure strengthened the recall of the four items similarly across the conditions. Bauml and Aslan argued that this finding shows that being re-exposed to items and strengthening them does not induce forgetting of the noncue items. Rather forgetting relied upon whether participants retrieved the cues. We will return to the critical role of retrieval in causing memory impairment in the next section on retrieval-induced forgetting.

If people's instinct to be helpful and provide cues sometimes harms memory, what would happen if a group of people got together and tried to collaboratively remember things that they had all experienced or learned? Would one person's recounting prompt others to remember more than they would have, or might it cause part-set cuing impairment? Recent work indicates that when people get together to remember material that they each learned, they remember less when recalling the information as a group than they do when each person recalls information separately and their results are combined into a common score. This phenomenon, known as collaborative inhibition may arise from the mechanisms that produce part-set cuing inhibition (Weldon & Bellinger, 1997). If group members are generating lots of items while you are listening, the interference this causes may disrupt your retrieval. Thus, research on part-set cuing may help to understand the effects of group effort on generating a diversity of new ideas and recollections.

Retrieval-induced forgetting

An ironic feature of human memory is that the very act of remembering can cause forgetting. Of course, it's not that remembering harms memory for the retrieved experience itself. Rather, retrieval can harm recall of other memories or facts related to the retrieved item. Anderson et al. (1994) have referred to this phenomenon as retrieval-induced forgetting.

Retrieval-induced forgetting is usually studied with a procedure known as the retrieval practice paradigm (Anderson et al., 1994), illustrated in Figure 9.8. In this procedure, people first study simple verbal categories,

like *fruits*, *drinks*, and *trees* for a later memory test. People would then be asked to repeatedly recall some of the examples that they just studied, from some of the categories. For example, participants might receive the cues *fruit–or—* to help them retrieve the item *orange*. Following this "retrieval practice," a test is given in which people are asked to recall all examples that they remember seeing from every category. Clearly, on this final test, people will recall the examples that they practiced quite well. More interesting, however, is how well they recall the remaining unpracticed examples (e.g. *fruit–banana*), compared to unpracticed items from baseline categories that are also studied, but none of whose examples receive retrieval practice (e.g. *drinks–wine*). Strikingly, as can be seen in Figure 9.8, retrieval practice enhances recall of practiced items (e.g. *fruit–orange*), but it impairs related items (e.g. *fruit–banana*). So, it seems that the very act of remembering can cause forgetting. This observation fits well with our earlier discussion of Bauml and Aslan's (2004) finding that retrieval was an important factor in causing part-set cuing impairment.

If retrieval causes forgetting, students might have reason to be concerned about how they study for exams. Consider the plight of students who have limited time to prepare. You must prioritize your time, and the issue arises as to what to pass over. Research on

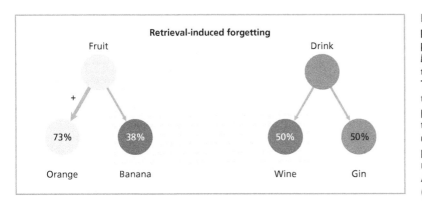

Figure 9.8 In this example, participants perform retrieval practice on *orange* but not *banana* or any members from the *drink* category (baseline). The final test scores indicate that, relative to baseline, practice facilitates recall of the practiced items, whereas unpracticed items from practiced categories suffer retrieval-induced forgetting. Adapted from Anderson (2003).

retrieval-induced forgetting suggests that selectively reviewing facts impairs nonreviewed material, particularly related material. Neil Macrae and Malcolm MacLeod (1999) tested this idea by giving students facts like those they might learn in a classroom. Participants studied ten geography facts about each of two fictitious islands (*Tok* and *Bilu*; e.g. *The official language of Tok is French* or *Bilu's only major export is copper*). Students then performed retrieval practice. For one island, they practiced retrieving five of its ten facts. A final test followed, cued by the name of each island. Macrae and MacLeod found that practice facilitated the later recall of practiced facts (70%) over baseline facts about the unpracticed island (38%), but at the cost of impairing retention of related but unpracticed facts (23%). Similar effects have been demonstrated with complex textual materials when the test involved either short answer or essay tests, though not on multiple-choice exams (Carroll, Campbell-Ratcliffe, Murnane, & Perfect, 2007). So, one must be careful about what one leaves out whilst studying, because omitting material will hasten its forgetting.

Selective retrieval occurs often in daily life. One situation of concern arises when members of law enforcement, detectives, and lawyers interview a witness after a crime. Answering interrogators, of course, requires retrieval. John Shaw, a psychologist who had once been a Los Angeles public defender, thought that such questioning might harm witness's memories for nonquestioned material, an intuition based on experiences with some of his own clients. To examine this possibility, Shaw, Bjork, and Handal (1995) told a group of participants

to imagine that they had attended a party and that, upon leaving, they noticed that their wallet was missing. Participants then watched slides of a student's apartment and paid attention to the details contained therein so that they might assist the police in an investigation. The slides contained a number of household items plus two categories of critical items (i.e. college sweatshirts and schoolbooks). Participants were then given structured questions about some of the objects (e.g. sweatshirts) during the *interrogation phase*. Consistent with Shaw's experience, they found that interrogating people about some stolen items impaired their memory for related items. Supporting this conclusion, Malen Migueles and Elvira Garcia-Bajos found similar retrieval-induced forgetting effects using a naturalistic bank robbery videotape, showing that questioning

Retrieval-induced forgetting suggests that selectively reviewing facts impairs nonreviewed material. What implications could this have for the questioning procedures used, for example, in a court of law?

could disrupt memory for offender characteristics (Migueles & Garcia-Bajos, 2007), and such forgetting effects have been found to last as long as a week (Garcia-Bajos, Migueles, & Anderson, 2009). So, retrieval-induced forgetting may have significant implications for how witnesses should be questioned.

If retrieval impairs memory, then simply discussing an experience with someone might alter whether people will remember what was omitted. Conroy and Salmon (2006) examined this idea by having young children participate in a staged event at school called *Visiting the Pirate*, during which the children engaged in a number of activities across a variety of scenes. For example, in the *Becoming a Pirate* scene, the children were asked to hoist a sale, bang a drum, put on pirate clothes, greet a pirate, and put their name in the pirate's book, whereas in the *Winning the Key* scene, they might have fed a bird, looked through a telescope, steered the pirate ship, and done a dance. On the next 3 days, the children discussed the event with another experimenter, who asked them questions about only some parts, such as, "Tell me about the animal that you fed." On the final day, the children recalled the nondiscussed elements less well than did a control group of children, who engaged in no discussion at all. Conroy and Salmon speculated that children's memory of their growing up years will be shaped by the way in which parents and family members reminisce, with nondiscussed aspects growing appreciably less accessible over time.

If discussions with other people about a shared past can lead one to forget what is not discussed, then forgetting can, in a sense, be contagious. If a friend has forgotten some parts of an experience, then they will leave the forgotten parts out while reminiscing about it. Might selective remembering on the part of one person cause forgetting of the nondiscussed material in others? Alexandru Cuc, Jonathan Koppel, and William Hirst (2007) looked at this possibility in recent work on socially shared retrieval-induced forgetting. One study replicated the experiment of Anderson et al., (1994; discussed earlier) with a twist: they had two people, seated side by side, studying the same pairs. In the retrieval practice phase, however, one participant performed retrieval practice, whereas

the other sat silently and observed, monitoring their partner's recollections for accuracy. Both then took the final test. As expected, the participant who performed retrieval practice showed retrieval-induced forgetting. Surprisingly, however, the silent observer also showed this effect. Cuc and colleagues observed the same effect when they used stories as materials; they even observed it when people were allowed to discuss the stories freely with one another: the nondiscussed elements of the story for one person were more likely to be forgotten by the other. It seems that when we are amongst others discussing past events, we spontaneously recall those events along with the person doing the recounting, and, in doing so, subject ourselves to retrieval-induced forgetting for whatever the speaker remains silent about. If so, then retrieval-induced forgetting may be one mechanism by which a society's collective memory of an event comes to be more uniform over time. It may also provide a means of political manipulation, when silences about certain facts or events are deliberate, and mass media is used to trumpet certain elements of the past. As Cuc and colleagues remark, "Silence is not always golden." Charles Stone and colleagues make a fascinating case that "mnemonic silences," which arise when one selectively retrieves some aspects, experiences, or knowledge, and not others, play a large role in shaping individual and collective memories (Stone, Coman, Brown, Koppel, & Hirst, 2012).

Retrieval thus appears to be a powerful force that shapes memory, for the better and for the worse. As discussed, Marigold Linton's observations indicate that retrieval greatly enhances the longevity of a memory, but the current results show that when retrieval is incomplete the benefits may be offset by the forgetting of other things. To understand the importance of this finding, one need only consider how pervasive this basic process is in our daily cognitive experience. That is, any cognitive act that makes reference to traces stored in memory, which is likely to be all processes, employs retrieval. If retrieval is a source of forgetting, then accessing what we already know might contribute to forgetting, independent of the encoding of new experience. The role of retrieval in causing forgetting has led to a new perspective on why the situation

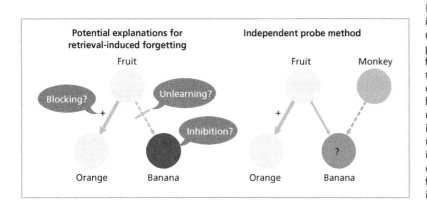

Figure 9.9 Left: Practiced items could block target recall during the final test, producing retrieval-induced forgetting. Alternatively, the connection between cue and target could have been unlearned during retrieval practice. Inhibition involves a reduction in the target memory's activation, itself. Right: Only inhibition correctly predicts that forgetting generalizes to independent cues.

of interference is associated with forgetting. We discuss this perspective shortly.

Interference mechanisms

As the preceding discussion illustrates, many "interference" situations impair retention. Although these phenomena describe *when* forgetting will arise, they do not say *how* forgetting occurs. Why does presenting cues impair recall? Why does retrieval-induced forgetting occur? Why does introducing new learning impair retention of previously acquired material? First we consider classical mechanisms proposed to explain interference, and show how they can be extended to explain phenomena like part-set cuing and retrieval-induced forgetting (Figure 9.9). Then we consider a more recent view in which inhibitory processes associated with retrieval cause forgetting.

Associative blocking

Once, while recalling the British term for what Americans call a "Christmas ornament," I persistently recalled "Christmas balls" (what Belgians call Christmas ornaments), instead of "Christmas baubles." "Christmas balls" kept intruding until I gave up. In essence, "Christmas balls" blocked "Christmas baubles." After drifting off to other activities, the right answer "popped" to mind. Perhaps something like this tip-of-the-tongue experience might explain interference. For instance, in retroactive interference, people may forget first-list responses because the cues used to access them now elicit the second-list

responses. In part-set cuing, presenting exemplar cues may strengthen their association to the category, leading them to intrude when people try to retrieve noncue exemplars. In each case, a cue elicits a stronger competitor, leading us to helplessly perseverate on something that we know to be incorrect. The idea that such a process explains interference was proposed by McGeoch in his (1942) *response competition theory*, modern versions of which are known as associative blocking (see Anderson et al., 1994).

The core assumption of the blocking hypothesis is the idea that memories compete for access to awareness when their shared cue is provided. The degree of interference should increase as the cue grows more strongly associated to the competitor, exhibiting what Anderson et al. (1994) refer to as *strength-dependent competition*. But how does a stronger competitor impair recall? Consider an example from retrieval-induced forgetting, in which you are trying to recall *banana* after having practiced *fruit–orange*. According to the blocking theory, the cues on the final test (e.g. *fruit*) to recall *banana* lead the person to accidentally retrieve the stronger practiced item, *orange*.

KEY TERM

Associative blocking: A theoretical process hypothesized to explain interference effects during retrieval, according to which a cue fails to elicit a target trace because it repeatedly elicits a stronger competitor, leading people to abandon efforts to retrieve the target.

Once accidentally retrieved, *orange* will achieve greater prominence, having been practiced again, making it even more likely to be accidentally retrieved. And so the cycle would continue, because, with each accidental retrieval, the wrong answer grows stronger. Eventually, people may simply give up. So, according to the blocking theory, people forget unpracticed exemplars of practiced categories because associations to the practiced memories dominate retrieval. Blocking can also explain the cue-overload principle: The more memories associated to a cue, the more likely it should be to accidentally retrieve a wrong answer, setting the blocking process in motion. If so, the reason you can't remember your dinner 4 months ago is because retrieval calls to mind recent dinners to such an extent that you give up.

Associative unlearning

Associative unlearning is another theoretical account of interference effects, which can be illustrated intuitively with a real-life example. Suppose that your acquaintance describes a conversation at a party several years ago. You may recall, in good detail, elements of the party, including your friend's attendance, various conversations, as well as several amusing events. However, you may forget discussing a topic with your friend, despite your friend's most confident confirmations—even when you clearly recollect discussing the topic. Subjectively, it seems as though your memory has become fragmented, impairing your judgment about how elements of the experience go together. This apparent fragmentation may reflect damage to the associations between elements of that event caused by storing subsequent experiences. Perhaps such damage underlies my inability to recollect knocking over the Christmas tree.

Research on the unlearning hypothesis of retroactive interference (Melton & Irwin, 1940)

is relevant to these ideas. According to the hypothesis, the association between a stimulus and a trace will be weakened whenever that trace is retrieved inappropriately. In effect, the bond between the cue and the target gets "punished." For example, suppose that you try to retrieve the new password to your email account. According to the unlearning view, if you recall your old password and realize the mistake, the association between the cue "password" and the original password details will get weakened, decreasing the chances that it will pop up again in the future. If the old password is punished often enough, the association may grow so weak that the cue "password" will no longer activate that trace; the stimulus will be decoupled from the response. This view can explain retrieval-induced forgetting, if we assume that during retrieval practice, competing items intrude and are punished. It explains retroactive interference in the same way. So whereas blocking attributes forgetting to very strong practiced competitors, unlearning says that associations into the target are too weak.

The unlearning and blocking hypotheses are not incompatible. In fact, according to the classical two-factor model of retroactive interference (Melton & Irwin, 1940), both mechanisms are needed. It is worth emphasizing, however, that proof of unlearning is difficult to establish, for the same reasons that it is difficult to prove that memories are permanently forgotten, as discussed earlier in this chapter. And although blocking explains why forgetting appears to grow as competitors are strengthened, there are reasons to doubt whether strengthening a competitor, by itself, produces forgetting, as will be illustrated shortly. For these reasons, an alternative view has emerged that attributes the forgetting arising from interference to inhibitory processes.

Inhibition as a cause of forgetting

The preceding discussion raises an important point: Sometimes it is maladaptive for a trace to be accessible. The goal of retrieving a target memory can be disrupted by highly accessible competitors, and people need a way to limit

---

KEY TERM

Unlearning: The proposition that the associative bond linking a stimulus to a memory trace will be weakened when the trace is retrieved in error when a different trace is sought.

this distraction. Although unlearning is one way to accomplish this, another is to inhibit the offending trace. Consider an analogy. Suppose that you normally wear a watch, but one day the wristband breaks, and you can't wear it. If someone then asks you what time it is, you may look at your wrist reflexively, even when you know the watch is absent. This may happen several times before you learn to look at the clock instead. Clearly, what is normally a useful and overlearned habit has, for the time being, become an inappropriate response that must be shut down, so that an alternative but more appropriate response may be given. Humans and other organisms have the ability to terminate responses, either so that an alternative may be given, or so that all responding may be stopped. Stopping is thought to be accomplished by a mechanism that inhibits the response. Inhibition reduces the activity level of the response, ceasing its production in a manner analogous to how inhibiting a neuron would reduce its influence on other neurons.

The same demands confronted in shutting down interfering responses occur for internal actions, such as retrieval. As discussed in the section on proactive interference, if somebody asks for our telephone number, we may automatically remember our old number even though we have switched phones. Recalling the new number requires that we stop retrieval of the old one, which may be accomplished by inhibition. If the old number is inhibited, however, it will grow harder to recall, even if it remains available. In the context of retrieval-induced forgetting, *banana* may become activated and intrude during the retrieval of *fruit-or—*. To facilitate the retrieval of *orange*, perhaps *banana* is inhibited, with persisting inhibition making it harder to retrieve that item. *Banana*, like the habit of looking at one's wrist, may be inhibited to support the current goals. Are inhibitory processes engaged during retrieval?

The role of inhibition during retrieval has often been studied through the phenomenon of retrieval-induced forgetting (Levy & Anderson, 2002). Inhibition makes several predictions about retrieval-induced forgetting that are not made by either the blocking or unlearning theories. According to inhibition, performing retrieval practice on *fruit-orange* impairs the recall of *banana* because

banana, as the competing memory (like looking at the wristwatch), is inhibited by activation-reducing mechanisms. If *banana* is truly inhibited, one might imagine that *banana* would be harder to recall generally, whether one tests it with *fruit* as a cue, or, say, another unrelated associate, such as *monkey-b—*. In other words, inhibition predicts that retrieval-induced forgetting should generalize to new cues, thus exhibiting cue independence. In contrast, both blocking and unlearning attribute forgetting to problems with the associations linking *fruit* to either *banana* or *orange*. Hence, according to these theories, retrieval-induced forgetting should be cue dependent. That is, as long as you switch to another cue, like *monkey*, which circumvents the stronger association from *fruit* to *orange* and the potentially weaker association from *fruit* to *banana*, no impairment should be found for *banana*. Cue-independent forgetting has been observed many times (Anderson & Spellman, 1995; see Anderson, 2003, Weller, Anderson, Gomez-Ariza, & Bajo, 2013, for reviews), indicating that inhibition does play a role in causing retrieval-induced forgetting.

According to the inhibition hypothesis, the need to overcome interference during retrieval triggers inhibition. If so, then active retrieval on practiced items should be necessary to induce forgetting of competitors. For example, simply replacing retrieval practice trials (e.g. *fruit-or—*) with a chance to re-study *fruit-orange* multiple times should eliminate later forgetting of competitors like *banana*. Forgetting should disappear because giving people *fruit-orange* to study eliminates any struggle to retrieve *orange*, and thus, any need to resolve interference from *banana*. This retrieval-specificity property is a consistent feature of retrieval-induced forgetting (see Anderson, 2003; Storm & Levy, 2012). Thus, even though both retrieval practice and extra study exposures strengthen memory for the practiced items to the same degree, only retrieval practice impairs retention of the unpracticed competitors. There appears to be something special about the need to reach into memory and retrieve something that induces forgetting, consistent with the idea that inhibition is involved. This finding doesn't favor the blocking hypothesis, however, which predicts that strengthening practiced shapes should impair recall of competitors, regardless of whether strengthening is accomplished by retrieval or study. Inhibitory processes engaged during retrieval can also explain the part-set cuing findings of Bauml and Aslan (2004) discussed earlier.

One important feature of retrieval-induced forgetting that speaks against blocking theories of this phenomenon is that the amount of forgetting appears unrelated to how strong the practiced associations become as a result of practice. Research on retrieval specificity, for example, shows that it is possible to greatly strengthen practiced items through repeated study, without impairing unpracticed competitors. If strengthening practiced items were enough to cause forgetting, one should have observed forgetting under these circumstances. Indeed, strengthening a competitor may not be necessary at all, to trigger retrieval-induced forgetting. In one study, Benjamin Storm, Elizabeth Bjork, Robert Bjork, and John Nestojko (2006) had the clever idea to see whether it was merely the retrieval attempt that created retrieval-induced forgetting. Participants in this retrieval practice paradigm were, for some categories, given retrieval practice cues that were impossible to complete. So, for example, they might have received the cue *fruit-lu—* to complete during retrieval practice, even though no fruit begins with *lu*. Strikingly, even though people could not complete any of these retrieval practice tests, they showed as much retrieval-induced forgetting for the remaining unpracticed exemplars as they did for categories in which retrieval practice trials could be completed. So the struggle to extract a trace from memory in the face of interference is the important trigger for retrieval-induced forgetting, not the strengthening of the practiced items. This property is referred to as *strength independence*.

If inhibition overcomes interference from competitors, the amount of retrieval-induced forgetting a person suffers should depend on the presence of interference during retrieval practice. If the other associates of a cue don't cause interference, inhibition should be unnecessary. In an early demonstration of

this, Anderson et al. (1994) varied whether competing items were high-frequency examples of their respective categories (e.g. *fruit–banana*) or were low-frequency examples (e.g. *fruit–guava*). Intuitively, one might imagine that a high-frequency example like *banana* would be resistant to forgetting, whereas a low frequency item might be vulnerable. The analogy to the wristwatch example, however, suggests that the opposite may be true. It's precisely because one reflexively checks one's wrist when the watch is not there that one must inhibit that response to prevent it from occurring. If so, then high-frequency examples, like *fruit–banana* might be prime targets for inhibition because they come to mind so readily, whereas low-frequency exemplars might not need to be inhibited. This is exactly what Anderson and colleagues found. This property is known as *interference dependence*, or the tendency for retrieval-induced forgetting to be triggered by interference from a competing memory (see Anderson & Levy, 2011; Storm, 2011; Storm & Levy, 2012 for reviews).

Research on retrieval-induced forgetting suggests that selectively retrieving facts or events places demands on attentional control processes like inhibition, to overcome interference from distracting memory traces. In our wristwatch example, it takes attention to suppress the tendency to look at your wrist reflexively when someone asks you what time it is. If inhibition truly requires attention, then retrieval-induced forgetting might be reduced if people are distracted during retrieval practice, and can't devote the full resources needed to suppress distracting memories. This prediction was confirmed by Patricia Roman, Felipa Soriano, Carlos Gomez-Ariza, and Teresa Bajo (2009), who studied what happens when attention is divided during retrieval practice (Figure 9.10A. After studying a list of categories like fruits and drinks, participants performed retrieval practice according to the typical retrieval-induced forgetting procedure used by Anderson et al. (1994). Crucially, whereas some participants performed retrieval practice with full attention, others had to do a concurrent attention-demanding task: they listened to an audio recording of a speaker reading a series of digits, and had to press a button each time they heard three odd digits in a row. Remarkably, participants in the two groups were equally successful in performing retrieval practice, despite the differing attention demands. However, when it came to the final memory test, participants in the divided attention condition showed significantly less retrieval induced forgetting than full attention participants. Indeed, they showed no retrieval-induced forgetting at all. Relatedly, Koessler, Engler, Riether, and Kissler (2009) found that giving people a highly stressful task (having to give a presentation unexpectedly to a group of strangers) just before they performed retrieval practice abolished retrieval-induced forgetting (Figure 9.10B). Storm and White (2009) further found that participants with attention deficit disorder showed significantly reduced

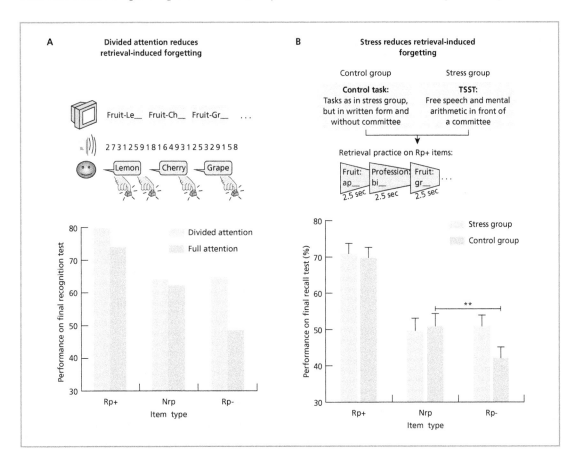

Figure 9.10 The effects of divided attention and stress on retrieval-induced forgetting. Panel A illustrates findings from Roman et al., who manipulated whether participants performed retrieval practice on category exemplars under full attention, or while simultaneously performing a digit monitoring task (described in the text). Participants in the full attention condition showed facilitation of practiced (Rp+) items and impaired retention of competitors (Rp- items) on a final recognition test; in contrast, participants who had their attention divided showed facilitation of practiced items, but no impairment for Rp- items. A similar pattern was shown by Koessler et al. (Panel B), though the stress manipulation was introduced before retrieval practice. In the experimental group, participants were asked to give an unannounced presentation in front of a committee. Thus, in both cases, inhibition effects could be selectively abolished without affecting practice benefits, by manipulations likely to compromise attention. Panel A from Román et al. (2009), copyright © Association for Psychological Science. Panel B from Koessler et al. (2009), copyright © Association for Psychological Science.

retrieval-induced forgetting. Taken together, these findings suggest that retrieval-induced forgetting is attention dependent. This feature is consistent with the role of inhibitory processes in suppressing distracting memories during retrieval practice.

It makes sense that suppressing distraction from competing memories might require focused attention and effort. Does suppressing particular competing memories grow easier with each time that we retrieve the memory we want? In our wristwatch analogy, one is less likely to look at one's watchless wrist with each successive occasion of being asked for the time. The increasing ease with repetitions may indicate that the habit that was once distracting has been inhibited, and so no longer demands effort to control. Research using brain imaging suggests that this process may also happen with inhibiting memories. Brice Kuhl and his colleagues used fMRI to scan people during retrieval practice. As in most retrieval-induced forgetting experiments, they asked participants to retrieve the same to-be-practiced items on three occasions, and they wondered what brain areas would be more engaged during the first retrieval practice compared to the

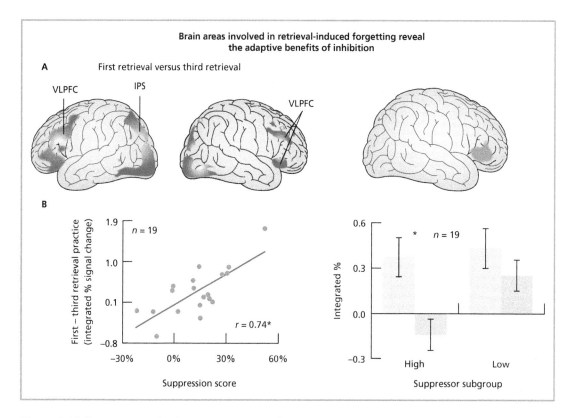

Figure 9.11 Brain areas involved in retrieval-induced forgetting in the study by Kuhl et al. Participants were scanned with fMRI as they performed retrieval practice trials on studied items. Panel A illustrates brain areas that were more active during the first retrieval practice compared to the third, which includes both left and right ventrolateral prefrontal cortex (VLPFC). This finding is consistent with a role for VLPFC in overcoming competition, which subsides over repetitions, as memories are inhibited. Consistent with this view, activation in a subregion of right VLPFC (Panel A, right side) predicted the amount of retrieval-induced forgetting (Panel B). Panel C illustrates how high suppressors (people who show a lot of retrieval-induced forgetting) show a steeper decline in VLPFC activation from the first to the third practice trial than do low suppressors (people who show little retrieval-induced forgetting). Thus, people who are good at forgetting via inhibition, exert less neural effort over time, as interfering memories are suppressed. From Kuhl et al. (2007) copyright © Nature Publishing.

third. On the first practice trial, competing memories are yet to be inhibited, and so produce substantial interference that needs to be resolved by engaging interference resolution mechanisms. By the third trial, any interference caused by competitors should be much reduced, eliminating the need for control. Intriguingly, Kuhl and colleagues observed more activation in the left and right ventrolateral prefrontal cortex and anterior cingulate cortex on early trials compared to later trials (Figure 9.11A). These brain regions previously have been associated with cognitive control and the resolution of response conflict, suggesting that the attentional demands of retrieval practice indeed declined over repetitions, consistent with a diminished need to overcome distraction. Importantly, the steeper the decline in activation in these areas from the first to the third retrieval practice trial, the greater was the retrieval-induced forgetting observed on the final test. Kuhl and colleagues argued

that this finding revealed the adaptive advantage of forgetting: by reducing distraction from competing memories, people expended less neural effort during retrieval practice to retrieve the things they wanted to recall (Kuhl, Dudukovic, Kahn, & Wagner, 2007; see Levy, Kuhl, & Wagner, 2010 for a review). Other research has since built on this fascinating finding to show that a person's ability to engage the ventrolateral prefrontal cortex to inhibit competing memories is related to genetically linked variation in the availability of dopamine in the prefrontal cortex (Wimber et al., 2011).

Taken together, the properties of cue independence, retrieval specificity, strength independence, interference dependence and attention dependence converge to support a role of inhibition as a source of forgetting. If so, it suggests that many of our experiences with forgetting may arise from the need to control interference. It's precisely because we are distracted by momentarily irrelevant

TABLE 9.1 Properties of retrieval-induced forgetting

Property of retrieval-induced forgetting	Description
Cue independence	The tendency for forgetting caused by inhibition to generalize to novel test cues on the independent probe test (e.g. *monkey–b—* for *banana*, which was originally studied with the cue *fruit*).
Retrieval specificity	Active retrieval from long-term memory is necessary to induce forgetting of related information. For example, having to retrieve *orange*, given *fruit–or—* generates retrieval-induced forgetting of unpracticed competitors (e.g. *banana*), whereas simply studying the intact pairing (*fruit–orange*) does not.
Strength independence	The degree to which competitors are strengthened by retrieval practice is unrelated to the size of the retrieval-induced forgetting deficit. Thus, strengthening an item by presenting the intact pairing (*fruit–orange*) does not induce retrieval-induced forgetting, whereas engaging in an impossible retrieval attempt (e.g. *fruit–lu—*) still results in forgetting of unpracticed competitors.
Interference dependence	Interference by competitors during retrieval of targets is necessary for retrieval-induced forgetting of those competitors to occur. Therefore, high-frequency competitors (e.g. *fruit–banana*), which pose greater competition than low-frequency competitors (e.g. *fruit–guava*) are more likely to be inhibited than vice versa.
Attention dependence	During retrieval of a target, competitors are only inhibited if attentional control is available to suppress those distracting memories. Reduced attention during retrieval reduces inhibition aftereffects.

information in our memories—those unintended looks at our "mental wristwatch"—that we engage inhibition to refocus on what we hope to retrieve from memory. On the one hand, it may seem ironic that the mechanisms we use to direct retrieval are the ones that ultimately contribute to forgetting. On the other hand, as Robert Bjork suggests, such forgetting may be adaptive because it helps to reduce interference from information that may no longer be as relevant as it once was (Bjork, 1989). If information remains in memory and can be revived (e.g. by re-exposure), forgetting may be very functional.

A FUNCTIONAL VIEW OF INCIDENTAL FORGETTING

Experimental psychologists have traditionally focused on passive mechanisms of forgetting, including trace decay, contextual fluctuation, the use of inappropriate retrieval cues, and interference processes such as blocking. The presumption has been that people are passive victims of forgetting, with memory loss arising from factors that simply happen to us, such as random changes in the environment, and the addition of traces into memory. Although such processes contribute to forgetting, research on inhibition suggests a different outlook.

According to the inhibitory control view, much of the forgetting that we experience arises from the need to control the retrieval process in the face of competition. It is the process by which we combat interference—inhibition of competing traces—that precipitates forgetting, not the mere presence of other traces in memory. By this view, reducing the accessibility of competing traces is adaptive because it facilitates retrieval, but also because it makes subsequent retrievals of the same information easier, reducing future competition. These observations highlight the fact that inhibitory processes can be quite adaptive. This functional view conceptualizes forgetting as a positive outcome, and highlights how a properly functioning memory system must be as good at forgetting as it is at remembering (Bjork, 1988; Anderson & Spellman, 1995; Anderson, 2003; Bjork, Bjork, & Macleod, 2006). Thus, rather than being victims of forces beyond our control, many cases of forgetting may be tied to the very mechanisms that enable the effective control of cognition.

SUMMARY

Whether we like it or not, the vast majority of life's experiences are forgotten. How can experiences that, in the present moment, are in the full focus of consciousness, be completely forgotten? What mechanisms underlie forgetting? To address these fundamental questions, we must first understand the characteristics of forgetting, including the scope of the problem, and what constitutes forgetting. In this chapter, we have reviewed what is presently known about incidental forgetting, and different ideas about its causes. Some of the key ideas reviewed here are summarized below. In the next chapter, we consider the phenomenon of motivated forgetting.

- Forgetting increases over time, though not at a constant rate. The function relating forgetting to time is known as a forgetting curve, and it follows a logarithmic function.
- At the same time, synaptic and systemic consolidation processes make memories more resilient over time, though consolidated memories need to undergo reconsolidation when accessed.

- Repeated retrieval of memories slows their forgetting.
- The availability of a memory in the system (i.e. whether it remains in storage) must be distinguished from its accessibility (i.e. whether one can retrieve it).
- Permanent memory loss is very difficult to establish through behavior, as lack of availability and inaccessibility both predict memory failure.
- Neurobiological changes over time, such as degradation of synaptic connections, cell death, and, in fact, neurogenesis, likely degrade availability of a memory over time, supporting a decay process, even if this may be hard to establish behaviorally.
- Other factors correlated with time (apart from decay) make potent contributions to the forgetting function, including interference, inhibition, and fluctuations in physical and mental context.
- Interference arises when the retrieval cues used to access a memory become associated to other experiences that compete for access to conscious awareness. The more competitors that are attached to a cue, the worse recall of any one item becomes, a generalization known as the cue-overload principle.
- When previously learned experiences (or knowledge) disrupt retention of more recently acquired experiences, it is known as proactive interference.
- When more recently acquired experiences (or knowledge) disrupt retention of previously acquired experiences, it is known as retroactive interference.
- When one has learned a set of material, presenting part of the set as cues for the recall of the remainder typically impairs the ability to recall the remainder, a phenomenon known as part-set cuing impairment.
- The very act of remembering can cause forgetting, a phenomenon known as retrieval-induced forgetting. Retrieval-induced forgetting happens when one tries to selectively retrieve some memories associated to a cue, a process which generally impairs the remaining associates.
- Blocking theories attribute interference to the tendency for stronger traces to persistently intrude during retrieval of weaker ones, leading the person to abandon the search.
- Unlearning theories propose that interference causes destructive changes to the associations that underlie a trace, as a result of learning mechanisms that punish inappropriate retrievals.
- Inhibition theories propose that forgetting arises from the suppression of interfering traces by inhibitory mechanisms that resolve competition.
- Research using the retrieval-induced forgetting paradigm has provided specific evidence supporting the existence of inhibition.
- Retrieval-induced forgetting exhibits key properties that favor the involvement of inhibition, including interference dependence, cue independence, strength independence, retrieval specificity, and attention dependence.
- Retrieval engages cognitive control processes mediated by the ventrolateral prefrontal cortex that have been linked to the suppression of interfering memories and the induction of retrieval-induced forgetting.
- Forgetting may often be adaptive, if it reduces demands on cognitive control processes that would otherwise be needed to suppress interference from competing memories. Thus, adaptive forgetting may increase cognitive efficiency.

Sometimes one's forgetting can be very costly in terms of time, money, embarrassment, or inconvenience to others. Pick the top three most significant examples of forgetting that you have experienced. Use the concepts described in this chapter to explain, in detail, why the forgetting happened to you.

You are trying to remember someone's name, and a well-meaning friend tries to help by supplying guesses, all of them wrong. Using your knowledge of interference mechanisms, describe how you would explain to your friend why they should stop doing this.

Cuc and colleagues colorfully noted that "Silence is not always golden" in their article on socially shared retrieval-induced forgetting. Explain what this means, and why socially shared retrieval-induced forgetting is important.

What are the key findings that suggest that inhibition mechanisms contribute to retrieval-induced forgetting?

FURTHER READING

Anderson, M. C., & Neely, J. H. (1996). Interference and inhibition in memory retrieval. In E. L. Bjork & R. A. Bjork (Eds.), *Memory. Handbook of perception and cognition* (2nd edn., pp. 237–313). San Diego, CA: Academic Press.

Frankland, P. W., Köhler, S., & Josselyn, S. A. (2013). Hippocampal neurogenesis and forgetting. *Trends in Neurosciences, 36*, 497–503.

Levy, B. J., & Anderson, M. C. (2002). Inhibitory processes and the control of memory retrieval. *Trends in Cognitive Sciences, 6*, 299–305.

Levy, B. J., Kuhl, B. A., & Wagner, A. D. (2010). The functional neuroimaging of forgetting. *Forgetting*, 135–163.

Smith, S. M., & Vela, E. (2001). Environmental context-dependent memory: A review and meta-analysis. *Psychonomic Bulletin and Review, 8*(2), 203–220.

Storm, B. C., & Levy, B. J. (2012). A progress report on the inhibitory account of retrieval-induced forgetting. *Memory and Cognition, 40*, 827–843.

REFERENCES

Altmann, E. M., & Schunn, C. D. (2012). Decay versus interference: A new look at an old interaction. *Psychological Science, 23*(11), 1435–1437.

Anderson, M. C. (2003). Rethinking interference theory: Executive control and the mechanisms of forgetting. *Journal of Memory and Language, 49*(4), 415–445.

Anderson, M. C., & Levy, B. J. (2011). On the relationship between interference and inhibition in cognition. In A. S. Benjamin (Ed.), *Successful remembering and successful forgetting: A festschrift in honor of Robert A. Bjork* (pp. 107-132). New York: Psychology Press.

Anderson, M. C., & Neely, J. H. (1996). Interference and inhibition in memory retrieval. In E. L. Bjork & R. A. Bjork (Eds.), *Memory. handbook of perception and cognition* (pp. 237–313). San Diego, CA: Academic Press.

Anderson, M. C., & Spellman, B. A. (1995). On the status of inhibitory mechanisms in cognition: Memory retrieval as a model case. *Psychological Review, 102*, 68–100.

Anderson, M. C., Bjork, R. A., & Bjork, E. L. (1994). Remembering can cause forgetting: Retrieval dynamics in long-term memory. *Journal of Experimental Psychology: Learning, Memory, and Cognition, 20*, 1063–1087.

Baddeley, A. D. (1986). *Working memory*. New York: Oxford University Press.

Baddeley, A. D., & Hitch, G. (1977). Recency re-examined. In S. Dornic (Ed.), *Attention and performance*. (pp.647–667). Hillsdale, NJ: Lawrence Erlbaum Associates.

Bahrick, H. P. (1984). Semantic memory content in permastore: Fifty years of memory for Spanish learning in school. *Journal of Experimental Psychology: General, 113*, 1–29.

Bahrick, H. P., Bahrick, P. O., & Wittlinger, R. P. (1975). Fifty years of memory for names and faces: A cross-sectional approach. *Journal of Experimental Psychology: General, 104*(1), 54–75.

Bailey, C. H., & Chen, M. (1989). Structural plasticity at identified synapses during long-term memory in *Aplysia*. *Journal of Neurobiology, 20*(5), 356–372.

Barnes, J. M., & Underwood, B. J. (1959). Fate of first-list association in transfer theory. *Journal of Experimental Psychology, 58*(2), 97–105.

Bäuml, K.-H., & Aslan, A. (2004). Part-list cuing as instructed retrieval inhibition. *Memory and Cognition, 32*(4), 610–617.

Berman, M. G., Jonides, J., & Lewis, R. L. (2009). In search of decay in verbal short-term memory. *Journal of Experimental Psychology: Learning, Memory, and Cognition, 35*(2), 317.

Bjork, E. L., Bjork, R. A., & Macleod, M. D. (2006). Types and consequences of forgetting: Intended and unintended. In L. Nilsson & O. Nobuo (Eds.), *Memory and society: Psychological perspectives* (pp. 141–165). New York: Psychology Press.

Bjork, R. A. (1988). *Retrieval practice and the maintenance of knowledge*. Oxford: John Wiley & Sons.

Bjork, R. A. (1989). Retrieval inhibition as an adaptive mechanism in human memory. In H. L. Roediger & F. I. Craik (Eds.), *Varieties of memory and consciousness: Essays in honour of Endel Tulving* (pp. 309–330). Hillsdale, NJ: Lawrence Erlbaum Associates.

Broadbent, D. E. (1958). *Perception and communication*. New York: Pergamon Press.

Carroll, M., Campbell-Ratcliffe, J., Murnane, H., & Perfect, T. J. (2007). Retrieval-induced forgetting in educational contexts: Monitoring, expertise, text integration and test format. *European Journal of Cognitive Psychology, 19*, 580–606.

Conroy, R., & Salmon, K. (2006). Talking about parts of a past experience: The influence of elaborative discussion and event structure on children's recall of nondiscussed information. *Journal of Experimental Child Psychology, 95*, 278–297.

Cowan, N. (1988). Evolving conceptions of memory storage, selective attention, and their mutual constraints within the human information-processing system. *Psychological Bulletin, 104*(2), 163–191.

Crowder, R. G. (1976). *Principles of learning and memory*. Oxford: Lawrence Erlbaum.

Cuc, A., Koppel, J., & Hirst, W. (2007). Silence is not golden: A case for socially shared retrieval-induced forgetting. *Psychological Science, 18*(8), 727–733.

Delaney, P. F., Sahakyan, L., Kelley, C. M., & Zimmerman, C. A. (2010). Remembering to forget: The amnesic effect of daydreaming. *Psychological Science, 21*, 1036–1042.

Dudai, Y. (2004). The neurobiology of consolidations, or, how stable is the engram. *Annual Review of Psychology, 55*, 51–86.

Ebbinghaus, H. (1913). *Memory: A contribution to experimental psychology*. (H. A. Ruger & C. E. Bussenius, Trans.). New York: Teachers College, Columbia University.

Eichenbaum, H. (1994). The hippocampal system and declarative memory in humans and animals: Experimental analysis and historical origins. In D. L. Schacter & E. Tulving (Eds.), *Memory Systems*. (pp.143-99). Cambridge, MA: MIT Press.

Frankland, P. W., Köhler, S., & Josselyn, S. A. (2013). Hippocampal neurogenesis and forgetting. *Trends in neurosciences, 36*(9), 497–503.

Garcia-Bajos, E., Migueles, M., & Anderson, M.C. (2009). Script knowledge modulates retrieval-induced forgetting for eyewitness events. *Memory, 17*(1), 92–103.

Gold, J. M., Murray, R. F., Sekuler, A. B., Bennett, P. J., & Sekuler, R. (2005). Visual memory decay is deterministic. *Psychological Science, 16*(10), 769–774.

Hardt, O., Einarsson, E. Ö., & Nader, K. (2010). A bridge over troubled water: Reconsolidation as a link between cognitive and neuroscientific memory research traditions. *Annual Review of Psychology, 61*, 141–167.

Josselyn, S. A., & Frankland, P. W. (2012). Infantile amnesia: A neurogenic hypothesis. *Learning and Memory, 19*(9), 423–433.

Karpicke, J. D., and Roediger, H. L. (2008). The critical importance of retrieval for learning. *Science, 319*(5865), 966–968.

Koessler, S., Engler, H., Riether, C., & Kissler, J. (2009). No retrieval-induced forgetting under stress. *Psychological Science, 20*(11), 1356–1363.

Kuhl, B. A., Dudukovic, N. M., Kahn, I., & Wagner, A. D. (2007). Decreased demands on cognitive control reveal the neural processing benefits of forgetting. *Nature Neuroscience, 10,* 908–914.

Levy, B. J., & Anderson, M. C. (2002). Inhibitory processes and the control of memory retrieval. *Trends in Cognitive Sciences, 6,* 299–305.

Levy, B. J., Kuhl, B. A., & Wagner, A. D. (2010). The functional neuroimaging of forgetting. *Forgetting,* 135–163.

Linton, M. (1975). Memory for real-world events. In D. A. Norman & D. E. Rumelhart (Eds.), *Explorations in cognition.* San Francisco: Freeman.

Macrae, C. N., & MacLeod, M. D. (1999). On recollections lost: When practice makes imperfect. *Journal of Personality and Social Psychology, 77*(3), 463–473.

McGeoch, J. A. (1942). *The psychology of human learning: An introduction.* New York: Longmans.

McKone, E. (1998). The decay of short-term implicit memory: Unpacking lag. *Memory and Cognition, 26*(6), 1173–1186.

Meeter, M., Murre, J. M., & Janssen, S. M. (2005). Remembering the news: Modeling retention data from a study with 14,000 participants. *Memory and Cognition, 33*(5), 793–810.

Melton, A., & Irwin, J. (1940). The influence of degree of interpolated learning on retroactive inhibition and the overt transfer of specific responses. *American Journal of Psychology, 53,* 173–203.

Migueles, M., and García-Bajos, E. (2007). Selective retrieval and induced forgetting in eyewitness memory. *Applied Cognitive Psychology, 21*(9), 1157–1172.

Mueller, J. H., & Brown, S. C. (1977). Output interference and intralist repetition in free recall. *American Journal of Psychology, 90*(1), 157–164.

Müller, G. E., & Pilzecker, A. (1900). Experimentalle beitrage zur lehre com gedachtnis. *Zeitschrift fur Psychologie, 1,* 1–288.

Nader, K. & Hardt, O. (2009). A single standard for memory: The case for reconsolidation. *Nature Reviews Neuroscience, 10,* 224–234.

Nader, K., Schafe, G. E., & Le Doux, J. E. (2000). Fear memories require protein synthesis in the amygdala for reconsolidation after retrieval. *Nature, 406*(6797), 722–726.

Nairne, J. S. (2002). Remembering over the short-term: The case against the standard model. *Annual Review of Psychology, 53,* 53–81.

Nickerson, R. S. (1984). Retrieval inhibition from part-set cuing: A persisting enigma in memory research. *Memory and Cognition, 12*(6), 531–552.

Oberauer, K., & Lewandowsky, S. (2013). Evidence against decay in verbal working memory. *Journal of Experimental Psychology: General, 142*(2), 380.

Page, M. P., & Norris, D. (1998). The primacy model: A new model of immediate serial recall. *Psychological Review, 105*(4), 761–781.

Parker, E. S., Cahill, L., & McGaugh, J. L. (2006). A case of unusual autobiographical remembering. *Neurocase, 12*(1), 35–49.

Polyn, S. M., Norman, K. A., and Kahana, M. J. (2009). A context maintenance and retrieval model of organizational processes in free recall. *Psychological Review, 116*(1), 129–156.

Postman, L. (1971). Transfer, interference and forgetting. In J. W. Kling, & L. A. Riggs (Eds.), *Woodworth and Schlosberg's experimental psychology* (pp.1019–1132). New York: Holt, Rinehart and Winston.

Román, P., Felipa Soriano, M., Gómez-Ariza, C. J., & Teresa Bajo, M. (2009). Retrieval-induced forgetting and executive control. *Psychological Science, 20,* 1053–1058.

Shaw, J. S., Bjork, R. A., & Handal, A. (1995). Retrieval-induced forgetting in an eyewitness-memory paradigm. *Psychonomic Bulletin and Review, 2*(2), 249–253.

Slamecka, N. J. (1968). A methodological analysis of shift paradigms in human discrimination learning. *Psychological Bulletin, 69*(6), 423–438.

Squire, L. R. (1992). Memory and the hippocampus: A synthesis from findings with rats, monkeys, and humans. *Psychological Review, 99*(2), 195–231.

Stone, C. B., Coman, A., Brown, A. D., Koppel, J., & Hirst, W. (2012). Toward a science of silence: The consequences of leaving a memory unsaid. *Perspectives on Psychological Science, 7*(1), 39–53.

Storm, B. C. (2011). Retrieval-induced forgetting and the resolution of competition. In A. S. Benjamin (Ed.), *Successful remembering and successful forgetting: A festschrift in honor of Robert A. Bjork* (pp. 89–105). New York: Psychology Press.

Storm, B. C., & Levy, B. J. (2012). A progress report on the inhibitory account of retrieval-induced forgetting. *Memory and Cognition, 40,* 827–843.

Storm, B. C. & White, H. (2010). ADHD and retrieval-induced forgetting: Evidence for a deficit in the inhibitory control of memory. *Memory, 18*(3), 265–271.

Storm, B. C., Bjork, E. L., Bjork, R. A., & Nestojko, J. F. (2006). Is retrieval success a necessary condition for retrieval-induced forgetting? *Psychonomic Bulletin and Review, 13*, 1023–1027.

Towse, J. N., Hitch, G. J., & Hutton, U. (2000). On the interpretation of working memory span in adults. *Memory and Cognition, 28*(3), 341–348.

Underwood, B. J. (1957). Interference and forgetting. *Interference and Forgetting, 64*, 49–60.

Watkins, M. J. (1978). Engrams as cuegrams and forgetting as cue-overload: A cueing approach to the structure of memory. In C. R. Puff (Ed.), *The structure of memory* (pp. 347–372). New York: Academic Press.

Weldon, M. S., & Bellinger, K. D. (1997). Collective memory: Collaborative and individual processes in remembering. *Journal of Experimental Psychology: Learning, Memory, and Cognition, 23*(5), 1160–1175.

Weller, P. D., Anderson, M. C., Gomez-Ariza, C., & Bajo, M. T. (2013). On the status of cue independence as a criterion for memory inhibition: Evidence against the covert blocking hypothesis. *Journal of Experimental Psychology: Learning, Memory, and Cognition, 39*, 1232–1245.

Wimber, M., Schott, B. H., Wendler, F., Seidenbecher, C. I., Behnisch, G., Macharadze, T. et al. (2011) Prefrontal dopamine and the dynamic control of human long-term memory. *Translational Psychiatry, 1*(7), e15.

Yonelinas, A. P., & Levy, B. J. (2002). Dissociating familiarity from recollection in human recognition memory: Different rates of forgetting over short retention intervals. *Psychonomic Bulletin and Review, 9*(3), 575–582.

Contents

Life is good, or memory makes it so   266

Terminology in research on motivated
forgetting   267

Factors that predict motivated forgetting   268

Factors that predict memory recovery   281

Recovered memories of trauma: Instances of motivated
forgetting?   287

Summary   292

Points for discussion   293

Further reading   294

References   294

CHAPTER 10

MOTIVATED FORGETTING

Michael C. Anderson

People usually think of forgetting as something bad. It is to lose our cherished past, to forget friends' names, and to neglect our responsibilities. But as Jill Price's remarkable memory (discussed in Chapter 9) illustrates, forgetting may be more desirable than we think. Price often yearns to forget, so that she can avoid continually reliving the events and emotions of terrible times. She has difficulty "letting go" and 'getting past" things that most of us get over quickly. These sentiments reveal that more often than we realize, forgetting is exactly what we need to do. Sometimes we confront reminders of experiences that sadden us, as when after the death of a loved one, or after a broken relationship, objects and places evoke memories of the lost person. Other times, reminders trigger memories that make us angry, anxious, guilty, ashamed, or embarrassed; a face may remind us of an argument that we hope to get past; an envelope may bring to mind a very unpleasant task we are avoiding; or an image of the World Trade Center in a movie may elicit upsetting memories of 11 September. In the popular film, *Eternal Sunshine of the Spotless Mind*, the main character, Joel, suffers so badly from memories of his lost love, Clementine, he seeks out a memory deletion clinic, to have all memories of her removed from his brain. Unfortunately, though we might at times yearn for them, no such clinics exist, and we cannot avoid life's tendency to insert memories we wish were not there.

People do not take this situation lying down, however. They do something about it.

Jim Carrey's character, Joel, in Michel Gondry's film, *Eternal sunshine of the spotless mind* hires a service to permanently erase painful memories of his ex-girlfriend from his mind. While such technology is science fiction, our desire and ability to control our memory is very much a reality.

When we confront reminders to unwanted memories, a familiar reaction often occurs—a flash of experience and feeling followed rapidly by an attempt to exclude the memory from awareness. Unlike in most other situations, retrieval is unwanted, and must be shut down. Suppressing retrieval shuts out the intrusive memories, restoring control over the direction of thought and our emotional well-being. Indeed, for veterans, witnesses of terrorism, and countless people experiencing personal traumas, the day-to-day reality of the need to control intrusive memories is all too clear. Any serious and general treatment of forgetting therefore needs to consider the motivated involvement of individuals as conspirators in their own memory failures. Is my failure to remember knocking over the Christmas tree (see Chapter 9) simply an accident of normal forgetting? Is the fact that you "forgot" to do that unpleasant task, *yet again*, truly an innocent mistake? In this chapter, we consider what is known about how people forget things that they would prefer not to remember.

LIFE IS GOOD, OR MEMORY MAKES IT SO

With surprising consistency, people across the world, of all ages, ethnicities, and income levels report being generally happy with their lives. This feeling of well-being is widespread, and often defies people's objective circumstances. It is found in people with physical or mental disabilities, people with low incomes, and in members of minority groups (Diener & Diener, 1996; Lykken & Tellegen, 1996). Research suggests that memory may contribute to this perceived well-being. Our assessment of how we are doing in life relies on what we remember. For example, people show a strong positivity bias in what they remember over the long-term. In an early illustration of this bias, Waldfogel (1948) gave participants 85 minutes to generate as many memories as they could recall from the first 8 years of their lives. Of these memories, people rated 50% as pleasant, 30% as unpleasant, and 20% as neutral, suggesting that, for whatever reason, positive memories were simply more accessible. A similar finding occurs when, instead of asking people to generate memories intentionally, you ask them to note memories that "spontaneously" pop into mind over a longer time period. Of the involuntary reminders reported in a study by Bernsten (1996), 49% were pleasant, 32% neutral, and 19% unpleasant. This positivity bias increases as we get older, and grow to focus more on emotional goals, and on maintaining a sense of well-being. Why do such effects occur? Are memories of positive events more frequent because those types of events are more common, or might people's motivations have something to do with it?

Susan Charles, Mara Mather, and Laura Carstensen (2003) conducted a simple and compelling study suggesting that our memory biases are no accident. They asked younger and older adults to view 32 scenes. The scenes included a mixture of pleasant, neutral, and rather unpleasant images. After a 15-minute delay, participants recalled as many of the pictures as they could. As illustrated in Figure 10.1, pictures with emotional content were recalled better, in general, than were neutral pictures, and older adults recalled fewer pictures than did younger adults. Importantly, however, as participants got older, their memories became progressively more biased in favor of positive scenes over negative ones, even though all scenes were viewed for the same amount of time: Whereas young participants recalled positive and negative scenes with equal frequency, older adults recalled nearly twice as many positive as negative scenes. A subsequent test revealed that older adults could recognize the positive and negative scenes equally well, indicating that they both made it into memory. For some reason, however, negative events were not recalled as well. Similar age-related emotional biases have been observed with words and faces (Leigland, Schulz, & Janowsky, 2004). In a review of research on aging and positivity effects, Mather and Carstensen (2005) build a compelling case that as we get older and life grows short, people focus more on maintaining a sense of well-being, and less on goals concerning knowledge and the future. As a result, people grow skilled in emotion regulation, which includes, in part, controlling what we remember. How could this possibly happen? What processes contribute to motivated forgetting?

KEY TERM

Positivity bias: The tendency, increasing over the lifespan, to recall more pleasant memories than either neutral or unpleasant ones.

Emotion regulation: Goal-driven monitoring, evaluating, altering, and gating one's emotional reactions and memories about emotional experiences.

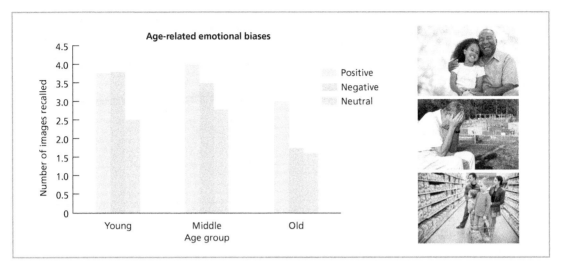

Figure 10.1 Although memory overall tends to decline with age, older adults tend to remember fewer negative memories relative to positive ones, demonstrating an age-related positivity bias. From Charles, Mather, and Carstensen (2003). Copyright © American Psychological Association. Reproduced with permission. Right: Examples of positive, negative, and neutral images used in the study.

TERMINOLOGY IN RESEARCH ON MOTIVATED FORGETTING

It is important to clarify certain terms and distinctions that will arise in our discussion of how motives alter our memories. Perhaps the most well-known term relating to motivated forgetting is repression, popularized by Sigmund Freud through his psychoanalytic theory. In Freud's framework, repression refers to a psychological defense mechanism that banishes unwanted memories, ideas, and feelings into the unconscious to reduce conflict and psychic pain. It is one in an arsenal of defensive processes, including rationalization, projection, and many others. Although

KEY TERM

Repression: In psychoanalytic theory, a psychological defense mechanism that banishes unwanted memories, ideas, and feelings into the unconscious in an effort to reduce conflict and psychic pain. Theoretically, repression can either be conscious or nonconscious.

Freud used repression in a number of ways, he offered the following simple definition: "The essence of repression lies simply in the function of rejecting and keeping something out of consciousness" (Freud, 1917, p. 147).

Within this framework, repressed contents were not eliminated from the mind, but were excluded from conscious awareness. They could still influence behavior unconsciously, manifesting themselves in our dreams, preferences, choice of topics we discuss, and even our emotional reactions. Moreover, repressed contents were not guaranteed to remain unconscious, but were thought to pop up again on later occasions, a phenomenon Freud referred to as the *return of the repressed* (e.g. Freud, 1900, 1917).

A distinction is sometimes drawn between *repression* and *suppression*, with the former being an unconscious process, and the latter being conscious and intentional. By this view, repression is an automatic, defensive process by which a memory is excluded from consciousness without a person ever being aware of its presence. Suppression, on the other hand, refers to the intentional, goal-directed exclusion of ideas or memories from awareness. Although the modern psychoanalytic field maintains this distinction, Mathew Erdelyi (2006) has shown that the distinction was introduced by Anna Freud, Sigmund Freud's daughter. He argues that Freud used the terms interchangeably, and that the distinction distorts his theoretical viewpoint. In this chapter, the term repression can refer to either sense, but when the term suppression is used, we intend to refer specifically to a voluntary process.

Several other terms often arise that are not linked to Freudian theory, including intentional forgetting and motivated forgetting. Intentional forgetting refers to forgetting arising from processes initiated by a conscious goal to forget. It includes conscious strategies to forget, such as suppression and intentional context shifts. Although we discuss intentional forgetting, this term omits cases when forgetting is nonaccidental, but not consciously intended. The broader term *motivated forgetting* encompasses these potential cases. For example, if every time you see someone associated to an unpleasant event, your mind steers towards topics unrelated to that event, this motivated bias may induce forgetting without being generated by an intention to forget. Nevertheless, this type of forgetting would clearly be motivated.

Motivated forgetting encompasses the term psychogenic amnesia, which means any forgetting that is psychological in origin, and not attributed to neurological damage or dysfunction—forgetting that is psychological in genesis. Although psychogenic amnesia and motivated forgetting might be treated synonymously, the term psychogenic amnesia is generally used for cases of profound and surprising forgetting of major chunks of one's life, or to profound forgetting of a particular event that ought to be remembered. The term is theoretically and mechanistically neutral in that it does not presume Freud's theoretical framework, nor does it say how forgetting is accomplished, merely that the source is psychological rather than biological. Motivated forgetting includes these cases, but it also includes more ordinary, day-to-day examples in which people forget unpleasant things in a way that would not call for clinical evaluation.

FACTORS THAT PREDICT MOTIVATED FORGETTING

Theoretically, controlling unwanted memories may be accomplished by manipulating any stage of memory. The simplest way to avoid remembering unpleasant events is to limit encoding. You might literally look away from a stimulus, or focus instead on only its pleasant aspects; or, if you are unfortunate enough to have looked at something unpleasant, you might cease elaborative thoughts. If an unwanted experience gets encoded, you might avoid reminders to prevent retrieval. Or, if reminders are inescapable, you might endeavor to stop retrieval. In all of these examples, mechanisms involved in "normal forgetting" are engaged in the service of your emotional goals. Research on motivated forgetting has addressed all of these factors, which we discuss next.

Instructions to forget

Have you ever told someone to "Forget about it?" Does saying that make a difference? When you recommend this, you presumably have reason to believe that the person can do it. We often have good reason to put things out of mind, even when they are not emotionally significant. Consider R. A. Bjork's (1970) example of a short-order cook, who during a typical morning breakfast shift must process dozens of similar orders. Having completed an order such as, "Scramble two eggs, crisp bacon, and an English muffin," the cook's performance can only suffer if prior orders have not been forgotten. Similarly, we have all experienced times when, after completing a demanding activity, such as an examination, we must "let go" of the information so that our minds may shift to new endeavors. When we return to the

---

KEY TERM

Psychogenic amnesia: Profound and surprising episodes of forgetting the events of one's life, arising from psychological factors, rather than biological damage or dysfunction.

"dropped" material, we are often surprised that the knowledge once readily available now eludes us. These examples suggest that forgetting may sometimes be initiated to reduce the tendency for proactive interference to impede our concentration. This idea is often studied with the directed forgetting procedure (Bjork, 1970, 1989; see Sahakyan , 2013, Anderson & Hanslmayr, 2014, for reviews), in which participants are overtly instructed to forget recently encoded materials. There are two variants of the directed forgetting procedure, and each involves different forgetting processes: the item method, and the list method.

Item-method directed forgetting

In *item-method directed forgetting*, a participant receives a series of items to remember, one at a time. After each item, an instruction appears indicating that the participant should either continue to remember it or to forget it, because they will no longer need to remember it. After the list ends, participants are given a test of *all* of the to-be-remembered and to-be-forgotten words. Interestingly, recall for to-be-forgotten words is often substantially impaired, relative to to-be-remembered items. For example, Basden and Basden (1996) observed worse recall for to-be-forgotten than for to-be-remembered items regardless of whether the items presented were pictures (78% versus 36% for remember and forget items, respectively), words (72% versus 46%) or words for which participants were asked to construct imagery (85% versus 42%).

Informatively, directed forgetting effects observed with the item method also occur on recognition tests (Basden, Basden, & Gargano, 1993). For these reasons, many theorists believe that item-method directed forgetting effects reflect differential episodic encoding. If you were a participant in such a procedure, you would, in all likelihood refrain from elaborate rehearsal, for example, until you knew whether it was to be remembered or to be forgotten. The *remember instruction* would trigger elaborate semantic encoding, whereas the *forget instruction* would give you permission to simply release attention from the word. This finding illustrates one way in which people exercise control over what they permit into memory—by regulating whether a stimulus is granted elaborative processing. Mather and Carstensen's (2005) participants might have employed some version of this strategy, though their encoding was apparently deep enough to support subsequent recognition.

Although most researchers agree that item-method directed forgetting leads to differences in encoding quality across remember and forget items, it less clear what mechanisms cause those differences. Naturally, when you ask a person to remember something, they are likely to rehearse and elaborate the item more than something you tell them to forget. This *selective rehearsal hypothesis* predicts better memory for remember items. But is it also possible that the *forget* instruction has a detrimental effect as well? Recent work on item-method directed forgetting suggests that a forget instruction engages an active process that disrupts encoding. According to the selective rehearsal account, people exert more cognitive effort after a remember instruction than after a forget instruction. If so, people should have less of their attention to spare when they are trying to implement a remember instruction compared to when they are trying to forget, because in the latter case they don't have to rehearse or elaborate the item. Interestingly, however, the opposite appears to be true. In one example, Jonathan Fawcett and Tracey Taylor (2008) gave participants a secondary task to perform right after the remember/forget instruction. After the memory instruction, an asterisk briefly appeared on the screen, and participants simply were asked to press a button as quickly as possible when they saw it. Contrary to the selective rehearsal account, people were significantly slower to perform this secondary task when it appeared after the forget instruction than after the remember instruction, indicating that implementing the forget instruction required more attention. This surprising pattern—greater effort

---

KEY TERM

Directed forgetting: The tendency for an instruction to forget recently experienced items to induce memory impairment for those items.

associated with forgetting—has been found a number of times, raising the possibility of an active forgetting process. The existence of this additional *encoding suppression* process is supported by recent neuroimaging studies of item-method directed forgetting that point to an inhibitory control process that disrupts episodic encoding (see Anderson & Hanslmayr, 2014 for discussion). This encoding suppression process may involve similar neural processes as those involved in retrieval suppression, to be discussed shortly.

Research on item-method directed forgetting illustrates how people often can regulate which experiences they allow into memory by intentionally limiting encoding. One can imagine that people might use such processes to reduce the footprints in memory of life's less pleasant moments. For example, it may not come as much surprise to you to learn that people generally don't like to hear negative feedback about themselves, and greatly prefer to hear positive things. People's memory, it turns out, reflects this bias well. In one nice example, Constantine Sedikides and Jeffrey Green gave participants a mock personality inventory that asked them to provide ratings on various personality questions. Afterwards, the supposedly sophisticated program provided its analysis, and listed 32 behaviors that the participant was likely to exhibit. Each behavior pertained to key personality dimensions such as trustworthiness, kindness, modesty, and tendency to complain. Critically, some behaviors reflected well upon the participant, whereas others were rather more negative. After carefully reviewing their report, participants were tested on their memory for these behaviors following a short delay. As one might guess, people recalled significantly more of the positive than the negative behaviors. This bias does not arise simply because the negative behaviors are intrinsically less memorable: When people were instead told that the behaviors in the report were from another participant's analysis, people showed no such bias, remembering the positive and negative behaviors comparably. This *mnemonic neglect effect* (Sedikides & Green, 2000) suggests that people's desire to view themselves favorably leads them to limit the encoding of negative feedback. People seem to regulate their memory to protect their self-image (Sedikides & Green, 2009).

The list-method of directed forgetting

The *list-method directed forgetting* procedure presents the instruction to forget only after half of the list (often 10 to 20 items) has been studied, and usually as a surprise. Typically, deception is employed, in which the experimenter tells the participant that the list they just studied was for "practice," and that the real list is about to be presented. Other times, the experimenter may pretend that the participant had received the wrong list, which they should "forget about." Following this instruction, a second list is presented. A final test is then given, quite often for both lists, but sometimes only for the first list. Participants are asked to disregard the earlier instruction to forget, and to remember as much as they can. Performance in this *forget group* is contrasted with a *remember group* who follows the same procedure, except that the instruction after the first list simply reminds people that they should continue remembering the first list. Two findings are consistently observed. First, when participants believe that they can forget the first list, they often do much better at recalling the second list on the final test, compared to the remember group. In other words, the proactive interference one finds from the first list often disappears when people believe that they can forget that list, providing a clear *benefit* of an instruction to forget. Second, forget instructions impair people's recall of items from the first list, compared to performance in the remember condition, reflecting a *cost* of a forget instruction. An illustration of the different varieties of directed forgetting is provided in Figure 10.2, along with a classic example of directed forgetting taken from a study by Geiselman, Bjork, & Fishman (1983) in Figure 10.3.

List-method directed forgetting effects exhibit interesting properties that distinguish them from effects observed with the item method. First, it is unlikely that participants use shallow encoding to forget first-list items. Participants do not receive any hint that they will have to forget anything until the

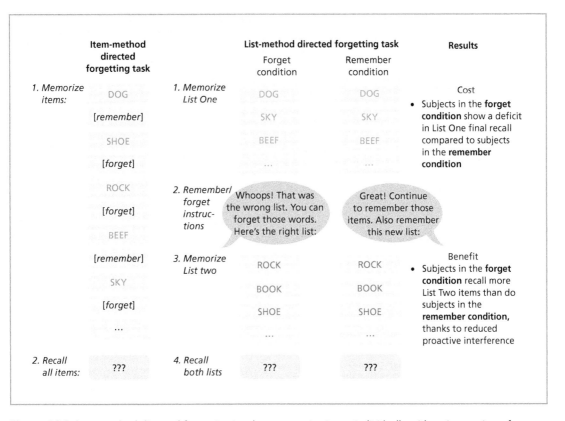

Figure 10.2 Item-method directed forgetting involves presenting items individually with an instruction, after each, to remember or forget. List-method directed forgetting presents many items before some participants receive an instruction to forget it and learn a second list. Memory is impaired for the first list in the forget condition; second-list performance is augmented.

entire first list has been studied, and so have no motive to not encode effectively. Thus, list-method directed forgetting more likely engages a process that hinders later retrieval. Consistent with this idea, list-method directed forgetting effects usually disappear when recognition is tested. Second, unlike in the item-method (Basden & Basden, 1996), items in the list method reveal their presence on implicit memory tests. Indeed, to-be-forgotten items can sometimes exert a greater influence on behavior when memory is tested implicitly. For example, Bjork and Bjork (2003) found that when some to-be-forgotten names were included on a later (apparently unrelated) *fame judgment test* presenting a set of famous and nonfamous names, to-be-forgotten (non-famous) names were judged as more famous than were to-be-remembered (nonfamous)

names in the remember condition. Presumably, participants had forgotten where they knew the name from, due to directed forgetting, and misattributed its familiarity to fame. This finding illustrates how Freud may not have been far off when he claimed that intentionally forgotten materials influence behavior outside of people's awareness.

List-method directed forgetting illustrates how, when people no longer wish to remember events, they can intentionally reduce their accessibility. Can such processes be engaged to forget more realistic personal experiences with emotional content? Susan Joslyn and Mark Oakes took a novel approach to this issue. They asked students to record in a diary two unique events that happened to them each day over a 5-day period (Joslyn & Oakes, 2005). Participants wrote a brief narrative and a title

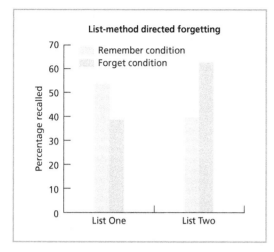

Figure 10.3 A classic example of results from a list-method directed forgetting experiment. Note that, relative to the remember condition, recall of List One is decremented in the forget condition, while List-Two recall is superior, thereby illustrating the cost and benefit of the instruction to forget. Data from Geiselman, Bjork, and Fishman (1983).

summarizing each experience, and they also rated the events for emotional valence and intensity. For example, one student recorded this event, entitled *Crow Chase.*

A few friends and I were walking through campus when we suddenly saw a crow running around on the ground following a squirrel. It was so funny! We stood and watched them for a few minutes, exchanging funny squirrel stories and other animal stories.

(Joslyn & Oakes, 2005, p. 4)

After the first week of recording, students turned in their diaries. The forget group was told that the events recorded on the first 5 days would be used for a different study and that they should forget them, so that they could focus on events from the second week, which they would have to remember. The remember group was told that they would have to remember the events from the first week, as well as the ones from the upcoming week. Over the next 5-day period, the students then recorded

a new set of events. After the second week ended, participants turned in their diaries and were then asked to remember all of the events they had recorded during both weeks. Joslyn and Oaks found that participants instructed to forget had poorer memory for events from the first week than did participants instructed to remember. This pattern was even observed for a group of "practice memories" that participants recorded in their first week that neither group believed they would have to recall. Interestingly, impairment was even found with negative and positive mood events. Related findings were observed by Amanda Barnier and colleagues (Barnier, Conway, Mayoh, & Speyer, 2007) for personal memories learned outside of the experiment.

There are two leading theories of list-method directed forgetting. According to the retrieval inhibition hypothesis, an instruction to forget the first list inhibits list-1 items, impairing recall. This inhibition does not, however, do permanent damage, and memories remain available. Inhibition merely limits retrieval by reducing activation of unwanted items. This view explains why intentionally forgotten items are difficult to recall, but can be recognized, if we assume that re-presentation of forgotten items restores their activation levels. In contrast, according to the context shift hypothesis (Sahakyan & Kelley, 2002), instructions to forget mentally separate the to-be-forgotten items from the second list. If

KEY TERM

Retrieval inhibition hypothesis: A proposed mechanism underlying list-method directed forgetting suggesting that first-list items are temporarily inhibited in response to the instruction to forget and can be reactivated by subsequent presentations of the to-be-forgotten items.

Context shift hypothesis: An alternative explanation for list-method directed forgetting, positing that forget instructions separate first-list items into a distinct context, which unless reinstated during the final test will make the later context a relatively ineffectual retrieval cue.

a person's mental context changes between the first and the second lists and if the second list context remains active during the final test, to-be-forgotten items should be recalled more poorly because the new context is a poor retrieval cue for them, similar to the notion of cognitive context discussed in Chapter 8.

To test the context shift hypothesis, Sahakyan and Kelley varied the mental context in between two lists of words. Might such a context shift produce the pattern observed in directed forgetting? In their context shift condition, participants encoded a first list of words, and then performed a simple task designed to shift their "frame of mind." Participants were asked to imagine, for 1 minute, what their life would be like if they were invisible. The reasoning was that by performing such a bizarre task, participants would enter into studying the second list in a different mental context than was present while they were studying the first list (perhaps one in which they thought the experimenters were crazy). If the context shift hypothesis is correct, this simple manipulation should impair people's memory for the first list, even in the absence of any instruction to forget it. This in fact occurred: Participants given this context shift task showed much poorer retention of the first list on a later test. These findings suggest that part of the directed forgetting effect may arise from a shift in mental context induced by the intention to forget. This hypothesis is not inconsistent with the retrieval inhibition hypothesis, however, if mental context shifts are accomplished by inhibiting the unwanted context instead of individual items (Anderson, 2003). In either case, the deficit induced by instructions to forget (in laboratory studies) is produced by diminished access to the context in which forgotten events were encoded.

Research on directed forgetting establishes that people have some ability to intentionally forget recently experienced events. One method is to deprive experiences of rehearsal and elaboration, and to suppress the encoding process (item-method directed forgetting), increasing the chances that those memories will be forgotten quickly. The consequence of this method is a generalized deficit in recall or recognition, including diminished influence of the experience on indirect tests.

Alternatively, unwanted memories can be rendered less accessible by a process that impairs access to the context to which to-be-forgotten memories are associated. The to-be-forgotten items can continue to influence participants on indirect tests, suggesting that even in the absence of awareness, intentionally forgotten items might make their presence known. Both item-method and list-method directed forgetting can impair neutral as well as emotionally negative materials.

Motivated context shifts and changes in stimulus environment

The preceding discussion illustrates how simply changing one's mental context (e.g. intentionally shifting to a new line of thought) can diminish access to past events. If changing mental context can induce forgetting, perhaps changing other elements of incidental context might work as well. People know this intuitively. For example, when something traumatic happens in one context, people avoid returning to that context to prevent them from being reminded. If the location is a home or a town of residence, people will often change homes or towns to get over the unpleasant incident. When the unwanted memory concerns a person, people often avoid exposure

Sometimes people are so motivated to control their memories that they alter the physical environment to remove retrieval cues. Such was the case at Columbine High School in Colorado. Following the shootings, families of the victims lobbied to demolish and rebuild the library where the incident took place.

to that person. If people cannot remove themselves from an environment, they will sometimes seek to change the environment itself. For example, in the aftermath of the fatal shootings at Columbine High School in Colorado, families of the victims lobbied to have the school library at which the shootings took place torn down and replaced with an entirely different structure, removing reminders to the horrible events.

Motivated context shifts are likely to occur when it is too late to minimize encoding. To limit awareness of the memory, people avoid reminders. The avoidance of cues, especially shifts in environmental context, might facilitate normal forgetting processes in several ways. First, by avoiding reminders, the person deprives a memory of retrievals that ordinarily strengthen and preserve it (Erdelyi, 2006). Essentially, retrieval practice is prevented. Preventing reactivation of the trace should encourage decay processes. Second, by changing the physical environment, the mental context within which one operates will come to mismatch the one in which the event took place, hindering retrieval. If the new context allows a person to recover, mood context will change, making spontaneous retrieval of the event less likely.

Intentional retrieval suppression

Sometimes we cannot avoid reminders to unpleasant events. When this happens, we only have two choices: be reminded, or stop retrieval. To see how people might stop retrieval, consider the following example. Suppose that you have an argument with a significant other. The next time you see them, chances are you will be reminded of the argument, recreating the upset feelings. If you are motivated to "get past" the argument, and sustain a good feeling about the person, you might put the memory out of mind, especially if the argument was not of great consequence. You might find this difficult at first, requiring concentration to redirect your thoughts and emotions to more constructive ends. With repeated encounters, however, the reminders often grow less frequent. After much time, you may be unable to recollect the argument. Such forgetting is not a bad thing. Healthy

relationships require at least some "forgive and forget." Without this, people dwell on small transgressions, never forgetting any upset or wrongdoing. Hyperthymestics wish that they could forget, because unpleasant memories trouble them long past when others would have succeeded in banishing them from mind. People often confront reminders to difficult memories that can make them sad, angry, anxious or ashamed, and they quickly adjust their thoughts.

How do people suppress retrieval? To shed light on these issues, Collin Green and I considered an analogy between how people control unwanted memories and how they control action. We noted that unwanted memories have an "intrusive" quality, seeming to "leap" to awareness in response to reminders, despite our intention to avoid them. This reflexive quality seems similar to reflexive actions. Importantly, we clearly have the ability to stop physical actions. Consider the time that I knocked a potted plant off of my kitchen windowsill. As my hand darted to catch the falling object, I realized that the plant was a

People reflexively try to catch a falling object. But in certain situations (if the object is a cactus, for example), this prepotent motor response would be painfully inappropriate. We are fortunate to have the ability to stop ourselves in mid-action. Can we also stop ourselves from retrieving memories?

cactus. Mere centimeters from it, I stopped myself from catching the cactus. The plant dropped and was ruined, but I was relieved to have avoided being pierced with little needles. This illustrates the need to override a reflexive response to a stimulus. Without the capacity to override reflexive responses, we could not adapt behavior to changes in our goals or circumstances. If we can stop reflexive actions, perhaps we have the machinery to stop retrieval. Indeed, controlling retrieval may build upon these mechanisms of behavioral control to achieve cognitive control.

Retrieval suppression: Basic findings

How do we control reflexive actions? As discussed in Chapter 9, suppressing action may be accomplished by inhibition. Might suppressing retrieval be accomplished in the same way? To look at this, Collin Green and I (Anderson, 2001) developed a procedure modeled after the go/no-go task, which is used to measure people's ability to stop motor responses. In a typical go/no-go task, people press a button as quickly as possible whenever they see a letter appear on a computer screen, *except* when the letter is an X, for which they are to withhold their response. The tendency to withhold the response measures inhibitory control over action (e.g. how well a person could avoid catching the cactus). To see whether people's attempts to stop retrieval might engage inhibitory control, we adapted this procedure to create the think/no-think paradigm.

The think/no-think procedure is intended to mimic those times in life when we stumble upon a reminder to a memory we would prefer not to think about, and try to keep it out of mind. In the simplest version, people study a set of cue-target pairs (e.g. *ordeal–roach*), and are then trained to recall the second word (e.g. *roach*) whenever they encounter the first word as a reminder (e.g. *ordeal*). By training participants to recall pairs in this way, we hoped that the left-hand word would serve as a powerful reminder. In the next step, participants enter the think/no-think phase, which requires them to exert control over retrieval. Most of the trials require the person to recall the response whenever they see the reminder, but for certain reminders (colored in red), participants are admonished to avoid retrieval. So, for example, upon seeing the word *ordeal*, participants are asked to stare directly at this reminder, but nevertheless willfully prevent the associated memory from entering consciousness. It is emphasized that it is insufficient to avoid *saying* the response, and that preventing the memory from entering awareness is crucial. Can people recruit inhibitory control to prevent an unwanted memory from intruding into consciousness? If so, this procedure may capture the essence of repression, which, as Freud said, "Lies simply in the function of rejecting and keeping something out of consciousness" (Freud, 1917, p. 147).

Of course, we cannot observe people's conscious awareness, so it is difficult to know whether someone prevents a memory from entering consciousness. Instead, the think/no-think procedure measures the after-effects of stopping retrieval. If inhibition persists, perhaps stopping retrieval repeatedly might cause forgetting, much like the memory of the argument grows less accessible with repeated encounters with your friend. To measure this behavioral footprint of suppression, participants receive the studied cues (*ordeal*) on a final test and are asked to recall the target memory (*roach*) for every one.

As Figure 10.4 reveals, there is a sizable difference in people's ability to recall "think" and "no-think" items on the final test. This difference, known as the total memory control effect (Levy & Anderson, 2008; Anderson & Levy, 2009), illustrates how a person's intention to control retrieval alters retention. Exactly how intention influences performance is not clear from this effect alone, however. Including a third set of pairs that are studied initially, but

---

KEY TERM

Cognitive control: The ability to flexibly control thoughts in accordance with our goals, including our ability to stop unwanted thoughts from rising to consciousness.

Think/no-think (TNT) paradigm: A procedure designed to study the ability to volitionally suppress retrieval of a memory when confronted with reminders.

that do not appear during the think/no-think phase (i.e. baseline items), allows us to measure the positive control effect, and the negative control effect. The *positive control effect* can be seen in Figure 10.4 as the enhanced memory for "think" items above baseline recall, and is caused by intentional retrieval. This effect confirms that when people are inclined to be reminded, cues enhance memory. The *negative control effect* can be seen in the memory deficit for "no-think" items below baseline recall, and this is due to participants intentionally shutting down retrieval. Thus when people avoid reminders, presenting cues triggers inhibitory processes that impair memory. This

negative control effect is also often referred to as *suppression-induced forgetting*. Most people would expect that repeatedly encountering reminders would improve memory. But clearly this outcome depends on people's disposition as to whether they wish to be reminded. As can be seen in Figure 10.4, suppression-induced forgetting is also seen when people are tested with a novel test cue, showing that impairment is cue-independent. As discussed in Chapter 9, this suggests that the item was inhibited.

Much is now known about suppression-induced forgetting (Anderson & Huddleston, 2012; Anderson & Hanslmayr, 2014). First, the amount of forgetting generally increases

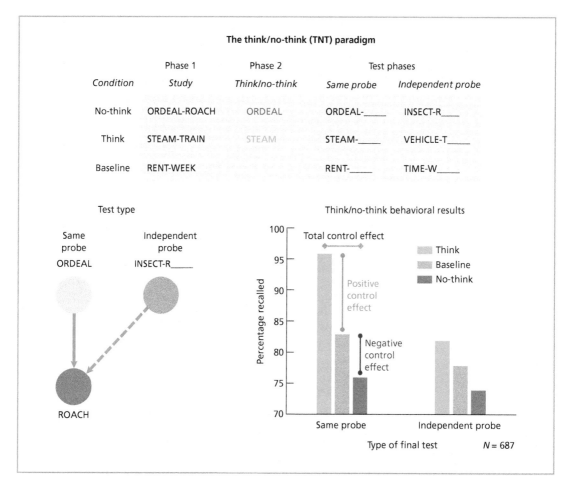

Figure 10.4 Top: After learning word pairs, participants in a think/no-think (TNT) experiment are asked to either think or not think about an item's associate. Participants' memory for all items is then assessed. Lower left: A depiction of the two types of final tests. Lower right: Results of a TNT meta-analysis by test type.

the more times people suppress a given item. Suppression-induced forgetting arises with many stimuli including word pairs, face–scene pairs and various other kinds of stimuli. Forgetting effects occur whether the memory is a neutral or negatively valenced word or scene, though it is unclear whether emotional memories are more or less suppressible compared to neutral memories. Importantly, suppression-induced forgetting has even been observed with autobiographical experiences. For example, Saima Noreen and Malcolm MacLeod (2012) found suppression-induced forgetting for both negative and neutral personal experiences from participants' own lives, though suppression mainly affected participants' memory for details of these events. Although few studies have examined how long forgetting lasts, one study found that a single suppression session produces forgetting that lasts at least 24 hours (Hotta & Kawaguchi, 2009). Interestingly, people who have challenges with cognitive control processes like inhibition appear to be less able to suppress the retrieval of unwanted memories. For instance, adults with attention deficit disorder show diminished suppression-induced forgetting compared to control participants (Depue et al., 2010). This suggests that there may be something important in common between the processes underlying suppression-induced forgetting and broader control mechanisms, a possibility supported by brain-imaging studies that we discuss next.

Brain mechanisms underlying retrieval suppression

Might people really control intrusive memories in the same way they control overt action? One way to look into this is to see whether common brain regions are involved in stopping retrieval and stopping action. In one example, with John Gabrieli, Kevin Ochsner, Brice Kuhl, and colleagues, I conducted a fMRI study contrasting brain activity during no-think and think trials (Anderson, Ochsner, Cooper, Robertson, Gabrieli, Glover, et al., 2004). If suppressing retrieval is similar to motor stopping, more activation should be found in motor stopping regions during no-think trials, in which stopping is required, than during think trials. Consistent with this hypothesis,

we found that suppressing retrieval recruited a network of brain regions including the right lateral prefrontal cortex, and anterior cingulate cortex. This network overlaps with that involved in motor inhibition, even though people doing the no-think task never have to stop motor actions. The right lateral prefrontal cortex plays an especially critical role in stopping reflexive motor action (e.g. Aron, Fletcher, Bullmore, Sahakian, & Robbins, 2003). In fact, stimulation of this brain region during a "go" motor response induces monkeys to stop their movement (Sasaki, Gemba, & Tsujimoto, 1989). This overlap is consistent with the possibility that stopping unwanted actions and memories engages a common inhibition process.

One can compare those moments when we want to avoid retrieval of unwanted memories to how we might avoid crashing into a car that has had an accident on the road ahead of us. When you initially detect the danger on the road ahead, you have a short time window to respond quickly, and slam on the brakes and bring your car to a halt. If stopping retrieval is similar, how do people "slam on the brakes" to prevent retrieval from moving forward? Interestingly, the answer lies in a brain region that is targeted by control: the hippocampus. As discussed in Chapter 16 in this volume, the hippocampus is essential for forming new episodic memories (Squire, 1992). Importantly, however, neuroimaging studies have linked increased hippocampal activation to retrieving one's past, suggesting it is important to that process. If increasing hippocampal activity is important to consciously retrieving a memory, then perhaps suppressing awareness of a memory involves decreasing hippocampal activity. This appears to be true: Anderson et al. (2004) found reduced hippocampal activity when participants suppressed retrieval (Figure 10.5) compared to when they engaged in retrieval. Later studies have shown that this reduction arises because the right lateral prefrontal cortex actively reduces hippocampal activity during no-think trials (Benoit & Anderson, 2012). Thus, slamming on the "mental brakes" to prevent retrieval from unfolding appears to involve an active termination of hippocampal processes that would otherwise carry the retrieval process forward. A similar modulation of hippocampal activity by the right lateral prefrontal cortex may contribute to encoding suppression in the item-method directed forgetting procedure (Rizio & Dennis, 2013; see Anderson & Hanslmayr, 2014, for a review).

Of course, we generally want to stop retrieval when memories are particularly unpleasant, and unpleasant experiences have a tendency to intrude often, especially right after they happen. Are retrieval stopping mechanisms effective for more complex emotional memories? Recent studies indicate that suppressing negative memories also causes suppression-induced forgetting. For example, in two studies by Brendan Depue, Marie Banich, and Tim Curran ((Depue, Banich, & Curran, 2006; Depue, Curran, &, Banich, 2007), participants learned to pair certain unfamiliar faces with unpleasant scenes. One face might have served as the reminder for a scene of a bad car accident, and another might have been paired with a badly deformed infant. Depue and colleagues found that presenting the face reminders and asking people to suppress retrieval impaired later recall of the aversive pictures, replicating suppression-induced forgetting effects observed with word pairs. Depue et al. (2007) also replicated the activation of the right lateral prefrontal cortex

and the reduced hippocampal activity during "no-think" trials. Thus, inhibitory control can be effective at suppressing more naturalistic memories, suggesting it might be a fruitful model for how people regulate awareness of unpleasant memories. One open issue, however, is whether emotionally aversive memories are harder to suppress, compared to emotionally neutral memories (Anderson & Hanslmayr, 2014).

Stopping the retrieval process is not the only way people try to control unwanted memories, however. Following on from our driving analogy, one can avoid crashing into the car ahead either by slamming on the brakes, or by steering quickly out of harm's way, to a different lane. Interestingly, it turns out that when reminders start to trigger an unpleasant memory, one has similar options: to either slam on the mental "brakes" and stop the retrieval process from bringing the memory fully to mind, or, instead, to redirect retrieval processes to other thoughts. Recently, several authors have shown that both approaches to preventing unwanted awareness of a memory cause forgetting (Bergstrom, de Fockert, & Richardson-Klavehn, 2009; Hertel & McDaniel, 2010; Benoit & Anderson, 2012). In one study, Roland Benoit and I wanted to see whether these *direct suppression* and *thought substitution* mechanisms truly engaged different mechanisms, and whether we might be able to identify the brain systems underlying them. Again using the think/no-think procedure, we had two groups of people who were given different instructions on how to prevent retrieval of a memory on no-think trials, when given the reminder. The direct suppression group were asked to look straight at the reminder and to prevent the memory from coming to mind, without distracting themselves with substitute thoughts. They were told that if the memory started to come to mind, they should stop this retrieval process as soon as they could (i.e. slam on the brakes). In contrast, the thought substitution group was told to avoid retrieval on no-think trials by retrieving an alternative association to the reminder as a way to redirect their minds away from the unwanted memory (quickly steering the car into another lane).

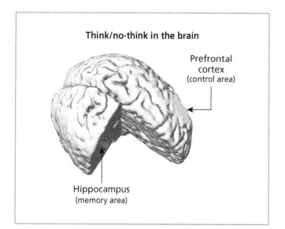

Think/no-think in the brain

Prefrontal cortex (control area)

Hippocampus (memory area)

Figure 10.5 A rendering of the neuroimaging results of Anderson et al. (2004). The lateral prefrontal cortex (depicted in green) is recruited during no-think trials to suppress neural activity in the hippocampus (in red), thereby preventing unwanted memories from coming to mind.

The results of this simple change in instructions were striking. On the one hand, we observed very similar amounts of forgetting for the no-think items in both groups, regardless of approach, as had been found before (Bergstrom et al., 2009). Despite this highly similar memory recall pattern, the two groups differed in how the brain accomplished forgetting. The direct suppression participants recruited the right lateral prefrontal cortex area typically linked with stopping retrieval and this caused reduced hippocampal activity, as found in previous retrieval suppression studies. In stark contrast, the participants using thought substitution engaged areas in the left prefrontal cortex, and the more they engaged these areas, the higher was the hippocampal activity. Thus, thought substitution had the opposite influence on the hippocampus (increased activity) to what we found for direct suppression. This pattern makes sense, given that activation in the hippocampus increases in general when one is remembering the past: Suppressing retrieval (slamming on the brakes) reduces hippocampal activity that might have lead a person to remember the unwanted memory, whereas retrieving an alternate thought (redirecting the car) engages retrieval processes that help to recollect the substitute memory and keep it in awareness, distracting oneself. These findings illustrate how the same goal (avoiding retrieval of an unwanted memory) can be achieved in two fundamentally different (in fact opposite) ways.

It thus appears that when people want to not "catch their mental cacti" and avoid an unwelcome reminder, they can engage at least two systems. One, which performs retrieval stopping, engages systems that are also necessary for motor stopping. For this system, the difference between motor and memory stopping appears to be the area of the brain that is stopped by control; with motor inhibition, motor areas are modulated by the right lateral prefrontal cortex, but with memory inhibition, people instead "close down memory lane" by down-regulating activation in the hippocampus (Anderson & Weaver, 2009). The second is involved in retrieving a substitute memory itself, to keep oneself distracted from the unwanted memory. This process not only does not suppress the retrieval process in general, it engages retrieval actively, but steers it in another direction. It is likely that in real-life settings, some combination of these mechanisms is used to suppress memories, rather than just one or the other: When an unwelcome memory pops to mind, direct suppression may purge the memory from mind (Levy & Anderson, 2012), but thought substitution processes may ensure that one's mind is quickly refocused.

Extreme emotional distress

Perhaps amongst the most striking and unusual form of motivated forgetting arises in *psychogenic amnesia*. Consider the dramatic case of AMN, a 23-year-old insurance worker (Markowitsch, Kessler, Van Der Ven, Weber-Luxenburger, Albers, & Heiss, 1998). AMN discovered a small fire in his basement and left the house to call for help. He did not inhale smoke, and he smashed the cellar door and immediately ran out of the house. That evening, he appeared dazed and frightened, and the next morning, when he awoke, he no longer knew what his profession was, or where he lived. After three weeks, he entered hospital. Upon examination, it became clear that his memories only extended until the age of 17. He barely recognized his partner, whom he had known for three years, and did not recognize his friends or co-workers. After 3 weeks of therapy, he reported one of his earliest memories as a child: at the age of 4, he saw a car crash which set another car in flames; he was then witness to the driver's screams and his death in the flames, with his head pressed against the window. Since that time, fire had been AMN's worst fear. Despite this, AMN showed normal psychological and physical development, and, throughout his life, showed no evidence of psychological illness. A full examination revealed no obvious evidence of brain damage, though greatly reduced metabolism was discovered in memory-related areas. Eight months later, at the time of the report, AMN's deficits in personal memory remained.

Cases like this illustrate several characteristics of psychogenic amnesia. First, psychogenic amnesia is triggered by severe psychological stressors. For AMN, a particular event makes contact with a trauma, and triggers a massive reaction. The stressful event can cause a profound loss of personal memories, often despite a lack of observable neurobiological causes. In striking contrast, memory for public events and general knowledge is often intact. Unlike in AMN's case, amnesia can be *global*, in that it affects the entirety of a person's history. Indeed, in a form of psychogenic amnesia known as psychogenic fugue state (Hunter, 1968), people forget their entire history, including who they are. In such cases, people are often found wandering, not knowing where to go or what to do. Triggering events include such things as severe marital discord, bereavement, financial problems, or criminal offense. A history of depression and also head injury make a person more vulnerable to fugue states, when coupled with acute stress and trauma. Fugue typically lasts a few hours or a few days, and when the person recovers, he/she remembers his/her identity and history once again. However, he/she often have persisting amnesia for what took place during the fugue.

Functional amnesia can also be situation specific, with the person experiencing severe memory loss for a particular trauma. Committing homicide, experiencing or committing a violent crime such as rape, or torture; experiencing combat violence; attempting suicide; and being in automobile accidents, and natural disasters have all induced cases of situation-specific amnesia (Arrigo & Pezdek, 1997; Kopelman, 2002). As Kopelman (2002) notes, however, care must be exercised in interpreting cases of psychogenic amnesia, when there are compelling motives to feign memory deficits for legal or financial reasons. Although some fraction of psychogenic amnesia cases can be explained in this fashion, it is generally acknowledged that true cases are

Members of the military, like many nonuniformed individuals, suffer unimaginable traumas all too often. Such events have the potential to spark psychogenic amnesia, in which memories for the trauma become inaccessible.

not uncommon. Both global and situation-specific amnesia are often distinguished from the organic amnesic syndrome (discussed in Chapter 11) in that the capacity to store new memories and experiences remains intact.

Although the mechanisms of psychogenic amnesia remain poorly understood, one recent study suggests an intriguing connection between at least some cases of this condition and the mechanisms studied in research on retrieval suppression. Hirokazu Kikuchi and colleagues studied two psychogenic amnesia patients, with amnesia extending years prior to scanning (Kikuchi et al., 2009). Both patients were well educated, and neurologically normal, and of normal intelligence, but both had undergone a recent stressful event or period of time that led to extensive retrograde amnesia. Patient 1, a 27-year-old businessman exhibited focal retrograde amnesia for all events, people, and activities that took place in the 4.5 year period prior to the onset of his amnesia, even though he could recall experiences and people from before that period. Patient 2 presented a similar, but more extensive, retrograde amnesia. No neurological abnormalities could be detected, and they appeared to remember all new experiences that happened to them after the onset of the amnesia, showing normal new learning.

Both these patients were scanned with fMRI as they identified faces. Some faces were of strangers (novel faces). Others were of people the patients knew, with half of them drawn from people they met prior to their window of amnesia (identifiable faces), and the other half from during the window of time affected by amnesia (unidentifiable faces). Unsurprisingly, patients did not recognize the novel faces, and could recognize all of the identifiable faces. Intriguingly, although neither patient remembered any of the unidentifiable faces, these faces elicited increased activation in the right lateral prefrontal cortex, together with reduced activity in the hippocampus, as observed in laboratory studies of retrieval suppression. After treatment, one patient recovered his memories, and upon rescanning, no longer exhibited the suppression pattern. These findings suggest that extreme psychological distress may lead retrieval suppression to be engaged involuntarily in reaction to certain stimuli. Much more work remains to be done to understand this phenomenon, however.

Given the dramatic nature of memory loss in such cases, there is usually a concerted effort to help the person recover their identity and history, as in the study by Kikuchi and colleagues. Deliberate attempts to remind the person of their past and identity rarely work, however. Memories can sometimes be recovered spontaneously when particular cues are encountered (Abeles & Schilder, 1935; Schacter, Wang, Tulving, & Freedman, 1982). For example, Kopelman (1995) reported a patient who spontaneously recalled, upon seeing the name of an author on the spine of a book, that he had a friend who was dying of cancer who shared that name. Although some patients appear to recover spontaneously or with supportive therapy, Kritchevsky, Chang, and Squire (2004) found that only two of the ten patients they studied recovered fully, even 14 months after onset. Clearly, the conditions under which memories may be recovered need to be more fully understood.

FACTORS THAT PREDICT MEMORY RECOVERY

As the preceding discussion highlights, people may be motivated to forget at one time, but then wish to recall forgotten memories later.

Although the need for recovery is dire in psychogenic amnesia, it is also an important goal in less dramatic instances of forgetting. At some point, you need to face that unpleasant task that you keep suppressing; to do so, you need to extract it from memory when making your to-do list. Or you may encounter people who remember some embarrassing event that occurred to you that you simply cannot recall (like knocking over a Christmas tree), and, in your astonishment, may seek to release it from the dungeons to which it has been banished. Perhaps you are undergoing therapy and need to discuss past experiences. In this section, we consider factors that predict when motivated recovery can occur.

Passage of time

The passage of time is, of course, associated with forgetting. In some cases, however, memory paradoxically improves with delay even when no effort to retrieve is made. The classic demonstration comes from Ivan Pavlov, in his studies of classical conditioning. Pavlov found that when a classically conditioned salivary response was extinguished, the response gained in strength again after 20 minutes (Pavlov, 1927). Pavlov referred to this finding as spontaneous recovery. Spontaneous recovery is a robust phenomenon (Rescorla, 2004), including in research on conditioned emotional responding. After a conditioned response has been extinguished, spontaneous recovery increases with time, though conditioned responses do not generally return to full strength. Moreover, with repeated recovery/extinction cycles, the conditioned response recovers less each time. Spontaneous recovery illustrates that some types of memory, when seemingly forgotten, can once again return unbidden.

KEY TERM

Spontaneous recovery: The term arising from the classical conditioning literature given to the reemergence of a previously extinguished conditioned response after a delay; similarly, forgotten declarative memories have been observed to recover over time.

Similar findings have been observed for declarative memory. The idea that memory might improve over time originated in research on retroactive interference, and was premised on an analogy between retroactive interference and extinction in conditioning (Underwood, 1948). In particular, according to the unlearning hypothesis discussed in Chapter 9, whenever a "response" is retrieved by accident, the association between the cue and the mistaken response is punished via a process akin to extinction. If so, retroactive interference should dissipate. Consistent with this hypothesis, Underwood (Underwood, 1948) found significant retroactive interference at short delays, but performance on the first list improved at longer delays. Spontaneous recovery has been observed in a large number of retroactive interference studies since that

time (see Brown, 1976; Wheeler, 1995, for reviews).

Mark Wheeler (1995) reported several nice illustrations of spontaneous recovery in episodic memory. In one study, Wheeler presented students with twelve pictures, giving them three opportunities to study the items. The students were then told that the list had been for practice, and that the real lists would begin. They then received two additional lists of twelve pictures, with a free-recall test occurring after each. After the third list was presented, students were given a free-recall test for the pictures studied on the first list either immediately, or after about 30 minutes. As can be seen in Figure 10.6, recall from the first list suffered significant retroactive interference from learning two intervening lists, compared to a control group who performed irrelevant

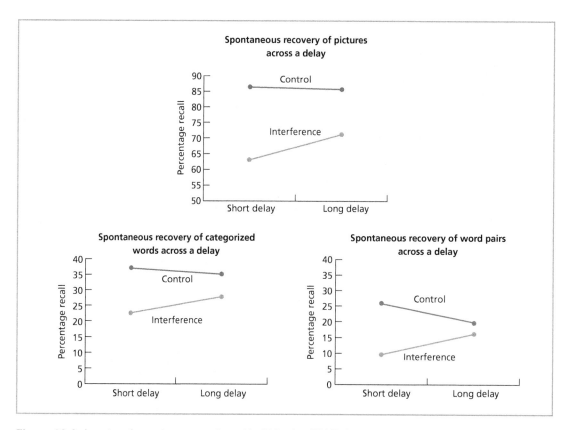

Figure 10.6 A series of experiments conducted by Wheeler (1995) demonstrating that the retroactive interference produced by intervening lists of pictures, words, or word pairs observed at short delays is diminished after a longer delay. Note that memory for items in the interference condition improves with delay in each case. From Wheeler (1995). Copyright © American Psychological Association. Reproduced with permission.

distractor activities instead of learning the second and third lists. Notice, however, that after about 30 minutes, free recall of the first-list pictures actually gets better. Wheeler demonstrated the same effect with lists of categorized words, and also with word pairs, showing that recovery is general. Although most studies of spontaneous recovery have examined intervals up to 30 minutes, some have found recovery after several days. The stronger memories are, the more likely they will be to exhibit recovery (Postman, Stark, & Henschel, 1969).

Why does episodic memory improve over time when the overwhelming majority of research indicates the opposite relationship? One feature shared by spontaneous recovery in both classical conditioning and episodic memory is the explicit rejection of particular responses that had previously been relevant. As discussed earlier, the need to stop unwanted responses is one of the main conditions thought to engage inhibition. If retroactive interference reflects the persisting effects of inhibition, perhaps forgotten items recover because inhibition is gradually released. Thus, the factor that differentiates when memory will improve and when it will decline may be the involvement of inhibition. Consistent with this, Malcolm MacLeod and Neil Macrae (2001) found that retrieval-induced forgetting was significantly reduced after a 24-hour delay, suggesting that in some cases inhibition may dissipate over time. Given the tendency for emotionally unpleasant experiences to come back and haunt us, even after frequent suppression, spontaneous recovery seems likely to be a force behind the reappearance of forgotten traces.

Repeated retrieval attempts

After a long struggle trying to recall an experience, is it worth continuing to search even when your intuition tells you that there is nothing to be recalled? Doesn't that feeling mean that the event has been lost forever? Perhaps not. Consider my experience trying to remember the location of my passport. After strenuous effort, I had no recollection whatsoever of storing this item, and felt that I would never remember. Yet, the moment I found it, I instantly recalled placing it in that location, showing that the memory was there. On the other hand, my efforts to remember knocking over the Christmas tree discussed in the last chapter have proven fruitless, despite prolonged recall attempts, stretching over months. When you fail to recall numerous times, doesn't it mean that the memory will never be recovered?

Interestingly, the answer this question often is "no." Repeated retrieval attempts typically increase the amount recalled, even when the person feels that he/she cannot recall more. This phenomenon was first discovered by Ballard (1913), who asked young school children to memorize poetry. Over successive recalls, Ballard found that the children would often recall new lines of poetry that they had failed to recall previously. Ballard referred to this phenomenon as reminiscence, which he defined as, "the remembering again of the forgotten without relearning," or "a gradual process of improvement in the capacity to revive past experiences" (Ballard, 1913). Ballard noted that even when the overall number of lines of poetry did not increase across retrievals, students often included newly recalled lines in later attempts not present in earlier ones. Overall recall sometimes didn't improve, however, because the benefits of recalling new lines were countered by students' failures to recall lines previously recalled. Nevertheless, often the amount of reminiscence exceeded this inter-test forgetting, yielding improvement overall. When overall recall improves through repeated testing (when reminiscence exceeds inter-test forgetting), a person has exhibited hypermnesia, a term introduced by Mathew Erdelyi to contrast this with the amnesia normally arising from the passage of time.

KEY TERM

Reminiscence: The remembering again of the forgotten, without learning or a gradual process of improvement in the capacity to revive past experiences

Hypermnesia: The improvement in recall performance arising from repeated testing sessions on the same material.

Although neglected for decades, Mathew Erdelyi and colleagues revived interest in this phenomenon through striking demonstrations. In an amusing example, Erdelyi tricked a psychology PhD student, Jeff Kleinbard, into becoming a participant in a week-long study of hypermnesia. The student was interested in pursuing research on hypermnesia. To help him get a feel for the phenomenon, Erdelyi had Kleinbard join participants in a testing session. Participants studied 40 line drawings of objects. Participants then spent 5 minutes recalling as many of the pictures as possible (by writing the name of the object) on a blank sheet with 40 lines. If they could not recall all 40 items, the students were required to make educated guesses about what the remaining unrecalled pictures might be. This testing procedure continued for five recall attempts. When Kleinbard went to Erdelyi's office to score his recall, Erdelyi challenged him to continue his recall efforts over an entire week—a challenge that Kleinbard accepted. Each day, Kleinbard filled out recall sheets as many times as he cared to. When done, he inserted each sheet into an envelope and did not review them again. As can be seen in Figure 10.7, Kleinbard's total recall improved dramatically over the testing days, starting at 48% on the first day and rising to 80% by the final day. Indeed, when one considers his cumulative recall (i.e. giving him credit for each item recalled at any point up until and including a given test), Kleinbard's recall went from 48% to 90%. This occurred despite the fact that on the first day, Kleinbard had tried his hardest to recall as many items as possible. Thus, Erdelyi and Kleinbard had essentially reversed Ebbinghaus' forgetting curve, by which memory gets progressively worse over time.

How might hypermnesia come about? Kleinbard stated that one of the most important factors was by visualization and reconstruction. In his own words:

By far, the most interesting subjective experience was getting a general "visual feeling" in my mind for a particular shape such as a length or roundness. I remember seeing a vague, oblong shape in my mind from which I was able to extract such items as gun, broom, and baseball bat; from an oval shape—football and pineapple; from an inverted cup form—bell, funnel, and bottle (the bottle in the stimulus resembled a bell-jar); from a rectangular box—table and book. Just before many of these recoveries, I often experienced what might best be described as a "tip-of-the-eye" phenomenon, in which I was certain a particular item was on the verge of recovery but which would take its time before suddenly coalescing into an image in consciousness.
(Erdelyi & Kleinbard, 1978, p. 280)

Erdelyi and Kleinbard (1978) found the same pattern with a group of six additional participants, three of whom studied pictures, and three of whom studied words. Participants who studied words, however, showed modest hypermnesia compared to those who studied pictures, suggesting that imagery plays an important role in determining whether traces can be unearthed with repeated recall. Indeed, several participants noted "tip of the eye" experiences much like that of Kleinbard.

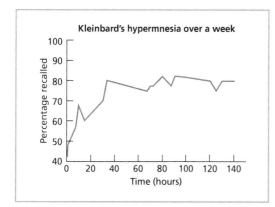

Figure 10.7 The recall data of an unwitting participant in an investigation of hypermnesia. Repeated retrieval attempts over a period of about a week led to a striking improvement in the percentage of pictures recalled. Data from Erdelyi and Kleinbard (1978).

Hypermnesia is a robust phenomenon, and can be observed in simple laboratory sessions lasting less than an hour (Payne, 1987). Hypermnesia is largest on free-recall tests, but has been found on cued-recall and recognition tests. The effect has been found with both verbal and visual materials, though effects are consistently larger with imageable materials. Of course, hypermnesia increases with increasing numbers of recall tests, and several investigations indicate that this effect does not simply reflect increases in time *per se*, as giving a single long test often does not yield as much benefit as many repeated tests. Nor does hypermnesia seem to reflect participants guessing more loosely as time goes on, because the frequency of false recalls often does not go up with repeated testing.

But can hypermnesia be found with complex, realistic memories? In one interesting illustration, Susan Bluck, Linda Levine, and Tracy Laulhere (1999) studied memory for a public event that many people had witnessed, and for which objective verification of details was possible: the televised reading of the verdict in the O. J. Simpson murder trial. The reading of the verdict took place at 10.04 a.m. on 2 October, 1995 in Los Angeles, and the 14.5 minute proceedings were televised by a single courtroom camera shared by all television networks. Eight months after the verdict had been televised, Bluck et al. recruited people who viewed the coverage, and asked them to remember as much as they could, including details that occurred before, during, and after the reading of the verdict. Participants were interviewed three times in a row to obtain their complete recollection of every detail. Within each interview, participants were prompted several times with requests for further details, making sure that they had recalled everything they could. Significant hypermnesia occurred, with the number of verifiable details remembered increasing from 27% to 52% across the three attempts.

But can hypermnesia occur for memories that people have deliberately tried to forget? On the one hand, the motivation to not remember may engage processes that have a special impact, making memories difficult to recall. Moreover, the same motivational factors that led to the memories being forgotten may

also come into play during retrieval, undermining recovery. On the other hand, if someone decides to remember something he/she had previously tried to forget, might the change in disposition undo avoidant tendencies, and render forgotten material subject to hypermnesia? I may initially have been motivated to not think about knocking over the Christmas tree, but my motivations certainly changed years later. Although research examining hypermnesia for intentionally forgotten memories is rare, several studies using the directed forgetting procedure demonstrated that hypermnesia does occur for intentionally forgotten items (Goernert & Wolfe, 1997; Goernert, 2005).

It is natural to worry whether repeated retrievals may introduce persisting errors that come to be attributed to actual experience. In a nice illustration, Linda Henkel (2004) showed participants slides that contained either line drawings with their names (e.g. an image of a lollipop, plus the word *lollipop*), or simply the names with no picture. For each slide, participants were asked to think of functions of the object, and when a drawing was absent, to try to visualize a typical example. Participants then received three recall tests. Participants exhibited robust hypermnesia, but also showed an increase in source misattribution errors. With each test, participants grew more likely to falsely claim that they had *seen* an image of an object that they had only imagined. This tendency was especially likely when participants had seen physically or conceptually similar objects on the list. However, the overall rate of erroneous recalls is often surprisingly low, compared to accurate recall, in studies examining repeated recall of emotional eyewitness events (Bornstein, Liebel, & Scarberry, 1998) or autobiographical memory (Bluck et al., 1999).

Cue reinstatement

After putting unwanted memories out of mind, we sometimes stumble upon reminders. Walking around a corner, you may see a car matching the model your former partner used to drive. Rummaging through a box, you may find a gift from a loved one who has died. Veterans of Iraq may see someone make a sudden movement alongside the road while driving, transporting them back to the roadside bomb attack they experienced. Unintended reminders illustrate the power of cues to reinstate unwanted memories. Cues have the same power, of course, when one reverses course and intends to remember something that one previously wished to forget.

Steve Smith and Sarah Moynan (2008) compellingly demonstrated how people may come to forget, and then later recover experiences, given the right cues. Very often one may need to confront reminders of unpleasant experiences on a recurring basis. One way of handling this might be to think about or discuss only some aspects of the experience while avoiding the unpleasant parts, perhaps rendering the nondiscussed elements less accessible. To simulate this, Smith and Moynan presented people with a categorized word list. The 21 categories included things such as *furniture*, *fruit*, *drinks*, but also emotional categories like *disease*, *death*, and *gross*. Following encoding, the experimental group made judgments about the examples from 18 of the 21 categories, three times each, encouraging selective reprocessing of parts of the list. In the control group, the same time was spent on irrelevant tasks. Participants were then asked to recall all of the category names, including ones that were left out of the intervening phase. As can be seen in the top portion of Figure 10.8, participants exhibited truly remarkable forgetting of the three category names omitted from the intervening phase. Importantly, this occurred even when categories involved emotional items such as curse words or words concerning death. In some cases, recall of the avoided categories was 70% lower than the control group, despite comparable delays and demands on attention in the intervening phase. Clearly, biasing attention to certain elements of an experience can induce dramatic rates of forgetting.

What happened to the forgotten items? Participants in the experimental condition clearly had difficulty recalling the omitted categories. If asked, they might feel as though they could not recall any more. Smith and Moynan (2008) showed that this was not true, however. After participants tried to recall the categories, they were given the category names, in turn, and asked to recall the examples. As can be seen at the bottom of Figure 10.8, once the category names were given, the

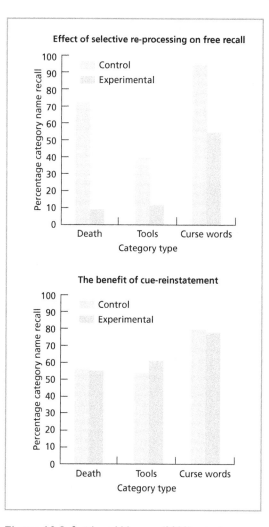

Figure 10.8 Smith and Moynan (2008) asked participants to selectively review a subset of categorized word lists. Top: The free-recall test revealed forgetting for nonreviewed categories. Bottom: Exemplars from categories participants failed to generate during free recall could often still be retrieved using category cues. From Smith and Moynan (2008). Copyright © Blackwell Publishing. Reproduced with permission.

control and experimental participants recalled exactly the same number of items per category, and recalled these at a very high rate. Thus, retention of the items was preserved, once the right cue appeared. Indeed, of the ten death words experimental participants had encountered, they recalled nearly 60% when cued with the category (an amount identical to that recalled by the control group), even though moments earlier only 10% of the participants could even recall seeing death words on the list (compared with 70% of the participants in the control condition). This illustrates that unpleasant experiences can sometimes be forgotten, given the right motivated biases in reminiscing about the event, and later recovered, given the right reminders.

But can cues really help recover memories that were intentionally forgotten? In one example, Goernert and Larson (1994) found that directed forgetting could be "released" by simply presenting a subset of the items participants studied on the first list as cues. Without any cues, participants showed a directed forgetting effect, with those people instructed to remember recalling 44% of the first-list words, and those instructed to forget only recalling 21%. If participants were given either four or eight cues, their first-list recall increased to 29% and 31%, respectively. Bauml and Sameneih (2012a, 2012b) also observed these beneficial effects and further found recovery of to-be-forgotten items when some were retrieved instead of being presented as cues. Of course, the potency of cueing is also shown when people receive to-be-forgotten items on a recognition test, in which directed forgetting effects are not usually observed (with the list-method). Seeing the item itself is a potent reminder, much like seeing a videotape of an experience we have tried to forget would prove an alarmingly effective cue.

Reinstating context can also help to recover memories intentionally forgotten. For example, Sahakyan and Kelley (2002) showed that reinstating mental context can undo the effects of instructions to forget in the list-method directed forgetting procedure. Participants were exposed to an unusual context just prior to encoding the first list of words: the presentation of the theme from the Star Wars® soundtrack. Later, on the final test, Sahakyan and Kelley asked participants to reinstate the mental context that they had been in upon entering the room, including anything that they could remember about how they felt or what they thought. Would reinstating the incidental context bring back intentionally forgotten material? When the context was not reinstated,

participants showed a 22% deficit in the forget condition compared with the remember condition. The context-reinstatement group, however, showed only an 8% directed forgetting effect. These findings demonstrate that motivated forgetting processes often reduce the accessibility of unwanted memories, but do not alter their availability in storage. Often, these memories remain, awaiting a time when they are sought and when the right cues are available. One question that arises is whether experiences can reside in memory, untouched and inaccessible, and be reinstated after a long delay, given the right cues? Next, we consider an important societal issue on which our understanding of these processes bear, and illustrate recovery in real life.

RECOVERED MEMORIES OF TRAUMA: INSTANCES OF MOTIVATED FORGETTING?

Most people have heard stories in which a person claims to have recovered a memory of a deeply unpleasant event, after years of being unaware of it. Sometimes famous cases receive media attention because they have led to legal charges of childhood sexual abuse against priests or parents. Other times, fictionalized cases appear on television or film, with a recovered memory as a plot device. Some people hear about recovered memories through friends or family who have had such experiences. As a memory instructor for many years, I have been approached by many students claiming to have recovered memories of abuse (several times a year). The idea that people can repress disturbing experiences is a central tenet of psychoanalytic theory. Indeed, many therapists would say that they routinely see repression and recovery in their clients. Can an unpleasant experience be forgotten and then recovered years later?

There are good reasons to be cautious in interpreting such reports. Retrieval is imperfect. When people have difficulty remembering, they may engage in reconstruction and inference that adds things to memory that may not have taken place. Moreover, people sometimes confuse the sources of their memories, failing to distinguish things that they have imagined, heard about, read, dreamt, or seen in a film with things that truly happened. The risks of such possibilities grow when people participate in therapies that have, as their objective, the goal of uncovering repressed memories. Using hypnosis, guided imagery, and other suggestive techniques may create an environment in which discerning fact from fiction may prove difficult. The cost of a memory error might be the accusation of a family member of childhood abuse when none has occurred.

The possibility of false memories and concern over their consequences does not, however, imply that recovered memories are untrue. One should place equal emphasis on the possibility that such experiences may reflect true events, and that failure to acknowledge this will have consequences for the victim and others who may suffer abuse at the hands of the perpetrator. In this section, we consider reports of recovered memories and the possible mechanisms by which such experiences might come about. We begin by describing several case reports in which the memory recovery experience came about in different ways.

Cases of recovered memories

The following are real recovered memory cases, although the names have been changed. In Case 1, a person recovers a memory gradually, in suggestive therapy. Case 2 recounts a woman who abruptly remembered an abuse memory, outside of therapy, when confronted with powerful reminders. Case 3 is the story of a woman who recovered a series of deeply unpleasant events outside of therapy, and who, as a result, sought therapy.

Case 1
As reported by Geraerts (2006), Elizabeth Janssen became very depressed. Her marriage was falling apart and she even quit her job for a while. Elizabeth and Carl went to a marriage counselor to solve their problems. After several sessions, the therapist referred them to a colleague because she could not figure out why

they stopped caring for each other and why their sex life was unsatisfactory. Elizabeth and Carl then started individual therapy with a psychiatrist. Almost immediately, Elizabeth was diagnosed with a major depressive disorder. She was told that she had to uncover her repressed memories of early childhood abuse, as this was the underlying cause of her disorder.

At first, Elizabeth vehemently denied having been abused, and certainly not by her beloved father, as her psychiatrist insinuated. Her psychiatrist insisted that a childhood trauma must have happened to her; he had seen the same symptoms in so many patients. He started using guided imagery, instructing Elizabeth to imagine scenes of the supposed abuse even though Elizabeth continued to deny, although less fervently, that she had such memories. Because no abuse memories were surfacing, Elizabeth was given books about child abuse survivors to read; she was told that if something felt uncomfortable while reading these books, this would indicate that similar things happened to her. To help Elizabeth remember the abuse, hypnosis was used. After 2 months of intense therapy, Elizabeth gradually recovered vivid images of being abused. She said that she could see herself lying in bed as her father came into her room at night. While she was very anxious, he performed terrible and painful sexual acts on her. "Yes, even penetration." These traumatic events allegedly continued until she went to boarding school at age 12. Meanwhile, Elizabeth's husband Carl had been in therapy with the same psychiatrist. He was told that he also suffered from depression. After several weeks, Carl had recovered being sexually abused by several priests at boarding school.

When asked how she had felt after recovering these abuse memories, Elizabeth said that she had never felt such a relief. It turned out that not she, but her father, was responsible for her depression. She broke off all contact with her parents. Contact with her sister and brother also became infrequent since they did not believe her story.

Case 2
Another report by Geraerts (2006) describes Mary de Vries, who had been working in the

hospital as a pediatric nurse. She had a happy marriage and a 3-year old daughter. She had been very happy, that after several years of trying, she had finally become pregnant. However, the birth of her daughter Lynn elicited serious problems. When Mary came home with Lynn from the hospital, she felt uncomfortable when her husband was taking care of their baby. She almost never left him alone with their daughter; she always wanted to be there when he was washing her or changing her nappies. She really could not stand the thought of her husband doing something bad to Lynn. Her mistrust resulted in heavy arguments between the couple. Mary did not even know why she mistrusted him.

Almost at the same time, her mother fell ill. Her mother had been living alone on the coast since her second husband, Mary's stepfather, had left her. Mary reassured her mother and told her that she would come over for a couple of days with her baby and would help her with the housekeeping. While she was cleaning, she entered her former bedroom. Mary said that she suddenly had a complete recollective experience in which "a whole series of pictures were running through my head." The cascade of memories horrified, shocked, overwhelmed, surprised, and baffled her at the same time. Suddenly she remembered vulgar events that occurred in that room. She remembered that her stepfather had approached her several times while she was playing there. He had fondled her genitals several times. Mary just could not talk with her mother about these horrible memories. A few days later, when Mary got home, she called her sister. Mary told her what had happened at their mother's place. First, her sister said nothing. After a couple of minutes, she told Mary that she had always vividly remembered that she had been molested by their stepfather as well.

Case 3
Herman and Schatzow (1987) report the following case, which subsequently appeared in *Science News* (Bower, 1993). After losing more than 100 pounds in a hospital weight-reduction program she had entered to battle severe obesity, Claudia experienced flashbacks of sexual abuse committed by her older brother. She joined a therapy group for incest survivors, and memories of abuse flooded back. Claudia told group members that from the time she was 4 years old to her brother's enlistment in the Army 3 years later, he had regularly handcuffed her, burned her with cigarettes, and forced her to submit to a variety of sexual acts. Claudia's brother had died in combat in Vietnam more than 15 years before her horrifying memories surfaced. Yet Claudia's parents had left his room and his belongings untouched since then. Returning home from the hospital, Claudia searched the room. Inside a closet she found a large pornography collection, handcuffs, and a diary in which her brother had extensively planned and recorded what he called sexual 'experiments' with his sister.

What do we make of such cases?

The previous cases make several important points. First, memories can be recovered in many ways. In some cases, memories are recovered gradually, through active search and reconstruction, sometimes targeted at remembering abuse the person is not sure ever occurred. In other cases, the experience comes to mind spontaneously, without active search. Memories sometimes are recovered outside of therapy, triggered by a compelling need to explain some powerful reaction or feeling. Indeed, of the 634 cases of recovered memories reported by a sample of 108 British clinical psychologists in a study by Andrews, Brewin, Ochera, Morton, Bekerian, Davies, et al. (1999), 32% reported recovering their memories prior to therapy of any kind.

These cases also illustrate that corroboration is sometimes lacking. In Case 1, no evidence was produced to prove that the abuse had occurred, other than the conviction of the therapist, and, eventually, of the patient. It is common for corroboration to be lacking, as the hypothetical event is usually thought to have taken place years earlier, outside the view of anyone other than the accuser, who, at the time of the event, is usually a child. In such cases, it is impossible to know whether corroboration is missing because the event is not real, or because care was taken to conceal it. Corroboration has often been possible, however, as illustrated in the latter cases. Indeed, there any many cases of individuals recovering memories that have been objectively corroborated (see the web resource, "Recovered memory archive," listed under Further readings at the end of this chapter). These cases provide compelling proof of the phenomenon of recovery: It is possible to forget an emotionally significant event over many years and later recover it.

The cases also highlight a serious concern about some reports of recovered memories. Case 1 illustrates that some reports come through therapeutic techniques that are overly suggestive. Elizabeth Janssen had no predisposition to believe that her father had abused her, but her therapist was very insistent. In fact, the therapist appears eager to apply repression of abuse as a diagnosis. Despite her protests, Janssen was asked to repeatedly imagine and try to remember abuse she did not believe occurred, in some cases under hypnosis. Only then did Janssen come to believe in the event. Although repeated retrievals might have revealed real memories, as suggested by work on hypermnesia, it also seems possible that Janssen could no longer distinguish her previous imaginings from true memories, as suggested by the Henkel (2004) work discussed earlier. When a therapist has conviction in a memory's reality, and a client starts to feel as though he/she is remembering (even if the remembering is of previous imaginings), it may become difficult to discount the possibility that the memory is real. Thus, some cases of memory recovery may be false memories unwittingly encouraged by therapists who intend to help the patient.

Differing origins of recovered memory experiences

The preceding discussion suggests that memories recovered under differing circumstances may be produced by different processes. On the one hand, memories recovered through suggestive therapy may be more likely to reflect suggestions by the therapist rather than true recovery. On the other hand, memories recovered spontaneously, outside of therapy or in therapy, without suggestion, may be more likely to be genuine. These memories could have been forgotten by any of the mechanisms outlined

in this chapter. If so, corroboration should be more likely for memories recovered spontaneously than for memories recovered through suggestive therapy.

Elke Geraerts, Jonathan Schooler, Harald Merckelbach, and colleagues (2007) sought to corroborate abuse memories of people who have always remembered their abuse, and people who have recovered it. After filling out a questionnaire about their memory of the abuse, participants were queried about sources of corroboration. Independent raters, blind to the group in which a participant fell, used this information to seek evidence that would corroborate the event. A memory was considered corroborated if: (1) another individual reported learning about the abuse within a week after it happened; (2) another individual reported having been abused by the same perpetrator; or (3) the perpetrator admitted to committing the abuse. Strikingly, memories recovered spontaneously, outside of therapy, were corroborated at a rate (37%) that was comparable to that observed for people with continuously accessible memories (45%). Memories recovered through suggestive therapy, however, could never be corroborated (0%). Although the lack of corroboration does not imply that those recovered memories are false, the lack of evidence does not permit confidence in their reality, and recommends caution in interpretation. More generally, these findings suggest that discontinuous memory does not make an experience any less real than something a person has always remembered.

The foregoing findings suggest that recovered memories may originate in different ways for people who recollect the abuse spontaneously, and for those who recall it through suggestive therapy. Geraerts and colleagues hypothesized that memories recalled through suggestive therapy may be more likely to be false, a possibility consistent with the lack of corroboration. People recalling memories spontaneously, by contrast, may have genuinely forgotten the experience, and later remembered it. Alternatively, the spontaneously recovered group may have recalled the event, but may have forgotten that they have recalled it before. The latter possibility is suggested by a case reported by Jonathan Schooler (Schooler, Ambadar, & Bendiksen, 1997), in which a woman "recovered" a memory of childhood abuse for "the first time," only to be informed by her spouse that they had discussed the event at length years earlier. Might people who have spontaneous recovery experiences simply be forgetting prior occasions of thinking about it?

To explore these possibilities, Geraerts, Arnold, Lindsay, Merckelbach, Jelicic, and Hauer (2006) first investigated whether people reporting recovered memories had a tendency to underestimate prior remembering. They invited people with recovered or continuous memories to write down a memory from their childhood for each of 25 titles. The titles described common things that happen to children like *being home alone* or *going to the dentist*. For some of these titles, participants were asked to concentrate on emotionally negative aspects of the event (e.g. for *being home alone* this might be the feeling of being frightened), but for others, the positive aspects (e.g. for the home alone title, this might be getting to do whatever you want). Everyone returned 2 months later and generated the same memories, yet again. There was one switch, however: Sometimes people retrieved the events in the same emotional frame as before, but for other titles, they were asked to retrieve the event in the opposite emotional frame. So, for example, if they had recalled *being home alone* in a positive light during the first visit, they recalled the same event again, but focused on the negative aspects. When this second visit was complete, people returned to the laboratory for a third

and final time 2 months later. They recalled all of the events yet again, but this time they recalled each one in the same emotional frame in which they had recalled it during the first visit. Critically, after recalling each memory, people were asked to remember whether they had recalled that same memory during the second (i.e. middle) visit. Interestingly, when the emotional framing on the final visit differed from the one on the second visit, people were quite likely to forget having remembered the event during that second visit, compared to when the emotional framing remained the same. Thus, shifting the way that people thought about the same memory (whether positively or negatively) from one occasion to the next made them forget thinking about the memory before. Importantly, this tendency was much greater for people reporting recovered memories than it was for people reporting continuous memories, or people without any history of abuse (Figure 10.9).

So it seems that one reason why people may have a recovered memory experience is that they simply forget having remembered the event before. They may forget prior cases of remembering if, for example, the mental context present when they are having their recovery experience differs from the mental context on prior occasions in which they thought of the event. By this view, it is not that people have forgotten the event for all those years; it is that they simply can't remember having remembered, perhaps due to context-dependent memory.

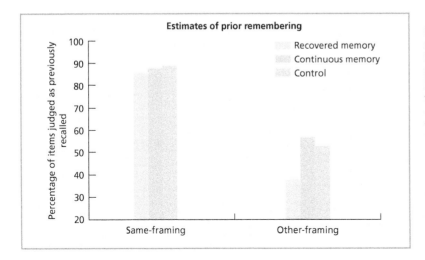

Figure 10.9 The ability to recall prior remembrances is diminished if the retrieval perspective differed between them (other-framing condition). Geraerts et al. (2006) found that this tendency is greatest in individuals who previously reported recovered memories of abuse, distinguishing them from abuse victims who reported continuous memories of their trauma and controls. Data from Geraerts et al. (2006).

The discussion thus far does not explain why some people might show greater susceptibility to forgetting prior remembering. One possibility is that people with authentic abuse experiences may engage some of the motivated forgetting processes discussed in this chapter in order to limit intrusive reminders of the unwanted experience. So, for example, they might learn to engage inhibitory control to suppress intrusive thoughts. If so, perhaps the reason why these people cannot remember their prior incidences of remembering is that these memories have been disrupted by the same processes at work in retrieval-induced forgetting or the think/no-think procedure discussed earlier. This hypothesis has received some support (Geraerts et al., 2007). People with spontaneously recovered memories are better at suppressing thoughts of unpleasant experiences than are people with memories recovered through suggestive therapy, or people with continuously accessible memories. Thus people may learn to habitually suppress reminders of those events, causing them to forget their prior thoughts.

If the thought suppression hypothesis is correct, does this present an alternative to the idea that memories can be repressed, and later recovered? It depends. On the one hand, if a memory must be consistently inaccessible over many years for it to count as repression, this research suggests a different mechanism. On the other hand, Freud emphasized the *return of the repressed* and the idea that repression needed to be actively maintained. If repression requires continual reinstatement, then suppressing intrusive reminders over the span of many years simply reflects reinstatement. Further work is required to establish the mental and biological mechanisms that account for these, and other cases of motivated forgetting. It is clear, however, that what we remember is not random, and aligns with our motivations, and goals of emotional regulation (Anderson & Huddleston, 2011; Anderson & Hanslmayr, 2014).

SUMMARY

When we try to understand why we remember what we do, we cannot disregard our motivations. We often have compelling reasons for limiting retrieval of certain experiences. Sometimes, those reasons relate to functional goals, like concentration or ensuring that we access only current knowledge; other times, they concern the regulation of emotions. People don't like to feel sad, anxious, afraid, ashamed, or embarrassed. Yet, we sometimes confront reminders to memories that make us feel these feelings. When the world calls to mind such memories, people regulate their feelings by intentionally controlling memory. If such experiences are forgotten, it aids our long-term objective of maintaining a positive emotional state. The results of these ongoing efforts can be seen in people's remarkable capacity for selective remembering. In this chapter, we have reviewed what experimental psychology has revealed about motivated forgetting and its biological underpinnings, a topic that has received increased attention in psychology and neuroscience. Research in this area will help to clarify how people's motivations and emotions, and our efforts to deliberately control how we feel, influence what elements we retain of our past. Some of the key points in this chapter are summarized below.

- People exhibit a pronounced positivity bias in their autobiographical memory, which may contribute to perceptions of life satisfaction.
- Having good memory for the past can sometimes be a problem.
- People are motivated to forget unpleasant events, to regulate their emotions, maintain a positive outlook, and a positive self-image, or simply to concentrate.
- Motivation to forget can alter the way that memories are encoded or retrieved.
- Item-method directed forgetting research shows that people can limit encoding intentionally, both through selective rehearsal, and encoding suppression.

- List-method directed forgetting research shows that people can reduce access to encoded memories by intentionally suppressing access to a whole context of events.
- People will avoid reminders to an unwanted memory as a way to avoid retrieving experiences they'd rather not think about.
- When people cannot avoid reminders, they can suppress retrieval of the unwanted memory.
- Retrieval suppression may build on basic mechanisms of behavioral control that help us to stop actions, to stop retrieval.
- Retrieval suppression impairs memory for suppressed events.
- Retrieval suppression can be accomplished by direct suppression, a process of shutting down the retrieval process, or thought substitution, a process of retrieving alternate distracting thoughts.
- Direct suppression is accomplished by down-regulating hippocampal activation, achieved by the right lateral prefrontal cortex. Thought substitution is achieved by retrieval processes supported by the left prefrontal cortex.
- Extreme emotional distress can induce dramatic loss of access to large chunks of one's personal past, and sometimes one's entire identity, a phenomenon known as psychogenic amnesia.
- Sometimes people wish to recover memories they had deliberately forgotten.
- A number of factors can contribute to the recovery of forgotten memories, including the passage of time, repeated retrieval efforts, provision of appropriate cues, or physical context.
- Recovered memories of abuse have frequently been reported.
- Many documented cases of recovered memories have been demonstrated, with objective corroboration that the forgotten event had occurred, demonstrating the reality of the phenomenon.
- Concern has been raised about the reality of some recovered memories, and the possibility that overly suggestive therapeutic practices may be responsible for creating false memories of abuse.
- False memories constitute a significant hazard of overly suggestive therapeutic practices, because research has shown that people can be highly suggestible.
- Both true and false recovered memories are likely to exist.
- The mechanisms underlying cases of true recovered memories are unclear at present, though some of the mechanisms identified in laboratory studies of motivated forgetting, including retrieval suppression and changes in context, have been proposed.

POINTS FOR DISCUSSION

With the advent of affordable life-recording devices such as Google Glass™ and Momenta™, one could, theoretically record photos or video of every moment of our lives. If you could do this, would you? Would remembering everything in your life make you happier? Why or why not? Can you think of cases in your life which you wished you could forget?

What are the main factors that predict when motivated forgetting will occur? Have you ever used any of the strategies or mechanisms described in this chapter to forget, or take your mind off something?

What has laboratory research shown about the conditions under which it might it be possible to recover a memory that you have tried to forget?

FURTHER READING

Anderson, M. C., & Hanslmayr, S. (2014). Neural mechanisms of motivated forgetting. *Trends in Cognitive Sciences, 18*, 279–292.

Anderson, M. C., & Huddleston, E. (2011). Towards a cognitive and neurobiological model of motivated forgetting. In R. F. Belli (Ed.), *True and false recovered memories: Toward a reconciliation of the debate*, Vol. 58: *Nebraska Symposium on Motivation*. New York: Springer.

Anderson, M. C., & Levy, B. J. (2009). Suppressing unwanted memories. *Current Directions in Psychological Science, 18*(4), 189–194.

Bjork, R. A. (1989). Retrieval inhibition as an adaptive mechanism in human memory. In H. L. Roediger & F. I. Craik (Eds.), *Varieties of memory and consciousness: Essays in honour of Endel Tulving* (pp. 309–330). Hillsdale, NJ: Lawrence Erlbaum Associates.

Cheit, R. E. (Director) *Recovered memory archive.* Online. Available: www.RecoveredMemory.org.

Erdelyi, M. H. (2006). The unified theory of repression. *Behavioral and Brain Sciences, 29*(5), 499–551.

Johnson, M. K., Raye, C. L., Mitchell, K. J., & Ankudowich, E. (2011). The cognitive neuroscience of true and false memories. In R. F. Belli (Ed.), *True and false recovered memories: Toward a reconciliation of the debate. Vol. 58: Nebraska Symposium on Motivation* (pp. 15–52). New York: Springer.

Loftus, E. F., & Davis, D. (2006). Recovered memories. *Annual Review of Clinical Psychology, 2*, 469–498.

MacLeod, C. M. (1998). Directed forgetting. In J. M. Golding & C. M. MacLeod (Eds.), *Intentional forgetting: Interdisciplinary approaches* (pp. 197–218). Mahwah, NJ: Lawrence Erlbaum Associates.

REFERENCES

Abeles, M., & Schilder, P. (1935). Psychogenic loss of personal identity: Amnesia. *Archives of Neurology and Psychiatry, 34*, 587–604.

Anderson, M. C. (2001). Active forgetting: Evidence for functional inhibition as a source of memory failure. *Journal of Aggression, Maltreatment and Trauma, 4*(2), 185–210.

Anderson, M. C. (2003). Rethinking interference theory: Executive control and the mechanisms of forgetting. *Journal of Memory and Language, 49*(4), 415–445.

Anderson, M.C. & Hanslmayr, S. (2014). Neural mechanisms of motivated forgetting. *Trends in Cognitive Sciences, 18*, 279–292.

Anderson, M. C., & Huddleston, E. (2011). Towards a cognitive and neurobiological model of motivated forgetting. In Belli, R. F. (Ed.), *True and false recovered memories: Toward a reconciliation of the debate, Vol. 58: Nebraska Symposium on Motivation.* New York: Springer.

Anderson, M. C., & Levy, B. J. (2009). Suppressing unwanted memories. *Current Directions in Psychological Science, 18*(4), 189–194.

Anderson, M. C., & Weaver, C. (in press). Inhibitory Control over Action and Memory.

In L. R. Squire (Ed.), *The new encyclopedia of neuroscience* (Vol. 5, pp. 153–163). Oxford: Elsevier Ltd.

Anderson, M. C., Ochsner, K. N., Cooper, J., Robertson, E., Gabrieli, S. W., Glover, G. H., et al. (2004). Neural systems underlying the suppression of unwanted memories. *Science, 303*, 232–235.

Andrews, B., Brewin, C. R., Ochera, J., Morton, J., Bekerian, D. A., Davies, G. M., et al. (1999). Characteristics, context and consequences of memory recovery among adults in therapy. *British Journal of Psychiatry, 175*, 141–146.

Aron, A. R., Fletcher, P. C., Bullmore, E. T., Sahakian, B. J., & Robbins, T. W. (2003). Stop-signal inhibition disrupted by damage to right inferior frontal gyrus in humans. *Nature Neuroscience, 6*(2), 115–116.

Arrigo, J. M., & Pezdek, K. (1997). Lessons from the study of psychogenic amnesia. *Current Directions in Psychological Science, 6*(5), 148–152.

Ballard, P. B. (1913). Oblivescence and reminiscence. *British Journal of Psychology Monograph Supplements, 1*, 1–82.

Barnier, A. J., Conway, M. A., Mayoh, L., & Speyer, J. (2007). Directed forgetting of recently recalled autobiographical memories. *Journal of Experimental Psychology: General, 136*(2), 301–322.

Basden, B. H., & Basden, D. R. (1996). Directed forgetting: Further comparisons of the item and list methods. *Memory, 4*(6), 633–653.

Basden, B. H., Basden, D. R., & Gargano, G. J. (1993). Directed forgetting in implicit and explicit memory tests: A comparison of methods. *Journal of Experimental Psychology: Learning, 19*(3), 603–616.

Bäuml, K. H. T., & Samenieh, A. (2012a). Influences of part-list cuing on different forms of episodic forgetting. *Journal of Experimental Psychology: Learning, Memory, and Cognition, 38*(2), 366.

Bäuml, K. H. T., & Samenieh, A. (2012b). Selective memory retrieval can impair and improve retrieval of other memories. *Journal of Experimental Psychology: Learning, Memory, and Cognition, 38*(2), 488.

Benoit, R. G., & Anderson, M. C. (2012). Opposing mechanisms support the voluntary forgetting of unwanted memories. *Neuron, 76*(2), 450–460.

Bergström, Z. M., de Fockert, J. W., & Richardson-Klavehn, A. (2009). ERP and behavioural evidence for direct suppression of unwanted memories. *NeuroImage, 48*(4), 726–737.

Bernsten, D. (1996). Involuntary autobiographical memories. *Applied Cognitive Psychology, 10*(5), 435–454.

Bjork, E. L., & Bjork, R. A. (2003). Intentional forgetting can increase, not decrease, residual influences of to-be-forgotten information. *Journal of Experimental Psychology: Learning, Memory, and Cognition, 29*(4), 524–531.

Bjork, R. A. (1970). Positive forgetting: The noninterference of items intentionally forgotten. *Journal of Verbal Learning and Verbal Behavior, 9*(3), 255–268.

Bjork, R. A. (1989). Retrieval inhibition as an adaptive mechanism in human memory. In H. L. Roediger & F. I. Craik (Eds.), *Varieties of memory and consciousness: Essays in honour of Endel Tulving.* (pp. 309–330). Hillsdale, NJ: Lawrence Erlbaum Associates.

Bluck, S., Levine, L. J., & Laulhere, T. M. (1999). Autobiographical remembering and hypermnesia: A comparison of older and younger adults. *Psychology and Aging, 14*(4), 671–682.

Bornstein, B. H., Liebel, L. M., & Scarberry, N. C. (1998). Repeated testing in eyewitness memory: A means to improve recall of a negative emotional event. *Applied Cognitive Psychology, 12*(2), 119–131.

Bower, B. (1993). Sudden recall: Adult memories of child abuse spark a heated debate. Retrieved May 5, 2008, from: http://www.thefreelibrary.com/ Sudden recall: adult memories of child abuse spark a heated debate.-a014458675

Brown, A. S. (1976). Spontaneous recovery in human learning. *Psychological Bulletin, 83*(2), 321–338.

Charles, S. T., Mather, M., & Carstensen, L. L. (2003). Aging and emotional memory: The forgettable nature of negative images for older adults. *Journal of Experimental Psychology: General, 132*(2), 310–324.

Depue, B. E., Banich, M. T., & Curran, T. (2006). Suppression of emotional and nonemotional content in memory. Effects of repetition on cognitive control. *Psychological Science, 17*(5), 441–447.

Depue, B. E., Burgess, G. C., Willcutt, E. G., Ruzic, L., & Banich, M.T. (2010) Inhibitory control of memory retrieval and motor processing associated with the right lateral prefrontal cortex: Evidence from deficits in individuals with ADHD. *Neuropsychologia, 48*, 3909–3917. doi:10.1016/j.neuropsychologia.2010.09.013

Depue, B. E., Curran, T., & Banich, M. T. (2007). Prefrontal regions orchestrate suppression of emotional memories via a two-phase process. *Science, 317*, 215–219.

Diener, E., & Diener, C. (1996). Most people are happy. *Psychological Science, 7*(3), 181–185.

Erdelyi, M. H. (2006). The unified theory of repression. *Behavioral and Brain Sciences, 29*(5), 499–551.

Erdelyi, M. H., & Kleinbard, J. (1978). Has Ebbinghaus decayed with time? The growth of recall (hypermnesia) over days. *Journal of Experimental Psychology: Human Learning and Memory, 4*(4), 275–289.

Fawcett, J. M. and Taylor, T. L. (2008) Forgetting is effortful: Evidence from reaction time probes in an item-method directed forgetting task. *Memory and Cognition, 36*, 1168–1181.

Freud, S. (1900). The interpretation of dreams. In J. Strachey (Ed.), *The standard edition of the complete psychological writings of Sigmund Freud.* London: Hogarth Press.

Freud, S. (1917). Repression. In J. Riviere (Ed.), *A general introduction to psychoanalysis* (p. 147). New York: Liveright.

Geiselman, R. E., Bjork, R. A., & Fishman, D. L. (1983). Disrupted retrieval in directed forgetting: A link with posthypnotic amnesia. *Journal of Experimental Psychology General, 112*(1), 58–72.

Geraerts, E. (2006). Remembrance of things past. The cognitive psychology of remembering and forgetting trauma. Unpublished PhD Thesis, Maastricht University, The Netherlands.

Geraerts, E., Arnold, M. M., Lindsay, D. S., Merckelbach, H., Jelicic, M., & Hauer, B. (2006). Forgetting of prior remembering in persons reporting recovered memories of childhood sexual abuse. *Psychological Science, 17*(11), 1002–1008.

Geraerts, E., Lindsay, D. S., Merckelbach, H., Jelicic, M., Raymaekers, L., Arnold, M. M., et al. (2009). Cognitive mechanisms underlying recovered memory experiences of childhood sexual abuse. *Psychological Science, 20*, 92–98.

Geraerts, E., Schooler, J. W., Merckelbach, H., Jelicic, M., Hauer, B. J., & Ambadar, Z. (2007). The reality of recovered memories: Corroborating continuous and discontinuous memories of childhood sexual abuse. *Psychological Science, 18*(7), 564–568.

Goernert, P. N. (2005). Source-monitoring accuracy across repeated tests following directed forgetting. *British Journal of Psychology, 96*(2), 231–247.

Goernert, P. N., & Larson, M. E. (1994). The initiation and release of retrieval inhibition. *The Journal of General Psychology, 121*(1), 61–66.

Goernert, P. N., & Wolfe, T. (1997). Is there hypermnesia and reminiscence for information intentionally forgotten? *Canadian Journal of Experimental Psychology, 51*(3), 231–240.

Henkel, L. A. (2004). Erroneous memories arising from repeated attempts to remember. *Journal of Memory and Language, 50*(1), 26–46.

Herman, J., & Schatzow, E. (1987). Recovery and verification of memories of childhood sexual trauma. *Psychoanalytic Psychology, 4*, 1–14.

Hertel, P., & McDaniel, L. (2010) The suppressive power of positive thinking: Aiding suppression-induced forgetting in repressive coping. *Cognition and Emotion, 24*, 1239–1249.

Hotta, C. and Kawaguchi, J. (2009) Self-initiated use of thought substitution can lead to long term forgetting. *Psychologia, 52*, 41–49.

Hunter, I. M. L. (1968). *Memory.* Harmondsworth, UK: Penguin Books.

Joormann, J., Hertel, P. T., Brozovich, F., & Gotlib, I. H. (2005). Remembering the good, forgetting the bad: Intentional forgetting of emotional material in depression. *Journal of Abnormal Psychology, 114*(4), 640–648.

Joslyn, S. L., & Oakes, M. A. (2005). Directed forgetting of autobiographical events. *Memory and Cognition, 33*(4), 577–587.

Kikuchi, H., Fujii, T., Abe, N., Suzuki, M., Takagi, M., Mugikura, S., et al. (2009). Memory repression: Brain mechanisms underlying dissociative amnesia. *Journal of Cognitive Neuroscience, 22*(3), 602–613.

Kopelman, M. D. (1995). The Korsakoff syndrome. *The British Journal of Psychiatry, 166*(2), 154–173.

Kopelman, M. D. (2002). Disorders of memory. *Brain, 125*(10), 2152–2190.

Kritchevsky, M., Chang, J., & Squire, L. R. (2004). Functional amnesia: Clinical description and neuropsychological profile of 10 cases. *Learning and Memory, 11*(2), 213–226.

Leigland, L. A., Schulz, L. E., & Janowsky, J. S. (2004). Age related changes in emotional memory. *Neurobiology of Aging, 25*(8), 1117–1124.

Levy, B. J., & Anderson, M. C. (2008). Individual differences in the suppression of unwanted memories: The executive deficit hypothesis. *Acta Psychologica, 127*, 623–635.

Levy, B. J. and Anderson, M. C. (2012) Purging of memories from conscious awareness tracked in the human brain. *Journal of Neuroscience, 32*, 16785–16794. doi:10.1523/JNEUROSCI.2640–12.2012

Lykken, D., & Tellegen, A. (1996). Happiness is a stochastic phenomenon. *Psychological Science, 7*(3), 186–189.

MacLeod, M. D., & Macrae, C. N. (2001). Gone but not forgotten: The transient nature of retrieval-induced forgetting. *Psychological Science, 12*(2), 148–152.

Markowitsch, H. J., Kessler, J., Van Der Ven, C., Weber-Luxenburger, G., Albers, M., & Heiss, W. D. (1998). Psychic trauma causing grossly reduced brain metabolism and cognitive deterioration. *Neuropsychologia, 36*(1), 77–82.

Mather, M., & Carstensen, L. L. (2005). Aging and motivated cognition: The positivity effect in attention and memory. *Trends in Cognitive Sciences, 9*(10), 496–502.

Noreen, S., & MacLeod, M. D. (2012). It's all in the detail: Intentional forgetting of autobiographical memories using the autobiographical think/no-think task. *Journal of Experimental Psychology: Learning, Memory, and Cognition.* doi:10.1037/a0028888

Pavlov, I. P. (1927). *Conditioned reflexes; An investigation of the physiological activity of the cerebral cortex* (G. V. Anrep, Ed.). London: Oxford University Press.

Payne, D. G. (1987). Hypermnesia and reminiscence in recall: A historical and empirical review. *Psychological Bulletin, 101*(1), 5–27.

Postman, L., Stark, K., & Henschel, D. M. (1969). Conditions of recovery after unlearning. *Journal of Experimental Psychology, 82*(1, Pt. 2), 1–24.

Rescorla, R. A. (2004). Spontaneous recovery varies inversely with the training-extinction interval. *Learning and Behavior: A Psychonomic Society Publication, 32*(4), 401–408.

Rizio, A. A. and Dennis, N. A. (2013). The neural correlates of cognitive control: Successful remembering and intentional forgetting. *Journal of Cognitive Neuroscience. 25*, 297–312.

Sahakyan, L. (2013). List-method directed forgetting in cognitive and clinical research: A theoretical and methodological review. In B. H. Ross (Ed.), *Psychology of Learning and Motivation* (Vol. 59, pp. 131–189). New York: Elsevier.

Sahakyan, L., & Kelley, C. M. (2002). A contextual change account of the directed forgetting effect. *Journal of Experimental Psychology: Learning, Memory, and Cognition, 28*(6), 1064–1072.

Sasaki, K., Gemba, H., & Tsujimoto, T. (1989). Suppression of visually initiated hand movement by stimulation of the prefrontal cortex in the monkey. *Brain Research, 495*(1), 100–107.

Schacter, D. L., Wang, P. L., Tulving, E., & Freedman, M. (1982). Functional retrograde amnesia: A quantitative case study. *Neuropsychologia, 20*(5), 523–532.

Schooler, J. W., Ambadar, Z., & Bendiksen, M. A. (1997). A cognitive corroborative case study approach for investigating discovered memories of sexual abuse. In J. D. Read & D. S. Lindsay (Eds.), *Recollections of trauma: scientific evidence and clinical practice* (pp. 379–88). New York: Plenum.

Sedikides, C., & Green, J. D. (2000). On the self-protective nature of inconsistency/negativity management: Using the person memory paradigm to examine self-referent memory. *Journal of Personality and Social Psychology, 79*, 906–922.

Sedikides, C., & Green, J. D. (2009). Memory as a self-protective mechanism. *Social and Personality Psychology Compass, 3*, 1055–1068.

Smith, S. M., & Moynan, S. C. (2008) Forgetting and recovering the unforgettable. *Psychological Science, 19*(5), 462–468.

Squire, L. R. (1992). Memory and the hippocampus: A synthesis from findings with rats, monkeys, and humans. *Psychological Review, 99*(2), 195–231.

Underwood, B. J. (1948). Retroactive and proactive inhibition after five and forty-eight hours. *Journal of Experimental Psychology, 38*, 29–38.

Waldfogel, S. (1948). The frequency and affective character of childhood memories. *Psychological Monographs, 62*(291, whole issue).

Wheeler, M. A. (1995). Improvement in recall over time without repeated testing: Spontaneous recovery revisited. *Journal of Experimental Psychology: Learning, 21*(1), 173–184.

Contents

Why do we need autobiographical memory?   299

Methods of study   300

Theories of autobiographical memory   306

Psychogenic amnesia   318

Organically based deficits   320

Summary   322

Points for discussion   322

Further reading   322

References   323

CHAPTER 11

AUTOBIOGRAPHICAL MEMORY

C an you remember your first school? The names of your teachers? Your friends? An incident at school, pleasant or unpleasant?

To answer these questions, you need autobiographical memory. Autobiographical memory refers to the memories that we hold regarding ourselves and our interactions with the world around us. Is it important? Certainly. But is it a separate kind of memory? Yes and no. No, given that it almost certainly depends on the episodic and semantic memory systems we have already discussed. Yes, because the role that it plays in our lives differs in interesting and important ways from other functions of memory. Remembering facts about ourselves, such as our name, when we went to school, and where we live, is autobiographical but forms a personal aspect of semantic memory. Remembering what you had for breakfast today is also autobiographical but involves recollecting a specific episodic experience. The fact that autobiographical memory involves both of these inevitably means that it is complex, and much that constitutes this chapter is descriptive rather than theory driven. This is meant not as a criticism

but as an account of the relatively early stage of development of our understanding of this intriguing area. Happily, theory-driven basic research is increasingly able to throw light on the nature of autobiographical memory and its disorders, with issues discussed in the chapter on motivated forgetting (Chapter 10), being particularly relevant.

We will begin by discussing the function of autobiographical memory and why it is important, leading on to the thorny question of how to study it. The problem here is that, unlike most of the research we have discussed so far, the experimenter typically has no control over the learning situation, which makes it difficult to analyze the processes involved in either the acquisition or forgetting of autobiographical memories.

WHY DO WE NEED AUTOBIOGRAPHICAL MEMORY?

Williams, Conway, and Cohen (2008) propose four functions of autobiographical memory. These include *directive* functions, for example what happened the last time you tried to change a car tire, and a more *social* function; sharing autobiographical memories can be a very pleasant and socially supportive activity (Neisser, 1988). In my own case, hearing my sons reminisce about childhood family holidays is an example. Conversely,

KEY TERM

Autobiographical memory: Memory across the lifespan for both specific events and self-related information.

when autobiographical memory is disrupted by amnesia or dementia, this can be one factor that impairs relationships (Robinson & Swanson, 1990), leading to the feeling that "This is not the person I married." Autobiographical memories can also play an important role in creating and maintaining our *self-representation*, hence the value of reminiscence therapy (Woods, Spector, Jones, Orrell, & Davies, 2005), a process described in Chapter 16 whereby elderly patients with memory problems are encouraged to build up a set of reminders of their earlier life based on photographs and personal mementos—items that bring back memories of their younger days. Finally, autobiographical recollection can be used to help us cope with adversity. One of the problems of depression is that patients find it difficult to recollect positive life experiences when depressed, whereas negative recollections are more readily available, a retrieval effect known as *mood-congruent memory*, which is one form of context-dependent memory discussed in more detail in Chapter 8 (p. 213).

However, although these functions might be plausible, they are largely speculative. In an attempt to obtain empirical evidence on this matter, Hyman and Faries (1992) questioned people about memories they frequently talked about, and the situations in which they were discussed. They found very few reports of autobiographical memory being used directively to solve problems, with the sharing of experience and passing on of advice being more common. In a subsequent study, they used cue words to prompt memories, finding a distinction between memories that were used internally for self-related functions and those used in interacting with others, but again little evidence of directive use of autobiographical memory.

Bluck, Alea, Habermas, and Rubin (2005) devised the Thinking About Life Experiences (TALE) questionnaire, specifying particular situations and then categorizing the resulting reports as: directive, self-related, nurturing existing social relationships, or developing new social relationships. The factor analysis of the results found considerable overlap between the directive function, the self-related function, and those related to nurturing and

developing relationships (e.g. *I enjoyed talking to John; so I think I'll accept his party invitation*). Hence, although it remains plausible that autobiographical memory has a number of different functions, it is doubtful that they are clearly separable into different categories in actual practice.

One weakness with the research described so far is the problem of adequate methodology. The studies assume, for example, that participants are aware of the function of such memories and can remember their autobiographical memories and the situations that evoked them in sufficient detail to categorize them. In an area as complex as autobiographical memory, there is clearly a need for the development of a range of methods of study. This is discussed next.

METHODS OF STUDY

One method of tackling this problem is to use diaries in which participants record events, and subsequently try to remember them. This is a useful approach but one that places onerous and persistent demands on the participants. A second approach is to probe memory, for example asking for a memory associated with a cue word such as *river*, then analyzing the nature of the responses. A third method is to ask for memories associated with either a specific time period, or a major public event such as the 9/11 attack on New York. Finally, as in the case of semantic and episodic memory, we can learn a good deal from what happens when autobiographical memory breaks down, as the result either of brain damage or emotional stress. Each of these approaches is discussed in turn.

Diaries

One problem in studying autobiographical memory is that of knowing what was initially experienced, and one solution to this is to record events in a diary that allows later memories to be objectively checked. Linton (1975) used this method to study her own autobiographical memory. She kept a diary for over 5 years, recording two events per day,

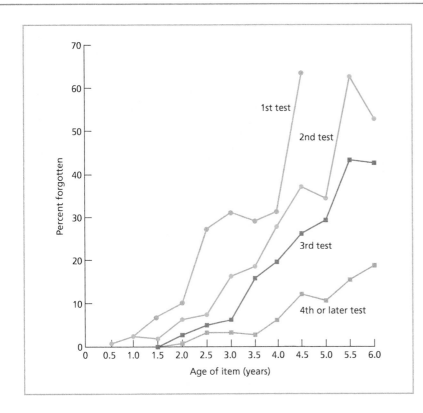

Figure 11.1 Probability of forgetting an autobiographical diary item as a function of elapsed time and number of prior tests. From Linton (1975). Copyright W.H. Freeman. Reproduced with permission.

each being briefly described and written on an index card. She tested herself each month by randomly picking out two index cards and deciding whether she could remember the order in which incidents occurred and the date. Because she chose cards at random and then replaced them, she would sometimes test herself on the same incident on several occasions. As Figure 11.1 shows, she observed a powerful effect: The more often an event was probed, the better it was retained. This provided further evidence for the value of retrieval practice on long-term learning as discussed in Chapter 5 (see p. 113).

A classic diary study was carried out by the Dutch psychologist Willem Wagenaar (1986), who kept a diary for over 6 years, on each day recording two events, together with four features or cues to that event. As shown Figure 11.2, he recorded *who* was involved, *what* the event was, *where* it occurred, and *when*. He also rated the incident for its saliency and whether it was something that happened frequently or was rather unusual, in addition to

recording the degree of emotional involvement and whether this was pleasant or unpleasant. He recorded a total of 2400 incidents. He then tested his memory by selecting an incident at random and cueing himself with one, two or three retrieval cues, randomizing the order in which the *who*, *what*, *where*, and *when* cues were presented. Figure 11.3 shows the mean percentage of questions answered correctly as a function of number of cues. Wagenaar found that the *who*, *what*, and *where* cues tended to be equally good at evoking a memory, whereas the *when* cue, which simply provided the date, was much less efficient. This is perhaps not surprising. Can you remember where you were on 19 July last year? Neither can I, although as we shall see later, some people can.

Wagenaar reports that he found the task to be surprisingly difficult and unpleasant, but that given sufficient cues he could recollect most of the incidents eventually. In a number of cases, he could not remember anything, despite all his recorded cues. However, in those cases where another person was

No. 3329

WHO   Leonardo da Vinci

WHAT I went to see his 'Last Supper'

WHERE In a church in Milano

WHEN Saturday, September 10, 1983

SALIENCE

1 = 1/day
2 = 1/week
☒ 3 = 1/month
4 = 2/year
5 = 1/three years
6 = 1/fifteen years
7 = 1/lifetime

EMOTIONAL INVOLVEMENT

☒ 1 = nothing
2 = little
3 = moderate
4 = considerable
5 = extreme

PLEASANTNESS

1 = extr. unpleasant
2 = very unpleasant
3 = unpleasant
4 = neutral
☒ 5 = pleasant
6 = very pleasant
7 = extr. pleasant

CRITICAL DETAIL

QUESTION   Who were with me?

ANSWER   Beth Loftus and Jim Reason

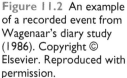

Figure 11.2 An example of a recorded event from Wagenaar's diary study (1986). Copyright © Elsevier. Reproduced with permission.

involved, they would typically be able to evoke a recollection, which could be verified by his providing additional information. Does that mean that we never forget anything? Almost certainly not. Wagenaar selected events that were most likely to be highly memorable; for example, going to see Leonardo da Vinci's painting of *The Last Supper*, accompanied by scientific colleagues (incidentally including Elizabeth Loftus whose classic work on eyewitness testimony you will encounter in Chapter 14). The process of selecting the event would in itself involve retrieval, and in effect a rehearsal, while the process of deciding on his *who*, *where*, *what*, and *when* cues would involve a relatively deep level of processing (Craik & Lockhart, 1972). This degree of selection and implicit rehearsal is a

problem for diary studies, because they result in memories that are atypically well encoded.

A somewhat more naturalistic approach to encoding of autobiographical memories is to use events reported in letters. I myself have used this based on a series of letters sent to my widowed mother during a year in California some 40 years ago (Baddeley, 2012). I went through the letters, identifying anything that could be regarded as an integrated episode, then classifying each on the basis of the extent to which I could remember it. I distinguished three degrees of vividness of the recollection, together with episodes that "I knew" had happened but of which I had no recollective experience, and those that were completely forgotten. Of 62 episodes identified in the letters, I judged that I could remember 23, about half

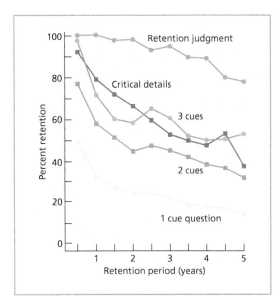

Figure 11.3 Recall of autobiographical incidents as a function of time, given one, two, or three retrieval cues. From Wagenaar (1986). Copyright © Elsevier. Reproduced with permission.

of these vividly. One example that springs to mind is losing my voice on a lecturing trip, then having a lively dinner with Endel Tulving, and the frustration of being unable to croak my own opinions with adequate vigor. The vivid memories were of nontrivial unique events that I remembered having told others about. Of the 62 total recorded episodes, I had forgotten 26 completely, nearly all trivial, with no recollection of retelling. Retelling of course is a form of rehearsal that, as Linton's (1975) diary indicated, has a major effect on subsequent recall.

The experience of re-reading my letters changed my view of my own autobiographical memory. Instead of seeing it as a landscape of potential memories extending into the distance with striking peaks of vivid memories and less clear valleys, the experience seemed much more analogous to perceiving a limited series of islands of memory in a sea of forgetting. Furthermore, the fact that the "islands" appear to depend on retelling over the years implies that they themselves may not be true memories, but rather memories of memories, a rather sobering thought!

But perhaps this is only true of distant memories? Why should we want to remember

relatively trivial events that happened 40 years ago? And perhaps it is not surprising that surviving memories are rather special, or at least worth telling others about. Would nonselected relatively trivial memories survive over a much shorter period than those reported in diary studies? Brewer (1988) tried to avoid the biased selection of recorded memories in a study that sampled events at random. His ten participants were each given a beeper and a tape recorder. The beeper went off at random intervals, at which point participants were to say what they were doing, where, what the significance of their activity was, its goal-directedness, and their emotional state. The incidents were tested at delays ranging from 0 to 46 days, using one or other of their ratings as a cue. A total of 414 events were recorded. When subsequently tested, 26% were correctly recalled, 28% were wrong, and 46% evoked a blank. It is likely that, given more cues, more would be recalled but it seems very unlikely that all of the 74% failed memories would be recollected. Note also that the act of providing the features to serve as subsequent cues would again involve atypically deep encoding.

A more detailed analysis of the nature of the items recalled was made by Conway, Collins, Gathercole, and Anderson (1996) in a study involving two participants who kept diaries over a period of months, recording both "events" and "thoughts." These were then mixed with plausibly invented alternatives and recognition was required. This was followed by a categorization as to whether the item was "remembered," meaning that recognition was accompanied by a feeling of recollecting the initial experience, or simply "known" (see Chapter 8 p. 221 for discussion of this distinction). True events were more likely to evoke a remember response than invented but plausible foils, with items classified as "events" being twice as likely to evoke recollection as entries that were "thoughts."

In conclusion, diary studies have been useful in giving some idea of the richness of autobiographical memory, and of the relative importance of different types of event and experience. They do, however, suffer from problems of sampling bias in the events recorded, together with a tendency for the event reporting process itself to result in the enhanced learning of the events selected. Finally, the method requires considerable perseverance from the diarists, who are therefore likely to be a small and atypical sample of the general population.

The memory probe method

An alternative to the diary method is that of cued recall, a method first used by Galton (1879). It was subsequently revived by Crovitz and Shiffman (1974), who gave their participants a word and asked them to recollect an autobiographical memory associated with that word. For example, given the cue word *horse*, this might evoke a memory of the first time you rode a horse. The method has also been adapted to probe for memories from a given time period such as childhood, or of a particular type of incident, for example a happy memory. Despite its simplicity and relative lack of control, this method has been used widely, and productively.

A prominent feature of probed autobiographical memories is their distribution across the lifespan. When left free to recall memories from any period in their life, all healthy participants, whether young or old, tend to recall few autobiographical memories from the first 5 years of life, termed *infantile amnesia* (see Chapter 14, p. 394). They also tend to produce plenty of memories from the most recent period. Those over the age of 40, however, also show a marked increase of memories from the period between the ages of 15 and 30, the so-called reminiscence bump (Rubin, Wetzler, & Nebes, 1986). A cross-cultural study illustrated in Figure 11.4 shows a similar pattern across participants from China, Japan, Bangladesh, England, and the US (Conway, Wang, Hanyu, & Haque, 2005). However, there are cultural differences in the average date for the first memory, which occurs at an average age of 3.8 for US and 5.4 for Chinese participants (Wang, 2006a, 2006b). This might reflect differences in the way that mothers talk to their children, with the US interaction tending to be more elaborate, emotionally oriented, and focused on the past than occurs in Chinese culture (Leichtman, Wang, & Pillemer, 2003). This might also account for a tendency for US recollections of early memories to be longer, more elaborate, and more emotionally toned and self-focused than occurs with Chinese respondents, whose recollections tend to be briefer and to have a stronger collective than individual emphasis (Wang, 2001).

There have been a number of attempts to explain the pattern of autobiographical memories across the lifespan. It probably reflects both a recency effect (see Chapter 3, p. 49)

Sir Francis Galton (1822–1911), a Victorian polymath, who in addition to his classic study of autobiographical memory, was a tropical explorer, geographer, meteorologist, anthropologist, and statistician.

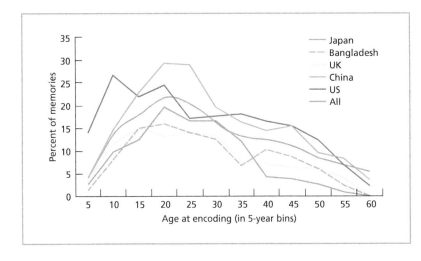

Figure 11.4 Lifespan retrieval curves for participants from five countries. From Conway et al. (2005). Copyright © 2005 Sage Publications. Reprinted by permission.

and at least two other processes, one accounting for infantile amnesia (the lack of memories from the first 1 or 2 years of life) and the other concerned with the high rate of recalling episodes from the teens and twenties. A number of interpretations of infantile amnesia have been proposed. These include Freudian repression, the late development of the hippocampus, and the undeveloped nature during infancy of a coherent *self*, something that is gradually built up on the basis of memories and experiences. The intriguing topic of infantile amnesia is discussed in Chapter 14 (p. 394).

Most interpretations of the reminiscence bump tend to focus on the fact that this is a period when many important things in our lives tend to happen. Berntsen and Rubin (2004) asked their participants to rate a number of important life events, finding that the average age for first falling in love was 16 years, college memories tended to be a rather later 22 years, marriage at an average age of 27, and children at 28. All fell within the period of the bump, making this an important period within what is sometimes known as the life narrative. This represents a coherent account that we create for ourselves as we progress through life—the story of who we are and how we got to this point in our life. Events that influence this are likely to be important to us, to be more likely to be retrieved, and to be more deeply encoded. Furthermore, such events as beginning college, making new friends, and falling in love are all likely to be relatively emotionally intense, a factor that increased the accessibility of memories (Dolcos, LaBar, & Cabeza, 2005), particularly when these are positive and occur in young adulthood (Berntsen & Rubin, 2002).

Glück and Bluck (2007) further elaborate the life narrative hypothesis. They collected a total of 3541 life events from 659 participants aged

KEY TERM

Life narrative: A coherent and integrated account of one's life that is claimed to form the basis of autobiographical memory.

The reminiscence bump occurs in early adulthood and reflects memories from a period when many important life events, such as falling in love, getting married and having children, tend to happen.

between 50 and 90 years. Participants were asked to rate their memories on emotional *valence*, their *personal* importance, and the extent to which the rememberer felt that they had *control* over events. A reminiscence bump was found, but only for positive events over which participants felt that they had a high degree of control, a result that they interpret as consistent with the importance of autobiographical memory in creating a positive life narrative (Figure 11.5).

An intriguing exception to the observation of a reminiscence bump in a person's early twenties occurs when memories are cued by smell. Despite an initial report by Rubin, Groth, and Goldsmith (1984), of equivalence across verbal, visual, and olfactory cues, Chu and Downes (2002) found that memories evoked by smell peaked at an earlier age (6–10 years) than the typical verbally cued reminiscence bump. Willander and Larsson (2006) replicated this using a sample of 93 volunteers ranging in age from 65 to 80 years. They cued with items that could not only be represented as a word, but also as a picture or a smell (e.g. *violet, tobacco, soap, whiskey*). Like Chu and Downes, they found a distinct tendency for smells to evoke memories that are rated by their participants as earlier than visually or verbally cued events. How could we explain this? Are odor-induced memories more emotional? Both Herz (2004) and Willander and Larsson (2007) found that they were.

It is, of course, the case that the probe studies described all depend to some extent on the accuracy with which participants can date events. As we saw from Wagenaar's diary study, memory for dating of an incident was the weakest of all the cues. This also presents a problem for the many practically oriented survey studies that are retrospective in nature, requiring respondents to remember, for example, when they last went to the doctor. A study by Means, Mingay, Nigam, and Zarrow (1988) asked patients who had made at least four medical visits in the last year to recall and report them, subsequently checking against the doctor's records. Performance was poor, particularly for visits that had clustered (25% correct versus 60% for more isolated occasions). People tend to date events indirectly, either by recollecting incidental features such as the weather or "the trees were bare," or by linking it to some other event that can itself be dated, such as holiday in Paris or the eruption of Mount St. Helens (Baddeley, Lewis, & Nimmo-Smith, 1978; Loftus & Marburger, 1983). These, in turn, are likely to be located within the broader context of a life narrative.

THEORIES OF AUTOBIOGRAPHICAL MEMORY

The systematic study of autobiographical memory began more recently than most other

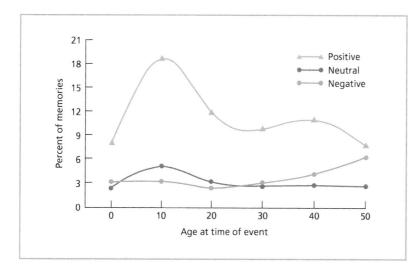

Figure 11.5 Distribution of involuntary memories for participants who were over 40 years old. Only positive memories show the reminiscence bump. From Glück and Bluck, (2007). Copyright © The Psychonomic Society. Reproduced with permission.

aspects of episodic memory and, as a result, much of what has been described could be regarded as operating at a level of natural history. That is not intended as a criticism. Good natural history leads to soundly based theory that in turn should result in the creation and testing of specific hypotheses. One influential attempt to develop an overall theory of autobiographical memory is that proposed by Martin Conway (2005).

Conway defines autobiographical memory as a system that retains knowledge concerning the *experienced self*, the "me." It is always addressed by the content of the memory but does not always produce recollective experience; hence you might know that you had a trip to Paris last year, but only recollect the episodic detail later, or indeed not at all. Such recollective experiences occur when autobiographical knowledge, our personal semantic memory, retains access to associated episodic memories, for example when the knowledge that you went to Paris connects with a specific recollection, such as seeing the Eiffel Tower in the rain.

Such autobiographical memories are transitory and are constructed dynamically on the basis of the autobiographical knowledge base. The knowledge base itself ranges from very broad-brush representations of lifetime periods to sensory–perceptual episodes, which are rapidly lost. Finally, the whole system depends on the interaction between the knowledge base and the *working self*. The working self is assumed to play a similar role in autobiographical memory to that played by working memory in cognition more generally (Conway & Pleydell-Pearce, 2000). These broad ideas were developed by Conway (2005) into a more detailed account of the way in which the self interacts with memory (Figure 11.6).

The working self comprises a complex set of active goals and self-images. For example, I have the active goal of describing Conway's ideas and am doing so by dictating this while walking along a country road with the sun on my face. The working self modulates access to long-term memory, and is itself influenced by LTM. To write this, I need to access my knowledge of Martin Conway's views. The working self comprises both conceptual self-knowledge—my occupation, my family background, and my professional aims—which in turn are socially constructed on the basis of my family background, the influence of peers, school, myths, and other factors that make up the complex representation of myself.

To summarize, the working self is a way of encoding information about *what is*, *what has been*, and *what can be*. To be effective, however, it needs to be both coherent and to correspond reasonably closely with outside reality. When this link is lost, problems occur, which might—in extreme cases—lead to confabulation or delusion (see Chapter 16 p. 446). Conway and Tacchi (1996), for example, describe a patient suffering frontal-lobe damage following a road traffic accident who had comforting but totally false memories of the support provided by his family.

The *autobiographical knowledge base* has a broadly hierarchical structure, with an *overall life story* being linked to a number of broad themes; work and personal relationships, for example. These in turn split up into different time periods: for example, *When I was an undergraduate*; *My first job*; *My hopes for the future*. These comprise a number of general "events," which can include individuals and institutions as well as activities: for example, *The psychology department*; *Professor Smith*; *Departmental talks*; *Promotion*. These are still conceptualized at a relatively abstract level but can lead to specific episodic memories; for example, my interview with Professor Smith on applying for a job, or the last departmental research talk I heard. These in turn might have been stored at a more fundamental level containing more detailed sensory–perceptual information; for example, the room where the interview was held, the weather outside, or Professor Smith's tone of voice in offering me the job. In recollecting an event, it is this essentially

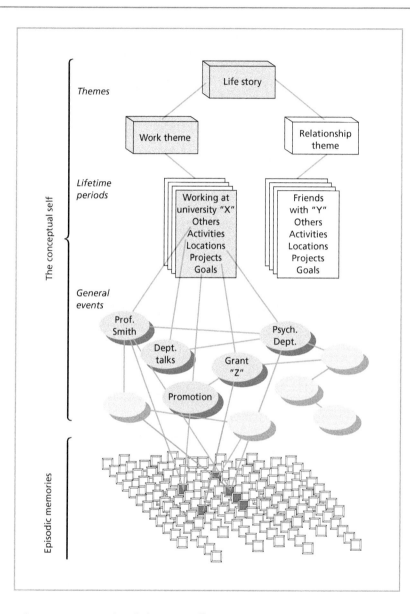

Figure 11.6 The knowledge structures within autobiographical memory, as proposed by Conway (2005). Copyright © Elsevier. Reproduced with permission.

arbitrary sensory detail that typically convinces us that we have a genuine memory rather than a confabulation (Johnson, Foley, Suengas, & Raye, 1988). Such detail is often visual in character, which is one reason why vivid visual flashbacks are so convincing and potentially so disturbing.

Following Tulving (1989), Conway refers to the process of recollecting such detail and recognizing it as familiar as being based on autonoetic consciousness, the capacity to reflect on our thoughts. This ability to reflect on our memories is of course essential in deciding whether a recollection is an accurate record of our past or a confabulation.

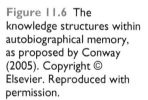

KEY TERM

Autonoetic consciousness: A term proposed by Tulving for self-awareness, allowing the rememberer to reflect on the contents of episodic memory.

Accessing such detailed knowledge tends to be relatively slow, typically taking several seconds, whereas access to semantic memory is often performed almost immediately (Haque & Conway, 2001). As we saw in Chapter 4 (p. 79), patients with frontal-lobe damage can have difficulty both in accessing autobiographical memories and also, once accessed, in evaluating them.

In a later account of the model, Conway and Jobson (2012) discuss the role in autobiographical memory of factors such as the parents' reminiscing style and subsequent discussion of memories with peers, as well as broader social factors such as the manner of thought in the local culture, local heroes and role models, myths and general attitudes as to what is good and right. Such influences, in which the inner processes of autobiographical memory are shaped by the surrounding sociocultural world, are depicted in Figure 11.6.

Conway and Jobson stress that the operation of autobiographical memory is goal-related, and that different goals tend to predominate in different cultures. There is, for example, considerable evidence for differences between individualistic cultures that tend to dominate in the West, and more communal and collective attitudes that are characteristic of many Asian cultures. Wang (2008) studied autobiographical memory in US participants who come from an Asian background, probing autobiographical memory related to their US or Asian identity and finding the latter generated more socially oriented memories in contrast to the greater self-focus for US-related memories. Marian and Kaushanskaya (2004) interviewed Russian–English bilingual participants in both languages. Regardless of the language of encoding of a specific autobiographical memory, recollections in Russian were more collectivist than those in English. At a more extended and integrated level, life scripts are also influenced by culture; hence a celebration such as a Bar Mitzvah is likely to tie participants into traditional Jewish culture and a first communion into a Catholic context (Berntsen & Rubin, 2004).

Conway's theory provides a useful framework that pulls together what we know about autobiographical memory, which in turn is likely to lead to further more theoretically oriented questions. For example, how might we test the assumption that the autobiographical database is divided in the way proposed by Conway (2005)? A further challenge is offered by the need to explain the increasingly rich evidence accumulating from situations in which autobiographical memory might appear to be atypical, either because it appears to be unusually detailed or because it is impaired or distorted by stress or disease. A range of such instances is described next.

Calendrical autobiographical memory

A couple of years ago I was contacted by a lady who claimed that her husband had a remarkable memory and wondered if I would like to test him. I was somewhat skeptical; people are, in general, not very good at estimating the quality of their memory, but since they lived locally I agreed to visit. I took along a few standard tests and an autobiographical inventory (AMI), which probes for information from different periods of life. I was welcomed by a sociable chap (RM) in his early 40s, who worked in an administrative post in local government. RM's performance on standard episodic memory tests proved to be good but not outstanding, unlike his autobiographical memory, which seemed to be rich and quite detailed. However, as he pointed out, we had no way of knowing whether his recollections were accurate.

The next step therefore was to test him on verifiable information. One example that I subsequently chose was based on his support for Bradford City, a local soccer team with a long string of not very successful managers. He proved adept at recalling managers, together with dates, when they had been appointed and when sacked, sometimes coming up with further information as to where he first heard about the sacking. At this point I decided to enlist the help of Martin Conway, a friend and ex-colleague who is an expert in that field. Martin drew up a list of dates; on half of them some dramatic item of news had occurred, and on half this was not the case. I tested both RM and Martin on a sample of such dates. Below is a typical example:

AB: *"What happened on the 17th of January 1991?"*

Martin: *"Well I have to think to myself what was happening in life at the time. I was a young university lecturer in Lancaster and we would have been back at work after the Christmas break. I taught a course on consciousness. I do remember that (but not much else!)."*

RM: *"It was a Thursday and I do believe it was the first day of the Gulf War (correct). I was working for the Department of Employment at the time and was involved in a training course at Hebden Bridge, I can't recall whether I was actually on the training course or whether I was contributing to the training, but I recall the day quite clearly."*

AB: *"Can you remember hearing about the news?"*

RM: *"Yes I think I stayed up late to watch something on TV and I heard about it before I went to bed either later on the Wednesday night or the early hours of Thursday morning."*

RM was also good at generating the date on which events had happened, provided it was something within his interest. This included general elections, where he could provide the date of each British election together with the results in terms of which party had attained the majority of seats and how large the majority. He could reel off the last 34 UK prime ministers and the last 21 US presidents, mentioning that as a child he had carefully copied out and illustrated the many kings of England in chronological order.

He could not always remember particular days however, so given *19th December 2006* he responded:

It was a Tuesday and I have absolutely no idea what I was doing, but on the Monday I was offered a new job in the company where I was working at the time, I remember the guy ringing me and offering me a job.
I remember on the Thursday we had a Christmas party and Friday we had friends around, then obviously into Christmas.

He was accurate in his dating of public events, pointing out that the date that a popular comedian had died of heart attack on TV was not the date recorded in our book of notable events. We checked the date online, and he was correct.

When asked about his memory he remarked that for many years he had assumed it was just like everyone else's. He said that for him dates provided an important cue to memories and that this process depended on his capacity to work out the relevant day of the week. He reported that his memories typically involved visual imagery, mentally observing himself in a particular situation rather than re-experiencing the event from within. Finally we asked him whether his remarkable memory was useful in any way. "Not very" he replied, "though it makes me a popular member of our pub quiz team!" probably not much of an evolutionary advantage for homo sapiens!

I have described testing RM in some detail in order to give a flavor of the way in which he remembers. He is very different from JP, described in Chapter 9. You may recall that JP appears to remember every day in her life since her teens in intricate detail, experienced like a continuous movie that is full of emotion. None of this is true of RM whose memories seem very much like those you or I might have in recalling, for example, Wednesday of last week, with the exception that he can do this for specific days over many years.

How does he do it? My own view (Baddeley, 2012) relies on the difference between the two types of organizational structure described in Chapter 6 (p. 149). One is hierarchical, beginning with a general concept and systematically splitting it into subconcepts; the example we gave was minerals which were then split into metals and stones with the metals then dividing into precious versus nonprecious, etc. Broadbent, Cooper and Broadbent (1978) contrasted this with an equally helpful matrix structure comprising a series of categories, each split into subcategories. An example might be a set of countries, with, for each, the capital city, a river, a mountain and a language. For most of us, our autobiographical memory is likely, as Conway suggested, to be hierarchically organized, starting at a broad general level and moving to the more particular. In the above date-based example, Martin Conway began with a broad period of his life, followed by his job, followed by a course he was teaching, whereupon everything stopped because he could not map the course onto specific days. In contrast, RM uses a date-based calendar framework, encoding information on the basis of dates, rather as if he were able to consult his diary for that year. This, if successful, gives him a precise day, which if the information was of sufficient interest at encoding, gives a reasonable chance of retrieval. This only works of course if you are sufficiently interested in dates to use an encoding strategy, which RM certainly is, and apparently has been since childhood as indicated by his careful noting of the dates of the kings and queens of England. He mentioned also that in idle moments, such as when shaving, he notes the date and reflects on other things that have happened on that date in his life, a form of rehearsal that is not available to most of us.

At the same time as we were carrying out our somewhat fragmentary investigation of RM's memory, the group in California who had discovered the remarkable autobiographical memory of JP were conducting an extensive investigation into the generality of their earlier results (LePort, Mattfeld, Dickinson-Anson, Fallon, Stark, Kruggel, et al., 2012). They advertised widely for people with what they describe as Highly Superior Autobiographical Memory (HSAM), and were contacted by 150 adults who claimed this capacity. A series of telephone screening tests followed, using a public event quiz which led to a more demanding test based on dates; 31 contacts passed this test, of whom 11 were invited to their laboratory in Irvine, California to take part in a range of further tests which were also performed by a matched control group.

So, were they like JP, plagued by an uncontrollable stream of memories, or were they like RM, or were they different again? Their autobiographical memory was first tested by asking them to recall five personal events for which the answers could be verified for accuracy. These included the first day at university, at elementary school, an 18th birthday celebration, and so forth. They then had a series of more standard memory tests, including learning to associate names with faces, visual memory for unrelated objects, forward and backward digit span, recall of a prose passage, and paired associate learning. They were tested then for depression and for obsessionality, together with an interview and behavioral questionnaire about how they use their memory, their knowledge of calendars dates, etc. Finally, the 11 HSAM participants and controls were examined by MRI to look for possible anatomical differences in the structure of their brains.

So what were the results? First of all none of the HSAM group resembled JP in experiencing the stressful continuous stream of lifetime experiences. They were extremely good at recalling public events and dates; they had of course been selected on this basis. They were in addition very much better then controls in their autobiographical performance, both in terms of verified details and in terms of the richness of detail recalled. Like RM, their performance on standard tests of episodic memory was unremarkable. They were slightly better than controls at remembering face–name associations and the array of visual stimuli, but did not differ from controls on backward or forward digit span, or memory for prose or paired associates. In short, their episodic LTM was unremarkable.

There were no clear personality differences. The HSAM group showed no evidence of depression, although there was a tendency for the group to be somewhat higher in obsessionality. The neuroimaging results identified no fewer than nine structures that appeared to differ from those of control participants. However, given the small sample size, it is probably premature to place too much weight on such apparent differences.

Nine out of eleven of the HSAM group reported organizing their memories chronologically, sometimes retrieving events, on the basis of day, and date and year, with six reporting that they habitually recall their memories in this way as a means of passing time or going to sleep. LePort et al. conclude that:

Calendric ability is a unique and defining characteristic of the HSAM population. We speculate that this ability allows for application of a temporal order to their memory, an organisation that possibly facilitates the retrieval of details from their daily life.
(Leport et al., 2012 p86)

This does not of course preclude my own matrix retrieval hypothesis.

Flashbulb memories

Do you remember where you were when you first heard of the 9/11 attack on the World Trade Center? Unlike humdrum events such as routine visits to the doctor, certain occasions appear to give rise to remarkably clear detailed and persistent memories. Brown and Kulik (1977) asked people to recall how and when they had first heard of the assassination of President Kennedy. They found a degree of vividness and detail that was surprising, leading them to propose a new kind of memory system, which they termed flashbulb memory. They argued for a separate process that, given appropriate conditions, leads to a special mechanism resulting

Flashbulb memories are typically vivid, clear and persistent. What were you doing when you heard about the World Trade Center attacks on September 11th 2001?

in a qualitatively different memory record. They termed this process the "now print" mechanism, whereby extreme emotion was assumed to lead to an almost photographic representation of the event and its physical context. In subsequent years, this has proved to be an extremely popular area of study. It now seems that whenever a disaster occurs, a cognitive psychologist somewhere will be devising a questionnaire to establish whether flashbulb memories have occurred, and trying to answer some of the questions raised by Brown and Kulik's claim.

There is no doubt that people do report very vivid recollections of the point at which they remember hearing about major disasters. It is also the case that the probability of report of a flashbulb memory depends on the degree to which the rememberer was likely to be affected by the event. Black people were more likely to have a flashbulb memory concerning the deaths of Martin Luther King and Malcolm X than were white participants (McCloskey, Wible, & Cohen, 1988), and Danes who reported an involvement with the Danish resistance movement were more likely to have a flashbulb experience, and be able to report on the weather, time of day, and day of the week for the invasion and liberation of Denmark than did those who were less directly involved (Berntsen & Thomsen, 2005).

KEY TERM

Flashbulb memory: Term applied to the detailed and apparently highly accurate memory of a dramatic experience.

But do we need to assume a special mechanism to account for these results? The Brown and Kulik conclusions have been challenged on two fronts. First is the question of whether flashbulb memories are as accurate as they seem, and second whether one needs a special mechanism to explain them. In a study based on the Challenger space disaster, Neisser and Harsch (1992) compared the recall of the experience of learning about the event, testing people after 1 day and retesting after 2½ years, finding a substantial drop in accuracy. For example, after 1 day, 21% reported first hearing about the disaster on TV, whereas after 2½ years this had increased to 45%. Similarly, Schmoick, Buffalo, and Squire (2000) reported considerable forgetting of the experience of hearing the result of the OJ Simpson trial over a period of 32 months.

A further problem is the question of what should be the baseline against which one judges whether a memory is unusually accurate or vivid. Rubin and Kozin (1984) report that memories of high-school graduation or of an early emotional experience can be just as clear and vivid. I myself have a very vivid memory of an incident at my wedding some 50 years ago; sitting nervously in the church front pew, waiting for things to begin, I was approached by the minister loudly whispering "you did arrange the organist? Well he's not here!" He'd forgotten to come. The best I could come up with was a friend who played honky-tonk piano. Miraculously, the call of "Is there an organist in the congregation?" worked. A young man we did not know stepped forward and saved the day. He was an organ scholar at a Cambridge college, who had come with a friend of my future wife. Flashbulb memories don't need to be life-threatening.

Davidson, Cook, and Glisky (2006) contrasted memory for the 9/11 World Trade Center attack with everyday memories, finding that after a year there was a correlation of .77 between the initial and subsequent recollection for the 9/11 incident, indicating very good retention, compared with a correlation of only .33 for more everyday memories. By contrast, however, Talarico and Rubin (2003) found the same degree of loss of detail of 9/11 for flashbulb and everyday memories, although participants *believed* that their

memory of 9/11 was clearer. The crucial difference between these two studies might be that, whereas Talarico and Rubin's participants themselves produced and recorded their everyday events, and hence generated their own retrieval cues, in the Davidson et al. study, the experimenters chose the events to be recalled. Cueing an exceptional event in an unambiguous way is much easier for the experimenter than providing an adequate cue for an everyday event in someone else's life.

However, although there is doubt as to whether the degree of recall is quite as impressive as suggested by Brown and Kulik, there is no doubt that people do have vivid autobiographical memories of flashbulb incidents. In terms of interpretation, however, the problem is that there are a number of reasons why this might be. First of all, such incidents are highly distinctive, with little danger of their being confused with other events, which is not the case for most everyday memories. Second, we tend to talk about such events and watch them repeatedly on TV; in effect, rehearsing them. Third, they tend to be important events that potentially change some aspect of our lives and surroundings; and fourth, they tend to give rise to emotions.

Given that all of these are likely to enhance memory in one way or another, do we need an additional quite separate theory? Perhaps not. And if not, is it worthwhile attempting to untangle these various contributions that operate under conditions that are by their very nature hard to control? But no doubt such studies will continue, if only because the phenomenon is dramatic and intriguing. My own inclination, however, is to attempt to understand the possible contributions independently, perhaps subsequently attempting to bring them to bear on the phenomenon of flashbulb memory. One such potential contributor concerns the effect of social and emotional influences on autobiographical memory.

Social and emotional influences

As we saw in Chapter 6, we tend to construct our memories rather than simply calling them up like a book being chosen from a library.

Consequently, memory in general, and autobiographical memory in particular, is likely to be influenced by our hopes and needs. This is illustrated very clearly in a classic study by Neisser (1981) of the testimony of John Dean, one of the Watergate conspirators, whose testimony against President Nixon was so detailed that the press labeled him "the man with the tape-recorder memory." In this case, however, there was a real tape recording against which his memory could be compared. Dean's memory proved to be very accurate in terms of broad gist, but there was a persistent tendency for his account to exaggerate his own role and significance.

A tendency to place ourselves center-stage probably plays a part in many of our memories, perhaps because it helps us maintain our self-esteem. We are not lacking in ways of defending ourselves against challenges to our self-esteem. We readily accept praise but tend to be skeptical of criticism (Wyer & Frey, 1983; Kunda, 1990), often attributing criticism to prejudice on the part of the critic (Crocker & Major, 1989). We are inclined to take credit for success when it occurs but deny responsibility for failure (Zuckerman, 1979). If this stratagem fails, we are rather good at selectively forgetting failure and remembering success and praise (Crary, 1966). Although this tendency to preserve our self-esteem can seem pathological, there is evidence to suggest that it serves a useful function. As noted in our

discussion of mood-congruent memory, there is a tendency for a depressed mood to bias recollection, leading to the differential recall of negative memories from one's past (see Chapter 8, p. 213). This process of rumination tends to become self-perpetuating, hence deepening the depression. Perhaps as a defense against this process, there is a tendency for depressed patients to retrieve much less rich and detailed—and hence perhaps less distressing—autobiographical memories (Williams & Scott, 1988).

This tendency for depressed patients to have less rich autobiographical memories is linked to their preoccupation with negative thoughts (Healy & Williams, 1999; Dalgleish, Spinks, Yiend, & Kuyken, 2001). This was first reported in studies of people who had recently attempted suicide. When asked to generate an autobiographical memory in response to cue words, depressed patients would respond with a very general response. Hence, given the cue *angry*, they might respond "When I've had a row," whereas control participants are more specific, for example "With my supervisor last Monday." This tendency is reversed when depression is successfully treated (Williams, Watts, MacLeod, & Mathews, 1997).

A good experimental example of the tendency to preserve self-esteem is provided by Conway (1990), who asked his students prior to an exam to report their expected grades, the importance of such grades, their hours of study, how well they had prepared, and how valid the test would be. Two weeks after results were announced, he asked each student the same set of questions. For those who got better results than expected, the amount of work reported was the same but the importance of the result was increased. Those who had underperformed reported doing less work, resulting in the claim by the student that the grade was less important and less valid.

Of course, the levels of emotion involved in exam results, although significant, are not massive. It is difficult and ethically dubious to carry out experiments involving extreme emotions, but occasionally the opportunity arises for studying such emotions in a naturalistic context. Wagenaar and Groeneweg (1990) were able to do so in connection with the trial of John Demanjuk who, in the early 1980s,

When testifying to the Watergate Committee in June 1973, John Dean's recall of specific events consistently exaggerated his own role and significance.

was accused of being a particularly brutal concentration camp guard, known as Ivan the Terrible, during the Second World War. In this connection, they were able to re-interview victims who had first testified some 40 years before. Most witnesses claimed to recognize Demanjuk as Ivan the Terrible, with 74% of his victims and 58% of those who had not suffered directly claiming recognition, a high rate given the amount of elapsed time. Two separate subgroups had seen Demanjuk on television. In both groups, 80% reported recognition, indicating an important potential source of eyewitness error when accused persons are shown in the media.

In general, the unprompted information that the camp survivors produced was accurate when compared to earlier accounts. Twelve of the thirteen who spontaneously mentioned whether Jews were housed in tents or barracks were accurate, whereas only fourteen out of twenty-five who did not volunteer this information were correct. Somewhat surprisingly, even quite dramatic events such as being beaten up or witnessing another prisoner being murdered, often appeared to have been forgotten, although there was no clear evidence that such very negative emotional memories were harder to recall than more neutral information. The influence of emotion on memory is of course a very challenging and clinically important issue that has already been discussed in the chapter on motivated forgetting (see Chapter 10, p. 266), which also has links to my next topic, *post-traumatic stress disorder*.

Post-traumatic stress disorder

The term post-traumatic stress disorder (PTSD) applies to the symptoms that can follow from situations of extreme stress such as rape, near

KEY TERM

Post-traumatic stress disorder (PTSD): Emotional disorder whereby a dramatic and stressful event such as rape results in persistent anxiety, often accompanied by vivid flashback memories of the event.

drowning, or a horrific traffic accident. PTSD often involves "flashbacks," extremely vivid memories of the scene of the initial terror. This might be accompanied by nightmares and a more general state of anxiety (Foa, Rothbaum, Riggs, & Murdock, 1991). Whereas there is often a life-threatening aspect to the experience generating the flashback, this is not essential. As a student, I worked for a time as a hospital porter. We occasionally had to wheel bodies to the morgue, not something I found easy to adapt to, although the body was covered by a device known locally as the "tureen." Then, on one trip, I had to pass through the autopsy room and suddenly caught sight of the body of a naked woman ripped open. The image kept coming back at apparently random moments, and I can still "see it" over 50 years later, although happily with considerably less vividness. My own experience was relatively mild and certainly not directly threatening. How much worse must it be continually to re-experience a rape, or being surrounded by people being burned in a fire, or drowning in a shipping disaster (Cardena & Spiegel, 1993, Foa & Rothbaum, 1998)?

Do flashbacks represent a different kind of memory? Brewin (2001) suggests a distinction between *verbally accessible memory*, which links with the normal memory system, and *situationally accessible memory*, which is highly detailed when it occurs as a flashback but cannot be called to mind intentionally. It is certainly the case that considerable memory for detail can occur in the context of amnesia for other aspects of the situation. Harvey and Bryant (2000) describe a patient who was a passenger involved in a road traffic accident and who has vivid flashback memories of the car they hit, its color, the floral hat worn by one of its occupants, and a soft toy in the rear window, but who could recall nothing after that point. He was a skilled professional driver and felt considerable guilt at not having called out to warn the driver. Eventually, it was demonstrated to him that his perception of the time available was illusory, and that he had absolutely no possibility of influencing the accident. He subsequently recovered from his PTSD, but never went back to driving as a professional.

The precise mechanism underlying memory disturbance in PTSD remains uncertain.

One possibility is that it is based on classical conditioning, with the environmental stimuli associated with the horrific moment being powerfully associated with the feeling of terror. As a result, incidental stimuli or thoughts can act as a conditioned stimulus that can trigger off the emotional response, bringing back the associated memory. Indeed, some treatments of PTSD use this model, focusing on the extinction of the fear response. The response is cued by having the patient imagine the scene under safe conditions controlled by the therapist, leading gradually to the extinction of the fear response (Rothbaum & Davis, 2003). Sometimes, virtual reality techniques are used; for example, having a pilot who has developed PTSD under combat conditions, fly a simulated helicopter sortie over "virtual Vietnam."

In many cases, such treatment leads to a reduction of the symptoms. However, this is not always the case. Furthermore, it is of course the case that, given an equivalent level of stress, not everyone develops PTSD, and those who do sometimes recover spontaneously. Figure 11.7 shows the approximate proportion of people responding in each of these ways following exposure to a traumatic event such as a terrorist attack or the death of a spouse (Bonanno, 2005). What makes the difference?

The answer to this question might lie in the response of the autonomic nervous system (ANS) to stress. In a threatening situation, the amygdala signals the ANS to release adrenalin and cortisol, stress hormones that alert the organism for flight or fight. When the danger passes, the brain normally signals the adrenal glands to stop producing stress hormones, gradually bringing the body back to normal. It is suggested that in PTSD patients, this corrective process is reduced, leading to a more prolonged period of stress. There is some evidence that treatment with propranolol, which aids this recovery process, might reduce the likelihood of PTSD (Pitman, Sanders, Zusman, Healy, Cheema, Lasko et al., 2002; Vaiva, Ducrocq, Jezequel, Averland, Levestal, Brunet, & Marmar, 2003). This does not lead to forgetting of the traumatic event but it does reduce the emotional impact of the associated memories.

There is also some evidence that patients with PTSD might have a somewhat smaller hippocampal volume than those without. This raises the question of whether the stress has actively reduced the size of the hippocampus, or whether a small hippocampus has made the patient more vulnerable. Animal studies have suggested that prolonged stress can disrupt the operation of the hippocampus, possibly even leading to neuronal death (Sapolsky, 1996; McEwen, 1999). An ingenious study by Gilbertson, Shenton, Ciszewski, Kasai, Lasko, Orr and Pitman. (2002) tackled this problem by studying Vietnam veterans who had developed PTSD, and who had a twin who had not experienced Vietnam. Both PTSD veterans and their unexposed twins had smaller hippocampi than veterans who had experienced stress in Vietnam without developing PTSD and their unexposed twins. It appears to be the case, therefore, that a reduced hippocampus makes one more vulnerable to PTSD, presumably because a smaller hippocampus is less able to recover from the huge surge in adrenalin associated with extreme stress.

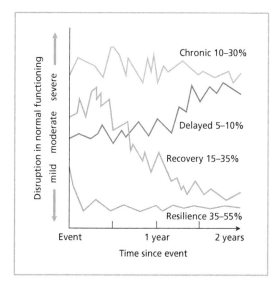

Figure 11.7 Patterns of recovery function following post-traumatic stress disorder (PTSD), with the approximate percentage of patients following each pattern. Data from Bonanno (2005).

Involuntary memories

Do the flashbacks that occur in PTSD represent a different kind of memory? They are clearly atypical in their negativity and emotional intensity, but do they imply a different mechanism from normal recall? A recent study by Berntsen and Rubin (2008) suggests that this might not be the case.

This study begins with an analysis of PTSD in a sample of 118 Danes who were tourists in Thailand or Sri Lanka at the time of the tsunami catastrophe in December 2004. About half had experienced or witnessed danger to life and had experienced intense fear, helplessness, or horror. Some 40% of respondents reported recurrent memories, with the likelihood of this increasing for those who were close to the threatening wave. As expected, the frequency of the recurrent memories tended to coincide with the point of maximum emotional impact, with those directly threatened by the wave having recurrent memories of escaping, whereas those who had heard about the tragedy rather than directly witnessing it, tending to have recurrent memories of searching for loved ones or of the possible worst-case scenario. Broadly speaking, the pattern of recurrent memories was characteristic of those found in PTSD cases more generally.

A standard clinical interpretation of such involuntary memories is in terms of what Neisser (1967) refers to as the reappearance hypothesis, which implies that "the same memory image, or other cognitive unit, can disappear and reappear over and over again." An example is that of a man who kept seeing headlights coming towards him because he had seen the same thing shortly before a car crash in which he was involved (Ehlers, Hackmann, & Michael, 2004). Note that this type of repeated and stereotyped memory, if it occurs, differs greatly from the reconstructive view of memory that is associated with normal remembering.

Berntsen and Rubin (2008) noted that the evidence for the unchanging nature of such

memories is based only on clinical report, and went on to investigate the extent to which intrusive memories in PTSD follow the same course as intrusive memories more generally. They proposed that such memories will also occur in the general population, and will follow the same pattern as is found in autobiographical memory more generally. More specifically, they proposed that such intrusive normal memories, will be more accessible for a number of reasons, including that they are: (1) more recent (Rubin & Wenzel, 1996); (2) more arousing (McGaugh, 2003); (3) more likely to occur for positive events (Walker, Skowronski, & Thompson, 2003); and (4) likely to show the reminiscence bump, at least in older participants.

Berntsen and Rubin (2008) began with a telephone survey of 1504 Danes aged between 18 and 96, asking each about the frequency of recurrent memories and recurrent dreams. As Figure 11.8 shows, such memories are frequent, and decline somewhat with age. Recurrent dreams are less frequent and show a modest correlation with recurrent memories. As panel (b) in Figure 11.8 shows, as we get older, we tend to have more positive recurrent memories, which are also more intense. Panel (c) of Figure 11.8 shows that recent recurrent memories are more likely, whereas panel (d), which is based on respondents over the age of 40, indicates that such positive recurrent memories are likely to come from late childhood and adolescence, namely that they show a characteristic reminiscence bump.

A final study was concerned with the extent to which recurrent memories were identical across repetitions. Berntsen and Rubin carried out a diary study in which nine participants nominated their most traumatic experience when filling in a PTSD questionnaire, after which they kept an involuntary memory diary for the next few weeks. Each participant recorded from two to seven recurrent memories of the traumatic incident. Eight of the nine cases showed no evidence of exact repetition of either time or of the precise features of the incident. Berntsen and Rubin conclude that the flashbacks that are observed in PTSD do not comprise a special type of memory but have the same characteristics as recurrent memories in the

KEY TERM

Reappearance hypothesis: The view that under certain circumstances, such as flashbulb memory and PTSD, memories can be created that later reappear in exactly the same form.

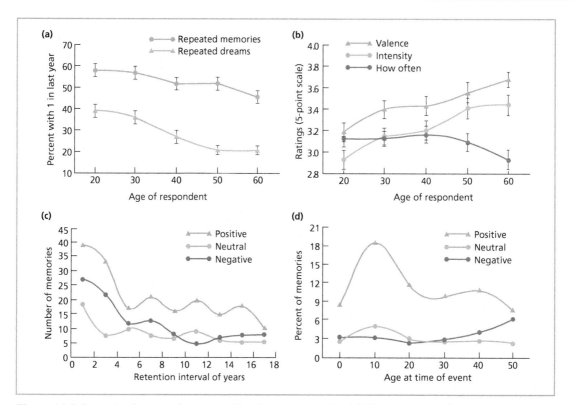

Figure 11.8 Retention functions for repeated involuntary memories. (a) The percentage of participants with a repeated memory or dream in the last year as a function of the age of the participant. (b) The mean ratings of valence, intensity, and frequency as a function of the age of the participant. (c) The retention function for positive, neutral, and negative repeated involuntary memories for all participants. (d) The distribution of positive, neutral, and negative repeated involuntary memories from age 0 to 50 for those participants who were 40 years old or older. From Berntsen and Rubin (2008). Copyright © The Psychonomic Society. Reproduced with permission.

normal course of life, and that both reflect the same basic principles as are found across all types of autobiographical memory.

PSYCHOGENIC AMNESIA

As described in Chapter 10 on motivated forgetting (p. 279), emotion can have a marked effect on the capacity to remember events and experiences. Such effects are particularly marked in the case of autobiographical memory, when emotionally based disruption of memory can have a dramatic effect on everyday life, as in the case of fugue states, (see also Chapter 10, p. 280).

Fugue

The main characteristics of fugue states are that: (1) they are typically preceded by stress, for example an accusation of embezzlement (Kopelman, Green, Guinan, Lewis, & Stanhope, 1994), and are more common in wartime (Sargeant & Slater, 1941); (2) depressed mood is common; (3) there is often a history of transient organically based amnesia; and (4) it is often difficult to discount the possibility of ulterior motive. As an example of this last feature, Kopelman (1987) describes a somewhat extreme case of a man who had experienced some ten to twelve prior fugue episodes, was depressed, had attempted suicide, and had claimed amnesia for a road traffic accident that occurred while he was driving disqualified, uninsured, and drunk. Potential ulterior motives are usually rather more subtle than this but do need to be taken into account.

As might be expected, the symptoms of psychogenic amnesia are somewhat varied. General semantic knowledge and intelligence are normally well preserved and there might be islands of autobiographical memory. New learning, for example of word lists, is typically severely impaired. Attempts to cue memory directly tend to be unsuccessful. The use of amytal or hypnosis to access forgotten memories is typically not effective, but if the patient is intentionally simulating amnesia then the use of drugs or hypnosis could allow the patient to "recover" without loss of face (Kopelman, 2002).

Situation-specific amnesia

A dramatic example of the type of amnesia that could readily be dismissed as malingering occurs in cases of violent crime and murder, with approximately 30% of perpetrators claiming to be amnesic for the incident (Kopelman, 2002; Pyszora, Barker, & Kopelman, 2003). Amnesia is most common in association with extreme emotion, for example in crimes of passion, with the probability of amnesia increasing with the violence of the offence (Yuille & Cutshall, 1986). It is also more likely when alcohol is a factor, possibly because of "blackout" effects, which might indicate either a failure of memory consolidation, or a retrieval-based deficit reflecting state dependency (see Chapter 8, p. 211). What you encode when drunk is best recalled when drunk (Goodwin, Powell, Bremer, Hoine, & Stern, 1969). Yuille and Cutshall (1986) report that some 33% of cases recover the relevant memory during a 3-year follow-up, with a further 26% showing partial recovery, suggesting that in these cases at least, the problem is one of retrieval rather than consolidation.

Are such instances genuine cases of amnesia, or simply evidence of malingering? Schacter (1986) inclines to the latter view that psychogenic amnesia often reflects an intentional strategy. There are, however, a number of features that suggest that violence-related amnesia is a genuine phenomenon rather than a form of malingering. First of all, it can occur with prisoners who have spontaneously reported their crime to the police and make no attempt to evade capture. Second, amnesia is not accepted as a mitigating factor in UK law, or in many other countries, so there would be no practical advantage. Third, a similar pattern occurs in the case of victims or eyewitnesses of violent crime who have no reason to dissimulate (Kuehn, 1974). Finally, there does seem to be a consistency across accounts with comments like "so horrifying … that I just can't remember anything" or "it seems to be forming a picture and then … my head hurts and it gets all jumbled up again" (O'Connell, 1960).

Multiple person disorder

The idea that one person could contain two or more very different personalities was popularized by Robert Louis Stevenson's book *Dr Jekyll and Mr Hyde*. This disorder is described by Kihlstrom and Schacter (2000) as "the crown jewel … of the functional amnesias," generating over 2000 papers, two-thirds of them in the decade before their review. And yet Kopelman (2002), a London neuropsychologist and psychiatrist, describes the disorder as rare. The reason is that, like crown jewels in general, it is not distributed evenly around the world. Indeed, Merskey (1992) suggests that it simply reflects a fashion for certain symptoms, encouraged in patients by "reinforcing behavior" from psychologists, psychiatrists, and the outside world.

Such "fashions" in psychiatric symptoms do seem to occur. A good example is the classic hysterical symptom of *glove anesthesia*, when the patient reports a pattern of lack of feeling in the hand that involves the whole of the hand up to the wrist, something that is anatomically very unlikely, given the pattern of innervation of the hand. This symptom was relatively widespread in the early years of the twentieth century, but seems to be very rare now. Another example is catatonia, a rigid immoveable posture that once was common in schizophrenic patients but is now rarely if ever seen.

The different multiple personalities displayed by a patient might or might not be mutually aware. A study by Nissen, Ross, Willingham, MacKenzie, and Schacter (1988), of a woman with 22 personalities, found 8 of

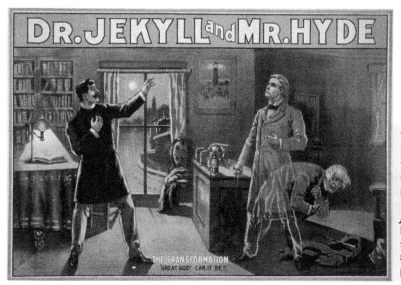

The concept that one person could contain two or more very different personalities was popularized by Robert Louis Stevenson's book *Dr Jekyll and Mr Hyde*. There have been dozens of major stage and film adaptations, and countless references in popular culture.

them to be mutually amnesic. In those personalities that are mutually amnesic it is typically possible to demonstrate common implicit memory, for example by presenting words to one personality and requiring stem completion from another (Eich, Macauley, Loewenstein, & Dihle, 1997), whereas explicit recall across personalities might be absent.

It is not clear what produces multiple person disorder and why it differs from one culture to another. One possibility suggested by Kopelman (2002) is that patients might be trying out a new mode of life. But if so, you might have expected Nissen et al.'s (1988) patient to have found something suitable before needing 22 attempts.

ORGANICALLY BASED DEFICITS

Whereas psychogenic amnesia can often have an organic component, other sources of loss of autobiographical memory are very clearly the result of brain damage of a particular kind. Organically based amnesia differs from psychogenic amnesia in that a sense of personal identity is rarely lost. For that reason it will be discussed in the context of organic amnesia (Chapter 16) rather than the current context of autobiographical memory.

Autobiographical memory and the brain

Greenberg and Rubin (2003) note that patients with damage to the areas involved in visualization tend to have poor autobiographical memory, suggesting—as others have—that visual imagery might play an important role. Conway, Pleydell-Pearce, Whitecross, and Sharpe (2003) used EEG to study the cortical activation associated with the task of reading a cue word, evoking a related autobiographical memory, holding it, and then reporting the memory. They found that the early stages involved the left prefrontal cortex, presumably reflecting the verbal and executive processes involved in evoking the memory, followed by activation that spread back to the occipital and temporal lobes, consistent with an important role for visual imagery, a pattern that was broadly similar to that subsequently found by Addis, Moscovitch, Crawley, and McAndrews (2004a, 2004b).

Although not as extensively investigated as episodic memory more generally, an increasing number of neuroimaging studies are focusing on autobiographical memory. An overview combining data from 24 different studies (Svoboda, McKinnon, & Levine, 2006) concludes that the evidence supports a distinction between episodic and semantic aspects of autobiographical memory, together with a tendency for the presence of emotion to shift the balance of activation between the right and left hemispheres. In one study, Cabeza, Prince, Daselaar, Greenberg, Budde, Dolcos, et al. (2004) had their student participants take photographs at specified locations on the Duke University campus. These were then mixed in with photographs taken by other undergraduates, and presented in an event-related fMRI study. Both types of photograph activated a common episodic memory network that involved the medial temporal and prefrontal regions. In addition, the self-generated photographs activated areas of the medial prefrontal cortex that were known to be associated with self-referential processing, as well as areas associated with recollection (hippocampus) and visuo-spatial memory (visual and parahippocampal regions).

It might be argued that the autobiographical significance of your own versus someone else's photograph of a familiar scene could be somewhat minimal. Another study (Greenberg, Rice, Cooper, Cabeza, Rubin, & LaBar (2005) used a more conventional technique in which participants first generated cue words for 50 of their own autobiographical memories, recording their subjective responses to each. An fMRI study then presented each of the cue words, requiring the participants to press a button when they retrieved the relevant memory. This condition was contrasted with a semantic retrieval task in which participants were asked to give an appropriate response to a series of category names (e.g. the cue *animal* might evoke *elephant*). Autobiographical retrieval led to more activation of the amygdala, which is related to emotion; the hippocampus, related to episodic memory; and the right inferior frontal gyrus, linked to self-related processing. The semantic retrieval condition led to more prolonged activation of the left frontal region (Figure 11.9).

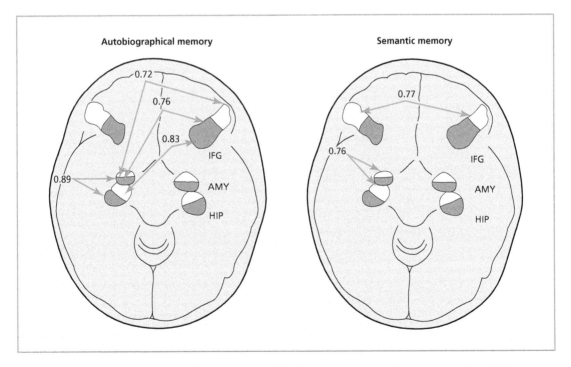

Figure 11.9 Patterns of activation during autobiographical memory and semantic memory retrieval. The numbers represent correlation between the activity in areas linked by the arrows. White and brown represent separate areas of each structure. Based on Greenberg et al. (2005). AMY, amygdala; HIP, hippocampus; IFG, inferior frontal gyros.

SUMMARY

Autobiographical memory helps us create a coherent representation of ourselves and our lives.

- It is difficult to study because we often have no record from the time that the memories are initially encoded.
- Diary studies are informative but suffer from a number of limitations.
- Much research involves the probe method, whereby autobiographical memories are evoked either by presenting a cue word or by asking for memories from a specified life period.
- For people over the age of 40, the temporal distribution of recalled events typically shows a peak extending from the late teens to early thirties, the reminiscence bump, probably reflecting an important period in building up a life narrative.
- Much autobiographical memory research is still concerned with individual phenomena, such as flashbulb memories and post-traumatic stress disorder (PTSD).
- In both, a highly emotional event appears to lead to a very specific and detailed memory.
- There is controversy as to whether either of these represents a special type of memory or are explicable using the same processes as is assumed in normal autobiographical memory.
- Psychogenic amnesia occurs when strong negative emotion disrupts retrieval from auto-biographical memory.
- Neuroimaging techniques suggest that autobiographical memory depends on several brain regions, including the frontal lobes, the hippocampus, and areas involved in visual memory.

POINTS FOR DISCUSSION

Would it matter if you lost access to your autobiographical memory? If so, in what way?
What are the relative strengths and weaknesses of diary studies and probe methods for studying autobiographical memory?
How might Conway's model account for PTSD and psychogenic amnesia?

FURTHER READING

Conway, M. A., Pleydell-Pearce, C. W., Whitecross, S., & Sharpe, H. (2002). Brain imaging autobiographical memory. *The Psychology of Learning and Motivation, 41,* 229–263. A review of some of the contributions made by neuroimaging to the study of autobiographical memory.

Gardiner, M. (2006). The memory wars, parts two and three. *Skeptical Enquirer, 30,* 246–250. Discusses the controversies surrounding reports of memories of abuse recovered during therapy, and evaluates the evidence and the resulting controversies.

Neisser, U. (1981). John Dean's memory: A case study. *Cognition, 9,* 1–22. A classic study of autobiographical memory in which it proved possible to compare the recollection of a series of important events by the participants in the Watergate affair, in which Dean's conversations with President Nixon were recorded, and hence could subsequently be checked.

Rubin, D. C. (1996). *Remembering our past: Studies in autobiographical memory.* Cambridge: Cambridge University Press. A collection of chapters describing various approaches to autobiographical memory. Edited by David Rubin, who has been one of the most active and innovative contributors to the study of autobiographical memory.

Williams, H. L., Conway, M. A., & Cohen, G. (2008). Autobiographical memory. In G. Cohen and M. Conway (Eds.), *Memory in the real world* (3rd edn., pp. 21–90). Hove, UK: Psychology Press. An extensive review of research on autobiographical memory, which incorporates Conway's theoretical approach.

REFERENCES

Addis, D. R., Moscovitch, M., Crawley, A. P., & McAndrews, M. P. (2004a). Qualities of autobiographical memory modulate hippocampal activation during retrieval: Preliminary findings of an fMRI study. *Brain and Cognition, 54,* 145–147.

Addis, D. R., Moscovitch, M., Crawley, A. P., & McAndrews, M. P. (2004b). Recollective qualities modulate hippocampal activation during autobiographical memory retrieval. *Hippocampus, 14,* 752–762. doi: 10.1002/hipo.10215

Baddeley, A. D. (2012). Reflections on autobiographical memory. In D. Berntsen & D. C. Rubin (Eds.), *Understanding autobiographical memory: Theories and approaches* (pp. 70–88). Cambridge: Cambridge University Press.

Baddeley, A. D., Lewis, V. J., & Nimmo-Smith, I. (1978). When did you last...? In M. M. Gruneberg, P. E. Morris, & R. N. Sykes (Eds.), *Practical Aspects of Memory* (pp. 77–83). London: Academic Press.

Berntsen, D., & Rubin, D. C. (2002). Emotionally charged autobiographical memories across the life span: The recall of happy, sad, traumatic and involuntary memories. *Psychology and Ageing, 17,* 636–652.

Berntsen, D., & Rubin, D. C. (2004). Cultural life scripts structure recall from autobiographical memory. *Memory and Cognition, 32,* 427–442.

Berntsen, D., & Rubin, D. C. (2008). The reappearance hypothesis revisited: Recurrent involuntary memories after traumatic events and in everyday life. *Memory and Cognition, 36,* 449–460.

Berntsen, D., & Thomsen, D. K. (2005). Personal memories for remote historical events: Accuracy and clarity of flashbulb memories related to World War II. *Journal of Experimental Psychology: General, 134,* 242–257.

Bluck, S., Alea, N., Habermas, T., & Rubin, D. C. (2005). A TALE of three functions: The self-reported uses of autobiographical memory. *Social Cognition, 23,* 91–117.

Bonanno, G. (2005). Resilience in face of potential trauma. *Current Directions in Psychological Science, 14,* 135–138.

Brewer, M. B. (1988). A dual process model of impression formation. In T. Srull & R. Wyer (Eds.), *Advances in Social Cognition* (Vol. 1). Hillsdale, NJ: Lawrence Erlbaum Associates.

Brewin, C. R. (2001). A cognitive neuroscience account of posttraumatic stress disorder and its treatment. *Behaviour Research and Therapy, 39,* 373–393.

Broadbent, D. E., Cooper, P. J., & Broadbent, M. H. (1978). A comparison of hierarchical retrieval schemes in recall. *Journal of Experimental Psychology: Human Learning and Memory, 4,* 486–497.

Brown, R., & Kulik, J. (1977). Flashbulb memories. *Cognition, 5,* 73–99.

Cabeza, R., Prince, S. E., Daselaar, S. M., Greenberg, D. L., Budde, M., Dolcos, F., LaBar, K. S., & Rubin, D. C. (2004). Brain activity during episodic retrieval of autobiographical and laboratory events: An fMRI study using a novel photo paradigm. *Journal of Cognitive Neuroscience, 16,* 1583–1594.

Cardena, E., & Spiegel, D. (1993). Dissociative reactions to the San Francisco Bay area earthquake of 1989. *American Journal of Psychiatry, 150*, 474–478.

Chu, S., & Downes, J. J. (2002). Proust Nose Best: Odors are better cues of autobiographical memory. *Memory and Cognition, 30*, 511–518.

Conway, M. A. (1990). *Autobiographical memory: An introduction*. Philadelphia, PA: Open University Press.

Conway, M. A. (2005). Memory and the self. *Journal of Memory & Language, 53*, 594–628.

Conway, M. A., & Jobson, L. (2012). On the nature of autobiographical memory In D. Berntsen & D. C. Rubin (Eds.), *Understanding autobiographical memory: Theories and approaches*. Cambridge, UK.: Cambridge University Press.

Conway, M. A., & Pleydell-Pearce, C. W. (2000). The construction of autobiographical memories in the self-memory system. *Psychological Review, 107*, 262–288.

Conway, M. A., & Tacchi, P. C. (1996). Motivated confabulation. *Neurocase, 2*, 325–338.

Conway, M. A., Collins, A. F., Gathercole, S. E., & Anderson, S. J. (1996). Recollection of true and false autobiographical memories. *Journal of Experimental Psychology: General, 125*, 69–95.

Conway, M. A., Pleydell-Pearce, C. W., Whitecross, S., & Sharpe, H. (2003). Neurophysiological correlates of autobiographical memory: On the universality of the reminiscence bump. . *Neuropsychologia, 41*, 334–340.

Conway, M. A., Wang, Q., Hanyu, K., & Haque, S. (2005). A cross-cultural investigation of autobiographical memory. *Journal of Cross-Cultural Psychology, 36*, 739–749.

Craik, F. I. M., & Lockhart, R. S. (1972). Levels of processing. A framework for memory research. *Journal of Verbal Learning and Verbal Behavior, 11*, 671–684.

Crary, W. G. (1966). Reactions to incongruent self-experiences. *Journal of Consulting Psychology, 30*, 246–252.

Crocker, J., & Major, B. (1989). Social stigma and self-esteem: The self-protective properties of stigma. *Psychological Review, 96*(4), 608–630.

Crovitz, H. F., & Shiffman, H. (1974). Frequency of episodic memories as a function of their age. *Bulletin of the Psychonomic Society, 4*, 517–518.

Dalgleish, T., Spinks, H., Yiend, J., & Kuyken, W. (2001). Autobiographical memory style in seasonal affective disorder and its relationship to future symptom remission. *Journal of Abnormal Psychology, 110*, 335–340.

Davidson, P. S. R., Cook, S. P., & Glisky, E. L. (2006). Flashbulb memories for September 11th can be preserved in older adults. *Aging, Neuropsychology, and Cognition, 13*, 196–206.

Dolcos, F., LaBar, K. S., & Cabeza, R. (2005). Remembering one year later: Role of the amygdala and the medial temporal lobe memory system in retrieving emotional memories. *Proceedings of the National Academy of Sciences of the USA, 102*, 2626–2631.

Ehlers, A., Hackmann, A., & Michael, T. (2004). Intrusive reexperiencing in posttraumatic stress disorder: Phenomenology, theory, and therapy. *Memory, 12*, 403–415.

Eich, E., Macauley, D., Loewenstein, R. J., & Dihle, P. H. (1997). Memory, amnesia and dissociative identity disorder. *Psychological Science, 8*, 417–422.

Foa, E. B., & Rothbaum, B. O. (1998). *Treating the trauma of rape: Cognitive behavioral therapy for PTSD*. New York: Guilford Press.

Foa, E. B., Rothbaum, B. O., Riggs, D. S., & Murdock, T. (1991). Treatment of posttraumatic stress disorder in rape victims: A comparison between cognitive behavioral procedures and counseling. *Journal of Consulting and Clinical Psychology, 59*, 715–723.

Galton, F. (1879). Psychometric experiments. . *Brain: A Journal of Neurology, II*, 149–162.

Gilbertson, M., Shenton, M., Ciszewski, A., Kasai, K., Lasko, N., Orr, S., & Pitman, R. (2002). Small hippocampal volume predicts pathologic vulnerability to psychological trauma. *Nature Neuroscience, 5*, 1242–1247.

Glück, J., & Bluck, S. (2007). Looking back across the life span: A life story account of the reminiscence bump. *Memory and Cognition, 35*, 1928–1939.

Goodwin, D. W., Powell, B., Bremer, D., Hoine, H., & Stern, J. (1969). Alcohol and recall: State dependent effects in man. *Science, 163*, 135–138.

Greenberg, D. L., & Rubin, D. C. (2003). The neuropsychology of autobiographical memory. *Cortex, 39*, 687–728.

Greenberg, D. L., Rice, H. J., Cooper, J. J., Cabeza, R., Rubin, D. C., & LaBar, K. S. (2005). Co-activation of the amygdala, hippocampus and inferior frontal gyros during autobiographical retrieval. *Neuropsychologia, 43*, 659–674.

Haque, S., & Conway, M. A. (2001). Sampling the process of autobiographical memory construction. *European Journal of Cognitive Psychology, 13*, 529–547.

Harvey, A. G., & Bryant, R. A. (2000). Memory for acute stress disorder symptoms: A two-year prospective study. *Journal of Nervous and Mental Disease, 188*, 602–607.

Healy, H., & Williams, J. M. G. (**Eds.**). (1999). *Autobiographical memory*. Chichester, UK: Wiley.

Herz, R. S. (2004). A naturalistic analysis of autobiographical memories triggered by olfactory, visual and auditory stimuli. *Chemical Senses 29,* 217–224.

Hyman, I. E., Jr., & Faries, J. M. (1992). The functions of autobiographical memories. In M. A. Conway, D. C. Rubin, H. Spinnler, & W. A. Wagenaar (Eds.), *Theoretical perspectives on autobiographical memory.* (pp. 207–221). Dordrecht, The Netherlands: Kluwer Academic Publishers.

Johnson, M. K., Foley, M. A., Suengas, A. G., & Raye, C. L. (1988). Phenomenal characteristics of memory for perceived and imagined autobiographical events. *Journal of Experimental Psychology: General, 117,* 371–376.

Kihlstrom, J. F., & Schacter, D. L. (2000). Functional amnesia. In F. Boller & J. Grafman (Eds.), *Handbook of Neuropsychology.* (Vol. 2, pp. 409–427). Amsterdam: Elsevier.

Kopelman, M. D. (1987). Crime and amnesia: A review. *Behavioural Sciences and the Law, 5,* 323–342.

Kopelman, M. D. (2002). Psychogenic amnesia. In A. D. Baddeley, M. D. Kopelman, & B. A. Wilson (Eds.), *Handbook of memory disorders* (2nd edn., pp. 451–472). Chichester, UK: Wiley.

Kopelman, M. D., Green, R. E. A., Guinan, E. M., Lewis, P. D. R., & Stanhope, N. (1994). The case of the amnesic intelligence officer. *Psychological Medicine, 24,* 1037–1045.

Kuehn, L. L. (1974). Looking down a gun barrel: Person perception and violent crime. *Perceptual and Motor Skills, 39,* 1159–1164.

Kunda, Z. (1990). The case for motivated reasoning. *Psychological Bulletin, 108,* 480–498.

Leichtman, M., Wang, Q., & Pillemer, D. P. (2003). Cultural variations in interdependence and autobiographical memory: Lessons from Korea, China, India, and the United States. In R. Fivush & C. Haden (Eds.), *Autobiographical memory and the construction of a narrative self: Developmental and cultural perspectives* (pp. 73–98). Hillsdale, NJ: Lawrence Erlbaum Associates.

LePort, A. K., Mattfeld, A. T., Dickinson-Anson, H., Fallon, J. H., Stark, C. E., Kruggel, F., Cahill, L., & McGaugh, J. L. (2012). Behavioral and neuroanatomical investigation of Highly Superior Autobiographical Memory (HSAM). *Neurobiology of Learning and Memory, 98,* 78–92. doi: 10.1016/j.nlm.2012.05.002

Linton, M. (1975). Memory for real-world events. In D. A. Norman & D. E. Rumelhart (Eds.), *Explorations in cognition* (pp. 376–404). San Francisco: Freeman.

Loftus, E. F., & Marburger, W. (1983). Since the eruption of Mount St. Helens, has anyone beaten you up? Improving the accuracy of retrospective reports with landmark event. *Memory and Cognition, 11,* 114–120.

Marian, V., & Kaushanskaya, M. (2004). Self-construal and emotion in bicultural bilinguals. *Journal of Memory and Language, 51,* 190–201.

McCloskey, C. G., Wible, C. G., & Cohen, N. J. (1988). Is there a special flashbulb-memory mechanism? *Journal of Experimental Psychology: General, 117,* 171–181.

McEwen, B. (1999). Stress and hippocampal plasticity. *Annual Review of Neuroscience, 22,* 105–122.

McGaugh, J. L. (2003). *Memory and emotion: The making of lasting memories.* New York: Columbia University Press.

Means, B., Mingay, D. J., Nigam, A., & Zarrow, M. (1988). A cognitive approach to enhancing health survey reports of medical visits. In M. M. Gruneberg, P. E. Morris, & R. N. Sykes (Eds.), *Practical aspects of memory: Current research and issues* (pp. 537–542). Chichester, UK: John Wiley & Sons.

Merskey, H. (1992). The manufacture of personalities. The production of multiple personality disorder. . *British Journal of Psychiatry, 160,* 327–340.

Neisser, U. (1967). *Cognitive psychology.* New York: Appleton-Century Crofts.

Neisser, U. (1981). John Dean's memory: A case study. *Cognition, 9,* 1–22.

Neisser, U. (1988). Five kinds of self-knowledge. *Philosophical Psychology, 1,* 35–59.

Neisser, U., & Harsch, N. (1992). Phantom flashbulbs: False recollections of hearing the news about challenger. In E. Winograd & U. Neisser (Eds.), *Affect and accuracy in recall: Studies of 'flashbulb' memories* (pp. 9–31). New York: Cambridge University Press.

Nissen, M. J., Ross, J. L., Willingham, D. D., MacKenzie, T. B., & Schacter, D. L. (1988). Memory and awareness in a patient with multiple personality disorder. *Brain and Cognition, 8,* 117–134.

O'Connell, B. A. (1960). Amnesia and homicide. *British Journal of Delinquency, 10,* 262–276.

Pitman, R., Sanders, K., Zusman, R., Healy, A., Cheema, F., Lasko, N., Cahill, L., & Orr, S. (2002). Pilot study of secondary prevention of post traumatic stress disorder with propranolol. *Biological Psychiatry, 51,* 189–192.

Pyszora, N. M., Barker, A. F., & Kopelman, M. D. (2003). Amnesia for criminal offences: A study of life sentence prisoners. *Journal of Forensic Psychiatry and Psychology, 14,* 475–490.

Robinson, J. A., & Swanson, K. L. (1990). Autobiographical memory: The next phase. *Applied Cognitive Psychology, 4,* 321–335.

Rothbaum, B. O., & Davis, M. (2003). Applying learning principles to the treatment of post-trauma reactions. *Annals of the New York Academy of Sciences, 1008*, 112–121.

Rubin, D. C., & Kozin, M. (1984). Vivid memories. *Cognition, 16*, 81–95.

Rubin, D. C., & Wenzel, A. E. (1996). One hundred years of forgetting: A quantative description of retention. *Psychological Review, 103*, 734–760.

Rubin, D. C., Groth, E., & Goldsmith, D. J. (1984). Olfactory cuing of autobiographical memory. *American Journal of Psychology, 97*, 493–507.

Rubin, D. C., Wetzler, S. E., & Nebes, R. D. (1986). Autobiographical memory across the adult lifespan. In D. C. Rubin (Ed.), *Autobiographical memory* (pp. 202–221). Cambridge: Cambridge University Press.

Sapolsky, R. (1996). Why stress is bad for your brain. *Science, 273*, 749–750.

Sargant, W., & Slater, E. (1941). Amnesic syndromes of war. *Proceedings of the Royal Society of Medicine, 34*, 757–764.

Schacter, D. L. (1986). On the relation between genuine and simulated amnesia. *Behavioural Sciences and the Law, 4*, 47–64.

Schmoick, H., Buffalo, E. A., & Squire, L. R. (2000). Memory distortions develop over time: Recollections of the O. J. Simpson trial verdict after 15 and 32 months. *Psychological Science, 11*, 39–45.

Svoboda, E., McKinnon, M. C., & Levine, B. (2006). The functional neuroanatomy of autobiographical memory: A meta-analysis. *Neuropsychologia, 44*, 2189–2208.

Talarico, J. M., & Rubin, D. C. (2003). Confidence, not consistency, characterizes flashbulb memories. *Psychological Science, 14*, 455–461.

Tulving, E. (1989). Memory: Performance, knowledge and experience. *European Journal of Cognitive Psychology, 1*, 3–26.

Vaiva, G., Ducrocq, F., Jezequel, K., Averland, B., Levestal, P., Brunet, A., & Marmar, C. (2003). Immediate treatment with propranolol decreases post traumatic stress two months after trauma. . *Biological Psychiatry, 54*, 947–949.

Wagenaar, W. A. (1986). My memory: A study of autobiographical memory over six years. *Cognitive Psychology, 18*, 225–252.

Wagenaar, W. A., & Groeneweg, J. (1990). The memory of concentration camp survivors. *Applied Cognitive Psychology, 4*, 77–87.

Walker, W. R., Skowronski, J. J., & Thompson, C. P. (2003). Life is pleasant—and memory helps to keep it that way! *Review of General Psychology, 7*, 203–210.

Wang, Q. (2001). Cultural effects on adults' earliest childhood recollection and self-description: Implications for the relation between memory and the self. *Journal of Personality and Social Psychology, 81*, 220–233.

Wang, Q. (2006a). Relations of maternal style and child self-concept to autobiographical memories in Chinese, Chinese immigrant, and European American 3-year-olds. *Child Development, 77*, 1799–1814.

Wang, Q. (2006b). Earliest recollections of self and others in European American and Taiwanese young adults. *Psychological Science, 17*, 708–714.

Wang, Q. (2008). Emotion knowledge and autobiographical memory across the preschool years: A cross-cultural longitudinal investigation. *Cognition, 108*, 117–135.

Willander, J., & Larsson, M. (2006). Smell your way back to childhood: Autobiographical odour memory. *Psychonomic Bulletin and Review, 13*, 240–244.

Willander, J., & Larsson, M. (2007). Olfaction and emotion: The case of autobiographical memory. *Memory and Cognition, 35*, 1659–1663.

Williams, H. L., Conway, M. A., & Cohen, G. (2008). Autobiographical memory. In G. Cohen & M. A. Conway (Eds.), *Memory in the real world* (3rd edn.). London: Psychology Press.

Williams, J. M. G., & Scott, J. (1988). Autobiographical memory in depression. *Psychological Medicine, 18*, 689–695.

Williams, J. M. G., Watts, F. N., MacLeod, C., & Mathews, A. (1997). *Cognitive psychology and emotional disorders* (1 edn.). Chichester, UK: Wiley.

Woods, B., Spector, A., Jones, C., Orrell, M., & Davies, S. (2005). Reminiscence therapy for dementia. *Cochrane Database of Systematic Reviews*. doi: 10.1002/14651858.CD001120.pub2

Wyer, S. R., Jr., & Frey, D. (1983). The effects of feedback about self and others on the recall and judgments of feedback-relevant information. *Journal of Experimental Social Psychology, 19*, 540–559.

Yuille, J. C., & Cutshall, J. L. (1986). A case study of eyewitness memory of a crime. *Journal of Applied Psychology, 71*, 291–301.

Zuckerman, M. (1979). *Sensation seeking: Beyond the optimal level of arousal*. Hillsdale, NJ: Lawrence Erlbaum Associates.

Contents

Introduction	329
Major factors influencing eyewitness accuracy	330
Anxiety and violence	338
Age and eyewitness accuracy	340
Remembering faces	341
Police procedures with eyewitnesses	346
From laboratory to courtroom	349
Summary	352
Points for discussion	354
Further reading	354
References	354

CHAPTER 12

EYEWITNESS TESTIMONY

Michael W. Eysenck

INTRODUCTION

You are a juror in a case involving serious assault. You are finding it very hard to decide whether the defendant is indeed the person who carried out the assault. This is because nearly all the evidence is indirect or circumstantial, and so not really very convincing. However, one piece of evidence *does* seem to be very direct and revealing. The person who was assaulted identified the defendant as her assailant in a lineup. When you see this eyewitness being questioned in court, you are impressed by the fact that she is very confident that she has correctly identified the person who attacked her so viciously. As a result, you and your fellow jurors find the defendant guilty of serious assault and he is sentenced to several years in prison.

It is not uncommon for a guilty verdict to depend heavily on eyewitness testimony. For example, a thorough analysis of trials in England and Wales many years ago revealed nearly 350 cases in which eyewitness identification was the only real evidence of guilt. In 74% of these cases the defendant was found guilty, which indicates the substantial weight given to eyewitness testimony.

Is it safe to rely on eyewitness testimony? Many people give a "Yes" answer to that question. Simons and Chabris (2011) found 37% of Americans believe the testimony of a single confident eyewitness should be sufficient to convict a criminal defendant. That figure rose to 48% among Americans with no college education.

The increased use of DNA testing in recent years has made it easier to answer the question posed in the previous paragraph. These tests often help to establish whether the person convicted of any given crime was actually the culprit. Note, however, that DNA tests are not infallible. They can indicate that a given individual was present at the scene of the crime but not necessarily that he/she committed the crime.

In the US, over 200 people have been shown to be innocent by DNA tests. Of these more than 75% were found guilty on the basis of mistaken eyewitness identification. Let's consider the case of Charles Chatman. He was 20 years old when a young woman who had been raped picked him out from a lineup. As a result of her eyewitness testimony, Chatman was sentenced to 99 years in prison in Dallas County, Texas. DNA testing led to Chatman being released after 26 years in prison. Chatman claimed that race was a factor: "I was convicted because a black man committed a crime against a white woman."

There have been several other cases in Dallas in which guilty verdicts have been overturned on the basis of DNA evidence. This has happened because those involved in administering the law in Dallas are more likely to store the original evidence than in most other areas. This raises the disturbing prospect that the lack of stored DNA evidence means that numerous innocent individuals languishing in prison have no chance of their guilty verdict being overturned. More generally, Smalarz and

Charles Chatman walking out from Frank Crowley Courts Building in Dallas after he was cleared of his rape charge.

Wells (2012) estimated that in only approximately 5% of cases is DNA evidence potentially available that might show eyewitnesses have mistakenly identified an innocent person.

Knowledge about limitations of eyewitness memory

It seems reasonable to assume that most judges would be knowledgeable about potential problems with eyewitness testimony and that they would use this knowledge to ensure a fair trial. These assumptions do not seem to be justified. Wise and Safer (2004) asked 160 American judges to indicate their agreement or disagreement with various statements about eyewitness testimony on which psychologists have obtained relevant evidence.

Worryingly, the judges were correct on only 55% of the items and most believed jurors knew less about the limitations of eyewitness testimony than they did themselves. Judges minimized the factors causing eyewitness testimony

to be inaccurate. As a result, only 23% agreed with the following statement: "Only in exceptional circumstances should a defendant be convicted of a crime solely on the basis of eyewitness testimony."

Wise and Safer (2010) compared the knowledge of factors influencing the accuracy of eyewitness testimony in American judges, law students, and undergraduate students. Judges' knowledge was comparable to that of undergraduate students and less than that of law students. The findings suggested strongly that the number of wrongful convictions based on eyewitness testimony would be reduced if judges had increased relevant knowledge.

Jurors in most countries are drawn more or less at random from the total population of that country. How good is their knowledge of the factors that determine the accuracy (or otherwise) of eyewitness testimony? The first step is to establish the current state of knowledge. This can be done by making use of the opinions of eyewitness experts. When Kassin, Tubb, Hosch, and Memon (2001) did this, they found there were several factors on which at least 80% of the experts agreed about their reliability or unreliability. For example, 100% agreed that an eyewitness's expectations influence their memory and 95% agreed that information provided after an event can distort eyewitness memory.

Desmarais and Read (2011) combined the findings from 23 studies to establish the opinions of ordinary members of the public with respect to the factors studied by Kassin et al. (2001). It was somewhat reassuring that most of these lay respondents agreed with the expert consensus on about two-thirds of the factors. However, it is of concern that lay knowledge differed from expert knowledge on one-third of the factors. In what follows, we will focus much of our attention on those factors where conventional wisdom is probably wrong.

MAJOR FACTORS INFLUENCING EYEWITNESS ACCURACY

How reliable (or should it be unreliable?) is eyewitness testimony? This is the central issue we will address in this chapter. We have seen that DNA evidence means that such testimony is sometimes seriously flawed. In fact, as we will see, eyewitness testimony is often very unreliable.

Change blindness

Our powers of observation are worse than we like to think. This was shown strikingly in a well-known study by Simons and Chabris (1999). All the participants watched a video, with some of them counting the number of times that students dressed in white threw a ball to each other. At some point a woman in a gorilla suit walks right into camera shot, looks at the camera, thumps her chest, and then walks off (see Figure 12.1). Altogether she is on the screen for 9 seconds.

Wouldn't you guess that virtually everyone shown the video would spot the "gorilla" taking several seconds to stroll across the scene? In fact, 50% of the observers did not notice the "gorilla" at all! This failure to notice an unexpected object in a visual display is known as inattentional blindness.

Figure 12.1 Frame showing a woman in a gorilla suit in the middle of a game of passing the ball. From Simons and Chabris (1999). Figure provided by Daniel Simons. www.Simonslab.com.

KEY TERM

Inattentional blindness: The failure to perceive the appearance of an unexpected object in the visual environment.

There is a related phenomenon known as *change blindness*, which involves a failure to detect changes in an object (e.g. it has been replaced). This phenomenon is discussed in Chapter 5. Change blindness is extremely common. Informal evidence of this comes from the mistakes that occur in movies when the same scene is shot more than once with parts of each shot being combined in the finished version. Have you seen the movie *Titanic*? If so, you probably failed to notice any of the numerous such mistakes in it. There is one scene in which Rose has a scarf in her left hand, then it is missing, and then it magically returns! In the movie *Grease*, while John Travolta is singing, *Greased Lightning*, his socks change color several times between black and white.

It is often assumed that inattentional blindness and change blindness are very similar phenomena. It is certainly the case that attentional failures are frequently involved. However, in general terms, more complex processing is typically required to avoid change blindness than to avoid inattentional blindness (Jensen, Yao, Street, & Simons, 2011).

Change blindness blindness

Direct evidence that we are often wildly optimistic about our own observational powers was reported by Levin, Drivdahl, Momen, and Beck (2002). Participants, who had been forewarned of the changes, saw videos of two people having a conversation in a restaurant. In one video the plates on their table changed from red to white, and in another a scarf worn by one of them disappeared. A third video showed a man sitting in his office and then walking into the hall to answer the telephone. When the view switches from the office to the hall, the first person has been replaced by another man wearing different clothes.

The above videos had previously been used by the researchers, who found that none of their participants detected any of the changes. Levin et al. (2002) asked their participants to indicate whether they thought they would have noticed the changes if they had not been forewarned. The percentages claiming they would have noticed the changes were as follows: 78% for the disappearing scarf; 59% for the changed man; and 46% for the change in color of the plates. Levin et al. used the term change blindness blindness to describe our misplaced confidence in our ability to detect visual changes.

What causes change blindness blindness? We generally think we are processing the entire visual scene reasonably thoroughly and so can detect visual changes. In fact, we are much better at detecting changes in objects we have previously looked at directly than those we haven't (Hollingworth & Henderson, 2002). Thus, we underestimate the importance of fixating objects if we are to remember them and detect how they have changed.

Loussouam, Gabriel, and Proust (2011) identified two other relevant factors. First, people show greater change blindness blindness when they appear to detect object changes rapidly and effortlessly rather than slowly and effortfully. Second, change blindness blindness is stronger when people are led to believe they have previously been very successful in detecting changes.

Expectations

Our memory for events is often influenced by our expectations. This is notoriously the case with sporting contests—supporters of the two teams often have almost diametrically opposed memories of crucial moments in the game! Consider a classic study carried out by Hastorf and Cantril (1954) on a football game between two American universities (Princeton and Dartmouth). A film of the game was shown to Dartmouth and Princeton students, and they were instructed to detect infringements of the rules. Unsurprisingly, Princeton students detected more than twice as many rule infringements by Dartmouth players than did Dartmouth students.

The findings of Hastorf and Cantril (1954) show confirmation bias—event memory is influenced and distorted by the observer's expectations. Confirmation bias was also probably present in a study by Lindholm and Christianson (1998). Swedish and immigrant students saw a videotaped simulated robbery in which the perpetrator seriously wounded a cashier with a knife. The perpetrator was either Swedish (with blond hair and light skin) or an immigrant (with black hair and brown skin).

After watching the video, eyewitnesses were shown color photographs of eight men (four Swedes and four immigrants). The actual perpetrator was selected 30% of the time, with the eyewitnesses performing slightly better when the perpetrator was ethnically similar to themselves. However, the central finding was that both immigrant and Swedish eyewitnesses were *twice* as likely to select an innocent immigrant as an innocent Swede. Immigrants are overrepresented in Swedish crime statistics, and this fact probably influenced participants' expectations about the likely ethnicity of the perpetrator.

Bartlett (1932) explained *why* expectations color our memories. According to him, we possess numerous schemas or packets of knowledge stored in long-term memory. These schemas lead us to form certain expectations (see Chapter 7). For example, our bank-robbery schema includes the following information: robbers are male; they wear disguises; they wear dark clothes; they make demands for money; and they have a getaway car with a driver (Tuckey & Brewer, 2003a).

According to Bartlett's (1932) schema theory, recall involves a process in which all relevant information (including schema-based information) is used to *reconstruct* the details of an event based on "what must have been true." Thus, eyewitnesses' recall of a bank robbery should be systematically influenced by the information contained in their bank-robbery schema.

KEY TERM

Change blindness blindness: Individuals' exaggerated belief that they can detect visual changes and so avoid *change blindness*.

Confirmation bias: Distortions of memory caused by the influence of expectations concerning what is likely to have happened.

Can you imagine elderly ladies like these committing a robbery? According to Bartlett (1932) our stereotypical schemas may influence expectations which color our memories.

recall was better for information relevant to the bank-robbery schema than for irrelevant information (e.g. the color of the getaway car). Thus, eyewitnesses used schematic information to assist in their recall of the bank robbery.

A major prediction from Bartlett's theory is that eyewitness memory would often be *distorted* to conform to the relevant schemas. Support for this was reported by Tuckey and Brewer (2003b). Of central interest was how eyewitnesses remembered ambiguous information. For example, some eyewitnesses saw a robber's head covered by a balaclava so that the robber's gender was ambiguous.

As predicted, eyewitnesses generally interpreted the ambiguous information as being consistent with their crime schema (see Figure 12.2). Thus, for example, they tended to recall the robber whose head was covered by a balaclava as being male.

Shapiro (2009) studied the effects of gender schema on eyewitness memory. For example, some eyewitnesses saw a simulated crime involving a male criminal whose features, clothing, and behavior were 'feminine'. The eyewitnesses tended to misremember such gender-inconsistent information—they used their male gender schema to infer that the criminal's features, clothing, and behavior were 'masculine' rather than 'feminine'.

Post-event misinformation

Perhaps the most obvious explanation for the inaccurate memories of eyewitnesses is that

Tuckey and Brewer (2003a) showed eyewitnesses a video of a simulated bank robbery, followed by a memory test. As predicted,

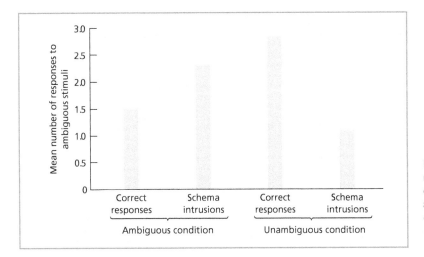

Figure 12.2 Mean correct responses and schema-consistent intrusions in the ambiguous and unambiguous conditions with cued recall. Data from Tuckey and Brewer (2003b).

they often fail to pay sufficient attention to the crime and to the criminal(s). After all, the crime they observe typically occurs suddenly and unexpectedly. However, Elizabeth Loftus and John Palmer argued that what matters is *not* only what happens at the time of the crime. According to them, eyewitness memories are fragile and can surprisingly easily be distorted by what happens after observing the crime.

In their well-known study (Loftus & Palmer, 1974), participants watched a film of a car accident. After viewing the film, they described what had happened and then answered some specific questions. Some participants were asked, "About how fast were the cars going when they hit each other?" Others were asked the same question but with the word "hit" replaced by "collided," "bumped," "contacted," or "smashed into,"

What did Loftus and Palmer (1974) find? Speed estimates were highest (40.8 mph) when the word smashed was used, lower with collided (39.3 mph), and lower still with bumped (38.1 mph), hit (34 mph), and contacted (31.8 mph). One week later, all the participants were asked, "Did you see any broken glass?" Although there was no broken glass, 32% of those previously asked about speed using the verb "smashed" said they had seen broken glass. In contrast, only 14% of the participants asked using the verb "hit" said they had seen broken glass. Thus, our memory for events is so fragile it can be systematically distorted by changing one word in one question!

The findings of Loftus and Palmer (1974) have been repeated many times. It is clear that eyewitness memory can be easily influenced by misleading information presented after a crime or other incident. For example, Eakin, Schreiber, and Sergent-Marshall (2003) showed participants slides of a maintenance man repairing a chair in an office and stealing money and a calculator. Some of the eyewitnesses received misleading information presented after the slides. For example, the slides showed the maintenance man hiding the calculator under a screwdriver, whereas the subsequent information referred to a wrench.

Eyewitness memory was impaired by misleading information presented after the eyewitnesses had seen the slides. More strikingly, memory was impaired even when the eyewitnesses were warned about the presence of misleading information very shortly after it had been presented. Ecker, Lewandowsky, and Tang (2010) confirmed that explicit warnings do not eliminate the negative effects of misinformation on memory. However, such warnings did serve to reduce the misinformation effect.

The above findings indicate that information acquired between original learning (at the time of the event) and the subsequent memory test can disrupt performance on that test. This is a clear example of *retroactive interference* (the disruption of memory by the learning of other material during the retention interval; see Chapter 9).

Can eyewitness memory also be distorted by proactive interference (learning occurring *prior* to observing the critical event)? Evidence that the answer is positive was reported by Lindsay, Allen, Chan, and Dahl (2004). Participants saw a video of a museum burglary. On the previous day they listened to a narrative thematically similar (a palace burglary) or thematically dissimilar (a school field-trip to a palace) to the video.

The eyewitnesses made many more errors when recalling information from the video when the narrative was thematically similar than when it was dissimilar. This is potentially important. In the real world, eyewitnesses often have previous experience of relevance to the questions they are asked about the event or crime. These experiences may well distort some of their answers. More generally, evidence that inaccurate eyewitness recall can depend on retroactive and proactive interference suggests that eyewitnesses often have problems with retrieval and forgetting (see Chapter 10).

Are there individual differences in susceptibility to misinformation effects? The answer is "Yes." Zhu, Chen, Loftus, Lin, He, Chen, et al. (2010a) found that eyewitnesses with higher intelligence and greater working memory capacity were better at resisting misinformation. This is consistent with much evidence indicating that more intelligent individuals have generally superior memories to those of less intelligence.

Personality characteristics associated with resisting misinformation include being high in

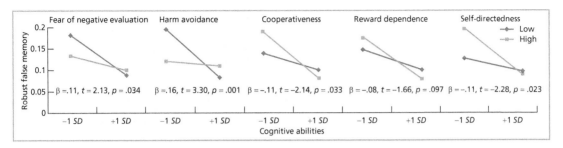

Figure 12.3 False memory as a function of cognitive abilities (low = − 1 SD; high = + 1 SD) and various personality characteristics. From Zhu et al. (2010b). Copyright © American Psychological Association. Reprinted with permission.

fear of negative evaluation and low in cooperativeness and reward dependence (Zhu, Chen, Loftus, Lin, He, Chen, et al., 2010b). Of interest, the effects of most personality characteristics were greater in those of lower intelligence (see Figure 12.3). It remains to be determined *why* misinformation effects depend on personality.

The discovery that eyewitness memory can be systematically distorted by information presented before or after they have observed a crime or other incident is worrying. However, such distorting effects may be less damaging than might be imagined. Memory distortions are more common for peripheral or minor details (e.g. presence of broken glass) than for central details (e.g. features of the criminal) (Heath & Erickson, 1998).

Theoretical explanations

How does misleading information distort what eyewitnesses report? The evidence indicates that several factors are involved. One such factor is source misattribution (Johnson, Hashtroudi, & Lindsay, 1993; Lindsay, 2008). In essence, a memory probe (e.g. a question) activates memory traces overlapping with it in terms of the information they contain. The eyewitness decides on the probable source of any activated memory on the basis of the information it contains.

Source misattribution is most likely when the memories from one source resemble those from a second source. Supporting evidence was reported by Lindsay, Allen, Chan, and Dahl (2004). In spite of the fact that the participants were led to believe that the narrative and the

video belonged to two different experiments, they often showed source misattribution by intruding information from the narrative into their memory of the video. As predicted by the source misattribution account, such intrusions were much more common when the two events were similar.

A simple explanation for the effects of misleading post-event information is that eyewitnesses are responding to social pressure (e.g. to please the experimenter). Loftus (1979) rejected this explanation, arguing that the information from misleading questions permanently alters the memory representation of an incident, with the previously formed memory being "overwritten" and destroyed.

Loftus (1979) provided evidence for the above viewpoint in a study in which eyewitnesses saw a pedestrian accident involving a car stopping at either a stop sign or a yield sign. Two days later, participants were asked questions about the incident, one of which biased them away from what had actually happened. More specifically, if they had seen a stop sign, the biasing question referred to a yield sign, and vice versa.

Their memory of the incident was then tested by showing them pairs of slides and asking them which sign they had seen (see Figure 12.4). In the critical pair of slides, one showed a stop sign and the other a yield sign. Loftus argued that if her participants genuinely remembered the correct version but simply responded otherwise to please the experimenter, the bias could be removed by offering a high enough pay-off for making a correct response. One group was given no reward, another was promised $1 each if they decided correctly, a third group was offered $5, and a fourth was told that the person in the experiment scoring the highest would receive $25. In spite of these incentives, between 70% and 85% of those tested selected the wrong response. This suggests (but does not prove) that the original memory trace had been altered.

Other researchers have reported some evidence that the original memory trace does survive. For example, consider a study by Bekerian and Bowers (1983). They found the standard Loftus procedure of asking questions in a fairly unstructured way led to the same biasing effect of misleading information she had reported. However, the biasing effect disappeared when participants were questioned systematically starting with earlier incidents and working through to later ones.

Loftus (1992) argued for a less extreme position than the one she had previously adopted. She emphasized the notion of misinformation acceptance: Eyewitnesses "accept"

Figure 12.4 Two slides from the study by Loftus, Millerm, and Burns (1978). Copyright © American Psychological Association. Reprinted with permission.

misleading information presented to them after an event, and subsequently regard it as forming part of their memory for that event. Accepting post-event information in this way becomes more common as the time since the event increases.

Finally, we consider an explanation of the effects of misleading post-event information based on the notion that it is generally adaptive to *update* and change existing memory traces by incorporating new relevant information into them (Schacter, Guerin, & St. Jacques, 2011). Updating is important. For example, there is generally little or no point in students remembering their lecture schedule for last semester—it is much better to *replace* that information in long-term memory with information about the current lecture schedule.

This explanation was tested in a study by Edelson, Sharot, Dolan, and Dudai, 2011). Most participants showed accurate memory for crime events when they were tested on their own. However, their memories subsequently became severely distorted when they were informed that their fellow participants remembered the events differently. The key finding was that this misinformation effect was associated with significant changes in memory representations in the brain. This finding suggests that the original memory traces had been "overwritten" by subsequent information. It involves retroactive interference in which memory for the original event (i.e. the crime event) was disrupted or interfered with by information presented subsequently. Retroactive interference is discussed in detail in Chapter 9.

Interventions

What can be done to reduce the negative impact of misleading post-event information on eyewitness memory? Gabbert, Hope, Fisher, and Jamieson (2012) argued that an early opportunity to recall the details of a witnessed crime would strengthen the relevant memory traces by protecting them from distortion by misleading information.

In their study, Gabbert et al. (2012) showed participants a video of a bank robbery. Some participants then completed a self-administered interview in which they provided all the details of the crime that they could remember. One week later, all participants were provided with misinformation followed by recall of the crime event. Participants who had previously completed the self-administered interview recalled many more correct details at this one-week recall than did control participants. More importantly, they were more resistant to the misinformation.

Eyewitness confidence

Jurors are often influenced by how confident the eyewitness seems to be that he/she has correctly identified the culprit. This seems entirely reasonable on the face of it. However, Kassin, Tubb, Hosch, and Memon (2001) found that more than 80% off eyewitness experts agreed that an eyewitness's confidence is *not* a good predictor of his/her identification accuracy!

We need to strike a balance here, because confidence is often moderately associated with accuracy. Sporer, Penrod, Read, and Cutler (1995) combined the findings from numerous studies in which eyewitnesses' confidence was assessed immediately after they had chosen a suspect from a lineup. They distinguished between *choosers* (eyewitness making a positive identification) and *nonchoosers* (those not making a positive identification). There was practically no correlation or association between confidence and accuracy among nonchoosers. However, the mean correlation was +.41 among choosers, indicating that choosers' confidence predicted their accuracy to a moderate extent.

Is confidence correlated with accuracy among eyewitnesses to a real-life crime as well as in the laboratory? Odinot, Wolters, and van Koppen (2009) addressed this issue in a study on eyewitnesses of a supermarket robbery in the Netherlands. There was a moderate correlation of +.38 between eyewitness confidence and accuracy.

Note that the strength or the relationship between eyewitness confidence and accuracy is *variable*—it depends on various factors. Here we will consider two factors that reduce the association between confidence and accuracy. First, there is confirming feedback, which involves telling eyewitnesses that they have identified the suspect. Bradfield, Wells, and Olson (2002) found that confirming feedback increased eyewitnesses' confidence in the accuracy of their identification much more when it was incorrect

than when it was correct. As a result, the relationship between confidence and accuracy was reduced.

Confirming feedback may play a role when eyewitnesses provide evidence in a court of law. If they have been led by police officers to believe that their identification of the culprit was correct, this may lead them to appear highly confident in their identification even when it is wrong.

Second, there is the "dud" effect, which can occur when eyewitnesses are trying to identify the culprit from a lineup. Charman, Wells, and Joy (2011) considered the effects on eyewitness performance when the lineup included several individuals very dissimilar to the culprit (duds). In one experiment, eyewitnesses observed a mock crime. This was followed by a lineup of two individuals resembling the culprit or a lineup consisting of the same two individuals plus four more very dissimilar to the culprit (duds) (see Figure 12.5). Note that the actual culprit was not present in either lineup.

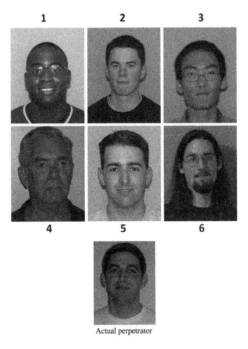

Figure 12.5 Dud lineup and actual perpetrator from one of Charman et al.'s (2011) experiments. Copyright © American Psychological Association. Reprinted with permission.

When eyewitnesses made a mistaken identification, they were much more confident in the correctness of their choice when duds were present—this is the dud effect. What seemed to be happening is that the presence of duds increased the perceived similarity of the other members of the lineup to the culprit.

What mechanisms determine the relationship between eyewitness confidence and accuracy? There is no simple answer to that question. However, eyewitness confidence probably depends on the amount of information retrieved, familiar knowledge, and expectations.

Brewer and Sampaio (2012) showed the importance of familiar knowledge in a study on American participants. They were given deceptive items such as, "Minneapolis, Minnesota is north of Hamilton, Ontario." Familiar knowledge that nearly all of Canada is north of nearly all of the United States creates the expectation that the statement is incorrect. In fact, however, it is correct. On such items, participants' performance was typically inaccurate but high in confidence. As a result, the correlation between accuracy and confidence was -.52.

The findings were very different with nondeceptive items (e.g. "Pennsylvania is east of Las Vegas"). On these items, familiar knowledge produced the correct answer and the correlation between accuracy and confidence was +.68.

In sum, the accuracy of eyewitness memory typically correlates moderately positively with confidence. However, there are many exceptions, and factors such as confirming feedback and the dud effect can reduce the effect. More generally, the relationship between accuracy and confidence can vary considerably between moderately positive and moderately negative (Brewer & Sampaio, 2012).

KEY TERM

Dud effect: An eyewitness's increased confidence in his/her mistaken when the lineup includes individuals very dissimilar to the culprit.

ANXIETY AND VIOLENCE

One of the authors (Alan Baddeley) was phoned one Sunday night by a caller announcing himself as a detective with the San Diego Police Force. He was investigating a multiple throat-slasher whose seventh victim had escaped. The woman claimed she would be able to recognize her attacker. What, the detective asked, was the likely effect of extreme emotion on the reliability and accuracy of her testimony?

This is an important (and very controversial) issue on which experts' opinions vary dramatically. When 235 American lawyers were asked whether high levels of emotion would impair facial recognition, 82% of the defense lawyers argued that recognition would be impaired. In contrast, only 32% of prosecution lawyers believed that high emotion impairs facial recognition.

Who is right? Does extreme emotion brand the experience indelibly on the victim's memory, or does it reduce his/her capacity for recollection. We will shortly turn to the relevant evidence. Bear in mind, however, that laboratory studies have for obvious reasons not exposed participants to extremely stressful conditions. For example, not even the most zealous experimenters try to convince their participants that they are about to have their throats cut!

Deffenbacher, Bornstein, Penrod, and McGorty (2004) combined the findings from numerous studies focusing on the effects of stress and anxiety on eyewitness memory. In their first analysis, they found face recognition was correct on average 54% of the time in low anxiety or stress conditions, compared to 42% in high anxiety or stress conditions. Thus, heightened anxiety and stress have a negative impact on eyewitness identification accuracy.

In their second analysis, Deffenbacher et al. (2004) considered the effects of anxiety and stress on eyewitness recall of culprit details, crime scene details, and the actions of the central characters. The average correct recall of details was 64% in the low anxiety or stress conditions compared to 52% in the high anxiety or stress conditions.

Deffenbacher et al.'s (2004) findings were supported in a field study by Valentine and

Mesout (2009). Participants encountered somebody in the Horror Labyrinth at the London Dungeon and then tried to describe and identify that person. Memory performance was worse among those participants who experienced the most anxiety while in the Labyrinth.

Weapon focus

Much of the research on anxiety and eyewitness memory has focused on the weapon focus effect, where the presence of a weapon causes eyewitnesses to fail to recall details about the assailant and the environment. Loftus (1979) discussed a study in which each participant waited outside a laboratory before taking part in an experiment. There were two conditions. In the "no weapon" condition, the participants overheard a harmless conversation about equipment failure in the experimental room, after which someone emerged holding a pen and with grease on his hands, uttered a single statement, and left. In the "weapon" condition, participants heard a hostile exchange between two people, ending with broken bottles, chairs crashing, and someone leaving the experimental room holding a letter opener covered in blood. Again the person uttered a single line before leaving.

All the participants were subsequently given an album containing 50 photographs and asked whether the person who had emerged from the room was represented there. In the "no weapon" condition, participants located the correct photograph 49% of the time compared to only 33% in the "weapon" condition. This is a clear example of the weapon focus effect. However, it seems strange in a way, because it was more important for eyewitnesses to focus on the person's face when a crime had possibly been committed.

Weapon focus is the phenomenon in which eyewitnesses are so distracted by the weapon used in a crime that they will fail to recall other details of the event.

Is weapon focus found in eyewitnesses to real-life crimes as well as in the laboratory? The evidence is mixed. Valentine, Pickering, and Darling (2003) found across 300 real lineups that the presence of a weapon had no effect on the probability of an eyewitness identifying the suspect. Bear in mind, however, that the suspect was not always the culprit! In contrast, Tollestrup, Turtle, and Yuille (1994) found significant evidence for weapon focus in their analysis of police records of real-life crimes. The reasons for the discrepancy in the findings are unknown.

The most obvious explanation of the weapon focus effect is that eyewitnesses tend to focus on the weapon at the expense of other aspects of the situation. Support for this explanation was reported by Loftus, Loftus, and Messo (1987). They asked participants to watch one of two sequences:

KEY TERM

Weapon focus: The finding that eyewitnesses have poor memory for details of a crime event because they focus their attention on the culprit's weapon.

1 A person pointing a gun at a cashier and receiving some cash.
2 A person holding a check to the cashier and receiving some cash.

As expected, eyewitnesses looked more at the gun than they did at the check. As a consequence, memory for details unrelated to the gun/check was poorer in the weapon condition.

Pickel (2009) pointed out that people often attend to stimuli that are *unexpected* in a situation. This impairs their memory for other stimuli. This led Pickel to argue that the weapon focus effect will be greater when the presence of a weapon is very unexpected. As predicted, there was a stronger weapon focus effect when a criminal carrying a folding knife was female, because it is more unexpected to see a woman with a knife. Also as predicted, the weapon focus effect was greater when a criminal with knitting needle was male rather than female.

Fawcett, Russell, Peace, and Christie (2013) carried out a meta-analysis based on numerous studies on weapon focus. Overall, there was a moderate effect on eyewitness memory of weapon focus. Importantly, the size of this effect was similar regardless of whether the event occurred in the laboratory or in the real world.

Why does stress impair memory?

There are various reasons why stress might impair memory. An especially influential approach is based on Easterbrook's (1959) hypothesis. According to this hypothesis, stress or anxiety causes a narrowing of attention on central or important stimuli which, in turn, causes a reduction in people's ability to remember peripheral details. In other words, anxious or stressed individuals exhibit "tunnel vision," which makes sense when the situation is potentially threatening or dangerous.

Yegiyan and Lang (2010) presented people with distressing pictures. As picture stressfulness increased, recognition memory for the central details improved progressively. In contrast, memory for peripheral details was much worse with highly stressful pictures than with moderately stressful ones. Thus, the findings supported Easterbrook's hypothesis.

AGE AND EYEWITNESS ACCURACY

Do you think an eyewitness's age is relevant when deciding whether his/her memory for an event is likely to be accurate? If you have already read Chapter 14, then your answer should be "Yes!" The reason is that evidence indicating that young children generally make less accurate eyewitnesses than older ones was discussed in that chapter.

There is another reason why your answer should have been affirmative. As we will see, there is evidence that the eyewitness testimony of older adults is less accurate than that of young ones. Brewer, Williams, and Semmler (2005) reviewed research on eyewitness identification in older people (60- to 80-year-old range). Older people were more likely than younger adults to choose someone from a lineup even when the culprit was not present.

Older people are more strongly influenced than younger adults by misleading suggestions. Jacoby, Bishara, Hessels, and Toth (2005) presented misleading information to younger and older adults. On a subsequent recall test, older adults had a 43% chance of producing false memories compared to only 4% for younger ones.

Dodson and Krueger (2006) showed a video to younger and older adults, who later completed a questionnaire that misleadingly referred to events not shown on the video. The older adults were more likely to produce false memories triggered by the misleading suggestions. Worryingly, the older adults tended to be very confident about the correctness of their false memories. In contrast, the younger adults were generally rather uncertain about the accuracy of their false memories.

Garcia-Bajos, Migueles, and Aizpurua (2012) clarified the reasons why older adults produce more false memories than younger ones and are more confident about those false memories. They examined the effects of the bank-robbery script on recall and recognition. Several findings (including high confidence in their false memories) occurred because the older eyewitnesses relied more than did younger ones on the bank-robbery script when details of the actual robbery did not correspond to the script or schema.

Differences in the accuracy of eyewitness memory between younger and older adults depend in part on characteristics of the culprit. Wright and Stroud (2002) presented crime videos and then asked eyewitnesses to identify the culprit. They found an own-age bias, with both groups being more accurate at identification when the culprit was of a similar age to themselves.

What causes own-age bias? Harrison and Hole (2009) found it was due to the greater *exposure* most people have to people of their own age. Teachers (who spend hours a day exposed to children's faces) showed no evidence of own-age bias—they recognized children's faces as well as those of people of their own age.

REMEMBERING FACES

The culprit's face is often easily the most important information that eyewitnesses may or may not remember. In what follows, we will consider in detail the processes involved in remembering faces, and factors that can make it hard to do so.

"I never forget a face!" One often hears people making such claims, but how justifiable are they? In view of the huge importance that accurate face perception plays in our everyday lives, you might imagine that most people would be real experts at identifying other people's faces. The substantial problems caused by being very poor at identifying faces can be seen most clearly in patients suffering from prosopagnosia or face-blindness. They can recognize most objects reasonably well in spite of their enormous difficulties with faces. A young prosopagnosic Swedish woman called Cecilia Berman has described the strategies she uses to minimize social embarrassment:

Many face-blind people will greet within a second, in spite of not having had enough time to recognize someone ... We have to greet everyone who might be a friend, which can be pretty much everyone we meet ... Some face-blind people ... become experts at pretending they knew all along who someone was when they finally learn about it ... Many face-blind people go to great lengths to avoid using names ... I probably use other people's names in their presence less than once a month, and always with a rush of adrenaline.
(Berman, 2004, pp. 4–5)

How well do we remember faces?

In spite of the importance of face recognition, it seems that most of us are not especially good are remembering faces, or more precisely, unfamiliar faces. Bruce, Henderson, Greenwood, Hancock, Burton, and Miller (1999) investigated this issue. In view of the dramatic increase in the number of closed-circuit television (CCTV) cameras in the US, the UK, and elsewhere, they decided to focus on people's ability to identify someone on the basis of CCTV images. Participants were presented with a target face taken from a CCTV video,

---

KEY TERM

Own-age bias: the tendency for eyewitnesses to identify individuals of the same age as themselves for accurately than those much older or younger.

Prosopagnosia: A condition, also known as face-blindness, in which there is extremely poor face recognition combined with reasonable ability to recognize other objects.

together with an array of ten high-quality photographs (see Figure 12.6). Their task was to select the matching face or to indicate that the target face was not present in the array.

Bruce et al. (1999) found that performance was disappointingly poor. When the target face was present in the array, it was selected only 65% of the time. When it was NOT present, 35% of participants nevertheless claimed that one of the faces in the array matched the target face. Allowing participants to watch a 5-second video segment of the target person as well as a photograph of their faces failed to improve identification performance.

Dramatic evidence that we have much greater problems with *unfamiliar* faces than *familiar* ones was reported by Jenkins, White, van Montfort, and Burton (2011). Participants were presented with 40 photographs (20 each of two Dutch celebrities unknown in the UK). Their task was to sort the photographs into a separate pile for each person shown in the photographs. When this task was given to Dutch participants, the faces were familiar and their performance was almost perfect: They sorted the photographs into two piles with 20 of one celebrity in each pile.

In another experiment by Jenkins et al. (2011), the same task was given to British participants for whom the faces were unfamiliar. On average, the participants thought 7½ different individuals were shown across the 40 photographs! Note that this very poor performance was obtained without the need for the participants to remember the faces they were sorting—we would obviously expect performance to be even worse if memory were involved.

The above findings mean that two photographs of the same person often look as if they come from two different individuals, and so passport photographs have limited value. The

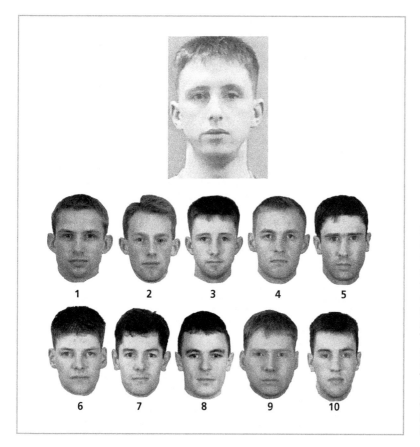

Figure 12.6 Example of full-face neutral target with an array used in the experiments. Readers might want to try the task of establishing whether the target is present in this array and which one it is. The studio and video images used are from the Home Office Police Information Technology Organisation. Bruce et al. (1999). Copyright © American Psychological Association. Reprinted with permission.

fact that a single photograph of an unfamiliar face conveys limited information helps to explain why eyewitnesses often have difficulties in identifying the person responsible for a crime.

We have seen that *average* face-recognition performance is poor. However, we might imagine that there would be large individual differences, with some people displaying good performance. Bindemann, Avetisyan, and Rakow (2012) found that this was the case using a face-matching task on which participants had to decide on each trial whether two faces showed the same person. Surprisingly, however, they found that any given individual's face-recognition performance on the same unfamiliar faces often fluctuated considerably from day to day. Thus, many people show a lack of *consistency* in their performance over time.

Patterson and Baddeley (1977) identified various factors that influence face-recognition performance. Participants were presented with photographs of individuals photographed undisguised or wearing a beard, wig, spectacles, or any combination thereof. The photographs were taken either full face or in profile. Their participants were familiarized with one photograph of each person in any one combination of disguised features. This was repeatedly presented until it was consistently recognized and the person's name given correctly. The participants were then presented with photographs consisting of the target individuals in all possible combinations of disguise, either in full frontal view or in profile, together with a number of similarly disguised but unfamiliar people. Their task was to detect and name the target individuals.

What did Patterson and Baddeley (1977) find? The effect of disguise was dramatic. Every time an item of disguise was added or removed the probability of correct recognition decreased. Performance ranged from extremely good when the face was presented in its originally learned form to virtually guesswork when the maximum number of disguised features was changed. These findings suggest that criminals are well-advised to wear masks or other forms of disguise even if this makes them look very conspicuous!

Is face recognition affected by more subtle forms of disguise? Moniz, Righi, Peissig, and Tarr (2010) addressed this issue by investigating what they called the Clark Kent effect—the mystery that Superman became unrecognizable as Clark Kent when he put on a pair of glasses. Moniz et al. showed the existence of this effect. Adding or removing glasses between the initial encoding and the subsequent recognition memory test impaired performance.

Righi, Peissig, and Tarr (2012) confirmed the earlier findings of Moniz et al. (2010). They also found that a change in hairstyle produced by a wig reduced face recognition. Why do such apparently minor changes have reasonably large effects on face-recognition performance? Face recognition involves holistic processing, meaning that information from several different regions of the face is integrated (e.g. Richler, Cheung, & Gauthier, 2011). Thus, adding or removing glasses influences how other parts of the face are processed.

Righi et al. (2010) investigated what they called the Clark Kent effect—the mystery that Superman became unrecognizable as Clark Kent when he put on a pair of glasses.

Unconscious transference

Eyewitnesses are sometimes better at remembering faces than they are at remembering the precise circumstances in which they previously saw the face. This can have serious consequences. More specifically, it can cause eyewitnesses to correctly recognize a face as having been seen before but to incorrectly judge that person to be responsible for a crime. This effect is known as unconscious transference.

Davis, Loftus, Vanous, and Cucciare (2008) studied unconscious transference using a video of a simulated crime in a supermarket. There were two innocent bystanders. One walked down the liquor aisle and then passed behind a stack of boxes from which the criminal emerged and stole a bottle of liquor. The other bystander was shown in the produce aisle. Eyewitnesses subsequently inspected a lineup from which the criminal was absent. Worryingly, 23% of the eyewitnesses selected the innocent bystander who had passed behind the boxes and 29% selected the innocent bystander who had been in the produce aisle.

You may be wondering whether unconscious transference happens in real life. One real-life case occurred in Australia. A psychologist (Donald Thomson) took part in a live television discussion on the unreliability of eyewitness testimony. Sometime later, he was picked up by the police, who refused to explain why they were arresting him. He assumed he was being unofficially harassed because of his strong views on eyewitness unreliability.

At the police station, Donald Thomson was placed in a lineup. A very distraught woman identified him and Donald Thomson was then told he was being charged with rape. When he asked for details, it became clear that the rape had been committed at the same time as he had been taking part in the television discussion. He said he had a perfectly good alibi, and numerous witnesses including an official of the Australian Civil Rights Committee and an Assistant Commissioner of Police. To this, the policeman taking his statement replied: "Yes, and I suppose you've got Jesus Christ and the Queen of England, too!" It turned out that the woman had been raped while watching the program. For Thomson himself, it was an especially unpleasant way of discovering just how right he was to worry about eyewitness unreliability!

Verbal overshadowing

Suppose you are a police officer and you have arrived at the scene of a crime that occurred only a few minutes ago. You find an eyewitness and have to decide whether to ask him/her to provide a verbal description of the culprit. You would probably assume that doing so would improve the eyewitness's subsequent ability to identify the culprit. In fact, however, eyewitnesses' recognition memory for faces is often *worse* if they have previously provided a verbal description! This effect is known as verbal overshadowing.

Schooler and Engstler-Schooler (1990) provided the first demonstration of verbal overshadowing. Eyewitnesses watched a film of a crime. After that, some eyewitnesses provided a detailed verbal report of the criminal's appearance, whereas others did an unrelated task. Those who had provided the detailed verbal report performed worse than the other eyewitnesses on this test.

Verbal overshadowing has also been obtained in several others studies (see Nakabayashi, Burton, Brandimonte, & Lloyd-Jones, 2012, for a review). However, there are also several studies in which describing faces verbally has had the opposite effect of enhancing face-recognition memory.

How can we account for these positive and negative effects of verbally describing

---

KEY TERM

Unconscious transference: The tendency of eyewitnesses to misidentify a familiar (but innocent) face as belonging to the culprit.

Verbal overshadowing: The reduction in recognition memory for faces that often occurs when eyewitnesses provide verbal descriptions of those faces before the recognition-memory test.

faces? In their own research, Nakabayashi et al. (2012) obtained beneficial effects when participants engaged in subvocal verbal processing during the initial presentation of faces. They argued that this occurred because verbal processing played a role in directing attention to the most important visual features of faces. In contrast, producing verbal descriptions after faces had been presented impaired subsequent recognition performance on unfamiliar faces. This occurred because it increased participants' attention to general semantic information about the faces, but reduced the extent to which they focused on the subtle perceptual and spatial information that is of major importance in discriminating among faces.

Cross-race effect

We will consider one final issue relating to eyewitnesses' ability to recognize faces. This is the cross-race effect—same-race faces are typically recognized more accurately than cross-race faces (see Young, Hugenberg, Bernstein, & Sacco, 2012, for a review). This effect depends on various factors, one of which is expertise. As might be expected, eyewitnesses having the

most experience with members of another race have a smaller cross-race effect than those with less experience (Hugenberg, Young, Bernstein, & Sacco, 2010).

Social psychologists distinguish between ingroups (i.e. those groups with which we identify) and outgroups (i.e. those groups with which we do not identify). It has been argued that the faces of ingroup members are processed more thoroughly than those of outgroup members. It follows that face recognition should be better for ingroup faces than outgroup ones.

Shriver, Young, Hugenberg, Bernstein, and Lanter (2008) investigated the above prediction. The cross-race effect disappeared when white, middle-class American students saw photographs of white men in impoverished contexts (e.g. ramshackle housing). This happened because these white faces were not regarded as belonging to the students' ingroup.

It has generally been assumed that the cross-race effect occurs because we find it hard to *remember* the faces of individuals who belong to a different race. That assumption is undoubtedly true in part, but it is by no means a complete explanation.

Megreya, White, and Burton (2011) found the cross-race effect depends importantly on *perceptual* processes. British and Egyptian participants were presented with a target face and an array of ten faces (see Figure 12.7). They were instructed to decide whether the target face was in the array. If it was in the array, they had to identify which face it was. Note that this task imposes minimal demands on memory because all the photographs remained visible.

KEY TERM

Cross-race effect: The finding that recognition memory for same-race faces is generally more accurate than for cross-race faces.

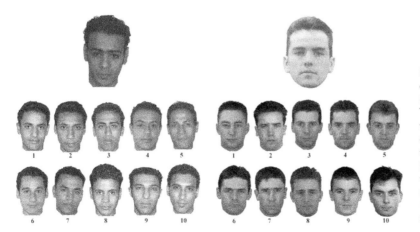

Figure 12.7 An example of Egyptian (left) and UK (right) face-matching arrays. The person shown at the top may or may not be one of the ten below. Subjects' task is to decide whether he is present, and, if so, which he is. From Megreya et al. (2011) Copyright © Experimental Psychology Society.

Even though perception rather than memory was involved, Megreya et al. (2011) found evidence of the other-face effect. When the target face was present, correct identification occurred on 70% of trials with same-race faces compared to 64% for other-race faces. When the target face was absent, a face in the array was mistakenly identified as the target on 34% of trials with same-race faces compared to 47% for other-race faces.

How can face recognition be improved?

A very useful starting point when addressing the above question is to return to research we discussed earlier. It has been found consistently (e.g. Jenkins et al., 2011; Megreya et al., 2011) that people are surprisingly poor at deciding whether photographs presented at the same time represent the same person. The take-home message from such research is that photographs of the same face often differ considerably from each other and this causes major problems in face recognition. These problems are much greater with unfamiliar faces (which is typically the case when eyewitnesses observe a crime) than with familiar ones.

Jenkins and Burton (2011) argued that we can enhance face recognition by *combining* information from multiple photographs of the same face to create an average. When they did this, they discovered with familiar faces that averaged ones were recognized significantly faster than single photographs.

Jenkins et al. (2011) used a computer-based system to study face recognition. This system recognized 100% of averaged faces compared to only 54% when individual photographs were used. There was thus a dramatic superiority for averaged faces, and this approach holds considerable promise for increasing the accuracy of eyewitnesses' face recognition.

POLICE PROCEDURES WITH EYEWITNESSES

The police obviously have no control over the circumstances at the time of a crime. They have to try to identify the culprit on the basis of the often limited and inaccurate memories of eyewitnesses. However, the police have considerable control over the ways in which eyewitnesses are treated. Here we will focus on two of the most important of such elements of control: (1) lineups; and (2) interview techniques used with eyewitnesses.

Lineups

What happens in a lineup is that the suspect is present along with various nonsuspects of broadly similar characteristics (e.g. age, race, height). The witness is asked if he/she recognizes any member of the lineup as the culprit. It is essential that the suspect is not obviously different from the other members of the lineup if the evidence obtained is to be at all valid. In days gone by, it was not unknown for this simple requirement to be ignored. In one extreme case, for example, the suspect was Asian but the lineup included only one Asian!

Evidence that the performance of eyewitnesses is rather fallible when they try to select the suspect from a lineup was reported by Valentine et al. (2003). They analyzed the findings from 640 eyewitnesses who tried to identify suspects in 314 real lineups organized by the Metropolitan Police in London. Only 40% of witnesses identified the suspect, 20% identified a nonsuspect, and the remaining 40% failed to make an identification.

Lineups can be *simultaneous* (the eyewitness sees everyone at the same time) or *sequential* (the eyewitness sees only one person at a time). There has been some controversy as to which type of lineup is preferable. Steblay, Dysart, and Wells (2011) combined the data from 27 experimental tests on this issue. When the culprit was present, he/she was selected 52% of the time with simultaneous lineups compared to 44% with sequential ones.

When the culprit was absent, eyewitnesses mistakenly selected someone with simultaneous lineups more often than with sequential ones (54% vs. 32%, respectively). Thus, eyewitnesses tend to adopt a more lenient criterion when deciding whether to identify someone as the culprit with simultaneous lineups.

What should we conclude from these findings? Steblay et al. pointed out that sequential lineups are more *diagnostic*; that is, better at distinguishing between guilty and innocent individuals. There is admittedly a small reduction in the number of correct identifications (8%) for sequential lineups compared to simultaneous ones. However, this is more than outweighed by the substantial reduction in the number of misidentifications (22%). Misidentifications with sequential lineups can be reduced further by explicitly providing eyewitnesses with a not-sure option. This reduces misidentifications from 22% to only 12% (Steblay & Phillips, 2011).

Another way of minimizing identification errors is to warn eyewitnesses that the culprit may not be in the line-up. Steblay (1997) found in a meta-analysis that such warnings reduced mistaken identification rates in culprit-absent lineups by 42%, while reducing accurate identification rates in culprit-present lineups by only 2%.

Cognitive interview

Much of this chapter has been devoted to identifying the limitations of eyewitness memory. It is obviously important to recognize those limitations in order to minimize the probability of innocent individuals being wrongly convicted solely on the basis of eyewitness testimony. However, it is also important for the police to make use of effective interviewing techniques

It is also important for the police to make use of effective interviewing techniques so as to obtain as much accurate information as possible from eyewitnesses. The cognitive interview is a method developed by psychologists for effectively obtaining information from eyewitnesses.

so as to obtain as much accurate information as possible from eyewitnesses.

Historically, the police in many countries tended to use inadequate interviewing techniques. For example, they would often ask closed-ended questions (e.g. "What color was the car?") which generally elicit very limited and specific information. A preferable approach is to ask open-ended questions (e.g. "What can you tell me about the car?").

Police in the past would often interrupt eyewitnesses when they were in the middle of saying something. Such interruptions disrupt eyewitnesses' concentration and make it harder to retrieve relevant information. A third inadequacy with the interviewing techniques that used to be common was the tendency of police to ask questions in a predetermined order. Such an approach took no account of the answers provided by the eyewitness.

Psychologists have produced increasingly effective ways of eliciting information from eyewitnesses. Of particular note is the cognitive interview which was originally devised by Geiselman, Fisher, MacKinnon, and Holland (1985). This approach is based on four general retrieval rules:

1   Mental reinstatement of the environment and any personal contact experienced during the crime.
2   Encouraging the reporting of every detail regardless of how peripheral it might seem to the main incident or crime.
3   Describing the incident in several different orders.
4   Reporting the incident from different viewpoints including those of other participants or witnesses.

Why might we expect the cognitive interview to be effective? In short, it makes direct use of our knowledge of human memory. The first two rules are based on the encoding specificity principle (Tulving, 1979). According to this principle, eyewitnesses will remember most when there is maximal overlap or match between the context in which the crime was witnessed and the context in which the recall attempt is made.

The third and fourth rules are based on the assumption that memory traces are usually complex and contain various kinds of information (e.g. the person's mood at the time of learning). As a result, information about a crime can be retrieved using various routes, each of which may provide information about rather different aspects of the original experience.

Fisher, Geiselman, Raymond, Jurkevich, and Warhaftig (1987) devised an enhanced cognitive interview. This included all four rules discussed above. In addition, it also requires investigators to minimize distractions, to persuade the eyewitness to speak slowly, to reduce eyewitness anxiety, and to review the eyewitness's descriptions.

Findings

Memon, Meissner, and Fraser (2010) combined the findings from numerous studies to compare the effectiveness of the cognitive interview against that of the standard police interview. The number of details correctly recalled by eyewitnesses with the cognitive interview was much greater than with the standard interview. This increase was comparable whether the crime or incident was viewed live or via videotape.

Memon et al. (2010) found the beneficial effects of the cognitive interview were reduced when the situation was highly arousing. They were also reduced when there was a long interval of time between the incident and the interview. However, the cognitive interview remained effective even with high arousal and a long retention interval.

Memon et al. (2010) reported only one negative effect of the cognitive interview on eyewitness memory performance. There was a fairly small (but significant) increase in recall of incorrect details compared to the standard interview.

Advocates of the cognitive interview often claim that the eyewitness should recall the event with his/her eyes closed. Vredeveldt, Hitch, and Baddeley (2011) found this enhanced recall. Why was eye closure beneficial? It reduced cognitive load on the eyewitness and also reduced distraction.

Does the cognitive interview reduce the adverse effects of misleading information on eyewitness memory? Memon, Zaragoza, Clifford, and Kidd (2009) found the answer was "No" when the misleading information

was presented *before* the cognitive interview. However, the negative impact of misleading information on eyewitness memory was reduced when it was presented *after* the cognitive interview.

Are *all* the components of the cognitive interview equally useful? Colomb and Ginet (2012) addressed this issue. Mental reinstatement of the situation and reporting all the details both enhanced recall. However, altering the eyewitness's perspective and changing the order in which the information was recalled were ineffective.

Dando, Ormerod, Wilcock, and Milne (2011) found that requiring eyewitnesses to recall information in a backward temporal order actually *reduced* the number of correct details recalled and *increased* recall errors. These negative effects occurred because backward recall disrupted the temporal organization of eyewitness memory for the crime.

Evaluation

The cognitive interview is a very effective method for obtaining as much accurate information as possible from eyewitnesses. It remains effective even when the incident was arousing and the eyewitness's memory is assessed only after a fairly long interval of time. Importantly, the components most responsible for the effectiveness of the cognitive interview have been identified.

What are the limitations with the cognitive interview? First, the small increased amount of incorrect information recalled by eyewitnesses can lead detectives to misinterpret the evidence.

Second, recreating the context at the time of the incident is a key ingredient in the cognitive interview. However, context has less effect on recognition memory than on recall (see Chapter 8), and so does not improve face recognition from photographs or lineups (Fisher, 1999).

Third, the cognitive interview is less effective when the event was stressful. It is also less effective when there is a long delay between the event and the interview.

Fourth, the cognitive interview is ineffective in reducing the negative effects of misleading information when it is conducted after that information is presented (Memon et al., 2009).

It is thus very important to ensure that eyewitnesses are not exposed to misleading information ahead of being questioned via cognitive interview.

FROM LABORATORY TO COURTROOM

We have seen that psychologists have identified numerous reasons why jurors should be wary of accepting the validity of eyewitness testimony. These reasons include change blindness, witnesses' prior expectations, pre- and post-event information, misplaced witness confidence, unconscious transference, verbal overshadowing, and weapon focus.

The accumulating psychological evidence led Handberg (1995) to argue in a review of legal opinion that, "Courts should admit eyewitness expert testimony to correct the misperceptions that many jurors have about the reliability of eyewitness identifications." Most psychologists would agree that our knowledge of the strengths and limitations of eyewitness memory has reached a point at which it is wholly appropriate for experts on eyewitness testimony to testify in court.

Some skeptics doubt whether our knowledge of eyewitness memory is sufficient to justify its extensive use in court cases. For example, Ebbesen and Konecni (1997, p. 2) concluded as follows:

Handberg (1995) argued that many jurors have misperceptions about the reliability of eyewitness testimony and that admitting eyewitness expert testimony would help address this issue.

There is no evidence that the experts who testify would be any better at detecting witness inaccuracy than uninformed jurors ... the nature of what is known about human memory is so complex that an honest presentation of this knowledge to a jury would only serve to confuse rather than improve their decision-making.
(Ebbesen & Konecni, 1997, p. 2)

In view of these differing opinions, we need to consider what conclusions can validly be drawn from the available evidence. Two issues are of importance. First, there is *ecological validity*—do laboratory findings on eyewitness memory generalize to real life? If laboratory findings on eyewitness testimony lack ecological validity, it would be inappropriate to provide jurors with such findings.

Second, suppose we find that laboratory research possesses ecological validity. It does not necessarily follow that eyewitness expert testimony should be presented to jurors. For example, it might lead jurors to become so skeptical of the value of eyewitness testimony that they become excessively reluctant to find defendants guilty.

Laboratory findings are not relevant!

It is indisputable that there are several important differences between eyewitnesses' typical experiences in the laboratory and those they have when observing a real-life crime. Below we will consider some of the main ones.

First, in the overwhelming majority of laboratory studies, the event in question is observed by eyewitnesses rather than by the victim or victims. In contrast, eyewitness evidence in real crimes is more likely to be provided by the victim than by bystanders.

Second, it is obviously less stressful and anxiety-provoking to watch a video of a violent crime than to experience a real-life violent crime (especially from the perspective of the victim). As we saw earlier in the chapter, high levels of anxiety and stress typically reduce eyewitness recall of details of a crime (Deffenbacher et al., 2004).

Third, eyewitnesses in the laboratory generally observe the event from a *single* perspective in an essentially passive fashion. In contrast, eyewitnesses to a real-life crime are likely to move around and may be forced to interact with the individual or individuals committing the crime.

Fourth, with real-life crimes, eyewitnesses often have somewhere between 5 and 10 minutes' exposure to the criminal (Moore, Ebbesen, & Konecni, 1994). In contrast, eyewitnesses under laboratory conditions typically spend much less time observing the criminal.

Fifth, the consequences if an eyewitness makes a mistaken identification in the laboratory are trivial (e.g. minor disappointment at his/her poor memory). In contrast, the consequences in an American court of law can literally be a matter of life or death.

Findings

We will shortly be considering research that compares laboratory and real-life eyewitness testimony. To anticipate, reasonable comparability of findings is generally obtained in such comparisons. However, there are some concerns about the reliability or consistency of some of the research results. Here we will consider findings on the effects of arousal on eyewitness memory.

Deffenbacher (1983) reviewed 21 studies concerned with the relationship between arousal and eyewitness memory. The findings from 10 studies suggested that high arousal *increases* eyewitness accuracy but the remaining 11 studies suggested it *decreases* accuracy. However, many of these studies are only of marginal relevance to crime situations because arousal was created by sources (e.g. electric shock, white noise) totally separate from the event itself.

Evidence that the *source* of arousal is important was obtained by Dutton and Carroll (2001). They compared the effects on memory of physiological arousal (produced by varying amount of exercise) and emotional arousal (produced by varying the content of a video).

Physiological arousal had no effect on recall of central or peripheral details. In contrast, medium emotional arousal improved recall of central and peripheral details, whereas high emotional arousal impaired recall of central details. Thus, the apparent inconsistencies in the effects of arousal on memory reported by Deffenbacher (1983) can be explained by focusing on the source of arousal.

A key issue is whether the presentation of expert testimony improves the accuracy of jurors' decisions. Suggestive evidence that it does not was reported by Leippe, Eisenstadt, Rauch, and Seib (2004). They considered the impact of expert testimony concerning eyewitness memory introduced toward the end of a murder-trial transcript. This was followed by a reminder about this testimony in the judge's final instructions.

The case used by Leippe et al. (2004) involved a holdup at night that led to a fatal stabbing. There were three versions of the case in which the evidence against the defendant was very strong, moderately strong, or weak. In all three versions, the prosecution case depended in part on eyewitness testimony from a man observing the crime from a bedroom window. In the very strong condition, DNA results indicated a 94% probability that a blood sample taken from the defendant's jacket was that of the victim. In addition, there was clear evidence the defendant had been in a struggle (e.g. swollen eye, scraped knuckles), and the victim's wallet was found in a trash can on the block where the defendant lived.

The key findings related to the percentage of mock jurors who decided the defendant was guilty. The presence of expert testimony produced a relatively large reduction in guilty verdicts regardless of the strength of the case. Even when the overall case was very strong, expert testimony reduced guilty verdicts from 74% to 59%. This suggests that exposing mock jurors to expert testimony made them focus too much on possible inaccuracies in the eyewitness's evidence at the expense of the otherwise strong evidence against the defendant.

Martire and Kemp (2011) reviewed the available evidence on the effects of expert evidence on jurors' decision making. They argued that there is an important distinction between sensitivity and skepticism. *Sensitivity* refers to the ability to weigh up accurately the quality of evidence provided by an eyewitness. *Skepticism* refers to the tendency to disbelieve an eyewitness regardless of the quality of his/her evidence. Expert evidence would be very valuable if it increased jurors' sensitivity without increasing their skepticism. In fact, however, the typical finding is the exact opposite—the main effect of expert evidence is to increase jurors' skepticism (as was found by Leippe et al., 2004).

Laboratory findings are relevant!

In the previous section, we identified some major differences between eyewitnesses' experiences in the laboratory and in real life. What is of crucial importance is whether these differences have large and systematic effects on the accuracy of eyewitness memory. Lindsay and Harvie (1988) had eyewitnesses watch an event via slide shows, video films, or live staged events. There were only small differences in the accuracy of culprit identification across these three conditions, suggesting that artificial laboratory conditions do *not* lead to distortions in the findings obtained.

Ihlebaek, Løve, Eilertsen, and Magnussen (2003) made use of a staged robbery involving two robbers armed with handguns. In the live condition, the eyewitnesses were ordered repeatedly to "Stay down." A video taken during the live condition was presented to eyewitnesses in the video condition. There were important similarities in memory in the two conditions. For example, participants in both conditions exaggerated the duration of the event, and the patterns of memory performance (i.e. what was well and poorly remembered) were similar. However, eyewitnesses in the video condition recalled more information than those in the live condition. They estimated the robbers' age, height, and weight more closely, and they also identified the robbers' weapons more accurately.

Ihlebaek et al.'s (2003) findings suggest that witnesses to real-life events are more inaccurate in their memories of those events than are those observing the same events under laboratory conditions. This finding (if confirmed) is important. The implication is that the inaccuracies and distortions in eyewitness memory obtained under laboratory conditions

provide an *underestimate* of eyewitnesses' memory deficiencies for real-life events. If so, it is legitimate to regard laboratory research as providing evidence of genuine relevance to the legal system.

More support for the relevance of laboratory findings for the legal system was reported by Pozzulo, Crescini, and Panton (2008). Eyewitnesses observed a staged theft live or via video. Identification accuracy of the culprit was comparable in the two conditions. However, eyewitnesses in the live condition reported more stress and arousal.

Tollestrupp et al. (1994) analyzed police records concerning the identifications by eyewitnesses to crimes involving fraud and robbery. What they discovered were that factors found to be important in laboratory studies (e.g. exposure duration, weapon focus, retention interval) were also important in real-life crimes. Thus, for example, identification accuracy was higher when the eyewitness was exposed to the culprit for a relatively long period of time and when the interval of time between the crime and the initial questioning was short.

In spite of the negative findings discussed by Martire and Kemp (2011), the use of expert evidence sometimes enhances jurors' decision making. Cutler, Penrod, and Dexter (1989) carried out a study in which mock jurors viewed a realistic videotaped trial concerning an armed

In Pozzulo et al.'s (2008) study eyewitnesses observed a staged theft live or via video. Identification accuracy of the culprit was comparable in the two conditions. However, eyewitnesses in the live condition reported more stress and arousal.

robbery of a liquor store. The main evidence was the victim's identification of the defendant. The witnessing and identification conditions were good or poor. In the poor condition, the robber was disguised, he brandished a handgun, the identification took place 14 days after the robbery, and the lineup instructions were suggestive (the office in charge didn't explicitly provide the witness with the option of not choosing anyone). In the good witnessing and identification condition, the robber was not disguised, his handgun was hidden throughout the robbery, the identification took place 2 days after the robbery, and the lineup instructions were not suggestive.

Cutler et al. (1989) found that the quality of the witnessing and identification conditions had a significant impact on jurors' judgments as to the accuracy of the witness's identification when they were presented with eyewitness expert testimony. However, the conditions had practically no effect when this expert testimony was not presented. In addition, the verdict was much more influenced by the witnessing and identification conditions when expert testimony was presented than when it was not. Thus, jurors not exposed to eyewitness expert testimony were fairly insensitive to the quality of the witnessing and identification conditions to which the eyewitness was exposed.

Another approach can be taken when assessing the usefulness of the knowledge of eyewitness memory obtained by psychologists in laboratory studies. Eyewitnesses view a simulated crime and their subsequent testimony about that crime is videotaped. Simulated jurors then view the videotapes and judge the witness's accuracy. After that, half of the jurors hear expert testimony based on laboratory findings concerning factors that influence eyewitness identification, whereas the other half do not. Finally, all of the jurors reach a decision. The typical finding is that jurors who have heard the expert testimony make more accurate decisions than those who have not (see Cutler & Penrod, 1995, for a review).

Conclusions

It seems reasonable to conclude that the evidence obtained by eyewitness researchers is relevant and should be presented to juries. The single strongest argument in favor of this conclusion is that the findings from police records and from naturalistic research are generally very much in agreement with those obtained under typical laboratory conditions. However, the presentation of this evidence to jurors by eyewitness experts needs to be done very carefully. What often happens is that expert evidence leads jurors to be excessively skeptical about the value of eyewitness testimony and thus unwilling to accept even high-quality eyewitness testimony.

In sum, we have a frustrating situation. On the one hand, we know a considerable amount about the factors influencing the accuracy of eyewitness testimony. On the other hand, when this knowledge is communicated to jurors, they often misinterpret it as indicating that eyewitness memory is always very fallible.

SUMMARY

- There is compelling evidence (some based on the use of DNA) that many innocent people have been sent to prison primarily on the basis of eyewitness testimony.
- It is a matter of concern that the beliefs of judges and jurors often differ from those of the expert consensus with respect to the factors influencing the accuracy of eyewitness memory.
- Eyewitnesses tend to exaggerate their ability to notice and remember changes in the environment.
- What eyewitnesses claim to remember is influenced by their expectations concerning what is likely to have happened based on their schemas or packets of knowledge.

- Misleading information presented after (or before) an event can cause eyewitness memory for that event to be distorted.
- Stress and anxiety typically reduce the ability of eyewitnesses to remember faces and other details of the situation.
- Eyewitnesses sometimes attend so closely to the criminal's weapon that their memory for his/her features is impaired; this is weapon focus.
- Weapon focus has been found with real-life crimes as well as in the laboratory. It occurs in part because of attentional narrowing or "tunnel vision."
- Children and older eyewitnesses both have less accurate memory for events than young and middle-aged adults.
- Older adults often produce false memories and are strongly influenced by misleading suggestions.
- There is an own-age bias in which eyewitnesses are more accurate at identification when the culprit is of a similar age to themselves.
- Eyewitnesses are often poor at recognizing unfamiliar faces and even at deciding whether two photographs show the same person.
- Face-recognition memory is much reduced by disguise even when this involves apparently small changes such as adding or removing glasses.
- Face processing is holistic and so altering one feature can alter the way in which the entire face is perceived.
- Eyewitnesses often identify an innocent bystander as the culprit because his/her face seems familiar in a process of unconscious transference.
- Eyewitnesses tend to be better at recognizing same-race faces than other-race faces. This occurs, in part, because eyewitnesses engage in more processing of ingroup faces than of outgroup ones.
- Sequential lineups are generally preferable to simultaneous ones. Accurate identification is slightly lower with sequential lineups, but there is a substantial reduction in the number of misidentifications. As a result, sequential lineups have greater diagnostic value than simultaneous ones.
- More information is obtained from eyewitnesses using cognitive interviews than standard ones.
- The most useful components of the cognitive interview are the use of mental reinstatement of the crime scene and the requirement for eyewitnesses to recall every detail no matter how apparently trivial.
- The main disadvantage with the cognitive interview is that there is a small increase in the number of incorrect details recalled.
- There are many differences between eyewitnesses' experiences when in the laboratory and in real life. In the laboratory, the event is typically observed by eyewitnesses rather than victims, there is little or no stress, and eyewitnesses have only a few seconds to study the culprit. In contrast, in real life the event is generally observed by the victim, there may be extremely high levels of stress, and eyewitnesses and victims on average observe the culprit for between 5 and 10 minutes.
- The factors found to influence the accuracy of eyewitness memory in the laboratory also do so with more naturalistic studies and with real-life crimes.
- Jurors informed of the findings from eyewitness research tend to become more skeptical about the accuracy of eyewitness memory rather than more sensitive to factors influencing eyewitness memory.

Why is eyewitness memory often inaccurate and/or distorted?

What effects do anxiety and stress have on the accuracy of eyewitness recall?

Why is it often difficult for eyewitnesses to remember faces? What can be done to enhance face recognition?

What are the characteristics of the most successful interviewing techniques used by the police with eyewitnesses?

How relevant is laboratory research on eyewitness testimony to the courtroom?

FURTHER READING

Frenda, S. J., Nichols, R. M., & Loftus, E. F. (2011). Current issues and advances in misinformation research. *Current Directions in Psychological Science, 20,* 20–23. This article contains a useful, reader-friendly account of developments in eyewitness memory research.

Memon, A., Meissner, C. A., & Fraser, J. (2010). The cognitive interview: A meta-analytic review and study space analysis of the past 25 years. *Psychology, Public Policy and Law, 16,* 340–372. Amina Memon and her colleagues provide a statistically based evaluation of the strengths and limitations of the cognitive interview.

Steblay, N. K., & Loftus, E. F. (2013). Eyewitness identification and the legal system. In E. Shafir (Ed.), *The behavioral foundations of public policy.* Princeton, NJ: Princeton University Press. This chapter discusses the many ways in which the legal system has benefitted (and could benefit further) from making use of the insights of psychological research.

Wells, G. L., & Loftus, E. F. (2013). Eyewitness memory for people and events. In R. K. Otto & I. B. Weiner (Eds.), *Handbook of psychology: Forensic psychology.* Hoboken, NJ: John Wiley & Sons. Gary Wells and Elizabeth Loftus, two of the leading experts in the field, discuss the contributions that psychologists have made to our understanding of eyewitness memory.

REFERENCES

Bartlett, F. C. (1932). *Remembering.* Cambridge: Cambridge University Press.

Bekerian, D. A., & Bowers, J. M. (1983). Eyewitness testimony: Were we misled? *Journal of Experimental Psychology: Learning, Memory, and Cognition, 9,* 139–145.

Berman, C. (2004). *Welcome to my pages on prosopagnosia.* Available online at: http://www.prosopagnosia.com

Bindemann, M., Avetisyan, M., & Rakow, T. (2012). Who can recognize unfamiliar faces? Individual differences and observer consistency in person identification. *Journal of Experimental Psychology: Applied, 18,* 277–291.

Bradfield, A. L., Wells, G. L., & Olson, E. A. (2002). The damaging effect of confirming feedback on the relation between eyewitness certainty and identification accuracy. *Journal of Applied Psychology, 87,* 112–120.

Brewer, N., Williams, K. D., & Semmler, C. (2005). Psychology and law research. In N. Brewer and K. D. Williams (Eds.), *Psychology and the Law: An Empirical Perspective.* New York: Guilford Press.

Brewer, W. F., & Sampaio, C. (2012). The metamemory approach to confidence: A test using semantic memory. *Journal of Memory and Language*, 67, 59–77.

Bruce, V., Henderson, Z., Greenwood, K., Hancock, P., Burton, A.M., & Miller, P. (1999). Verification of face identities from images captured on video. *Journal of Experimental Psychology: Applied*, 5, 339–360.

Charman, S. D. Wells. G. L., & Joy, S. W. (2011). The dud effect: Adding highly dissimilar fillers increases confidence in lineup identifications. *Law and Human Behavior*, 35, 479–500.

Colomb, C., & Ginet, M. (2012). The cognitive interview for use with adults: An empirical test of an alternative mnemonic and of a partial protocol. *Applied Cognitive Psychology*, 26, 35–47.

Cutler, B. L., & Penrod, S. D. (1995*). Mistaken identifications: The eyewitness, psychology, and the law*. New York: Cambridge University Press.

Cutler, B. L., Penrod, S. D., & Dexter, H. R. (1989). The eyewitness, the expert psychologist, and the jury. *Law and Human Behavior*, 13, 311–332.

Dando, C. J., Ormerod, T. C., Wilcock, R., & Milne, R. (2011). When help becomes hindrance: Unexpected errors of omission and commission in eyewitness memory resulting from changes in temporal order at retrieval? *Cognition*, 121, 416–421.

Davis, D., Loftus, E. F., Vanous, S., & Cucciare, M. (2008). "Unconscious transference" can be an instance of "change blindness". *Applied Cognitive Psychology*, 22, 605–623.

Deffenbacher, K. A. (1983). Identification evidence: A psychological evaluation. *American Journal of Psychology*, 96, 591–595.

Deffenbacher, K. A., Bornstein, B. H., Penrod, S. D., & McGorty, E. K. (2004). A meta-analytic review of the effects of high stress on eyewitness memory. *Law and Human Behavior*, 28, 687–706.

Desmarais, S. L., & Read, J. D. (2011). After 30 years, what do we know about what jurors know? A meta-analytic review of lay knowledge regarding eyewitness factors. *Law and Human Behavior*, 35, 200–210.

Dodson, C. S., & Krueger, L. E. (2006). I misremember it well: Why older adults are unreliable eyewitnesses. *Psychonomic Bulletin and Review*, 13, 770–775.

Dutton, A., & Carroll, M. (2001). Eyewitness testimony: Effects of source of arousal on memory, source-monitoring, and metamemory judgments. *Australian Journal of Psychology*, 53, 83–91.

Eakin, D. K., Schreiber, T. A., & Sergent-Marshall, S. (2003). Misinformation effects in eyewitness memory: The presence and absence of memory impairment as a function of warning and misinformation accessibility. *Journal of Experimental Psychology: Learning, Memory, and Cognition*, 29, 813–825.

Easterbrook, J. A. (1959). The effect of emotion on cue utilization and the organization of behavior. *Psychological Review*, 66, 183–201.

Ebbesen, E. B., & Konecni, V. J. (1997). Eyewitness memory research: Probative vs. prejudicial value. *The International Digest of Human Behavior, Science, and the Law*, 5, 2–28.

Ecker, U. K. H., Lewandowsky, S., & Tang, D. T. W. (2010). Explicit warnings reduce but do not eliminate the continued influence of misinformation. *Memory and Cognition*, 38, 1087–1100.

Edelson, M., Sharot, T., Dolan, R. J., & Dudai, Y. (2011). Following the crowd: Brain substrates of long-term memory conformity. *Science*, 333, 108–111.

Fawcett, J. M., Russell, E. J., Peace, K. A., & Christie, J. (2013). Of guns and geese: A meta-analytic review of the "weapon focus" literature. *Psychology, Crime & Law*, 19, 35–66.

Fisher, R. P. (1999). Probing knowledge structures. In D. Gopher & A. Koriat (Eds.), *Attention and performance XVII: Cognitive regulation of performance: Interaction of theory and application*. Cambridge, MA: MIT Press.

Fisher, R. P., Geiselman, R .E., Raymond, D. S., Jurkevich, L .M., & Warhaftig, M. L. (1987). Enhancing enhanced eyewitness memory: Refining the cognitive interview. *Journal of Police Science and Administration*, 15, 291–297.

Gabbert, F., Hope, L., Fisher, R. P., & Jamieson, K. (2012). Protecting against misleading post-event information with a self-administered interview. *Applied Cognitive Psychology*, 26, 568–575.

Garcia-Bajos, E., Migueles, M., & Aizpurua, A. (2012). Bias of script-driven processing on eyewitness memory in young and older adults. *Applied Cognitive Psychology*, 26, 737–745.

Geiselman, R. E., Fisher, R. P., MacKinnon, D. P., & Holland, H. L. (1985). Eyewitness memory enhancement in police interview: Cognitive retrieval mnemonics versus hypnosis. *Journal of Applied Psychology*, 70, 401–412.

Handberg, R. B. (1995). Expert testimony on eyewitness identification: A new pair of glasses for the jury. *American Criminal Law Review*, 32, 1013–1064.

Harrison, V., & Hole, G. J. (2009). Evidence for a contact-based explanation of the own-age bias in face recognition. *Psychonomic Bulletin and Review*, 16, 264–269.

Hastorf, A. A., & Cantril, H. (1954). They saw a game: A case study. *Journal of Abnormal and Social Psychology*, 97, 399–401.

Heath, W. P., & Erickson, K. R. (1998). Memory for central and peripheral actions and props after varied post-event presentation. *Legal and Criminal Psychology*, 3, 321–346.

Hollingworth, A., & Henderson, J. M. (2002). Accurate visual memory for previously attended objects in natural sense. *Journal of Experimental Psychology: Human Perception and Performance, 28*, 113–136.

Hugenberg, K., Young, S. G., Bernstein, M. J., & Sacco, D. F. (2010). The categorization individuation model: An integrative account of the other-race recognition deficit. *Psychological Review, 117*, 1168–1187.

Ihlebaek, C., Løve, T., Eilertsen, D. E., & Magnussen, S. (2003). Memory for a staged criminal event witnessed live and on video. *Memory, 11*, 310–327.

Jacoby, L. L., Bishara, A. J., Hessels, S., & Toth, J. P. (2005). Aging, subjective experience, and cognitive control: Dramatic false remembering by older adults. *Journal of Experimental Psychology: General, 134*, 131–148.

Jenkins, R., & Burton, A. M. (2011). Stable face representations. *Philosophical Transactions of the Royal Society B: Biological Sciences, 366*, 1671–1683.

Jenkins, R., White, D., van Montfort, X., & Burton, A. M. (2011). Variability in photos of the same face. *Cognition, 121*, 313–323.

Jensen, M. S., Yao, R., Street, W. N., & Simons, D. J. (2011). Change blindness and inattentional blindness. *Wiley Interdisciplinary Reviews: Cognitive Science, 2*, 529–546.

Johnson, M. K., Hashtroudi, S., & Lindsay, D. S. (1993). Source monitoring. *Psychological Bulletin, 114*, 3–28.

Kassin, S. M., Tubb, V. A., Hosch, H. M., & Memon, A. (2001). On the "general acceptance" of eyewitness testimony research. *American Psychologist, 56*, 405–416.

Leippe, M. R., Eisenstadt, D., Rauch, S. M., & Seib, H. M. (2004). Timing of eyewitness expert testimony, jurors' need for cognition, and case strength as determinants of trial verdicts. *Journal of Applied Psychology, 89*, 524–541.

Levin, D. T., Drivdahl, S. B., Momen, N., & Beck, M. R. (2002). False predictions about the detectability of visual changes: The role of beliefs about attention, memory, and the continuity of attended objects in causing change blindness blindness. *Consciousness and Cognition, 11*, 507–527.

Lindholm, T., & Christianson, S.-A. (1998). Intergroup biases and eyewitness testimony. *Journal of Social Psychology, 138*, 710–723.

Lindsay, D. S. (2008). Source monitoring. In H. L. Roediger (Ed.), *Cognitive Psychology of Memory* (Vol. 2, pp. 325–348). Oxford: Elsevier.

Lindsay, D. S., Allen, B. P., Chan, J. C. K., & Dahl, L. C. (2004). Eyewitness suggestibility and source similarity: Intrusions of details from one event into memory reports of another event. *Journal of Memory and Language, 50*, 96–111.

Lindsay, R. C. L., & Harvie, V. (1988). Hits, false alarms, correct and mistaken identifications: The effects of method of data collection on facial memory. In M. Gruneberg, P. Morris, & R. Sykes (Eds.), *Practical Aspects of Memory: Current Research and Issues, Vol. 1: Memory in Everyday Life* (pp. 47–52). Chichester, UK: Wiley.

Loftus, E. F. (1979). *Eyewitness testimony.* Cambridge, MA: Harvard University Press.

Loftus, E. F. (1992). When a lie becomes memory's truth: Memory distortions after exposure to misinformation. *Current Directions in Psychological Science, 13*, 145–147.

Loftus, E. F., & Palmer, J. C. (1974). Reconstruction of automobile destruction: An example of the interaction between language and memory. *Journal of Verbal Learning and Verbal Behavior, 13*, 585–589.

Loftus, E. F., Loftus, G. R., & Messo, J. (1987). Some facts about "weapons focus". *Law and Human Behavior, 11*, 55–62.

Loftus, E. F., Miller, D. G., & Burns, H. J. (1978). Semantic integration of verbal information into a visual memory. *Journal of Experimental Psychology: Human Learning, 1*, 19–31.

Loussouam, A., Gabriel, D., & Proust, J. (2011). Exploring the informational sources of metaperception: The case of change blindness blindness. *Consciousness and Cognition, 20*, 1489–1501.

Martire, K. A., & Kemp, R. I. (2011). Can experts help jurors to evaluate eyewitness evidence? A review of eyewitness expert effects. *Legal and Criminological Psychology, 16*, 24–36.

Megreya, A. M., White, D., & Burton, A. M. (2011). The other-race effect does not rely on memory: Evidence from a matching task. *Quarterly Journal of Experimental Psychology, 64*, 1473–1483.

Memon, A., Meissner, C. A., & Fraser, J. (2010). The cognitive interview: A meta-analytic review and study space analysis of the past 25 years. *Psychology, Public Policy and Law, 16*, 340–372.

Memon, A., Zaragoza, M., Clifford, B. R., & Kidd, L. (2009). Inoculation or antidote? The effects of cognitive interview timing on false memory for forcibly fabricated events. *Law and Human Behavior, 34*, 105–117.

Moniz, E., Righi, G., Peissig, J. J., & Tarr, M. J. (2010). The Clark Kent effect: What is the role of familiarity and eyeglasses in recognizing disguised faces? *Journal of Vision, 10*(7), Article 615.

Moore, P. J., Ebbesen, E. B., & Konecni, V. J. (1994). *What does real eyewitness testimony* look like? *An archival analysis of witnesses to adult felony crimes.* Technical Report: University of California, San Diego, Law and Psychology Program.

Nakayabayashi, K., Burton, A. M., Brandimonte, M. A., & Lloyd-Jones, T. J. (2012). Dissociating positive and negative influences of verbal processing on the recognition of faces and objects. *Journal of Experimental Psychology: Learning, Memory, and Cognition, 38,* 376–390.

Odinot, G., Wolters, G., & van Koppen, P. J. (2009). Eyewitness memory of a supermarket robbery: A case study of accuracy and confidence after 3 months. *Law and Human Behavior, 33,* 506–514.

Patterson, K. E., & Baddeley, A. D. (1977). When face recognition fails. *Journal of Experimental Psychology: Human Learning and Memory, 3,* 406–417.

Pickel, K. L. (2009). The weapon focus effect on memory for female versus male perpetrators. *Memory, 17,* 664–678.

Pozzulo, J. D., Crescini, C., & Panton, T. (2008). Does methodology matter in eyewitness identification research? The effect of live versus video exposure on eyewitness identification of accuracy. *International Journal of Law and Psychiatry, 31,* 430–437.

Richler, J. J., Cheung, O. S., & Gauthier, I. (2011). Holistic processing predicts face recognition. *Psychological Science, 22,* 464–471.

Righi, G., Peissig, J. J., & Tarr, M. J. (2012). Recognizing disguised faces. *Visual Cognition, 20,* 143–169.

Schacter, D. L., Guerin, S. A., & St. Jacques, P. L. (2011). Memory distortion: An adaptive perspective. *Trends in Cognitive Sciences, 15,* 467–474.

Schooler, J. W., & Engstler-Schooler, T. Y. (1990). Verbal overshadowing of visual memories: Some things are better left unsaid. *Cognitive Psychology, 22,* 36–71.

Shapiro, L. R. (2009). Eyewitness testimony for a simulated juvenile crime by male and female criminals with consistent or inconsistent gender-role characteristics. *Journal of Applied Developmental Psychology, 30,* 649–666.

Shriver, E. R., Young, S .G., Hugenberg, K., Bernstein, M. J., & Lanter, J . R. (2008). Class, race, and the face: Social context modulates the cross-race effect in face recognition. *Personality and Social Psychology Bulletin, 34,* 260– 274.

Simons, D. J., & Chabris, F. (1999). Gorillas in our midst: Sustained inattentional blindness for dynamic events. *Perception, 28,* 1059–1074.

Simons, D.J., & Chabris, C. F. (2011). What people believe about how memory works: A representative survey of the US population. *Public Library of Science One, 6,* e22757.

Smalarz, L., & Wells, G. L. (2012). Eyewitness-identification evidence: Scientific advances and the new burden on trial judges. *Court Review: The Journal of the American Judges Association,* Paper 385.

Sporer, S. L., Penrod, S., Read, D., & Cutler, B. (1995). Choosing, confidence, and accuracy: A meta-analysis of the confidence-accuracy relation in eyewitness identification studies. *Psychological Bulletin, 118,* 315–327.

Steblay, N. M. (1997). Social influence in eyewitness recall: A meta-analytic review of line-up instruction effects. *Law and Human Behavior, 21,* 283–298.

Steblay, N. K., & Phillips, J. D. (2011). The not-sure response option in sequential lineup practice. *Applied Cognitive Psychology, 25,* 768–774.

Steblay, N. K., Dysart, J. E., & Wells, G. L. (2011). Seventy-two tests of the sequential lineup superiority effect: A meta-analysis and policy discussion. *Psychology, Public Policy, and Law, 17,* 99–139.

Tollestrup, P. A., Turtle, J. W., & Yuille, J. C. (1994). Actual victims and witnesses to robbery and fraud: An archival analysis. In D. F. Ross, J. D. Read, & M. P. Toglia (Eds.), *Adult eyewitness testimony: Current trends and developments.* New York, NY: Wiley.

Tuckey, M. R., & Brewer, N. (2003a). How schemas affect eyewitness memory over repeated retrieval attempts. *Applied Cognitive Psychology, 7,* 785–800.

Tuckey, M. R., & Brewer, N. (2003b). The influence of schemas, stimulus ambiguity, and interview schedule on eyewitness memory over time. *Journal of Experimental Psychology: Applied, 9,* 101–118.

Tulving, E. (1979). Relation between encoding specificity and levels of processing. In L. S. Cermak & F. I. M. Craik (Eds.), *Levels of processing in human memory.* Hillsdale, NJ: Lawrence Erlbaum Associates.

Valentine, T., & Mesout, J. (2009). Eyewitness identification under stress in the London Dungeon. *Applied Cognitive Psychology, 23,* 151–161.

Valentine, T., Pickering, A., & Darling, S. (2003). Characteristics of eyewitness identification that predict the outcome of real lineups. *Applied Cognitive Psychology, 17,* 969–993.

Vredeveldt, A., Hitch, G. J., & Baddeley, A. D. (2011). Eyeclosure helps memory by reducing cognitive load and enhancing visualization. *Memory and Cognition, 39,* 1253–1263.

Wise, R. A., & Safer, M. A. (2004). What US judges know and believe about eyewitness testimony. *Applied Cognitive Psychology*, *18*, 427–443.

Wise, R. A., & Safer, M. A. (2010). A comparison of what US judges and students know and believe about eyewitness testimony. *Journal of Applied Social Psychology*, *40*, 1400–1422.

Wright, D. B., & Stroud, J. N. (2002). Age differences in lineup identification accuracy: People are better with their own age. *Law and Human Behavior*, *26*, 641–654.

Yegiyan, N. S., & Lang, A. (2010). Processing central and peripheral detail: How content arousal and emotional tone influence encoding. *Media Psychology*, *13*, 77–99.

Young, S. G., Hugenberg, K., Bernstein, M. J., & Sacco, D. F. (2012). Perception and motivation in face recognition: A critical review of theories of the cross-race effect. *Personality and Social Psychology Review*, *16*, 116–142.

Zhu, B., Chen, C., Loftus, E. F., Lin, C., He, Q., Chen, C., et al. (2010a). Individual differences in false memory from misinformation: Cognitive factors. *Memory*, *18*, 543–555.

Zhu, B., Chen, C., Loftus, E. F., Lin, C., He, Q., Chen, C., et al. (2010b). Individual differences in false memory from misinformation: Personality characteristics and their interactions with cognitive abilities. *Personality and Individual Differences*, *48*, 889–894.

Contents

Introduction   361

Prospective memory in everyday life   365

Types of prospective memory   369

Theoretical perspectives   371

Improving prospective memory   373

Summary   375

Points for discussion   375

Further reading   376

References   376

CHAPTER 13

PROSPECTIVE MEMORY

Michael W. Eysenck

INTRODUCTION

Has the following ever happened to you? You are introducing two people to each other but suddenly realize you have forgotten the name of one of them. If you have experienced that, you will know how acutely embarrassing it can be. Frustration is another emotion we can experience when forgetting occurs, as when a student sitting an examination goes blank and can't remember what he/she knows about a topic. These are failures of retrospective memory, which involves remembering events, words, and so on from the past typically (but not always) when deliberately trying to do so.

There is an important distinction between retrospective memory and prospective memory. This is a type of memory that involves remembering to carry out intended actions without being instructed to do so. Failures of prospective memory (absent-mindedness when action is required) can also be embarrassing, as when you completely forget you had arranged to meet a friend at a coffee shop. Freud (1901, p. 157), in his usual over-the-top style, argued that the motive behind many of our missed appointments is "an unusually large amount of unavowed contempt for other people."

There are several types of prospective memory. However, the most important distinction is between time-based and event-based prospective memory. Time-based prospective memory is assessed by tasks that involve remembering to perform a given action at a given time (e.g. phone a friend at 8pm). In contrast, event-based prospective memory is assessed by tasks that involve remembering to perform an action in the appropriate circumstances (e.g. passing on a message when you see someone). As we will see later, most research has focused on event-based prospective memory.

KEY TERM

Retrospective memory: Memory for people, words, and events experienced in the past.

Prospective memory: Remembering to carry out some intended action in the absence of any explicit reminder to do so; see retrospective memory.

Time-based prospective memory: A form of prospective memory in which time is the cue indicating that a given action needs to be performed.

Event-based prospective memory: A form of prospective memory in which some event provides the cue to perform a given action.

Why is prospective memory important?

Most human behavior is *goal-directed*. If we are to attain our goals, it is often essential that actions intended to facilitate goal attainment are performed at the appropriate time. This requires successful prospective memory. For example, if you set yourself the goal of having a vacation during a given week, you need to remember to book the flights, a hotel to stay at, and so on, in good time.

Many failures of prospective memory have trivial consequences. For example, if you forget to put milk back in the fridge after using it, the worst that is likely to happen is that you subsequently find yourself throwing sour milk away. However, failures of prospective memory can sometimes result in serious injury or even death. Einstein and McDaniel (2005) gave this tragic example of what can happen when prospective memory fails:

After a change in his usual routine, an adoring father forgot to turn toward the daycare center and instead drove his usual route to work at the university. Several hours later, his infant son, who had been quietly asleep in the back seat, was dead.
(Einstein and McDaniel, 2005, p. 286)

Failures of prospective memory also play an important part in many aircraft accidents. In the mid-1990s, a DC-9 landed in Houston without the landing gear in place. The crew failed to notice the gear wasn't down because they hadn't switching the hydraulic pumps to high. Why did this failure in prospective memory occur? The crew had been concentrating on coping with an unstabilized approach to the landing strip— they prioritized this task over ensuring that the landing gear was in place. There is more on the role of prospective memory in fatal aircraft accidents a little later in the chapter.

We conclude this section with a very common everyday situation in which prospective memory is very important. In the US and the UK, millions of individuals suffer from chronic health conditions requiring regular medication. Surprisingly, about 50% of these individuals show partial failure to adhere to their recommended schedule of medication. There are numerous reasons for this nonadherence to medication schedules. However, deficient prospective memory is an important factor. Zogg, Woods, Sauceda, Wieber, and Simoni (2012) reviewed research showing the importance of prospective memory in the treatment of several conditions including HIV/AIDS, rheumatoid arthritis, and diabetes. For example, Woods, Dawson, Weber, Gibson, Grant, Atkinson, et al. (2009) found among patients with HIV/AIDS that those making errors on a laboratory task of prospective memory were nearly *six times* more likely to be nonadherent to their medication regime than those making no errors.

Prospective vs. retrospective memory

The most important difference between prospective and retrospective memory is their respective emphasis on the future versus the past. However, there are several other important differences. First, retrospective memory generally involves remembering *what* we know about something and can be high in informational content. In contrast, prospective memory focuses on *when* to do something and has low informational content. This low informational content helps to ensure that nonperformance of the prospective memory task is *not* due to retrospective memory failure.

Second, more external cues are typically available with retrospective memory than with prospective memory. For example, retrospective memory can be tested by asking someone a question about the past. Third, as Moscovitch (2008, p. 309) pointed out, "Research on prospective memory is about the only major enterprise in memory research in which the problem is not memory itself, but the uses to which memory is put." Fourth, prospective memory (but not retrospective memory) is relevant to the plans or goals we form for our daily activities

Fifth, people interpret failures of the two types of memory in different ways. Failures of prospective memory involving promises to another person are regarded by other people as indicating poor motivation and reliability (Graf, 2012). In contrast, failures of retrospective memory are attributed to a poor memory rather than deficient motivation or unreliability. Thus, deficient prospective memory means "flaky person" whereas deficient retrospective memory means "faulty brain" (Graf, 2012, p. 7).

Remembering and forgetting in our everyday lives often involve a mixture of prospective and retrospective memory. Suppose you agree to buy various goods at the supermarket for yourself and the friends with whom you share an apartment. Two things need to happen. First, you must remember your intention to go to the supermarket (prospective memory). Even if you remember to go to the supermarket, you then have to remember precisely what you had agreed to buy (retrospective memory).

Assessing prospective memory: Self-report measures

How good are your retrospective and prospective memories? You can answer that question by completing the questionnaire in Box 13.1 (taken from Crawford, Smith, Mayloe, Della Sala, and Logie (2003)).

Box 13.1 The Prospective and Retrospective Memory Questionnaire (PRMQ)

1   Do you decide to do something in a few minutes' time and then forget to do it?
2   Do you fail to recognize a place you have visited before?
3   Do you fail to do something you were supposed to do a few minutes later even though it's there in front of you, like take a pill or turn off the kettle?
4   Do you forget something that you were told a few minutes before?
5   Do you forget appointments if you are not prompted by someone else or by a reminder such as a calendar or diary?
6   Do you fail to recognize a character in a radio or television show from scene to scene?
7   Do you fail to buy something you planned to buy, like a birthday card, even when you see the shop?
8   Do you fail to recall things that have happened to you in the last few days?
9   Do you repeat the same story to the same person on different occasions?
10 Do you intend to take something with you, before leaving a room or going out, but minutes later leave it behind, even though it's there in front of you?
11 Do you mislay something that you have just put down, like a magazine or glasses?
12 Do you fail to mention or give something to a visitor that you were asked to pass on?
13 Do you look at something without realizing you have seen it moments before?
14 If you tried to contact a friend or relative who was out, would you forget to try again later?
15 Do you forget what you watched on television the previous day?
16 Do you forget to tell something you had meant to mention a few minutes ago?

Retrospective memory items: 2, 4, 6, 8, 9, 11, 13, and 15
Prospective memory items: 1, 3, 5, 7, 10, 12, 14, and 16

On the basis of administering the PRMQ to 551 people, Crawford et al. (2003) reported the following statistics (approximately 68% of participants had scores within 1 standard deviation of the mean):

- Prospective memory: Mean = 20.18; standard deviation = 4.91
- Retrospective memory: Mean = 18.69; standard deviation = 4.98
- Total score: Mean = 38.88; standard deviation = 9.15

From Crawford et al. (2003). Copyright © Psychology Press.

In order to show that a questionnaire is valid (i.e. measures what it claims to be measuring) it is important to demonstrate that what people *say* on the questionnaire corresponds to their actual *behavior*. This issue was investigated by Mäntylä (2003) with respect to the Prospective and Retrospective Memory Questionnaire (PRMQ; Box 13.1). Women claiming to have significant problems with prospective memory were compared against control women not reporting such problems. The former group scored higher on the prospective memory items on the PRMQ. The two groups were then given various tasks to assess prospective memory (e.g. remind the experimenter to sign a paper when the experimenter indicated the session was over). As predicted, women reporting problems with prospective memory performed worse than controls on the prospective memory tasks.

There is other evidence that the PRMQ is valid. Zimprich, Kliegel, and Rast (2011) confirmed in a study on older adults that this questionnaire contains separable (although highly correlated) factors of prospective and retrospective memory. In addition, individuals reporting the greatest number of problems with prospective memory performed worse than those reporting few such problems on prospective memory tasks. In similar fashion, individuals reporting many problems with retrospective memory performed worse than those with few problems on a retrospective memory task.

In spite of Zimprich et al.'s (2011) positive findings, the relationship between self-reported prospective memory problems and prospective memory performance was fairly modest. That suggests our knowledge of our own prospective memory abilities is limited. This issue was investigated by Schnitzspahn, Zeintl, Jäger, and Kliegel (2011). Their participants' judgments of their future prospective memory performance on a task were reasonably accurate. However, there was a general tendency to *underestimate* that performance.

The knowledge that we have about our own memory abilities (known as metamemory)

is important in our everyday lives. So far as prospective memory is concerned, the less likely we are to believe that we will remember to carry out an intended action, the more time and effort we generally devote to ensuring we do remember.

Nature of prospective memory

Prospective memory involves several separate processes or stages. Zogg et al. (2012) provided a conceptual model of the component processes involved (see Figure 13.1). A major implication of this stage- or process-based approach is that there are several different ways prospective memory can fail. We will work through this model stage by stage:

1 *Intention formation*: At this stage, the individual forms or encodes the intention that is linked to a specific cue. This cue may be a specific event (e.g. I will talk to my friend when I see him) or it may be time-related (e.g. I will phone my friend at 8 o'clock).

2 *Retention interval*: There is typically a delay of between several minutes and weeks between intention formation and intention execution. During that time, there is typically some monitoring of the environment for task-relevant cues (i.e. event cues or time cues). This monitoring may involve automatic or strategic (resource-requiring) processes (see theoretical perspectives section later in this chapter).

3 *Cue detection and intention retrieval*: This stage requires the individual to detect and recognize the relevant cue (event or time), followed by the self-initiated retrieval of the appropriate intention. As Zogg et al. (2012) pointed out, this is the defining stage of prospective memory that most clearly distinguishes it from retrospective memory.

4 *Intention recall*: The individual successfully retrieves the intention from retrospective memory. There may be problems at this stage because of the complexity of the intention, its relationship to other stored intentions, or the presence of other competing intentions.

KEY TERM

Metamemory: Knowledge about one's own memory and an ability to regulate its functioning.

5   *Intention execution*: This is typically a fairly automatic and undemanding process.

PROSPECTIVE MEMORY IN EVERYDAY LIFE

How common are failures of prospective memory in everyday life? Marsh, Hicks, Landau (1998) found people reported an average of 15 plans for the forthcoming week of which 25% were not completed. The main reasons for these noncompletions were rescheduling and reprioritization, with only 3% of plans that had been made being forgotten.

In this section, we consider prospective memory in various groups of people. First, we consider people (e.g. pilots) for whom forgetting intended actions can easily prove fatal. Second, we consider people generally regarded as having very poor prospective memory.

Why do plane crashes occur?

Fatal accidents involving aircraft occur for many reasons, some of which are of relevance to psychology and some of which are not. Detailed information on the causes of 1085 fatal aircraft accidents between 1950 and 2010 is contained in the PlaneCrashInfo.com.accident database. According to this database, 57% of these fatal accidents were due at least in part to human error. We can break this figure down into various subcategories. When we do this, we see that 29% of fatal aircraft accidents were due solely to pilot error. A further 16% were due to a combination of pilot error and poor weather conditions, and 5% to pilot error and mechanical problems. Finally, 7% were due to errors by nonpilot humans (e.g. air traffic controllers).

Dismukes (2012) pointed out that there are various important differences between prospective memory studied in the laboratory and that in natural settings (e.g. pilots flying planes). For example, there is much less emphasis on habitual tasks in the laboratory. In addition, while laboratory research typically makes use of predictable, experimenter-defined cues, pilots often encounter unanticipated cues.

Pilot errors

Dismukes and Nowinski (2006) carried out two studies to identify those airline flight

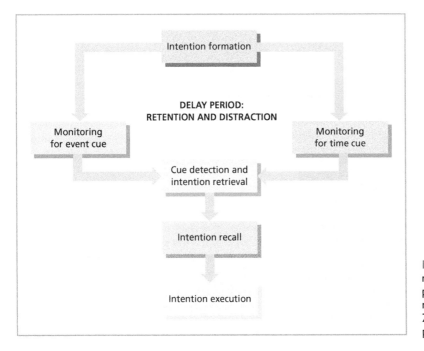

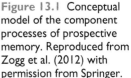
Figure 13.1 Conceptual model of the component processes of prospective memory. Reproduced from Zogg et al. (2012) with permission from Springer.

operations most clearly requiring prospective memory. In the first one, they considered in detail the Boeing 737. They observed numerous flights from the cockpit jump-seat, they watched flight-simulation training, and they read carefully through the written operating procedures. In the second study, they analyzed reports on the 19 major airline accidents between the years 1990 and 2001 that were attributed to crew errors. In the third study, they sampled 20% of all air carrier reports that had been submitted to the Aviation Safety Reporting System (ASRS) over a 1-year period in order to study in detail those involving memory failures.

The most striking finding emerged from the ASRS study. Dismukes and Nowinski (2006) uncovered 75 reports in which the nature of the memory failure that had caused the incident or accident could be identified. In 74 cases, there was a failure of prospective memory, with only *one* case involving retrospective memory! Why were there practically no failures of retrospective memory? The main reason is that airline pilots receive lengthy and demanding training. As a consequence, they have excellent knowledge and memory of all the operations needed to fly a plane. Unfortunately, however, their training provides less protection against failures of prospective memory.

Dismukes and Nowinski (2006) discovered that there are *five* main types of situations associated with flying an airplane in which significant demands are placed on prospective memory:

1   *Episodic tasks*: Pilots have to remember to perform later a task that is not typically performed at that time (e.g. reporting when the plane passes below 10,000 feet).
2   *Habitual tasks*: Pilots and crew need to remember to perform habitual tasks in the correct order. Note that approximately 100 actions are needed to prepare a large aircraft for departure.
3   *Atypical actions substituted for habitual ones*: Crews need to deviate from standard procedures in certain circumstances (e.g. heavy air traffic; unusual weather conditions).
4   *Interrupted tasks*: Pilots and crew have to remember to return to a task after they have been interrupted by flight attendants, mechanics, or jump-seat riders.
5   *Interleaving tasks*: Pilots and crew often have to carry out two (or more) tasks together. For example, the first officer may be re-programming the flight management system, monitoring the plane's taxiing, and handling radio communications at the same time.

Why do pilots and crew exhibit failures of prospective memory when flying aircraft? Pilots and crew typically form an explicit intention to carry out a given operation later in the sequence of operations. They then turn their attention to other tasks, relying on some prompt or cue to remind them to carry out the given operation at the appropriate time. This strategy works well under normal circumstances. However, problems can arise when there are *deviations* from the typical sequence of operations, as happens when atypical actions have to be substituted for habitual ones or when pilots are interrupted.

For example, when a plane is due to land shortly, the crew is generally instructed by approach control to switch radio frequencies to tower frequency and to contact the tower immediately. This instruction provides a very specific cue or prompt. However, crews are sometimes instructed by approach controllers to delay switching their radios to tower frequency until the aircraft reaches a specified distance from

Dismukes and Nowinski's (2006) study showed that although airline pilots have excellent knowledge and memory of all the operations needed to fly a plane, their training provides less protection against failures of prospective memory.

the airport. The ASRS data indicated that 12 out of 13 crash landings that occurred without tower clearance occurred when the normal prompt was missing.

Dismukes and Nowinski (2006) found pilots were most likely to show failures of prospective memory if interrupted while carrying out a plan of action. Interruptions often occur so rapidly and forcefully that individuals do not think explicitly about producing a new plan or intention to deal with the changed situation.

Dodhia and Dismukes (2009) found interruptions can seriously impair prospective memory. Participants were instructed to return to an interrupted task after completing a different task. When there was a 10-second pause after the interruption, 88% of participants returned to the interrupted task. The comparable figure was 65% when there was a 4-second pause just before the interruption, but only 48% when there was no pause before or after the interruption (see Figure 13.2).

What do the above findings mean? It is important that people have a few seconds to form a new plan when an interruption changes the situation. It is also important to have a few seconds at the end of the interruption

to retrieve the intention of returning to the interrupted task.

Air traffic controller errors

Dismukes and Nowinski (2006) give the following concrete example of air traffic controller error causing a fatal aircraft accident. At Los Angeles International airport at dusk one evening in 1991, a tower controller cleared one aircraft to position and hold on runway 24L while she cleared other aircraft to cross the other end of the runway. Unfortunately, there were various communication delays because one of the other aircraft was on the wrong radio frequency. In addition, visibility was poor because of the haze and glare.

The tower controller forgot to clear the first aircraft to take off but did clear another aircraft to land on runway 24L. This aircraft crashed into the stationary plane on that runway, destroying both planes and killing 34 people. It is highly probable that the tower controller could have recalled what she had planned to do with the holding aircraft (retrospective memory) if she had been asked after the accident occurred. The error was forgetting to carry out that planned intention at the

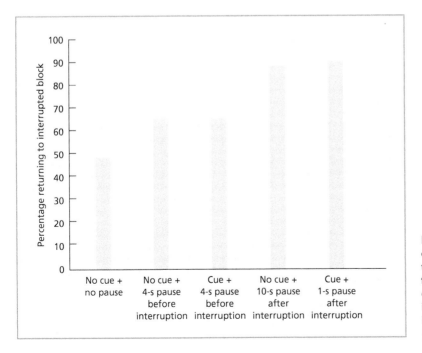

Figure 13.2 Percentage of participants returning to an interrupted task as a function of cuing and pause duration before or after interruption. Based on data in Dodhia and Dismukes (2005).

right time, and was thus a failure of prospective memory.

Air traffic control is an excellent example of an occupation in which individuals have to remember to perform intended actions while monitoring a display (Loft, Smith, and Bhaskara, 2011). It is thus no surprise that 38% of the memory errors reported by controllers involve failures to complete intentions (Shorrock, 2005).

Loft and Remington (2010) used a simulated air traffic control task under laboratory conditions. They distinguished between well-practiced or strong routines and less practiced weak routines. Prospective memory errors were more common when participants had to deviate from strong rather than weak routines. This effect is known as *habit capture*.

Obsessive-compulsive disorder and checking behavior

One might well argue that individuals suffering from obsessive-compulsive disorder have especially poor memory. Many patients with this disorder have so little confidence in their memory (and such an inflated sense of personal responsibility) that they check

It is possible that excessive checking followed by repetition of an action leads to poor prospective memory! Obsessionals may be uncertain, for example, whether they have washed their hands today, or on one of the many times in the past.

repeatedly they have locked their front door, that the gas stove has been turned off, and so on. In spite of all this repeated checking, obsessive-compulsive patients (and healthy individuals with obsessive-compulsive symptoms) tend to be uncertain whether they have actually performed the actions they intended to perform.

How can we explain such checking behavior? One obvious explanation is that obsessional individuals have poor retrospective memory ability, which causes them to forget whether they have recently engaged in checking behavior. As a result, they feel the need to perform the checking behavior repeatedly. In fact, this explanation is generally incorrect. Cuttler and Graf (2009a) found in a review of relevant studies that compulsive checkers did not differ from controls in retrospective memory.

An alternative explanation of compulsive checking is that checkers have poor prospective memory. There is increasing support for this explanation. Cuttler and Graf (2009b) found that compulsive checkers had impaired performance on various prospective memory tasks. A major reason for such performance impairments depends on *metamemory*, which consists of the knowledge and beliefs we have about our own memory. Cuttler, Sirois-Delisle, Alcolado, Radomsky and Taylor (2013) provided participants with fake feedback indicating their prospective memory performance was poor. This caused diminished confidence in their prospective memory ability and an increased urge to engage in checking behavior.

It seems reasonable to assume that poor prospective memory causes obsessional individuals to engage in excessive checking. However, it is also possible that the causality goes the other way, so that excessive checking leads to poor prospective memory. Suppose you check several times every day that you have locked your front door. You would obviously remember that you have checked your front door hundreds or even thousands of time. However, your long-term memory would contain so many very similar memories of checking your front door that you might be confused as to whether you have checked your front door *today*.

Van den Hout and Kindt (2004) carried out an experiment in which some participants engaged in repeated checking of a virtual gas stove whereas others did not. Those who had checked repeatedly had less vivid and detailed memories of what had happened on the final trial. Thus, repeated checking can impair long-term memory.

Linkovski, Kalanthroff, Henik, and Anholt (2013) carried out a similar study to that of van den Hout and Kindt (2004). In addition, they assessed participants' level of inhibitory control. They did this because obsessional individuals have deficient inhibitory control that can lead to intrusive thoughts and memory problems. Linkovski et al. found repeated checking reduced memory vividness and detail and also lowered participants' confidence in their memory. Most importantly, these effects were all much stronger in participants with poor inhibitory control (see Figure 13.3).

In sum, the memory problems experienced by compulsive checkers involve predominantly prospective rather than retrospective memory. Individuals who engage in compulsive checking tend to have low confidence in their memory abilities. There is interesting evidence that, as well as poor prospective memory helping to cause excessive checking, it is also the case that excessive checking can cause impaired memory.

TYPES OF PROSPECTIVE MEMORY

Most of the research has indicated that prospective memory is better with event-based tasks than with time-based ones. For example,

Kim and Mayhorn (2008) compared the two types of prospective memory in naturalistic settings as well as in the laboratory. Performance on event-based tasks was superior to that on time-based tasks, and this was especially the case under laboratory conditions. Time-based tasks were performed better in naturalistic settings than in the laboratory for an obvious reason—participants often used alarm clocks or reminders from friends in the former setting.

Why is performance generally better on event-based tasks than time-based ones? Probably the main reason is that environmental cues to perform the appropriate action are more likely to be present on event-based tasks. In contrast, time-based tasks often require extensive self-initiated processing. As a result, event-based tasks are typically less demanding than time-based ones.

Hicks, Marsh, and Cook (2005) confirmed that the processing demands of event-based tasks are less than those of time-based ones. However, they also found that both kinds of tasks were more demanding when the task was ill-specified (e.g. detect animal words) than when it was well-specified (e.g. detect the words *nice* and *hit*). A well-specified time-based task was no more demanding than an ill-specified event-based task.

How similar are the strategies used during the retention interval by individuals given event- and time-based prospective memory tasks? Since time-based tasks tend to be harder than event-based ones, we might suppose that people performing time-based tasks would be more likely to use deliberate self-initiated

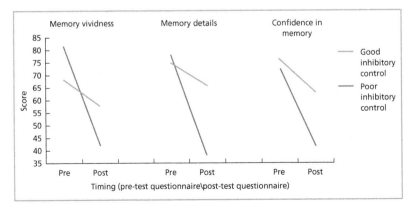

Figure 13.3 Mean scores for the pre-test and post-test repeated-checking questionnaire for participants with good and poor inhibitory control. Reprinted from Linkovski et al. (2013), Copyright © 2013, with permission from Elsevier.

processes to rehearse intended actions. In fact, however, Kvavilashvili and Fisher (2007) found the strategies were remarkably similar. In their study, participants made a phone call at a given time after an interval of 1 week (time-based task) or when they received a certain text message (event-based task) which arrived after 1 week.

Participants averaged nine rehearsals over the week with the time-based task and seven with the event-based task. About 50% of the rehearsals with both tasks occurred automatically (i.e. the task simply popped into the participant's head for no apparent reason) and very few (6% with the time-based task and 3% with the event-based tasks) involved deliberate retrieval of the task. Performance was better on the event-based task than the time-based task (100% vs. 53% punctual phone calls) because the text message in the event-based task provided a useful external cue.

Other evidence suggests that the differences between event-based and time-based prospective memory tasks can be much greater than appeared in the study by Kvavilashvili and Fisher (2007). Tarantino, Cona, Bianchin, and Bisiacchi (2010) argued that a crucial difference is that the occurrence of the prospective memory cue is typically much more *predictable* on time-based tasks than on event-based ones. As a result, people tend to engage in only sporadic monitoring of prospective memory cues on time-based tasks. This monitoring increased as the occurrence of the cue approaches. In contrast, there was much more evidence for continuous monitoring on event-based tasks.

Cona, Arcara, Tarantino, and Bisiacchi (2012) also reported clear-cut differences between event- and time-based prospective memory tasks. On the ongoing task, five letters were presented and participants decided whether the second and fourth letters were the same or different. At the same time, they performed an event-based task (detect the letter 'B' in the second or fourth position) or a time-based task (respond every 5 minutes). Cona et al. assessed processing activities by using *event-related potentials (ERPs)*, which reveal the electrophysiological reaction of the brain to specific stimuli over time.

What did Cona et al. (2012) discover? The effects of event-based and time-based tasks on event-related potentials are shown in Figure 13.4. Overall, the amplitude of the ERPs was greater in the event-based condition than in the time-based condition. The increased amplitude between 130–180 milliseconds after stimulus onset in the event-based condition may reflect the greater use of attentional resources in that condition. In contrast, the greater amplitude between 400–600 milliseconds in the event-based condition may be due to the greater frequency of target checking in the event-based condition.

Conclusions

Event-based prospective memory is generally (but not always) superior to time-based prospective memory. The main reason why event-based prospective memory is better is because responding is typically triggered by the presentation of environmental cues. However, prospective memory performance is also influenced by whether the task is well- or ill-specified. Continuous monitoring (involving attentional processes and

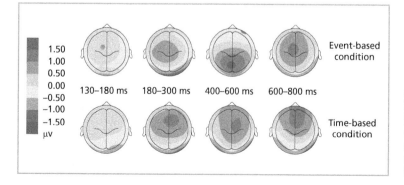

Figure 13.4 Scalp distribution of ERP differences in event-based and time-based prospective-memory conditions. From Cona et al. (2012). Copyright © G. Cona, G. Arcara, V. Tarantino, and P. S. Bisiacchi.

target checking) occurs more often with event-based than time-based prospective memory. In many cases, differences in monitoring and processing between event-based and time-based prospective memory occur because the cue for responding is more predictable with the latter type of prospective memory.

THEORETICAL PERSPECTIVES

One of the major theoretical controversies in the area of prospective memory concerns the appropriate answer to this question: Does successful prospective memory performance *always* involve active and capacity-consuming monitoring (e.g. attention)? Some theorists (e.g. Smith & Bayen, 2005) argue that the answer is "Yes," whereas others (e.g. Einstein & McDaniel, 2005) claim the answer is "No."

Preparatory attentional and memory processes (PAM) theory

We will start with Smith and Bayen's (2005) preparatory attentional and memory processes (PAM) theory. According to the PAM theory, two types of processes are always involved in successful prospective memory performance. First, there is a *monitoring process* that starts when someone forms an intention and is maintained until the required action is performed. Monitoring makes use of capacity-consuming processes such as those involved in attention.

Second, *retrospective memory processes* are involved. These processes are needed to discriminate between prospective memory targets and nontargets and in the recollection of the intended action. Retrospective memory is needed to ensure we remember *what* we are supposed to be doing in the future. In contrast, the monitoring process is needed so we perform the required action *when* the appropriate circumstances occur.

Smith, Hunt, McVay, and McConnell (2007) accepted that we are not constantly engaged in preparatory attentional processing over long periods of time. However, they argued that retrieval of intentions on prospective memory tasks always incurs a cost and is never automatic: "Successful performance of a prospective memory task accompanied by convincing evidence of no disruption of a sufficiently sensitive and demanding background task ... would falsify the PAM theory" (Smith et al., 2007, p. 735).

Findings

There is much support for the hypothesis that prospective memory tasks often require the use of attentional processes. McDaniel, Robinson-Riegler, and Einstein (1998) tested this hypothesis in a study in which participants performed a prospective memory task on its own (i.e. with full attention) or while performing a second demanding task (i.e. with divided attention). Prospective memory performance was much better with full than with divided attention, indicating that attentional processes can be important in prospective memory.

Are prospective memory tasks attentionally demanding even during periods of time in which no target stimuli requiring response are presented? Smith (2003) addressed this issue and answered "Yes" to the question. On trials when a target word was *not* presented, performance on the main task was much slower (approximately 45%) for participants performing the prospective memory task than for those not doing it.

In spite of the above findings, it is implausible that we *always* use preparatory attentional processes when trying to remember some future action. In fact, it often seems as if an intention to perform a predetermined action simply "pops" into our minds. Indeed, Kvavilashvili and Fisher (2007) found precisely that in the study discussed earlier.

Knight, Meeks, Marsh, Cook, Brewer, and Hicks (2011) obtained findings inconsistent with the PAM theory. The main task involved lexical decision (deciding whether strings of letters formed words), and the prospective memory task was to detect animal names starting with "C," The novel twist was that participants were told the prospective memory task would *only* be required later in the experiment. This was done to see what would happen when monitoring and attentional processes were not involved.

What did Knight et al. (2011) find? Knowing a prospective memory task would be required later had no effect on overall performance speed on the lexical decision task. Thus, there was *no* active monitoring of the letter strings on the lexical decision task. However, targets from the subsequent prospective memory task (e.g. "cougar") were spontaneously noticed and were recognized on a recognition memory test. Thus, as predicted by multi-process theory (but not by PAM theory), prospective memory cues can be noticed without conscious monitoring.

Multi-process theory

Einstein and McDaniel (2005) put forward a multi-process theory, according to which various cognitive processes (including attentional processes) *can* be used to perform prospective memory tasks. However, the detection of cues for response will typically be *automatic* (and thus not involve attentional processes) when the following criteria (especially the first one) are fulfilled:

1   The ongoing task (performed at the same time as the prospective memory task) stimulates processing of the target event on the prospective memory task.
2   The cue and the to-be-performed action are highly associated.
3   The cue is conspicuous or salient.
4   The intended action is simple.

Einstein and McDaniel (2005) argued that there is an important distinction between ongoing tasks that encourage processing of the target event on the prospective memory task (*focal* tasks) and those that do not (*nonfocal* tasks).

McDaniel and Einstein (2011) expanded on this argument. In essence, they argued that people engage in much more planning and monitoring for cues when performing nonfocal ongoing tasks than focal ones. They also argued that frontal brain systems are associated with such planning and monitoring activities.

Findings

There is much evidence (reviewed by McDaniel and Einstein, 2011) showing that frontal functioning is impaired in older individuals. It follows theoretically that aging should have a large effect on prospective memory when people are performing nonfocal ongoing tasks. In contrast, the negative effects of aging should be much less when focal ongoing tasks are being performed.

Kliegel, Phillips, and Jaeger (2008) carried out a meta-analysis of relevant studies. As predicted by the multi-process theory, the decline in prospective memory performance as a function of increasing age was greater when nonfocal ongoing tasks were used rather than focal ones. However, the difference was relatively small.

Uttl (2011) challenged the findings reported by Kliegel et al. (2008). He carried out his own meta-analysis and discovered that the age-related reduction in prospective memory performance with focal tasks was much larger than reported by Kliegel et al. (2008). The most likely reason why Uttl found a large effect of age even with focal tasks is that they typically involve the use of cognitive resources (e.g. retrieval of the intention). Whatever the precise explanation, Uttl's findings are inconsistent with the multi-process theory.

In spite of the negative findings discussed so far, much evidence supports the notion that targets on prospective memory tasks can sometimes be detected in the absence of monitoring. Indeed, the Knight et al. (2011) study discussed earlier provides such support. Another supportive study was carried out by Scullin and Bugg (2013). Participants carried out a main or ongoing task and a prospective memory task at the same time. They were then told that the prospective memory task had finished. In spite of that, 25% of the participants continued to respond to cues for the prospective memory task. This happened in the absence of any monitoring.

We have seen that Knight et al. (2011) and Scullin and Bugg (2013) found evidence that prospective memory targets can be responded to in the absence of monitoring. This is consistent with multi-process theory. That theory is further supported by the fact that focal ongoing tasks were used in both studies. These are precisely the tasks that theoretically should maximize the chances that prospective memory targets can be responded to automatically and without monitoring. Some of the research discussed in the next section (e.g. Bugg, Scullin, & McDaniel, 2013) also shows automatic detection of prospective memory targets.

Evaluation

There is much empirical support for both theories discussed in this section. As predicted by the PAM theory, cognitively demanding monitoring processes are typically involved on prospective memory tasks. These processes disrupt performance on ongoing tasks performed at the same time, also as predicted by the PAM theory. However, increasing evidence is inconsistent with the PAM theory and supports multi-process theory. This research evidence (e.g. Knight et al., 2011; Scullin & Bugg, 2013) indicates that prospective memory targets (especially with focal ongoing tasks) can sometimes be detected *automatically*. According to the multi-process theory, older individuals should show little or no impairment of prospective memory with focal ongoing tasks. It remains unclear why this prediction has not been supported by the evidence.

In sum, the research evidence overall is somewhat more consistent with the multi-process theory than with the PAM theory. One reason is that the former theory is more flexible and so can accommodate a wider range of findings. Gilbert, Hadjipaviou, and Raoelison (2013) provided additional support for the multi-process approach. They developed a computational model based on multi-process theory. This model (which included the assumption that prospective memory performance can sometimes be successful even with no monitoring) accounted successfully for ongoing and prospective memory task performance.

IMPROVING PROSPECTIVE MEMORY

There are several ways we can try to improve our prospective memory. For example, we saw earlier that failures of prospective memory often occur when we are interrupted when carrying out a plan of action (Dodhia & Dismukes, 2009). This problem can largely be overcome by forming an explicit intention to resume the interrupted task as soon as feasible.

Dismukes (2012) identified several other practical measures we can take to enhance prospective memory. One measure is to create salient and distinctive reminder cues and place them in locations where they are likely to be seen at the appropriate time for execution of the intention. Another measure is to avoid performing several other tasks at the same time because this will distract attention away from the prospective memory task.

Implementation intentions

One of the most effective techniques for enhancing prospective memory is based on the notion of implementation intentions. Implementation intentions "specify the when, where, and how of responses leading to goal attainment" (Gollwitzer, 1999, p. 494). More specifically, implementation intentions are of the following form: "If situation X is encountered, then I will initiate goal-directed behaviour X!" (Gollwitzer & Sheeran, 2006, p. 69).

We can see what is involved in implementation intentions by considering a study by Gollwitzer and Brandstätter (1997). Participants were instructed to write a report on how they spent Christmas Eve within 48 hours of that day. The intended goal (i.e. writing the report very shortly after Christmas) was achieved by 75% of those who formed

---

KEY TERM

Implementation intentions: Plans spelling out in detail how individuals are going to achieve the goals they have set themselves.

implementation intentions but by only 33% of those who did not.

Gollwitzer and Sheeran (2006) carried out a meta-analysis based on numerous studies. Overall, there was a moderately strong positive effect of implementation intentions on the probability of successfully completing the intention. Why are implementation intentions so effective? There are several reasons. Of most relevance here, explicitly linking cues to intentions during encoding should facilitate prospective memory by increasing the probability these cues will subsequently be detected and trigger retrieval of the appropriate intention. In addition, implementation intentions often enhance an individual's motivation to complete the intention.

Findings

Gollwitzer (1999) argued that forming an implementation intention is like forming an "instant habit." As a result, we might expect that the use of implementation intentions would reduce the processing costs when people retrieve their intentions on a prospective memory task. Supporting evidence was reported by McFarland and Glisky (2012). Participants were asked trivia questions as the main task. The prospective memory task involved detecting occasional usage of the word "state" within these questions, with some of the participants having received implementation intentions beforehand. At the same time as the other two tasks, participants listened to digits and responded when they heard two consecutive odd ones.

What did McFarland and Glisky (2012) find? First, performance on the prospective memory task was better in the implementation intention condition than in the control condition (54% detection rate vs. 31%, respectively). Second, participants in the implementation intention condition detected more pairs of odd digits than those in the control condition (59% vs. 35%, respectively). These findings suggest that implementation intentions led to relatively automatic identification of targets on the prospective memory task, thereby freeing up processing resources to detect pairs of odd digits.

Rummel, Einstein, and Rampey (2012) found that participants who had received

implementation intention instructions performed better than controls on a prospective memory task incorporated within an ongoing task. They identified two possible explanations for the performance advantage associated with implementation instructions: (1) these instructions increased attentional monitoring for prospective memory targets; (2) these instructions produced relatively automatic and spontaneous retrieval of intentions.

Rummel et al. (2012) obtained support for the second explanation. They used a series of trials on which participants were instructed *not* to respond when target words from the prospective memory task were presented. These target words caused more disruption to the ongoing task for participants previously given implementation intentions because participants were more likely to retrieve their intentions automatically.

Rummel et al.'s (2012) findings suggest that people find it hard to switch off implementation intentions when they are no longer required. Stronger evidence was reported by Bugg et al. (2013). Participants carried out a prospective memory task using implementation intentions or with standard instructions. After that, they were told that the prospective memory task had finished. Participants previously given implementation intentions were twice as likely as those given standard instructions to mistakenly continue to respond to prospective memory cues.

Conclusions

Performance on prospective memory tasks is generally improved by the use of implementation intentions. This probably happens because implementation intentions strengthen the associations between cues and intentions and thus permit intentions to be retrieved automatically. Implementation intentions may prove valuable in encouraging patients to adhere to their medication schedule (Zogg et al., 2012).

The main limitation associated with the use of implementation intentions is that it is hard to deactivate them when they are no longer required. This is unsurprising since it is generally difficult to alter automatic processes.

SUMMARY

- Prospective memory focuses on the future, whereas retrospective memory focuses on the past.
- Another important difference between the two forms of memory is that only prospective memory is intimately related to our plans and goals.
- Remembering and forgetting in the real world typically involve a mixture of prospective memory and retrospective memory.
- Prospective memory can be event-based (respond when some event occurs) or time-based (respond at a given time).
- Failures of prospective memory can have serious consequences (e.g. fatal airplane crashes; impaired health if medication is not taken).
- Prospective memory involves a series of stages: intention formation; retention interval; cue detection and intention retrieval; intention recall; and intention execution.
- Our knowledge of the effectiveness (or otherwise) of our own prospective memory is limited.
- Pilot errors are due far more to failures of prospective memory than of retrospective memory. Such prospective memory errors are especially likely to occur when a pilot is interrupted while carrying out a sequence of actions and fails to generate a new plan of action.
- Memory problems in compulsive checkers involve prospective memory and are due in part to low confidence in their memory ability. Poor prospective memory partly causes excessive checking and that excessive checking partly causes poor prospective memory.
- Event-based prospective memory is generally better than time-based prospective memory because the former involves explicit environmental cues. However, performance differences between the two types of prospective memory depend in part on how well-specified the task is.
- Continuous monitoring is more common with event-based tasks than time-based tasks because the occurrence of the cue for response is more predictable in the latter case.
- According to the preparatory attentional and memory processes (PAM) theory, successful prospective memory always requires a capacity-demanding monitoring process and retrospective memory.
- In contrast, it is claimed in the multi-process theory that monitoring is required with nonfocal ongoing tasks but can be automatic with focal ongoing tasks. On balance, the evidence is more supportive of the multi-process theory than of the PAM theory.
- The use of implementation intentions typically enhances prospective memory. It does this by strengthening the associations between cues and intentions and thus producing automatic retrieval of intentions. The downside is that implementation intentions can be hard to switch off when no longer of relevance.

POINTS FOR DISCUSSION

What are the main differences between retrospective memory and prospective memory?
What are the main types of prospective memory? How do they differ?
What role does monitoring play in prospective memory?
What can be done to enhance our prospective memory?

FURTHER READING

Dismukes, R. K. (2010). Remembrance of things future: Prospective memory in laboratory, workplace, and everyday settings. In D. H. Harris (Ed.), *Reviews of human factors and ergonomics* (Vol. 6, pp. 79–122). Santa Monica, CA: Human Factors and Ergonomics Society. R. Key Dismukes, a leading expert in aviation psychology, provides a comprehensive account of research in laboratory and real-life settings.

Einstein, G. O., & McDaniel, M. A. (2005). Prospective memory: Multiple retrieval processes. *Current Directions in Psychological Science, 14,* 286–290. In this article, Gilles Einstein and Mark McDaniel present their influential multi-process theory of prospective memory.

Graf, P. (2012). Prospective memory: Faulty brain, flaky person. *Canadian Psychology, 53,* 7–13. Peter Graf identifies several reasons why prospective memory is of major importance in everyday life.

Smith, R. E. (Ed.) (2011). *Prospective memory.* Göttingen: Hogrefe Verlag. This edited book contains chapters by leading experts on prospective memory.

REFERENCES

Bugg, J. M., Scullin, M. K., & McDaniel, M. A. (2013). Strengthening encoding via implementation intention formation increases prospective memory commission errors. *Psychonomic Bulletin and Review, 20,* 522–527.

Cona, G., Arcara, G., Tarantino, V., & Bisiacchi, P. S. (2012). Electrophysiological correlates of strategic monitoring in event-based and time-based prospective memory. *PLoS ONE, 7*(2): e31659 doi: 0.1371/journal.pone.003 1659

Crawford, J. R., Smith, G., Maylor, E. A., Della Sala, S., & Logie, R. H. (2003). The Prospective and Retrospective Memory Questionnaire (PRMQ): Normative data and latent structure in a large non-clinical sample. *Memory, 11,* 261–275.

Cuttler, C., & Graf, P. (2009a). Checking-in on the memory deficit and meta-memory deficit theories of compulsive checking. *Clinical Psychology Review, 29,* 393–409.

Cuttler, C., & Graf, P. (2009b). Sub-clinical compulsive checkers show impaired performance on habitual, event- and time-cued episodic prospective memory tasks. *Journal of Anxiety Disorders, 23,* 813–823.

Cuttler, C., Sirois-Delisle, V., Alcolado, G. M., Radomsky, A. S., & Taylor, S. (2013). Diminished confidence in prospective memory causes doubts

and urges to check. *Journal of Behavior Therapy and Experimental Psychiatry, 44,* 329–334.

Dismukes, R. K. (2012). Prospective memory in workplace and everyday situations. *Current Directions in Psychological Science, 21,* 215–220.

Dismukes, R. K., & Nowinski, J. L. (2006). Prospective memory, concurrent task management, and pilot error. In A. Kramer, D. Wiegmann, & A. Kirlik (Eds.), *Attention: From theory to practice.* Oxford: Oxford University Press.

Dodhia, R. M., & Dismukes, K. R. (2009). Interruptions create prospective memory tasks. *Applied Cognitive Psychology, 23,* 73–89.

Einstein, G. O., & McDaniel, M. A. (2005). Prospective memory: Multiple retrieval processes. *Current Directions in Psychological Science, 14,* 286–290.

Freud, S. (1901). *The psychopathology of everyday life.* New York: W. W. Norton.

Gilbert, S. J., Hadjipaviou, N., & Raoelison, M. (2013). Automaticity and control in prospective memory: A computational model. *PLoS ONE, 8*(3), e59852.

Gollwitzer, P. M. (1999). Implementation intentions. *American Psychologist, 54,* 493–503.

Gollwitzer, P. M., & Brandstätter, V. (1997). Implementation intentions and effective goal pursuit. *Journal of Personality and Social Psychology, 73,* 186–199.

Gollwitzer, P. M., & Sheeran, P. (2006). Implementation intentions and goal achievement:

A meta-analysis of effects and processes. *Advances in Experimental Social Psychology, 38,* 69–119.

Graf, P. (2012). Prospective memory: Faulty brain, flaky person. *Canadian Psychology, 53,* 7–13.

Hicks, J. L., Marsh, R. L., & Cook, G. I. (2005). Task interference in time-based, event-based, and dual intention prospective memory conditions. *Journal of Memory and Language, 53,* 430–444.

Kim, P. Y., & Mayhorn, C. B. (2008). Exploring students' prospective memory inside and outside the lab. *American Journal of Psychology, 121,* 241–254.

Kliegel, M., Phillips, L. H., & Jaeger, T. (2008). Adult age differences in event-based prospective memory: A meta-analysis on the role of focal versus nonfocal cues. *Psychology and Aging, 23,* 203–208.

Knight, J. B., Meeks, J. T., Marsh, R. L., Cook, G. I., Brewer, G. A., & Hicks, J. L. (2011). An observation on the spontaneous noticing of prospective memory event-based cues. *Journal of Experimental Psychology: Learning, Memory, and Cognition, 37,* 298–307.

Kvavilashvili, L., & Fisher, L. (2007). Is time-based prospective remembering mediated by self-initiated rehearsals? Role of incidental cues, ongoing activity, age, and motivation. *Journal of Experimental Psychology: General, 136,* 112–132.

Linkovski, O., Kalanthroff, E., Henik, A., & Anholt, G. (2013). Did I turn off the stove? Good inhibitory control can protect from influences of repeated checking. *Journal of Behavior Therapy and Experimental Psychiatry, 44,* 30–36.

Loft, S., & Remington, R. W. (2010). Prospective memory and task interference in a continuous monitoring dynamic display task. *Journal of Experimental Psychology: Applied, 16,* 145-157.

Loft, S., Smith, R. E., & Bhaskara, A. (2011). Prospective memory in an air traffic control simulation: External aids that signal when to act. *Journal of Experimental Psychology: Applied, 17,* 60–70.

Mäntylä, T. (2003). Assessing absentmindedness: Prospective memory complaint and impairment in middle-aged adults. *Memory and Cognition, 31,* 15–25.

Marsh, R. L., Hicks, J. L., & Landau, J. D. (1998). An investigation of everyday prospective memory and executive control of working memory. *Journal of Experimental Psychology: Learning, Memory and Cognition, 24,* 336–349.

McDaniel, M. A., & Einstein, G. O. (2011). The neuropsychology of prospective memory in normal aging: A componential approach. *Neuropsychologia, 49,* 2147–2155.

McDaniel, M. A., Robinson-Riegler, B., & Einstein, G. O. (1998). Prospective remembering:

Perceptually driven or conceptually driven processes? *Memory and Cognition, 26,* 121–134.

McFarland, C., & Glisky, E. (2012). Implementation intentions and imagery: Individual and combined effects on prospective memory among young adults. *Memory and Cognition, 40,* 62–69.

Moscovitch, M. (2008). Commentary: A perspective on prospective memory. In M. Kliegel, M. A. McDaniel, & G. O. Einstein (Eds.), *Prospective memory: Cognitive, neuroscience, developmental, and applied perspectives* (pp. 309–320). New York: Lawrence Erlbaum Associates.

Rummel, J., Einstein, G. O., & Rampey, H. (2012). Implementation-intention encoding in a prospective memory task enhances spontaneous retrieval of intentions. *Memory, 20,* 803–817.

Schnitzspahn, K. M., Zeintl, M., Jäger, T., & Kliegel, M. (2011). Metacognition in prospective memory: Are performance predictions accurate? *Canadian Journal of Experimental Psychology, 65,* 19–26.

Scullin, M. K., & Bugg, J. M. (2013). Failing to forget: Prospective memory commission errors can result from spontaneous retrieval and impaired executive control. *Journal of Experimental Psychology: Learning, Memory, and Cognition, 39,* 965–971.

Shorrock, S. T. (2005). Errors of memory in air traffic control. *Safety Science, 43,* 571–588.

Smith, R. E. (2003). The cost of remembering to remember in event-based prospective memory: Investigating the capacity demands of delayed intention performance. *Journal of Experimental Psychology: Learning, Memory, and Cognition, 29,* 347–361.

Smith, R. E., & Bayen, U. J. (2005). The effects of working memory resource availability on prospective memory: A formal modeling approach. *Experimental Psychology, 52,* 243–256.

Smith, R. E., Hunt, R .R., McVay, J. C., & McConnell, M. D. (2007). The cost of event-based prospective memory: Salient target events. *Journal of Experimental Psychology: Learning, Memory, and Cognition, 33,* 734–746.

Tarantino, V., Cona, G., Bianchin, M., & Bisiacchi, P. S. (2010). Monitoring mechanisms in time- and event-based prospective memory: Third International Conference on Prospective Memory, Vancouver, Canada, July 28–30.

Uttl, B. (2011). Transparent meta-analysis: Does aging spare prospective memory with focal vs. non-focal cues? *PLoS ONE, 6*(2): e16618. doi:10.1371/journal.pone.0016618

Van den Hout, M., & Kindt, M. (2004). Obsessive-compulsive disorder and the paradoxical effects of perseverative behavior on experienced uncertainty.

Journal of Behavior Therapy and Experimental Psychiatry, 35, 165–181.

Woods, S. P., Dawson, M. S., Weber, E., Gibson, S., Grant, I., Atkinson, J .H., et al. (2009). Timing is everything: Antiretroviral nonadherence is associated with impairment in time-based prospective memory. *Journal of the International Neuropsychological Society, 15,* 42–52.

Zimprich, D., Kliegel, M., & Rast, P. (2011). The factorial structure and external validity of the Prospective and Retrospective Memory Questionnaire in older adults. *European Journal of Ageing, 8,* 3–48.

Zogg, J. B., Woods, S. P., Sauceda, J. A., Wiebe, J. S., & Simoni, J .M. (2012). The role of prospective memory in medication adherence: A review of an emerging literature. *Journal of Behavioral Medicine, 35,* 47–62.

Contents

Introduction   381

Memory in infants   383

Developmental changes in memory during childhood   387

Implicit memory   392

Autobiographical memory and infantile amnesia   394

Children as witnesses   398

Summary   404

Points for discussion   405

Further reading   405

References   406

CHAPTER 14

MEMORY IN CHILDHOOD

Michael W. Eysenck

INTRODUCTION

Think back to your early childhood. What is the earliest memory you can bring to mind? What age were you at the time? What else can you remember from that period? Perhaps you remember only one or two isolated incidents.

Don't worry if you find it hard to think of any very early memories. Most people remember very little (if anything) of what occurred before the age of 2 or 3. For example, Rubin (2000) combined data from numerous studies in which adults reported autobiographical memories (memories of specific events that had happened to them in the past). Of those memories based on events occurring before the age of 11, only 1% occurred before the age of 3.

More generally, systematic studies of autobiographical memory suggest that adults have a dearth of memories before the age of about 4 years. This phenomenon is known as *infantile amnesia* (alternatively, childhood amnesia), and is also discussed in Chapter 11.

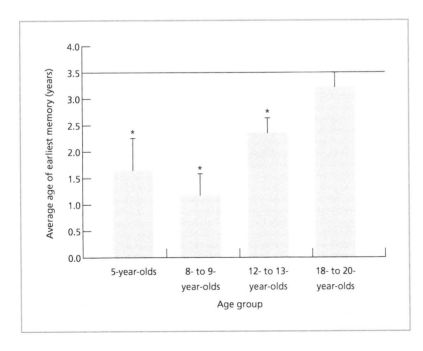

Figure 14.1 Findings from Tustin and Hayne's (2010) study of the earliest memories of children between the ages of 5 and 9 were from about 1½ years. From Tustin and Hayne (2010). Copyright © American Psychological Association. Reprinted with permission.

Most studies on infantile amnesia have asked *adults* to think of memories from early childhood. What would happen if we asked children and adolescents to provide early memories? Tustin and Hayne (2010) did precisely that. The earliest memories of children between the ages of 5 and 9 were from about 1½ years on average, those of adolescents were from 2½ years, and those of adults were from just over 3 years (see Figure 14.1).

What do the above findings mean? First, the boundaries of childhood amnesia are more *flexible* that has often been assumed. Second, one reason why most adults cannot recall any memories from the first 3 years of life is simply because those memories have been forgotten over the years.

Although the existence of infantile amnesia has been known for a very long time, it remains fairly hard to study. One problem is that it is not easy to assess the accuracy of adults' claimed memories of early childhood given that several decades might have passed since the events allegedly occurred.

One way forward is to focus on significant events that can be precisely dated and verified by a third party. The birth of a brother or sister falls into this category and has been investigated in several studies. In one study, Sheingold and Tenney (1982) asked college students and children aged 4, 6, 8, and 12 to recall the birth of a brother or sister that occurred when they were aged between 3 and 11 years. They were asked questions such as, "Who took care of you while your mother was in hospital?", "Did the baby receive presents?" The mothers were asked the same questions.

There was surprisingly little forgetting among participants who had been at least 3 years old at the time, regardless of the length of time that had elapsed since the event (see Figure 14.2). However, children who were under 3 years old when their brother or sister was born remembered very little.

Another issue is deciding whether adults' reported memories of early childhood are *genuine* recollections or are based on knowledge obtained from others (e.g. parents). In a study by Crawley and Eacott (2006), adults recalled events from their childhood. Memories the adults believed to be genuine differed in several ways from *those* based on second-hand

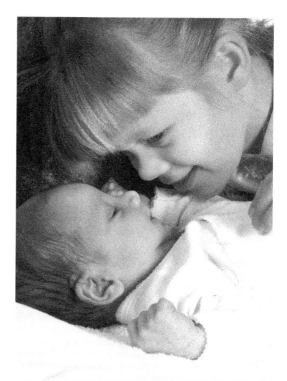

In Sheingold and Tenney's (1982) study, children who had been under 3 years old when their brother or sister was born remembered virtually nothing, providing strong evidence for infantile amnesia. Children older than 3 at the time had surprisingly strong memories for the event.

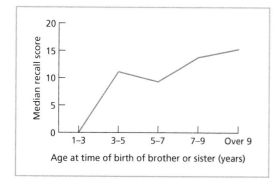

Figure 14.2 When college students were asked to recall the birth of a sibling, they remembered virtually nothing if the event had occurred before they were 3 years old: an example of infantile amnesia (Sheingold & Tenney, 1982).

knowledge. The former memories were more pictorial and less verbal than the latter ones; they involved more feelings, and were more complex. These findings suggest that most of their childhood memories that adults regard as true recollections may well actually be genuine.

MEMORY IN INFANTS

It is easier said than done to assess the memory abilities of infants. The most serious problem is that infants' language abilities are either virtually nonexistent or very limited in scope. As a result, experimenters cannot use verbal instructions to tell infants what they are to learn. Another issue is that (as you may have noticed) infants constantly shift their attention from one object to another.

In addition, tests of memory (unlike those in studies on older children and adults) typically require infants to produce certain motor responses, in view of their inability to report verbally what they have learned. Even when memory is assessed by motor responses, the limited motor skills possessed by infants under the age of 12 months means there are real constraints on the kinds of memory tasks that are suitable. As we will see, however, ingenious experimenters have surmounted all these problems.

There is a further, more intractable, problem. The necessary reliance on nonverbal memory responses when testing infants means it is very hard (or impossible) to assess the extent to which they are consciously aware of what they remember. More specifically, how do we decide whether infants' memories on any given task involve implicit memory (not involving conscious recollection) or explicit memory (involving conscious recollection)? Various criteria for identifying a task as one involving explicit memory have been proposed (Rovee-Collier & Cuevas, 2009). These include memory formation in one trial, long-term memory in the absence of practice immediately after learning, and impaired performance on the task by amnesic patients.

Theoretical considerations

Rovee-Collier and Cuevas (2009) contrast traditional views about memory development in infancy with their own ecological model. Traditionally, it was assumed that infants during the first year of life were capable only of simple implicit learning and memory for perceptual and motor skills. Such learning was acquired gradually by providing positive reinforcement or reward for correct responses. In contrast, it was argued that infants could not form explicit or declarative memories until toward the end of the first year. For example, Richmond and Nelson (2007, p. 351) argued that maturation of the hippocampus in infancy results in "adult-like explicit memory capabilities at around 8 months of age." This maturational hypothesis is discussed more fully later on.

Rovee-Collier and Cuevas's (2009) ecological model makes very different assumptions. They argued that basic memory processes do not change with increasing age. Instead, *what* infants learn differs considerably from what is learned by slightly older children. Infants during the first several months of life cannot move independently. Partly as a result of this, such infants are very good at associating whatever they see together in a *nonselective* fashion. In the words of Rovee-Collier and Giles (2010, p. 205), infants up to the age of about 8 months experience "a period of rapid and exuberant learning."

When infants achieve independent locomotion (i.e. crawling) at around 9 months of age, they encounter a substantially greater number of objects. This leads them to become increasingly selective in the associations they form.

What differences in infant learning and memory are predicted by these two theoretical approaches? First, the traditional approach predicts that infants under the age of 1 should have very limited learning and memory abilities. In contrast, the ecological model predicts that "very young infants spontaneously and rapidly associate stimuli that merely appear together in their surround" (Rovee-Collier, Mitchell, & Hsu-Yang, 2013, p. 4).

Second, the traditional approach predicts that all forms of learning and memory will tend to improve with increasing age. In contrast, the ecological model predicts that younger infants should *surpass* older infants when learning and remembering certain kinds of information (e.g. associating two stimuli presented together).

Various memory tasks have been used to test the above differing predictions of the two theoretical approaches. Here we will focus on three such tasks: the mobile conjugate reinforcement task; deferred imitation; and sensory preconditioning. Research using all of these tasks with infants is reviewed by Rovee-Collier and Cuevas (2009).

Findings: Mobile and train tasks

Rovee-Collier (1989) argued that it is important when assessing learning in babies to use situations that interest and motivate them; otherwise there is a real danger of underestimating how much they can learn and remember. She achieved this by suspending a mobile over the baby's crib and attaching it to the baby's foot via a ribbon (see Figure 14.3). When the baby kicked, the mobile moved. Young babies seem to enjoy this because they rapidly learn to kick when the mobile is present.

The task used by Rovee-Collier (given the unwieldy name of the mobile conjugate reinforcement task) has three distinct phases. First, there is a baseline phase during which the ribbon attached to the infant's foot is also attached to the side of the crib but not the mobile.

Second, there is the learning phase during which the ribbon attached to the infant's foot is also attached to the mobile. During this phase, the infant learns that kicking (a response) causes the mobile to move (the reward or reinforcement).

Finally, there is the test phase. In this phase, the ribbon is once again attached to the side of the crib but not to the mobile. Memory is shown when the infant's rate of kicking is greater than in the baseline phase. The strength of the infant's memory can be assessed by varying the length of time between the learning and test phases.

Rovee-Collier (1989) found that the level of kicking responses of 2-month-olds dropped to the baseline level when there was a gap of 2 days between learning and test. This indicates that they remembered what they had learned for a relatively short period of time. In contrast, the 3-month-olds still showed a reliable effect of learning after a week.

Rovee-Collier (1989) also considered the effect of presenting a *reminder*. This consisted of a moving mobile (controlled by the experimenter) presented to the infants some time before being tested. This reminder resulted in memory returning virtually to its initial level even when testing took place after a delay of 2 weeks. More strikingly, the reminder reactivated a significant amount of kicking at a delay of 1 month. These findings indicate that even very young infants can show good long-term memory.

A limitation of the mobile conjugate reinforcement paradigm is that it is only suitable for use with infants up to the age of about 7 months. However, a similar task known as the train task is suitable for older infants. On this task, infants learn to press a lever to make a miniature train move around a track.

The most dramatic findings using the train task were reported by Hartshorn (2003). Infants aged 6 months learned this task and then received five reminders (2-minute additional reinforcement sessions) at 7, 8, 9, 12, and 18 months of age. Their retention of what they had learned at 6 months was tested when they were 24 months old. There was significant evidence of long-term memory 18 months after learning even though the infants had received only one reminder in the preceding 12 months.

How can we explain the strongly beneficial effects of reminders on infants' long-term memory? Hsu (2010) argued that the reminder triggers retrieval of the original memory and the

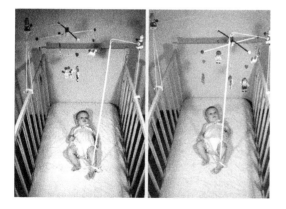

Figure 14.3 An infant in Rovee-Collier's causal contingency paradigm (left) during baseline, when kicking cannot activate the mobile and (right) during acquisition, when the ankle ribbon is attached to the mobile. From Rovee-Collier, Sullivan, Enright, Lucas, and Fagen (1980). Copyright © 1980 AAAS. Reprinted with permission.

two memories are then integrated. Of key importance, this integration process can occur *only* when the reminder is presented before the original memory has been forgotten. Thus, there is a time period after the original memory is formed (which Hsu calls a *time window*) during which reminders enhance infants' long-term memory.

Hsu (2010) tested the notion of a time window using the train task with infants aged between 6 and 18 months. These infants were given a reminder (brief second training session) just inside the time window or just outside it. After that, all of the infants were given a memory test on the train task. Hsu's findings are shown in Figure 14.4. As predicted, the reminder failed to enhance long-term memory when presented *outside* the time window. In contrast, the reminder had a strong enhancing effect on memory when presented *inside* the time window.

In sum, the findings from the mobile and train tasks indicate that long-term memory can be exhibited at surprisingly young ages. Of special note is the finding (Hartshorn, 2003) that 6-month-olds can retain information over an 18-month period. When a reminder is provided within the time window (period during which the original memory is still accessible), it triggers retrieval of the original memory and memory integration. Overall, these findings indicate that very young infants can have longer-lasting memories than predicted with the traditional approach.

Findings: Deferred imitation

What happens with deferred imitation tasks is that infants observe target actions. Long-term memory is shown if the infants can reproduce some (or all) of these actions after a delay (i.e. deferred imitation). It has been argued (e.g. Richmond & Nelson, 2007) that deferred imitation is an explicit memory task. If so, it would be expected with the traditional approach that infants under the age of approximately 9 months would show little or no deferred imitation.

Early studies suggested that the length of delay over which 6-month-olds showed deferred imitation was only 1 day. However, it has proved relatively easy to obtain deferred imitation at much longer retention intervals. Consider, for example, research by Barr, Rovee-Collier, and Campanella (2005). When 6-month-olds saw the target actions modeled for a second time 1 day after the original presentation, they showed evidence of deferred imitation over a 10-day period. When they had the opportunity to engage in repeated

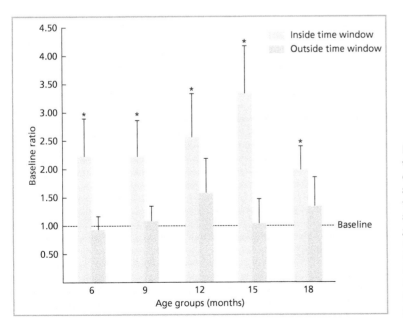

Figure 14.4 Memory for the train task in children of different ages who received a reminder inside or outside the time window (TW). The asterisk indicates that a given group showed significantly memory compared to the baseline control condition. Results from Hsu (2010). Copyright © John Wiley & Sons, reproduced with permission.

retrieval of the actions, deferred imitation was found 10 weeks after learning.

Rovee-Collier and Cuevas (2009) combined the data from ten studies on 6-month-olds. Deferred imitation was found in 83% of these infants 7 days after learning. However, what 6-month-old infants learn is more limited than what 9- and 12-month-old infants learn. Patel, Gaylord, and Fagen (2013) found that 6-month-olds only showed deferred imitation when the testing environment was *identical* to the one in which learning occurred. In contrast, the learning of older infants was more extensive. As a result, they continued to show deferred imitation even when the testing environment was not identical to the learning one.

Can infants younger than 6 months show deferred imitation? One obstacle to answering this question is that younger infants are not sufficiently coordinated to perform the target actions. However, Campanella and Rovee-Collier (2005) presented target actions to 3-month-olds and then provided them with periodic reminders of those actions over the following 3 months. When these infants were tested at the age of 6 months, they showed evidence of deferred imitation.

In sum, deferred imitation has been found in infants as young as 3 months at the time of learning. There is substantial evidence that 6-month-olds can retain memory of target actions over periods of several weeks. These findings are more consistent with the ecological model than with the traditional approach.

Findings: Sensory preconditioning

As mentioned earlier, the ecological model assumes that infants during the first 6 months of life exhibit a good ability to associate stimuli that are presented close to each other, even when they are not rewarded or reinforced for so doing. This form of association is known as sensory preconditioning.

KEY TERM

Sensory preconditioning: An association between two stimuli that is established prior to the start of conditioning.

Sensory preconditioning in infants of 6 and 9 months was studied by Giles and Rovee-Collier (2011). In Phase 1, the infant formed an association between a pink rabbit and a yellow duck (see Figure 14.5). The infants were exposed to the two animals together for 60 minutes in one experiment and for two 30-minute sessions with the two animals on a single day in another experiment. In Phase 2, the infant saw three target actions modeled on the rabbit. Finally, in Phase 3, the infant was tested with the duck to see whether he/she could imitate the actions previously modeled on the rabbit (see Figure 14.5). It was assumed that an ability to do so indicated memory for the initial association between the rabbit and the duck in Phase 1 and was thus evidence for sensory preconditioning.

What did Giles and Rovee-Collier (2011) find? First, the infants retained information about the association between the two animals far longer when the animals were presented for two 30-minute sessions than when they were presented once for 60 minutes. It is known that memories are strengthened simply by retrieving them (see earlier discussion and section on the testing effect in Chapter 17). Thus, retrieval of what had been learned in the first 30-minute session at the outset of the second 30-minute session likely explains this finding.

Second, the 6-month-old infants showed *longer* retention of the association between the two animals than the 9-month-olds. This was especially the case when the animals were initially presented for two 30-minute sessions.

Figure 14.5 These photos show infants with the pink rabbit and yellow duck used by Giles and Rovee-Collier in their study of sensory preconditioning. Reprinted from Giles and Rovee-Collier (2011), Copyright © 2011, with permission from Elsevier.

In this condition, the 6-month-olds showed long-term memory for 28 days whereas the 9-month-olds only did so for 14 days.

In sum, the various findings generally support the ecological model. They show that young infants have very good long-term memory for associations between objects that are seen together. Strikingly, younger infants remember such associations for *longer* periods of time than older ones. This suggests that forming associations between adjacent objects is of particular importance to infants before they reach the stage of independent locomotion.

DEVELOPMENTAL CHANGES IN MEMORY DURING CHILDHOOD

We have seen that young children show considerable improvements in declarative memory (memory involving conscious recollection) over the first 2 or 3 years of life. There is overwhelming evidence that the development of declarative memory continues for many years after infancy, at least until adolescence. In this section, we first consider explanations for the progressive improvements in declarative memory throughout childhood. Then, we consider circumstances in which errors in memory actually *increase* as children develop! Finally, we discuss differences in the development of declarative and implicit memory.

Development of declarative memory

Why does declarative memory in children become progressively better during the process of development? Siegler (1998) identified *four* possible answers to this question:

1   The capacity of short-term memory or working memory may increase over the years.
2   Children develop more memory strategies (e.g. rehearsing the to-be-remembered information) as they develop, and they also learn to use these strategies more efficiently.

3   Older children possess much more knowledge than younger ones which makes it easier for them to learn and to remember new information.
4   There is *metamemory*, which is the knowledge we possess about our own memory and how it works. Metamemory develops during the course of childhood, and it is likely that children with good metamemory can use their memory systems more effectively than those with poor or nonexistent metamemory.

Bear in mind that the above four factors are *not* entirely separate from each other. All aspects of the memory system are connected in some way with all the other aspects. As a result, what we will do is consider the memory system in children from various perspectives. We return to this interconnectedness issue at the end of the section.

Basic capacity

As we saw in Chapter 4, the working memory system as described by Baddeley (e.g. 1986, 2007) originally consisted of three components. There was a central executive (resembling an attentional system), a phonological loop (used for verbal rehearsal), and a visuo-spatial sketchpad that stores visual and spatial information briefly. There is substantial evidence that the working memory system is of crucial importance for the processing and performance of numerous tasks (see Chapter 3). More recently, Baddeley (2001) added a fourth component (the episodic buffer) that integrates information from the other components.

The working memory model has mostly been tested on adults. In view of the general significance of the working memory system, it is thus of considerable importance to see whether there are developmental changes in some (or all) of its components. We will ignore the episodic buffer because there is, as yet, relatively little information concerning developmental changes in its capacity.

The first issue to be addressed is whether the structure of the working memory system remains reasonably constant as a function of age. This issue was addressed by Michalczyk, Malstädt, Worgt, Könen, and

Hasselhorn (2012) in a study on children aged between 5 and 12 years. They found the same three components originally identified by Baddeley were also present in children throughout the age range 5 to 12. In addition, the strength of the relationships among the three components was very similar across that age range.

The most thorough investigation of developmental changes in the capacity of the three original components of the working memory system was reported by Gathercole, Pickering, Ambridge, and Wearing (2004). They studied boys and girls between the ages of 4 and 15 who performed a range of memory tasks relevant to working memory.

What did Gathercole et al. (2004) discover? First, there were progressive improvements year by year in all three components of the working memory system (see Figure 14.6). It seems reasonable that much of the enhanced overall memory performance during childhood is attributable to the large increases in the capacity of these three components. Second, the structure of working memory was fairly constant (a finding subsequently confirmed by Michalczyk et al., 2012). Thus, even children as young as 6 have a functioning phonological loop, visuo-spatial sketchpad, and central executive.

What causes these age-related changes in the capacity of the various components of

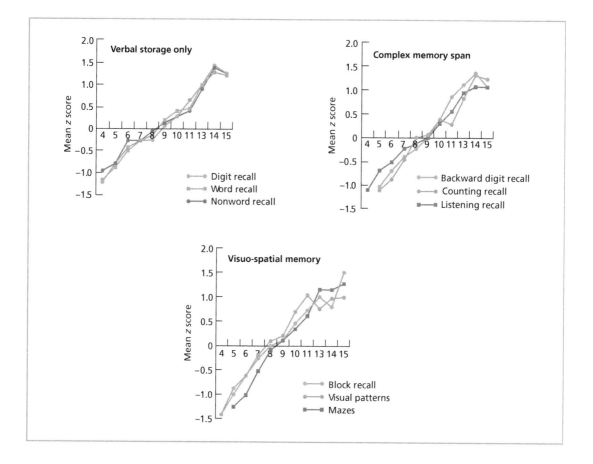

Figure 14.6 Developmental changes in verbal storage only (phonological loop), complex memory span (central executive), and visuo-spatial memory (visuo-spatial sketchpad) between the ages of 4 and 15 expressed in mean z-scores. From Gathercole et al. (2004). Copyright © American Psychological Association. Reprinted with permission.

working memory? Many factors are undoubtedly involved. However, structural changes in the brain involving a fronto-parietal network are probably of special importance. The limitation with most research in this area is that the data obtained typically reveal associations or correlations between enhanced working memory functioning and maturation of brain structures.

More direct evidence was reported by Tamnes, Walhovd, Grydeland, Holland, Ostby, Dale, et al. (2013) in a study on children and adolescents. They assessed working memory functioning (mainly the central executive) and structural changes in the brain at two points in time. Their key finding was that improvement in working memory over time was related to structural changes within the fronto-parietal network. As Tamnes et al. (2013, p. 1611) concluded, these findings "provide the first direct evidence that structural maturation of a fronto-parietal network supports working memory development."

Content knowledge

One of the most obvious differences between older and younger children is that older ones possess much more knowledge of nearly all kinds. This is undoubtedly of major importance to understanding the development of memory because memory is generally better when the learner can relate what he/she is learning to relevant stored knowledge (see Chapter 7). It is also the case that many mnemonics designed to enhance long-term memory involve making use of pre-existing knowledge to organize new to-be-learned information (see Chapter 17).

If the amount of knowledge possessed by the learner is a key determinant of memory performance, then a well-informed child might remember some things better than an ill-informed adult. This prediction was tested by Chi (1978), who studied digit recall and reproduction of chess positions in 10-year-olds skilled at chess and adults knowing little about chess. The adult performed better than the children in digit recall. However, the children's recall of chess positions was over 50% higher than that of the adults (see Figure 14.7).

Schneider, Gruber, Gruber, Gold, and Opwis (1993) compared children and adults with similar chess expertise. Both groups remembered

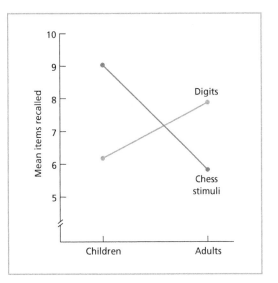

Figure 14.7 Immediate recall of chess positions and digits in children (mean age 10 years 6 months) with expert knowledge of chess and in adults with limited knowledge of chess. Adapted from Chi (1978).

chess positions equally well and much better than nonexpert children and adults. Thus, memory for chess positions depends largely on expertise and very little on age.

Memory strategies

When adults try to remember information, they typically use various memory strategies (e.g. verbal rehearsal, mnemonics) to assist

Schneider, Gruber, Gruber, Gold, and Opwis (1993) discovered that memory for chess positions depends largely on expertise and hardly at all on age.

them. Unsurprisingly, older children are much more likely than younger ones to use a range of memory strategies in their learning. Much research in this area has involved categorized list recall, and so we will focus on that task here. What typically happens is that participants are presented with a certain number of words belonging to various categories (e.g. four-footed animals, articles of clothing). These words are presented in *random* order and the list presentation is followed by free recall (recall of the list words in any order).

Most adults given the above task use an organizational strategy in which they rehearse the words category by category. Their subsequent recall is also organized strongly on a categorical basis. This organizational strategy is effective because adults whose rehearsal and recall are strongly organized in categories recall more than those whose rehearsal and recall are less organized (Weist, 1972).

What do children do when learning categorized word lists with the items presented in random order? Schneider, Knopf, and Stefanek (2002) addressed this issue in a longitudinal study on children between the ages of 8 and 17. The children were presented with four pictures belonging to each of six categories (e.g. animals, food) and could arrange these pictures as they wished. After that, they recalled as many pictures as possible.

Free recall increased steadily with age, being approximately 50% higher when the children were 17 than when they were 8. At the older ages, there was more sorting of the pictures into their categories during learning and recall was category by category to a greater extent. The enhanced free recall with increasing age was probably due in large part to the greater organization of the pictures at learning and at retrieval.

Schleepen and Jonkman (2012) used a similar memory task with children aged between 6 and 12. The children were presented with 12 pictures consisting of four members of the categories of fruit, animals, and clothes. Free recall increased progressively with age. Only the oldest children spontaneously organized the material into categories at learning and at recall. Schleepen and Jonkman assessed individual differences in working memory capacity. Children with high working memory

capacity used categorical organization more successfully at learning and at retrieval than those with low capacity.

Metamemory

As children grow older, they show increasing evidence of metamemory. Metamemory includes "knowledge and beliefs about the capacities, functioning, limitations and development of one's own memory and the human memory system in general" (Pierce & Lange, 2000, p. 277).

Does metamemory knowledge generally predict memory performance? Schneider and Pressley (1998) found in a meta-analysis of 60 studies that the correlation between metamemory and memory performance was +.41. Thus, there is a moderate tendency for children with good metamemory knowledge to have superior memory performance to children with poor metamemory.

There are various possible reasons why the relationship between metamemory and memory performance is not stronger. Children may not always be motivated (or able) to use effective memory strategies they possess. Metcalfe and Finn (2013) addressed this issue in Grade 3 children (7 or 8 years old) and Grade 5 children (9 or 10 years) who studied definition–word pairs (i.e. a definition was followed by the correct word). Both groups showed good metamemory when subsequently judging whether they knew what the word was when presented with the definition. In spite of this, the younger children (but not the older ones) made random choices when asked to select the items they would like to restudy. Thus, children aged 7 or 8 seem unable to make effective use of metamemory information.

Our understanding of metamemory has increased over the years. Fritz, Howie, and Kleitman (2010) drew a distinction between declarative metamemory and procedural metamemory. Declarative metamemory refers to conscious knowledge about factors influencing memory performance. It can include knowing not only *that* various factors influence memory but also knowing *why* they have that influence. In contrast, procedural metamemory is concerned with the application of metamemory during memory performance. It includes processing such as monitoring, controlling, and regulating memory activity.

Fritz et al. (2010) obtained evidence for the above distinction and also discovered an important difference between them. Declarative metamemory increased steadily between the ages of 6 and 10. In contrast procedural metamemory improved considerably between the ages of 6 and 10 but changed relatively little between the ages of 8 and 10.

Summary

There are several reasons why older children generally remember much more than younger ones. The main components of the working memory system all increase in capacity during childhood; children's knowledge increases, their use of effective strategies increases, and they develop a greater awareness of their own memory system (metamemory). However, as we have seen, younger children typically fail to use the metamemory information they possess.

As mentioned at the beginning of this section, the above factors are all interconnected. We will consider two examples. First, organizational strategies (e.g. rehearsing category by category) are increasingly used by children as they grow older. Part of the reason for this is the development of working memory capacity over time (Schleepen & Jonkman, 2012). Second, children possessing the most relevant content knowledge on a learning task are likely to have acquired this additional knowledge partly as a result of having high working memory capacity and having previously used effective learning strategies.

Verbatim and gist memory

Does declarative or explicit memory on *all* memory tasks improve throughout childhood? It seems reasonable to assume the correct answer is positive, but in fact it is negative.

As we will see, it is instructive to consider the circumstances in which declarative memory is actually more error prone as children grow up.

The key research in this area is based on a theoretical approach put forward by Brainerd and Reyna (2004). They argued that there are two kinds of memory trace. First, there are *verbatim* traces, which contain accurate and detailed information about to-be-remembered material (e.g. the font in which a word is printed).

Second, there are *gist* memory traces. These traces often contain much semantic information about to-be-remembered material (e.g. associating the word "France" with information that it is a country that produces wine and cheese). In essence, gist traces contain the learner's "understanding" of his/her experiences whereas verbatim traces reflect the learner's "actual" experiences.

Fuzzy-trace theory (discussed by Brainerd, Reyna, & Ceci, 2008) is based on various assumptions. First, verbatim memory and gist memory improve considerably during development. As a result, there is a substantial increase in *accurate* memory during childhood. However, there is also an increase in *false* memory with age under certain conditions. More specifically, the superior gist memory of older children increases the likelihood of false recall and recognition of information very similar in meaning to the to-be-remembered information.

Findings

As predicted by fuzzy-trace theory, verbatim memory and gist memory both show marked improvements during childhood. Much of the relevant research is reviewed by Brainerd, Reyna, and Ceci (2008). Verbatim memory was considered by Brainerd and Reyna (2004). Children aged 11 showed much better recognition memory for nonwords (e.g. *cexib*, *zuteg*) than those aged 5.

It is unsurprising that verbatim memory and gist memory both improve with age. The most dramatic prediction from fuzzy-trace theory is that older children will often show an increase in *false* memory. Brainerd et al. (2008) reviewed research relevant to this prediction. Here we will consider a study by Brainerd and Mojardin (1998). Children aged 6, 8, and 11 listened to sets of three sentences (e.g. "The coffee is hotter than the cocoa," "The cocoa is hotter than the soup"). On the subsequent recognition test, participants decided whether the test sentences had been presented in precisely that form initially. The key condition was one in which sentences having the same meaning as the original sentences were presented (e.g. "The cocoa is cooler than the tea"). As predicted, false recognition on these sentences increased steadily as a function of age (see Figure 14.8).

Fuzzy-trace theory has often been tested by focusing on the Deese–Roediger–McDermott task (also discussed in Chapter 7). In this task, word lists constructed in a particular way are presented. A common word (e.g. *doctor*) is selected and then the 15 words most closely associated with it (e.g. *nurse, sick, hospital*) are identified. Those 15 words (but *not* the original word) are then presented followed by a test of free recall or recognition.

What is of key interest with the above task is the extent to which participants falsely recall or recognize the original or target word (e.g. *doctor*). According to fuzzy-trace theory, older children engage in more gist processing leading to an increased probability of false recall and recognition for the target word.

Brainerd and Reyna (2012) reviewed the findings from 35 studies using the Deese–Roediger–McDermott task. As predicted, the typical finding was that false memory (recall and recognition) for the target word was more common among older than among younger

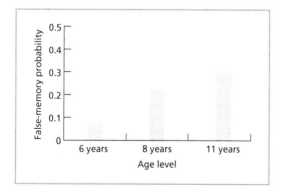

Figure 14.8 False recognition of gist-consistent sentences at 6, 8, and 11 years of age. Based on data from Brainerd and Mojardin (1998).

children. For example, Verkoeijen and Bouwmeester (2012) obtained false recall in 4% of Grade 3 children, 10% of Grade 5 children, and 20% of college students. For false recognition, the figures were 32%, 37%, and 68%, respectively. Of most importance, participants with high levels of gist processing had more false recalls than those with low levels of gist processing. This is exactly as predicted by fuzzy-trace theory. Note that high levels of gist processing were associated with the production of a greater number of correct recalls as well, indicating that gist processing is generally valuable.

In sum, there is compelling evidence that it is important to distinguish between verbatim memory traces and gist memory traces. The fact that older children form more gist memory traces than younger ones is generally an advantage. However, it becomes a disadvantage when a memory test requires verbatim recall or recognition.

IMPLICIT MEMORY

We have seen at various places in this chapter that declarative or explicit memory (memory involving conscious recollection) shows substantial age-related changes during infancy and childhood. However, it is less clear that the same is true of implicit memory (memory inferred from performance rather than conscious recollection).

Here is an example of implicit memory taken from Murphy, McKone, and Slee (2003). Children were presented with members of categories (e.g. *frog* for the category *animal*) and decided whether the member belonged to that category. On the memory test, the children generated members of various categories (e.g. "Tell me the first five animals you can think of"). Implicit memory was shown if children were more likely to say *frog* when they had been presented with the word earlier in the experiment than when they had not.

Murphy et al. (2003) reviewed studies on implicit memory in children. Nonsignificant effects of age on memory performance were obtained in 15 out of 18 studies. Since that review, mostly small or nonsignificant effects of age on implicit memory have been reported. Amso and Davidow (2012) obtained especially striking findings. They argued it is very important for infants to be sensitive to environmental regularities and to violations of those regularities. Sensitivity to these factors was equally present at all ages from 7 months of age to 30 years.

Sauzéon, Déjos, Lestage, Pala, and N'Kaoua (2012) focused on the distinction between *associative* links (e.g. *monkey–banana*; *rabbit–carrot*) and *categorical* links (e.g. *animal–monkey*; *fruit–banana*). Young children prefer (and make more extensive use of) associative links whereas older children have a preference for categorical links. They predicted that implicit memory based on associative links would not show age-related differences in performance. In contrast, younger children should perform worse than older ones when implicit memory was based on categorical links. Both predictions were supported by the evidence (see Figure 14.9).

Sauzéon et al. (2012) also considered explicit memory for associatively and categorically related information. Performance on both tasks improved progressively between the ages of 7 and 16, thus showing the typical age-related changes in explicit or declarative memory.

Maturation and cognitive processes

Why are age effects on implicit memory typically much smaller than those on explicit or declarative memory? One approach to this question is to focus on maturational processes within the brain. So far as implicit memory is concerned, there is reasonable agreement that parts of the striatum, the cerebellum, and the brainstem are all involved in implicit learning and memory (Richmond & Nelson, 2007). What is important here is that these brain structures mature very early in life.

The brain structures of most importance to declarative or explicit memory are the hippocampus and parahippocampal cortex (Lavenex & Lavenex, 2013). Much of this brain system is formed before birth or matures rapidly (e.g. CA1; see Figure 14.10). However, there is prolonged postnatal maturation and addition of neurons in the dentate gyrus (DG) within the hippocampal formation. Maturation is also slow in various areas downstream

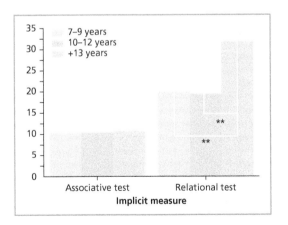

Figure 14.9 Sauzéon et al.'s (2012) results support the predictions that implicit memory based on associative links would not show age-related differences in performance and that younger children should perform worse than older ones when implicit memory was based on categorical links. From Sauzéon et al. (2012). Copyright © Taylor & Francis.

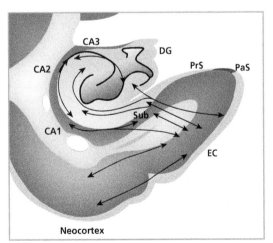

Figure 14.10 The brain structures of most importance to declarative or explicit memory are formed before birth or mature rapidly (e.g. CA1; shown in this figure). Reprinted from Lavenex and Lavenex (2013). Copyright © 2013, with permission from Elsevier.

from the dentate gyrus (especially CA3). These late-developing parts of the hippocampal formation could help to explain why declarative memory develops greatly over the early years of life. As we will see later, the slow development of the hippocampus helps to explain infantile amnesia (very poor ability to recall early memories).

We can also approach the greater age effects on explicit memory than on implicit memory from a more psychological perspective. In general terms, implicit memory involves more basic processes than declarative or explicit memory and so is less affected by children's developing cognitive skills and abilities. More specifically, the factors known to influence improvements in declarative memory during childhood (i.e. basic working memory capacities; content knowledge; memory strategies; and metamemory) are generally of much less importance in implicit memory.

Conclusions

There are clear-cut differences between implicit and explicit or declarative memory. Of special importance, age-related differences are typically much greater with explicit memory than with implicit memory. There are two main reasons for this. First, the brain areas most associated with episodic memory mature much more slowly than those most associated with implicit memory. Second, explicit memory involves more complex cognitive processes than implicit memory and these processes take several years to develop fully.

What are the limitations with research in this area? As we saw earlier, the notion that episodic memory depends on slowly maturing brain areas leads to the prediction that infants should exhibit very poor long-term memory for their experiences. However, research on the mobile, train, deferred imitation, and sensory preconditioning tasks indicates that infants sometimes have surprisingly long-lasting memories. Overall, the distinction between implicit memory and explicit memory has proved valuable in understanding the development of human memory. However, it clearly does not account for all the findings.

AUTOBIOGRAPHICAL MEMORY AND INFANTILE AMNESIA

We have seen that learning can occur during the first few months of life, and that infants can display memory over relatively long periods of time. However, these studies shed little or no light on causes of infantile amnesia (people's inability to recall childhood memories for the first 3 or 4 years of life). Of much more relevance are studies concerned with infants' ability to remember the events of their own lives.

Findings

Katherine Nelson (1989) described the intriguing singular case of Emily, a child who had developed the rather convenient habit of talking to herself in her cot before she went to sleep. Her nightly monolog between the ages of 21 and 36 months was recorded and analyzed. At 21 months, she already recalled events from 2 months before (e.g. the family car breaking down). Her monolog was mostly very unstructured and generally did not relate to particularly salient or important events such as Christmas or the birth of a baby brother.

Many of Emily's reminiscences were from the previous day, but some went back as far as 6 months. At about 24 months, she began to construct explicit rules and generalizations (e.g. "You can't go down the basement with jamas on"). At about 36 months of age, Emily stopped producing monologs at bedtime and the study ended. However, she provided us with compelling evidence that 2-year-olds can remember specific events.

Subsequent research has confirmed that most 2-year-olds have some autobiographical memory for events occurring several months previously (see Peterson, 2012, for a review). However, infants under the age of 2 have much more limited long-term autobiographical recall even for emotional events. For example, Peterson and Rideout (1998) studied young children taken to a hospital emergency room for treatment of a traumatic injury. Their memories for their injuries and hospital treatment were assessed 6 months, 1 year, and 1½ to 2 years afterward. Recall was much worse and more error prone in children who were 1-year-olds when the injury occurred than in those who were 2-year-olds. Indeed, half the children between 12 and 18 months of age at the time of the injury could remember nothing at all about it 18 months later. What was of crucial importance in determining how much children could remember was whether they possessed the language skills to talk about the injury at the time it happened.

Peterson (2011) investigated long-term autobiographical memory in children initially aged between 2 and 13 years who had been injured and admitted to a hospital emergency room. These children were interviewed about the injury event a few days after it happened and then 1 year and 2 years later. Memory for the overall structure of the event remained

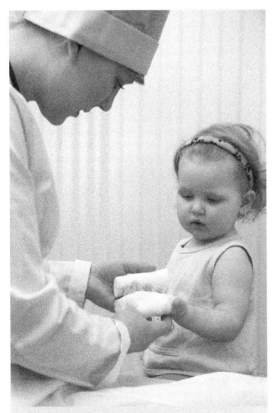

Peterson and Rideout (1998) concluded that how much children could remember about their injury and hospitalization depended on whether they possessed the language skills to talk about the event at the time it happened.

very similar over the 2-year period. Strikingly, this was so even for the children who were 2 years old at the time of the injury event (although their initial recall was significantly more limited than that of older children). However, children at every age tended to show an increase in the production of false details over time.

Some of the most impressive evidence that 2-year-olds can remember unique events over long periods of time was reported by Jack, Simcock, and Hayne (2012). Children aged between 27 and 51 months played a game with a "magic shrinking machine"— large objects went into it and small ones came out. When the children were tested 6 years later, 20% of those who had originally been 2 years old managed to recall a reasonable amount of information about their experiences.

The most-used method by far to assess children's memory is verbal report. However, if young children produce limited verbal reports of personal events, this may reflect their inability to express what they remember in words rather than poor event memory. Limitations with verbal report were shown by Simcock and Hayne (2003). Children aged between 24 and 48 months played with the magic shrinking machine and their memory of what happened was tested 24 hours later. Memory was tested by verbal recall, by photograph recognition (i.e. recognizing objects that had been placed in the machine), or by behavioral re-enactment (show how the machine works). Memory performance (especially among the younger children) was best with the photograph recognition test and worst with verbal recall.

Conclusions

From the age of 2 onwards, young children often show reasonably good long-term memory for emotional and/or dramatic events. A key difference between young children who recall autobiographical memories a long time after an event and those who do not is the language ability possessed at the time of the event. Studies in which there is exclusive reliance on verbal recall to assess what children can remember of past events often underestimate their memory ability.

Infantile amnesia

As mentioned already, infantile amnesia is a striking phenomenon. Research discussed earlier (Tustin & Hayne, 2010) found that infantile amnesia extends further into childhood when adults' childhood memories are tested compared to older children and adolescents.

Infantile amnesia could occur for two very different reasons. First, childhood amnesia may occur because infants are very poor at encoding and storing autobiographical information in long-term memory. Second, infants may form long-term autobiographical memories but these memories are forgotten before their memory is tested several years later.

Relevant evidence was reported by Gross, Jack, Davis, and Hayne (2013). Young children aged between 2 and 5 years tried to recall the birth of a sibling that had occurred within the previous 2 months. They found 85% of 2-year-olds could not provide any information about the birth of their sibling during free recall. However, 3-year-olds could generally provide a few details about the birth of their sibling. These findings suggest that childhood amnesia for events during the first 2 or 3 years of life is mostly due to a failure to encode the event effectively.

Gross et al. (2013) also studied adults who tried to recall the birth of a sibling when they were aged between 2 and 5 years. The adults recalled more information about the birth of a sibling than the young children. This suggests that adults' recall of early childhood events is augmented by additional sources of information (e.g. family photographs).

The most famous (or perhaps it should be notorious!) account of childhood or infantile amnesia was provided by Sigmund Freud (1915/1957; see Chapter 11). He argued that childhood amnesia occurs through repression, with threat-related thoughts and experiences (e.g. sexual feelings toward one's parents) being consigned to the unconscious. More specifically, Freud claimed that such threatening memories are changed into more innocuous memories (which he called screen memories).

The most obvious problem with Freud's repression theory is that it fails to explain why adolescents and adults cannot remember *positive* and *neutral* events from early childhood.

This is mystifying from Freud's perspective because such events should not be subject to repression.

Several cognitive theories have been advanced to explain childhood amnesia and the development of autobiographical memory. We will focus on two major theories. One emphasizes the role played by the development of the cognitive self (Howe & Courage, 1997). The other (the social cultural approach) is based on the assumption that social and cultural factors are of prime importance in the development of autobiographical memory (Fivush & Nelson, 2004).

Finally, we discuss an alternative approach (the neurogenic hypothesis) based on the notion that the slow development of brain areas central to long-term memory is of crucial importance in explaining infantile amnesia. This approach has considerable potential and has become influential.

Cognitive self

According to Howe and Courage's (1997) theoretical approach, infants can only form autobiographical memories *after* they have developed a sense of self to whom events having *personal* significance can occur (see Howe, 2013, for a review). This sense of self appears to develop towards the end of the second year of life. For example, Lewis and Brooks-Gunn (1979) carried out a study in which infants

When infants can recognize their own reflection, by reaching for their own nose rather than the one in the mirror, they are considered to have developed a sense of self-awareness.

who had a red spot applied surreptitiously to their nose were held up to a mirror. Those recognizing their own reflection and so reaching for their own nose were claimed to show some self-awareness. Practically no infants in the first year of life showed self-awareness but 70% of infants between 21 and 24 months of age did so.

The crucial assumption of Howe and Courage's (1997) theory is as follows:

The development of the cognitive self late in the second year of life (as indexed by visual self-recognition) provides a new framework around which memories can be organised. With this cognitive advance ... we witness the emergence of autobiographical memory and the end of infantile amnesia.
(Howe and Courage, 1997, p. 499)

Evidence that the cognitive self plays a role in the onset of autobiographical memory around or shortly before a child's second birthday was reported by Howe, Courage, and Edison (2003). They worked with infants aged between 15 and 23 months and found self-recognizers had better memory for personal events than those who were not self-recognizers. They also followed a group of infants from the age of 15 to 23 months. Not a single child showed good performance on a memory test for personal events before achieving self-recognition.

Social cultural theory

The social cultural developmental theory (Fivush & Nelson, 2004; Fivush, 2010) provides a rather different account of childhood amnesia. According to this theory, language and culture both play central roles in the early development of autobiographical memory. Language is important in part because we use it to communicate our memories. Experiences occurring before children develop language are hard to express in language later in childhood.

Parents' use of language is also very important when an event occurs and when discussing it subsequently. Nelson (1989) focused on interactions between mothers and their children while wandering around a museum. These interactions were categorized as "freely interacting" or "practical." The former interactional style was freewheeling and reminiscing, and involved mothers relating what was seen in the museum to previous experiences shared with their child. In contrast, the practical style involved the mother asking questions such as, "What do you think this is for?"; "What do you think this statue is made of?" When tested a week later, the mothers and children who had freely interacted answered an average of 13 out of 30 questions whereas the more practical group could answer only 5.

Mothers differ considerably in how they naturally reminisce about the past with their young children. Some have a very elaborate reminiscing style (i.e. discussing the past in great detail with their children), whereas other mothers do not. As predicted by the social cultural theory, the age of first memory reported by 12-year-olds was earlier in children whose mothers had had a very elaborate reminiscing style when they were preschoolers (Jack, MacDonald, Reese, & Hayne, 2009). Additional support to the theory was provided by Kingo, Berntsen, and Krøjgaard (2013) using a large sample of 1043 participants between 20 and 70 years of age. Participants whose parents had had an elaborate reminiscing style reported slightly earlier first memories than those whose parents lacked this reminiscing style.

The language skills available at the time of an experience determine what children can recall about it subsequently. Simcock and Hayne (2003) asked 2- and 3-year-olds to describe their memories for complex play activities up to 12 months later. The children only used words already known at the time of the event. This is impressive evidence given that the children had acquired hundreds of new words between having the experience and subsequently describing it.

A major prediction from the social cultural theory is that children's autobiographical memories will depend in part on the particular culture in which they grow up. Accumulating evidence supports this prediction. Han, Leichtman, and Wang (1998) compared the reported memories of early childhood in children from Korea, China, and America. The memories of the American children were most elaborated and emotional, probably because of cultural differences in the mothers' reminiscing style.

Two-stage theory

Jack and Hayne (2010) argued that the common assumption of a gradual decline in childhood amnesia during the preschool period is incorrect. In their study, they asked young adults (19 years of age) to recall early autobiographical memories. The participants' earliest memory dated from approximately 23 months of age. However, their memories for the first 4–6 years of life were sparse. These findings suggested to Jack and Hayne that childhood amnesia is a two-stage process—there is absolute amnesia for the first 2 years of life followed by relative amnesia for the remaining preschool years.

How can we account for these two stages? According to Jack and Hayne (2010), the period of absolute amnesia ends with the onset of the cognitive self. After that, the development of language leads to the end of relative amnesia. There was a strong tendency for the amount of information recalled about a childhood event to increase as the participant's age at the time of the event increased. This may well reflect children's rapid development of language over the early years of life.

Evaluation

Three points about infantile amnesia need to be emphasized. First, the cognitive self and social cultural theories are not mutually exclusive. The *onset* of autobiographical memory in infants may depend on the emergence of the self. However, its *subsequent* expression may be heavily influenced by social factors, cultural factors, and infants' development of language. Jack and Hayne's (2010) two-stage theory provides a useful synthesis of these theoretical viewpoints. Second, there is reasonable research evidence indicating that all the main factors identified in the two theories are involved in the development of autobiographical memory.

Third, most of the research evidence is limited in that it shows an association or correlation in time between, for example, the mother's reminiscing style and autobiographical memory performance in her child. The presence of an *association* or correlation does not demonstrate the memory performance was *caused* by the reminiscing style.

Neurogenic hypothesis

Josselyn and Frankland (2012) pointed out that infantile amnesia has been observed in several nonhuman species. As a result, it cannot be explained fully using human concepts (e.g. the cognitive self, language development). How, then, can we account for infantile amnesia? Josselyn and Frankland noted that the hippocampus (crucially involved in declarative memory including autobiographical memory) shows protracted postnatal development. Of special importance, there is a process of neurogenesis in which new neurons are generated in the hippocampus (especially the dentate gyrus) during the early years of life (see Figure 14.10).

According to Josselyn and Frankland's (2012) neurogenic hypothesis, "High neurogenesis levels negatively regulate the ability to form enduring memories, most likely by replacing synaptic connections in pre-existing hippocampal memory circuits" (p. 423). There is indirect supporting evidence for this hypothesis. For example, mice with high levels of neurogenesis in the dentate gyrus have especially fast rates of forgetting (see Josselyn & Frankland, 2012). Conversely, it has been found in several species that the ability to form long-lasting memories increases substantially when neurogenesis declines.

In sum, there is as yet little definitive evidence to support the neurogenic hypothesis. However, the central role of the hippocampus in the formation of long-term declarative memories means that it provides a very plausible explanation of the almost complete absence of long-term memories for the first 3 years of life.

CHILDREN AS WITNESSES

Throughout this chapter, we have focused mainly on basic research designed to understand how and why children's memory abilities improve substantially during the course of childhood. However, research on children's memory also has important practical applications. For example, in legal cases children are increasingly asked to provide reports of their experiences as victims or witnesses of a crime (see Chapter 12 for a discussion of eyewitness testimony in adults).

Two key topics will be discussed. First, there is the issue of the accuracy and reliability of children's reports of crimes. Second, there is the issue of how we can maximize the accuracy of such reports.

How accurately do children recall events?

As we saw earlier, young children have reasonable memory for specific events, especially when suitable cues are provided. For example, Fivush, Hudson, and Nelson (1984) studied 5-year-olds' memories of a visit to the Jewish Museum in New York. The visit included an explanation of archeological methods and the chance to dig in a sandbox to find artifacts. Recall of this event showed considerable forgetting. However, 6 years later, the children successfully recalled 87% of the original information when given appropriate cues.

Children are, increasingly, called to give evidence in legal cases and an important practical application of research is how we can maximize their accuracy in recalling events.

The issue of how well children can remember events has become increasingly important as the extent of child physical and sexual abuse is more fully acknowledged. In such cases, the evidence typically depends on the children's testimony. In 1983, for example, a 36-year-old woman who ran a nursery school was convicted of murder and of 12 counts of child abuse mainly on eyewitness testimony from 29 children who had attended the school.

Brainerd and Reyna (2012, p. 225) pointed out that the traditional view concerning the accuracy of children's memory was that "children are highly unreliable witnesses—so unreliable that early researchers had claimed that children's evidence can only mislead jurors." Hundreds of experiments support this view. However, there are also several experiments finding the opposite. Most of these disconfirming findings can be understood with reference to fuzzy-trace theory (discussed earlier in the chapter). Its key explanatory principle was expressed by Brainerd (2013, p. 339): "False memories that are rooted in understanding meaning connections among events ... are apt to increase with age because formation of such connections improves dramatically between childhood and young adulthood."

Some evidence that older children can produce more false memories than younger ones was discussed earlier. For example, there are many studies using the Deese–Roediger–McDermott task in which a nonpresented target word associated with all the list words is falsely remembered as being on the list. Older children are more susceptible to this illusion than younger ones.

It could be argued that such laboratory-based research may not be relevant to children's memory for criminal events they have experienced. However, increased false memories as a function of increasing age have been reported in several more naturalistic studies (see Brainerd and Reyna, 2012, for a review). For example, Odegard, Cooper, Lampinen, Reyna, and Brainerd (2009) carried out a study in which children aged between 5 and 12 attended four birthday parties. The key finding was that false memories for nonexistent events associated with parties increased progressively with age.

In sum, older children do not always exhibit more accurate memory for events and experiences than younger ones. Older children process events in more elaborate ways than younger ones, and this additional processing can lead to inaccurate recall subsequently.

Memory for traumatic events

Since children are often asked to provide evidence about traumatic events such as physical and/or sexual abuse, we need to consider whether their memory for such events is likely to be better or worse than their memory for neutral or positive events. According to Freud's repression theory (discussed earlier), children should tend to repress memory of traumatic events. As a result, these events should be harder to recall than nontraumatic ones.

In contrast, much research discussed in this book indicates that significant and distinctive experiences are generally better remembered than those that are trivial and/or nondistinctive. As the great majority of traumatic events are both significant and distinctive, it follows that traumatic memories should typically be remembered *better* than nontraumatic ones.

Cordón, Pipe, Sayfan, Melinder, and Goodman (2004) reviewed studies on children's memory for traumatic and nontraumatic events. They concluded that the similarities between memories for the two types of event greatly outweigh the differences:

Memories of traumatic and non-traumatic experiences have much in common ... the same variables that influence memory for non-traumatic events, such as age, delay, and the nature of the event, are also important determinants of memory for early childhood trauma. Age at the time of the event emerges as a crucial factor in the ability to consciously access memory for traumatic events.

(Cordón et al., 2004, p. 122)

Suggestibility

A central concern with using children to provide eyewitness testimony is that they tend to be suggestible, and this can lead to systematic errors in their recall of events. It has typically been assumed that children become less suggestible throughout the course of development. Below we discuss the relevant research starting with a study by Ceci, Baker, and Bronfenbrenner (1988).

Ceci et al. (1988) read children aged between 3 and 12 a story about a little girl called Lauren on her first day at school. Lauren eats eggs for breakfast, then has a stomachache which she forgets about when allowed to play with another child's toy. Misleading information was introduced by asking the question: "Do you remember the story about Lauren, who had a headache because she ate her cereal too fast? Then she felt better when she got to play with her friend's game?" This is a leading question because it carries with it an implication as to the correct answer.

The children were tested individually for their understanding of the story and then the experimenter left. Two days later the children were again tested individually and chose between pairs of pictures. One picture showed Lauren eating eggs and the other eating cereal; another pair portrayed Lauren with a stomachache or a headache. Memory performance was only slightly affected by age when no misleading information (i.e. the leading question) was provided (see Figure 14.11). By contrast, memory accuracy was much lower in younger children than in older children when misleading information was given.

The first systematic review of age-related changes in suggestibility was provided by Ceci and Bruck (1993). They discovered that memory suggestibility decreased with age in 83% of studies and did not increase in any of the studies. Brainerd and Reyna (2012) discussed research on age-related reductions in suggestibility including many studies published since Ceci and Bruck's review. Such reductions have been found for implanted false memories of thefts, personal traumatic experiences, and physically and emotionally painful events involving children's bodies.

Why are younger children more suggestible than older ones? There are two main reasons (Ceci & Bruck, 2006). First, younger children are more likely than older ones to yield to social pressure and a lack of social support even when their own recollection is accurate. Second, there is cognitive incompetence. Younger children are less likely to have

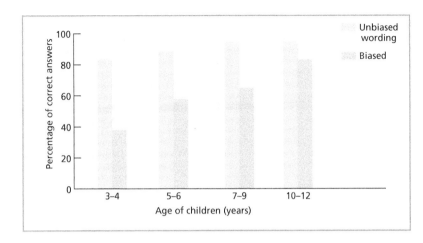

Figure 14.11 This graph shows the effects of misleading information on the memory of children of different ages. When unbiased wording is used, recall is more or less equally high across the age range, but under biased conditions younger children are more easily misled (Ceci et al., 1988).

cognitive processing and language abilities to challenge suggestive influences.

What can be done?

From a practical point of view, it is important to maximize the accuracy of children's eyewitness reports. Perhaps the most obvious approach is to reduce problems of social compliance by ensuring that those involved in interviewing children avoid leading questions. That is certainly desirable. However, as we will see shortly, interviewer bias can manifest itself in several ways other than through the use of leading questions.

An obstacle to obtaining complete and accurate information from child witnesses is the extensive use of cross-examination in the courtroom (Zajac, O'Neill, & Hayne, 2012). Cross-examination is part of a legal system basically designed *by* adults *for* adults. As we will see, cross-examination has many limitations when applied to child witnesses but various steps can be adopted to improve its usefulness.

Reducing interviewer bias

The most obvious way to reduce interviewer bias is to ensure that those involved in interviewing children avoid leading questions (i.e. questions that suggest a given answer). That is certainly desirable. However, interviewer bias can manifest itself in several other ways. For example, an interviewer can display bias by rewarding desired answers,

criticizing nondesired answers, repeating specific questions within an interview, and so on.

In a study by Garven, Wood, and Malpass (2000), kindergarten children recalled details about a visitor called Paco who came to their classroom. They were later asked misleading questions about plausible events (e.g. "Did Paco break a toy?") and about bizarre events (e.g. "Did Paco take you to a farm?"). Children who received praise for answering such questions positively but were criticized for answering them negatively agreed with 35% of the plausible questions and 52% of the bizarre ones. In contrast, children receiving no feedback agreed with only 13% of the plausible questions and 5% of the bizarre ones. This was not simply due to social pressure, because the children exposed to interviewer bias continued to provide false answers to the misleading questions when interviewed later by different neutral interviewers.

Sparling, Wilder, Kondash, Boyle, and Compton (2011) instructed an interviewer to respond with approving statements when children produced inaccurate answers and disapproving statements when they produced accurate answers. This manipulation caused an increase in the number of inaccurate answers produced by the children.

Improving cross-examination techniques

Cross-examination by lawyers is a fundamental part of criminal trials in many countries. It was originally designed for use with adults and is often regarded as inappropriate when used with children (Zajac et al., 2012). Children often find cross-examination intimidating and distressing—they are often accused of lying, they are questioned in an aggressive fashion, and the questions they are asked can be very complex and hard to understand.

What can be done to improve cross-examination techniques to increase the accuracy of the testimony provided by child witnesses? Zajac et al. (2012) make several useful suggestions, including reducing time delays between the event and cross-examination, and using a third party to put the lawyers' questions to the child in a simple and nonthreatening way. Another useful approach is to use a pretrial intervention to prepare child witnesses for subsequent cross-examination. O'Neill and Zajac (2013) gave some children aged between 5 and 10 practice at answering cross-examination-style questions and provided them with feedback. Cross-examination accuracy was greater for those children receiving the pretrial intervention.

Improving source monitoring

Most children watch television for several hours every week. As a consequence, one reason why children's eyewitness testimony is often distorted may be because they tend to confuse real-life and television events. For example, they might see disturbing sexual scenes on television and then include some elements of what they have seen in their answers when questioned about real-life experiences. In other words, young children may be poor at monitoring the source of events.

The above considerations led Thierry and Spence (2002) to study the effects of training in source monitoring on the eyewitness memory of 3- and 4-year-olds. All the children initially watched as the experimenter (Mrs. Science) presented live and video-taped demonstrations of science experiments. Then all the children watched live and video puppet shows. After that, some children received training in source monitoring. Finally, the children were questioned about events from the initial live and video-taped demonstrations featuring Mrs. Science. On average, children receiving no training made five times as many errors in attributing events correctly to the live and video-taped sources as those who had been trained.

Thierry, Lamb, Pipe, and Spence (2010) argued that child witnesses providing testimony in real life are most likely to experience source confusions between experienced events and events they have heard about. Accordingly, they gave training in source monitoring to some children who watched live events and also heard stories about other similar events. Training enhanced the ability to distinguish between the two types of events even in children as young as 3 years old.

Reinstating context

Memory for events can be improved by putting the person back into the situation in which the event took place. For example, I spent my early years in south London close to Crystal Palace Football Club. I have often driven along the streets I knew as a boy, and this acts as an effective trigger to recall childhood events. This can be explained in terms of Tulving's encoding specificity principle (see Chapter 8). According to this principle, we generally store away contextual information about events, and memory should be maximal when the information available at the time of retrieval (including context) matches that in the memory trace.

Priestley, Roberts, and Pipe (1999) considered the possible beneficial effects of reinstating context on children's memory for an event. Children between 5 and 7 years of age participated in an event that involved pretending to be a pirate and their memory was then tested 6 months later. Children in the context condition were tested with the pirate props present whereas other children were tested in the absence of relevant context. The key finding was that children in the context condition recalled approximately 40% more items of information.

Levy-Gigi and Vakil (2010) initially presented a list of items to children aged 9 and 12 years in the form of pictures. This was followed by presenting a list of words to the children. Finally, there was a recognition memory test for information contained in the first list. This test involved either the presentation of pictures (same context: PWP condition) or of words (different context: PWW condition).

What did Levy-Gigi and Vakil (2010) find? First, memory performance was better in the same-context than in the different-context condition (see Figure 14.12). Second, there was no effect of age on the number of correct recognition responses in the same-context condition. Third, the younger children had significantly fewer correct recognition responses than the older ones in the different-context condition. There was a very similar pattern for errors—there was no age effect on errors in the same-context condition but younger children made more errors than older ones in the different-context condition. The above findings indicate that context reinstatement is more important for younger than for older children. Younger children have less developed cognitive skills than older ones for coping with contextual changes between learning and testing.

Accessing nonverbal information

Some of the information children store in long-term memory after witnessing an event is likely to be in nonverbal form. As a result, interviews with child witnesses might often fail to access all of the relevant information they possess about events. Gross and Hayne (1999) tested this idea in a study on 5- and 6-year-old children who visited a chocolate factory. They were taken there by a woman wearing a purple suit who called herself "Charlie Chocolate." The children's memory for this event was tested by asking them to provide a verbal report after 1 day, 6 months, and 1 year. Some children drew what they could remember prior to the verbal report.

What did Gross and Hayne (1999) find? At the two shorter retention intervals (1 day and 6 months), children in the drawing condition recalled 30% more information in their verbal reports than those who provided only verbal reports. The effects were even stronger after 1 year—the children who drew in addition to providing a verbal report recalled almost twice as much information about the visit to the chocolate factory as those in the control condition. These beneficial effects were obtained with no increase in errors. Thus, including drawing in memory interviews may be a very effective way of obtaining accurate and reasonably complete accounts of events.

Katz and Hamama (2013) explored the usefulness of drawing in the context of alleged sexual abuse. Three children aged between 6 and 9 provided narrative accounts of the alleged abuse before and after spending several minutes drawing the incident. The narrative following drawing was much richer and more detailed than the narrative preceding drawing. However, a note of caution is in order—there was no direct evidence concerning the accuracy of the details that were recalled.

Conclusions

The good news so far as using children as witnesses is that there are several ways of

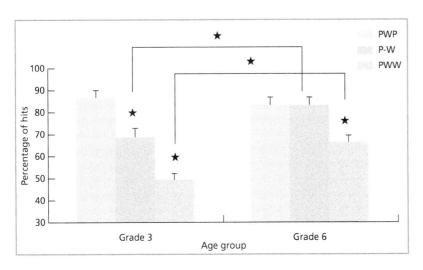

Figure 14.12 Mean percentages of hits as a function of age group and contextual condition. Error bars show standard errors. Stars represent significance p < 0.005. Reprinted from Levy-Gigy, E. and Vakil, E. (2010). Copyright © 2010, with permission from Elsevier.

increasing how much they can recall accurately about events that have happened to them. It is very important for interviewers and lawyers to avoid bias (including the use of leading questions). Children can be trained in source monitoring so their recall of a crucial event does not include aspects of a different event. Two further useful general approaches are to reinstate the context in which the event in question happened and to provide children with the opportunity to produce drawings of the event prior to verbal recall.

SUMMARY

- According to traditional theories, infants have very limited long-term memory because key brain structures are slow to mature. In contrast, it is argued within the ecological model that infants have very good long-term memory for certain kinds of information (e.g. associations between objects seen together).
- Findings from the mobile, train, deferred imitation, and sensory preconditioning tasks provide some support for the ecological model. The duration of infants' long-term memory is especially impressive when they are provided with reminders permitting integration of information from the original memory with information provided by the reminder.
- There are several reasons why explicit or declarative memory improves greatly during childhood:

  ○ All the main components of the working memory system show increased capacity during development.
  ○ Older children have more relevant knowledge.
  ○ Older children make use of a wider range of learning strategies than younger ones.
  ○ Older children have greater metamemory or knowledge concerning their own memory.

  The above four factors are interconnected.
- In spite of the general substantial improvement in declarative memory during childhood, older children sometimes produce more false memories than younger ones when verbatim memory (rather than gist memory) is required.
- Implicit memory typically (but not always) does not show age-related changes during childhood, in contrast to the large age-related changes shown in declarative or episodic memory.
- Implicit memory relies more than explicit memory on brain structures that mature early. It also involves simpler processes than explicit memory and relies much less on working memory, relevant knowledge, memory strategies, and metamemory.
- Children from the age of 2 years upward show good long-term memory for emotional or unique events and can sometimes remember such events for at least 6 years.
- Children under 2 years of age typically have very poor long-term memory for autobiographical experiences, especially if they have very limited language ability. Young children generally have poorer memory performance if their memory is assessed by verbal report rather than via other methods (e.g. drawing).
- The term 'infantile amnesia' refers to the inability of older children and adults to remember any childhood events before the age of 3 or 4 years. One explanation for infantile amnesia is that infants can only form autobiographical memories after developing a sense of self toward the end of the second year of life.
- An alternative explanation for infantile amnesia is that the development of autobiographical memory depends heavily on language and culture. This explanation receives support

from the finding that children whose parents discuss the past with them in great detail have more memories of early childhood than those whose parents do not.

- The onset of autobiographical memory may depend on the emergence of the self, whereas its subsequent development may depend on social and cultural factors, and the child's development of language.
- The slow development of the hippocampus (central to long-term memory) probably plays a crucial role in infantile amnesia.
- Older witnesses typically produce more accurate recall than younger ones. However, they tend to process events in more elaborate ways and this sometimes makes their memory more error prone.
- Younger children are more suggestible than older ones because they yield more to social pressure and have limited cognitive competence.
- Interviewer bias can be reduced if interviewers avoid leading questions, and do not reward desired answers or criticize nondesired ones.
- Child witnesses can recall more information if they have received training in source monitoring, provide some information nonverbally (e.g. through drawing), and the context of the event is reinstated.

POINTS FOR DISCUSSION

What is the ecological model of memory development? To what extent is this model supported by the evidence?

Why is it difficult to study long-term memory in infants?

What are some of the main factors causing declarative or explicit memory to increase with age?

Why are the effects of age typically smaller with implicit memory than with explicit or declarative memory?

Describe the phenomenon of infantile amnesia and discuss *two* theoretical explanations of it.

What can be done to maximize the accuracy with which child witnesses remember events?

FURTHER READING

Brainerd, C. I., & Reyna, V. F. (2012). Reliability of children's testimony in the era of developmental reversals. *Developmental Review*, 32, 224–267. Charles Brainerd and Valerie Reyna discuss in detail research showing that younger children's testimony is sometimes less prone to error than that of older ones.

Fivush, R. (2010). The development of autobiographical memory. *Annual Review of Psychology*, 62, 2–24. Robyn Fivush provides a comprehensive account of childhood amnesia and the ways in which autobiographical memory develops during childhood.

(Continued)

(Continued)

Ghetti, S., & Lee, J. (2011). Children's episodic memory. *Wiley Interdisciplinary Reviews: Cognitive Science*, 2, 365–373. This article provides a short, readable account of the main findings with respect to the development of episodic memory in children.

Josselyn, S. A., & Frankland, P. W. (2012). Infantile amnesia: A neurogenic hypothesis. *Learning and Memory*, 19, 423–433. The hypothesis that infantile amnesia can be largely explained in terms of the slow development of the hippocampus during the early years of life is discussed in detail in this article.

Mitchell, P., & Ziegler, F. (2013). *Fundamentals of developmental psychology* (2nd edn.). This textbook by Peter Mitchell and Fenja Ziegler includes a readable account of the development of memory during childhood.

Rovee-Collier, C., & Cuevas, K. (2009). Multiple memory systems are unnecessary to account for infant memory development: An ecological model. *Developmental Psychology*, 45, 160–174. Carolyn Rovee-Collier argues persuasively that infants' learning abilities are much greater than is commonly supposed.

Zajac, R., O'Neill, S., & Hayne, H. (2012). Disorder in the courtroom? Child witnesses under cross-examination. *Developmental Review*, 32, 181–204. This review article considers how complete and accurate eyewitness testimony can be obtained from children, and the ways in which this conflicts with typical courtroom cross-examination.

REFERENCES

Amso, D., & Davidow, J. (2012). The development of implicit learning from infancy to adulthood: Item frequencies, relations, and cognitive flexibility. *Developmental Psychobiology*, 54, 664–673.

Baddeley, A. D. (1986). *Working memory*. New York: Oxford University Press.

Baddeley, A. D. (2001). Is working memory still working? *American Psychologist*, 56, 851–864.

Baddeley, A. D. (2007). *Working memory, thought, and action*. Oxford: Oxford University Press.

Barr, R., Rovee-Collier, C., & Campanella, J. (2005). Retrieval protects deferred imitation by 6-month-olds. *Infancy*, 7, 263–283.

Brainerd, C. J. (2013). Developmental reversals in false memory: A new look at the reliability of children's evidence. *Current Directions in Psychological Science*, 22, 335–341.

Brainerd, C. J., & Mojardin, A. H. (1998). Children's and adults' spontaneous false memories: Long-term persistence and mere-testing effects. *Child Development*, 69, 1361–1377.

Brainerd, C. J., & Reyna, V. F. (2004). Fuzzy-trace theory and memory development. *Developmental Review*, 24, 396–439.

Brainerd, C. J., & Reyna, V. F. (2012). Reliability of children's testimony in the era of developmental reversals. *Developmental Review*, 32, 224–267.

Brainerd, C. J., Reyna, V. F., & Ceci, S. J. (2008). Developmental reversals in false memory: A review of data and theory. *Psychological Bulletin*, 134, 343–382.

Campanella, J., & Rovee-Collier, C. (2005). Latent learning and deferred imitation at 3 months. *Infancy*, 7, 243–262.

Ceci, S. J., & Bruck, M. (1993). The suggestibility of the child witness: A historical review and synthesis. *Psychological Bulletin*, 113, 403–439.

Ceci, S. J., & Bruck, M. (2006). Children's suggestibility: Characteristics and mechanisms. *Advances in Child Development and Behavior*, 34, 247–281.

Ceci, S. J., Baker, J. E., & Bronfenbrenner, U. (1988). Prospective remembering and temporal calibration. In M. M. Gruneberg, P. E. Morris, & R. N. Sykes (Eds.), *Practical Aspects of Memory:*

Current Research and Issues (Vol. 1). Chichester, UK: Wiley.

Chi, M. T. (1978). Knowledge, structure and memory development. In R. S. Siegler (Ed.), *Children's thinking: What develops?* Hillsdale, NJ: Lawrence Erlbaum Associates.

Cordón, I. M., Pipe, M. E., Sayfan, L., Melinder, A., & Goodman, G. S. (2004). Memory for traumatic experiences in early childhood. *Developmental Review, 24,* 101–132.

Crawley, R. A., & Eacott, M. J. (2006). Memories of early childhood: Qualities of the experience of recollection. *Memory and Cognition, 34,* 287–294.

Fivush, R. (2010). The development of autobiographical memory. *Annual Review of Psychology, 62,* 2–24.

Fivush, R., & Nelson, K. (2004). Culture and language in the emergence of autobiographical memory. *Psychological Science, 15,* 573–577.

Fivush, R., Hudson, J., & Nelson, K. (1984). Children's long-term memory for a novel event: An exploratory study. *Merrill-Palmer Quarterly Journal of Developmental Psychology, 30,* 303–316.

Freud, S. (1915/1957). In *Freud's collected papers* (Vol. IV). London: Hogarth Press.

Fritz, K., Howie, P., & Kleitman, S. (2010). "How do I remember when I got my dog?" The structure and development of children's metamemory. *Metacognition Learning, 5,* 207–228.

Garven, S., Wood, J. M., & Malpass, R. S. (2000). Allegations of wrongdoing: The effects of reinforcement on children's mundane and fantastic claims. *Journal of Applied Psychology, 85,* 38–49.

Gathercole, S. E., Pickering, S. J., Ambridge, B., & Wearing, H. (2004). The structure of working memory from 4 to 15 years of age. *Developmental Psychology, 40,* 177–190.

Giles, A., & Rovee-Collier, C. (2011). Infant long-term memory for associations formed during mere exposure. *Infant Behavior and Development, 34,* 327–338.

Gross, J., & Hayne, H. (1999). Drawing facilitates children's verbal reports after long delays. *Journal of Experimental Psychology: Applied, 5,* 265–283.

Gross, J., Jack, F., Davis, N., & Hayne, H. (2013). Do children recall the birth of a younger sibling? Implications for the study of childhood amnesia. *Memory, 21,* 336–346.

Han, J. J., Leichtman, M. D., & Wang, Q. (1998). Autobiographical memory in Korean, Chinese, and American children. *Developmental Psychology, 34,* 701–713.

Hartshorn, K. (2003). Reinstatement maintains a memory in human infants for 1½ years. *Developmental Psychology, 42,* 269–282.

Howe, M. L. (2013). The co-emergence of the self and autobiographical memory: An adaptive view of early memory. In P. J. Bauer & R. Fivush (Eds.), *Wiley-Blackwell Handbook on the development of children's memory.* New York: Wiley Blackwell.

Howe, M. L., & Courage, M. L. (1997). The emergence and early development of autobiographical memory. *Psychological Review, 104,* 499–523.

Howe, M. L., Courage, M. L., & Edison, S. C. (2003). When autobiographical memory begins. In M. Conway, S. Gathercole, S. Algarabel, A. Pitarque, & T. Bajo (Eds.), *Theories of memory, Vol. III.* Hove, UK: Psychology Press.

Hsu, V. C. (2010). Time windows in retention over the first year-and-a-half of life: Spacing effects. *Developmental Psychobiology, 52,* 764–774.

Jack, F., & Hayne, H. (2010). Childhood amnesia: Empirical evidence for a two-stage phenomenon. *Memory, 18,* 831–844.

Jack, F., MacDonald, S., Reese, E., & Hayne, H. (2009). Maternal reminiscing style during early childhood predicts the age of adolescents' earliest memories. *Child Development, 80,* 496–505.

Jack, F., Simcock, G., & Hayne, H. (2012). Magic memories: Young children's verbal recall after a 6-year delay. *Child Development, 83,* 159–172.

Josselyn, S. A., & Frankland, P. W. (2012). Infantile amnesia: A neurogenic hypothesis. *Learning and Memory, 19,* 423–433.

Katz, C., & Hamama, L. (2013). "Draw me everything that happened to you": Exploring children's drawings of sexual abuse. *Children and Youth Services Review, 35,* 877–882.

Kingo, O. S., Berntsen, D., & Krøjgaard, P. (2013). Adults' earliest memories as a function of age, gender, and education in a large stratified sample. *Psychology and Aging, 28,* 646–653.

Lavenex, P., & Lavenex, P. B. (2013). Building hippocampal circuits to learn and remember: Insights into the development of human memory. *Behavioural Brain Research, 254,* 8–21.

Levy-Gigi, E., & Vakil, E. (2010). Developmental differences in the impact of contextual factors on susceptibility to retroactive interference. *Journal of Experimental Child Psychology, 105,* 51–62.

Lewis, M., & Brooks-Gunn, J. (1979). Toward a theory of social cognition: The development of self. *New Directions for Child Development, 4,* 1–20.

Metcalfe, J., & Finn, B. (2013). Metacognition and control of study choice in children. *Metacognition and Learning, 8,* 19–46.

Michalczyk, K., Malstädt, N., Worgt, M., Könen, T., & Hasselhorn, M. (2012). Age differences and measurement invariance of working memory in

5- to 12-year-old children. *European Journal of Psychological Assessment, 29,* 220–229.

Murphy, K., McKone, E., & Slee, J. (2003). Dissociations between implicit and explicit memory in children: The role of strategic processing and the knowledge base. *Journal of Experimental Child Psychology, 84,* 124–165.

Nelson, K. (1989). *Narratives from the Crib.* Cambridge, MA: Harvard University Press.

Odegard, T. N., Cooper, C. M., Lampinen, J. M., Reyna, V. F., & Brainerd, C. J. (2009). Children eyewitness memory for multiple real-life events. *Child Development, 80,* 1877–1890.

O'Neill, S., & Zajac, R. (2013). Preparing children for cross-examination: How does intervention timing influence efficacy? *Psychology, Public Policy and Law, 19,* 307–320.

Patel, S., Gaylord, S., & Fagen, J. (2013). Generalization of deferred imitation in 6-, 9-, and 12-month-old infants using visual and auditory contexts. *Infant Behavior and Development, 36,* 25–31.

Peterson, C. (2011). Children's memory reports over time: Getting both better and worse. *Journal of Experimental Child Psychology, 109,* 275–293.

Peterson, C. (2012). Children's autobiographical memories across the years: Forensic implications of childhood amnesia and eyewitness memory for stressful events. *Developmental Review, 32,* 287–306.

Peterson, C., & Rideout, R. (1998). Memory for medical emergencies experienced by 1- and 2-year-olds. *Developmental Psychology, 34,* 1059–1072.

Pierce, S. H., & Lange, G. (2000). Relationships among metamemory, motivation and memory performance in young school-age children. *British Journal of Developmental Child Psychology, 18,* 121–135.

Priestley, G., Roberts, S., & Pipe, M. E. (1999). Returning to the scene: Reminders and context reinstatement enhance children's recall. *Developmental Psychology, 35,* 1006–1019.

Richmond, J., & Nelson, C. A. (2007). Accounting for change in declarative memory: A cognitive neuroscience perspective. *Developmental Review, 27,* 349–373.

Rovee-Collier, C. (1989). The joy of kicking: Memories, motives, and mobiles. In P. R. Solomon, G. R. Goethals, C. M. Kelley, & B. R. Stephens (Eds.), *Memory: Interdisciplinary Approaches* (pp. 151–180). New York: Springer.

Rovee-Collier, C., & Cuevas, K. (2009). Multiple memory systems are unnecessary to account for memory development: An ecological model. *Developmental Psychology, 45,* 160–174.

Rovee-Collier, C., & Giles, A. (2010). Why a neuromaturational model of memory fails:

Exuberant learning in early infancy. *Behavioural Processes, 83,* 197–206.

Rovee-Collier, C., Mitchell, K., & Hsu-Yang, V. (2013). Effortlessly strengthening infant memory: Associative potentiation of new learning. *Scandinavian Journal of Psychology, 54,* 4–9.

Rovee-Collier, C., Sullivan, M. W., Enright, M., Lucas, D., & Fagen, J. W. (1980). Reactivation of infant memory. *Science, 208,* 1159–1161.

Rubin, D. C. (2000). The distribution of early childhood memories. *Memory, 8,* 265–269.

Sauzéon, H., Déjos, M., Lestage, P., Pala, P. A., & N'Kaoua, B. (2012). Developmental differences in explicit and implicit conceptual memory tests: A processing view account. *Child Neuropsychology, 18,* 23–49.

Schleepen, T. M. J., & Jonkman, L. M. (2012). Children's use of semantic organizational strategies is mediated by working memory capacity. *Cognitive Development, 27,* 255–269.

Schneider, W., & Pressley, M. (1998). The development of metacognition: Introduction. *European Journal of Psychology of Education, 13,* 3–8.

Schneider, W., Gruber, W., Gruber, H., Gold, A., & Opwis, K. (1993). Chess expertise and memory for chess positions in children and adults. *Journal of Experimental Child Psychology, 56,* 328–349.

Schneider, W., Knopf, M., & Stefanek, J. (2002). The development of verbal memory in childhood and adolescence: Findings from the Munich Longitudinal Study. *Journal of Educational Psychology, 94,* 751–761.

Sheingold, K., & Tenney, Y. J. (1982). Memory for a salient childhood event. In U. Neisser (Ed.), *Memory observed* (pp. 201–212). New York: Freeman.

Siegler, R. S. (1998). *Children's thinking* (3rd. edn.). Upper Saddle River, NJ: Prentice Hall.

Simcock, G., & Hayne, H. (2003). Age-related changes in verbal and nonverbal memory during early childhood. *Developmental Psychology, 39,* 805–814.

Sparling, J., Wilder, D. A., Kondash, J., Boyle, M., & Compton, M. (2011). Effects of interviewer behavior on accuracy of children's responses. *Journal of Applied Behavior Analysis, 44,* 587–592.

Tamnes, C. K., Walhovd, K. B., Grydeland, H., Holland, D., Ostby, Y., Dale, A. M., et al. (2013). Longitudinal working memory development is related to structural maturation of frontal and parietal cortices. *Journal of Cognitive Neuroscience, 25,* 1611–1623.

Thierry, K. L., & Spence, M. J. (2002). Source-monitoring training facilitates preschoolers' eyewitness memory performance. *Developmental Psychology*, *38*, 428–437.

Thierry, K. L., Lamb, M. E., Pipe, M.-E., & Spence, M. J. (2010). The flexibility of source-monitoring training: Reducing young children's source confusions. *Applied Cognitive Psychology*, *24*, 626–644.

Tustin, K., & Hayne, H. (2010). Defining the boundary: Age-related changes in childhood amnesia. *Developmental Psychology*, *46*, 1049–1061.

Verkoeijen, P. P. J. L., & Bouwmeester, S. (2012). Gist processing in free recall and recognition: Latent variable modeling of children's and adults' true and false memories. *Journal of Cognitive Psychology*, *24*, 633–646.

Weist, R. M. (1972). The role of rehearsal: Recopy or reconstruct? *Journal of Verbal Learning and Verbal Behavior*, *11*, 440–445.

Zajac, R., O'Neill, S., & Hayne, H. (2012). Disorder in the courtroom? Child witnesses under cross-examination. *Developmental Review*, *32*, 181–204.

Contents

Approaches to the study of aging   411

Working memory and aging   414

Aging and long-term memory   416

Theories of aging   424

The aging brain   426

Summary   428

Points for discussion   428

Further reading   429

References   429

CHAPTER 15

MEMORY AND AGING

Alan Baddeley

We all complain about the fallibility of our memories and, as we get older, we complain more. This is what Patrick Stewart, most widely known for his role in *Star Trek*, says about learning his lines on returning to the stage in *Macbeth* and as Malvolio in *Twelfth Night* (Box 15.1).

Box 15.1 Patrick Stewart, *The Observer*, 29 July 2007, p. 37

With every year that passes I am more and more puzzled—and dismayed—by the mental process of learning, absorbing, internalizing and finally speaking lines of dialogue. It has become the only labour in this marvellous job I love so much.

Learning lines used to be a breeze. In rep. I'd do the show, go to the pub, knock back a couple of pints, and then home and head down, into the script, knocking off an act or so before bedtime.

Not any more. Now, learning has to be planned, soberly, in advance of rehearsals and—for me—usually undertaken early in the morning.

APPROACHES TO THE STUDY OF AGING

It is difficult to compare one's own memory with that of others, and comparing it with the state of one's own memory years ago itself involves memory. There is also evidence that we become somewhat less good at reporting memory lapses as we get older (Sunderland, Watts, Baddeley, & Harris, 1986), and that complaints about memory in the elderly relate more closely to depression than to actual memory performance (Rabbitt & Abson, 1990). We clearly need better evidence than our subjective feelings of progressive memory failure, especially given that impaired memory is the earliest and most powerful predictor of the onset of Alzheimer disease, an increasingly serious problem with the gradual aging of the Western population. So what can you expect if you remain healthy but get older, and how will it differ from the onset of Alzheimer's?

The longitudinal approach

The study of aging involves the study of change, as opposed to most of the research described so far, which assumes a system that is relatively stable, although of course one that can change as a result of learning or forgetting. There are two principal methods of studying aging, the *longitudinal* and the *cross-sectional*. In a longitudinal study, a sample of people, preferably selected so as to reflect the full range of the population, will be tested repeatedly, for example every 5 years, preferably over many decades (Rönnlund, Nyberg, Bäckman, & Nilsson, 2005; Rönnlund & Nilsson, 2006). The advantage of this approach is that the effects of age on the performance of each individual can be studied, subsequently allowing specified individuals, such as those developing Alzheimer disease, to be singled out and their performance *before* the onset of the disease compared with that of more fortunate, healthy people. Such studies are expensive in time and funding but are already yielding crucial information about the development of a range of diseases and their genetic, physiological, and cognitive precursors.

Longitudinal designs do, however, have two major problems. The first stems from the fact that some participants will almost certainly drop out, because they move house or perhaps because they lose interest. Furthermore, people who drop out might be atypical of the rest of the sample, gradually making it less representative. There are statistical methods of attempting to correct for drop-out, but this is inevitably a complex and potentially controversial issue. A second problem concerns measures of cognition in general, and memory in particular. Even though test sessions are separated by as much as 5 years, substantial learning occurs, not just because patients learn the particular items comprising the test but also because there are more general practice effects that can be sufficient to counteract any decrement due to aging.

This problem is avoided if one uses a cross-sectional design in which different groups of people are sampled across the age range and their performance is measured on a single occasion. The drawbacks of this approach are that one cannot, of course, relate performance to earlier data, nor can one relate performance to the future development of the individual, without at least including a later test that will be influenced by practice effects from the first test session. A further problem with both designs is the so-called cohort effect, reflecting the very substantial changes in education, society,

health, and nutrition that have occurred across decades, that might well have a major influence on performance. Average scores on the Raven's Matrices intelligence test have, for example, been increasing steadily since 1940 (Flynn, 1987) in many Western societies, and the health and longevity of the general population have also steadily increased in many parts of the world. Hence, comparing people currently in their twenties with 80-year-olds involves more than a simple effect of aging.

A solution to these problems is to combine longitudinal and cross-sectional approaches by adding a new cohort of participants at each test point. In due course, comparison of these initial test groups across the years will provide a measure of any cohort effects, while comparing them with the relevant longitudinal group of that age will give a clear indication of learning effects. This approach has been used by a number of studies including the Betula Study carried out in Northern Sweden and named after the birch tree that predominates at those latitudes (Nilsson, Adolfsson, Bäckman, de Frias, Molander, & Nyberg, 2004). The study emphasizes memory and is beginning to show some very interesting results. One of these is that both practice effects (Figure 15.1), and cohort effects (Figure 15.2) are very substantial (Rönnlund et al., 2005).

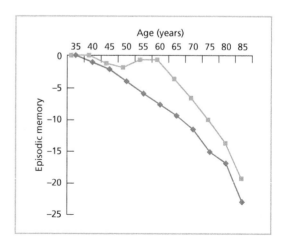

Figure 15.1 Decline in episodic memory performance between ages 35 and 85 as measured by a longitudinal (filled squares) or cross-sectional (diamonds) method. Based on Rönnlund et al. (2005).

KEY TERM

Longitudinal design: Method of studying development or aging whereby the same participants are successively tested at different ages.

Cohort effect: The tendency for people born at different time periods to differ as a result of historic changes in diet, education and other social factors.

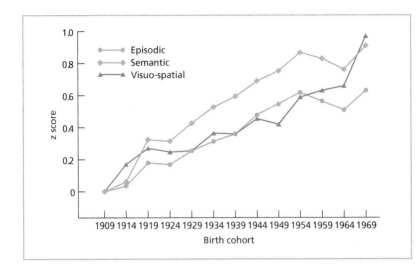

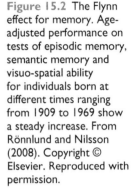

Figure 15.2 The Flynn effect for memory. Age-adjusted performance on tests of episodic memory, semantic memory and visuo-spatial ability for individuals born at different times ranging from 1909 to 1969 show a steady increase. From Rönnlund and Nilsson (2008). Copyright © Elsevier. Reproduced with permission.

Using a correlational approach it is possible to identify some of the causes of enhanced performance in more recent cohorts. The Rönnlund et al. (2005) evidence suggests an important role for nutrition, as reflected in the gradual increase over the years in average height. Years of education also appear to be associated with memory performance, independent of age. Number of children in the family, which is tentatively interpreted as reflecting the amount of attention an individual child might receive within the family, is also linked to memory performance (Figure 15.3). As each sample includes participants across the age range, it is possible to study the way

in which such variables influence the process of aging within different cohorts. Finally, the very large numbers involved are beginning to allow genetic studies to be carried out, with the potential for identifying not only the genetic precursors to diseases, but also whether genetic links influence different aspects of memory in different ways (Nilsson, Adolfsson, Bäckman, Cruts, Nyberg, Small, & van Broeckhoven, 2006).

The Betula study, in common with most similar studies, focuses on the specific part of the life span involved in aging. A longitudinal study extending over the whole lifespan would, of course, take a lifetime to complete. Even so,

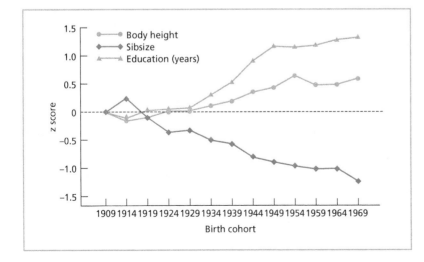

Figure 15.3 Age-adjusted height, family size, and years of education for Swedish people born between 1909 and 1969. People have become taller and better educated, while families have become smaller. From Rönnlund and Nilsson (2008). Copyright © Elsevier. Reproduced with permission.

some studies that commence with pregnancy and test at regular intervals are ongoing, although they are—for the most part—not focused on cognition and have not yet been running for a lifetime. It was therefore with great excitement that Ian Deary, an Edinburgh psychologist with an interest in intelligence, discovered that well-validated IQ tests had been given to every child in Scotland who was 11 years old in 1932 (N = 89,498) and that these results were still available (Deary, Whiteman, Starr, Whalley, & Fox, 2004). Through local records and press advertising, they were able to contact 550 people in the Edinburgh area who had been born in 1921 and tested 11 years later. These volunteers were retested using the original IQ measure, together with a number of other psychological and physical measures.

People originally tested in 1932 would be 80 at the time of retest and, by that point, many of the original sample had died. Deary et al. (2004) found that, for both men and women, the lowest IQ quartile had the lowest life expectancy; mortality differences between the remaining quartiles were small. A slight discrepancy in the general pattern occurred in the case of men during the 1940s and 1950s, which probably results from the effect of the Second World War, where certain dangerous operations such as aircrew tended to differentially select for a higher ability.

In terms of mental testing there proved to be a very high correlation between score at 11 and at age 80 (r = .66), although, as expected, level of performance at 80 was lower. In an attempt to identify factors that led to successful aging, IQ at 11 was correlated with a range of cognitive and physical fitness measures, namely grip strength, lung function, and time to walk to 6 meters (Deary, Whalley, Batty, & Starr, 2006). Physical fitness at 80 was predicted by IQ at 11 and was influenced by sex, social class and the *APOE* gene, which Nilsson et al. (2006) had also found to be related to episodic and semantic memory performance in their elderly sample in the Betula study.

Cross-sectional studies

Despite the growing importance of such large-scale longitudinal projects, much of the research in the field so far has relied on cross-sectional studies, typically involving the comparison of a young and an elderly sample, approximately matched for educational and socioeconomic status. We will begin by viewing the results of such studies, looking in turn at the various components of memory, then moving on to theories of aging and attempts to optimize cognition in old age. We conclude by discussing what is known about the link between the structure and functioning of the brain and aging.

WORKING MEMORY AND AGING

Although both verbal and visual memory span tend to decline with age, the decline is far from dramatic, with mean digit span dropping from 6.6 items to 5.8 over the course of an adult life (Parkinson, Inman, & Dannenbaum, 1985) and spatial span using the Corsi block tapping task dropping from 5.1 to 4.7 blocks (Spinnler, Della Sala, Bandera, & Baddeley, 1988). Craik (1986) found a minimal drop in memory span for unrelated words in the elderly, a difference that increased substantially when the task was changed to one in which the words had to be recalled in alphabetic order (e.g. hear *pen dog zoo hat* , recall *dog hat pen zoo*). The crucial difference, of course, is the need to simultaneously hold and manipulate the material, in short, to use working memory.

There is broad general agreement that working memory is susceptible to the effects of age, although it is not always clear exactly which aspects are most vulnerable (Box 15.2). Whereas sentence span in which participants must process a sequence of sentences and then recall the final word does tend to be sensitive to aging, the pattern of results is less marked than one might expect. Verhaeghen, Marcoen, and Goossens (1993) reviewed a range of studies of the effects of age on working memory span, concluding that a decrement occurs, but is rather small. May, Hasher, and Kane (1999) suggest that this decline could largely be the result of the build-up of interference from earlier sequences, reflecting a problem with inhibiting irrelevant material rather than one of combining storage and processing *per se* (May et al., 1999). This is consistent with the suggestion by Hasher and Zacks (1988; Hasher, Zacks, & May, 1999) that a major cognitive effect of aging is the reduced capacity to inhibit irrelevant stimuli.

Box 15.2 Memory and aging

There is saying that "you are as old as you feel." But how old is that? A study by Rubin and Berntsen (2006) suggests that, from their mid forties, people begin to feel younger than their age, with the perceived age being an average of 20% younger than their actual age. Why should this be? Is it a memory effect, or just that we view the world through rose-tinted spectacles?

An intriguing example of the decline of the capacity to inhibit irrelevant information with age comes from a study carried out by Bäckman and Molander (1986), who tested groups of competitive miniature golf players who were matched in skill under practice conditions. During competition, however, the 50-year-old senior group showed a decline in performance in contrast to younger competitors. Under practice conditions, a heart-rate monitor indicated that both groups of players showed a slowing of the heart rate when making a shot, reflecting higher concentration; during competition this effect occurred with the young golfers but was not seen in the older group. When subsequently asked to describe specific shots, the older group showed a greater tendency to recall irrelevant information than the young, who appeared to be able to shut out potential distractions and concentrate on the stroke. Bäckman and Molander note, however, that very large individual differences occur.

There tends to be a decline in performance with age in many skills that involve intense concentration, including those that do not involve physical strength, such as chess, where adapting to age appears to involve a gradual change in strategy. Charness (1985) studied the performance of chess players who differed in age but were matched for expertise. He found that the young players tended to scan a wide range of options, whereas the older players scanned fewer but in greater depth. This could reflect an increasing difficulty in keeping track of multiple sources of information.

There is considerable evidence to suggest that age impairs the capacity to divide attention between two sources. There is no doubt that dual-task performance is often more affected by age than performance on the two components separately (see Riby, Perfect, & Stollery, 2004, for a review). The results of many such studies might, however, simply reflect the increased overall load rather than a specific deficit in the ability to coordinate two simultaneous tasks. If an elderly person has

As we get older, it becomes harder at times of stress to shut out distractions, making it more likely that the older golfer will 'choke' on the final putt that would have won the championship.

greater difficulty with each of the individual tasks, it is hardly surprising that he/she has even more difficulty in performing both at the same time.

To demonstrate a deficit in task combination *per se*, it is necessary to ensure that level of performance on the individual tasks is equal for the young and old groups, if necessary by making the tasks easier for the elderly. In a series of studies to be described in the section on Alzheimer disease (see Chapter 16, p. 454), digit span and a visuo-spatial tracking task were combined (Spinnler et al., 1988; Baddeley, Bressi, Della Sala, Logie, & Spinnler, 1991). Provided level of performance on the individual tasks was equated, no reliable age decrement occurred, although there was a marked detrimental effect of dementia. Broadly speaking, however, it is probably wise to assume that working memory is progressively impaired, particularly when it involves tasks comprising either speed of processing or episodic long-term memory, which we consider next.

AGING AND LONG-TERM MEMORY

Episodic memory

There is no doubt that performance on tasks involving episodic memory declines steadily through the adult years. Although many studies have used relatively artificial material, such as the acquisition of pairs of unrelated words or the retention of geometric figures, the effects are by no means limited to such material. The Doors and People test described in Chapter 16 (p. 441) uses relatively realistic material, such as people's names and pictures of doors, and shows a decline for both recall and recognition of visual and verbal materials. A similar decline is shown in the Rivermead Behavioural Memory Test (see Chapter 16, p. 454), which was designed to mirror everyday memory situations (Wilson, Cockburn, Baddeley, & Hiorns 1989b), and Salthouse (1991) reviews over 40 real-world activities, from actors learning lines, through recall of bridge hands to memory for conversations, all of which show a decline with age.

What, then, is the nature of the episodic memory decline with age? The magnitude of the decline varies depending on the nature of the memory task and the method of testing retention. Fergus Craik and his collaborators identify three factors as crucial determinants of episodic memory performance in the elderly. The first of these is the overall decline in *episodic memory per se*. This is modulated by two other variables, one being the *processing capacity* of the learner and the other concerning the level of environmental support provided during retrieval (Craik, 2005).

Most learning experiments involve presenting material under time constraints, and, given that age tends to slow processing, then the elderly may take longer to perceive and process the material, and also be less likely to be able to develop and utilize complex learning strategies. Craik and colleagues have explored this aspect of learning by using a secondary task to reduce the available attention in younger participants, demonstrating that under some conditions at least, performance by the young then resembles that of the elderly (Craik & Byrd, 1982).

However, the fact that both age and an attentionally demanding task impair learning does not mean that they necessarily do so by influencing the same memory process. For example, it might be that the main source of impairment in the elderly is a basic memory deficit at the neurophysiological level, possibly reflecting poorer consolidation of the memory trace, whereas the deficit shown by the young when their attention is distracted might reflect a reduction of time spent on learning because of competition from the secondary task. This was tested in a series of experiments by Naveh-Benjamin (2000) in which young and older participants were presented with pairs of words that differed in whether they were semantically associated or not (e.g. *dog–bone* versus *cat–book*). Performance was then tested by recognition. There was found to be a substantial difference

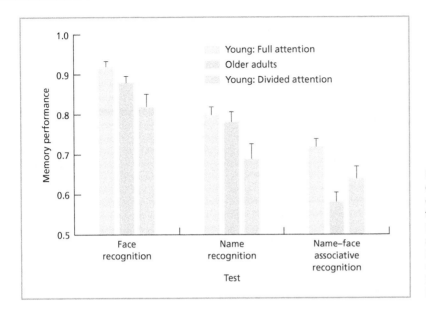

between the two age groups for the unrelated items, but not for associated pairs.

The initial interpretation of these results by Naveh-Benjamin (2000) was that their impaired attentional capacity meant that the elderly were less able to form associative links than the young. This was subsequently tested using young participants given an attentionally demanding concurrent task, with the prediction that the pattern of performance of the young would than resemble that of the elderly. This was not supported by subsequent experiments (Naveh-Benjamin, Guez, & Marom 2003a; Naveh-Benjamin, Hussain, Guez, & Bar-On, 2003b). The secondary task impaired both related and unrelated pairs to the same extent, suggesting that the difference between the young and old groups was attributable to basic learning capacity, rather than to attentional or strategic differences. Naveh-Benjamin refers to this as the associative deficit hypothesis.

KEY TERM

Associative deficit hypothesis: Proposal that the age deficit in memory comes from an impaired capacity to form associations between previously unrelated stimuli.

A series of later studies has investigated the associative deficit hypothesis across a range of materials involving both words and pictures (Naveh-Benjamin et al., 2003a, 2003b), in each case replicating the relative preservation of the capacity to recognize which items had been presented, together with a substantial deficit in the capacity to bind or associate unrelated word pairs. The fact that this deficit was not attributable to an attentional deficit was shown particularly clearly in a study by Naveh-Benjamin, Guez, Kilb, and Reedy (2004a) using face–name pairs. Participants were shown 40 name–face pairs for 3 seconds each and instructed to try to remember them. Three groups were tested—an elderly group and two young groups—one of which involved a demanding concurrent task that required participants to discriminate between tones and to respond as rapidly as possible. Two aspects of memory were tested. The first involved recognizing which names and faces had been presented and which were new. As the first two sets of data in Figure 15.4 show, this recognition task showed little or no effect of age, but a clear effect of the concurrent task. The second memory test involved deciding which name went with which face. As this dataset shows, there was a substantial age effect, which was reliably greater than the effect of the demanding concurrent task. The fact that the age effect was not found for recognition but is clearly present in the name–face binding condition suggests an *associative* deficit that does not appear to be explicable in attentional terms.

A striking feature of the studies by Naveh-Benjamin is the observation that the associative deficit shown by the elderly is much reduced when pairs of items are related rather than arbitrary, suggesting that there might be other situations in which the effects of aging on episodic memory may be minimized. This occurs in the case of the *self-performed task* effect. This involves a subject attempting to remember a list of objects, each accompanied by an instruction, for example "break the matchstick" and "shake the pen," each of which has to be either passively heard or performed. Performing the act leads to substantially better subsequent free recall than simply hearing the experimenter provide the action instructions, greatly reducing the age difference (Bäckman & Nilsson, 1984; Engelkamp, 1998). The current view is that this procedure gains its advantage from providing an enriched level of coding involving auditory, visual, manual, and—perhaps importantly—self-related codes, with the multiple coding reducing reliance on any given feature or cue.

The third aspect of Craik's classification concerns the amount of environmental support provided at retrieval. It is in general the case that age effects show up most clearly in free recall, where there are no external cues; age decrements are somewhat less when retrieval cues are provided, and are least under recognition conditions (Craik, Byrd, & Swanson, 1987). However, although it is often the case that recognition memory can be relatively preserved in the elderly, in many such studies (as shown by the previously described studies by Naveh-Benjamin, 2000) this might reflect the tendency of recall tests to involve an associative component, either explicitly, as in paired-associated learning, or implicitly, as in free recall, which is likely to depend on creating and retrieving associated chunks. As data from the Doors and People test show, clear effects of age can be found using carefully matched recall and recognition measures (Baddeley, **Emslie**, & Nimmo-Smith, 1994). However,

recognition tests typically *are* less demanding than recall, and tend to show less of a difference between younger and older groups.

Remembering and knowing

An interesting feature of the effects of age on recognition memory is that older people appear to be much better at recognizing that an item has occurred than in remembering the context in which it occurred (Park & Puglisi, 1985; Chalfonte & Johnson, 1996). You might recall from Chapter 8 that recognition appears to be based on two separable processes: "remembering," in which the participant recollects the learning incident and its context (for example, remembering that the word *dog* reminded you of your childhood pet); and "knowing," in which a positive identification is based on a feeling of familiarity rather than a specific recollection. Parkin and Walter (1992) presented young, middle-aged, and elderly participants with a sequence of 36 words, each printed on a flash card. Next, participants were shown the 36 old items together with 36 new items for recognition. They were required to categorize any recognized items as members of the "remember" or "know" category. There was no difference between the young and old groups in the number of words correctly identified as "known." By contrast, however, correctly "remembered" responses were greatest for the young and least for the elderly group.

This result was subsequently replicated by Rajaram (1993), who ruled out the possibility that it simply reflected a difference in level of confidence between the age groups. Hay and Jacoby (1999) applied the process dissociation method described in Chapter 8 to groups of young and old participants, finding that the old were impaired on the recollection but not on the familiarity component. Reviewing the literature on this issue, Light, Prull, LaVoie, and Healy (2000) conclude that there is strong evidence that the recollective process declines with age. Given that recollection is likely to depend on retrieving an association between the item and the context or experience of learning, this is consistent with the associative deficit hypothesis of aging and episodic long-term memory proposed by Naveh-Benjamin et al. (2003b). Whether the familiarity mechanism is entirely free from any age effect is, however, more controversial. Conclusions depend on the assumptions made in computing the familiarity measure, and in particular on whether these two mechanisms are assumed to be independent or not.

So is recognition memory spared in the elderly? The answer would seem to depend on the precise nature of the task. To the extent that recollection of the original experience is involved in the recognition decision, it clearly is not spared. However, if a general sense of familiarity is sufficient then recognition in the elderly is relatively well preserved.

Prospective memory

One of the most frustrating features of memory failure occurs when we plan or agree to do something and then forget to carry out that action, whether it is a relatively simple error, such as failing to pick up bread on the way home from work, or more serious, such as missing an important appointment. There is no doubt that as we get older we complain more about such everyday lapses, but are we in fact less reliable?

The easiest way to study prospective memory is in a constrained laboratory situation, such as that developed by Einstein and McDaniel (1990), in which participants perform an ongoing task and are instructed to respond either after a specified time or when a specific cue occurs (for further discussion, see Chapter 13). Their initial study (Einstein & McDaniel, 1990) found little evidence of age effects, whereas a later investigation (Einstein, McDaniel, Richardson, Guynn, & Cunfer, 1995) found a decrement for time-based but not for event-based tasks; a result they interpreted on the grounds that time-based prospective memory required more self-initiated processing. However, later research suggests that both types of prospective memory tend to be impaired in the elderly.

One large-scale study involved 100 participants in each of 10 cohorts ranging from 35 to 80 years in age. The task was simply to remember to sign a form on completion of the test session. Whereas 61% of the younger 35- to 45-year-olds remembered, only 25% of 70- to 80-year-olds were successful (Mäntylä

& Nilsson, 1997). Similar major declines in prospective memory have been reported by Cockburn and Smith (1991), and Maylor (1996) found that both time-based and event-based prospective memory declined with age. Some studies find a greater decline in time-based performance (Park, Hertzog, Kidder, Morrell, & Mayhorn 1997), but the opposite result was found by d'Ydewalle, Luwel, & Brunfaut (1999), suggesting that the time-versus event-based categorization might not be a particularly useful one in this context.

It is important to bear in mind that the term "prospective memory" refers to a class of situations, not necessarily mapping onto any single type of memory. To perform a prospective memory task, it is necessary to encode two things: The first is the action to be performed; the second is the time or event when that action must be retrieved. Given that the material and retrieval plan have been adequately encoded, it is then necessary to maintain this information over a delay and perform the relevant action at an appropriate time. In certain laboratory-based tasks, continuous active maintenance might be possible while performing the concurrent task, provided that participants have sufficient working memory capacity. Such continuous maintenance is much less likely, however, under many real-world situations, in which it might be necessary to maintain an intention over several days. Rehearsal could still occur, but this will presumably be intermittent, involving periodic retrieval from long-term memory. In line with Craik's rule of thumb regarding memory tasks, the presence of a retrieval cue in the event-based case might be expected to enhance performance in the elderly, although the evidence suggests that this is often not sufficient to guarantee success.

So far, we have discussed experimental results in which prospective memory virtually always appears to be poorer in the elderly. Somewhat surprisingly perhaps, this is not always the case in more realistic contexts. One class of prospective memory task involves instructing the participant to post a card or make a telephone call at a specific future time, and under these arguably more ecologically relevant situations, older subjects often perform better than the young. For example, Rendell and Thomson (1999) tested adults in their twenties, sixties and eighties, and found that when the tasks were embedded in their daily life, the older participants out-performed the young ones, whereas when the task was simulated in the laboratory the opposite occurred. This was replicated by Rendell and Craik (2000) using a laboratory board game called *Virtual Week* to simulate everyday life more closely; again the elderly performed better than the young outside the laboratory context, but poorly within.

This discrepancy between everyday life and laboratory results is often attributed to older people being aware of the limitations of their memory and using various strategies, such as diaries and reminders, to compensate, whereas the young tend to rely more on their still-fallible memory. Rendell and Craik, however, explicitly instructed their subjects not to use external aids, and attribute the difference to the fact that their older participants lived more ordered and structured lives, making it easier to form a well-ordered plan. It could also be the case that a test of their memory was a more important feature of the lives of the elderly than it was for the younger prospective rememberers. Motivation in the real world is probably a very important variable in prospective memory. I suspect most of us forget more dental appointments than parties, and to fail to get married because one forgot to turn up would not be regarded as a very plausible excuse. Indeed, one of the reasons why forgetting appointments might be so embarrassing is because of the suggestion that the event, and by implication the person involved, was not regarded as very important.

Direct evidence for the influence of importance on prospective memory comes from a recent study by Ihle, Schnitzpahn, Rendell, Luong and Kliegel (2012) who suggested that even the studies requiring remembering outside the laboratory tend to be somewhat artificial in setting up a specific separate task such as sending a postcard at a particular time. In order to obtain a more realistic assessment of prospective memory, they used a diary-based approach where, over a sequence of 5 successive days, a younger and an older group were required to list their intentions for the following day and indicate their relative importance. On the day after, they were required to report whether the actions had in fact been completed, and if not, whether this was because they forgot or because they downgraded its importance. They were also asked to report their use of reminders. The results are shown in Figure 15.5 from which two main conclusions can be drawn. First of all, there is a clear relationship been rated importance and probability of forgetting, with both groups being virtually perfect for items they regard as very important. Second, there is a clear advantage to the older group. There was no overall difference in number of reminders used, although the young reported a significantly higher stress level than the retired elderly. Ihle et al. suggest that the setting and regulation of goals may be something that develops with age and enhances prospective memory, despite declining episodic memory.

Semantic memory

Unlike the steady decline in episodic memory as we grow older, semantic memory is maintained, at least as measured by vocabulary knowledge, which even continues to grow slightly with age and which hence is typically somewhat more extensive in the elderly than in the young (Giambra, Arenberg, Zonderman, & Kawas, 1995). Knowledge of historical facts

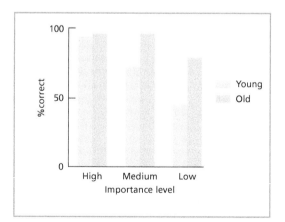

Figure 15.5 Results from Ihle et al., which suggest that the setting and regulation of goals may be something that develops with age and enhances prospective memory, despite declining episodic memory. Data from Ihle et al. (2012).

also increases with age (Perlmuter, Scharff, Karsh, & Monty, 1980), although speed of access declines (Burke, MacKay, Worthley, & Wade, 1991).

Vocabulary scores are sometimes regarded as providing a "hold" test, because they tend to be relatively resistant to the effects of brain damage, age, or disease, whereas speed measures tend to be highly sensitive. Both these features are measured in the SCOLP (Speed and Capacity of Language Processing) test (Baddeley, Emslie, & Nimmo-Smith, 1992). Vocabulary is tested using the spot-the-word test in which the participant must choose between pairs of items, one a word and the other a pseudo word. These range from very obvious, for example *rabbit–flotter*, to more obscure pairs such as *lapidary–halitation*. Performance correlates highly with other measures of vocabulary and verbal intelligence and is resistant to the effects of age, or indeed Alzheimer disease (Baddeley, Baddeley, Bucks, & Wilcock, 2001; Baddeley & Crawford, 2012).

The second component of the SCOLP test involves a task based on the original semantic memory studies of Collins and Quillian (1969), who you may recall from Chapter 7, required participants to verify simple statements about the world as rapidly as possible. Sentences are either obviously true or obviously false, e.g. *snakes travel on their bellies* versus *beefsteaks travel on their bellies*. Errors are uniformly low, indicating that the problem is not lack of knowledge but speed of access to that knowledge. This is highly sensitive to a range of factors, including age.

Although vocabulary is well preserved, the use of language can be constrained by age in other more subtle ways. This was shown in an ingenious study by Kemper (1990), involving a study of diaries kept over a period of 70 years by pioneers settling the American Midwest. Because the diaries were written by the same individual over a long period of time, they provide a naturalistic longitudinal study of language.

The diaries tend to show an increase in ambiguity over the years through the use of indeterminate pronouns such as "he" as in "Cousins Robert and John visited us last week, despite the terrible weather. He was full of

stories about the old days..." As they became older, diarists seemed to attempt to avoid this source of ambiguity by reducing the number of pronouns used. Later diaries also tended to avoid left-branching sentences such as "A roof over his head is the right of every man," which tend to place a heavier load on working memory than their right-branching equivalent "Every man has a right to a roof over his head." Despite the more constrained nature of the later diaries, independent judges tended to rate them as better written and more interesting (Kemper, Kynette, & Norman, 1992).

Implicit learning and memory

Given that implicit learning and memory involve a range of different processes, it is perhaps unsurprising that the effects of aging are not uniform. Reviewing the extensive literature, Light et al. (2000) conclude that, on balance, there is evidence for a clear but moderate age effect on priming tasks that involve response production, such as stem completion in which a list of words is presented and then tested by giving participants the first few letters of a word and asking them to produce a possible completion. They contrast this with *identification* tasks, such as deciding whether an item is a real word or not, or identifying a fragmented picture as rapidly as possible, where age effects tend to be smaller or absent. It may, however, reflect a contribution of episodic memory to production but not identification tasks. Reduced episodic memory may also be responsible for a tendency for the elderly to be more open to being misled by subsequent false information (Cohen & Faulkner, 1989; Schacter, Koutsaal, & Norman, 1997), perhaps failing to remember either its questionable source or the earlier correct version.

The effect of age on the acquisition of motor skills is also complex. There is no doubt that motor *performance* tends to decline as we get older, reflecting a decline in the speed of both perception and movement (Welford, 1985). This can lead to a slower rate of learning of time-based tasks such as pursuit tracking, which involves keeping a stylus in contact with a moving target (Wright & Payne, 1985). However, whereas skilled *performance* certainly can be impaired, it is less clear whether, given appropriate conditions, the rate of *learning* is necessarily slower. For example, the rate of learning a sequence of motor movements or a new stimulus–response mapping might not show an age difference (Wishart & Lee, 1997). Similarly, on a task involving responding serially to four separate stimuli under self-paced conditions, young and older adults showed a comparable rate of learning (Howard & Howard, 1989), whereas Willingham and Winter (1995) found that older adults, who had never used a computer mouse before, were as adept at learning to navigate a maze on a computer as were younger participants.

So can old dogs learn new tricks? It appears to depend on the tricks. As in the case of priming, it seems likely that in tasks in which the response is obvious, and performance is measured purely in terms of improved speed, the elderly will show slower initial performance with a preserved rate of subsequent learning, whereas tasks in which new and unobvious links must be learned are likely to create problems for the older adult. A good example of such a task was devised by Wilson, Baddeley, and Cockburn (1989), who required patients to learn how to enter the time and date into a small palm-computer. Rate of learning was extremely sensitive to episodic memory deficits. Although relatively few steps were involved, patients who had even relatively mild memory loss had great difficulty in acquiring them. Unfortunately, the rapid development of technology means that there a constant need to learn such basic and ever-changing skills.

Use it or lose it?

There is no doubt that individual differences become more marked as people get older, probably for a number of different reasons. One factor is certainly the general decline in health, which in turn is linked to both genetic and lifestyle differences. It appears to help if you are healthy, eat appropriately, take lots of exercise, and remain mentally active, in the sense that all of these tend to be correlated with comparative resistance to age impairment. However, a comparison of university professors and blue-collar workers in Sweden by Christensen, Henderson, Griffiths, and

Levings (1997) found no difference in rate of memory decline. A study of university professors in their thirties, fifties, and sixties by Shimamura, Berry, Mangels, Rustings, and Jurica (1995) found clear evidence of a decline in reaction time and paired-associate learning, but no difference in prose recall, suggesting that meaningful material might allow the active learner to compensate for declining episodic memory. A review by Hertzog, Kramer, Wilson and Lindenberger (2008) concludes that a reliable impact of lifestyle on aging has not, so far, been well established, with existing studies suffering from a number of problems of interpretation, including atypical samples of participants, unsatisfactory measures of cognition and the problem of other correlated variables such as socioeconomic status, nutrition and health. Hence, while many lifestyle factors correlate with preserved cognitive function, demonstrating clear and specific causal links is difficult.

A much more powerful way of demonstrating causation is, of course, to intervene by introducing training of each potentially relevant factor. This involves recruiting a sizable and representative sample of participants. One group then receives an intervention that is thought to be potentially helpful, while another group is provided with an intervention that is likely to be equally interesting, but unlikely to lead to delaying the normal aging process.

Given the increasing size of the aging population and the cost, both financial and in terms of suffering, imposed by Alzheimer's disease, there is considerable current interest in whether is it possible to slow the process of cognitive aging, to enhance levels of cognitive functioning and to reduce the likelihood or delay the onset of Alzheimer's disease. A number of studies have addressed this point, a good example being that of Ball, Berch, Helmers, Jobe, Leveck, Marsiske, et al. (2002), who divided a total of 2832 elderly participants into four groups, each of which underwent a 5- to 6-week training program. One group received memory training involving the teaching of strategies, accompanied by extensive practice on remembering words and shopping lists. A second group received training on a range of verbal reasoning tasks. A third group received speed training on visual search and divided attention tasks. Finally, a fourth group served as controls and received no explicit training.

All groups were subsequently tested on all three relevant areas, and in addition an attempt was made to assess the impact of the training on everyday functioning. Each of the three groups improved on the skills trained, even though tested using a different format. Happily, no change occurred for the untrained skills, indicating that only the specific training had been effective. Unfortunately, however, there was no reliable evidence that any of the gains transferred to everyday functioning, although the authors speculate, somewhat optimistically, that the training might have a protective effect in slowing subsequent age-related decline. The evidence from this and other related studies, however, does seem to suggest that one can certainly teach useful memory strategies to elderly participants, and that these can generalize to novel memory material. In principle, this could be useful in everyday life for acquiring new information such as PIN numbers and learning new names. At present, however, the evidence for a general impact on everyday cognition is not strong, leading Salthouse (2006) to a somewhat negative conclusion. This continues to be a very active field with new studies appearing

frequently, and a later review of the evidence by Hertzog et al. (2008), placing more emphasis on longitudinal studies, came to a more encouraging conclusion, that evidence of the effectiveness of cognitive training is becoming more convincing, particularly on executive functioning and working memory.

The evidence is much stronger for a positive effect of *exercise* on maintaining cognitive function. In a typical study, Kramer, Hahn, Cohen, Banich, McAuley, Harrison, et al. (1999) studied 124 sedentary but healthy older adults, randomizing them into two groups. One group received aerobic walking-based exercise, while the control group received toning and stretching exercises. The groups trained for about an hour a day for 3 days a week over a 6-month period. Cognition was measured by a number of tests including task switching, attentional selection, and capacity to inhibit irrelevant information. They found a modest increase in aerobic fitness, together with a clear improvement in cognitive performance. A subsequent meta-analysis of a range of available studies by Colcombe and Kramer (2003) found convincing evidence for a positive impact of aerobic exercise on a range of cognitive tasks, most notably those involving executive processing (see Figure 15.6).

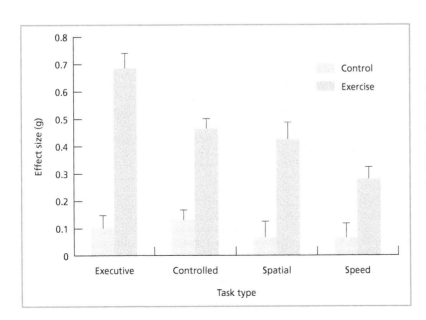

Figure 15.6 Effect sizes of mean differences in cognitive performance between older adults in aerobic fitness training (mauve bars) and those in a control condition (green bars) for different types of cognitive tasks. The greatest impact of training is on tasks involving executive processing. Adapted from Colcombe and Kramer (2003). From Hertzog et al. (2009). Copyright © American Psychological Association. Reprinted with permission.

It is, of course, easier to do controlled intervention studies with animals, and here the evidence is clear in showing beneficial effects of both environmental enrichment and exercise (see van Praag, Kempermann, & Gage, 2000 for a review). Rats raised in an enriched cage environment show less decline in learning with age than rats that have lived in comfortable but less interesting homes (Greenough, Black, & Wallis, 1987). Animal studies have the further advantage that it is possible to look for the mechanism whereby enrichment or exercise influence subsequent performance. A study by Black, Isaacs, Anderson, Alcantara and Greenough (1990) studied the effects on aging rats of both fitness training and motor skill learning. One group had access to activity wheels, resulting in aerobic training, while the other learned nonaerobic skills such as crossing rope bridges and climbing under and over obstacles. The motor skill group showed an increase in synapses in the cerebellum, an area that is important for motor behavior, whereas fitness training led to increased vascularization in other parts of the brain, potentially important in providing increased oxygen to such regions. Later studies reviewed by Kempermann (2008) present further evidence of

Greenough et al.'s (1987) study showed that rats who had lived in an enriched and interesting environment showed less cognitive decline than their counterparts who had lived in a more basic and less stimulating environment.

neurotrophic factors that enhance cell and neuron growth and facilitate synaptic plasticity, particularly in the dentate gyrus of the hippocampus, helping maintain and promote learning and memory.

So where do we stand on the use-it-or-lose-it question? Does more activity result in better memory, or does declining memory cause people to be less active? On balance, I myself would tend to favor the use-it-or-lose-it hypothesis; even if it does not protect you from cognitive decline, using it is likely to lead to a rather less boring old age.

THEORIES OF AGING

In recent years, there have been a number of attempts to account for the effects of aging on cognition in terms of one or other single factor. Probably the most influential of these macro theories has been the proposal by Salthouse (1996) that the cognitive effects of aging can all be explained by the reduced speed of processing that is a marked feature of aging. This conclusion is based on a very extensive series of correlational studies, which do indeed tend to show that the best overall prediction of performance in the elderly is provided by measures that depend on speed of processing, rather than processing accuracy or memory performance. There does, however, seem to be evidence that memory decline might be separable from a more general decline in cognitive function with age (Salthouse & Becker, 1998). Nonetheless, as Salthouse (1992, 1996) shows, it is possible to account for much of the influence of age on cognition in terms of a general speed factor.

One problem with such a conclusion is that it is not meaningful to talk about speed independent of the task on which it is assessed. If one combines speed across a wide range of tasks, then one could argue that one is sampling many aspects of performance, not just one. In response to this, Salthouse focused on an individual task, the Digit Symbol Substitution Test (DSST) taken from the Wechsler Adult Intelligence Scale (WAIS). This is indeed a good predictor of the effects of age on performance, but it is far from being a pure speed test. Good performance almost certainly involves strategy and working memory as well as perceptual speed. Given that it correlates highly with measures of both verbal and nonverbal intelligence, it should, according to Parkin and Java (2000), be regarded as a measure of working memory rather than simple perceptual speed. A test based on rate of number cancellation, which might be expected to provide a purer measure of perceptual speed, proved to be a poor predictor of age decrement in their study.

Another problem with using purely correlational methods is that many physical and intellectual capacities decline together as we age, making it difficult to assign a causal role to one over and above the remainder. The method used by Salthouse and many others in the field is to look for the most powerful and robust correlation, the measure that can account for most of the statistical variance in the results. However, this depends not only on the nature and purity of the measure as described above, but also on its reliability, which in turn depends on the number of observations on which it is based. Speed tests typically involve a large number of repetitions of a simple task, leading to results that are consistent across trials, as in the case of reaction time studies. Executive measures such as tests of reasoning are more likely to depend on fewer but more difficult subtasks that may need to be changed between test trials to prevent learning, resulting in less reliability and lower correlations with other measures. Finally, the best prediction of overall performance will depend crucially on the particular set of tasks chosen for inclusion, which will of course reflect the views of the investigator.

Whereas speed measures frequently do provide the highest correlations, this is not always the case. An extensive series of studies by Paul Baltes and his group in Berlin concentrated more attention on perceptual factors, finding initially that the best predictors were auditory and visual sensory thresholds, which depend on accuracy rather than speed (Baltes & Lindenberger, 1997). One might possibly argue that these would be influenced by such factors as neural transmission speed. However, Baltes and colleagues subsequently found that an even better predictor of the decline in cognition with age was grip strength, giving a whole

new meaning to the term "losing one's grip"! As Lindenberger and Pötter (1998) point out, there is a danger of forgetting that correlation does not equal causation.

Perhaps the time has come to abandon the search for the single factor that underpins the decline of cognition as we get older, returning to the Ford car (or in its UK version, the Woolworths' bicycle pump) hypothesis: An optimally engineered product will aim to manufacture all its parts to the same quality, rather than waste money on over-engineering some components. The result of this is that the parts all tend to last for about the same length of time before failing. Perhaps evolution is equally parsimonious?

The correlational approach is certainly not the only method of developing theories of cognitive aging. For example, Craik and colleagues, using an experimental approach, have emphasized the impact of reduced processing resources on learning and memory in the elderly, often finding that their young participants perform in a similar way to their elderly group when an attentionally demanding concurrent task reduces their available processing capacity (e.g. Craik & Byrd, 1982;

Henry Ford is said to have minimized the cost of his cars by carefully avoiding over-engineering any of the components, with the result that everything tended to wear out at the same time. Some claim that evolution took a similar approach to the process of aging, while others favor a weakest link view, claiming for example that the frontal lobes deteriorate faster than the rest of the brain.

Craik & Jennings, 1992). There is no doubt that attentional capacity is an important variable but, as the previously described studies by Naveh-Benjamin and colleagues indicate (Naveh-Benjamin et al., 2003a, 2003b 2004a, 2004b), reducing the attention available to the young does not always result in performance resembling the elderly. In the case of episodic memory, the aging deficit seems closer to a very mild amnesia, then to a purely attentional limitation. Similarly, whereas there might be a tendency for the elderly to have difficulty in inhibiting irrelevant material, as suggested by Hasher et al. (1999), it is not clear why this should influence free recall, one of the most sensitive tests of aging. One might expect increased susceptibility to inhibition to influence short-term forgetting performance on the Peterson and Peterson (1959) task, where forgetting appears to be principally the result of proactive inhibition (Keppel & Underwood, 1962). However, provided the initial level of performance is matched, there seems to be no difference in rate of forgetting between young and old (Parkinson et al., 1985). Hence, although age can reduce our inhibitory capacity, it seems unlikely that it is the principal cause of episodic memory decline.

A popular hypothesis over recent years has been to interpret the effects of aging in terms of the declining functions of the frontal lobes. Evidence in favor of this view has principally come from studies showing an association between the size of the aging effect and performance on tasks assumed to depend on frontal-lobe function. Such tasks are varied and numerous, typically involving the executive component of working memory, and possibly also the capacity for inhibition, together with a wide range of other executive functions that are themselves still poorly understood. At this stage, it is not clear how useful a general frontal hypothesis would be. The evidence supporting the frontal aging hypothesis was reviewed by Phillips and Henry (2005), who conclude that the direct evidence for a causal link between frontal-lobe atrophy and age-related cognitive decline is currently weak and that the present hypothesis relies on a simplistic interpretation of both the neuroanatomy

and the neuropsychology of the frontal lobes. That does not, of course, rule out an important role for the frontal lobes in normal aging, but it does suggest that any theory that assigns a special role to the frontal lobes in aging will need to be grounded more firmly both neuropsychologically and neuroanatomically.

THE AGING BRAIN

As we grow older, our brain shrinks. This shows most clearly in the expansion of the ventricles, the channels in the brain filled by cerebrospinal fluid, which take up more space as the brain becomes smaller. While this is a good overall measure of brain size, it is not a very good measure of function, as functional change depends—crucially—on what part of the brain is shrinking. As mentioned earlier, this tends to be the frontal lobes, with the temporal and occipital lobes shrinking more slowly. The hippocampus, crucial for memory, loses 20–30% of its neurons by the age of 80 (Squire, 1987), reflecting an initial slow decline, which subsequently accelerates, possibly as the result of disease (see Raz, 2000, for further discussion). The electrophysiological activity of the brain, as reflected in evoked response potential (ERP) measures (see Chapter 2, p. 30), slows steadily throughout the lifespan (Pelosi & Blumhardt, 1999), with the latency of the P300 component increasing at an average of 2 milliseconds per year, a rate of slowing that becomes more severe in dementia (Neshige, Barrett, & Shibasaki, 1988).

Studies of brain function using neuroimaging also tend to show age effects. Cabeza, Prince, Daselaar, Greenberg, Budde, Dolcos, et al. (2004), studying working memory and visual attention, observed that older subjects tended to show activation in both cerebral hemispheres, on tasks that activate a single hemisphere in young participants. A comparable result was observed by Maguire and Frith (2003) in a study of autobiographical memory, with the young showing predominantly left hippocampal involvement, while the involvement of the elderly was bilateral. Reuter-Lorenz (2002) and others have attributed the broader spread of activation to an attempt by the elderly to compensate for overload in one component of the brain by utilizing other brain structures.

It is not always the case that greater activation is shown in the elderly, particularly on tasks where it may be helpful to involve relatively complex strategies. A study by Iidaka, Sadato, Yamada, Murata, Omori, and Yonekura (2001) required participants to remember pairs of related or unrelated pictures. Both young and old showed more left frontal activation for the unrelated pictures, but only the young showed additional occipito-temporal activation. This probably indicates the active use of visual imagery, as this was an area observed by Maguire, Valentine, Wilding, and Kapur (2003) to be activated when using the method of loci, a classic visual-imagery-based mnemonic strategy. This method is itself very demanding, and while consistently aiding the young, only 50% of the elderly subjects tested by Nyberg, Sandblom, Jones, Neely, Petersson, Ingvar, and Bäckman (2003) were found to benefit from using the methods of loci. It appears to be the case, therefore, that older participants will attempt to compensate for cognitive decline by using additional strategies, reflected in a wider range of brain activation. However, this might no longer be possible when the task is already complex, potentially inducing reliance on a simpler strategy.

At this point the principal contribution of studies based on neuroimaging has been to identify the anatomical localization associated with different cognitive processes. An exciting new development is based on the capacity to image the distribution and operation of the neurotransmitters that play a crucial role in the neural basis of cognition. One such study concerns the link between aging and the neurotransmitter, dopamine. Postmortem studies have indicated that as we age, dopamine levels show a loss of 5–10% per decade. This finding has been confirmed by studies using positron emission tomography (PET) (see Chapter 2, p. 31), whereby the density of dopamine receptors is measured using the radioactive labeling of ligands, substances that selectively bind to specific types of dopamine receptor (Antonini, Leenders, Meier, Oertel, Boesiger, & Anliker, 1993).

It is known that dopamine is implicated in many cognitive functions, and that its depletion is associated with cognitive deficits in both Parkinson's disease (Brown & Marsden, 1990) and Huntington's disease (Bäckman, Almkvist, Andersson, Nordberg, Winblad, Reineck, & Langstrom, 1997). Pharmacological studies using healthy young participants confirm the importance of dopamine. Bromocriptine, which is known to facilitate dopamine function, is found to improve spatial working memory (Luciana & Collins, 1997), whereas haloperidol, which interferes with dopamine function,

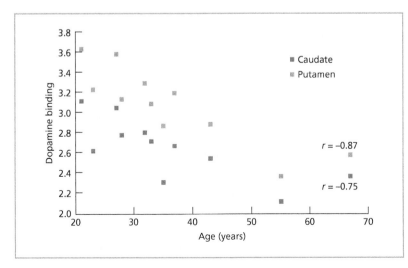

Figure 15.7 Relationship between the levels of dopamine in two brain areas (the caudate and the putamen) and aging. From Erixon-Lindroth et al. (2005). Copyright © 2005 Elsevier. Reproduced with permission.

has the opposite effect (Luciana & Collins, 1997; Ramaekers, Louwerens, Muntjewerff, Milius, de Bie, Rosenzweig, et al., 1999).

Bäckman, Ginovart, Dixon, Robins Wahlin, Wahlin, Halldin, and Farde (2000) used PET to measure dopamine binding in volunteers across the age range. They found a substantial correlation between dopamine levels in the brain and episodic memory that accounted for some 38% of the variance in performance on word recognition, and 48% in the case of face recognition (Figure 15.7). When the effect of dopamine level was removed statistically, age had only a minimal impact on memory performance, a result that has subsequently been replicated by Erixon-Lindroth, Farde, Robins Wahlin, Sovago, Halldin, and Backman (2005). At this early stage of the development of this line of work, it seems to show great promise, not only of developing a better understanding of how and why memory declines as we get older, but potentially also of providing pharmacological ways of easing this decline.

SUMMARY

- The study of aging is concerned with the study of change and can be pursued using two basic designs: longitudinal or cross-sectional.
- Longitudinal designs involve studying the same individuals across time.
- Cross-sectional studies involve testing people of different ages at a single point in time.
- Much current evidence on aging and memory comes from cross-sectional studies, which suggest the following:
- STM is relatively preserved (working memory is less so).
- Episodic memory certainly declines, but can benefit from environmental cues and support.
- The associative deficit hypothesis proposes that aging leads to a reduced capacity to form new associations.
- Prospective memory declines when tested under laboratory conditions, but in a real-world context is well preserved.
- The content of semantic memory continues to accumulate, as reflected in increasing vocabulary, but speed and reliability of access declines.
- Implicit memory tends to hold up reasonably well but varies with task.
- A number of unitary theories of cognitive decline with age have been proposed, but the tendency for many different measures to decline at the same time, makes strong conclusions questionable.
- The brain tends to shrink as we get older.
- Neuroimaging suggests that older people tend to show a wider spread of neural activation, possibly resulting from an attempt to compensate for a cognitive deficit.

POINTS FOR DISCUSSION

What are the relative strengths and weaknesses of longitudinal and cross-sectional approaches to the study of aging? How can they be tackled?

What impact on everyday life would you expect from the effects on memory of aging?

What are the effects of cognitive and physical training on memory and aging? How might these be linked to brain function?

Why do we become more forgetful as we become older?

What advice would you give to someone just about to retire?

FURTHER READING

American Journal of Geriatric Psychiatry: Special Issue on "Successful aging" (2006) Vol. 14, issue 1. Focuses on the developing research area of how we can best adapt to the inevitable process of aging.

Bäckman, L., Nyberg, L., Lindenberger, U., Li, S.-C., & Farde, L. (2006). The correlative triad among aging, dopamine, cognition: Current status and future prospects. *Neuroscience and Biobehavioral Reviews, 30*, 791–807. A review of the exciting developments in the neurobiology of aging. It suggests an important role for dopamine in determining the effects of age on cognition.

Perfect, T. J., & Maylor, E. A. (2000). Rejecting the dull hypothesis: The relationship between method and theory in cognitive aging research. In T. J. Perfect & E. A. Maylor (Eds.), *Models of cognitive aging* (pp. 1–18) Oxford: Oxford University Press. A discussion and critical evaluation of attempts to provide a general theory of cognitive aging.

Rabbitt, P. (2005). Cognitive gerontology and cognitive change in old age. Special issue of *Quarterly Journal of Experimental Psychology Section A*, Hove, UK. An overview of the cognitive psychology of aging by someone who has worked extensively using both experimental and longitudinal designs.

Salthouse, T. A. (1996). The processing-speed theory of adult age differences in cognition. *Psychological Review, 103*, 403–428. An influential attempt to provide a unitary theory of cognitive aging in terms of processing speed.

REFERENCES

Antonini, A., Leenders, K. L., Meier, D., Oertel, W. H.,Boesiger, P., & Anliker, M. (1993). T2 relaxation time in patients with Parkinson's disease. *Neurology, 43*, 697–700.

Bäckman, L., & Molander, B. (1986). Adult age differences in the ability to cope with situations of high arousal in a precision sport. *Psychology and Aging, 1*, 133–139.

Bäckman, L., & Nilsson, L.-G. (1984). Aging effect in free recall: An exception to the rule. *Human Learning, 3*, 53–69.

Bäckman, L., Almkvist, O., Andersson, J., Nordberg, A., Winblad, B., Reineck, R., & Langstrom, B. (1997). Brain activation in young and older adults during implicit and explicit retrieval. *Journal of Cognitive Neuroscience, 9*, 378–391.

Bäckman, L., Ginovart, N., Dixon, R. A., Robins Wahlin, T. B., Wahlin, A., Halldin, C., & Farde, L. (2000). Age-related cognitive deficits mediated by changes in the striatal dopamine system. *American Journal of Psychiatry 157*, 635–637.

Baddeley, A. D., & Crawford, J. (2012). *Spot the word* (2nd edn.). Oxford: Pearson.

Baddeley, A. D., Baddeley, H., Bucks, R., & Wilcock, G. K. (2001). Attentional control in Alzheimer's disease. *Brain, 124*, 1492–1508.

Baddeley, A. D., Bressi, S., Della Sala, S., Logie, R., & Spinnler, H. (1991). The decline of working memory in Alzheimer's disease: A longitudinal study. *Brain, 114*, 2521–2542.

Baddeley, A. D., Emslie, H., & Nimmo-Smith, I. (1992). *Speed and Capacity Of Language Processing Test (SCOLP)*. Bury St Edmunds: Thames Valley Test Company.

Baddeley, A. D., Emslie, H., & Nimmo-Smith, I. (1994). *Doors and people: A test of visual and verbal recall and recognition*. Bury St Edmunds, Suffolk: Thames Valley Test Company.

Ball, K., Berch, D. B., Helmers, K. F., Jobe, J. B., Leveck, M. D., Marsiske, M., et al. (2002). Effects of cognitive training intervention with older adults: A randomised control trial. *Journal of the American Medical Association, 288*, 2271–2281.

Baltes, P. B., & Lindenberger, U. (1997). Emergence of a powerful connection between the sensory and cognitive functions across the adult lifespan: A new window to the study of cognitive ageing? *Psychology and Ageing, 12*, 12–21.

Black, J. E., Isaacs, K. R., Anderson, B. J., Alcantara, A. A., & Greenough, W. T. (1990). Learning causes synaptogenesis, whereas motor activity causes angiogenesis, in cerebellar cortex of adult rats. *Proceedings of the National Academy of Sciences of the USA, 87*, 5568–5572.

Brown, R. G., & Marsden, C. D. (1990). Cognitive function in Parkinson's disease: From description to theory. *Trends in Cognitive Sciences, 13*, 21–29.

Burke, D. M., MacKay, D. G., Worthley, J. S., & Wade, E. (1991). On the tip of the tongue: What causes word finding failures in young and older adults. *Journal of Memory and Language, 30*, 542–579.

Cabeza, R., Prince, S. E., Daselaar, S. M., Greenberg, D. L., Budde, M., Dolcos, F., et al. (2004). Brain activity during episodic retrieval of autobiographical and laboratory events: An fMRI study using a novel photo paradigm. *Journal of Cognitive Neuroscience, 16*, 1583–1594.

Chalfonte, B. L., & Johnson, M. K. (1996). Feature memory and binding in young and older adults. *Memory and Cognition, 24*, 403–416.

Charness, N. (1985). Ageing and problem-solving performance. In N. Charness (Ed.), *Ageing and human performance* (pp. 225–260). Chichester, UK: John Wiley & Sons.

Christensen, H., Henderson, A. S., Griffiths, K., & Levings, C. (1997). Does ageing inevitably lead to declines in cognitive performance? A longitudinal study of elite academics. *Personality and Individual Differences, 23*, 67–78.

Cockburn, J., & Smith, P. T. (1991). The relative influence of intelligence and age on everyday memory. *Journal of Gerontology: Psychological Sciences, 46*, 31–36.

Cohen, G., & Faulkner, D. (1989). Age differences in source forgetting: Effects on reality monitoring and on eyewitness testimony. *Psychology and Aging, 4*, 10–17.

Colcombe, S., & Kramer, A. F. (2003). Fitness effects on the cognitive function of older adults: A meta-analytic study. *Psychological Science, 14*, 125–130.

Collins, A. M., & Quillian, M. R. (1969). Retrieval time from semantic memory. *Journal of Verbal Learning and Verbal Behavior, 8*, 432–438.

Craik, F. I. M. (1986). A functional account of age differences in memory. In F. Klix & H. Hagendorf (Eds.), *Human memory and cognitive capabilities: mechanisms and performances* (pp. 409–422). Amsterdam: Elsevier Science Publishers, North-Holland.

Craik, F. I. M. (2005). On reducing age-related declines in memory and executive control. In J. Duncan, P. Mcleod, & L. Phillips (Eds.), *Measuring the mind* (pp. 273–290). New York: Oxford University Press.

Craik, F. I. M., & Byrd, M. (1982). Aging and cognitive deficits: The role of attentional resources. In F. I. M. Craik & S. Trehub (Eds.), *Aging and cognitive processes* (pp. 191–211). New York: Plenum.

Craik, F. I. M., & Jennings, J. M. (1992). Human memory. In F. I. M. Craik & T. A. Salthouse (Eds.), *Handbook of ageing and cognition* (pp. 51–100). Hillsdale, NJ: Lawrence Erlbaum Associates.

Craik, F. I. M., Byrd, M., & Swanson, J. M. (1987). Patterns of memory loss in three elderly samples. *Psychology and Aging, 2*, 79–86.

d'Ydewalle, G., Luwel, K., & Brunfaut, E. (1999). The importance of on-going concurrent activities as a function of age in time- and event-based prospective memory. *European Journal of Cognitive Psychology, 11*, 219– 237.

Deary, I. J., Whalley, L. J., Batty, G. D., & Starr, J. M. (2006). Physical fitness and lifetime cognitive change. *Neurology, 67*, 1195–1200.

Deary, I. J., Whiteman, M. C., Starr, J. M., Whalley, L. J., & Fox, H. C. (2004). The impact of childhood intelligence on later life: Following up the Scottish mental surveys of 1932 and 1947. *Journal of Personality and Social Psychology, 86*, 130–147.

Einstein, G. O., & McDaniel, M. A. (1990). Normal aging and prospective memory. *Journal of Experimental Psychology: Learning, Memory, and Cognition, 16*, 717–726.

Einstein, G. O., McDaniel, M. A., Richardson, S. L., Cunfer, A. R., & Guynn, M. J. (1995). Aging and prospective memory: Examining the influence of self-initiated retrieval processes. *Journal of Experimental Psychology: Learning, Memory, and Cognition, 21*, 996–1007.

Engelkamp, J. (1998). *Memory for actions*. Hove, UK: Psychology Press.

Erixon-Lindroth, N., Farde, L., Robins Wahlin, T. B., Sovago, J., Halldin, C., & Bäckman, L. (2005). The role of the striatal dopamine transporter in cognitive aging. *Psychiatry Research: Neuroimaging 138*, 1–12.

Flynn, J. R. (1987). Massive IQ gains in 14 nations: What IQ tests really measure. *Psychological Bulletin, 101*, 171–191.

Giambra, L. M., Arenberg, D., Zonderman, A. B., & Kawas, C. (1995). Adult life span changes in immediate visual memory and verbal intelligence. *Psychology and Aging, 10*, 123–139.

Greenough, W. T., Black, J. E., & Wallace, C. S. (1987). Experience and brain development. *Child Development, 58*, 539–559.

Hasher, L., & Zacks, R. T. (1988). Working memory, comprehension, and aging: A review and a new view. In G. H. Bower (Ed.), *The psychology of learning and motivation.* (Vol. 22, pp. 193–225). San Diego, CA: Academic Press.

Hasher, L., Zacks, R. T., & May, C. P. (1999). Inhibitory control, circadian arousal, and age. In D. Gopher & A. Koriat (Eds.), *Attention and performance, XVII, Cognitive regulation of performance. Interaction of theory and application.* (pp. 653–675). Cambridge, MA: MIT Press.

Hay, J. F., & Jacoby, L. L. (1999). Separating habit and recollection in young and older adults: Effects of elaborative processing and distinctiveness. *Psychology and Aging, 14*, 122–134.

Hertzog, C., Kramer, A. F., Wilson, R. S., & Lindenberger, U. (2008). Enrichment effects on adult cognitive development: Can the functional capacity of older adults be preserved and enhanced. *Psychological Science in the Public Interest, 9*(1), 1–65.

Howard, D. V., & Howard, J. H., Jr. (1989). Age differences in learning serial patterns: Direct versus indirect measures. *Psychology and Aging, 4*, 357–364.

Ihle, A., Schnitzpahn, K., Rendell, P. G., Luong, C., & Kliegel, M. (2012). Age benefits in everyday prospective memory: The influence of personal task importance, use of reminders and everyday stress. *Aging, Neuropsychology, and Cognition, 19*, 84–101. doi: 10.1080/13825585.2011.629288

Iidaka, T., Sadato, N., Yamada, H., Murata, T., Omori, M., & Yonekura, Y. (2001). An fMRI study of the functional neuroanatomy of picture encoding in young and older adults. *Cognitive Brain Research, 11*, 1–11.

Kemper, S. (1990). Adults' diaries: Changes made to written narratives across the life-span. *Discourse Processes, 13*, 207–223.

Kemper, S., Kynette, D., & Norman, S. (1992). Age differences in spoken language. In R. West & J. Sinnott (Eds.), *Everyday memory and aging: Current research and methodology* (pp. 138–152). New York: Springer-Verlag.

Kempermann, G. (2008). The neurogenic reserve hypothesis: What is adult hippocampal neurogenesis good for? *Trends in Neurosciences, 31*(4), 163–169. Epub 2008 Mar 7.

Keppel, G., & Underwood, B. J. (1962). Proactive inhibition in short-term retention of single items. *Journal of Verbal Learning and Verbal Behavior, 1*, 153–161.

Kramer, A. F., Hahn, S., Cohen, N. J., Banich, M. T., McAuley, E., Harrison, C. R., et al. (1999). Aging, fitness and neurocognitive function. *Nature, 400*, 418–419.

Light, L. L., Prull, M. W., La Voie, D., & Healy, M. R. (2000). Dual process theories of memory in older age. In T. J. Perfect & E. Maylor (Eds.), *Theoretical debate in cognitive aging.* (pp. 238–300). Oxford: Oxford University Press.

Lindenberger, U., & Pötter, U. (1998). The complex nature of unique and shared effects in hierarchical linear regression: Implications for developmental psychology. *Psychological Methods, 3*, 218–230.

Luciana, M., & Collins, P. F. (1997). Dopaminergic modulation of working memory for spatial but not object cues in normal humans. *Journal of Cognitive Neuroscience, 9*, 330–367.

Maguire, E. A., & Frith, C. D. (2003). Lateral asymmetry in the hippocampal response to the remoteness of autobiographical memories. *Journal of Neuroscience, 23*, 5302–5307.

Maguire, E. A., Valentine, E. R., Wilding, J. M., & Kapur, N. (2003). Routes to remembering: The brains behind superior memory. *Nature Neuroscience, 6*, 90–95.

Mäntylä, T., & Nilsson, L.-G. (1997). Are my cues better than your cues? Recognition memory and recollective experience in Alzheimer's disease. *Memory, 5*, 657–672.

May, C. P., Hasher, L., & Kane, M. J. (1999). The role of interference in memory span. *Memory and Cognition, 27*, 759–767.

Maylor, E. A. (1996). Does prospective memory decline with age? In M. Brandimonte, G. O. Einstein, M. A. McDaniel, & N. J. Mahwah (Eds.), *Prospective memory: Theory and applications* (pp. 173–198). Hove, UK: Lawrence Erlbaum Associates.

Naveh-Benjamin, M. (2000). Adult age differences in memory performance: Tests of an associative deficit hypothesis. *Journal of Experimental Psychology: Learning, Memory, and Cognition, 26*, 1170–1187.

Naveh-Benjamin, M., Guez, J., Kilb, A., & Reedy, S. (2004a). The associative memory deficit of older adults: Further support using face–name associations. *Psychology and Aging, 19*, 541–546.

Naveh-Benjamin, M., Guez, J., & Marom, M. (2003a). The effects of divided attention at encoding on item and associative memory. *Memory and Cognition, 31*, 1021–1035.

Naveh-Benjamin, M., Guez, J., & Shulman, S. (2004b). Older adult's associative deficit in episodic memory: Assessing the role of decline in attentional resources. *Psychonomic Bulletin and Review, 11*, 1067–1073.

Naveh-Benjamin, M., Hussain, Z., Guez, J., & Bar-On, M. (2003b). Adult age differences in episodic memory: Further support for an associative deficit hypothesis. *Journal of Experimental Psychology: Learning, Memory, and Cognition, 29*, 826–837.

Neshige, R., Barrett, G., & Shibasaki, H. (1988). Auditory long latency event-related potentials in Alzheimer's disease and multi-infarct dementia.

Journal of Neurology, Neurosurgery, and Psychiatry, 51, 1120–1125.

Nilsson, L.-G., Adolfsson, R., Bäckman, L., Cruts, M., Nyberg, L., Small, B. J., & van Broeckhoven, C. (2006). The influence of APOE status on episodic and semantic memory: Data from a population-based study. *Neuropsychology, 20*, 645–657.

Nilsson, L.-G., Adolfsson, R., Bäckman, L., de Frias, C., Molander, B., & Nyberg, L. (2004). Betula: A prospective cohort study on memory, health and aging. *Aging, Neuropsychology and Cognition, 11*, 134–148.

Nyberg, L., Sandblom, J., Jones, S., Neely, A. S., Petersson, K. M., Ingvar, M., & Bäckman, L. (2003). Neural correlates of training-related memory improvement in adulthood and aging. *Proceedings of the National Academy of Sciences of the USA, 100*, 13728–13733.

Park, D. C., Hertzog, C., Kidder, D. C., Morrell, R. W., & Mayhorn, C. B. (1997). Effect of age on event-based and time-based prospective memory. *Psychology and Aging, 12*, 314–327.

Park, D. C., & Puglisi, J. T. (1985). Older adults' memory for the color of matched pictures and words. *Journal of Gerontology, 40*, 198–204.

Parkin, A. J., & Java, R. I. (2000). Determinants of age-related memory loss. In T. Perfect & E. Maylor (Eds.), *Debates in cognitive aging*. Oxford: Oxford University Press.

Parkin, A. J., & Walter, B. M. (1992). Recollective experience, normal aging and frontal dysfunction. *Psychology and Aging, 7*, 290–298.

Parkinson, S. R., Inman, V. W., & Dannenbaum, S. E. (1985). Adult age differences in short-term forgetting. *Acta Psychologica, 60*, 83–101.

Pelosi, L., & Blumhardt, L. D. (1999). Effects of age on working memory: An event-related potential study. *Cognitive Brain Research, 7*, 321–334.

Perlmuter, L. C., Scharff, K., Karsh, R., & Monty, R. A. (1980). Perceived control: A generalized state of motivation. *Motivation and Emotion, 4*, 35–45.

Peterson, L. R., & Peterson, M. J. (1959). Short-term retention of individual verbal items. *Journal of Experimental Psychology, 58*, 193–198.

Phillips, L. H., & Henry, J. D. (2005). An evaluation of the frontal lobe theory of cognitive aging. In J. Duncan, L. H. Phillips, & P. McLeod (Eds.), *Measuring the mind: Speed, control and age*. Oxford: Oxford University Press.

Rabbitt, P., & Abson, V. (1990). "Lost and found": Some logical and methodological limitations of self-report questionnaires as tools to study cognitive aging. *British Journal of Psychology, 81*, 1–16.

Rajaram, S. (1993). Remembering and knowing: Two means of access to the personal past. *Memory and Cognition, 21*, 89–102.

Ramaekers, J. G., Louwerens, J. W., Muntjewerff, N. D., Milius, H., de Bie, A., Rosenzweig, P., et al. (1999). Psychomotor, cognitive, extrapyramidal, and affective functions of healthy volunteers during treatment with an atypical (amisulspride) and a classic (haloperidol) antipsychotic. *Journal of Clinical Psychopharmacology, 19*, 209–221.

Raz, N. (2000). Aging of the bran and its impact on cognitive performance: Integration of structural and functional findings. In F. I. M. Craik & T. A. Salthouse (Eds.), *The handbook of aging and cognition*. (2nd edn., pp. 91–153). Mahwah, NJ: Erlbaum.

Rendell, P. G., & Craik, F. I. M. (2000). Virtual week and actual week: Age-related differences in prospective memory. *Applied Cognitive Psychology, 12*, S43–S62.

Rendell, P. G., & Thomson, D. M. (1999). Aging and prospective memory: Differences between naturalistic and laboratory tasks. *Journal of Gerontology: Psychological Sciences, 54*, 256–269.

Reuter-Lorenz, P. A. (2002). New visions of the aging mind and brain. *Trends in Cognitive Sciences, 6*, 394–400.

Riby, L. M., Perfect, T. J., & Stollery, B. (2004). The effects of age and task domain on dual task performance: A meta-analysis. *European Journal of Cognitive Psychology, 16*, 863–891.

Rönnlund, M., & Nilsson, L.-G. (2006). Adult life-span patterns in WAIS block design performance: Cross-sectional versus longitudinal age gradients and relations to demographic predictors. *Intelligence, 34*, 63–78.

Rönnlund, M., Nyberg, L., Bäckman, L., & Nilsson, L.-G. (2005). Stability, growth, and decline in adult life-span development of declarative memory: Cross-sectional and longitudinal data from a population-based sample. *Psychology and Aging, 20*, 3–18.

Rubin, D. C., & Berntsen, D. (2006). People over forty feel 20% younger than their age: Subjective age across the lifespan. *Psychonomic Bulletin and Review, 13*(5): 776–780.

Salthouse, T. A. (1991). *Theoretical perspectives on cognitive aging*. Hillsdale, NJ: Lawrence Erlbaum Associates.

Salthouse, T. A. (1992). *Mechanisms of age-cognition relations in adulthood*. Hillsdale, NJ: Lawrence Erlbaum Associates.

Salthouse, T. A. (1996). The processing-speed theory of adult age differences in cognition. *Psychological Review, 103*, 403–428.

Salthouse, T. (2006). Mental exercise and mental aging: Evaluating the validity of the "use it or lose it" hypothesis. *Perspectives on Psychological Science, 1*, 68–87.

Salthouse, T. A., & Becker, J. T. (1998). Independent effects of Alzheimer's disease on neuropsychological functioning. *Neuropsychology, 12*, 242–252.

Schacter, D. L., Koutsaal, W., & Norman, K. A. (1997). False memories and aging. *Trends in Cognitive Sciences, 1*, 229–236.

Shimamura, A. P., Berry, J. M., Mangels, J. A., Rustings, C. L., & Jurica, P. J. (1995). Memory and cognitive abilities in academic professors: Evidence for successful aging. *Psychological Science, 6*, 271–277.

Spinnler, H., Della Sala, S., Bandera, R., & Baddeley, A. D. (1988). Dementia, ageing and the structure of human memory. *Cognitive Neuropsychology, 5*, 193–211.

Squire, L. R. (1987). *Memory and brain.* New York: Oxford University Press.

Sunderland, A., Watts, K., Baddeley, A. D., & Harris, J. E. (1986). Subjective memory assessment and test performance in the elderly. *Journal of Gerontology, 41*, 376–385.

van Praag, H., Kempermann, G., & Gage, F. H. (2000). Neural consequences of environmental enrichment. *Nature Reviews Neuroscience, 1*, 191–198.

Verhaeghen, P., Marcoen, A., & Gossens, L. (1993). Facts and fiction about memory aging: A quantitative integration of research findings. *Journal of Gerontology: Psychological Sciences, 48*, 157–171.

Welford, A. T. (1985). Changes of performance with age: An overview. In N. Charness (Ed.), *Aging and human performance* (pp. 333–369). New York: Wiley.

Willingham, D. B., & Winter, E. (1995). Comparison of motor skill learning in elderly and young human subjects. *Society for Neuroscience Abstracts, 21*, 1440.

Wilson, B. A., Baddeley, A. D., & Cockburn, J. M. (1989a). How do old dogs learn new tricks: Teaching a technological skill to brain injured people. *Cortex, 25*, 115–119.

Wilson, B. A., Cockburn, J., Baddeley, A. D., & Hiorns, R. (1989b). The development and validation of a test battery for detecting and monitoring everyday memory problems. *Journal of Clinical and Experimental Neuropsychology, 11*, 855–870.

Wishart, L. R., & Lee, T. D. (1997). Effects of aging and reduced relative frequency of knowledge of results on learning a motor skill. *Perceptual and motor skills, 84*, 1107–1122.

Wright, B. M., & Payne, R. B. (1985). Effects of aging on sex differences in psychomotor reminiscence and tracking proficiency. *Journal of Gerontology, 40*, 184.

Contents

Amnesia: The patient and the psychologist   435

Episodic memory impairment   438

Traumatic brain injury   448

Alzheimer's disease   450

Rehabilitation of patients with
memory problems   456

Conclusion   460

Summary   460

Points for discussion   461

Further reading   461

References   462

We all have memory lapses, some more embarrassing than others. On one occasion, I agreed to talk about memory on a live radio phone-in program, the *Jimmy Mack Show* from Glasgow. As I lived in Cambridge at the time, it was agreed that I would participate from the local radio station. That morning I was reading the newspaper before checking my diary and setting off for work, when I glanced at the TV and radio section, prompting the awful realization that I should at that moment be telling the world about the wonders of memory. I leapt on my bike and arrived just before the end of the program, sheepishly muttering about the terrible traffic in Cambridge, to be asked by the host if I could give the listeners a few hints on how to improve their memory! On another occasion, I turned up to give an important lecture on amnesia, only to discover that I had forgotten my slides.

So we all have bad memories (though perhaps not as bad as mine), but what is it like to have a genuine memory problem—not the devastatingly dense amnesia experienced by Clive Wearing and described in Chapter 1, but the much more common level of memory deficit that accompanies many conditions, including stroke, Alzheimer's disease, and traumatic brain injury? A very good account of the problems associated with memory deficit is given by Malcolm Meltzer, a clinical psychologist who experienced memory problems following a heart attack that led to anoxia (Meltzer, 1983). Having given you some idea as to

what it is like to experience a serious memory problem, I will move on to a brief account as to the role that cognitive psychology can play in helping to deal with such problems. This will be followed by an account of what we know about *anterograde amnesia*, problems in acquiring new memories, and *retrograde amnesia*, problems in accessing premorbid memories. I will then discuss two major causes of memory problems, namely *traumatic brain injury* such as might occur following a road traffic accident, and Alzheimer's disease. The chapter will end with an account of ways in which the psychologist might help patients cope with their memory problems.

AMNESIA: THE PATIENT AND THE PSYCHOLOGIST

The patients' view

Meltzer's heart attack was followed by a period of coma lasting for 6 weeks before he finally recovered consciousness, knowing who he was and recognizing his family, but thinking he was 33 years old, whereas in fact he was 44. On returning home, he could not remember where things were kept and, unlike a pure amnesic patient, also had problems in remembering skills such as how to set an alarm clock, when bills should be paid, where was a good place to go for a vacation, and how one might get there. He also had problems with his working memory:

*Organization of thinking was
hampered ... I had trouble keeping the
facts in mind, which made it difficult to
organize them ... comparing things along a
number of variables is difficult to do when
you cannot retain the variables.*
(Meltzer, 1983, p. 4)

Meltzer found it hard work to watch films or TV because of the difficulty in remembering the plot or, in the case of sports, which team was which and which was ahead. He tended to find spatial orientation difficult and even walks in a familiar neighborhood were liable to result in his getting lost. A particular problem was the impact of his amnesia on his capacity to interact with people:

*Having conversations could become
a trial. Often in talking with people I was
acquainted with, I had trouble remembering
their names or whether they were married, or
what our relationship had been in the past.
I worried about asking where someone's wife
is and finding out that I had been at
her funeral two years before.*

*Often if I didn't have a chance to say
immediately what came to mind, it would
be forgotten and the conversation would
move to another topic. Then there was little
for me to talk about. I couldn't remember
much about current events or things I read
in the paper or saw on TV. Even juicy
tit-bits of gossip might be forgotten. So in
order to have something to say, I tended to
talk about myself and my "condition". My
conversation became rather boring.*
(Meltzer, 1983, p. 5)

Eventually, with considerable perseverance, Meltzer recovered sufficiently to return to work, and of course to write a paper, providing for carers and therapists a very clear insight into the problems that result from memory deficit.

The view from psychology

Some years ago, I and a number of cognitive psychologists, interested in what memory deficits could tell us about normal memory got together for a joint conference with a group of clinical neuropsychologists directly concerned with helping patients. I agreed to give the opening lecture, somewhat ambitiously attempting an overview of the whole of human memory in 55 minutes. The meeting was well attended and, to my relief, I managed my overview without too many in the audience going to sleep, and indeed had time for questions. A chap at the back then stood up and asked "How does all this help me when I see my next patient on Monday morning?" A fair question? Perhaps not at that point in the conference, but a question I have continued to bear in mind and use to guide my continuing interest in applying cognitive psychology to clinical questions.

As I hope you will have noticed from previous chapters, the study of patients with memory problems has made a very substantial contribution to our understanding of how memory works. Patient HM convinced people of the need to separate long-term and short-term memory (see Chapter 2, p. 25). Patients with impaired STM such as PV have played a crucial role in the fractionation of working memory and of the usefulness of the concept of a phonological loop (see Chapter 3, p. 58), while clinical evidence has been crucial in understanding both semantic memory (see Chapter 7) and autobiographical memory (see Chapter 11, p. 320). In my experience, patients are almost invariably generous in helping us understand the nature of their deficit, even though it is made clear to them that they themselves are unlikely to derive direct benefit. They typically report that if studying them can help others, then they are very happy to take part. But has cognitive psychology been clinically helpful? When and how has it been useful?

I want to try to answer this question by taking you through the various stages whereby a clinician might try to help a patient complaining of memory problems, highlighting the way in which the cognitive psychology of memory can contribute, and at the same time telling you something about the disorders that the clinician might encounter. I will illustrate some of the clinical tests commonly used and encourage you to try brief versions, not of the tests themselves, since making them generally available would compromise their clinical value, but using material of a similar type. As you will see, there are often clear links between many such tests and earlier research by cognitive psychologists (see Box 16.1a).

So if you were the clinician, seeing a patient next Monday morning, what would you need to do? You would be likely to begin by assessing the patient allowing you to contribute to diagnosis. In doing so, you would probably identify the patient's principle problems, leading in due course to treatment and

its subsequent evaluation. You would begin by talking to the patient and possibly an accompanying carer about their own views of the problem and what they hope to achieve, tactfully making it clear that a complete restitution of memory is very unlikely. The patient's account is important but not necessarily reliable; some patients are painfully aware of their difficulties while others are not. One of the first amnesic patients I tested responded to each failure to remember with the exclamation "How strange, I pride myself on my memory!"

Assessment is important in a number of ways. It contributes to the diagnosis of the clinical problem underlying the memory deficit, a process that will involve combining such test results with information from a number of other professionals and, if available, from neuroimaging techniques. Standardized test results will allow the patient's performance to be compared to healthy people using standardized norms, and to be related to the clinician's experience of others suffering from cognitive impairment. Such data are also important in communicating information about the patient to other professionals in a standardized way, and if the patient is to receive rehabilitation, then their pattern of strengths and weaknesses will be important in planning the treatment program. Finally, if the psychologist is conducting research, then specification of the patient is essential for any subsequent publication. Such assessment tests thus play an important role in treatment, and in addition provide a means whereby new discoveries can begin to influence clinical practice. Assessment is likely to depend ultimately on earlier research, much of it influenced by both concepts and methods that originated in the cognitive laboratory. This is also true of the methods devised to help the patient cope with memory problems that will be discussed later, although it is important to bear in mind that rehabilitation will need to call on knowledge and expertise that goes well beyond the remit of cognitive psychology.

Unlike many of the patients described because of their theoretical relevance in earlier chapters, a typical patient may have a range of perceptual, motor, cognitive and, potentially, also emotional problems. All need to be assessed and taken into account in planning

Box 16.1a

Test your memory

First copy the figure below:

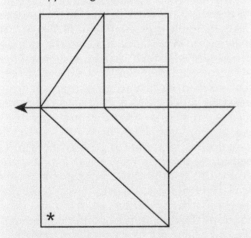

Read out each pair of words and try to remember which word goes with which.

head   – hair
bread – crust
dog   – cat
sheep – roof
house – sheep
fork   – carpet

Now turn to p. 442, Box 16.1c

further treatment. For present purposes, however, we will focus on memory deficits, referring to other factors only in as far as they interact with problems of memory.

Many of the most prevalent cognitive difficulties across a wide range of diseases result from impaired episodic memory. I will therefore begin by describing a pure case of impaired episodic memory as reflected in the classic amnesic syndrome, not because such a pure case is typical, but because it provides a very clear indication of types of problems that are likely to be encountered to a greater or lesser degree, by a wide range of patients.

Box 16.1b

Test your vocabulary

Each of these pairs contains a word and an invented nonword. Your task is to spot the word and mark it with a tick.

	a	b
1	porridge	brantle
2	implusion	estuary
3	venusial	osculate
4	fractious	jimble
5	ruminant	filliary
6	interpractic	episcopal
7	actuarial	strictive
8	exultist	trumpery
9	felucca	lapidism
10	autoplast	vacillating
11	imprecation	tuppler
12	asteroid	interfractive
13	phrenotide	trappist
14	interplosion	apparel
15	oboe	lentism
16	craster	vizier

Correct answers are given on p. 462.
[last page of chapter]

EPISODIC MEMORY IMPAIRMENT

Anterograde amnesia

A crucial distinction is that between anterograde amnesia and retrograde amnesia. Anterograde amnesia refers to a problem in encoding, storing or retrieving ongoing information that can be used in the *future*, hence the prefix *antero*. By contrast, retrograde amnesia refers to loss of access to events that happened in the *past*, typically before the onset of the disease. The densely amnesic patient HM, described in Chapter 2, is a classic case of anterograde amnesia because his capacity for new learning was greatly restricted and his ability to recall events from before his operation was far from perfect. You might recall in contrast that Clive Wearing, who was described in Chapter 1, showed dense anterograde amnesia together with retrograde amnesia, reflected in his very patchy access to earlier memories. However, as in the case of KI, a patient with dense but pure amnesia illustrates (Wilson & Baddeley, 1988) dense anterograde amnesia can occur in the absence of retrograde amnesia. Hence, these two forms of amnesia will be discussed separately.

There is general agreement that in its pure form, the amnesic syndrome involves grossly impaired episodic memory, together with preserved working memory, semantic memory, implicit memory and intelligence. In practice, however, although episodic memory deficits are relatively common, they will often be accompanied by other cognitive deficits that need to be taken into account in treating the patient. Nevertheless, the episodic memory deficit is often a central feature of the patient's problems; hence understanding its nature is important if the patient is to be helped. Attempts to explain the amnesic syndrome can operate at two separate but related levels. One of these concerns the psychological functions that are disturbed, while the other concerns their neurobiological underpinnings. We will begin with explanations of amnesia at the psychological level, moving on later to the role of neurobiology.

KEY TERM

Anterograde amnesia: A problem in encoding, storing, or retrieving information that can be used in the future.

Retrograde amnesia: A problem accessing events that happened in the past.

The 2001 film *Memento* chronicles the story of Leonard, an ex-insurance investigator who can no longer build new memories, as he attempts to find the perpetrator of a violent attack which caused his post-traumatic anterograde amnesia and left his wife dead. The attack is the last event he can recall.

Early hypotheses included greater susceptibility to interference leading to a retrieval deficit (Warrington & Weiskrantz, 1970), faster forgetting (Huppert & Piercy, 1979) and an incapacity for deep processing (Cermak, Butters, & Moreines, 1974), although all of these subsequently ran into problems (see Baddeley 1990, Chapter 16 for a discussion). It is, however, too soon to reject the possibility that faster forgetting, and/or susceptibility to interference may play a part in any final explanation. However, whatever the precise mechanism, it seems likely that amnesia disrupts the capacity to associate a *specific* event or episode with its *context*, its location in time and place.

An essential quality of episodic memory is that it allows individual specific memories to be retrieved. An influential theory as to what makes this possible proposes that individual episodes are linked to the specific time and place of the experience. This associative link provides a way of specifying that particular experience, and subsequently retrieving that memory rather than others occurring at a different time or place. Loss of the capacity to link experiences to their spatial and temporal context would therefore grossly disrupt subsequent recollection. In a study using rats, Winocur and Mills (1970) observed that animals with hippocampal lesions were particularly bad at making use of environmental context in a spatial learning task, suggesting to Winocur (1978) that a failure to associate memories with context may also apply to human amnesic patients.

Further evidence for a deficit in contextual memory came from an ingenious study by Huppert and Piercy (1978a, 1978b). They took advantage of the fact that people are very good at recognizing pictures that they have previously been shown, demonstrating first that the performance of amnesic and control patients can be roughly equated by giving the amnesic patients longer to encode the pictures than the controls. Their study involved presenting pictures either once or twice on each of two successive days. After the second day's presentation, participants were shown a sequence of pictures and asked to say whether they had seen each picture. If they recognized a picture they were then to decide on which day that picture had been shown.

The crucial comparison concerned the pictures that had been seen twice on day 1. Huppert and Piercy found that amnesic patients were more likely to say that items presented twice on day 1 had in fact been presented on day 2, presumably because the degree of familiarity was greater. The controls showed exactly the opposite pattern, being more accurate in assigning items to day 1 if they had been presented twice. Two presentations meant two chances of linking that picture to the day 1 context. In the absence of the link to context provided by episodic memory, the amnesic patients had to rely on a general feeling of familiarity. This did not allow them to distinguish between greater familiarity resulting from two presentations, and that resulting from a recent experience.

Schacter, Harbluk, and McLachlan (1984) showed a similar effect, using as their material the answers to trivial pursuit questions such as what was the favorite food of the comedian and film star Bob Hope, again finding that although amnesic patients may be able to recall the "fact," they are bad at recalling that they had just been given this information, tending to confuse recency with degree of familiarity. The term *source amnesia* has been applied to this characteristic difficulty that amnesic patients experience in recollecting the source of a given memory.

In Huppert and Piercy's (1978a, 1978b) study, amnesic patients were more likely to say that pictures presented twice on day 1 had in fact been presented on day 2 demonstrating a deficit in contextual memory.

You may recall from Chapter 6, Tulving's description of episodic memory as a system that allows "mental time travel." Amnesic patients clearly have problems in travelling to the recent past; what about the future? Amnesic patients may indeed have difficulty in imagining future activities, such as lying on a sandy tropical beach surrounded by palm trees. However, the patients *were* able to imagine the component experiences, but could not integrate them into a whole, a deficit that Hassabis, Kumaran, Vann and Maguire (2007) attribute to the importance of the hippocampus for spatial processing as well as memory. In a recent review of this issue, Mullally and Maguire (2013) conclude that, although the hippocampus plays a role in both episodic memory and the use of imagination to predict the future, these are best seen as separate functions.

A simplified model

In an attempt to pull together the overall pattern of data on the amnesic syndrome, I proposed what I termed a modal model of amnesia, a simple interpretation of the amnesic syndrome that appeared to capture most if not all of the evidence. This accepted a deliberately unspecified version of the consolidation hypothesis, whereby learning in episodic memory involved associating items with their context using some form of "mnemonic glue." This clearly nontechnical term was deliberately selected so as to indicate that it was *not* based on any sophisticated neurobiological evidence but simply accepted that a neurobiological interpretation of some form seemed necessary. This view is consistent with a contextual hypothesis, on the assumption that the essence of episodic memory is the capacity to "glue" experiences to a specific context, thus providing a contextual tag that allows individual experiences to be retrieved.

This simplified model of amnesia assumed that recall and recognition involve the same underlying storage processes, although they place different constraints on subsequent retrieval. It assumed that semantic memory represents the residue of many episodes. Over time, the capacity to retrieve individual experiences might have been lost through forgetting, but it was assumed that semantic memory, based on those common features that accumulated over repeated episodes, could be retrieved through a separate mechanism. Although this modal model seemed to give a plausible account of the classic amnesic syndrome, it was not clear how to test it and I myself ceased to work on amnesia.

Some years later, however, I was asked to talk about amnesia at a retirement symposium for the distinguished neuropsychologist Elizabeth Warrington. Because of our earlier work together, I agreed. I had not subsequently published anything on my speculative modal model of amnesia and thought it would be a good opportunity to obtain feedback from an expert audience. Despite absent-mindedly leaving my slides on the train en route, the talk seemed to go reasonably well. Then, shortly after the meeting, I was invited by Faraneh Vargha-Khadem, a neuropsychologist from the Institute of Child Health in London, to visit and test a patient, Jon. I accepted. Testing Jon convinced me that my modal model of amnesia was wrong, or at any rate far too simple.

Developmental amnesia

Jon had the misfortune to have been born prematurely and had to spend his early days in an incubator. He suffered breathing problems resulting in anoxia, and substantial damage to his hippocampus. Somewhat unusually, this appears to be the limit of the damage to his brain. It was, however, severe, with his hippocampus being less than half the normal size, and somewhat atypical in its structure.

At about the age of 5, Jon's parents began to suspect that he had memory problems, and this proved to be the case. However, despite having a degree of amnesia that made it difficult for him to cope independently, Jon has developed above average intelligence and good semantic memory skills. Furthermore, although his recall memory is clearly impaired, his recognition performance is within the normal range. Figure 16.1 shows the performance of Jon and two matched control participants on the Doors and People Test (Baddeley, Vargha-Khadem, & Mishkin, 2001b). This test was developed to provide a separate measure for visual and verbal recall and recognition, allowing each of these components to be assessed separately and then combined to give overall visual scores, overall verbal scores, and combined recall versus recognition. A similar level of relatively preserved recognition performance together with marked recall deficit was found on a wide range of other tests, confirming earlier observations on Jon and a number of other similar patients by Vargha-Khadem, Gadian, and Mishkin (2001).

Jon presents a number of problems for my proposed modal model of amnesia. First, if episodic memory is impaired, how can semantic memory develop if, as I assumed, it is based on an accumulation of episodes? Second, although the link between memory and intelligence is not

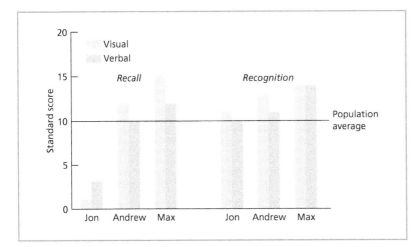

Figure 16.1 Performance on the Doors and People Test of visual and verbal recall by Jon, a developmental amnesic patient, and two controls. Jon is impaired on recall but not recognition. From Baddeley et al. (2001b). Copyright © 2001 MIT Press. Reproduced with permission.

clearly specified by the modal model, one might expect crystallized intelligence, based on prior learning, to be impaired, resulting for example, in reduced vocabulary. This was not the case. Subsequent research suggests, however, that although Jon's knowledge of the world is excellent, it might take him longer than controls to acquire new facts (Gardiner, Brandt, Baddeley, Vargha-Khadem, & Mishkin, 2008). Third, if recall and recognition involve essentially the same storage process, why, in Jon's case, can recognition be so well preserved and recall so impaired?

Box 16.1c

Testing your memory

First, try to remember and draw the figure you copied.

Now try to remember the words that were linked to each of the following:

dog?
fork?
head?
house?
sheep?
bread?

Turn back to p. 437 and check your answers.

A hint as to the answer to this question comes from the previously described distinction between "remembering" and "knowing." You will recall that "remembering" is based on the capacity to recollect an episode, "to travel backwards in time" to re-experience it, in contrast to the capacity to *know* that one has previously encountered an item, in the absence of such recollective experience (see Chapter 8, p. 221). We attempted to assess Jon's capacity to "remember," but had considerable difficulty teaching him the distinction between remembering and knowing. Eventually, he declared that he understood the distinction and we went ahead. Jon used the remember-and-know categories about as often as controls.

However, when control participants made a remember judgment they could describe their recollection, for example, *The word "dog" reminded me of my granny's dachshund.* Jon did not. He reported that he tried to form a visual image of the cards on which the words had been presented, and if his image of the word was clear and bright then he categorized this as remembering. In short, he appeared to be using a strength rather than a recollective criterion.

Further evidence on this point came from the electrophysiological response evoked in Jon's brain when attempting to recognize words that had previously been presented, and to categorize them as "remembered" or "known." This study took advantage of the fact that "remember" judgments are accompanied by a specific activation pattern that differs from that evoked by "know" responses. Jon proved to lack the remember component (Düzel, Vargha-Khadem, Heinze, & Mishkin, 2001). Finally, Maguire, Vargha-Khadem, and Mishkin (2001) succeeded in finding a few memories from Jon's life that seemed to evoke the crucial episodic experience of reliving an event. When such memories were evoked in a brain-imaging study, he finally showed the standard "remember" pattern of brain activation, indicating that he does have the capacity to recollect but has great difficulty in laying down the episodic memory traces on which such recollective experiences are based.

To summarize, it appears to be the case that Jon can learn, in the sense of building up familiarity, but that he is very impaired in his capacity to recollect. The fact that he has nonetheless acquired a rich semantic memory and above-average intelligence presents a clear challenge to theory and to widespread earlier assumptions regarding the role of the hippocampus.

There is no doubt that Jon is far from typical as an amnesic patient, most of whom are impaired on both recall and recognition tests. More specifically, Squire and colleagues have presented data from groups of amnesic patients who appear to have lesions limited to the hippocampus, and who behave in the standard way, with no evidence of preserved recognition memory (Reed & Squire, 1997; Manns & Squire, 1999). Why the difference?

One possibility is that Jon acquired his hippocampal damage at a very early age, whereas most amnesic patients become amnesic as adults. Subsequent research on developmental amnesia does not currently seem to support this, but this cannot yet be ruled out.

A second possibility is that the pattern of deficits shown by Jon reflects the specificity of the area of the damage within his brain, being limited to the hippocampus, whereas the surrounding regions comprising the *perirhinal* and *entorhinal* cortices appear to have been entirely spared. Such sparing is not common in amnesic patients, and seems clear that some of the earlier claims for the importance of the hippocampus stem in part from associated deficits. In animal lesion studies, it is very difficult to lesion the hippocampus without influencing these areas, and in brain-damaged patients the damage is very rarely both as extensive, as in Jon's case, and as clearly confined to the hippocampus. In the case of the patients reported by Squire and colleagues (Reed & Squire, 1997; Manns & Squire, 1999), it is possible that areas beyond the hippocampus might be compromised, in ways that are not readily detectable, although Squire and colleagues reject this view.

Aggleton and Brown (1999) proposed, prior to the study of Jon's memory, that whereas the hippocampus is important for episodic memory, familiarity-based recognition judgments might be based on the adjacent perirhinal regions that are preserved in Jon. They cite a number of cases from the literature with preserved recognition in the presence of clearly impaired recall, a pattern subsequently recorded by Mayes, Holdstock, Isaac, Hunkin, and Roberts (2002) in an adult-onset case in whom the sparing of recognition memory appeared to be associated with a lesion limited to the hippocampus.

Further evidence for this possibility comes from a recent study by Horner, Gadian, Fuentemilla, Jentschke, Vargha-Khadem, and Duzel (2012) used as an illustration in Chapter 2. You may recall that this involved recruiting 17 relatively pure amnesic patients with impaired memory and preserved intellect, together with 14 controls, who were shown a sequence of visual scenes, with a different word superimposed on each scene. Subsequent testing involved presenting word–scene combinations and requiring participants to judge first, whether the word had been shown before, a test of item memory, and then whether the word had been paired with that specific scene previously, a test of memory for context. Both the patients and controls varied in hippocampal volume reflecting normal variations in the controls and added variation due to lesions in the patients. This allowed correlational measures to be used to assess both item and context memory. Hippocampal volume had a minimal effect on memory for items, but a clear impact on context memory; the greater the volume of the hippocampus, the better the memory of which word went with which scene. During the retrieval process, the electrical activity of the brain was measured using MEG (see Chapter 2, p. 27). An early (350 ms) signal was found to depend on the hippocampus and was shown to be associated with memory for context, while a later component that is not hippocampus-dependent, was shown to be associated with item memory. So does this settle the issue? This is a potentially important and highly ambitious study, combining as it does, behavioral, anatomical and electrophysiological measures focused on answering a critical question. It is based on a substantial and carefully selected sample of patients and control participants, uses state of the art methodology, giving apparently clear results. However, given the complexity of this controversial area, it would be premature to assume that the issue has finally been resolved.

So, does Jon really present a challenge to a simple modal model of amnesia, as I initially concluded? Or does he reflect the danger of drawing overgeneral conclusions from developmental cases? No doubt, as more cases appear and as our methods of assessing the extent of anatomical damage improve, this issue will in due course be resolved, as too will the role of episodic memory in the development of the semantic system.

We have so far discussed the proposed focal deficit in amnesia, namely the binding of items to their context, and located this deficit principally in the hippocampus. We consider next the process that is most probably disrupted, namely consolidation of the memory trace.

Consolidation

The dominant explanation of both anterograde and retrograde amnesia at a neurobiological level rests on the concept of consolidation, the hypothesis that memory traces are initially fragile and become more resistant to forgetting as time progresses, a view that is at least a century old (Müller & Pilzecker, 1900). This was applied to the amnesic syndrome by assuming that consolidation depends crucially on the hippocampus and related areas, and that disruption to this system interferes with the consolidation process. Evidence in favor of the role of consolidation in learning comes from research on sleep as described in Chapter 5 (see p. 127). This shows that when learning is followed by a period of sleep, long-term retention is better than occurs when remaining awake during that time (e.g. Stickgold, James, & Hobson, 2000; Gaskell & Dumay, 2003).

Evidence consistent with the effects of both consolidation and interference comes from a group directed by Sergio Della Sala in Edinburgh. They report a number of studies demonstrating that the retention of information by amnesic patients was greatly enhanced if learning is immediately followed by removal of the patient to a quiet, dim interference-free room. In one study, four densely amnesic patients and six controls attempted to remember a story 1 hour later. When the hour was spent in a darkened room, patients performed almost as well as controls. However, when the hour was filled with the sort of cognitive tasks that would normally constitute patient assessment, the patients remembered virtually nothing (Dewar, Cowan, & Della Sala, 2010). Another study tested patients suffering from mild cognitive impairment (MCI), a condition typically reflecting poor memory and often a forerunner of Alzheimer's disease. It showed a similar improvement in retention by the patients when learning was followed by removal to a quiet dark room, whereas this made little difference to the healthy control group. An obvious interpretation of these findings is to suggest that amnesic patients are particularly susceptible to the disruption of the process of consolidation, particularly during the early stages. This was tested directly by Dewar, Fernandez-Garcia, Cowan and Della Sala (2009) in a study in which MCI patients and controls learned a list of words and

were tested after a delay of 9 minutes. The delay was divided into three, with interfering material presented during either the first, the second or the third part of the retention period. If the initial stages of consolidation are particularly vulnerable, then interference during the first stage should cause more forgetting than in the later phases. The results are shown in Figure 16.2, from which it is clear that this was the case. In addition to its obvious theoretical significance, this finding has considerable potential practical importance if it should prove widely applicable, and the learning observed reasonably robust. The process of hippocampal consolidation over this initial period is presumed to operate at the cellular and subcellular level, probably based on the mechanism of long-term potentiation (LTP) described briefly in Chapter 2 (p. 34). However, analysis of the amnesic syndrome at the subcellular level does not yet appear to be well advanced.

Retrograde amnesia

Whereas anterograde amnesia refers to the failure to acquire new memories, retrograde amnesia refers to the impaired capacity to retrieve old memories. Patients often suffer

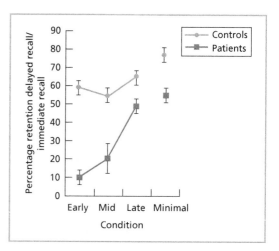

Figure 16.2 Dewar et al.'s (2009) study showed that amnesic patients are very susceptible to the disruption by later activity of the process of consolidation, particularly during its early stages. From Dewar et al. 2009. Copyright © American Psychological Association. Reprinted with permission.

from both; however, the severity of anterograde is not highly correlated with degree of retrograde amnesia, suggesting different origins (Shimamura & Squire, 1991; Greene & Hodges, 1996). For example, two patients studied by Baddeley and Wilson (1986) both had dense but pure amnesias with high and well-preserved intelligence, but one appeared to have excellent retrograde memory and could, for example, talk in great detail about his wartime experiences, whereas the other had at best only a hazy memory of his past. He knew he had been in the Navy and gone to university but could not remember in what order; he knew he had previously broken his arm, but could not recall how.

Measuring the degree of retrograde amnesia presents one problem that is not shared with anterograde amnesia, namely that the tester typically does not have control over the learning of the material to be recalled, as learning might have occurred many years before. An early attempt to quantify degree of retrograde amnesia was made by Sanders and Warrington (1971), who presented their patients with photographs of people who were famous for a limited period at different points in time, finding that their amnesic patients typically performed more poorly on this task than controls. They also observed that earlier memories were better preserved, so-called *Ribot's law*. This asserts that older memories are more durable than those acquired more recently (Ribot, 1882).

A number of similar scales have subsequently been developed using a range of material, including news events, winners of classic horse races, and TV shows that aired for a single season (e.g. Squire, Haist, & Shimamura, 1989). This general method suffers from two practical problems. First, the degree of knowledge of news events or horse races is likely to vary substantially across patients; second, scales of this sort are, of course, continually aging, as the recent events become progressively more remote in time, hence requiring a continuous process of revising and revalidating.

An alternative method is to probe the patient's memory of their earlier life by requesting autobiographical recollections, which can then if necessary be checked through a spouse or carer (Zola-Morgan, Cohen, & Squire, 1983).

Unfortunately, this is a somewhat laborious process; patients tend to produce large amounts of material, which must then be transcribed, checked and evaluated, not a very practical method in a busy clinical context.

In an attempt to reduce these methodological problems, Kopelman, Wilson, and Baddeley (1990) developed the Autobiographical Memory Interview (AMI), which involved asking people to remember specific information selected from a range of time periods. Some were remote, for example the name of their first school, others intermediate, such as their first job, yet others probed more recent events, such as where the patient spent last Christmas. These were essentially factual questions that could be regarded as probing a form of personal semantic memory. In addition, for each life period, participants were asked to recollect a specific personal event. An example from childhood might be winning a race at school. These episodic recollections were then rated in terms of amount and specificity of information retrieved.

The test was validated using both healthy people and a range of patients and was found to be sensitive and reliable. Even patients with Korsakoff syndrome, who are commonly believed to be inclined to confabulate, produced either accurate recall, as validated by relatives, or simply said they could not remember (Kopelman et al., 1990). This and related scales have been used increasingly widely in line with the increased interest in autobiographical memory and its disorders (see Chapter 11). Retrograde amnesia generally leads to impairment in autobiographical memory on both the personal and the semantic scales. However, cases who show differential impairment do occur. De Renzi, Liotti and Nichelli (1987) describe an Italian woman who could remember events of her personal life very well, but recalled virtually no public events, neither the war which she had lived through for example, nor the assassination of the Italian

> ## KEY TERM
>
> **Personal semantic memory:** Factual knowledge about one's own past.

Kopelman et al.'s (1990) Autobiographical Memory Interview (AMI) measured the extent of retrograde amnesia by asking people to remember specific information selected from a range of time periods, and to recall a temporally specific personal event, such as winning a race at school.

prime minister. The only public event that she seemed to remember was the wedding in England of Prince Charles to Lady Diana Spencer, who she described as a scheming girl just like the one that married her own son; a public event that she had personalized. Other studies have reported the opposite pattern. Dalla Barba, Cipolotti, and Denes (1990) describe a patient with alcoholic Korsakoff syndrome and a severe episodic memory deficit who was good at recalling famous people and events

KEY TERM

Alcoholic Korsakoff syndrome: Patients have difficulty learning new information, although events from the past are recalled. There is a tendency to invent material to fill memory blanks. Most common cause is alcoholism, especially when this has resulted in a deficiency of vitamin B1.

but could not remember aspects of personal autobiography.

Confabulation

Confabulation occurs when the reported autobiographical information is false but not intentionally misleading. A distinction can be made between spontaneous and provoked confabulation. Provoked confabulation can occur as a result of an amnesic patient's attempt to fill in a gap in knowledge, so as to avoid embarrassment. In one sense this is not too different from normal behavior, when we might produce a reasonably accurate account but include detail beyond what we can really remember, perhaps to make a better story. Spontaneous confabulation tends to be much more florid, is less common, and tends to be linked to frontal-lobe damage.

Consider, for example, patient RR, who had extensive bilateral damage to his frontal lobes following a driving accident (Baddeley & Wilson, 1988). When asked about the accident, he happily provided a detailed account that involved his getting out of his car and carrying out a polite but extremely repetitive conversation with the driver of the lorry that had hit him, with each apologizing to the other multiple times. He had in fact been unconscious for a lengthy period following the accident and could almost certainly not remember it. He was no longer capable of driving and gave a totally implausible account of how he had subsequently driven himself to the rehabilitation center, giving a lift to a fellow patient he rather ungallantly described as "a fat piece." Confabulation can also result in action. On one occasion, RR was found heading along the road outside the center pushing a fellow patient in a wheelchair to show his friend a sewage farm he was working on as an engineer. He had in fact worked on such a project, but it was many years ago and a good distance away.

Confabulation is typically found in patients with a dysexecutive syndrome, disruption to the operation of the central executive component of working memory (see Chapter 4, p. 78), resulting from damage, typically, to both frontal lobes. This probably interferes with autobiographical memory in two ways. First, such patients have difficulty in setting up appropriate retrieval cues. The previously described patient RR, for example, was very poor at generating items from semantic categories. Given the category *animals*, for example, he produced *dog ... animals ... there must be thousands of them! ... Did I say dog?* However, given appropriate retrieval cues, *an Australian animal that hops*, for example, he readily came up with the right answer.

A second problem is that of evaluating the outcome of a memory search, with the result that information that would clearly be implausible to most normal or indeed most brain-damaged people is accepted and elaborated. RR responded in an autobiographical memory study to the cue word *letter*. He described sending a letter to an aunt recounting the death of his brother Martin. When he was reminded that Martin visited him regularly, he accepted this, claiming falsely that his mother had had a later son, also called Martin (Baddeley & Wilson, 1986).

Explaining retrograde amnesia

There have been fewer studies of retrograde than anterograde amnesia, and less extensive theoretical analysis. This has begun to change in recent years with a number of models proposed, often accompanied by computer simulations to check that they are indeed able to predict the results claimed. Three of these models—those of Alvarez and Squire (1994); McClelland, McNaughton, and O'Reilly (1995); and Murre (1996)—differ in detail, but all assume that the hippocampus and surrounding regions play a crucial role in memory consolidation. They typically assume two types of consolidation. The first, *hippocampal consolidation*, a relatively rapid process, operates at the cellular and subcellular level and involves the initial encoding of new information within the hippocampus. A second more long-term process termed systems consolidation is subsequently

involved in gradually transferring information from the hippocampus to other brain regions for more long-term storage. These two types of consolidation are not, of course, mutually exclusive, although failure to consolidate at a cellular level will presumably interfere with any subsequent system consolidation.

The above three models differ in detail but all assume that the hippocampus and associated regions act as an intermediary, detecting and storing novel information at a relatively rapid rate, then holding it while it is gradually transferred to more cortical areas. Unlike hippocampal storage, which is relatively rapid but temporary, links within the cortex are assumed to take longer to set up, but are more durable. This consolidation process continues to progress within the neocortex after traces have been lost from the hippocampus, with the result that memory traces that have been in the brain for many years will be particularly robust, thus accounting for Ribot's law, the greater durability of early memory traces.

An alternative model is offered by the Multiple Trace Hypothesis, proposed by Nadel and Moscovitch (1997, 1998). They argue for the role of the hippocampus in *retrieval*, as well as encoding. They accept a version of the model just described, which they refer to as the "standard model" but assume that the process of long-term consolidation sets up recorded traces of experience within the hippocampal complex, leading to multiple replicas of earlier experiences. The temporal gradient in retrograde amnesia is assumed to result from partial damage to the hippocampus removing some of the available traces. Older traces, being more numerous, will be more likely to survive. However, complete damage to the hippocampus should lead to total retrograde amnesia. The question of whether this or one of the more standard models gives the better account of retrograde amnesia remain an open question.

The study of relative "pure" memory disorders and their links to clearly specified areas of the brain has proved enormously useful in developing both our theories of memory and our knowledge of brain function. However, the typical clinician is likely to encounter many more patients for whom a serious memory deficit is only one of a range of symptoms, and where

---

KEY TERM

Systems consolidation: Process of gradual reorganization of the regions of the brain that support memory. Information is consolidated within the brain by a process of transfer from one anatomically based system to another.

the association between the deficit and its anatomical localization is often unclear. From the patient's viewpoint, however, regardless of its origin, a memory deficit can be a crippling affliction. It is therefore important to study memory performance in diseases of this type, and to try to develop methods of helping patients to cope with the associated memory problems. Two such diseases will be described next, namely traumatic brain injury (TBI); and —Alzheimer's disease (AD).

TRAUMATIC BRAIN INJURY

Traumatic brain injury (TBI) occurs when the head receives a sharp blow, for example as a result of a fall, or is subject to a sudden acceleration or deceleration as in a car crash. The brain swirls around, resulting in damage from the bony protuberances within the skull, and from the twisting and shearing of fibers within the brain.

A few years ago I was waiting in a line of cars to leave a side road near a sea-coast resort when suddenly a blue figure arced in the air, to the horror and consternation of onlookers. It was a motorcyclist hit by a car turning into the side road, probably resulting in a serious head injury. Such injuries happen mainly to young men, and in the UK over 95% will survive with varying degrees of handicap. Other causes of TBI include falls, sports injuries and, in the case of Iraq war veterans, blast, with an estimated 10–20% of returnees suffering from TBI. Overall, it is estimated that some 5.3 million Americans are currently living with some degree of TBI (Langlois, Rutland-Brown, & Wald, 2006).

So what sort of memory problems might our unfortunate motorcyclist expect? First of all, if the brain injury was severe, he might be expected to be in a coma, sometimes for many weeks. Indeed in the most serious cases, the patient may be left in what is known as a *persistent vegetative state* in which physical functions continue to perform but mental functions do not. This in turn leads to the terrible ethical problem as to how long one should artificially maintain life in such a case. Fortunately, in most cases there will be a gradual recovery,

often so gradual that it can be missed by the medical support staff. To optimize this process of monitoring, Shiel, Wilson, McLellan, Horn, and Watson (2000) developed a scale entitled the Wessex Head Injury Matrix Scale (WHIM), which picks up the tiny changes that occur in behavior as the brain slowly recovers from major trauma.

Post-traumatic amnesia

On recovering consciousness, the patient is likely to move into a state of post-traumatic amnesia (PTA), in which attention can be disturbed and the capacity for new learning grossly impaired. Once again, it is important to be able to monitor this gradual recovery, and to do so a number of scales have been devised (Levin & Hanten, 2002). A study by High, Levin, and Gary (1990) monitored the progress through PTA of 84 patients whose brain injury was sufficient to lead to coma. They typically first recovered *personal knowledge*, who they were; followed by *place*, where they were; and finally *temporal orientation*. The estimated current date was typically displaced backwards, especially in more severe cases, where there could be an error of up to 5 years. As the patients recovered, the degree of error reduced, reflecting a shrinkage of their retrograde amnesia.

Length of time in PTA can vary considerably, and provides a rough, although not infallible, guide to level of probable recovery (Levin, O'Donnell, & Grossman 1979). Having recovered from PTA, the patient is likely to be left with a degree of retrograde amnesia. This might initially be quite extensive, but will shrink over time, as in the classic case described below.

A green-keeper, aged 22, was thrown from his motorcycle in August 1933. There was a bruise in the left frontal region and slight bleeding from the left ear but no fracture was seen on X-ray examination. A week after the accident he was able to converse sensibly and the nursing staff considered that he had fully recovered consciousness. When questioned, however, he said that the date was February 1922, and that he was a school boy. He had no recollection of 5 years spent in Australia and 2 years in the UK working on a golf course. Two weeks after the injury he remembered the 5 years spent in Australia and remembered returning to the UK; the past 2 years were, however, a complete blank as far as his memory was concerned. Three weeks after the injury, he returned to the village where he had been working for 2 years. Everything looked strange and he had no recollection of ever having been there before. He lost his way on more than one occasion. Still feeling a stranger to the district he returned to work; he was able to do his work satisfactorily but had difficulty in remembering what he had actually done during the day. About 10 weeks after the accident the events of the past 2 years were gradually recollected and finally he was able to remember everything up to within a few minutes of the accident.

(Russell, 1959, pp. 69–70)

The shrinkage in degree of retrograde amnesia is variable and typically less dramatic than that shown by our Australian green-keeper. The dense period of continuing amnesia immediately preceding the TBI is, however, very characteristic. Is the problem one of registering the experience in the first place, or consolidation of the memory trace? Light is thrown on this issue by a study by Yarnell and Lynch (1970) of American football players who have been "dinged." As they were led off, the investigator asked the name of the play that led to the collision (e.g. Pop 22).

Typically, the player could remember it immediately, but not when questioned later. Although other interpretations are possible, this certainly is consistent with a lack of early neural consolidation of the memory trace.

There has, in recent years, been a growing interest in the long-term effects of playing high-contact games like American football. Gina Geffen, an Australian neuropsychologist, was asked to examine an Australian-rules football player who had sustained a head injury. To obtain a comparison group, she tested a number of his colleagues using a test of speed of semantic processing developed by Baddeley, Emslie, and Nimmo-Smith (1992). This involves the patient in reading a series of brief sentences that are either obviously true or obviously false. Typical positive sentences are *Nuns have religious beliefs* and *Shoes are sold in pairs*. Negative sentences are created by recombining positive instances, as in *Shoes have religious beliefs* and *Nuns are sold in pairs*. Go to Box 7.2 in Chapter 7 to try the test yourself.

Geffen found that not only her patient but also his team-mates in this extremely vigorous sport were somewhat slowed on this sensitive speed test of semantic processing (Hinton-Bayre,

In Yarnell and Lynch's (1970) study of "dinged" American football players the player could generally recall the name of the play that had led to the collision immediately, but not when questioned later.

Box 16.2 The dementias

Dementia is an umbrella term describing symptoms that occur when the brain is affected by diseases. They are typically progressive and associated with aging, although earlier forms of dementia also occur. There is a range of types of which the following are more common.

Alzheimer's disease

The most common cause as discussed in the text.

Vascular dementia

Reduced oxygen supply to the brain may lead to cell death. This can occur either suddenly following a stroke, or more gradually through a series of strokes.

Dementia with Lewy bodies

Named from the small spherical structures that develop inside nerve cells leading to degeneration of the main tissue. Initial symptoms tend to be visual rather than memory problems. It is suggested it may be related to dementia that sometimes occurs with Parkinson's disease, for which motor symptoms are most common.

Fronto-temporal dementia

Involves deterioration of neurons in the frontal and/or temporal lobes resulting in changes in behavior and personality, and potentially leading to difficulties with language. Relatively rare.

Semantic dementia

Progressive loss of semantic memory involves failing comprehension of both words and pictures. Associated with atrophy of the temporal lobes, particularly in the left fronto-temporal region. Relatively rare but important theoretically because of its implication for understanding semantic memory (see Chapter 7).

Geffen, & McFarland, 1997). Others have found similar results in other high-contact sports players, and regular testing has now become an important feature within American football and increasingly in other sports (Sahler & Greenwald, 2012). This residual deficit is of course much less severe than that found in PTA, and in American college football players typically appears to resolve within a few days (McCrea, Guskiewicz, Marshall, Barr, & Randolph, Cantu, et al., 2003), although a too speedy return to playing can increase the chance of a further incident and lead to slower recovery particularly in the immature brain when it can prove fatal. A growing concern is that recurrent TBI may lead to later vulnerability to dementia. This is a particular problem in American football, where TBI may occur even at High school level where football is associated with 63% of reported TBI cases as opposed to 10% for wrestling and 6% for soccer (Powell & Barber-Foss, 1999). Clearly American football professionals are even more at risk; in a recent study, Randolph, Kazantzoulis and Guskiewicz (2013) contacted 513 retired NFL players aged 50 or older, finding preliminary evidence that some 35% showed signs of mild cognitive impairment (MCI) a condition that is predictive of progression to dementia. This is already giving rise to law suits in the US, and internationally to an increasing concern regarding sports-based concussive injuries.

While TBI represents a substantial problem, an even more serious problem is presented by the dementias, a problem that is ever more urgent as the life expectancy of the population increases. Dementia takes a number of forms (see Box 16.2), of which the most prevalent is Alzheimer's disease.

ALZHEIMER'S DISEASE

In 1907, Dr Alois Alzheimer first described the disease that bears his name. It is a devastating disease of the elderly with symptoms that vary but always include an increasingly severe deficit in episodic memory. Alzheimer's disease (AD) is the most prominent cause of senile dementia, comprising over 50% of cases of dementia. It occurs in about 10% of the population over the age of 65 with the rate increasing with age. Box 16.3 shows ten potential signs of dementia as described in a report by the US Academy of Neurology.

Box 16.3 Warning signs of Alzheimer's disease

The American Academy of Neurology proposed the following guidelines (Petersen, Stevens, Ganguli, Tangalos, Cummings, J. L., & DeKosky, 2001):

1   Memory loss that affects job skills
2   Difficulty performing familiar tasks
3   Problems with language
4   Disorientation to time and place (getting lost)
5   Poor or decreased judgment
6   Problems with abstract thinking
7   Misplacing things
8   Changes in mood or behavior
9   Changes in personality
10 Loss of initiative

It is suggested that people who show several of these should see their doctor for a thorough examination.

Diagnosis

Because of the varied range of symptoms, the early stages of AD can be difficult to diagnose; diagnosis requires that there is a memory impairment together with at least two other deficits, which can include problems of language, action control, perception, or executive function. The disease is progressive over time and, ultimately, diagnosis currently depends on a post-mortem examination of the brain tissue, revealing two cardinal signs of AD: amyloid plaques and neurofibrillary tangles. Plaques are created by faulty protein division. This results in the production of beta amyloid, which is toxic to neurons and leads to the formation of the clumps of amyloid that form the plaques. Neurofibrillary tangles occur within the neurons and are based on the microtubules that structure and nourish the cell. Abnormal proteins form, resulting in the twisting and collapse of the microtubules, and ultimately in cell death (St George-Hyslop, 2000). However, both plaques and tangles are often found in the normal aging brain. Cases of dementia have also been found in the absence of plaques and tangles, causing the previous assumption of their causal role to be questioned.

The disease typically develops through a series of stages (Braak & Braak, 1991) beginning in the medial temporal lobes and hippocampus, creating the initial memory problems, and then progressing to the temporal and parietal lobes and to other brain regions. Consistent with this anatomical diversity, a close examination of an extensive sample of well-studied patients indicated a wide and varied pattern of neuropsychological deficits (Baddeley, Della Sala, & Spinnler, 1991). A further extensive analysis of data from 180 patients and over a 1000 normal elderly individuals suggests that despite the potential presence of a varied range of other cognitive deficits, AD is basically characterized by a single overall feature, namely that of defective episodic memory (Salthouse & Becker, 1998). It is important to note, however, that a memory deficit is necessary for diagnosis, so this is perhaps unsurprising.

At the level of the individual patient, the disease can develop from an initial tendency to absentmindedness and memory failure, progressing to increasingly severe and potentially varied cognitive symptoms. These were well illustrated in a case study of the Oxford philosopher and novelist Iris Murdoch, as described by Garrard, Malony, Hodges, and Patterson (2005). They compared the sentence content and structure of one of Murdoch's early novels, *Flight from the Enchanter*, with a middle novel, *The Sea*, and her final novel, *Jackson's Dilemma*. They found that her last novel used considerably shorter sentences and more high-frequency words, suggesting that she was adapting to her growing language constraints. As the disease progressed, her linguistic problems increased, including word-finding difficulties, which she avoided by circumlocutions. She showed major problems

Box 16.4 The Nun Study

Nuns, from the Sisters of Notre Dame convent in Minnesota, who were participants in Snowden's (1997) longitudinal study of aging.

Some 678 nuns drawn from convents across the US have contributed to one of the most innovative studies on aging and dementia. Their ages range from 75 to 107, and over a period of 15 years they have received annual cognitive and physical function evaluations, followed eventually by post-mortem neuropathology. They show considerable variability, ranging from a cognitively and physically intact centenarian who has virtually no neuropathology to a 92 year old with both dementia and the expected neuropathology, and, perhaps most surprisingly, cases in which clear neuropathological and vascular signs occur in the absence of cognitive impairment, as in the case of Sister Mary who died at the age of 101, having maintained high cognitive capacity despite abundant neurofibrillary tangles and senile plaques. The assumption that these neuropathological signs are causal is now beginning to be questioned (Snowden, 1997). Nuns provide an ideal population for studying Alzheimer's disease because they have relatively simple and stable lives, allowing individual differences to be separated from the effects of external events. Surprisingly, a clear link was found between the quality of the essays each nun would write on entering the convent and the subsequent likelihood of developing dementia many years later. Those who packed more ideas into the sentences of their earlier autobiographies, and who expressed more positive emotions were likely to live up to 10 years longer that those who early efforts were more linguistically impoverished and less positive.

in word definition, for example describing a bus as "something carried along." Her spelling deteriorated, with a word such as *cruise* being written as *crewes*, and her capacity to name pictures or to generate items from a given semantic category such as animals was increasingly impaired.

Although the decline in cognitive performance in dementia can be very worrying, social and emotional deterioration can be even more distressing, sometimes leading to the feeling of a spouse that "this is not the person I married." In the case of Iris Murdoch, she appeared to maintain a very amiable disposition (Bayley, 1998), but sadly this is by no means always the case. For present purposes, however, we will limit discussion to the effects of AD on memory.

Episodic memory

By the time AD has been reliably diagnosed, patients are likely to show a substantial deficit in episodic memory, whether measured by recall or recognition, using verbal or visual material, or based on measures of everyday memory (Spinnler, Della Sala, Bandera, & Baddeley, 1988; Greene, Baddeley, & Hodges, 1996). As in the classic amnesic syndrome, the recency effect in free recall is relatively well preserved, although performance on earlier items is grossly impaired. There is evidence that as the disease progresses even recency tends to decline (Miller, 1971).

Forgetting

Despite the difficulty AD patients have in acquiring new information, once learned it appears to be forgotten no more rapidly than occurs in normal elderly people (Christensen, Kopelman, Stanhope, Lorentz, & Owen 1998). Kopelman (1985) took advantage of the fact that people tend to be very good at picture recognition, taking care to vary the exposure time so as to equate the performance of normal, AD, and elderly participants when tested after 5 minutes. He then retested them

Iris Murdoch was a famous novelist who suffered from Alzheimer's disease and displayed many typical cognitive symptoms and linguistic constraints. Her life story was turned into the 2001 film *Iris* starring Kate Winslet and Judy Dench as the younger and older Iris respectively. It went on to win an Oscar, a Golden Globe and a BAFTA, amongst many other awards.

KEY TERM

Everyday memory: Term applied to a movement within memory to extend the study of memory from the confines of the laboratory to the world outside.

after a 24-hour delay and found equivalent performance across the groups.

As noted in the case of Iris Murdoch, semantic memory declines as the disease progresses. Hodges and colleagues devised a battery for measuring semantic memory using a range of different tasks designed to ensure that any deficit observed is general, and not the result of perceptual or linguistic problems. A clear semantic deficit would be reflected in difficulties in naming pictures of objects or animals, in picking the appropriate picture given its name, in describing the characteristic of a named or pictured object, or in answering general questions such as whether an elephant has pricked up or floppy ears. In a series of studies, the Hodges group observed a steady decline in semantic memory in AD patients that was associated with degree of temporal lobe atrophy (Hodges, Patterson, & Tyler, 1994; Hodges & Patterson, 1995). The decline of semantic memory is even more precipitous in *semantic dementia*, a disease in which episodic memory is relatively well preserved, with atrophy occurring principally in the left temporal lobe rather than the more medial focus that tends to be found in AD (Snowden, Neary, & Mann, 1996).

Implicit memory

Perhaps unsurprisingly, given that implicit learning and memory can reflect a number of different systems, the pattern of deficit in AD is somewhat complex. Heindel, Salmon, Shults, Walicke, and Butters (1989) tested patients with AD on the pursuit rotor, which you may recall is a task which requires keeping a stylus in contact with a moving target. The patients performed less well initially, but improved at the same rate as an elderly control group. Similarly, Moscovitch (1982) found little impairment in the rate at which AD patients learned to read mirror-reversed words.

Fleischman, Vaidya, Lange, and Gabrieli (1997) found normal priming in a lexical decision task involving the speed of deciding whether a sequence of letters comprised a real word or not. However, unlike the classic amnesic syndrome, implicit memory was not spared when tested by stem completion, in which patients were shown a word (*stamp*) and later ask to "guess" a word beginning with *st*. In general, patients with AD tend to show intact priming on relatively automatic tasks but reduced priming on more complex tasks, for example when recall is primed by presenting associatively related cue words (Salmon, Shimamura, Butters, & Smith, 1988; Salmon & Heindel, 1992).

Working memory in Alzheimer's disease

A working memory deficit occurs but is typically less marked than that of episodic memory, with modest but reliable deficits in both digit span and on the Corsi block tapping test of visuospatial memory (Spinnler et al, 1988). Patients are able to maintain small amounts of material over an unfilled delay but, when the delay is filled with *articulatory suppression*, patients with AD rapidly forget, whereas normal elderly participants show a decline only when the interpolated task is intellectually demanding, such as counting backwards in threes (Morris, 1986; Morris & Baddeley, 1988). This suggests that maintenance by simple articulation remains, but that more complex or attention-demanding forms of rehearsal are lost.

To test the executive capacity of patients with AD, Baddeley, Logie, Bressi, Della Sala, and Spinnler, (1986) devised a series of tasks that combined auditory digit recall, like repeating a telephone number, with a concurrent nonverbal task. In one study, for example, the number of digits was adjusted so that AD, elderly, and young participants all performed at the same level of single-task accuracy. A similar matching occurred for a secondary tracking task in which participants had to keep a stylus in contact with a moving spot of light, with the difficulty modulated by varying the speed of movement of the spot. Having equated the two groups on the individual tasks, they were then required to perform the memory span and tracking tasks simultaneously. Young and normal elderly subjects both showed an equivalent small decrement under the combined condition, whereas the patients with AD showed a marked decline in performance, which became more marked as the disease progressed (Baddeley, Bressi, Della Sala, Logie & Spinnler, 1991). The AD deficit in dual-task performance was not simply due to task difficulty, as young, older, and AD groups responded in a similar way to an increase in difficulty level on a single task, while AD patients but not controls continued to show a dual-task deficit even when each of the combined tasks were very easy (Logie, Cocchini, Della Sala, & Baddeley, 2004). The fact that AD patients but not healthy elderly have difficulty in combining tasks is potentially useful for diagnosis. Memory testing is crucial but can be harder to

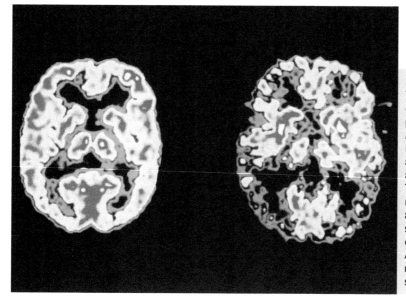

Positron Emission Tomography (PET) scans of the brain of a normal patient (left) versus an Alzheimer's disease patient. High brain activity displays as red and yellow; low activity as blue and black. The scan on the right shows reduction of both function and blood flow in both sides of the brain, a feature often seen in Alzheimer's. Alzheimer's disease is the most prominent cause of senile dementia.

interpret since performance is also likely to be impaired by a range of other conditions, including, of course, normal aging (see Chapter 15).

More recently, measures of visual working memory have been studied in AD, yielding a very striking new effect, namely a clear impairment in the capacity to bind features such as color and shape into remembered objects (see Chapter 3, p. 35). A series of studies by Mario Parra of the Edinburgh neuropsychology group has not only demonstrated this (Parra, Abrahams, Fabi, Logie, Luzzi, & Della Sala, 2009) but has extended his work to a rare genetic form of familial AD found in Colombia, in which any family member with the specific gene suffers early-onset AD, typically beginning in their forties. Parra was able to demonstrate the sensitivity of his binding measure to already diagnosed cases, but, remarkably, was also able to detect which family members possessed the fatal gene at a time when they appeared to have no other current symptoms of AD (Parra, Abrahams, Logie, Mendez, Lopera, & Della Sala, 2010). This task clearly also has the potential, given further development, to serve as an early detector of AD.

Other aspects of attentional control have been less thoroughly studied, but the evidence available suggests that some at least are comparatively spared. For example, the capacity for sustained attention or vigilance does not appear to be particularly compromised (see Perry & Hodges, 1999, for a review).

As we learn more about AD, we get better at early diagnosis, but then what?

Treatment

In an extensive review of available treatments, Doody, Stevens, Beck, Dubinsky, Kaye, Gwyther, et al. (2001) discuss both pharmacological and behavioral attempts to alleviate AD. At that time, they identified three drugs that appeared to have some effect in slowing the course of the disease, namely *donepezil*, *rivastigmine*, and *galantamine*. These operate as inhibitors of cholinesterase, a substance that breaks down the neurotransmitter acetylcholine. Acetylcholine tends to be depleted in AD, hence the value of drugs that resist further depletion. There is a huge interest in this area within the pharmaceutical industry, given that AD is a disease that inflicts enormous cost on society at both a financial and human level. This cost is increasing as the age structure of the population changes from the historic pattern in which the young greatly outnumbered the old, to one in which more and more of the population survive into old age. There is no doubt that pharmacological treatments will continue to be developed but, at present, they appear only to be able to slow the development of the disease, not to stop its progress.

In the meantime, there is considerable interest in behavioral approaches to patients with AD and to their carers. During the early stages of the disease, it is possible to use some of the methods described in the final section of this chapter to teach skills that will stand the patient in good stead as the disease advances (Clare, Wilson, Carter, Breen, Gosses, & Hodges, 2000). For example, patients can be taught to use simple memory aids, such as message boards or calendars, to avoid the need constantly to ask carers the same question, which is one of the most wearing features of supporting a densely amnesic patient. A related approach is to modify the environment in simple but useful ways. Moffat (1989), for example, describes the case of a patient who was constantly mislaying his spectacles and his pipe. His frustration level was reduced by a program training him always to return his spectacles and pipe to a bright orange bag (hopefully fire proof!). He would not remember where he left them, but could find them easily.

A number of programs have attempted to bring together techniques and skills aimed at helping the patient and the carer to cope as the disease progresses. Spector, Davies, Woods, and Orrell (2000) describe a program that improved performance on the specific areas trained, and tended to reduce levels of depression, although—as in the case of other programs of memory training for the elderly—this did not generalize to other aspects of performance.

As mentioned earlier, the purely cognitive aspects of AD are not typically the most distressing, and there is increasing interest in ways of helping patients and carers to cope with the social and emotional stresses it imposes. One disturbing feature of memory loss can be the problem of maintaining a sense of personal identity. This is particularly likely to be a problem for patients who need to move to a care home, and so are

Reminiscence therapy helps patients to maintain a sense of personal identity by recollecting their past by constructing a personal life-story book including photographs and other mementoes.

separated from their normal home environment and hence are surrounded by new and unfamiliar people. A number of approaches to this problem have been developed. One is reality orientation training (ROT), which involves helping patients maintain orientation in time and place, not necessarily a pleasant prospect given certain realities. An occupational therapist tells the story of an elderly man admitted to a hospital based in a rather grand Victorian building. He was densely amnesic and interpreted his situation as staying in a rather splendid hotel at the seaside. The overenthusiastic therapist carefully taught him to look at the calendar to say the date and to announce the name of the hospital where he was living, which he duly did, only to wink and say "But I know I am really at a grand hotel at the seaside!"

A rather more helpful approach is provided by a technique known as reminiscence therapy, which helps patients to maintain a sense of personal identity by recollecting their past (Woods & McKiernan, 2005). This can involve constructing a personal life-story book, including

KEY TERM

Reality orientation training (ROT): A method of treating patients in the latter stages of dementia who have lost their orientation in time and place.

Reminiscence therapy: A method of helping dementia patients cope with their growing amnesia by using photographs and other reminders of their past life.

photographs and other mementoes from earlier days. This not only has the advantage of reminding patients of their earlier life, but in a group context provides links with other patients who share experience of the past. It also provides things that they can tell the therapist, allowing a more natural interaction than might typically occur. However, although psychological approaches can be helpful, the best hopes for the future must lie with pharmacology, although progress has not been rapid.

REHABILITATION OF PATIENTS WITH MEMORY PROBLEMS

Attempting to enhance memory function in dementia is an uphill struggle, given the progressive nature of the disease and its tendency to impact on an increasingly wide range of cognitive, social and emotional capacities. Fortunately, many memory problems are not progressive, and here the psychologist can certainly help, not to restore memory function, but to enable the patient to make full use of remaining skills and capacities. Consider for example the biker I described in the TBI section. He would be expected to have a normal life expectancy accompanied by memory problems. How might a psychologist help him, and others suffering memory deficits from stroke or encephalitis or alcoholic Korsakoff syndrome? This will be discussed next.

How might a psychologist help a patient such as our biker? Although there is likely to be some spontaneous recovery of cognitive function, full recovery of episodic memory after serious TBI is unlikely. However, it is certainly possible to help him to make the most of his remaining memory capacity. An important aspect of any treatment is its evaluation, monitoring to check that it is actually leading to an improvement over and above any spontaneous recovery that would have occurred without treatment. What treatments are possible and how could they be evaluated?

External aids

For most patients, the main way of supplementing their impaired memory is through external aids, changing the environment in a way that helps them remember. Typical strategies for severe deficits such as occur in Alzheimer's disease might, as discussed earlier, involve labeling cupboards, drawers and doors, perhaps providing signposts from one room to the next. More generally, patients with severe memory problems benefit from building in a consistent routine, whereby objects are always kept in the same place, and everyday tasks always done in the same order. In all of these cases, of course, learning is necessary and the patient may well need considerable help from the psychologist, occupational therapist, or most importantly from a carer.

Fortunately, however, most patients subsequently develop at least some coping strategies independently or with the help of carers, but for patients with dense amnesia these are usually not enough to live independently, although there are occasional exceptions. One such case is that of JC, who was a first-year law student at Cambridge University; during a tutorial he experienced an epileptic seizure caused by a brain hemorrhage. This left him with a very pure but dense amnesia, but otherwise intellectually unimpaired. In due course he underwent rehabilitation, being taught to use external aids, mnemonics, and rehearsal strategies. He made very good use of both a diary and a notebook, and in due course recovered sufficiently to help in his father's shop. This potentially caused problems when he had to leave the counter and fetch a particular article for the customer. He coped here by subvocally verbalizing the item and a brief description of the customer for example, "Blue tights for Mrs. Big Nose."

He went on subsequently to develop what he described as "The Grand Plan" which involved a weekly sheet on his desk, a daily sheet with details from the weekly sheet, and one of appointments from his diary, using a Filofax™ with different colored sheets for different activities and different individuals. He supplements this using a Dictaphone on which he records events as they occur, carefully transferring them every evening. This is an abbreviated account of an extremely carefully devised and complex system that JC followed rigorously and remarkably successfully. Using it he was able to live independently, and to take a course in furniture renovation that enabled him to support himself (Wilson & Watson, 1996).

While the case of JC demonstrates that it is possible to live an independent and full life despite an extremely severe amnesia, he is clearly quite atypical in his intelligence, determination and preparedness to organize his life in extreme detail. What about the rest of us?

Help has come from the increasingly sophisticated development of electronic devices such as pagers and mobile phones. While these are used widely, there is often little effort to assess their usefulness. A valuable exception to this came from a study of NeuroPage™, a system developed by a neuropsychologist and an engineer who is the father of a young man who sustained a severe TBI (Hersh & Treadgold, 1994). Wilson, Evans, Emslie and Malinek (1997) sought to evaluate the system in the UK, initially starting with 15 patients with memory/ or planning problems. Each client selected a behavior he/she wanted to remember each day (e.g. "Take your tablets"; "Prepare your packed lunch"). Over a 6- week baseline, relatives monitored whether or not the targets had been achieved. The patients were then provided with the reminder system NeuroPage for a period of 12 weeks. NeuroPage is a simple paging device that can be set up to ring or buzz at prespecified times, at which one press of a button will present a message. The pager increased target behaviors from an average of 37% correct at baseline to over 85% during treatment. A major advantage of this approach is that is useable by a wide range of patients varying in their neurological problems and in their cognitive capacity. It is now of course possible to deliver a similar service by a mobile phone, although the simplicity of the original NeuroPage device is likely to make it easier to use for older patients.

So does this remove the need for the psychologist? Certainly not, since the NeuroPage experience showed that its effectiveness depended crucially on first of all establishing exactly *what* is important for the patient, programming it accordingly, and ensuring that the patient actually uses the system, not as straightforward as it might seem. It is important to recognize that almost any system for improving a patient's everyday memory will require some degree of new learning. So how can this be achieved?

Internal aids

This term refers to ways in which a patient can be helped by acquiring new habits or strategies, a task that becomes more difficult the more severe the amnesia, and the more extensive the accompanying problems. However, in practice, almost all patients have some preservation of episodic memory with truly dense amnesia being rare, so it is important to make full use of any residual memory capacity. Learning is likely to be difficult, and hence it is important to focus it on specific problems that particularly concern the individual patient, trying to ensure that steady progress is made, and for motivational reasons, that this is visible to the learner. As different patients will have different priorities and different preserved capacities, group evaluation is often not practical. However, a series of single-case methods originally derived from Skinnerian approaches to learning have been fruitfully adapted for clinical use.

All single-case treatment methods involve beginning with a measure of *baseline performance* across a series of trials before treatment is introduced. This baseline is used to determine whether genuine progress has been made by testing whether improvement begins or greatly accelerates *only* after treatment has begun. It may, however, be possible to treat several problems at the same time, in which case it is sensible to introduce different treatments at different points, to ensure that the patient is not simply showing a period of spontaneous recovery in overall cognition.

One such study is described by Wilson (1987) who attempted to teach amnesic patient TB, a 43-year-old man with Korsakoff Syndrome three relevant activities. The first activity involved finding his way around the rehabilitation center. This improved spontaneously, needing no further treatment. The second, reading and remembering a news story, applying a system known as PQRST to reading and remembering, is this case using as an example a newspaper paragraph. PQRST is an acronym for *Preview, Question, Read, State* and *Test*. Learning to apply this approach greatly improved performance. The third task of face-name learning was based on the use of imagery, for example remembering the name of a therapist called Stephanie might be remembered by imagining her sitting on a step and clutching her knee, a method which in this case, proved highly effective. Not all strategies suit all patients however; the use of imagery

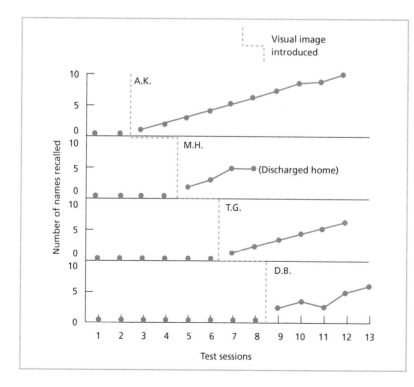

Figure 16.3 Demonstration of the effectiveness of a visual imagery strategy. Four patients were each taught the strategy and practiced over successive sessions. Note that in each case performance was flat until the strategy was introduced. The fact that across all four, performance improved only after introduction of the strategy suggests that it was the imagery strategy itself that led to improvement. From Wilson (1987). Copyright © Psychology Press.

can be too demanding for some patients, while another patient who was entirely capable of using it rejected it on the grounds that it was "silly".

Visual imagery can however often be helpful for name learning as shown in Figure 16.3. This uses another variant of single case design, in this example, by using the same imagery-based strategy but applying it to several patients, always establishing a flat baseline before subsequently introducing the imagery strategy. Note that in each case, improvement occurs only *after* the strategy is introduced, making clear its causal role in the improvement observed.

We have described two methods of enhancing learning, and, in general, approaches that facilitate learning in healthy people such as those described in Chapter 11 are also likely to be potentially useful for patients, although progress is likely to be slower. There is, however, one important exception to this. The retrieval practice effect described (in Chapter 5, p. 113) which proves so powerful for healthy learners can create problems for amnesic patients. Repeated attempts at retrieval may enhance learning in healthy young college students, but are not advisable for amnesic patients for whom errors made at retrieval can be particularly persistent and disruptive. This conclusion stems directly from the application of the results of basic research in cognitive psychology.

You will recall from Chapter 5 (p. 117) that a distinction can be made between explicit and implicit memory, with explicit episodic memory being impaired in amnesic patients, while a range of implicit learning tasks are preserved. We were tantalized by the question of whether these preserved capacities could be used to help the patient.

Reflecting on the characteristics of the preserved tasks, it seemed to us that many were either procedural tasks in which time rather than errors were the mark of success, or, as in the case of classical conditioning, a situation in which the correct response was evoked automatically by the test, as in the case of eye-blink conditioning. In contrast typical episodic memory tasks are measured in terms of error reduction. Could it be that the absence of episodic memory might make it particularly difficult for amnesic patients

to remember their earlier performance and use this to avoid future errors? We decided to test this by contrasting a learning situation in which people were encouraged to guess if uncertain, as a strategy encouraged by therapists, with one that minimized errors. Errorless learning had previously been shown in pigeons by Terrace (1963) and for a time was applied to assist learning-disabled people (Sidman & Stoddard, 1967). By this time, however, it appeared to have been abandoned clinically, or recommended as a final strategy only if normal learning had failed, by which time errors would of course already have become established.

Our own approach began with a task based on stem completion and involved presenting a series of five-letter words, cued by presenting the first two letters. Words were selected so that when given the first two letters there were several potential completions, for example *quote quiet queen* and *quite*. In the errorful condition participants were encouraged to guess the answer both initially and during learning. People in the errorless condition were told the answer each time, for example "I am thinking of a five-letter word beginning with QU and the word is QUOTE, please write it down."

We compared three groups, amnesic patients, elderly controls and young controls. They were tested over nine trials with rest points in between each group of three trials (Baddeley & Wilson, 1994). Results showed little difference between the two learning conditions for the young or normal elderly group, who seemed to have no difficulty in dealing with earlier guesses, while the errorless learning condition was substantially better for the amnesic patients.

It could of course be argued that we had used a very artificial task that might not generalize. We therefore moved on to a subsequent study using single-case treatment designs, in each case comparing errorless learning to the standard error correction approach. We studied a number of patients on several practically relevant learning tasks (Wilson, Baddeley, Evans, & Shiel, 1994). One task involved learning to use an electronic device; our amnesic patient succeeded using the errorless approach but failed completely to learn an

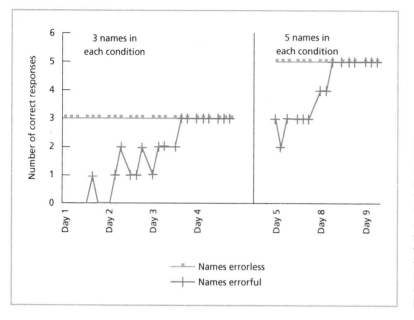

Figure 16.4 Rates of learning the names of rehabilitation staff members by ED a young man with very severe head injury using errorful and errorless learning strategies over a series of days. He began with three names and this then increased to five. From Wilson et al. (1994). Copyright © Psychology Press.

equivalent task using an error-prone approach. Other patients showed a clear errorless advantage in other tasks such as learning the names of staff, general knowledge, and information about their orientation in time and location (see Figure 16.4). Barbara Wilson immediately changed her clinical practice, which had previously been to encourage patients to guess if unsure.

The method has subsequently been widely used, not only with amnesic patients (Kessels & de Haan, 2003) but also with aphasic (Fillingham, Hodgson, Sage, & Lambon-Ralph, 2003) and schizophrenic patients (O'Carroll, Russell, Lawrie, & Johnstone, 1999). It is now widely used in memory rehabilitation, not because it guarantees learning but because it is a patient-friendly approach that facilitates learning by optimizing the use of implicit memory and minimizing the major source of difficulty and frustration in memory-impaired patients (Middleton & Schwartz, 2012).

CONCLUSION

Our understanding of human memory has benefited greatly from the study of patients with memory deficits, particularly in those cases where the deficit was limited to a specific memory system. This knowledge has fed back into the memory clinic, helping in the assessment, diagnosis, understanding, and treatment of the patient's memory problems. As such the cognitive study of memory provides one component of the array of clinical knowledge and skills available to the clinical neuropsychologist. Unfortunately, these will not "cure" the memory deficit, but they can maximize the capacity of patients to cope with their affliction.

SUMMARY

- Many kinds of disruption of normal brain function result in problems of learning and memory.
- These can be very severe and tend not to be reversible.
- Episodic memory is particularly vulnerable, reflected in its purest form in the amnesic syndrome.

- Its principal feature is anterograde amnesia, failure to lay down new memories.
- Implicit learning and memory are typically preserved.
- Anterograde amnesia is thought to result from failure to associate experiences with their context or location in time and space.
- This in turn is commonly thought to result from impaired consolidation of the memory trace.
- Retrograde amnesia involves failure to access earlier memories, including those acquired before the onset of amnesia.
- There is typically a gradient, with items acquired earlier in life being better preserved.
- Traumatic brain injury occurs when a blow or sudden deceleration causes damage to the white matter through sheering or twisting.
- In severe cases, a period of coma may be followed by post-traumatic amnesia, during which attention and new learning is disturbed.
- Both retrograde and anterograde amnesia will typically follow but become less severe over time.
- With an aging population, dementia is a growing problem.
- Alzheimer's disease is its most common form involving a memory deficit of increasing severity.
- While organic memory deficits cannot be reversed, patients can be helped to cope.
- External aids such as diaries, reminders and pagers offer the most extensive help.
- Patients still need to be trained to use these and to acquire other information; methods of achieving this are discussed.

POINTS FOR DISCUSSION

How does the amnesic syndrome differ from the cases of functional amnesia discussed in Chapter 11 on autobiographical memory?

What are the similarities and differences between anterograde and retrograde amnesia?

What might a psychologist do to help a patient, and how might this differ between a young man suffering TBI from a football injury and an elderly Alzheimer patient?

FURTHER READING

Baddeley, A. D., Kopelman, M. D., & Wilson, B. A. (Eds.) (2002). *The handbook of memory disorders* (2nd edn.). Chichester, UK: Wiley. A good source of evidence on specific types of memory disorder. It contains chapters on various types of memory deficit, and on ways of helping patients cope with memory problems.

Baxendale, S. (2004). Memories aren't made of this: Amnesia at the movies. *British Medical Journal, 329,* 1480–1483. An amusing analysis of the way in which amnesia is portrayed in movies, and a discussion of the implications of this for the public perception of memory and its deficits.

(Continued)

(Continued)

Parkin, A. J. (Ed.) (1997). *Case studies in the neuropsychology of memory*. Hove, UK: Psychology Press. Accounts of individual patients that give a feeling for the way in which different forms of memory disorder influence the lives of patients.

Parkin, A. J., & Leng, N. R. C. (1993). *Neuropsychology of the amnesic syndrome*. Hove, UK: Lawrence Erlbaum Associates. Although now somewhat dated, this presents a very clear account of the amnesic syndrome.

Wearing, D. (2005) *Forever today*. New York: Doubleday. Deborah Wearing's account of the devastating amnesia suffered by her husband, Clive, casting light on the human cost of severe memory disorder.

Box 16.1b Answers

1a, 2b, 3b, 4a, 5a, 6b, 7a, 8b, 9a, 10b, 11a, 12a, 13b, 14b, 15a, 16b.

REFERENCES

Aggleton, J. P., & Brown, M. W. (1999). Episodic memory, amnesia, and the hippocampal–anterior thalamic axis. *Behavioral and Brain Sciences, 22*, 425–489.

Alvarez, P., & Squire, L. R. (1994). Memory consolidation and the medial temporal lobe: A simple network model. *Proceedings of the National Academy of Sciences of the USA, 91*, 7041–7045.

Baddeley, A. D. (1990). *Human memory: Theory and Practice*. Hove, UK: Psychology Press.

Baddeley, A. D., & Wilson, B. (1986). Amnesia, autobiographical memory and confabulation. In D. Rubin (Ed.), *Autobiographical memory* (pp. 225–252). Cambridge: Cambridge University Press.

Baddeley, A. D., & Wilson, B. (1988). Frontal amnesia and the dysexecutive syndrome. *Brain and Cognition, 7*(2), 212–230.

Baddeley, A. D., & Wilson, B. (1994). When implicit learning fails: Amnesia and the problem of error elimination. *Neuropsychologia, 32*, 53–68.

Baddeley, A. D., Bressi, S., Della Sala, S., Logie, R., & Spinnler, H. (1991). The decline of working memory in Alzheimer's disease: A longitudinal study. *Brain, 114*, 2521–2542.

Baddeley, A. D., Della Sala, S., & Spinnler, H. (1991). The two-component hypothesis of memory deficit in Alzheimer's disease. *Journal of Clinical and Experimental Neuropsychology, 13*(2), 372–380.

Baddeley, A. D., Emslie, H., & Nimmo-Smith, I. (1992). Speed and Capacity Of Language Processing Test (SCOLP). Bury St Edmunds, UK: Thames Valley Test Company.

Baddeley, A. D., Logie, R., Bressi, S., Della Sala, S., & Spinnler, H. (1986). Dementia and working memory. *Quarterly Journal of Experimental Psychology, 38A*, 603–618.

Baddeley, A. D., Vargha-Khadem, F., & Mishkin, M. (2001b). Preserved recognition in a case of developmental amnesia: Implications for the acquisition of semantic memory. *Journal of Cognitive Neuroscience, 13*(3), 357–369.

Bayley, J. (1998). *Iris: A memoir of Iris Murdoch*. London: Duckworth.

Braak, H., & Braak, E. (1991). Neuropathological stageing of Alzheimer-related changes. *Acta Neuropathologica, 82* 239–259. doi: 10.1007/BF00308809

Cermak, L. S., Butters, N., & Moreines, J. (1974). Some analyses of the verbal encoding deficit of alcoholic Korsakoff patients. *Brain and Language, 1*, 141–150.

Christensen, H., Kopelman, M. D., Stanhope, N., Lorentz, L., & Owen, P. (1998). Rates of forgetting in Alzheimer dementia. *Neuropsychologia, 36*, 547–557.

Clare, L., Wilson, B. A., Carter, G., Breen, K., Gosses, A., & Hodges, J. R. (2000). Intervening with everyday memory problems in dementia of Alzheimer type: An errorless learning approach. *Journal of Clinical and Experimental Neuropsychology, 22*, 132–146.

Dalla Barba, G., Cipolotti, L., & Denes, G. (1990). Autobiographical memory loss and confabulation in Korsakoff's syndrome: A case report. *Cortex, 26*, 525–534.

De Renzi, E., Liotti, M., & Nichelli, P. (1987). Semantic amnesic with preservation of autobiographical memory: A case report. *Cortex, 23*, 575–597.

Dewar, M., Cowan, N., & Della Sala, S. (2010). Forgetting due to retroactive interference in amnesia: Findings and implications. . In S. Della Sala (Ed.), *Forgetting* (pp. 185–209). Hove, UK: Psychology Press.

Dewar, M., Fernandez Garcia, Y., Cowan, N., & Della Sala, S. (2009). Delaying interference enhances memory consolidation in amnesic patients. *Neuropsychology, 23*, 627–634.

Doody, R. S., Stevens, J. C., Beck, C., Dublinsky, R. M., Kaye, J. A., Gwyther, L., et al. (2001). Practice parameter: Management of dementia (an evidence-based review). Report of the Quality Standards Sub-Committee of the American Academy of Neurology. *Neurology, 56*, 1154–1166.

Düzel, E., Vargha-Khadem, F., Heinze, H. J., & Mishkin, M. (2001). Brain activity evidence for recognition without recollection after early hippocampal damage. *Proceedings of the National Academy of Sciences of the USA, 98*(14), 8101–8106.

Fillingham, J. K., Hodgson, C., Sage, K., & Lambon Ralph, M. A. (2003). The application of errorless learning to aphasic disorders: A review of theory and practice. *Neuropsychological Rehabilitation, 13*, 337–363.

Fleischman, D. A., Vaidya, C. J., Lange, K. L., & Gabrieli, J. D. E. (1997). A dissociation between visuoperceptual explicit and implicit memory processes. *Brain and Cognition, 35*, 42–57.

Gardiner, J. M., Brandt, K. R., Baddeley, A. D., Vargha-Khadem, F., & Mishkin, M. (2008). Charting the acquisition of semantic knowledge in the case of developmental amnesia. *Neuropsychologia, 46*, 2865–2868.

Garrard, P., Malony, L. M., Hodges, J. R., & Patterson, K. (2005). The effects of very early Alzheimer's disease on the characteristics of writing by a renowned author. *Brain, 128*, 250–260.

Gaskell, M. G., & Dumay, N. (2003). Lexical competition and the acquisition of novel words. *Cognition, 89*, 105–132.

Greene, J. D. W., & Hodges, J. R. (1996). The fractionation of remote memory: Evidence from a longitudinal study of dementia of Alzheimer type. *Brain, 119*, 129–142.

Greene, J. D. W., Baddeley, A. D., & Hodges, J. R. (1996). Analysis of the episodic memory deficit in early Alzheimer's Disease: Evidence from the Doors and People Test. *Neuropsychologia, 34*, 537–551.

Greene, J. D. W., Hodges, J. R., & Baddeley, A. D. (1995). Autobiographical memory and executive function in early dementia of Alzheimer type. *Neuropsychologia, 33*(12), 1647–1670.

Hassabis, D., Kumaran, D., Vann, S. D., & Maguire, E. A. (2007). Patients with hippocampal amnesia cannot imagine new experiences. *Proceedings of the National Academy of Sciences of the USA, 104*, 1726–1731.

Heindel, W. C., Salmon, D. P., Shults, C. W., Walicke, P. A., & Butters, N. (1989). Neuropsychological evidence for multiple implicit systems: A comparison of Alzheimer's, Huntington's and Parkinson's disease patients. *Journal of Neuroscience, 9*, 582–587.

Hersh, N., & Treadgold, L. (1994). Rehabilitation of memory dysfunction by prosthetic memory and cueing *Neurorehabilitation, 4*, 187–197.

High, W. M., Levin, H. S., & Gary, H. E. (1990). Recovery of orientation and memory following closed-head injury. *Journal of Clinical and Experimental Neuropsychology, 12*, 703–714.

Hinton-Bayre, A. D., Geffen, G., & McFarland, K. (1997). Mild head injury and speed of information processing: A prospective study of professional rugby league players. *Journal of Clinical and Experimental Neuropsychology, 19*, 275–289.

Hodges, J. R., & Patterson, K. (1995). Is semantic memory consistently impaired early in the course of Alzheimer's disease? Neuroanatomical and diagnostic implications. . *Neuropsychologia, 33*, 441–459.

Hodges, J. R., Patterson, K., & Tyler, L. (1994). Loss of semantic memory: Implications for the modularity of mind. *Cognitive Neuropsychology, 11*, 505–542.

Horner, A., Gadian, D. G., Fuentemilla, L., Jentschke, S., Vargha-Khadem, F., & Duzel, E. (2012). A rapid, hippocampus-dependent, item-memory signal that initiates context Memory in humans. *Current Biology, 22*, 2369–2374. doi: 10.1016/j.cub.2012.10.055

Huppert, F. A., & Piercy, M. (1978a). Dissociation between learning and remembering in organic amnesia. *Nature, 275*, 317–318.

Huppert, F. A., & Piercy, M. (1978b). Normal and abnormal forgetting in organic amnesia: Effect of locus of lesion. *Cortex, 15*, 385–390.

Huppert, F. A., & Piercy, M. (1979). Normal and abnormal forgetting in amnesia: Effect of locus of lesion. *Cortex, 15*, 385–390.

Kessels, R. P. C., & de Haan, E. H. F. (2003). Implicit learning in memory rehabilitation: A meta-analysis of errorless learning and vanishing cues methods. *Journal of Clinical and Experimental Neuropsychology, 25*, 805–814.

Kopelman, M. D. (1985). Rates of forgetting in Alzheimer-type dementia and Korsakoff's syndrome. *Neuropsychologia, 23,* 623–638.

Kopelman, M., Wilson, B. A., & Baddeley, A. D. (1990). Autobiographical memory interview. Bury St Edmunds, UK: Thames Valley Test Company.

Langlois, J. A., Rutland-Brown, W., & Wald, M. M. (2006). The epidemiology and impact of traumatic brain injury: A brief overview. *Journal of Head Trauma Rehabilitation, 21,* 375–378.

Levin, H. S., & Hanten, G. (2002). Post traumatic amnesia and residual memory deficit after closed head injury. In A. D. Baddeley, M. D. Kopelman, & B. A. Wilson (Eds.), *Handbook of memory disorders* (2nd edn., pp. 381–412). Chichester, UK: Wiley.

Levin, H. S., O'Donnell, V. M., & Grossman, R. G. (1979). The Galveston Orientation and Amnesia Test: A practical scale to assess cognition after a head injury. . *Journal of Nervous and Mental Disease, 167,* 675–684.

Logie, R. H., Cocchini, G., Della Sala, S., & Baddeley, A. (2004). Is there a specific capacity for dual task co-ordination? Evidence from Alzheimer's Disease. *Neuropsychology, 18*(3), 504–513.

Maguire, E. A., Vargha-Khadem, F., & Mishkin, M. (2001). The effects of bilateral hippocampal damage on fMRI regional activations and interactions during memory retrieval. *Brain, 124,* 1156–1170.

Manns, J. R., & Squire, L. R. (1999). Impaired recognition memory on the Doors and People Test after damage limited to the hippocampal region. *Hippocampus, 9,* 495–499.

Mayes, A. R., Holdstock, J. S., Isaac, C. L., Hunkin, N. M., & Roberts, N. (2002). Relative sparing of item recognition memory in a patient with adult-onset damage limited to the hippocampus. *Hippocampus, 12,* 325–340.

McClelland, J. L., McNaughton, B. L., & O'Reilly, R. C. (1995). Why there are complementary learning systems in the hippocampus and neocortex: Insights from the successes and failures of connectionist models of learning and memory. *Psychological Review, 102,* 419–457.

McCrea, M., Guskiewicz, K. M., Marshall, S. W., Barr, W., Randolph, C., Cantu, R. C., et al. (2003). Acute effects and recovery time following concussion in collegiate football players: The NCAA concussion study. *Journal of the American Medical Association, 290,* 2556–2563.

Meltzer, M. L. (1983). Poor memory: A case report. *Journal of Clinical Psychology, 39,* 3–10.

Middleton, E. L., & Schwartz, M. F. (2012). Errorless learning in cognitive rehabilitation: A critical review. *Neuropsychological Rehabilitation, 22,* 138–168.

Miller, E. (1971). On the nature of the memory disorder in presenile dementia. *Neuropsychologia, 9,* 75–78.

Moffat, N. (1989). Home-based cognitive rehabilitation with the elderly. In L. Poon, D. Rubin, & B. A. Wilson (Eds.), *Everyday cognition in adult and later life* (pp. 659–680). Cambridge: Cambridge University Press.

Morris, R. G. (1986). Short-term forgetting in senile dementia of the Alzheimer's type. *Cognitive Neuropsychology, 3,* 77–97.

Morris, R. G., & Baddeley, A. D. (1988). Primary and working memory functioning in Alzheimer-type dementia. *Journal of Clinical and Experimental Neuropsychology, 10,* 279–296.

Moscovitch, M. (1982). A neuropsychological approach to perception and memory in normal and pathological aging. In F. I. M. Craik & S. Trehub (Eds.), *Aging and cognitive processes* (pp. 55–78). New York: Plenum Press.

Mullally, S. L., & Maguire, E. A. (2013). Memory, imagination, and predicting the future: A common brain mechanism? *Neuroscientist.* Published online 11 July 2013, doi: 10.1177/1073858413495091

Müller, G. E., & Pilzecker, A. E. (1900). Experimentelle Beiträge zur Lehre vom Gedächtniss (Experimental contributions to the science of memory). *Zeitschrift für Psychologie. Ergänzungsband, 1,* 1–300.

Murre, J. M. J. (1996). TraceLink: A model of amnesia and consolidation of memory. *Hippocampus, 6,* 675–684.

Nadel, L., & Moscovitch, M. (1997). Memory consolidation, retrograde amnesia and the hippocampal complex. *Current Opinion in Neurobiology, 7,* 217–227.

Nadel, L., & Moscovitch, M. (1998). Hippocampal contributions to cortical plasticity. *Neuropharmacology, 37,* 431–439.

O'Carroll, R. E., Russell, H. H., Lawrie, S. M., & Johnstone, E. C. (1999). Errorless learning and the cognitive rehabilitation of memory-impaired schizophrenic patients *Psychological Medicine, 29,* 105–112.

Parra, M. A., Abrahams, S., Fabi, K., Logie, R., Luzzi, S., & Della Sala, S. (2009). Short-term memory binding deficits in Alzheimer's Disease. *Brain, 132,* 1057–1066.

Parra, M. A., Abrahams, S., Logie, R. H., Mendez, L. G., Lopera, F., & Della Sala, S. (2010). Visual short-term memory binding deficits in familial Alzheimer's disease. *Brain, 133,* 2702–2713. doi: 0.1093/brain/awq148

Perry, R. J., & Hodges, J. R. (1999). Attention and executive deficits in Alzheimer's disease: A critical review. *Brain, 122*, 383–404.

Petersen, R. C., Stevens, J. C., Ganguli, M., Tangalos, E. G., Cummings, J. L., & DeKosky, S. T. (2001). Practice parameter: Early detection of dementia: Mild cognitive impairment (an evidence based review). Report of the Quality Standards Subcommittee of the American Academy of Neurology. *Neurology, 56*, 1133–1142.

Powell, J. W., & Barber-Foss, K. D. (1999). Traumatic brain injury in high school athletes. *Journal of the American Medical Association, 282*(10), 958–963.

Randolph, C., Karantzoulis, S., & Guskiewicz, K. (2013). Prevalence and characterization of mild cognitive impairment in retired national football league players. *Journal of the International Neuropsychological Society, 19*, 873–880. doi: 10.1017/s1355617713000805

Reed, J. M., & Squire, L. R. (1997). Impaired recognition memory in patients with lesions limited to the hippocampal formation. *Behavioral Neuroscience, 111*, 667–675.

Ribot, T. (1882). *Diseases of the memory: An essay in the positive psychology.* New York, NY: D. Appleton and Company.

Russell, W. R. (1959). *Brain, memory, learning: A neurologist's view.* London: Oxford University Press.

Sahler, C. S., & Greenwald, B. D. (2012). Traumatic brain injury in sports: A review. *Rehabilitation Research and Practice,* 1–10. Retrieved from doi:http://dx.doi.org/10.1155/2012/659652

Salmon, D. P., & Heindel, W. C. (1992). Impaired priming in Alzheimer's disease: Neuropsychological implications. In L. R. Squire & N. Butters (Eds.), *Neuropsychology of memory.* (2 edn., pp. 179–187). New York: Guilford.

Salmon, D. P., Shimamura, A. P., Butters, N., & Smith, S. (1988). Lexical and semantic priming deficits in patients with Alzheimer's disease. . *Journal of Clinical and Experimental Neuropsychology, 10*, 477–494.

Salthouse, T. A., & Becker, J. T. (1998). Independent effects of Alzheimer's disease on neuropsychological functioning. *Neuropsychology, 12*, 242–252.

Sanders, H. I., & Warrington, E. K. (1971). Memory for remote events in amnesic patients. *Brain, 94*, 661–668.

Schacter, D. L., Harbluk, J. L., & McLachlan, D. R. (1984). Retrieval without recollection: An experimental analysis of source amnesia. *Journal of Verbal Learning and Verbal Behavior, 23*, 593–611.

Shiel, A., Wilson, B. A., McLellan, L., Horn, S., & Watson, M. (2000). *The Wessex Head Injury Matrix (WHIM).* Bury St Edmunds, UK: Thames Valley Test Company.

Shimamura, A. P., & Squire, L. R. (1991). The relationship between fact and source memory: Findings with amnesic patients and normal subjects. *Psychobiology, 19*, 1–10.

Sidman, M., & Stoddard, L. T. (1967). The effectiveness of fading in programming a simultaneous form discrimination for retarded children. *Journal of Experimental Analysis Behavior, 10*, 3–15.

Snowden, D. A. (1997). Aging and Alzheimer's disease: Lessons from The Nun Study. *The Gerontologist, 37*, 150–156.

Snowden, J. S., Neary, D., & Mann, D. M. A. (1996). *Frontotemporal lobar degeneration: Frontotemporal dementia, progressive aphasia, semantic dementia.* New York: Churchill Livingstone.

Spector, A., Davies, S., Woods, B., & Orrell, M. (2000). Reality orientation for dementia: A systematic review of the evidence of effectiveness from randomized controlled trials. *The Gerontologist, 40*, 206–212.

Spinnler, H., Della Sala, S., Bandera, R., & Baddeley, A. D. (1988). Dementia, ageing and the structure of human memory. *Cognitive Neuropsychology, 5*, 193–211.

Squire, L. R., Haist, F., & Shimamura, A. P. (1989). The neurology of memory: Quantitative assessment of retrograde amnesia in two types of amnesic patient. *Journal of Neuroscience, 9*, 828–839.

St George-Hyslop, P. H. (2000). Piecing together Alzheimer's. *Scientific American, 283*, 76–83.

Stickgold, R., James, L., & Hobson, J. A. (2000). Visual discrimination learning requires sleep after training. *Nature Neuroscience, 3*, 1237–1238.

Terrace, H. S. (1963). Discrimination learning with and without "errors". *Journal of the Experimental Analysis of Behavior, 6*, 1–27.

Vargha-Khadem, F., Gadian, D. G., & Mishkin, M. (2001). Dissociations in cognitive memory: The syndrome of developmental amnesia. *Philosophical Transactions of the Royal Society. B356*, 1435–1440.

Warrington, E. K., & Weiskrantz, L. (1970). Amnesic syndrome: Consolidation or retrieval? *Nature, 226*, 628–630.

Wilson, B. A. (1987). Single-case experimental designs in neuropsychological rehabilitation. *Journal of Clinical and Experimental Neuropsychology, 9*, 527–544.

Wilson, B. A. & Baddeley, A. D. (1988). Semantic, episodic and autobiographical memory in a post-meningitic amnesia patient. *Brain and Cognition, 8*, 31–46.

Wilson, B. A., & Watson, P. C. (1996). A practical framework for understanding compensatory behaviour in people with organic memory impairment. *Memory, 4*, 465–486.

Wilson, B. A., Baddeley, A. D., Evans, J., & Shiel, A. (1994). Errorless learning in the rehabilitation of memory-impaired people. *Neuropsychological Rehabilitation, 4*, 307–326.

Wilson, B. A., Evans, J. J., Emslie, H., & Malinek, V. (1997). Evaluation of NeuroPage: A new memory aid. *Journal of Neurology, Neurosurgery and Psychiatry, 63*, 113–115.

Winocur, G. (1978). Effects of interference on discrimination learning and recall by rats with hippocampal lesions. *Physiology and Behavior, 22*, 339–345.

Winocur, G., & Mills, J. A. (1970). Transfer between related and unrelated problems following hippocampal lesions in rats. *Journal of Comparative and Physiological Psychology, 73*, 162–169.

Woods, B., & McKiernan, F. (2005). Evaluating the impact of reminiscence on older people with dementia. In J. D. Webster & B. K. Haight (Eds.), *The art and science of reminiscing: Theory, research, methods, and applications* (pp. 233–242). Washington DC: Taylor & Francis.

Yarnell, P. R., & Lynch, S. (1970). Retrograde memory immediately after concussion. *Lancet, 1*, 863–865.

Zola-Morgan, S., Cohen, N. J., & Squire, L. R. (1983). Recall of remote episodic memory in amnesia. *Neuropsychologia, 21*, 487–500.

Contents

Introduction   469

Distinctive processing   470

Techniques to improve memory: Visual imagery   472

Techniques to improve memory: Verbal mnemonics   476

Why are mnemonic techniques effective?   477

Working memory training   478

Memory experts   479

Preparing for examinations   483

Learning verbatim   488

Summary   489

Points for discussion   490

Further reading   491

References   491

CHAPTER 17

IMPROVING YOUR MEMORY

Michael W. Eysenck

INTRODUCTION

Nearly everyone complains about their memory. In spite of the power and elegance of the human memory system, it is by no means infallible and we have to learn to live with that fallibility. It is regarded as much more acceptable to blame a social lapse on "a terrible memory," rather than to attribute it to stupidity or insensitivity.

How much do we actually know about our own memory? Obviously, we need to remember our memory lapses in order to know just how bad our memories are! One of the most amnesic patients ever tested by one of us (Alan Baddeley) was a woman suffering from Korsakoff's syndrome, which involves memory loss following chronic alcoholism. The test entailed presenting her with lists of words. After each list, she commented with surprise on her ability to recall the words, saying, "I pride myself on my memory!" In fact, she performed very poorly on the recall test compared to other people. She seemed to have forgotten just how bad her memory was.

A central problem when trying to evaluate our own memory is that in doing so we are effectively comparing it against other people's memories. We generally do not know very much about how good or bad their memories are, so it is very easy to have a distorted view of our own memory.

Evidence that many of us have poor memories for important information comes from the study of passwords. As you would expect, individuals who have many different passwords experience the greatest problems in terms of forgetting them or mixing them up. Pilar, Jaeger, Gomes, and Stein (2012) found 84% of people with between seven and nine different passwords had experienced memory problems with respect to their passwords. This figure dropped to 53% among those with between one and three passwords.

Brown, Bracken, Zoccoli, and Douglas (2004) found 31% of their sample of American students admitted to having forgotten one or more passwords. As Brown et al. (2004, p. 650) pointed out, "We are faced with a continuing dilemma in personal password construction between security and convenience: fool the password hacker and you are likely to fool yourself." They found 45% of students avoided this dilemma by using their own name in password construction, which hardly seems the best way to have a secure password!

Brown et al. (2004) provided tips to people constructing passwords. If security is important, select a password that is a transformation of some memorable cue involving a mixture of letters and symbols. In addition, keep a record of passwords in a place to which only you have access (e.g. a safe deposit box). Of course, you then need to remember where you have put your passwords! Research by Winograd and Soloway (1986) provides some guidance here. Students found it harder to remember the locations at which objects had been hidden when the locations were unlikely (e.g. hiding jewelry in the oven) than when they were likely (e.g. hiding a thermometer in the medicine chest).

DISTINCTIVE PROCESSING

Suppose you were presented with a list of 20 words to learn. All the words are printed in black except for the tenth word which is printed in bright red. Most people would guess that the word printed in red would be well remembered because it is distinctive or different from all the other words in the list. When experiments were done along these lines (von Restorff, 1933), it was indeed the case that there was a higher probability that the distinctive word would be recalled than other nondistinctive ones. For obvious reasons, this became known as the von Restorff effect.

von Restorff (1933) studied the effects of distinctiveness by manipulating the *visual* properties of stimuli, which presumably influenced internal processing. An alternative approach is to manipulate internal processing in a more direct way. Eysenck and Eysenck (1980) used nouns having irregular pronunciations (e.g. *comb* has a silent 'b'). In one condition, participants said these nouns in a distinctive way (e.g. pronouncing the 'b' in *comb*). In another condition, participants simply pronounced the same nouns as normally pronounced (nondistinctive processing). Long-term memory was much better for words processed distinctively than those processed nondistinctively.

It is tempting to regard distinctiveness as simply meaning that the processing of one or a few items is different from the processing of other items. However, Hunt (2013, p. 10) argued that distinctive processing should be defined as "the processing of difference in the context of similarity." Empirical support for this view of distinctiveness is discussed in Box 17.1.

KEY TERM

von Restorff effect: The finding that a to-be-remembered item that is distinctively different from other items is especially likely to be remembered.

Box 17.1 Demonstration of the effects of distinctiveness on long-term memory

Below is a list of 45 words with five words belonging to each of nine categories:

CHAIR	CAT	TANK
PIANO	ELEPHANT	KNIFE
CLOCK	GIRAFFE	POISON
TELEPHONE	MOUSE	WHIP
CUSHION	TIGER	SCREWDRIVER
APPLE	BICYCLE	DRESS
GRAPEFRUIT	TRACTOR	MITTENS
COCONUT	TRAIN	SWEATER
PEACH	CART	SHOES
BLUEBERRY	SLED	PYJAMAS
CARROTS	MICHAEL	DONNA
LETTUCE	DANIEL	PAULA
ASPARAGUS	JOHN	BETH
ONION	RICHARD	SUSAN
POTATO	GEORGE	ANNE

Ask a friend of yours to consider the list words category by category. The task is for him/her to write down one thing common to all five words within a category (Condition 1). When the task is completed, present your friend with everything that has been written down and ask him/her to recall as many list words as possible.

Ask another friend to consider the list words category by category. Beside each word, within each category, should be written one thing he/she knows about that word that is not true of any other word presented in that category (Condition 2). After that, present this friend with what has been written down, and ask him/her to recall as many words as possible.

This task is based closely on an experiment reported by Hunt and Smith (1996). They found recall was far higher in Condition 2 than Condition 1 (97% correct vs. 59%). The reason is that the instructions in Condition 2 led to much more distinctive or unique memory traces than those in Condition 1 because each word is processed differently from the others.

Distinctiveness is important with respect to learning face–name associations. Watier and Collin (2012) found names were more likely to be recognized or recalled when paired with a distinctive rather than a typical face. In similar fashion, faces were more likely to be recognized when paired with a distinctive name. Participants made judgments about their past and future memory performance with these face–name pairs. The key finding was that the predictive accuracy of participants' judgments was greater with distinctive names and faces than typical ones. Thus, distinctiveness increases the effectiveness of memory monitoring.

Theoretical considerations

How can we explain the effectiveness of distinctiveness in enhancing long-term memory? Eysenck (1979) argued that two factors are of special importance in determining long-term memory performance. First, there is informational overlap or match between the information available at retrieval and stored information. This is generally known as the *encoding specificity principle* (see Chapter 8). Second, there is the extent to which the information available at the time of retrieval allows us to *discriminate* between the correct memory trace and incorrect ones. This discrimination is greatest when the retrieval cue is uniquely associated with only one distinctive item.

Suppose you learn paired associates including *park–grove* and are later given the cue word *park* and asked to supply the target or response word (i.e. *grove*). The response words to the other paired associates are either associated with *park* (e.g. *tree, bench, playground, picnic*) or are not associated at all. In the latter case, the cue is uniquely associated with the target word and so your task should be easier. There is high overload (low distinctiveness) when a cue is associated with several response words and low overload (high distinctiveness) when it is only associated with one response word.

Goh and Lu (2012) tested the above predictions. Encoding–retrieval overlap was manipulated by using three types of items. There was maximal overlap when the same cue was presented at retrieval as at learning (e.g. *park–grove* followed by *park–???*); this

was an intra-list cue. There was moderate overlap when the cue was a strong associate of the target word (e.g. *airplane–bird* followed by *feather–???*). Finally, there was little overlap when the cue was a weak associate of the target word e.g. *roof–tin* followed by *armor–???*).

What did Goh and Lu (2012) find? As predicted from the encoding specificity principle, encoding–retrieval overlap was important (see Figure 17.1). However, cue overload was also important—memory performance was much better when each cue was uniquely or distinctively associated with a single response word. According to the encoding specificity principle, memory performance should be best when encoding–retrieval overlap is highest (i.e. with intra-list cues). However, that was *not* the case when there was high overload. Thus, high levels of memory performance required encoding–retrieval overlap plus high distinctiveness as predicted by Eysenck (1979).

Hunt, Smith, and Dunlap (2011) argued that distinctive processing at encoding constrains processing at test and thus reduces the incidence of false recall. They investigated this argument using the Deese–Roediger–McDermott task in which all the list words are associatively related to a word that is not presented (this task is also discussed in Chapter 14). Thus, for example, the list might contain the words *nurse, sick, hospital,* and *patient* but not the word *doctor*. The typical finding with this task is that the word not presented

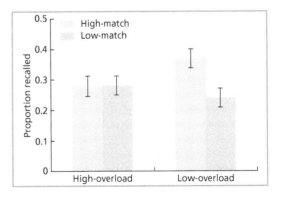

Figure 17.1 Positions recalled across overload and cue-type conditions. From Goh and Lu (2012). Copyright © The Psychonomic Society, reproduced with permission.

(e.g. *doctor*) is often falsely recalled. Hunt et al. found (as predicted) that false recall in this task was greatly reduced when list words were processed in a relatively distinctive fashion than when they were processed less distinctively.

TECHNIQUES TO IMPROVE MEMORY: VISUAL IMAGERY

In this section of the chapter, I will focus on some of the numerous techniques that can be used to improve your memory. As you may know, every self-help book designed to improve your memory provides many examples of effective mnemonic techniques (e.g. McPherson, 2004). Indeed, there are more such techniques than you can shake a stick at. Here I will consider a few of the most important mnemonic techniques, including an assessment of their strengths and limitations.

Here we will consider, primarily, mnemonics that rely on visual imagery. Mnemonics that are mostly word-based will be discussed in the next section. Bear in mind, however, that the distinction is only relative—many mnemonic techniques involve a combination of words and images.

As you read about the various mnemonic techniques, you may find yourself wondering *why* these techniques are so effective. What I have done is to describe the techniques before having a concluding section entitled, "Why are mnemonic techniques effective?" If you want to know the answer at any point, simply read this section, which starts on p. 477.

Method of loci

Mnemonics based on visual imagery have been common at least since classical times. According to Cicero, writing in the first century BC, the first such mnemonic was devised by the Greek poet Simonides in about 500 BC. A Greek who had won a wrestling victory at the Olympic Games gave a banquet at his house to celebrate. Simonides attended the banquet and gave a recitation in honor of the victor.

Shortly after completing his eulogy, Simonides was called away ... fortunately for him, because just after he left, the floor of the banqueting hall collapsed killing and mutilating the guests. Many bodies were unrecognizable.

How were the victims' relatives to identify them and give them a decent burial? Simonides found he could easily remember where most of the guests had been at the time he left, and so was able to identify the bodies. This set him thinking. If his visual memory was so good, couldn't he use it to help himself recall other material? He therefore devised a system in which he visualized a room in great detail and then imagined various items in special places in the room. Whenever he needed to remember those items, he would "look" at the appropriate location in his mind's eye and mentally recall them.

The system (known as the method of loci) became popular with classical orators such as Cicero and is still used today. As you will find if you give it a serious trial, it works very effectively and easily (see Box 17.2).

One of us (Alan Baddeley) has used the method of loci very often in student laboratory classes and it almost invariably works extremely well. It is much easier to use with concrete words such as names of objects, but is still effective when remembering abstract words such as *truth*, *hope*, and *patriotism*. The use of imagery can be prevented by introducing an interfering spatial task, so do not use this method while skiing down a mountain or driving a car!

Findings

The method of loci is often very effective. Bower (1973) compared recall of five lists of 20 nouns each, for groups using or not using the method of loci. The former group recalled 72% of the nouns on average against only 28% for the latter.

KEY TERM

Method of loci: A memory technique in which to-be-remembered items are associated with various locations well known to the learner.

Box 17.2 Method of loci: How it works

First of all, think of ten locations in your home, choosing them so the sequence of moving from one to the next is obvious; for example, front door to entrance hall to kitchen to bedroom, and so on. Check that you can imagine moving through your ten locations in a consistent order without difficulty. Now think of ten items and imagine them in those locations. If the first item is a pipe, you might imagine it poking out of the letterbox in your front door, and great clouds of smoke billowing into the street. If the second is a cabbage, you might imagine your hall obstructed by an enormous cabbage, and so on. When it comes to recall, all you need to do is to re-walk mentally the route around your house.

Now try to create similarly striking images associating your ten chosen locations with the words below:

shirt   eagle   paperclip   rose   camera
mushroom   crocodile   handkerchief
sausage mayor

The same set of locations can be used repeatedly, as long as only the most recent item in a particular location is remembered. Earlier items in that location will suffer from the usual interference effects, unless of course you deliberately link them into a coherent chain.

Try to recall the ten items listed two paragraphs ago. No, don't look! Rely on the images you created at various points around you.

It is certainly possible to create a system having more than ten locations; this was true of classical mnemonic systems and of the complex and somewhat mystical systems developed during the Middle Ages. Ross and Lawrence (1968) discovered that people using the method of loci could recall more than 95% of a list of 40 or 50 items after a single study trial.

The effectiveness of the method of loci depends on which locations are used. Massen, Vaterrodt-Plünnecke, Krings, and Hilbig (2009) found the method led to better recall when based on a route to work rather than one inside the participant's home. An individual's route to work is generally more constant than the ways he/she moves around his/her own home and thus easier to use. More specifically, recall is better when the retrieval cues (i.e. locations) are more accessible.

What would happen if someone used the same locations to learn several different lists of words? It seems likely he/she would become somewhat confused by the time each location has been associated with several different objects. Cast your mind back to Chapter 9 in which there was a discussion of proactive interference (the disruption of memory by previous learning). Proactive interference is especially great when the same stimulus is associated with several different responses, which is exactly the situation here.

The above issue was addressed by Massen and Vaterrodt-Plünnecke (2006). There was clear evidence of proactive interference (but not greater than with other learning strategies) when successive lists of words were composed of items from the same category. However, there was little or no evidence of proactive interference when each list consisted of words drawn from different categories because this made it easier to keep the lists separate in memory.

There are various limitations with the method of loci. It can be hard to recall any given item without working your way through the list in sequence until you come to the item you want. It is also often argued that the method of loci is not useful when people are trying to learn and remember in the real world. De Beni, Moè, and Cornoldi (1997) addressed this issue. They presented a 2000-word text orally or in written form to students who used the method of loci or rehearsed parts of the text. Memory was tested shortly after presentation and 1 week later.

The method of loci led to much better recall than rehearsal at both retention intervals following oral presentation (see Figure 17.2). Thus, it was very effective with a lecture-style presentation. In contrast, there was *no* effect

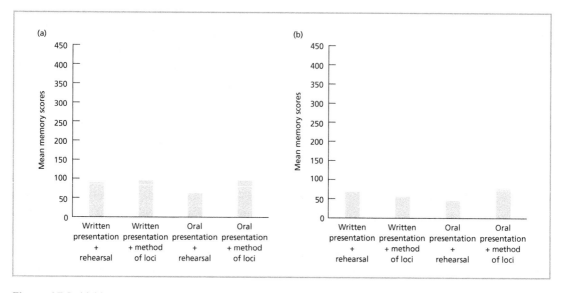

Figure 17.2 (a) Memory performance at a short retention interval as a function of type of presentation (written vs. oral) and learning strategy (rehearsal vs. method of loci). (b) Memory performance at a 1-week retention interval as a function of type of presentation and learning strategy. Data from De Beni et al. (1997).

of learning method when the text was in written form. Similar findings were reported by De Beni and Moè (2003). The method of loci was ineffective with written presentation because the visual nature of the presentation interfered with the use of visual imagery associated with the method of loci.

Do the above findings show the method of loci is useful in the real world? Not entirely. It is true that the learning situation De Beni and Moè used resembled the real world more than those used by previous researchers. However, the task of trying to remember the details of a 2000-word text is not something any of us often tries to do!

Pegword system

The pegword system resembles the method of loci in that it relies on visual imagery and allows you to remember sequences of ten unrelated items in the correct order. First of all, you memorize ten pegwords. Since each pegword rhymes with a number from one to ten, this is fairly easy. Try it for yourself:

One = *bun*   Two = *shoe*   Three = *tree*

Four = *door*

Five = *hive*   Six = *sticks*   Seven = *heaven*

Eight = *gate*

Nine = *wine*   Ten = *hen*

Having mastered this, you are ready to memorize ten unrelated words. Suppose these are as follows: *battleship, pig, chair, sheep, castle, rug, grass, beach, milkmaid, binoculars.* Take the first pegword (*bun* rhyming with one) and form an image of a bun interacting with *battleship*. You might, for example, imagine a battleship sailing into an enormous floating bun.

Now take the second pegword, *shoe*, and imagine it interacting with *pig*, perhaps a large shoe with a pig sitting in it. Pegword three is *tree*, and the third item is *chair*, so you might imagine a chair wedged in the branches of a

KEY TERM

Pegword system: A memory technique in which to-be-remembered items are associated with pegwords, each of which rhymes with a different number between one and ten.

tree. Work through the rest of the items, forming an appropriate interactive image in each case. We are reasonably confident that when you have completed the task, you will be able to recall all ten items in the correct order even though you have never before tried to remember ten unrelated items in a given order.

You may well feel that the pegword system closely resembles the method of loci, and you would be right. More specifically, they both produce distinctive encodings via elaborate processing and serial organization of the material, with the locations or pegwords providing a well-learned retrieval structure.

In view of the similarities between the pegword technique and the method of loci, it is reasonable to predict that it should be an effective method for enhancing long-term memory. All three authors of this book have tried the pegword technique. We were relieved to find it worked for us! Wang and Thomas (2000) found it was as effective as the method of loci.

Limitations

The first limitation with the pegword technique is that it requires extensive training to have reliable and rapid access to the pegwords. Second, it is more difficult to use the technique with abstract material than concrete material. For example, it is not easy to form interactive images involving abstract concepts such as *morality* or *insincerity*. Third, there are doubts about its applicability to real life, since we rarely need to remember a sequence of several unrelated items.

Remembering names

Most people have problems remembering names. As you have probably found, this can cause embarrassment at social occasions when you are introducing people to each other and suddenly realize you have forgotten one of their names. You can try to remember people's names based on a visual imagery mnemonic. For example, you start by searching for an imageable substitute for the person's name (e.g. *Eysenck* becomes *ice sink*). Then some prominent feature of the person's face is selected and the image is linked with that feature. For example, the nose might be regarded as a tap over the sink. Brief training in this method improved recall of names to faces by almost 80% (Morris, Jones, & Hampson, 1978) under laboratory conditions.

The imagery mnemonic for learning names works well in the peace and calm of the laboratory. However, that does not necessarily mean it is also effective in real-life social conditions in which being involved in conversation may make it difficult to find the time to construct good imagery mnemonics. Morris, Fritz, Jackson, Nichol, and Roberts (2005) invited first-year university students to attend a party having received instructions about learning the names of the other students there. One group was instructed in use of the imagery mnemonic. A second group was told to try to retrieve the names at increasing intervals after first hearing them (expanded retrieval practice). There was also a control group told simply to learn people's names.

Between 24 and 72 hours after the party, the students were given the task of writing the names under the photographs of the students who had been at the party. Morris et al.'s (2005) findings were clear-cut. Students in the expanded retrieval practice condition recalled 50% more names than those in the control condition (24 vs. 16, respectively). The imagery mnemonic was even less effective than no specific memorizing strategy, leading to an average recall of only 12 names. Thus, putting in the effort to recall the names of people you have just met at a party or other social occasion pays considerable dividends in enhanced long-term memory. However, trying to use the imagery mnemonic under severe time pressure is ineffective.

Helder and Shaughnessy (2011) also studied memory for names while participants concurrently carried out another cognitively demanding task. They found in line with Morris et al. (2005) that repeated retrieval practice for names greatly increased name recall. In addition, the beneficial effects of retrieval practice were greater when the times at which retrieval practice occurred were *self-generated* rather than being controlled by the experimenter. This probably occurred because participants could engage in self-generated retrieval practice at times when the demands of the other task were relatively low.

TECHNIQUES TO IMPROVE MEMORY: VERBAL MNEMONICS

The mnemonics devised approximately 2000 years ago relied mainly on visual imagery. However, this was by no means the case in later times. For example, the Puritans favored verbal systems over those based on visual imagery. They did so for a rather curious reason: They regarded images as wicked and liable to give rise to "depraved carnal affections"!

There are many situations in which verbal mnemonics are useful and widely used. Suppose, for example, you wanted to remember the colors of the spectrum (red, orange, yellow, green, blue, indigo, and violet). You start with the first letters of the colors (ROYGBIV) and use those first letters to construct a sentence (e.g. Richard Of York Gave Battle In Vain). Medical students learning anatomy often use verbal mnemonics to assist them. One of the best-known anatomy mnemonics refers to the names of the cranial nerves: On Old Olympia's Towering Top A Finn And German Vault And Hop (olfactory, optic, oculomotor, trochlear, trigeminal, abducens, facial, auditory, glossopharyngeal, vague, accessory, and hypoglassal). Such mnemonics are effective if we assume that medical students know the particular names but cannot reliably retrieve them in the correct order.

Story mnemonic

One of the most effective verbal mnemonics is the story mnemonic. It is used to remember a series of unrelated words in the correct order by linking them together within a story. Note that the story mnemonic often involves the use of visual imagery as well as producing sentences.

KEY TERM

Story mnemonic: A memory technique that involves constructing a story linking unrelated words together in the correct order.

We will show this method at work with the ten words we used earlier to illustrate use of the pegword technique (*battleship, pig, chair, sheep, castle, rug, grass, beach, milkmaid, binoculars*):

In the kitchen of the BATTLESHIP, there was a PIG that sat in a CHAIR. There was also a SHEEP that had previously lived in a CASTLE. In port, the sailors took a RUG and sat on the GRASS close to the BEACH. While there, they saw a MILKMAID watching them through her BINOCULARS.

Bower and Clark (1969) showed that the story mnemonic can be extremely effective. Participants were instructed to recall 12 lists of ten nouns each in the correct order when given the first words of each list as cues. Those who had constructed narrative stories recalled 93% of the words compared to only 13% for those who did not do so.

Hu, Ericsson, Yang, and Lu (2009) studied the mnemonist Chao Lu (discussed later in the chapter) who has recited the mathematical constant *pi* correctly to more places of decimals than anyone else. Chao Lu was asked to learn 40 words in order on a self-paced task. He recalled 100% of the words in the correct order having spent only 9 or 10 seconds learning each word. His memory performance depended on the story mnemonic—he mentally arranged the words into eight groups of five, and constructed a vivid story at a given location for each group.

Evaluation

The story mnemonic has the advantage over the method of loci and the pegword technique in that it does not require any prior learning (e.g. of pegwords). It also has the advantage that very different stories can be constructed for each list of words, thus reducing the likelihood of proactive interference from previous list learning.

What are the limitations of the story mnemonic? First, it requires fairly extensive training—I took a few minutes to construct the story given above! Second, you generally have to work your way through the list if you want to find a given item (e.g. the seventh one).

Third, even a renowned expert in mnemonics such as Chao Lu required approximately 10 seconds per word to construct stories to enable him to recall random-word sequences in order. That means it is impossible to utilize the story mnemonic effectively when information is presented rapidly.

WHY ARE MNEMONIC TECHNIQUES EFFECTIVE?

The success of techniques such as the method of loci, the pegword method, and the story method, owes much to the fact that they allow us to use our knowledge (e.g. about the layout of the world around us; about the sequence of numbers). However, the full story of what is involved is somewhat more complicated than that—detailed knowledge is not always enough.

Suppose, for example, we asked cab drivers and students to recall lists of streets in the city in which they lived. You might imagine that the taxi drivers (with their superb knowledge of the spatial layout of the city's streets) would always outperform the students. In fact, that is *not* the case. Kalakoski and Saariluoma (2001) asked Helsinki taxi drivers and students to recall lists of 15 Helsinki street names in the order presented. In one condition, the streets were connected, and were presented in an order forming a spatially continuous route through the city. In this condition, the taxi drivers recalled 87% of the street names correctly compared to only 45% by the students.

In another condition of the same study, the same street names (all from the same part of Helsinki) were presented in a *random* order. In this condition, the taxi drivers recalled 70% of the street names compared to 46% for the students. However, when *nonadjacent* street names taken from all over Helsinki were presented in a random order, there was no difference in recall between the taxi drivers and the students.

What can we conclude from the above study? The taxi drivers obviously knew considerably more than the students about the spatial structure of Helsinki's streets. This knowledge could be used effectively to facilitate learning and retrieval when all the streets were fairly close together in that spatial structure. However, the taxi drivers could not use their special knowledge effectively to organize the to-be-remembered information when the street names to be remembered were distributed randomly around the city.

Why are mnemonic techniques such as the method of loci and the pegword method so effective? According to Ericsson (1988), there are three requirements to achieving very high memory skills:

1 *Meaningful encoding*: The information should be processed meaningfully, relating it to pre-existing knowledge. This is clearly the case when you use known locations (the method of loci) or the num*ber* sequence (pegword method), or when taxi drivers use their knowledge of their own town of city. This is the *encoding principle*.

2 *Retrieval structure*: Cues should be stored with the information to aid subsequent retrieval. The connected series of locations or the number sequence both provide an immediately available retrieval structure, as does the knowledge of spatial layout possessed by taxi drivers. This is the *retrieval structure principle*.

3 *Speed-up*: Extensive practice allows the processes involved in encoding and retrieval to function faster and faster. The importance of extensive practice can be seen in the generally superior memory for street names shown by taxi drivers compared to students in the study by Kalkoski and Saariluoma (2001). This is the *speed-up principle*.

Ericsson and Kintsch (1995) developed the above ideas. They introduced the notion of a long-term working memory which can be used to store relevant information in long-term memory and access it through retrieval cues in working memory. Thus, information about retrieval structure stored in long-term memory can be accessed when required to enhance memory performance.

Evidence supporting the usefulness of long-term working memory was reported by Hu and Ericsson (2012) in a study on the mnemonist Chao Lu (discussed earlier). He showed almost perfect recall of a list of 300 digits. He associated each two-digit sequence with a unique image and then used the story mnemonic to combine these sequences. His ability to form an image for each two-digit sequence rapidly involved the use of long-term working memory. The involvement of long-term working memory is also shown by Chao Lu's use of the story mnemonic to provide a retrieval structure facilitating recall of the digits.

Hu and Ericsson (2012) wondered whether Chao Lu's ability to use long-term working memory effectively could be disrupted. Accordingly, they asked him to learn a long list of digits involving several repetitions of two-digit sequences. His recall remained very close to 100%. He achieved this by encoding groups of four digits with a single image, combined with use of the method of loci. Thus, he was able to use long-term working memory to prevent memory interference.

WORKING MEMORY TRAINING

As we have seen, most mnemonic techniques are limited in terms of their applicability. In addition, most of these techniques cannot readily be explained by the major theories of memory discussed in other chapters of this book. These limitations suggest it would be advantageous to focus on ways of improving memory that are based more directly on memory processes and/or structures known theoretically to be of general importance.

We saw in Chapter 4 that working memory is a crucially important part of the human memory system. Accordingly, one approach to improving memory would involve training designed to enhance the capacity and/or efficiency of the working memory system. As

Shipstead, Redick, and Engle (2012, p. 628) pointed out, "Many modern training programs are designed to specifically target WM [working memory]. … it is assumed that, if a person's WM can be strengthened, a constellation of related abilities will benefit." Such training programs typically focus almost exclusively on working memory tasks, emphasize strategies of potentially general applicability, and adapt the difficulty level of the tasks based on the individual's performance.

Why might we expect that working memory training would enhance long-term memory? First, such training might increase the capacity of the various components of the working memory system (the central executive, episodic buffer, phonological loop, visuospatial sketchpad). This would promote more effective learning and long-term memory.

Second, there is much evidence that individuals with high working memory capacity have greater attentional control than those with low capacity. For example, Unsworth and McMillan (2013) found that high-capacity individuals exhibited less mind wandering than low-capacity ones during a reading task. Enhanced attentional control during learning would undoubtedly increase long-term memory.

Shipstead et al. (2012) reviewed the literature on the effectiveness of working memory training. There was evidence that such training sometimes enhanced attention and also led to increased long-term free recall and recall of paired associates. However, the effects were small and often nonsignificant. More generally, research on working memory training has typically reported beneficial effects on tasks *similar* to those involved in training. However, it has rarely tested for transfer effects to working memory tasks *dissimilar* to the training tasks.

In research published after Shipstead et al.'s (2012) literature review, Thompson, Waskom, Garel, Cardenas-Iniguez, Reynolds, Winter, et al. (2013) obtained findings comparable to those contained in the review. They obtained substantial positive effects of working memory training on the trained tasks. However, there was no transfer of training to any of the nontrained measures.

In sum, there are grounds for arguing that working memory training might lead to enhanced long-term memory and other beneficial effects. So far, however, the findings have been somewhat disappointing and wide-ranging beneficial effects of such training have not been obtained. There is a need for training programs that teach a broader range of skills and abilities.

MEMORY EXPERTS

You have probably heard about the amazing memory feats performed by extremely gifted individuals. Some of these feats are so remarkable that you might have suspected that the claims made were grossly exaggerated. There have undoubtedly been some charlatans. However, solid evidence of truly outstanding memory powers has been obtained from some individuals (see Chapter 6 in Worthen and Hunt, 2011, for an interesting discussion of such individuals).

The Russian Shereshevskii was possibly the most extraordinary of all the mnemonists. This remarkable man was studied by the Russian psychologist A. R. Luria, who wrote a fascinating book about him, *The Mind of a Mnemonist* (Luria, 1968).

Shereshevskii was first discovered when he was a journalist. His editor noticed that however complex the briefing instructions he was given before going out on a story, he never took notes. In spite of this, he could repeat anything that was said to him word for word. His editor sent him to see Luria, who gave him a series of increasingly demanding memory tests.

There seemed to be no limit to the amount of information he could commit to memory—lists of more than 100 digits, long strings of nonsense syllables, poetry in unknown languages, complex figure, elaborate scientific formulae. According to Luria (1968), "He could repeat such material back perfectly, even in reverse order, and even years later!"

What was Shereshevskii's secret? He had exceptional imagery. Not only could he rapidly and easily create a wealth of visual images, he also had an amazing capacity for synesthesia, which is the capacity for a stimulus in one sense to evoke an image in another. For example, when presented with a tone having a pitch of 2000 cycles per second, he said, "It looks something like fireworks tinged with a pink-red hue. The strip of color feels rough and unpleasant, and it has an ugly taste—rather like that of a briny pickle."

You may envy Shereshevskii's memory powers. However, he found it extremely difficult to forget anything and so his memory was cluttered up with all sorts of information he didn't want to recall. Eventually, he hit on a very simple solution—he imagined the information he wished to remember written on a blackboard and then imagined himself rubbing it out. Strange to relate, this worked perfectly!

Naturals vs. strategists

Why do some individuals have memories far better than the rest of us? Is it simply that they are "naturally gifted," or is it rather that they have devoted much time and practice to developing effective mnemonic techniques?

Wilding and Valentine (1994) considered the above question. They assessed the memory performance of contestants at the World Memory Championships in London using two kinds of memory tasks:

1 Strategic tasks (e.g. associating names and faces) that seemed susceptible to the use of memory strategies.
2 Nonstrategic tasks (e.g. recognition of snow crystals).

Wilding and Valentine (1994) classified their participants into two groups: (1) *strategists*, who reported frequent use of memory strategies; and (2) *naturals*, who claimed naturally superior memory ability from early childhood, and who had a close relative exhibiting a similar level of memory ability.

As predicted, the strategists performed much better on strategic tasks than on nonstrategic ones, whereas the naturals did well on both kinds of memory tasks (see Figure 17.3). The data are plotted in percentiles so we can see how each group performed compared with a normal control sample (50th percentile = average person's score). Easily the most impressive memory performance (surpassing that of more than 90% of the population) was obtained by strategists on strategic tasks. That should provide hope and encouragement to all of us—an excellent memory can be developed through training.

Maguire, Valentine, Wilding, and Kapur (2003) used brain imaging to study superior memorizers, most of whom had performed outstandingly well at the World Memory Championships. These superior memorizers and control participants memorized three-digit numbers, faces, and snowflakes, with the superior memorizers outperforming the controls most with the three-digit numbers and least with the snowflakes.

Maguire et al.'s (2003) key finding was that during learning the superior memorizers had significantly more activity than the controls in areas of the brain involved in spatial memory and navigation. It is probably relevant that 90% of the superior memorizers reported using the method of loci (discussed earlier) on some or all the memory tasks. This method involves visualizing to-be-remembered information at various points along a known route, and so makes extensive use of spatial memory.

The evidence discussed in this section suggests that individuals with exceptional memory are made rather than born. In other words, the secret of their success is that they all spent numerous hours developing effective strategies on certain memory tasks. It follows that their performance might be surprisingly ordinary on memory tasks for which they have not developed specific strategies.

Supporting evidence for the above prediction was reported by Ericsson, Delaney, Weaver, and Mahadevan (2004). They studied Rajan Mahadevan, who for several years held the world record for memorizing the maximum number of digits of *pi* (31,811 digits). Rajan had previously been found to have a digit span of 59 digits for visually presented digits and of 63 for auditorily presented digits. Ericsson et al. obtained strikingly different findings when they assessed Rajan's symbol span using ten symbols (e.g. ?, @, #, and *). His initial symbol span was only six symbols, which is the same as college students. He managed to increase his symbol span to nearly 30 items. However, he did this by recoding each symbol into a different digit, and then used his usual strategies to remember the resulting string of digits.

Face recognition

Some recent research has focused on individuals having exceptional face-recognition ability. Russell, Duchaine, and Nakayama (2009) identified four individuals claiming to have extremely good face-recognition ability. For example, one of them said, "It doesn't matter how many years pass, if I've seen a face before I will be able to recall it. It only happens with faces" (p. 253). All four individuals performed at a very high level on several tasks involving face recognition. For example, one task involved identifying famous people when shown photographs of them before they were famous (often when they were children). Russell et al. called these individuals "super-recognizers."

How can we explain the memory abilities of super-recognizers? Russell, Chatterjee and Nakayama (2012) pointed out face

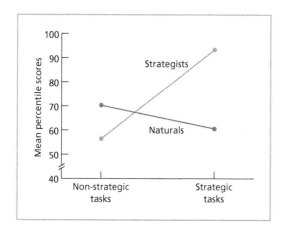

Figure 17.3 Memory performance strategists and naturals on strategic and nonstrategic tasks. Based on data in Wilding and Valentine (1994).

recognition depends on shape and surface reflectance (reflected light) information. In contrast, object recognition depends predominantly on shape information. Thus, we might expect that super-recognizers would be especially likely to make use of reflectance information. This was *not* the case. However, super-recognizers made very effective use of reflectance and shape information in face perception and recognition.

Genetic factors probably help to explain the existence of super-recognizers. Wilmer, Germine, Chabris, Chatterjee, Williams, Loken, et al. (2010) studied face recognition in monozygotic or identical twins (sharing 100% of their genes) and dizygotic twins (sharing only 50%). The face-recognition performance of identical twins was much more similar than that of fraternal twins, indicating that face-recognition ability is influenced in part by genetic factors.

In another twin study, Zhu, Song, Hu, Li, Tian, Zhen, et al. (2010) confirmed that face-recognition ability depends partly on genetic factors. However, there was no evidence that the ability to recognize houses was influenced by genetic factors, and there was a low correlation between face-recognition ability and IQ.

What do the above findings mean? They suggest that individual differences in face recognition are influenced by genetic factors *specific* to faces rather than more general. Thus, there are face-specific mechanisms, and these mechanisms have a genetic component.

Learning strategies

Several individuals have exhibited outstanding memory ability by reciting *pi* to thousands of decimal places. The current record holder is Chao Lu. On 20 November 2005, he recited *pi* to 67,890 digits without making any errors at a rate of 1.28 digits per second. His main strategy involved grouping digits into pairs, forming a visual image, and then turning these images into words. For example, the sequence 211480 became "At a volcano *cave, crocodile* ate one piece of *rose,* and found a *gourd.*" In spite of his outstanding performance, Chao Lu's visual digit span was only average. This

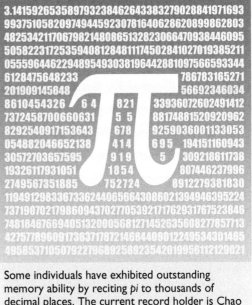

Some individuals have exhibited outstanding memory ability by reciting *pi* to thousands of decimal places. The current record holder is Chao Lu, and his main strategy involves grouping digits into pairs, forming a visual image, and then turning these images into words.

was probably because he had insufficient time to use his usual memory strategies.

Another individual, PI, recited *pi* to over 64,000 digits at the age of 22 (Raz, Packard, Alexander, Gerianne, Buhle, Zhu, et al., 2009). He used a modified form of the method of loci to learn this digit sequence, considering the digits two at a time. Sometimes he converted two-digit groups to words based on the similarity of their pronunciations. At other times he generated images resembling the physical characteristics of the digits (e.g. ten looks like a putter and a hole and led to the word golf). Then PI produced stories based on his earlier processing. Perhaps surprisingly, PI's visual memory for neutral faces and common events was very poor.

An important reason why PI was so successful at reciting *pi* is that his working memory abilities exceed those of 99% of the population. Raz et al. (2009) assessed PI's brain activity as he recited the first 540 digits of *pi*. Areas within the prefrontal cortex associated with working memory and attentional control were activated.

In sum, individuals such as Chao Lu and PI have a three-stage approach to memorizing huge numbers of digits. First, adjacent digits are formed into small groups or chunks. Second, a visual image or word is used to represent each chunk. Third, language is used to combine and integrate the information from successive chunks. Their memory strategies resemble an elaborated version of the story method (discussed earlier).

Having the ability to recite *pi* to thousands of places is a very specific skill and of extremely limited value in everyday life. It is potentially much more useful to have excellent memory for the events of one's own life (i.e. autobiographical memory; see Chapter 11). As we will see, researchers have uncovered several individuals with exceptional autobiographical memory (known as highly superior autobiographical memory: HSAM).

LePort, Mattfield, Dickinson-Anson, Fallon, Stark, Kruggel, et al. (2012) gave participants ten computer-generated dates (the 10 Dates Quiz). They had to identify the day of the week for each date, a verifiable event that happened within one month of the date, and a relevant autobiographical memory. There were 36 participants claiming to have HSAM (11 of whom appeared genuine) plus control participants. The findings are shown in Figure 17.4. The performance of those with HSAM was dramatically higher than that of the controls. However, the memory performance of those with HSAM was no better than that of controls on standard memory tasks such as digit span or verbal paired-associate learning.

How can we explain the outstanding autobiographical memory performance of participants with highly superior autobiographical memory? First, most have obsessional characteristics (e.g. hoarding things, being excessively germ-avoidant). These characteristics lead them to organize their autobiographical memories by time of events or by categories, and to spend much time recalling these memories.

Second, there were structural differences between those with HSAM and the other participants in those parts of the brain (e.g. the temporal lobe areas) forming part of the autobiographical memory network. These structural differences may help to explain the superior autobiographical memory of these individuals. Alternatively, however, it may be more the case that devoting large amounts of time to accessing autobiographical memories produces structural changes within the brain.

Having highly superior autobiographical memory has some disadvantages. One participant in the study by LePort et al. (2012) was Jill Price, a woman born in 1965 who had previously taken part in research by Parker, Cahill, and McGaugh (2006). According to her, "Most have called it a gift, but I call it a burden. I run my entire life through my head

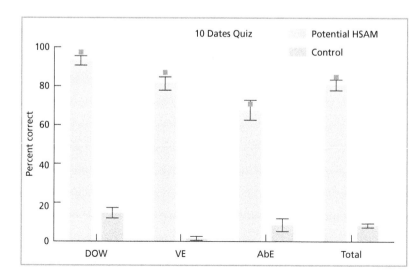

Figure 17.4 Performance on the 10 Dates Quiz for individuals claiming to have HSAM. From LePort et al. (2012). Copyright © 2012 Elsevier. Reproduced with permission.

Jill Price, a participant in LePort et al.'s (2012) study of highly superior autobiographical memory.

every day and it drives me crazy!!!" (Parker et al., 2006, p. 35).

Conclusions

What can we conclude from our discussion of memory experts? First, most have a *single* very specific memory ability, but their memory performance is generally only average. Such findings strongly indicate that outstanding memory depends very heavily on extensive, prolonged practice over a long period of time.

Second, the memory strategies used by memory experts involve elements of the mnemonic techniques discussed earlier in the chapter. More specifically, most of the strategists studied by Wilding and Valentine (1994) used the method of loci and other memorists (e.g. Chao Lu, PI) used a version

of the story method. More generally, visual imagery is an important ingredient in most memory strategies.

Third, there is suggestive evidence that structural brain differences between memory experts and other people may be of importance. Brain areas identified include those associated with spatial memory and navigation, prefrontal areas associated with working memory and attentional control, and those forming part of the autobiographical memory network. It is important for future research to decide the direction of causality between these structural brain differences and outstanding memory performance.

PREPARING FOR EXAMINATIONS

Students use numerous learning techniques to assist their learning and their ability to perform successfully in examinations. Ten such learning techniques were discussed in detail by Dunlosky, Rawson, Marsh, Nathan, and Willingham (2013) in light of the available research. Some techniques were rated as low in usefulness. These included summarization (writing summaries of texts), imagery for text (forming mental images of text materials), and re-reading (restudying text material after an initial reading).

Other techniques were rated as of moderate usefulness. These included elaborative interrogation (generating explanations for stated facts), self-explanation (explaining how new information is related to known information), and interleaved practice (studying different kinds of material within a single study session). Of course, what is of most interest to you (and also of most theoretical interest) is the technique rated the most useful. This technique (the testing effect) is discussed in detail after we have considered study skills.

Study skills

The SQ3R approach (Morris, 1979) provides an effective approach to studying and learning. SQ3R stands for *Survey, Question, Read,*

Recite, Review, and it is claimed that these represent the five stages in effective learning from texts. We will consider these five stages with respect to the task of reading a chapter of this book.

The *Survey stage* involves obtaining an overall view of how the information in the chapter is organized (e.g. using the chapter summary). The *Question stage* involves thinking of relevant questions to which you expect a given section of the chapter to provide answers. The *Read stage* involves trying to answer the questions generated during the previous stage and trying to integrate the information provided in that section to your pre-existing topic knowledge. The *Recite stage* involves trying to remember the key ideas contained in the chapter section you have been reading. Finally, the *Review stage* involves combining information from different sections into a coherent structure.

The research discussed by Dunlosky et al. (2013) provides empirical support for the SQ3R approach. For example, explaining how new information is related to pre-existing information and providing explanations for statements in the text both form part of the approach and were found by Dunlosky et al. to be moderately effective. These two strategies have two advantages: (1) they are applicable generally and (2) they require minimal training. However, most research has focused on short-term beneficial effects of self-explanation and elaborative integration, and little is known about whether these effects endure over long time periods.

Testing effect

Answer this question taken from research by Karpicke, Butler, and Roediger (2009). Imagine you are reading a textbook for an upcoming exam. After you have read the chapter one time, would you rather:

A   Go back and restudy either the entire chapter or certain parts of the chapter?
B   Try to recall the material from the chapter (without the possibility of restudying the material)?
C   Use some other study technique?

Karpicke et al. (2009) found 57% of students gave answer A, 21% gave answer C, and only 18% gave answer B. What is interesting about the pattern of responses is that the least frequent answer (B) is actually the correct one in terms of its effectiveness in promoting good long-term retention.

As Pyc and Rawson (2010, p. 335) pointed out, "An intuitive but incorrect assumption is that learning only occurs during study and that testing is useful only for evaluating the state of memory." In fact, practice in retrieving the to-be-remembered information during the learning period can enhance long-term memory more than simply engaging in study and restudy. This is known as the testing effect (see Roediger & Butler, 2011, for a review).

Findings

Convincing evidence of the testing effect was reported by Bangert-Drowns, Kulik, and Kulik (1991) in a review of 35 classroom studies. A significant testing effect was obtained in 83% of these studies. In addition, the size of the effect tended to increase as the number of testing occasions went up. Details of one of the first laboratory studies of the testing effect are to be found in Box 17.3.

How can we explain the testing effect? Zaromb and Roediger (2010) addressed this issue in a study in which participants learned lists consisting of words belonging to various categories (e.g. four-footed animals, articles of clothing). As expected, learners who had engaged in repeated retrieval practice performed better than those who had only engaged in study on a free-recall task two days later (39% correct vs. 17% correct, respectively). Of most theoretical importance, recall among those who had engaged in retrieval practice was more organized in terms of the categories contained in the lists. Thus, one reason for the existence of

KEY TERM

Testing effect: The finding that long-term memory is enhanced when much of the learning period is devoted to retrieving the to-be-remembered information.

Box 17.3 Testing effect (Roediger & Karpicke, 2006)

The basic set-up in the study by Roediger and Karpicke (2006) was that students read a prose passage covering a general scientific topic and tried to memorize it in one of three conditions:

1   *Repeated study:* The passage was read four times and there was no test.
2   *Single test:* The passage was read three times and then students recalled as much as possible from it.
3   *Repeated test:* The passage was read once and then students recalled as much as possible on three occasions.

Finally, memory for the passage was tested after 5 minutes or 1 week.

The findings are shown in Figure 17.5. Repeated study was the most effective strategy when the final test was given 5 minutes after learning, and the repeated test condition was the least effective. However, there was a dramatic reversal when the final test occurred 1 week after learning (this is the testing effect), and these findings are of most relevance to students preparing for an examination. What is striking is the size of the testing effect: average recall was 50% higher in the repeated test condition than the repeated study condition. That difference could easily make the difference between doing very well on an examination and failing it!

Why do so many students prefer repeated studying to repeated testing when revising for an examination? There are three main reasons. First, repeated studying produces short-term benefits, as can be seen in Figure 17.5. Second, Roediger and Karpicke (2006) found at the time of learning that students in the repeated study condition predicted they would recall more of the prose passage after 1 week than did those in the repeated test condition. Third, studying tends to be less effortful and demanding than testing, and this makes it more appealing to students.

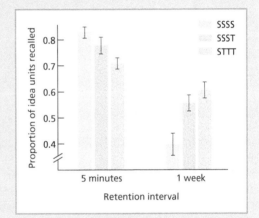

Figure 17.5 Memory performance as a function of learning conditions (S, study; T, test) and retention interval (5 minutes vs. 1 week). From Roediger and Karpicke (2006). Copyright © Blackwell Publishing. Reproduced with permission.

the testing effect is that repeated practice leads to enhanced organizational processes.

Suppose you were asked to learn Swahili–English pairs (e.g. *wingu–cloud*). You might try to learn *wingu–cloud* by thinking of a mediator (e.g. *bird*) to connect *wingu* and *cloud*, and this would probably enhance your ability to recall *cloud* (the target word) when presented with *wingu* (the cue word). According to Pyc and Rawson's (2010) mediator effectiveness hypothesis, testing supports the use of more effective mediators during learning and this leads to enhanced long-term memory.

Why does testing lead learners to use more effective mediators? Learners experience retrieval failures during testing, and these failures encourage them to seek mediators that are more effective than the ones they have previously been using.

Pyc and Rawson (2010) provided empirical support for their mediator effectiveness hypothesis. Some participants received a mixture of test and study trials (test–restudy group), whereas others received only learning trials (restudy group). There was a final memory test 1 week after the original session.

There were three main findings. First, the test–restudy group recalled almost *three* times as many target words as the restudy group. Second, members of the test-restudy group were better at recalling mediators when presented with cue words (51% vs. 34%). Third, the beneficial effects of recalling mediators on target recall was much greater for the test–restudy group (see Figure 17.6). Taken together, these findings suggest a major advantage of testing is that it leads to the use of effective mediators that are easily recalled and that lead to target retrieval.

Conclusions

The testing effect is typically associated with strong enhancement of long-term memory. In general terms, this effect occurs because repeated retrieval practice facilitates the development of an effective retrieval structure (based on effective mediators and organizational processes) to facilitate access to information stored in long-term memory. As we saw earlier in the chapter, the success of mnemonic techniques such as the method of loci and the pegword system depends in large measure on the fact that they provide a pre-existing retrieval structure that guides the retrieval process.

As Dunlosky et al. (2013) pointed out, the use of repeated retrieval practice has the advantage that it is generally applicable almost regardless of the nature of the to-be-learned material. In addition, it is a technique that is easy to use and does not require much training.

Concept maps and mind maps

There has been a substantial increase over the years in the use of techniques known as concept maps or mind maps. Both kinds of maps are similar in that they both show in visual form the links among several ideas or concepts (see Figure 17.7). However, there are some differences. Mind maps are more flexible and personal, and they are more likely than concept maps to contain images and color. In contrast, concept maps typically have general concepts at the top and more specific ones below. Concept maps have been used far more than mind maps in medical education.

A concrete example of a mind map is shown in Figure 17.7. As you can see, the interconnections among related concepts are shown. As mentioned above, the concepts are organized in a more-or-less hierarchical way with more specific concepts appearing lower down in the diagram than more general ones.

There are several potential reasons why concept maps and mind maps might enhance learning. First, students need to be actively involved in the learning process to produce adequate maps. Second, the concepts are shown as having several links or associations to each other. This is arguably more realistic (and also easier to remember) than the linear presentation of information in texts. Third, concepts are typically reduced to one or two

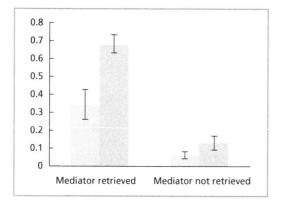

Figure 17.6 Proportion of items correctly recalled. From Pyc and Rawson (2010). Copyright © AAAS, reproduced with permission.

KEY TERM

Mind maps: Diagrams in which word concepts are linked in very flexible ways around a central key concept; they often contain images and color.

Concept maps: Diagrams in which the links among general concepts (at the top of the diagram) and specific concepts (lower down) are shown.

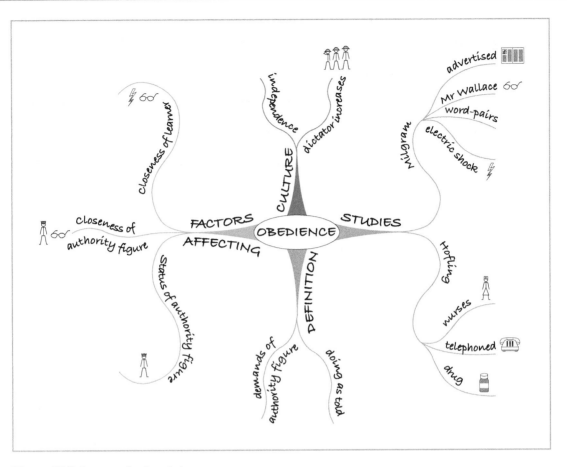

Figure 17.7 An example of a mind map.

words within concept and mind maps, extracting the *essence* of their meaning and ignoring trivial details. Fourth, mind maps (but not concept maps) provide striking visual images that may be easier to remember than conventional notes.

Findings

There is much evidence that concept maps are useful. Daley and Torre (2010) reviewed the evidence concerning the use of concept maps in medical education. The great majority of studies found medical students using concept maps showed an increase in meaningful learning, including improved integration of basic and clinical science information, and enhanced critical thinking abilities.

Many studies reviewed by Daley and Torre (2010) were limited in that they relied on students' self-reports of the effects of concept or mind maps. A study by Farrand, Hussain, and Hennessy (2002) was an exception in that they assessed medical students' recall of factual knowledge from a 600-word text. Students trained in the mind-map technique recalled 10% more than those who used their normal study techniques.

In more recent research, Veronese, Richards, Pernar, Sullivan, and Schwartzstein (2013) compared tutorials for medical students in which concept maps were or were not used. Students who used concept maps were better at integrating knowledge of physiological concepts and at identifying gaps in their knowledge. These beneficial effects lasted—students in the concept map tutorials had superior final examination scores to those not using concept maps.

Are there individual differences in the effectiveness of mind or concept maps? Most of the available evidence suggests there are only small individual differences. For example, Laight (2004) found that the self-reported usefulness of concept maps did not vary across students having a range of different learning styles. However, Budd (2004) argued that individual differences in learning style can help to explain why many students do not seem to be very motivated when using mind maps. Those students favoring a "doing" learning style felt they learned a lot from using mind maps and rated the use of mind maps as highly as lectures. In contrast, students preferring a "thinking" learning style were less sure about the value of mind maps, and rated lectures much more favorably than the use of mind maps.

As we have seen, one of greatest advantages of concept maps is that they increase students' ability to integrate information coherently. As a result, the beneficial effects of using concept maps should be especially large in problem-solving exams that require such integration. Gonzàlez, Palencia, Umaña, Galindo, and Villafrade (2008) tested this hypothesis in a study on medical students. The use of concept maps enhanced performance in a problem-solving exam but failed to do so in a multiple-choice exam.

LEARNING VERBATIM

Students on occasion must remember information verbatim (word for word). For example, English students may need to learn poems off by heart, and it is sometimes worthwhile for psychology students to learn key information (e.g. important quotations) verbatim.

We can gain insights into the processes involved in learning verbatim by focusing on the strategies used by actors and actresses. Whenever you go to a theatrical production, you have probably been very impressed by the ability of actors and actresses to remember hundreds (or even thousands) of lines when performing a play. You may have wondered whether what they are saying really corresponds to the words written down by the playwright. In fact, research shows this is nearly always the case (Oliver & Ericsson, 1986).

It seems perplexing that actors can fairly rapidly manage to memorize a script verbatim. We know that learners have much better memory for material that has been processed in terms of its meaning as is predicted by levels of processing theory (Craik & Lockhart, 1972; see Chapter 6). However, processing of meaning typically produces good recall of the gist of a text but not of its exact wording.

How long-lasting is an actor's memory for a script? Schmidt, Boshuizen, and van Breukelen (2002) addressed this question in a study in which actors recalled their parts from Sartre's *Huis Clos* (*No Exit*) 5 months after the end of the production. Overall, 53% of the script was recalled verbatim, with a further 28% being recalled in paraphrases capturing the meaning of the original script. In addition, 3% of what the actors said represented inferences based on the script. Thus, 85% of the text was retained in some form, with most inaccurately recalled material capturing the gist of the script.

Findings

One of the most surprising findings to emerge from research on professional actors is that they generally do *not* start by trying to learn the exact words of the script! Instead what they do is to focus on the needs and motivations of their characters.

Noice (1992) asked seven actors to describe how they learned their roles. Her central conclusion was as follows: "They [the actors] read the script many times, trying to infer the motivation behind each utterance. All the actors stressed the importance of identifying the underlying meaning and explaining why the character used those exact words."

We can see how this works in practice by considering the following example. An actor playing the part of a mayor says to a reporter, "Don't pester me now, please." (Noice & Noice, 1996). The actor assumed from the word *pester* that the mayor regarded the reporter as a bothersome child, which is why that word was in the script rather than *bother* or *annoy*. The mayor softens his statement by adding "please" at the end of the sentence, because he does not want to alienate the reporter.

Seamon, Punjabi, and Busch (2010) obtained similar findings in a study on JB, a 74-year-old man who had spent 3,000–4,000 hours learning Milton's *Paradise Lost*, which consists of over 60,000 words. He achieved verbatim recall via a deep conceptual understanding of the poem, which led him to become animated and emotional when reciting it (see www.paradiselostperformances.com).

Noice and Noice (1996) examined in detail how actors learn a script. They presented six actors with a scene from a play in which a man and a woman discuss love and possible infidelity. They were instructed to verbalize their thoughts as they worked through the script.

Over 40% of the thoughts belonged to the category of interactions ("statements concerning mental or emotional interactions between characters in which one character affects, tries to affect, or is affected by, another character"; Noice & Noice, 1996, p. 6). The second and third most common categories of utterances were metastatements (general statements regarding the actor's learning process) and memorization (the reasons why some lines are easier or harder to learn).

In sum, actors achieve verbatim memory for their lines by striving to obtain a deep understanding of why their character would use those precise words in context. As a result of achieving this deep understanding, actors can still remember most of their role several months later, mostly in verbatim or gist form.

SUMMARY

- Distinctive processing (the processing of difference in the context of similarity) is generally associated with enhanced long-term memory.
- Distinctive processing is also associated with increased ability to monitor one's own memory and to predict more accurately past and future memory performance.
- Distinctiveness enhances memory because it facilitates discrimination between the correct and incorrect responses on memory tests. As a result, it reduces false memory as well as increasing correct memory.
- Mnemonics based on visual imagery have been common since classical times. One of the oldest (and most effective) of such mnemonics is the method of loci. It can be used in lectures but is much harder to use with visually presented text.
- The pegword technique is similar to the method of loci and is also of proven effectiveness.
- Visual imagery can be effective when linking names to faces but works much better in the laboratory than social situations.
- The story mnemonic can be extremely effective. However, it typically requires much time to construct stories to link together words, and thus the mnemonic cannot be used effectively when to-be-remembered information is presented rapidly.
- There are three ingredients in most successful mnemonic techniques: meaningful encoding (relating what is to be learned to pre-existing knowledge), retrieval structure (cues are stored to assist subsequent retrieval), and speed-up (extensive practice allows encoding and retrieval to occur faster).
- Information about retrieval structure (of particular importance in long-term memory) is stored in long-term working memory from which it is easily accessed.
- It is plausible to argue that training designed to enhance the capacity and/or efficiency of working memory would improve long-term memory performance.

(Continued)

(Continued)

- There is some evidence that working memory training has small beneficial effects on long-term memory, and these effects may depend in part on increased attentional control. However, much research on working memory training has reported specific effects limited to tasks closely resembling those used during training.
- Many individuals have outstanding memory abilities, although these abilities are typically very limited in scope.
- Individuals with exceptional memories rely very heavily on learning strategies and extensive practice. More specifically, they typically combine information from two or more items into chunks and then use language to integrate the information across chunks.
- Individuals with exceptional autobiographical memory generally have obsessional characteristics and spend much time organizing information about their own lives.
- The limited evidence currently available suggests that expertise in face recognition may depend on genetic factors specific to faces.
- Study techniques that involve relating new knowledge to pre-existing knowledge have proved moderately effective. This forms an important part of the SQ3R approach based on the five stages of Survey, Question, Read, Recite, and Review.
- One of the most effective study techniques is based on the testing effect, which is the finding that retrieval practice enhances long-term memory much more than additional study.
- The testing effect occurs because repeated retrieval practice facilitates the development of an effective retrieval structure that makes it easier to access information stored in long-term memory.
- Mind maps and concept maps have both proved useful as techniques to promote understanding and long-term memory of information. Both types of maps can enhance the organization and integration of information about concepts which in turn promotes good long-term memory.
- Research on professional actors has shown they achieve word-for-word recall by trying to understand why their character used the precise words he/she did. This emphasis on understanding is shown by the finding that several months later actors who cannot remember lines verbatim typically nevertheless capture the underlying meaning or gist.

POINTS FOR DISCUSSION

Why does distinctiveness increase long-term memory?

Describe some mnemonic techniques based on visual imagery. What are the strengths and limitations of these techniques?

Describe training programs designed to enhance working memory. To what extent have these programs proved successful in increasing long-term memory?

How can we account for individuals who possess exceptional memory?

What is the testing effect? Why is it so effective?

How do actors learn their roles verbatim?

FURTHER READING

Dunlosky, J., Rawson, K. A., Marsh, E. J., Nathan, M. J., & Willingham, D. T. (2013). Improving students' learning with effective learning techniques: Promising directions from cognitive and educational psychology. *Psychological Science in the Public Interest, 14,* 4–58. John Dunlosky and his colleagues discuss and assess the effectiveness of several techniques designed to enhance learning and memory.

Hu, Y., & Ericsson, K. A. (2012). Memorization and recall of very long lists accounted for within the long-term working memory framework. *Cognitive Psychology, 64,* 235–266. Yi Hu and Anders Ericsson show how outstanding memory performance can be explained in terms of the notion of long-term working memory.

Hunt, R. R. (2013). Precision in memory through distinctive processing. *Current Directions in Psychological Science, 22,* 10–15. Reed Hunt discusses several reasons why memory is enhanced by distinctive processing.

Karpicke, J. D. (2012). Retrieval-based learning: Active retrieval promotes meaningful learning. *Current Directions in Psychological Science, 21,* 157–163. This article discusses some of the interesting findings to emerge from research on the testing effect.

Shipstead, Z., Redick, T. S., & Engle, R. W. (2012). Is working memory training effective? *Psychological Bulletin, 138,* 628–654. The authors provide a comprehensive review of training programs designed to enhance working memory.

Worthen, J. B., & Hunt, R. R. (2011). *Mnemonology: Mnemonics for the 21st century.* Hove, UK: Psychology Press (pp. 1–161). In this book, the authors provide a comprehensive and authoritative account of the best-known and most effective memory techniques.

REFERENCES

Bangert-Drowns, R. L., Kulik, J. A., & Kulik, C. L. C. (1991). Effects of frequent classroom testing. *Journal of Educational Research, 61,* 213–238.

Bower, G. H. (1973). How to … uh … remember! *Psychology Today, 7,* 63–70.

Bower, G. H., & Clark, M. C. (1969). Narrative stories as mediators for serial learning. *Psychonomic Science, 14,* 181–182.

Brown, A. S., Bracken, E., Zoccoli, S., & Douglas, K. (2004). Generating and remembering passwords. *Applied Cognitive Psychology, 18,* 641–651.

Budd, J. W. (2004). Mind maps as classroom exercises. *Journal of Economic Education, 35,* 35–46.

Craik, F. I. M., & Lockhart, R. S. (1972). Levels of processing: A framework for memory research. *Journal of Verbal Learning and Verbal Behavior, 11,* 671–684.

Daley, B. J., & Torre, D. M. (2010). Concept maps in medical education: An analytical literature review. *Medical Education, 44,* 440–448.

De Beni, R., & Moè, A. (2003). Imagery and rehearsal as study strategies for written or orally presented passages. *Psychonomic Bulletin and Review, 10,* 975–980.

De Beni, R., Moè, A., & Cornoldi, C. (1997). Learning from texts or lectures: Loci mnemonics can interfere with reading but not with listening. *Law and Human Behavior, 28,* 687–706.

Dunlosky, J., Rawson, K. A., Marsh, E. J., Nathan, M. J., & Willingham, D. T. (2013). Improving students' learning with effective learning techniques: Promising directions from cognitive and educational psychology. *Psychological Science in the Public Interest, 14*, 4–58.

Ericsson, K. A. (1988). Analysis of memory performance in terms of memory skill. In R. J. Sternberg (Ed.*), Advances in the psychology of human intelligence* (Vol. 4, pp. 137–179). Hillsdale, NJ: Lawrence Erlbaum Associates.

Ericsson, K. A., & Kintsch, W. (1995). Long-term working memory. *Psychological Review, 102*, 211–245.

Ericsson, K. A., Delaney, P. F., Weaver, G., & Mahadevan, R. (2004). Uncovering the structure of a mnemonist's superior "basic" memory capacity. *Cognitive Psychology, 49*, 191–237.

Eysenck, M. W. (1979). Depth, elaboration, and distinctiveness. In L. S. Cermak & F. I. M. Craik (Eds.), *Levels of processing in human memory*. Hillsdale, NJ: Lawrence Erlbaum Associates.

Eysenck, M. W., & Eysenck, M. C. (1980). Effects of processing depth, distinctiveness, and word frequency on retention. *British Journal of Psychology, 71*, 263–274.

Farrand, P., Hussain, F., & Hennessy, E. (2002). The efficacy of the "mind map" study technique. *Medical Education, 36*, 426–431.

Goh, W. D., & Lu, S .H. X. (2012). Testing the myth of encoding-retrieval match. *Memory and Cognition, 40*, 28–39.

Gonzàlez, H. L., Palencia, A. P., Umaña, L. A., Galindo, L., & Villafrade, M. L. A. (2008). Mediated learning experience and concept maps: A pedagogical tool for achieving meaningful learning in medical physiology students. *Advances in Physiology Education, 32*, 312–316.

Helder, E., & Shaughnessy, J. J. (2011). Self-generated retrievals while multitasking improve memory for names. *Memory, 19*, 968–974.

Hu, Y., & Ericsson, K. A. (2012). Memorization and recall of very long lists accounted for within the long-term working memory framework. *Cognitive Psychology, 64*, 235–266.

Hu, Y., Ericsson, K. A., Yang, D., & Lu, C. (2009). Superior self-paced memorization of digits in spite of a normal digit span: The structure of a memorist's skill. *Journal of Experimental Psychology: Learning, Memory, and Cognition, 35*, 1426–1442.

Hunt, R. R. (2013). Precision in memory through distinctive processing. *Current Directions in Psychological Science, 22*, 10–15.

Hunt, R. R., Smith, R. E., & Dunlap, K. D. (2011). How does distinctive processing reduce false memory? *Journal of Memory and Language, 65*, 478–389.

Kalakoski, V., & Saariluoma, P. (2001). Taxi drivers' exceptional memory of street names. *Memory and Cognition, 29*, 634–638.

Karpicke, J. D., Butler, A. C., & Roediger, H. L. (2009). Metacognitive strategies in student learning: Do students practice retrieval when they study on their own? *Memory, 17*, 471–479.

Laight, D. W. (2004). Attitudes to concept maps as a teaching/learning activity in undergraduate health professional education: Influence of preferred learning style. *Medical Teacher, 26*, 229–233.

LePort, A. K. R., Mattfield, A. T., Dickinson-Anson, H., Fallon, J. H., Stark, C. E. L., Kruggel, F., et al. (2012). Behavioral and neuroanatomical investigation of Highly Superior Autobiographical Memory (HSAM). *Neurobiology of Learning and Memory, 98*, 78–92.

Luria, A. R. (1968). *The mind of a mnemonist*. New York: Basic Books.

Maguire, E. A., Valentine, E. R., Wilding, J. M., & Kapur, N. (2003). Routes to remembering: The brains behind superior memory. *Nature Neuroscience, 6*, 90–95.

Massen, C., & Vaterrodt-Plünnecke, B. (2006). The role of proactive interference in mnemonic techniques. *Memory, 14*, 189–196.

Massen, C., Vaterrodt-Plünnecke, B., Krings, L., & Hilbig, B. E. (2009). Effects of instruction on learners' ability to generate an effective pathway in the method of loci. *Memory, 17*, 724–731.

McPherson, F. (2004). *The memory key: Unlock the secrets to remembering*. New York: Barnes & Noble.

Morris, P. E. (1979). Strategies for learning and recall. In M. M. Gruneberg & P. E. Morris (Eds.), *Applied problems in memory*. London: Academic Press.

Morris, P. E., Fritz, C. O., Jackson, L., Nichol, E., & Roberts, E. (2005). Strategies for learning proper names: Expanding retrieval practice, meaning and imagery. *Applied Cognitive Psychology, 19*, 779–798.

Morris, P. E., Jones, S., & Hampson, P. (1978). An imagery mnemonic for the learning of people's names. *British Journal of Psychology, 69*, 335–336.

Noice, H. (1992). Elaboration memory strategies of professional actors. *Applied Cognitive Psychology, 6*, 417–427.

Noice, H., & Noice, T. (1996). Two approaches to learning a theatrical script. *Memory, 4*, 1–17.

Oliver, W. L., & Ericsson, K. A. (1986). Repeating actors' memory for their parts. In *Proceedings of the 8th Annual Conference of the Cognitive Science Society*, Amherst, MA (pp. 399–406). Hillsdale, NJ: Lawrence Erlbaum Associates.

Parker, E. S., Cahill, L., & McGaugh, J. L. (2006). A case of unusual autobiographical remembering. *Neurocase, 12*, 35–49.

Pilar, D. R., Jaeger, A., Gomes, C. F. A., & Stein, L. M. (2012). Passwords usage and human memory limitations: A survey across age and educational background. *PLoS ONE, 7*(12).

Pyc, M. A., & Rawson, K. A. (2010). Why testing improves memory: Mediator effectiveness hypothesis. *Science, 330,* 335.

Raz, A., Packard, M. G., Alexander, G. M., Gerianne, M., Buhle, J. T., Zhu, H. T., et al. (2009). A slice of pi: An exploratory neuroimaging study of digit encoding and retrieval in a superior memorist. *Neurocase, 15,* 361–372.

Roediger, H. L., & Butler, A. C. (2011). The critical role of retrieval practice in long-term retention. *Trends in Cognitive Sciences, 15,* 20–27.

Roediger, H. L., & Karpicke, J. D. (2006). Test-enhanced learning: Taking memory tests improves long-term retention. *Psychological Science, 17,* 249–255.

Russell, R., Chatterjee, G., & Nakayama, K. (2012). Developmental prosopagnosia and super-recognition: No special role for surface reflectance processing. *Neuropsychologia, 50,* 334–340.

Russell, R., Duchaine, B., & Nakayama, K. (2009). Super-recognizers: People with extraordinary face recognition ability. *Psychonomic Bulletin and Review, 16,* 252–257.

Schmidt, H. G., Boshuizen, H. P. A., & van Breukelen, G. J. P. (2002). Long-term retention of a theatrical script by repertory actors: The role of context. *Memory, 10,* 21–28.

Seamon, J. G., Punjabi, P. V., & Busch, E. A. (2010). Memorizing Milton's Paradise Lost: A study of a septuagenarian exceptional memorizer. *Memory, 18,* 498–503.

Shipstead, Z., Redick, T. S., & Engle, R. W. (2012). Is working memory training effective? *Psychological Bulletin, 138,* 628–654.

Thompson, T. W., Waskom, M. L., Garel, K.-L. A., Cardenas-Iniguez, C., Reynolds, G. O., Winter, R., et al. (2013). Failure of working memory training to enhance cognition or intelligence. *PLoS ONE, 8*(5): e63614.

Unsworth, N., & McMillan, B. D. (2013). Mind wandering and reading comprehension: Examining working memory capacity, interest, motivation, and topic experience. *Journal of Experimental Psychology: Learning, Memory, and Cognition, 39,* 832–842.

Veronese, C., Richards, J. B., Pernar, L., Sullivan, A. M., & Schwartzstein, R. M. (2013). A randomized pilot study of the use of concept maps to enhance problem-based learning among first-year medical students. *Medical Teacher, 35,* E1478–E1484.

von Restorff, H. (1933). Über die Wirkung von Brieichsbildungen im Spurenfeld. *Psychologische Forschung, 18,* 299–542.

Wang, A. Y., & Thomas, M. H. (2000). Looking for long-term mnemonic effects on serial recall: The legacy of Simonides. *American Journal of Psychology, 113,* 331–340.

Watier, N., & Collin, C. (2012). The effects of distinctiveness on memory and metamemory for face–name associations. *Memory, 20,* 73–88.

Wilding, J., & Valentine, E. (1994). Memory champions. *British Journal of Psychology, 85,* 231–244.

Winograd, E., & Soloway, R. M. (1986). On forgetting the locations of things stored in special places. *Journal of Experimental Psychology: General, 115,* 366–372.

Worthen, J. B., & Hunt, R. R. (2011). *Mnemonology: Mnemonics for the 21st century.* Hove, UK: Psychology Press

Zaromb, F. M., & Roediger, H. L. (2010). The testing effect in free recall is associated with enhanced organizational processes. *Memory and Cognition, 3,* 995–1008.

Zhu, Q., Song, Y. Y., Hu, S. Y., Li, X. B., Tian, M. Q., Zhen, Z .L., et al. (2010). Heritability of the specific cognitive ability of face perception. *Current Biology, 20,* 137–142.

GLOSSARY

Accessibility/availability distinction: Accessibility refers to the ease with which a stored memory can be retrieved at a given point in time. Availability refers to the binary distinction indicating whether a trace is or is not stored in memory.

Activation level: The variable internal state of a memory trace that contributes to its accessibility at a given point.

Alcoholic Korsakoff syndrome: Patients have difficulty learning new information, although events from the past are recalled. There is a tendency to invent material to fill memory blanks. Most common cause is alcoholism, especially when this has resulted in a deficiency of vitamin B1.

Amygdala: An area of the brain close to the hippocampus that is involved in emotional processing.

Anterograde amnesia: A problem in encoding, storing, or retrieving information that can be used in the future.

Articulatory suppression: A technique for disrupting verbal rehearsal by requiring participants to continuously repeat a spoken item.

Associative blocking: A theoretical process hypothesized to explain interference effects during retrieval, according to which a cue fails to elicit a target trace because it repeatedly elicits a stronger competitor, leading people to abandon efforts to retrieve the target.

Associative deficit hypothesis: Proposal that the age deficit in memory comes from an impaired capacity to form associations between previously unrelated stimuli.

Autobiographical knowledge base: Facts about ourselves and our past that form the basis for autobiographical memory.

Autobiographical memory: Memory across the lifespan for both specific events and self-related information.

Autonoetic consciousness: A term proposed by Tulving for self-awareness, allowing the rememberer to reflect on the contents of episodic memory.

Binding: Term used to refer to the linking of features into objects (e.g. color red, shape square, into a red square), or of events into coherent episodes.

Category-specific deficits: Disorders caused by brain damage in which semantic memory is disrupted for certain semantic categories.

Cell assembly: A concept proposed by Hebb to account for the physiological basis of long-term learning, which is assumed to involve the establishment of links between the cells forming the assembly.

Change blindness: The failure to detect that a visual object has moved, changed, or been replaced by another object.

Change blindness blindness: Individuals' exaggerated belief that they can detect visual changes and so avoid *change blindness*.

Chunking: The process of combining a number of items into a single chunk typically on the basis of long-term memory.

Classical conditioning: A learning procedure whereby a neutral stimulus (e.g. a bell) that is paired repeatedly with a response-evoking stimulus (e.g. meat powder), will come to evoke that response (salivation).

Cognitive control: The ability to flexibly control thoughts in accordance with our goals, including our ability to stop unwanted thoughts from rising to consciousness.

Cohort effect: The tendency for people born at different time periods to differ as a result of historic changes in diet, education and other social factors.

Collaborative inhibition: A phenomenon in which a group of individuals remembers significantly less material collectively than does the combined performance of each group member individually when recalling alone.

Competition assumption: The theoretical proposition that the memories associated to a shared retrieval cue automatically impede one another's retrieval when the cue is presented.

Concept maps: Diagrams in which the links among general concepts (at the top of the diagram) and specific concepts (lower down) are shown.

Confabulation: Recollection of something that did not happen.

Confirmation bias: Distortions of memory caused by the influence of expectations concerning what is likely to have happened.

Consolidation: The time-dependent process by which a new trace is gradually woven into the fabric of memory and by which its components and their interconnections are cemented together.

Consolidation of memory: A process whereby the memory becomes more firmly established. It is commonly now divided into two processes, synaptic consolidation a process that is assumed to involve the hippocampus and operate over a 24 hour timescale, and *systems consolidation*. This is assumed to operate over a much longer period,

and to involve the transfer of information from the hippocampus to other parts of the neocortex (see Chapter 5, p. 127 for further discussion).

Context cues: Retrieval cues that specify aspects of the conditions under which a desired target was encoded, including (for example) the location and time of the event.

Context shift hypothesis: An alternative explanation for list-method directed forgetting, positing that forget instructions separate first-list items into a distinct context, which unless reinstated during the final test will make the later context a relatively ineffectual retrieval cue.

Context-dependent memory: The finding that memory benefits when the spatio-temporal, mood, physiological, or cognitive context at retrieval matches that present at encoding.

Contextual fluctuation: The gradual and persistent drift in incidental context over time, such that distant memories deviate from the current context more so than newer memories, thereby diminishing the former's potency as a retrieval cue for older memories.

Corsi block tapping: Visuo-spatial counterpart to digit span involving an array of blocks that the tester taps in a sequence and the patient attempts to copy.

Cross-race effect: The finding that recognition memory for same-race faces is generally more accurate than for cross-race faces.

Cue-overload principle: The observed tendency for recall success to decrease as the number of to-be-remembered items associated to a cue increases.

Depth of processing: The proposal by Craik and Lockhart that, the more deeply an item is processed, the better will be its retention.

Digit span: Maximum number of sequentially presented digits that can reliably be recalled in the correct order.

Direct/explicit memory tests: Any of a variety of memory assessments that overtly prompt participants to retrieve past events.

Directed forgetting: The tendency for an instruction to forget recently experienced items to induce memory impairment for those items.

Distributed practice: Breaking practice up into a number of shorter sessions; in contrast to massed practice, which comprises fewer, long, learning sessions.

Double dissociation: A term particularly used in neuropsychology when two patient groups show opposite patterns of deficit, e.g. normal STM and impaired LTM, versus normal LTM and impaired STM.

Dual-coding hypothesis: Highly imageable words are easy to learn because they can be encoded both visually and verbally.

Dual-process theories of recognition: A class of recognition models that assumes that recognition memory judgments can be based on two independent forms of retrieval process: recollection and familiarity.

Dud effect: An eyewitness's increased confidence in his/her mistaken when the lineup includes individuals very dissimilar to the culprit.

Echoic memory: A term sometimes applied to auditory sensory memory.

Ecological validity: The extent to which research findings (especially laboratory ones) can be generalized to everyday life.

Elaborative rehearsal: Process whereby items are not simply kept in mind, but are processed either more deeply or more elaborately.

Electroencephalogram (EEG): A device for recording the electrical potentials of the brain through a series of electrodes placed on the scalp.

Emotion regulation: Goal-driven monitoring, evaluating, altering, and gating one's emotional reactions and memories about emotional experiences.

Encoding specificity principle: The more similar the cues available at retrieval are to the conditions present at encoding, the more effective the cues will be.

Environmental support: Characteristics of a retention test that support retrieval.

Episodic buffer: A component of the Baddeley and Hitch model of working memory model that assumes a multidimensional code, allowing the various subcomponents of working memory to interact with long-term memory.

Episodic memory: A system that is assumed to underpin the capacity to remember specific events.

Event-based prospective memory: A form of prospective memory in which some event provides the cue to perform a given action.

Event-related potentials (ERPs): The pattern of electroencephalograph (EEG) activity obtained by averaging the brain responses to the same stimulus (or similar stimuli) presented repeatedly.

Everyday memory: Term applied to a movement within memory to extend the study of memory from the confines of the laboratory to the world outside.

Expanding retrieval: A learning schedule whereby items are initially tested after a short delay, with pretest delay gradually increasing across subsequent trials.

Explicit/declarative memory: Memory that is open to intentional retrieval, whether based on recollecting personal events (episodic memory) or facts (semantic memory).

Familiarity-based recognition: A fast, automatic recognition process based on the perception of a memory's strength. Proponents of dual process models consider familiarity to be independent of the contextual information characteristic of recollection.

Flashbulb memory: Term applied to the detailed and apparently highly accurate memory of a dramatic experience.

Forgetting curve/retention function: The logarithmic decline in memory retention as a function of time elapsed, first described by Ebbinghaus.

Fragment completion: A technique whereby memory for a word is tested by deleting alternate letters and asking participants to produce the word.

Frame: A type of schema in which information about objects and their properties is stored.

Free recall: A method whereby participants are presented with a sequence of items which they are subsequently required to recall in any order they wish.

Gestalt psychology: An approach to psychology that was strong in Germany in the 1930s and that attempted to use perceptual principles to understand memory and reasoning.

Hippocampus: Brain structure in the medial temporal lobe that is important for long-term memory formation.

Hypermnesia: The improvement in recall performance arising from repeated testing sessions on the same material.

Iconic memory: A term applied to the brief storage of visual information.

Immersion method: A strategy for foreign language teaching whereby the learner is placed in an environment where only the foreign language is used.

Implementation intentions: Plans spelling out in detail how individuals are going to achieve the goals they have set themselves.

Implicit/nondeclarative memory: Retrieval of information from long-term memory through performance rather than explicit conscious recall or recognition.

Inattentional blindness: The failure to perceive the appearance of an unexpected object in the visual environment.

Incidental forgetting: Memory failures occurring without the intention to forget.

Incidental learning: Learning situation in which the learner is unaware that a test will occur.

Infantile amnesia: Tendency for people to have few autobiographical memories from below the age of five.

Inhibition: A general term applied to mechanisms that suppress other activities. The term can be applied to a precise physiological mechanism or to a more general phenomenon, as in proactive and retroactive interference. The level of activation associated with a trace is actively reduced to diminish its accessibility.

Intentional learning: Learning when the learner knows that there will be a test of retention.

Interference: The phenomenon in which the retrieval of a memory can be disrupted by the presence of related traces in memory.

Irrelevant sound effect: A tendency for verbal STM to be disrupted by concurrent fluctuating sounds, including both speech and music.

Latent inhibition: Classical conditioning phenomenon whereby multiple prior presentations of a neutral stimulus will interfere with its involvement in subsequent conditioning.

Levels of processing: The theory proposed by Craik and Lockhart that asserts that items that are more deeply processed will be better remembered.

Life narrative: A coherent and integrated account of one's life that is claimed to form the basis of autobiographical memory.

Longitudinal design: Method of studying development or aging whereby the same participants are successively tested at different ages.

Long-term memory: A system or systems assumed to underpin the capacity to store information over long periods of time.

Long-term potentiation (LTP): A process whereby synaptic transmission becomes more effective following a cell's recent activation.

Long-term recency: A tendency for the last few items to be well recalled under conditions of long-term memory.

Long-term working memory: Concept proposed by Ericsson and Kintsch to account for the way in which long-term memory can be used as a working memory to maintain complex cognitive activity.

Magnetic resonance imaging (MRI): A method of brain imaging that relies on detecting changes induced by a powerful magnetic field.

Magnetoencephalography (MEG): A system whereby the activity of neurons within the brain is detected through the tiny magnetic fields that their activity generates.

Maintenance rehearsal: A process of rehearsal whereby items are "kept in mind" but not processed more deeply.

Masking: A process by which the perception and/or storage of a stimulus is influenced by events occurring immediately before presentation (forward masking) or more commonly after (backward masking).

Mental time travel: A term coined by Tulving to emphasize the way in which episodic memory allows us to relive the past and use this information to imagine the future.

Mere exposure effect: A tendency for a neutral stimulus to acquire positive value with repeated exposure.

Meta-analysis: A form of statistical analysis based on combining the findings from numerous studies on a given research topic.

Metamemory: Knowledge about one's own memory and an ability to regulate its functioning.

Method of loci: A memory technique in which to-be-remembered items are associated with various locations well known to the learner.

Mind maps: Diagrams in which word concepts are linked in very flexible ways around a central key concept; they often contain images and color.

Modal model: A term applied to the model of memory developed by Atkinson and Shiffrin (1968).

Model: A method of expressing a theory more precisely, allowing predictions to made and tested.

Mood-congruent memory: Bias in the recall of memories such that negative mood makes negative memories more readily available than positive, and vice versa. Unlike mood dependency, it does not affect the recall of neutral memories.

Mood-dependent memory: A form of context dependent effect whereby what is learnt in a given mood, whether positive, negative or neutral, is best recalled in that mood.

Motivated forgetting: A broad term encompassing intentional forgetting as well as forgetting triggered by motivations, but lacking conscious intention.

Nonsense syllable: Pronounceable but meaningless consonant-vowel-consonant items designed to study learning without the complicating factor of meaning.

Nonword repetition test: A test whereby participants hear and attempt to repeat back nonwords that gradually increase in length.

Object memory: System that temporarily retains information concerning visual features such as color and shape.

Own-age bias: the tendency for eyewitnesses to identify individuals of the same age as themselves for accurately than those much older or younger.

Part-set cuing impairment: When presenting part of a set of items (e.g. a category, a mental list of movies you want to rent) hinders your ability to recall the remaining items in the set.

Pegword system: A memory technique in which to-be-remembered items are associated with pegwords, each of which rhymes with a different number between one and ten.

Personal semantic memory: Factual knowledge about one's own past.

Phonological loop: Term applied by Baddeley and Hitch to the component of their model responsible for the temporary storage of speech-like information.

Phonological similarity effect: A tendency for immediate serial recall of verbal material to be reduced, when the items are similar in sound.

Positivity bias: The tendency, increasing over the lifespan, to recall more pleasant memories than either neutral or unpleasant ones.

Positron emission tomography (PET): A method whereby radioactively labeled substances are introduced into the bloodstream and subsequently monitored to measure physiological activation.

Post-traumatic amnesia (PTA): Patients have difficulty forming new memories. Often follows a severe concussive head injury and tends to improve with time.

Post-traumatic stress disorder (PTSD): Emotional disorder whereby a dramatic and stressful event such as rape results in persistent anxiety, often accompanied by vivid flashback memories of the event.

Primacy effect: A tendency for the first few items in a sequence to be better recalled than most of the following items.

Priming: The process whereby presentation of an item influences the processing of a subsequent item, either making it easier to process (positive priming) or more difficult (negative priming).

Proactive interference: The tendency for earlier memories to disrupt the retrievability of more recent memories.

Process dissociation procedure (PDP): A technique for parceling out the contributions of recollection and familiarity within a recognition task.

Prosopagnosia: A condition, also known as face-blindness, in which there is extremely poor face recognition combined with reasonable ability to recognize other objects.

Prospective memory: Remembering to carry out some intended action in the absence of any explicit reminder to do so; see retrospective memory.

Psychogenic amnesia: Profound and surprising episodes of forgetting the events of one's life, arising from psychological factors, rather than biological damage or dysfunction.

Psychogenic fugue: A form of psychogenic amnesia typically lasting a few hours or days following a severe trauma, in which afflicted individuals forget their entire life history, including who they are.

Rationalization: A term introduced by Bartlett to refer to the tendency in story recall to produce errors conforming to the rememberer's cultural expectations.

Reality orientation training (ROT): A method of treating patients in the latter stages of dementia who have lost their orientation in time and place.

Reappearance hypothesis: The view that under certain circumstances, such as flashbulb memory and PTSD, memories can be created that later reappear in exactly the same form.

Recency effect: A tendency for the last few items in a list to be well recalled.

Recognition memory: A person's ability to correctly decide whether he/she has encountered a stimulus previously in a particular context.

Recollection: The slower, more attention-demanding component of recognition memory in

dual process models, which involves retrieval of contextual information about the memory.

Reconstructive memory: An active and inferential process of retrieval whereby gaps in memory are filled-in based on prior experience, logic, and goals.

Reductionism: The view that all scientific explanations should aim to be based on a lower level of analysis: psychology in terms of physiology, physiology in terms of chemistry, and chemistry in terms of physics.

Remember/know procedure: A procedure used on recognition memory tests to separate the influences of familiarity and recollection on recognition performance. For each test item, participants report whether it is recognized because the person can recollect contextual details of seeing the item (classified as a "remember" response) or because the item seems familiar, in the absence of specific recollections (classified as "know" response).

Reminiscence: The remembering again of the forgotten, without learning or a gradual process of improvement in the capacity to revive past experiences.

Reminiscence bump: A tendency in participants over 40 to show a high rate of recollecting personal experiences from their late teens and twenties.

Reminiscence therapy: A method of helping dementia patients cope with their growing amnesia by using photographs and other reminders of their past life.

Repetition priming: Enhanced processing of a stimulus arising from recent encounters with that stimulus, a form of implicit memory.

Repression: In psychoanalytic theory, a psychological defense mechanism that banishes unwanted memories, ideas, and feelings into the unconscious in an effort to reduce conflict and psychic pain. Theoretically, repression can either be conscious or nonconscious.

Resource sharing: Use of limited attentional capacity to maintain two or more simultaneous activities.

Retrieval: The process of recovering a target memory based on one or more cues, subsequently bringing that target into awareness.

Retrieval-induced forgetting (RIF): The tendency for the retrieval of some target items from long-term memory to impair the later ability to recall other items related to those targets.

Retrieval inhibition hypothesis: A proposed mechanism underlying list-method directed forgetting suggesting that first-list items are temporarily inhibited in response to the instruction to forget and can be reactivated by subsequent presentations of the to-be-forgotten items.

Retrieval mode: The cognitive set, or frame of mind, that orients a person towards the act of retrieval, ensuring that stimuli are interpreted as retrieval cues.

Retrieval practice paradigm: A procedure used to study retrieval-induced forgetting.

Retroactive interference: The tendency for more recently acquired information to impede retrieval of similar older memories.

Retrograde amnesia: A problem accessing events that happened in the past.

Retrospective memory: Memory for people, words, and events experienced in the past.

Schema: Proposed by Bartlett to explain how our knowledge of the world is structured and influences the way in which new information is stored and subsequently recalled.

Scripts: A type of schema relating to the typical sequences of events in various common situations (e.g. having a meal in a restaurant).

Semantic coding: Processing an item in terms of its meaning, hence relating it to other information in long-term memory.

Semantic dementia: A progressive neurodegenerative disorder characterized by gradual deterioration of semantic memory.

Semantic memory: A system that is assumed to store accumulative knowledge of the world.

Sensory memory: A term applied to the brief storage of information within a specific modality.

Sensory preconditioning: An association between two stimuli that is established prior to the start of conditioning.

Short-term memory (STM): A term applied to the retention of small amounts of material over periods of a few seconds.

Signal detection theory: A model of recognition memory that posits that memory targets (signals) and lures (noise) on a recognition test posses an attribute known as strength or familiarity, which occurs in a graded fashion, with previously encountered items generally possessing more strength that novel items. The process of recognition involves ascertaining a given test item's strength and then deciding whether it exceeds a criterion level of strength, above which items are considered to be previously encountered. Signal detection theory provides analytic tools that separate true memory from judgment biases in recognition.

Source monitoring: The process of examining the contextual origins of a memory in order to determine whether it was encoded from a particular source.

Spatial working memory: System involved in temporarily retaining information regarding spatial location.

Spontaneous recovery: The term arising from the classical conditioning literature given to the reemergence of a previously extinguished conditioned response after a delay; similarly; forgotten declarative memories have been observed to recover over time.

Stem completion: A task whereby retention of a word is tested by presenting the first few letters.

Stereotypes: Schemas incorporating oversimplified generalizations (often negative) about certain groups.

Story mnemonic: A memory technique that involves constructing a story linking unrelated words together in the correct order.

Subjective organization: A strategy whereby a learner attempts to organize unstructured material so as to enhance learning.

Supervisory attentional system (SAS): A component of the model proposed by Norman and Shallice to account for the attentional control of action.

Synesthesia: The tendency for one sense modality to evoke another.

Systems consolidation: Process of gradual reorganization of the regions of the brain that support memory. Information is consolidated within the brain by a process of transfer from one anatomically based system to another.

Task switching: A process whereby a limited capacity system maintains activity on two or more tasks by switching between them.

Testing effect: The finding that long-term memory is enhanced when much of the learning period is devoted to retrieving the to-be-remembered information.

Think/no-think (TNT) paradigm: A procedure designed to study the ability to volitionally suppress retrieval of a memory when confronted with reminders.

Time-based prospective memory: A form of prospective memory in which time is the cue indicating that a given action needs to be performed.

Total time hypothesis: The proposal that amount learned is a simple function of the amount of time spent on the learning task.

Trace decay: The gradual weakening of memories resulting from the mere passage of time.

Transcranial magnetic stimulation (TMS): A technique in which magnetic pulses briefly disrupt the functioning of a given brain area; administration of several pulses in rapid succession is known as repetitive transcranial stimulation (rTMS).

Transfer-appropriate processing (TAP): Proposal that retention is best when the mode of encoding and mode of retrieval are the same.

Traumatic brain injury (TBI): Caused by a blow or jolt to the head, or by a penetrating head injury. Normal brain function is disrupted. Severity ranges from "mild" (brief change in mental status or consciousness) to "severe" (extended period of unconsciousness or amnesia after the injury).

Typicality effect: The finding that the time taken to decide a category member belongs to a category is less for typical than atypical members.

Unconscious transference: The tendency of eyewitnesses to misidentify a familiar (but innocent) face as belonging to the culprit.

Unlearning: The proposition that the associative bond linking a stimulus to a memory trace will be weakened when the trace is retrieved in error when a different trace is sought.

Verbal learning: A term applied to an approach to memory that relies principally on the learning of lists of words and nonsense syllables.

Verbal overshadowing: The reduction in recognition memory for faces that often occurs when eyewitnesses provide verbal descriptions of those faces before the recognition-memory test.

Visuo-spatial sketchpad: A component of the Baddeley and Hitch model that is assumed to be responsible for the temporary maintenance of visual and spatial information.

Visuo-spatial STM: Retention of visual and/or spatial information over brief periods of time.

von Restorff effect: The finding that a to-be-remembered item that is distinctively different from other items is especially likely to be remembered.

Weapon focus: The finding that eyewitnesses have poor memory for details of a crime event because they focus their attention on the culprit's weapon.

Word length effect: A tendency for verbal memory span to decrease when longer words are used.

Working memory: A memory system that underpins our capacity to "keep things in mind" when performing complex tasks.

Working memory capacity: An assessment of the how much information can be processed and stored at the same time.

Working memory span: Term applied to a range of complex memory span tasks in which simultaneous storage and processing is required.

Working self: A concept proposed by Conway to account for the way in which autobiographical knowledge is accumulated and used.

PHOTO CREDITS

Page 212 (left): © Sergiy Zavgorodny/Shutterstock.com; Page 212 (right): © Rich Carey/Shutterstock.com. Page 214: © Jose AS Reyes/Shutterstock.com. Page 216: Photo Courtesy of the Library of Congress.

Chapter 9

Page 231: © Lambert/Archive Photos. Page 247: Shutterstock.com. Page 249: © Tim Pannell/Corbis.

Chapter 10

Page 265: © AF archive/Alamy. Page 273: © Najlah Feanny/Corbis. Page 274: © Tim Flach. Page 280: © David Turnley/Corbis.

Chapter 11

Page 304: © Science Photo Library. Page 305: © the24studio/Shutterstock.com. Page 312: © Sean Adair/Reuters/Corbis. Page 314: © Bettmann/Corbis. Page 320: Image courtesy of the Library of Congress.

Chapter 12

Page 330: © Kye R. Lee/Dallas Morning News/Corbis. Page 333: Shutterstock.com. Page 339: © Daniel Wiedemann/Shutterstock.com. Page 343: © Bettmann/Corbis. Page 347: © Bubbles Photolibrary/Alamy. Page 349: © Royalty-free/Corbis. Page 351: © Jochen Tack/Alamy.

Chapter 13

Page 366: Shutterstock.com. Page 368: © Elena Elisseeva/Shutterstock.com.

Chapter 14

Page 382: © Anneka/Shutterstock.com. Page 389: © Stephen Mcsweeny/Shutterstock.com. Page 395: © Vadim Ponomarenko/Shutterstock. Page 396: © Alison Williams/Shutterstock.com. Page 399: © SCPhotos/Alamy.

Chapter 15

Page 415: Shutterstock.com. Page 424: © Maslov Dmitry/Shutterstock.com. Page 425: Photo by Hulton Archive/Getty Images.

Chapter 16

Page 439: © Corbis Sygma. Page 440: © BSIP, MENDIL/Science Photo Library. Page 446: © H. Armstrong Roberts/Corbis. Page 449: © Daniel Padavona/Shutterstock.com. Page 452: © RGB Ventures LLC dba SuperStock/Alamy. Page 453: © Sophie Bassouls/Sygma/Corbis. Page 454: Dr Robert Freidland/Science Photo Library. Page 456: © Don Mason/Corbis.

Chapter 17

Page 481: © Ivica Drusany/Shutterstock.com. Page 483: Photo by Dan Tuffs/Getty Images.

AUTHOR INDEX

A

Abel, T. 130
Abeles, M. 281
Aborn, M. 144
Abson, V. 411
Addis, D.R. 157, 320
Adlam, A. 74, 167
Aggleton, J.P. 156, 221, 443
Aizpurua, A. 340–1
Alberoni, M. 81
Alexander, M.P. 95, 167
Allen, R. 56, 57, 83
Alloway, T.P. 89
Allport, A. 81
Almeida, J. 181
Altmann, E.M. 238
Alvarez, G.A. 54
Alvarez, P. 447
Ambadar, Z. 290–1
Amso, D. 393
Anaki, D. 175
Anderson, J.R. 201
Anderson, M.C. 241, 242, 249, 250, 251, 253,
    254, 258, 269, 270, 273, 275, 276, 277–9, 292
Anderson, R. 206
Andrade, J. 82, 127
Andrews, B. 289
Antonini, A. 427
Aron, A.R. 277
Arrigo, J.M. 280
Ashbaugh, H. 109
Askew, C. 119
Aslan, A. 247–8, 254
Astin, A.W. 109
Atkinson, R.C. 9, 67, 221
Atran, S. 175
Averbach, E. 10
Avetisyan, M. 343

B

Baars, B.J. 82
Bäckman, L. 415, 418, 427, 428
Baddeley, A.D. 12, 13, 15, 26, 42, 44–5, 46, 47,
    49, 51, 52, 56, 59, 60, 68–9, 70, 71, 72, 73, 74,
    78, 79, 81, 82, 83, 85, 88, 92, 111, 114, 116,
    141, 150, 153, 169, 203, 212, 238, 245, 302–3,
    343, 348, 387, 416, 418, 421, 422, 439, 441,
    445, 446, 449, 451, 453, 454, 459, 472
Badre, D. 198, 204
Bahrick, H.P. 234–5, 237
Bahrick, P.O. 234
Bailey, C.H. 239
Baker, J.E. 400
Ball, K. 422–3
Ballard, P.D. 283
Baltes, P. 425
Banaji, M.R. 16
Bangert-Drowns, R.L. 484
Banich, M. 278
Bar, M. 185
Barber-Foss, K.D. 450
Barclay, J.R. 204
Barker, A.F. 319
Barnes, J.M. 244
Barnier, A. 272
Barr, R. 385
Barrett, G. 426
Barrouillet, P. 88
Barsalou, L.W. 176–7, 178–9
Bartlett, F. 8, 16, 138–41ff, 182, 185–6, 187,
    332–3
Basden, B.H. 269, 271
Basden, D.R. 269, 271
Basso, A.H. 59
Bauml, K.-H. 247–8, 254, 287
Bayley, J. 452
Bayley, P.J. 166

Bechara, A. 120
Becker, J.T. 424, 451
Bekerian, D. 116, 336
Bell, J.A. 77
Bellinger, K.D. 248
Bendiksen, M.A. 290–1
Benoit, R. 277, 278
Bentin, S. 175
Benton, S.L. 84
Bergstrom, Z.M. 278, 279
Berman, C. 341
Berman, M.G. 238
Berntsen, D. 266, 305, 309, 312, 317–18,
    397, 415
Berry, D.C. 125
Berryhill, M.E. 158
Bhaskara, A. 368
Bier, N. 183
Bindemann, M. 343
Binder, J.R. 165, 180
Bjork, E. 242, 258, 271
Bjork, R.A. 51, 111–12, 113, 114, 127, 208,
    209, 242, 249, 258, 268, 269, 270, 271
Black, J.B. 182
Black, J.E. 424
Blaney, P.H. 213
Bliss, T.V.P. 129
Bluck, S. 285, 300, 305–6
Blumhardt, L.D. 426
Bodenhausen, G.V. 185
Bonanno, G. 316
Boot, I. 178
Born, J. 128
Bornstein, B.H. 285
Bornstein, R.F. 119
Boshuizen, H.P.A. 488
Bourdais, C. 174
Bouwmeester, S. 392
Bower, B. 289
Bower, G.H. 141, 149, 182, 184, 476
Bowers, J.M. 336
Bowles, N. 220
Braak, E. 451
Braak, H. 451
Bradfield, A.L. 337
Brady, T.F. 54, 55
Brainerd, C.J. 391–2, 399, 400
Brandstätter, V. 373–4
Bransford, J.D. 146, 184
Brener, R. 81
Brewer, J.B. 156
Brewer, M.B. 303
Brewer, N. 332–3, 340
Brewer, W.F. 186, 338
Brewin, C.R. 315
Broadbent, D. 8, 125, 149, 238, 311
Broadbent, M.H. 149, 311

Bronfenbrenner, U. 400
Brooks, D.N. 15
Brooks, L.R. 125
Brooks-Gunn, J. 396–7
Brown, A.S. 282, 469
Brown, G.D.A. 49, 52
Brown, I.D. 80
Brown, M.W. 156, 221, 443
Brown, R. 196, 312, 313, 427
Brown, S.C. 247
Bruce, C.J. 92
Bruce, V. 341–2
Bruck, M. 400
Brunfaut, E. 419
Bryant, R.A. 315
Bub, D.N. 177–8
Buchanan, M. 45
Büchel, C. 121
Buckner, R. 157
Budd, J.W. 488
Buffalo, E.A. 313
Bugg, J.M. 372–3, 374
Bullemer, P. 124
Bunting, M.F. 87
Buonocore, A. 97
Burgess, N. 47, 49, 152, 153, 166
Burianova, H. 167
Burke, D.M. 421
Burke, K.A. 187–8
Burton, A.M. 345–6
Busch, E.A. 489
Bush, G. 94
Butcher, S.P. 130
Butler, A.C. 484
Butters, N. 439, 453
Byrd, M. 416, 418, 425

C

Cabeza, R. 305, 321, 426
Cahill, L. 232–3, 482
Camos, V. 88
Campanella, J. 385, 386
Campoy, G. 150
Cantril, H. 332
Caplan, D. 46
Cardena, E. 315
Carlesimo, G.A. 60
Carmichael, L. 140
Carpenter, P.A. 83, 87
Carroll. M. 249, 350
Carstensen, L. 266, 269
Carullo, J.W. 84
Ceci, S.J. 391, 400
Cermak, L.S. 439
Chabris, F. 329, 331
Chaigneau, S.E. 177

Chalfonte, B.L. 418
Chang, J. 281
Charles, S. 266
Charman, S.D. 337–8
Charness, N. 415
Chase, W. 150–1
Chassy, P. 165
Chater, N. 49
Chatterjee, G. 480–1
Chen, M. 239
Cheung, O.S. 343
Chi, M.T. 389
Chincotta, D. 74
Chiu, C.Y.P. 211
Christal, R.E. 84
Christensen, H. 422, 453
Christiaansen, R.E. 216
Christianson, S.-A. 332
Chu, S. 306
Chun, M.M. 57, 94, 97
Cipolotti, L. 446
Clare, L. 455
Clark, D.M. 213
Clark, J.J. 117
Clark, M.C. 476
Clayton, C.L. 76
Clayton, N.S. 155
Close, J. 175
Cockburn, J. 419, 422
Cohen, G. 137, 299, 421
Cohen, N. 15, 312, 445
Colcombe, S. 423
Coley, J.D. 175
Colle, H.A. 47
Collin, C. 471
Collins, A.M. 17, 169–72, 173, 421
Collins, K.W. 84
Colomb, C. 348
Cona, G. 370
Conezio, J. 54
Connell, L. 178
Conrad, C. 171
Conrad, R. 43
Conroy, R. 250
Conway, A.R.A 87
Conway, M. 137, 299, 303, 304–5, 307, 308,
    309–10, 311, 314, 320
Cook, G.I. 369
Cook, S.P. 313
Cooper, L.A. 122
Cooper, P.J. 149, 311
Cooper, R.P. 94–5
Copeland, S.M. 186
Cordón, I.M. 400
Corkin, S. 25
Cornoldi, C. 473–4
Cosentino, S. 183

Courage, M.L. 396–7
Cowan, N. 42, 45, 83, 85–6, 87, 98, 238, 444
Craik, F.I.M. 67, 144, 145, 146, 147, 202, 203,
    302, 414, 416, 418, 420, 425, 488
Craik, K. 8
Crary, W.G. 314
Crawford, J.R. 363
Crawley, R.A. 382
Cree, G.S. 177–8, 181
Crescini, C. 351
Crocker, J. 314
Crovitz, H.F. 304
Crowder, R.G. 12, 16, 51, 52, 241
Cuc, A. 250
Cuevas, K. 383, 386
Cunitz, A.R. 50
Curran, T. 278
Cutler, B.L. 351–2
Cutshall, J.L. 319
Cuttler, C. 368

D

Dale, H.C.A. 71
Daley, B.J. 487
Dalgliesh, T. 314
Dalla Barba, G. 446
Dallas, M. 221
Dallenbach, K.M. 127
Damasio, A.R. 126
Dando, C.J. 348
Daneman, M. 83, 87
Danker, J.F. 201
Dannenbaum, S.E. 414
Darling, S. 339
Davatzikos, C. 33
Dave, A.S. 129
Davidow, J. 393
Davidson, A.J. 126
Davidson, P.S.R. 313
Davis, D. 344
Davis, M.H. 153, 316
Davis, S. 130
De Beni, R. 473–4
de Fockert, J.W. 278
de Haan, E.H.F. 460
De Renzi, E. 445
Deary, I. 414
Deeprose, C. 127
Deese, J. 142, 148
Deffenbacher, K.A. 338, 349, 350
Delaney, P.F. 151, 240
Delaney, S.M. 122
Dell, G.S. 174
Della Sala, S. 48, 58, 97, 197, 444, 451
Denes, G. 446
Dennis, N.A. 278

Depue, B. 277, 278
Desai, R.H. 165
Desimone, R. 211
Desmarais, S.L. 330
Dewar, M. 444
Dexter, H.R. 351–2
DeZeeuw, C.I. 158
Di Vesta, F.J. 76
Dickinson, A. 155
Diener, C. 266
Diener, E. 266
DiGirolamo, G.J. 95
Dismukes, R.K. 365–7, 373
Dodhia, R.M. 367, 373
Dodson, C.S. 340
Dolan, R.J. 121
Dolcos, F. 305
Doody, R.S. 455
Dooling, D.J. 139–40, 216
Dreyer, F. 178
Druchman, D. 127
Duchaine, B. 480
Dudai, Y. 236
Dueck, A. 141
Dumay, N. 128
Duncan, J. 96
Dunlap, K.D. 471–2
Dunlosky, J. 483, 484, 486
Dunning, D.L. 91
Durmay, N. 444
Dutton, A. 350
Duyck, W. 153
Düzel, E. 442
d'Ydewalle, G. 419
Dysart, J.E. 346–7

E
Eacott, M.J. 382
Eakin, D.K. 334
Earhard, M. 154
Easterbrook, J.A. 340
Ebbesen, E.B. 349, 350
Ebbinghaus, H. 233–4
Ecker, U.K.H. 334
Edelson, M. 336
Edison, S.C. 396–7
Ehlers, A. 317
Eich, E. 213, 214, 320
Eichenbaum, H. 222, 238
Einarsson, E.Ö. 237
Einstein, G.O. 362, 371, 372, 374, 419
Eldridge, L. 222
Ellis, N.C. 125
Emerson, M.J. 75
Emslie, H. 418, 421, 449
Engel de Abreu, P.M.J. 73

Engelkamp, J. 418
Engle, R.W. 42, 84, 85, 86–8, 91, 119, 478
Engstler-Schooler, T.Y. 344
Erdelyi, M. 267–8, 273–4, 283–4
Erickson, K.R. 335
Ericsson, K.A. 109, 110, 150–1, 152, 477, 478, 480, 488
Erixon-Lindroth, N. 428
Eysenck, M.C. 470
Eysenck, M.W. 470, 471

F
Fagen, J. 386
Farag, C. 183–4
Faries, J.M. 300
Farrand, P. 487
Faulkner, D. 421
Fausey, C.M. 215
Fawcett, J. 269–70, 340
Feng, C. 76–7
Fernandes, M. 202
Fillingham, J.K. 460
Finke, R.A. 77
Finn, B. 390
Fischer, S. 128
Fischman, D. 76
Fisher, L. 370, 371
Fisher, R.P. 146, 348
Fishman, D.L. 270
Fivush, R. 396, 397, 399
Fleischman, D.A. 453
Flude, B. 153
Flynn, J.R. 413
Foa, E.B. 315
Fogarty, S.J. 213
Frackiowak, R.S.J. 93
Frankland, P. 239, 398
Franklin, N. 223
Franks, J.J. 146
Fraser, J. 348
Freud, A. 268
Freud, S. 267, 275, 292, 361, 396, 400
Frey, D. 314
Friedman, N.P. 87
Frith, C.D. 93, 426
Fritz, K. 390–1
Fukuda, K. 87
Funahashi, S. 92
Funnell, E. 182
Fuster, J.M. 92

G
Gabbert, F. 336–7
Gabriel, D. 332
Gabrieli, J.D. 211, 453

Gadian, D.G. 441
Gage, F.H. 424
Gais, S. 128
Galanter, E. 69
Galton, F. 304
Ganis, G. 33
Gao, Z. 158
Garcia Márques, G. 165–6
Garcia-Bajos, E. 249–50, 340–1
Gardiner, J.M. 221, 442
Gargano, G.J. 269
Garnham, A. 185
Garrard, P. 451
Garven, S. 401
Gary, H.E. 448
Gaskell, M.G. 128, 444
Gathercole, S. 72, 73, 85, 89, 91, 153, 388
Gauld, A. 139, 186
Gauthier, I. 343
Gaylord, S. 386
Geffen, G. 449–50
Geiselman, R.E. 270, 347–8
Gemba, H. 277
George, J. 220
Geraerts, E. 288–9, 290, 291, 292
Gershberg, F. 206
Giambra, L.M. 420
Gilbert, S.J. 373
Gilbertson, M. 316
Giles, A. 383, 386–7
Gilhooly, K.J. 77
Ginet, M. 348
Gladwell, M. 109
Glanzer, M. 50, 51, 220
Glaze, J.A. 141
Glenberg, A.M. 52, 147–8
Glisky, E.L. 313, 374
Gloor, P. 28
Glück, J. 305–6
Glucksberg, S. 172
Gobet, F. 165
Godden, D.R. 212
Goernert, P.N. 285, 287
Goh, W.D. 471
Gold, J.M. 238
Goldman-Rakic, P. 92
Goldsmith, D.J. 306
Gollwitzer, P.M. 373–4
Golomb, J.D. 94
Gomulicki, B. 139
Gonzàlez, H. 488
Goodwin, D.W. 213, 314
Goossens, L. 414
Gorman, A.M. 220
Grady, C.L. 167
Graf, P. 121, 362, 368
Grafton, S.T. 124

Green, C. 147–8, 274, 275
Green, D.M. 218
Green, J. 270
Greenberg, D.L. 167, 320, 321
Greene, J.D.W. 445, 453
Greenough, W.T. 424
Greenwald, B.D. 450
Grill-Spector, K. 211
Groeneweg, J. 314–15
Gross, J. 396, 403
Grossman, R.G. 448
Groth, E. 306
Gruneberg, M.M. 16
Guerin, S.A. 336
Guskiewicz, K. 450

H

Haber, R.N. 11, 54
Hackmann, A. 317
Hadjipaviou, N. 373
Haist, F. 445
Hall, J.F. 220
Hamama, L. 403
Hampson, P. 475
Han, J.J. 397–8
Handal, A. 249
Handberg, R.B. 349
Hanslmayr, S. 269, 270, 276, 278, 292
Hanten, G. 448
Haque, S. 309
Harbluk, J.L. 440
Hardman, E. 213
Hardt, O. 237
Harrison, S.A. 97
Harrison, V. 341
Harsch, N. 313
Hartley, T. 158
Hartshorn, K. 384, 385
Harvey, A.G. 315
Harvie, V. 351
Hasher, L. 414–15, 426
Hashtroudi, S. 223, 335
Hassabis, D. 158, 440
Hastorf, A.A. 332
Hatano, G. 77–8, 151
Haxby, J.V. 130
Hay, J.F. 418
Hayne, H. 381–2, 395, 396, 397, 398, 403
Hazeltine, E. 124
Healy, H. 314
Heath, W.P. 335
Hebb, D. 129
Hein, L. 88
Heindel, W.C. 453
Helder, E. 475
Hemmer, P. 186–7, 188

Henderson, J.M. 53, 332
Henkel, L. 285, 289
Henkel, L.A. 223
Hennessy, E. 487
Henry, J.D. 426
Henschel, D.M. 282
Henson, R. 211
Henson, R.N.A. 47
Herman, J. 289
Herron, J.E. 207
Hersh, N. 457
Hertel, P. 278
Hertzog, C. 422, 423
Herz, R.S. 306
Heuer, F. 76
Hicks, J.L. 365, 369
High, W.M. 448
Hinton-Bayre, A.D. 450
Hirst, W. 250
Hitch, G. 13, 42, 44–5, 47, 49, 51, 52, 56, 68–9,
    83, 88, 152, 153, 238, 245, 348
Hobson, J.A. 128
Hodges, J.R. 167, 445, 451,
    453, 455
Hogan, H.P. 140
Holding, D.H. 79–80
Hole, G.J. 341
Hollingworth, A. 53, 332
Holmes, J. 89, 90, 91
Holzman, P. 92
Hopkins, R.O. 166
Horner, A.J, 27
Horner, A.J. 30, 443
Hotta, C. 277
Howard, D.V. 422
Howard, J.H., Jr 422
Howe, M.L. 396–7
Howie, P. 390–1
Hsi, S. 77
Hsieh, S. 81
Hsu, V.C. 384–5
Hsu-Yang, V. 383
Hu, Y. 110, 476, 478
Hubel, D.H. 92
Huddleston, E. 276, 292
Hudson, J. 399
Hugenberg, K. 345
Hughes, R.W. 12
Hull, C. 4–5, 43
Hulme, C. 46, 49, 50, 91
Hunt, R.R. 470, 471–2, 479
Hunter, I.M.L. 280
Huppert, F.A. 439–40
Hussain, F. 487
Hutton, U. 88, 238
Hyde, T.S. 145, 150
Hyman, I.E. 300

I
Ihle, A. 420
Ihlebaek, C. 351
Iidaka, T. 427
Ingersoll, G. 76
Ingvar, D. 157
Inman, V.W. 414
Irion, A.L. 7
Irish, M. 167–8
Irwin, J. 252
Ivry, R. 124

J
Jack, F. 395, 397, 398
Jacoby, L.L. 221, 340, 418
Jaeger, T. 372
James, L. 128
James, W. 146–7
Janowsky, J.S. 266
Janssen, S.M. 234
Jarrold, C. 153
Java, R.I. 425
Jefferies, E. 180
Jenkins, J.G. 127
Jenkins, J.J. 142, 145, 150
Jenkins, R. 341–2, 346
Jennings, J.M. 426
Jensen, M.S. 331
Jobson, L. 309
Johnson, M.K. 57, 97, 184, 223, 308, 335, 418
Johnston, W.A. 81
Johnstone, K.M. 109
Jones, D. 12, 47, 48
Jones, O.D. 34
Jones, S. 475
Jonides, J. 93, 95, 238
Jonkman, L.M. 390
Joslyn, S. 271–2
Josselyn, S. 239, 398
Joy, S.W. 337–8
Jung, J. 141
Juola, J.F. 221

K
Kahana, M.J. 240
Kalakoski, V. 477
Kalm, K. 153
Kan, I.P. 167
Kandel, E.R. 130
Kane, M.J. 42, 86, 414–15
Karantzoulis, S. 450
Karlin, M.B. 141
Karlson, P. 57
Karpicke, J.D. 113, 237, 484, 485
Kassin, S.M. 330, 337

Katz, C. 403
Kaushanskaya, M. 309
Kawaguchi, J. 277
Kay, H. 114
Kelley, C.M. 272–3, 287
Kemp, R.I. 350–1
Kemper, S. 421
Kempermann, G. 424
Keppel, G. 426
Kessels, R.P.C. 460
Kiefer, M. 176
Kiewra, K.A. 84
Kihlstrom, J.F. 319
Kikuchi, H. 280–1
Kim, P. 369
Kindt, M. 368–9
Kingo, O.S. 397
Kinsbourne, M. 220
Kintsch, W. 83, 150, 477
Klauer, K.C. 48, 58
Kleinbard, J. 284
Kleitman, S. 390–1
Kliegel, M. 364, 372
Klingberg, T. 89–90, 91
Knight, J.B. 371–3
Knopf, M. 390
Knopman, D.S. 124
Koeppe, R.A. 93
Koessler, S. 255
Köhler, S. 239
Konecni, V.J. 349, 350
Konkle, T. 54
Kontis, T.C. 115
Kopelman, M.D. 280, 281, 318–19, 320, 445, 453
Koppel, J. 250
Kornell, N. 114
Koutsaal, W. 421
Kozin, M. 313
Kramer, A.F. 423
Krampe, R.T. 109
Kritchevsky, M. 281
Krøjgaard, P. 397
Krueger, L.E. 340
Kuehn, L.L. 319
Kuhl, B. 256–7
Kulik, C.L.C. 484
Kulik, J. 312, 313, 484
Kunda, Z. 314
Kunst-Wilson, W. 119
Kvavilashvili, L. 370, 371
Kyllonen, P.C. 84
Kynette, D. 421

L

LaBar, K.S. 305
Laight, D.W. 488

Lalumera, E. 178
Lambon Ralph, M.A. 167, 180
Lampinen, J.M. 186
Landau, J.D. 365
Landauer, T. 111–12, 113
Lang, A. 340
Lange, G. 390
Lange, K.L. 453
Langlois, J.A. 448
Larsen, J.D. 12
Larson, M.E. 287
Larsson, M. 306
Lashley, K. 49
Lattal, K.M. 130
Laulhere, T. 285
Lavenex, P. 393
Lavenex, P.B. 393
Lebovits, A.H. 127
LeDoux, J.E. 98, 120, 130, 131, 237
Lee, T.D. 422
Leichtman, M. 304, 397–8
Leigland, L.A. 266
Leippe, M.R. 350–1
Lépine, R. 88
LePort, A.K. 311–12, 482
Levin, D.T. 117, 331–2
Levin, H.S. 448
Levine, L. 285, 320–1
Levy, B.J. 238, 253, 254, 257, 275, 279
Levy-Gigi, E. 402–3
Lewandowski, S. 49
Lewandowsky, S. 238, 334
Lewis, M. 396–7
Lewis, R.L. 238
Lewis, V.J. 88
Lewis-Peacock, J. 97–8
Liebel, L.M. 285
Lieberman, K. 78
Light, L.L. 418, 421
Lindenberger, U. 425
Lindholm, T. 332
Lindsay, D.S. 223, 334, 335
Lindsay, R.C.L. 351
Linkovski, O. 369
Linn, M.C. 76, 77
Linton, M. 237, 250, 300–1, 303
Liotti, M. 445
Lockhart, R.S. 67, 144, 147, 302, 488
Loft, S. 368
Loftus, E.F. 17, 169, 173, 187, 302, 334, 335–6, 339–40
Loftus, G.R. 339–40
Logie, R.H. 48, 77, 78, 81, 97, 98, 454
Lomo, T. 129
Longman, D.J.A. 111
Loussouarn, A. 332
Lu, S.H.X. 471

Luciana, M. 427, 428
Luck, S.J. 53–4, 55, 56, 83
Luria, A. 75, 479
Luu, P. 94
Luwel, K. 419
Luzzatti, C. 60
Lykken, D. 266
Lynch, G. 130
Lynch, S. 449
Lynott, D. 178

M

Macauley, D. 214
McClelland, J.L. 447
McCloskey, C.G. 312
McCloskey, M.E. 172
McConnell, J. 78
McCrea, M. 450
McCullough, A.W. 55, 56
McDaniel, L. 278
McDaniel, M.A. 114, 362, 371, 372, 373, 419
McDermott, K.B. 114, 125
Macé, M. J,-M. 175
McEwan, B. 127
McEwen, B. 316
McFarland, C. 374
McFarland, K. 450
McGaugh, J. 232–3, 317, 482
McGeoch, J.A. 7, 251
Machizawa, M.G. 55
McIntosh, A.R. 167
Macken, W.J. 12, 47
McKenna, P. 92
McKiernan, F. 456
McKinnon, M.C. 320–1
Mackintosh, N. 34
Macko, K.A. 94
McKone, E. 238, 392–3
Mackworth, N.H. 187
McLachlan, D.R. 440
MacLeod, M.D. 249, 258, 277, 283
McMillan, B.D. 478
McNab, F. 90
McNamara, T.P. 173
McNaughton, B.L. 128, 447
McNeil, D. 196
McPherson, F. 472
Macrae, C.N. 185, 249, 283
McRae, K. 181
Maguire, E.A. 158–9, 166, 426, 427, 440, 442, 480
Major, B. 314
Malong, L.M. 251
Malpass, R.S. 401
Mamelak, A.N. 28

Mandler, G. 121, 150, 221
Mangels, J. 197
Mann, D.M.A. 453
Manns, J.R. 156, 166, 442, 443
Mäntylä, T. 364, 419
Marcoen, A. 414
Margoliash, D. 129
Marian, V. 214–15, 309
Markowitsch, H.J. 279
Marques, J.F. 181
Marsden, C.D. 427
Marsh, E.J. 114
Marsh, R.L. 365, 369
Martin, A. 130, 211
Martire, K.A. 350–1
Massen, C. 473
Masson, M.E.J. 177–8
Masters, R.S.W. 123
Mather, M. 266, 269
Matzel, L.D. 130, 131
May, C.P. 414–15
Mayberry, E.J. 167, 181
Mayes, A.R. 443
Mayhorn, C.B. 369
Maylor, E.A. 419
Mazzone, M. 178
Means, B. 306
Mechanic, A. 147–8
Medin, D.L. 175
Meeter, M. 234, 235
Megreya, A.M. 345–6
Meiser, T. 48
Meissner, C.A. 348
Melby-Lervåg, M. 91
Melton, A. 252
Meltzer, M. 435
Memon, A. 348
Merckelbach, H. 290
Merikle, P.M. 84
Merskey, H. 319
Mervis, C.B. 171
Mesout, J. 339
Messo, J. 339–40
Metcalf, J. 114
Metcalfe, J 390
Meteyard, L. 176
Meyer, D.E. 173
Michael, T. 317
Michalczyk, K. 387–8
Middleton, E.L. 460
Migueles, M. 249–50, 340–1
Miles, C. 213
Miller, E.K. 211
Miller, G.A. 69, 86
Miller, N.E. 453
Miller, R. 111, 131
Mills, J.A. 439

Milner, B. 159
Mishkin, M. 94, 158, 441, 442
Mitchell, K.A. 223, 383
Miyake, A. 13, 42, 74, 75, 85, 87
Moè, A. 473–4
Moffat, N. 455
Mojardin, A.H. 391–2
Molander, B. 415
Moniz, E. 343
Monsell, S. 81
Montaldi, D. 222
Moore, P.J. 350
Moreines, J. 439
Morris, C.D. 146
Morris, J. 121
Morris, P.E. 16, 475
Morris, R.G.M. 130, 454
Morton, S. 12
Moscovitch, M. 131, 202, 362, 447, 453
Mosse, E.K. 153
Moynan, S. 286–7
Mueller, J.H. 247
Mullaly, S.L. 440
Müller, G.E. 127, 241, 444
Murdock, B.B. Jr 11, 50
Murphy, K. 392–3
Murray, J.D. 187–8
Murre, J.M. 234, 447

N
Nadel, L. 131, 447
Nader, K. 131, 237
Nairne, J.S. 9, 46, 48–9, 238
Nakabayashi, K. 344, 345
Nakayama, K. 480–1
Naveh-Benjamin, M. 416–18, 426
Neary, S. 453
Neath, I. 9, 15, 46, 49, 125
Nebes, R.D. 304
Neely, J.H. 241
Neisser, U. 10, 11, 16, 35, 114, 139,
    214–15, 299, 313, 314, 317
Nelson, C.A. 385
Nelson, K. 393, 394, 396, 397, 399
Neshige, R. 426
Nestor, P.J. 180
Neuschatz, J.S. 184, 186
Nichelli, P. 445
Nickerson, R.S. 247
Nicolay, A. 73
Nilsson, L.-G. 114–15, 412, 413, 418, 419
Nimmo, L.M. 49
Nimmo-Smith, I. 418, 421, 449
Nissen, M.J. 124, 319–20
Noice, H. 488, 489
Noice, T. 488, 489

Noreen, S. 277
Norman, D. 78–9, 240
Norman, K.A. 421
Norman, S. 421
Norris, D. 47, 49, 152, 153, 238
Nowinski, J.L. 365–7
Nyberg, L. 427

O
Oakes, M. 271–2
Oakhill, J. 185
Oberauer, K. 88, 238
O'Carroll, R.E. 460
O'Connell, B.A. 319
Odegard, T.N. 399
Odinot, G. 337
O'Donnell, V.M. 448
Ohman, A. 121
Öhman, A. 98
Olesen, P. 90
Oliver, W.L. 152, 488
Olson, E.A. 337
O'Neill, S. 402
O'Regan, J.K. 117
O'Reilly, R.C. 447
Ornstein, T. 92
Osawa, K. 77–8, 151
Oschner, K.N. 211
Osler, S. 204
Oudiette, D. 129
Owen, A.M. 96

P
Pacteau, C. 124
Page, M.P.A. 47, 49, 152, 153, 238
Paivio, A. 142
Paller, K.A. 129, 205
Palmer, J. 334
Palmer, S.E. 185
Panton, T. 351
Papagno, C. 48, 70, 71, 73, 153
Park, D.C. 418, 419
Park, S. 92
Parker, E. 232–3, 482
Parkin, A.J. 418, 425
Parkinson, S.R. 414, 426
Parra, M. 455
Pashler, H. 112–13, 114
Patel, S. 386
Patterson, K. 167, 175, 180, 343,
    451, 454
Paulesu, E. 93
Pavlov, I.P. 118, 281
Payne, D.G. 285
Payne, J.D. 128

Payne, R.B. 421
Pearlstone, Z. 148
Pearson, D.G. 77
Pecher, D. 178
Pecheux, M.-C. 174
Pelosi, L. 426
Penrod, S.D. 351–2
Perfect, T.J. 119, 415
Perlmuter, L.C. 421
Perlovsky, L. 185
Pernet, C.R. 97
Perruchet, P. 124
Perry, R.J. 455
Pessi, J.J. 343
Petersen, A.C. 76
Petersen, R.C. 451
Peterson, C. 394–5
Peterson, L.R. 426
Peterson, M.J. 426
Pezdek, K. 280
Phillips, J.D. 346–7
Phillips, L.H. 372, 426
Phillips, L.W. 50
Phillips, W.A. 53, 54, 55, 56, 57
Pickel, K.L. 340
Pickering, A. 339
Pickering, S. 89
Pierce, S.H. 390
Piercy, M. 439–40
Piguet, O. 167–8
Pilar, D.R. 469
Pillemer, D.P. 304
Pilzecker, A.E. 127, 241, 444
Pinto, A. da Costa 51
Pipe, M.E. 402
Pitman, R. 316
Pleydell-Pearce, C.W. 307
Pobric, G. 180, 181
Poldrack, R.A. 24
Polyn, S.M. 240
Poncelet, M. 73
Posner, M.I. 94, 95, 96
Postle, B.R. 97–8
Postman, L. 50, 241, 282
Pothos, E.M. 175
Pötter, U. 425
Powell, J.W. 450
Pozzulo, J.D. 351
Pratte, M.S. 32
Prentice, W.C.H. 140
Pressley, M. 390
Pribram, K.H. 69
Priestley, G. 402
Pritchert, J. 206
Proust, J. 332
Puglisi, J.T. 418

Pulvermüller, F. 176
Punjabi, P.V. 489
Pyc, M.A. 484, 485–6
Pyszora, N.M. 319

Q

Quillian, M.R. 17, 169–72, 173, 421
Quinn, G. 78

R

Rabbitt, P. 411
Raeburn, V.P. 12
Rajaram, S. 418
Rakow, T. 343
Ramaekers, J.G. 428
Rampey, H. 374
Ramponi, C. 221
Randolph, C. 450
Ranganath, C. 222
Raoelison, M. 373
Raposo, A. 181
Rascovsky, K. 166
Rast, P. 364
Rawson, K.A. 484, 485–6
Raz, N. 426, 481
Read, J.D. 330
Reber, A.S. 124
Redelmeier, D.A. 81
Redick, T.S. 91, 478
Reed, J.M. 442, 443
Reisberg, D. 76
Remington, R.W. 368
Rendell, P.G. 419–20
Rensink, R.A. 117
Rescorla, R.A. 281
Reuter-Lorenz, P.A. 426–7
Reyna, V.F. 391–2, 399, 400
Reynolds, D.J. 185
Ribot, T. 445
Riby, L.M. 415
Richardson-Klavehn, A. 208, 209, 221, 278
Richler, J.J. 343
Richmond, J. 385, 393
Rideout, R. 394–5
Righi, G. 343
Rips, L.J. 171
Rissman, J. 96
Rizio, A.A. 278
Robbins, T. 80
Roberts, S. 402
Robinson, J.A. 300
Robinson-Riegler, B. 371
Rochon, E. 46
Roediger, H.L. 113, 114, 122, 125, 237, 484–5
Rogers, G. 130

Rogers, T.T. 175, 180
Rohrer, D. 202
Roman, P. 254
Rönnlund, M. 411, 412–13
Rosch, E. 171, 174
Rosiell, L.J. 117
Rothbart, M.K. 94
Rothbaum, B.O. 315, 316
Rovee-Collier, C. 383, 384, 385–7
Rowe, J.B. 92
Rubenstein, H. 144
Rubin, D.C. 115, 152, 205, 304, 305, 306, 309, 313, 317–18, 320, 381–2, 415
Ruchkin, D.S. 96
Rueda, M.R. 94
Rummel, J. 374
Rundus, D. 51
Russell, R. 480–1
Russell, W.A. 142
Russell, W.R. 449
Rutishauer, U. 28
Rutland-Brown, W. 448
Ryan, L. 214

S

Saariluoma, P. 477
Saeki, E. 75
Safer, M.A. 330
Sage, K. 167
Sahakyan, L. 269, 272–3, 287
Sahler, C.S. 450
Saito, S. 75
Salame, P. 47
Salmela, J.H. 109
Salmon, D.P. 453
Salmon, K. 250
Salthouse, T.A. 416, 423, 424–5, 451
Sameneih, A. 287
Sampaio, C. 338
Sanchez-Casas, R. 173
Sanders, H.I. 445
Sapolsky, R. 316
Sargeant, W. 318
Sasaki, K. 277
Sauzéon, H. 393
Scaggs, W.J. 117
Scarberry, N.C. 285
Schacter, D.L. 3, 121, 122, 124, 139, 157–8, 173–4, 208, 209, 211, 281, 319, 336, 421, 440
Schafe, G. 131, 237
Schatzow, E. 289
Schiffrin, R.M. 9
Schilder, P. 281
Schleepen, T.M.J. 390

Schmidt, H.G. 488
Schmoick, H. 313
Schneider, W. 389, 390
Schnitzspahn, K.M. 364
Schooler, J. 290–1, 344
Schott, B.H. 122
Schreiber, T.A. 334
Schulz, L.E. 266
Schulz, R.W. 141
Schuman, E.M. 28
Schunn, C.D. 238
Schvaneveldt, R.W. 173
Schwartz, M.F. 460
Scott, V. 125
Scullin, M.K. 372–3
Seamon, J.G. 489
Sebel, P.S. 126
Sedikides, C. 270
Semmler, C. 340
Serences, J. 96, 97
Sergent-Marshall, S. 334
Service, E. 73
Shah, P. 13, 42, 74
Shallice, T. 26, 48, 58, 67–8, 78–9, 94–5
Shapiro, L.R. 333
Shaughnessy, J.J. 475
Shaw, J. 249
Sheeran, P. 373
Sheingold, K. 382
Shen, F.X. 34
Shephard, R.N. 76–7
Shibaski, H. 426
Shiel, A. 448
Shiffman, H. 304
Shifrin, R.M. 67
Shimamura, A. 206, 422, 445
Shipstead, Z. 91, 478
Shoben, E.J. 171
Shorrock, S.T. 368
Shors, T.J. 130
Shrimp, T.A. 119
Shriver, E.R. 345
Shults, C.W. 453
Shute, R. 84
Sidman, M. 459
Siegler, R.S. 387
Simcock, G. 395, 397
Simmonds, D.C.V. 80
Simon, H. 109
Simons, D.J. 32, 117, 200, 329, 331
Sirigu, A. 183
Skowronski, J.J. 317
Slamecka, N.J. 247
Slater, E. 318
Slayton, K. 77
Slee, J. 392–3

Smalarz, L. 329–30
Smith, E. 93, 95, 171
Smith, P.T. 419
Smith, R.E. 368, 371, 470, 471–2
Smith, S. 286–7
Smith, S.M. 147–8, 212
Snowden, D.A. 452, 453
Soares, J.J.F. 98
Soloway, R.M. 469
Spaniol, J. 206, 222, 223
Sparling, J. 401
Spector, A. 455
Spellman, B.A. 253, 258
Spence, M.J. 402
Sperling, G. 10
Spiegel, D. 315
Spiers, H.J. 159, 166, 200
Spinnler, H. 414, 416, 451, 453
Spiro, R.J. 216
Sporer, L.S. 337
Springer, A.D. 130
Squire, L.R. 13, 15, 121, 137, 156, 158,
    166, 211, 236, 277, 281, 313, 442, 443,
    445, 447
Srinivas, K. 122
St George-Hyslop, P.H. 451
St Jacques, P.L. 336
Standing, L. 54, 55
Stanhope, N.M. 137
Stanley, W.B. 125
Stark, H.A. 122, 282
Staubli, U. 130
Steblay, N.M. 346–7
Stephanek, J. 390
Stephens, D.L. 84
Stephenson, G.M. 139, 186
Stewart, E.W. 119
Steyvers, M. 186–7, 188
Stickgold, R. 128, 444
Stoddard, L.T. 459
Stollery, B. 415
Stone, C. 250
Storm, B. 253, 254, 255–6
Storms, G. 172
Strayer, D.L. 81
Stroud, J.N. 341
Stuss, D.T. 166
Styles, E.A. 81
Sulin, R.S. 139–40
Sumby, W.H. 220
Sunderland, A. 411
Sunshine, P. 76
Suppes, P. 169
Surprenant, A. 9, 15, 49, 125
Svoboda, E. 320–1
Swanson, J.M. 418

Swanson, K.L. 300
Swets, J.A. 218
Sykes, R.N. 16
Szmalek, A. 153

T

Tacchi, P.C. 307
Talarico, J.M. 313
Tam, L. 51
Tamnes, C.K. 389
Tanaka, J.W. 175
Tang, D.T.W. 334
Tarantino, V. 370
Tarr, M.J. 343
Taylor, M.E. 175
Taylor, T. 269–70
Teasdale, J.D. 213
Tellegen, A. 266
Tenney, Y.J. 382
Terrace, H.S. 459
Tesch-Römer, C. 109
Thierry, K.L. 402
Thomas, M.H. 474–5
Thompson, C.P. 317
Thompson, T.W. 478
Thompson-Schill, S.L. 95
Thomsen, D.K. 312
Thomson, D.M. 220, 419–20
Thomson, J.A. 45
Thomson, N. 169
Tibshirani, R.J. 81
Tickner, A.H. 80
Tollestrup, P.A. 339, 351
Tolman, E. 5
Tong, F. 32, 97
Torgesen, J.K. 73
Torre, D.M. 487
Towse, J.N. 88, 238
Treadgold, L. 457
Treyens, J.C. 186
Triesman, A.M. 56
Tsujimoto, T. 277
Tuckey, M.R. 332–3
Tulving, E. 122, 137, 144, 145, 146, 148, 149,
    155, 157, 166, 204, 207, 221, 235, 308, 347–8,
    402, 440
Turk-Browne, N.B. 94
Turner, M.L. 86, 88
Turner, T.J. 182
Turtle, J.W. 339
Turvey, M. 10
Tustin, K. 381–2, 396
Twersky, T. 127
Twitmyer, E.B. 118
Tyler, L. 453

U

Underwood, B.J. 141, 244, 245–6, 282, 426
Ungerleider, L.G. 94, 130
Unsworth, N. 87–8, 478
Uttl, B. 372

V

Vaidya, C.J. 453
Vaiva, G. 316
Vakil, E. 402–3
Valentine, E. 479–80, 483
Valentine, T. 71, 338–9, 346
Vallar, G. 48, 59, 68, 70, 71, 88
van Beugen, B.J 158
van Breukelen, G.J.P. 488
Van Dantzig, S. 178
Van den Hout, M. 368–9
van Dyck, T. 83
van Koppen, P.J. 337
van Praag, H. 424
Vargha-Khadem, F. 156, 158, 222, 441, 442
Vaterrodt-Plünnecke, B. 473
Vela, E. 212
Velten, E. 213
Verfaellie, M. 167
Verhaeghen, P. 414
Verheyen, S. 172
Verkoeijen, P.P.J.L. 392
Veronese, C. 487
Vignal, J.P. 28
Vogel, E.K. 53–4, 55, 56, 83, 87
Vogt, S. 52–3
Vokey, J.R. 125
von Restorff, H. 470
Vredeveldt, A. 348
Vygotsky, L. 75

W

Wagenaar, W. 301–2, 306, 314–15
Wagner, A.D. 73, 96, 156–8, 198, 204, 205
Wald, M.M. 448
Waldfogel, S. 266
Walicke, P.A. 453
Walker, I. 50
Walker, M.P. 128
Walker, W.R. 317
Wallace, W.T. 205
Walter, A.A. 140
Walter, B.M. 418
Walter, W.G. 8
Wang, A.Y. 474–5
Wang, M. 127
Wang, Q. 304, 309, 397–8

Ward, G. 51
Warfield, T.D. 109
Warrington, E.K. 15, 26, 48, 58, 67–8, 121, 122, 439, 445
Waters, G.S. 46
Watier, N. 471
Watkins, M.J. 242
Watson, P.C. 457
Weaver, C. 279
Wei, G. 110
Weiner, N. 8
Weisel, T.N. 92
Weiskrantz, L. 15, 121, 122, 439
Weist, R.M. 390
Weldon, M.S. 248
Welford, A.T. 421
Weller, P.D. 253
Wells, G.L. 330, 337–8, 346–7
Wenzel, A.E. 317
Westerberg, H. 90
Wetzler, S.E. 304
Wheeler, M.A. 166, 282
Wheeler, M.E. 56
White, D. 345–6
White, H. 255–6
Whitten, W.B. 51
Wible, C.G. 312
Wickelgren, W.A. 43
Wiemer-Hastings, K. 178
Wilding, E.L. 207, 479–80, 483
Willander, J. 306
Williams, A.M. 110
Williams, H.L. 299
Williams, J.M.G. 314
Williams, K.D. 340
Willingham, D.B. 422
Wilson, B.A. 60, 79, 114, 416, 422, 445, 446, 457, 458, 459, 460
Wilson, M.A. 128
Wimber, M. 257
Winocur, G. 439
Winograd, E. 469
Winter, E. 422
Wise, R.A. 330
Wishart, L.R. 422
Wittgenstein, L. 172
Wittlinger, R.P. 234
Wolfe, T. 285
Wolters, G. 337
Wood, J.M. 401
Woodman, G.F. 55, 56, 83
Woods, B. 300, 456
Woods, S.P. 362
Woollett, K. 159
Worthen, J.B. 479
Wright, B.M 421

Wright, R.A. 341
Wu, L. 177
Wyer, S.R. 314

Y

Yardley, H. 185
Yarnell, P.R. 449
Yegiyan, N.S. 340
Yonelinas, A. 221, 222, 238
Young, A.W. 60
Young, B.W. 109
Young, S.G. 345
Yuille, J.C. 319, 339

Z

Zacks, R.T. 415
Zajac, R. 401, 402
Zajonc, R. 119
Zamani, M. 177
Zaromb, F.M. 484
Zhao, Z. 58
Zhu, B. 334, 335
Zhu, Q. 481
Zieman, K. 16
Zimprich, D. 364
Zogg, J.B. 362, 364, 374
Zola-Morgan, S. 445
Zuckerman, M. 314

SUBJECT INDEX

10 Dates Quiz 482

A

accessibility/availability distinction 235
acetylcholine 455
activation levels 199
active rehearsal 55
actors, learning lines 488–9
advertising 119–20
aeroplane crashes 365–9
age, and positivity bias 266–7
aging
  brain structure 426–8
  cross-sectional studies 412, 414
  depression 411
  diary research 420
  divided attention 415–17, 426
  effects on skills 415
  episodic memory 412–13, 416–19, 426
  implicit learning and memory 421–2
  and IQ 414
  laboratory vs. real life 420
  and language 421
  and long-term memory (LTM) 416–24
  longitudinal studies 411–14
  maintaining memory 422–4
  motor performance 421–2
  neuroimaging 427
  overview 411
  personal perception of 415
  prospective memory 419–20
  recognition memory 418–19
  and recollection 418
  remembering and knowing 418–19
  research approaches 411–14
  semantic memory 420–1
  social and demographic factors 413
  theories 424–6
  working memory (WM) 414–16
air traffic control 367–8
alcohol 319
alcoholic Korsakoff syndrome *see* Korsakoff
  syndrome
Alzheimer, Alois 450
Alzheimer's disease 411, 412, 422–3, 450–6
  attention division 81
  diagnosis 451
  episodic memory 452–3
  forgetting 453–4
  implicit memory 454
  pharmacological treatments 455
  positron emission tomography (PET) 453
  treatment 455–6
  working memory (WM) 454–5
ambiguity 140, 172
amnesia 14–15, 17, 26, 121, 122, 137, 156, 166,
  211 *see also* forgetting; memory failure
  anterograde amnesia 438–44
  childhood amnesia 398
  Clive Wearing 3–4
  consolidation of memory 444
  developmental amnesia 441–3
  H.M. (Henry Molaison) 25–6
  infantile amnesia 239, 304, 305, 381–2,
    394–5, 396–8
  modal model 440–2
  multiple person disorder 319
  organically based 320
  post-traumatic amnesia (PTA) 448–50
  psychogenic amnesia 268, 279–81, 318–20
  retrograde amnesia 166, 438, 444–8
  situation-specific 280, 319
  source amnesia 440
  violence-related 319
amygdala, role of 120–1

anesthesia, consciousness 126–7
anterior cingulate cortex 257, 277
anterograde amnesia 438–44
aplysia 32, 34
applied research 15–17
Aristotle 5
arousal, and eyewitness testimony 350
articulatory rehearsal 44, 45
articulatory suppression 45, 46, 49, 80
artificial grammars 124–5
associations 199
associative blocking 251–2
associative deficit hypothesis 417–18
associative links 439–40
associative unlearning 252
attention deficit disorder (ADD) 255–6
attention deficit hyperactivity disorder (ADHD)
　89, 90, 91–2
attention division 80–1
attention focus 97
attention slips 78–9
attention switching 81
attention to cues 202–3
attentional capacity 87–8
attentional control 79, 94
attentional focus 79–81, 88
auditory recency effect 11–12
autobiographical knowledge base 307–8
autobiographical memory *see also* infantile
　amnesia
　calendrical autobiographical memory 309–12
　in childhood 394–5
　confabulation 446–7
　cross-cultural differences 304, 309
　diaries 300–4, 317
　emotional influences 313–15
　flashbulb memories 312
　functions 299–300
　goal-related 309
　involuntary memories 316–17
　knowledge structures 308
　letters 302–3
　life narratives 305–6
　memory probes 303–4
　methods of study 300–6
　mood-congruence 314
　multiple person disorder 319–20
　neurobiology of 320–1
　organically based deficits 320–1
　overview 299
　post-traumatic stress disorder (PTSD) 315–18
　psychogenic amnesia 318–20
　reminiscence bump 304, 305–6, 317
　situation-specific amnesia 319
　social influences 313–15
　sociocultural influences 309
　theories 306–18

Autobiographical Memory Interview (AMI) 445
autonoetic consciousness 308
autonomic nervous system (ANS) 316
Ayer, A.J. 6

B
background sounds 46–7
Bartlett approach 138–41ff
Bartlett, Frederick 8
behavioral genetics 34–5
Berman, Cecilia 341
Betula Study 412–13
binding 56–7, 82–3
biological basis of memory 24
block tapping test 57
blocking 251–2, 253–4
blood flow based measures of brain activity 31–2
brain
　concept representations 179–80
　electrophysiological activity 426
　regions and functions 32
brain activity, working memory (WM) 90
brain damage, and classical conditioning 120
brain infection 3–4
brain mechanisms, of retrieval suppression 277–9
brain structure
　and aging 426–8
　and learning 110, 158
　maturation 393–4
brain surgery, patient reporting 28
brightness masking 10
bromocriptine 427
bus drivers 159

C
calendrical autobiographical memory 309–12
Canby, Martin 209
capacity, and resistance to distraction 87
cardboard cockpit 154
case examples
　autobiographical memory 309–11, 438
　childhood memory 394
　classical conditioning and brain damage 120
　Clive Wearing 3–4
　confabulation 446–7
　external aids 457
　H.M. (Henry Molaison) 25–6, 438
　Jill Price 232–3, 265, 310, 482–3
　Jon 156, 222, 441–3
　Korsakoff syndrome 458–9
　learning verbatim 489
　memory experts 476, 478, 481–2
　multiple person disorder 319–20
　post-traumatic amnesia (PTA) 448–9
　psychogenic amnesia 279–81
　PV 58–9, 70–1, 72

recovered memory 288–9, 290
RR 79
semantic dementia 182
SF 150–1
visuo-spatial short-term memory deficits 59–60
categorization 174–6, 177
category-specific deficits 181
cell assemblies 129
cellular basis of memory 32–3
central executive 57, 70, 78–81, 94, 95
chaining 47, 152
change blindness 116–17, 331–2
change blindness blindness 331–2
change detection 53–4
Changing State hypothesis 47
Chao Lu 476, 478, 481–2
chapter summaries
    aging 428–9
    autobiographical memory 322
    brain study techniques 35–7
    childhood memory 404–5
    episodic memory 159
    eyewitness testimony 352–3
    incidental forgetting 258–9
    learning 131
    memory failure 460–1
    memory improvement 489–90
    memory overview 17–18
    motivated forgetting 292–3
    prospective memory 375
    retrieval 224–5
    semantic memory 188–9
    short-term memory (STM) 60
    working memory (WM) 98–9
Chatman, Charles 329–30
checking behavior 368–9
chess players 165
childhood memory see also infantile amnesia
    accuracy of recall 399–400
    autobiographical memory 394–5
    brain maturation 393–4
    childhood amnesia 398
    children as witnesses 398–404
    cognitive self 396–7
    content knowledge 389
    context reinstatement 402–3
    cross-cultural differences 397–8
    cross-examination 401–2
    declarative memory 387–91
    developmental changes 387–92
    ecological mode 383
    gist memory 391–2
    implicit memory 392–4
    improving witness accuracy 401–4
    infants' memories 383–7
    interviewer bias 401
    language skills 397

    memory strategies 389–90
    metamemory 390–1
    neurogenic hypothesis 398
    nonverbal information 403
    reliability 382–3
    social cultural theory 397–8
    source monitoring 402
    suggestibility 400–1
    testing 384–7
    traumatic events 400
    two-stage theory 398
    verbatim memory 391–2
    working memory (WM) 387–91
children
    detecting learning problems 89
    language learning 73
    as witnesses 398–404
chunking 43, 82, 83, 148–9, 153, 154
Clark Kent effect 343
classical conditioning 15, 34, 118–21, 281
    advertising 119–20
    and brain damage 120
    and PTSD 316
Claudia 289
Cloze technique 143–4
Cogmed™ 89–90
cognitive context-dependent memory 214–15
cognitive control 275
cognitive interviews 347–9
cognitive maps 5
cognitive self 396–7
cohort effect 412
collaborative inhibition 248
color, memory for 56–7
Columbine High School 273–4
competition assumption 241–2
complex system control 125–6
complexity effects 56
computerized tomography (CT) 27
computers, as analogy 8
concept representations 176, 179–80
concepts 176–9, 182–4
conceptual hierarchies 149
confabulation 79, 446–7
confirmation bias 332
Conrad, R. 43, 44
consciousness 82, 126–9
consolidation of memory 127–8, 130, 236–7,
    444, 447
contact sports 449–50
content addressable memory 199
content knowledge 389
context 48
context-dependent memory 211–13, 291
context memory 443
context reinstatement 287, 402–3
context shift hypothesis 272–3

context signals 49
contextual fluctuation, and forgetting 239–40
contextual memory 439
controlled retrieval process 204
converging operations 26
core consciousness 126
correlational approach 84
corroboration, recovered memory 289–90
Corsi block tapping 58–9
Corsi span 57–8
cortical reinstatement 200
Craik, Kenneth 8
Crick, Francis 35
cross-examination 401–2
cross-race effect 345–6
cross-sectional studies 412, 414
cue detection 364
cue-maintenance 200
cue overload 242, 471
cue reinstatement 285–7
cue-specification 200
cue-target associative strength 204
cued recall 209
cues 121, 152, 153, 198–9, 241
    attention to 202–3
    context cues 207–8
    cue-target associative strength 204
    number of 204–5
    part-set cuing impairment 246–8
    relevance 203–4
    smell 306
cultural expectations 185
cultural factors, semantic memory 175

D

dates, memory for 301, 306, 310, 311
daydreaming 240
de Vries, Mary 288–9
Dean, John 314
declarative memory 13, 14–15, 118, 211, 282,
    387–91
declarative metamemory 390–1
declarative working memory (WM) 88
Deese–Roediger–McDermott task 173–4, 392,
    399, 471–2
deferred imitation 385–6
Dell's theory of speech production 174
Demanjuk, John 314–15
dementia with Lewy bodies 450
dementias 450 see also Alzheimer's disease;
    fronto-temporal dementia; semantic dementia
depression 411
depth of processing 144–5
description 76
developmental amnesia 441–3
diaries 300–4, 317, 420, 421

diffusion tensor imaging (DTI) 27, 28
digit span 41, 82, 150–1
Digit Symbol Substitution Test (DSST) 424–5
direct suppression 278
direct tests 208–9, 210
directed forgetting 269
discrimination 95, 471
discrimination ratio 52
discussion points
    aging 429
    autobiographical memory 322
    brain study techniques 37
    childhood memory 405
    episodic memory 160
    eyewitness testimony 354
    incidental forgetting 260
    learning 131
    memory failure 461
    memory improvement 490
    memory overview 18
    motivated forgetting 292–3
    prospective memory 375
    retrieval 224–5
    semantic memory 189
    short-term memory (STM) 61
    working memory (WM) 99
disease 3–4, 59–60
dissociation 26
distinctive processing 470–2
distraction, and forgetting 254–6
distributed practice 110–12
divided attention 57, 80–1, 202–3, 255–6
    and aging 415–17, 426
DNA evidence 329
Doors and People test 416, 418, 441
dopamine 427–8
double dissociation 26
Dr Jekyll and Mr Hyde 319–20
driver inattention 81
droodles 141
drugs, and learning 130
dual coding hypothesis 142–3
dual-task deficit 80–1
dud effect 337–8
dysexecutive syndrome 446–7

E

Ebbinghaus, Herman 6–7, 107–8, 138
Ebbinghaus tradition 138
echoic memory 11
ecological model of infant memory 383
ecological validity 53, 186, 349
educational applications, working memory
    (WM) 89–90
effort after meaning 139
elaboration 146

elaborative rehearsal 147
electrodes 28
electroencephalography 28–9
embedded processes model 85–6
emotion regulation 266
encoding 8, 144
encoding-retrieval overlap 471
encoding specificity principle 203–4, 347, 402, 471
encoding speed 55
encoding suppression 270
entorhinal cortex 443
environmental context 212
environmental enrichment 424
environmental support 416, 418
epigenetics 35
episodic buffer 81–4, 96
episodic memory 14–15
    Alzheimer's disease 452–3
    deeper processing 146–8
    effects of aging 412–13, 416–19, 426
    expertise 150–2
    healthy brain research 156–9
    impairment 438–48
    improvement over time 282–3
    intention to learn 150
    levels of processing hypothesis 144–5
    meaning and memory 141–3
    neuropsychology 155–9
    in non-human animals 155–6
    organization and memory 148–50
    overview 137–8
    predictability 143–4
    vs. semantic memory 166–8
    seriation 152–4
    transfer-appropriate processing 145–6
errorless learning 459–60
errors 139–40
Eternal Sunshine of the Spotless Mind 265
eugenics 34–5
event-based prospective memory 361
event-related potentials (ERPs) 30, 55, 370
everyday memory 453
evoked response potential (ERP) 87, 426
exam preparation 483–9
    concept maps 486–8
    learning verbatim 488–9
    mind maps 486–8
    SQ3R 483–4
    study skills 483–6
    testing effect 484–6
examinations, studying for 248–9
executive capacity 454
exercise 423–4
expanded retrieval 112–13, 475
expectations 184, 185, 332
experienced self 307
expertise 150–2

explicit memory 13, 14–15, 118, 211, 282
    development 387–91
explicit memory tests 208–9
external aids, for memory failure 456–7
extinction 118
eye movement 53
eyewitness testimony 17, 341
    accuracy factors 330–8
    age and accuracy 340–1
    anxiety and violence 338–40
    change blindness 331–2
    children as witnesses 398–404
    cognitive interviews 347–9
    conclusions 352
    cross-race effect 345–6
    dud effect 337–8
    ecological validity 349
    effects of arousal 350
    expectations 332
    faces 341–3
    feedback effects 337
    improving face recognition 346
    laboratory vs. real life 349–52
    limitations 330
    line-ups 346–7
    overview 329–30
    police procedure 346–9
    post-event misinformation 333–8
    stress effects 340
    unconscious transference 344
    verbal overshadowing 344–5
    weapon focus 339–40
    witness confidence 337–8

F
face-blindness 341
face–name associations 471
faces 341–6
facial recognition, memory experts 480–1
fame judgment test 271
familiarity 218–20
familiarity-based recognition 221
Feature model 48–9
feature units 200
feedback, and learning 114
flashbulb memories 312
Flynn effect 35, 413
forced-choice recognition test 217
forgetting 10 *see also* amnesia; incidental
    forgetting; memory failure; motivated forgetting
    adaptive advantage 257
    Alzheimer's disease 453–4
    associative blocking 251–2
    associative unlearning 252
    collaborative inhibition 248
    and contextual fluctuation 239–40

discouraging 236–8
and distraction 254–6
and inhibition 252–8
and initial learning 235
intentional forgetting 268
and interference 240–2
interference effects 243
interference mechanisms 251
interference phenomena 242
nature of 235
over time 7, 233–5, 236
part-set cuing impairment 246–8, 254
proactive interference (PI) 245–6
problems of measuring 235–6
retrieval-induced forgetting (RIF) 248–51,
    252, 253–4, 257, 283
retroactive interference 242–5, 252
forgetting curves 233–5
fragment completion 121
fragmentation, and forgetting 46
frames 182
free recall 49–52, 142, 209
    serial position curve 50
Freud, Sigmund 267–8
frontal lobes 198
    and aging 426
    damage 96
    functions 79, 94, 95–6, 156–8
fronto-temporal dementia 183, 450
fugue 318–19
functional imaging 27–8
functional magnetic resonance imaging (fMRI)
    31–2, 95
fuzzy-trace theory 391–2

G

Galton, Sir Francis 6, 34, 76, 304
gender
    eyewitness testimony 333
    and spatial manipulation 76–7
general theory of learning 4–5
generation effect 112
genetics 34–5
    and facial recognition 481
    and learning 130
Gestalt psychology 7
gist memory 391–2
glove anaesthesia 319
go/no-go task 275
goal-setting 420
grammar acquisition 73
grammatical reasoning test 69
grand theories 7
grip strength 425
group studies 23–6
grouping 43

H

habit capture 368
habituation 32, 34
haloperidol 427–8
happiness 266
Harrison, George 209
head injury 23, 59–60
health 422
Hebb, Donald 129, 152–3
Hebb effect 152–3
Hebbian learning 129
hierarchical network model 169–72
hierarchies 149
high contact sports 449–50
Highly Superior Autobiographical Memory
    (HSAM) 233, 311–12, 482
hippocampal consolidation 447
hippocampal stimulation 28
hippocampus
    effects of neurogenesis 239
    maturation 393–4, 398
    role of 120, 129–30, 156–8, 205, 222, 236,
        277–8, 279, 316, 439, 440, 442–3, 447
H.M. (Henry Molaison) 25–6, 438
hub-and-spoke model 180–2
human genome 35
hypermnesia 283–5
hyperthymestic syndrome 233

I

iconic memory 10–11
identification tasks 421
image manipulation 76–7
imagery, working memory (WM) 82
immersion method 125
implementation intentions 373–4
implicit memory 13, 15, 117–18, 126
    Alzheimer's disease 453
    in childhood 392–4
    effects of aging 421–2
inattentional blindness 331
incidental context 211–17
incidental forgetting
    functional view 258
        see also forgetting
    over time 238–9
    overview 231–2
incidental learning 146
incidental retrieval 200
indirect tests 209–11
infantile amnesia 239, 304, 305, 381–2,
    394–5, 396–8
infants' memories 383–7
inferences 184
information processing 9
information, updating and replacing 336

information uptake, visuo-spatial short-term memory 55
ingroups 345
inhibition 86–7, 252–8
inhibitory control 369
inhibitory control model 86–7
intelligence quotient (IQ), and aging 414
intention execution 365
intention formation 364
intention recall 364
intention retrieval 364
intention to learn 150
intentional forgetting 268
intentional learning 147
intentional retrieval 200
intentional retrieval suppression 274–9
interference
    and forgetting 240–2
    proactive interference (PI) 245–6, 334
    retroactive interference 242–5, 252, 282, 334, 336
interference dependence 254
interference effects 243
interference mechanisms 251
interference phenomena 242
interference resolution processes 200
internal aids, for memory failure 457–60
interviewer bias 401
introspection 6
involuntary memories 316–17
irrelevant sound effect 46–7, 48, 49
irrelevant speech effect 47
item-method directed forgetting 269–70

J
Jacobs, John 41
James, William 118
Janssen, Elizabeth 288, 290
Jost's Law 236
journals 7

K
Kahneman, Daniel 150
Kandel, Eric 32
Keller, Helen 209, 216
Kleinbard, Jeff 284
Korsakoff syndrome 24–5, 445, 446, 458–9, 469

L
label effect 140–1
laboratory vs. real life
    effects of aging 420
    eyewitness testimony 349–52
language comprehension 84
language impairment 72

language learning 71–2, 73, 125
language, redundancy 143–4
language skills, and childhood memory 397
language use, and aging 421
latent inhibition 119
learning
    artificial grammars 124–5
    and brain structure 110, 158
    change blindness 116–17
    classical conditioning 118–21
    complex system control 125–6
    and consciousness 126–9
    distributed practice 110–12
    and drugs 130
    expanding retrieval 112
    and feedback 114
    and forgetting 235
    and genetics 130
    immersion method 125
    implicit learning 117
    incidental 146
    intentional 147, 150
    motivation 114–15
    neurobiology of 129–31
    and neurotransmitters 130
    overview 107–8
    of pairs 71
    practice 109–10
    procedural learning 122–4
    rate of 108–10
    and repetition 115–16
    and retention 108
    and sleep 127–9
    spacing effect 112–13
    and stress 123
    and testing 113–14
learning problems, detection 89
learning strategies, memory improvement 481–2
learning techniques, exam preparation 483–8
learning verbatim 488–9
letters 302–3
levels of processing 67
levels-of-processing effect 145
levels of processing hypothesis 144–8
lie detection 33–4
life narratives 305–6
lifestyle effects 422
line-ups 346–7
linguistic context 214–15
links 199
list-method directed forgetting 270–3
London bus drivers 159
London taxi drivers 158–9
long-term depression (LTD) 34
long-term memory (LTM) 9, 13
    and aging 416–24
    components 13

distinctive processing 470
interdependent systems 167–8
separate systems 166–7
and short-term memory 68–9
vs. visuo-spatial short-term memory 53–5
and working memory 82–3
working memory as 96–8
long-term potentiation (LTP) 34, 129–30
long-term recency effect 51
long-term working memory 151–2, 477
longitudinal studies 411–14
Luria, Alexander 75

M

magnetic resonance imaging (MRI) 27
H.M. (Henry Molaison) 25
magnetoencephalography (MEG) 30
Mahadevan, Rajan 480
Mailer, Norman 109
maintenance rehearsal 147
Mandler, George 7
masking 10–11, 47
meaning, and memory 141–3
meaningful encoding 477
mediator effectiveness hypothesis 485–6
Meltzer, Malcolm 435–6
Memento 439
memory aids 455
memory experts 479–83
memory failure *see also* amnesia; forgetting
    Alzheimer's disease 450–6
    anterograde amnesia 438–44
    assessment 437–8
    conclusions 460
    confabulation 446–7
    consolidation of memory 444
    dementias 450
    developmental amnesia 441–3
    episodic memory 438–48
    experience of 435–6
    external aids 456–7
    internal aids 457–60
    overview 435
    post-traumatic amnesia (PTA) 448–50
    psychological approach to 436–8
    rehabilitation 456–60
    retrograde amnesia 444–8
    traumatic brain injury (TBI) 448
memory improvement
    concept maps 486–8
    distinctive processing 470–2
    effectiveness of mnemonics 477–8
    exam preparation 483–8
    learning strategies 481–2
    learning verbatim 488–9
    memory experts 479–83

method of loci 472–4
mind maps 486–8
overview 469
pegword system 474–5
remembering names 475
story mnemonic 476–7
study skills 483–6
testing effect 484–6
verbal mnemonics 476–7
visual imagery 472–6
working memory training 478–9
memory load, and brain activity 56
memory probes 303–4
memory processes 9
memory recovery 281–7
    over time 281–3
    spontaneous recovery 281–3
memory span 42–3, 81–2 *see also* digit span
memory store 9
memory strategies 389–90
memory systems 8–9
mental calculation 77–8, 151
mental time travel 14, 137, 157–8, 440
mere exposure effect 119
meta-analysis 180
metamemory 364, 368
    childhood memory 390–1
    declarative metamemory 390–1
method of loci 472–4
microdistribution of practice 111–12
mild cognitive impairment (MCI) 444
misinformation acceptance 336
misinformation effects 333–5
mnemic neglect effect 270
mnemonic glue 440
mnemonic silences 250
mnemonics 150 *see also* memory improvement
    effectiveness 477–8
    method of loci 472–4
    pegword system 474–5
    remembering names 475
    story mnemonic 476–7
mobile conjugate reinforcement task 384
mobile phones, and driving 80
modal model 9, 67–9
modal model of amnesia 440–2
modality dependence/independence 48–9
models 8
mood-congruent memory 213–14, 300, 314
mood-dependent memory 214
motivated forgetting 232
    brain mechanisms of retrieval suppression 277–9
    context shift and environment change 273–4
    cue reinstatement 285–7
    emotional distress 279–81
    instructions to forget 268–9
    intentional retrieval suppression 274–9

item-method directed forgetting 269–70
list-method directed forgetting 270–3
memory recovery 281–7
overview 265–6
predictive factors 268–81
repeated retrieval attempts 283–5
terminology 267–8
trauma 287–92
use of term 268
motivation 114–15, 420
motor performance, and aging 421–2
motor stopping 277
multi-process theory 372–3
multi-voxel pattern analysis (MVPA) 32, 96–7
multicomponent model 69–76, 96, 151
multiple person disorder 319–20
Multiple Trace Hypothesis 447
multiple trace theory 131
Murdoch, Iris 452, 453
music, and recall 47

N

names, remembering 475
naming objects 174–6
Nazism 35
negative control effect 276
Neisser, Ulric 11, 16
neurogenesis 239
neurogenic hypothesis 398
neuroimaging 26–30
    aging 427
    and lie detection 33–4
    phonological loop 93
    of retrieval 256–7
    working memory (WM) 93–6
NeuroPage™ 457
neuropsychological approaches 23–6
neuroscience 17
neurotransmitters, and learning 130
nondeclarative memory 13, 15, 117, 126
    Alzheimer's disease 454
    in childhood 392–4
nonhuman primates, visual processing 94
nonsense syllables 107–8
nonword repetition test 72
now print mechanism 312
Nun study 451–2

O

object memory 52, 94
Object-Oriented Episodic Record (O-OER)
    hypothesis 47, 48
objects 56, 174–6
observation of brain 26–30
obsessive compulsive disorder 368–9
One Hundred Years of Solitude 165–6

operation span 86
organization, and memory 148–50
outgroups 345
own-age bias 341

P

paired-associate learning 141–2
pairs learning 71
Paivio, Allen 142
paper folding problems 77
parent–child interaction 397
part-set cuing impairment 246–8, 254
passwords 469
pattern completion 200
pattern masking 10–11
pattern span 58
patterns of activation 200
Pavlov, Ivan 118
pegword system 474–5
perceptual system, in conceptual processing 177
perirhinal cortex 222, 443
permastore 235
perseveration 79
persistent vegetative state 448
personal semantic memory 445
philosophy of mind 6
phonological and semantic similarity 44
phonological awareness 73
phonological loop 44, 47, 48, 69–76, 93, 153
phonological-loop-related models 47
phonological similarity effect 44–5, 49
PI (memory expert) 481–2
place cells 128
placebo 91
plane crashes 365–9
police procedure 346–9
population studies 35
positional marker model 152
positive control effect 276
positivity bias 266–7
positron emission tomography (PET) 31, 93,
    94, 453
post-event misinformation, and eyewitness
    testimony 333–8
post-retrieval monitoring 200
post-traumatic amnesia (PTA) 448–50
post-traumatic stress disorder (PTSD) 315–18
PQRST system 458–9
practice
    and learning 109–10
    and retrieval speed 477
precategorical acoustic store 12
predictability 143–4
predictive inferences 187–8
prefrontal cortex 183, 197, 206, 207, 222, 257,
    277, 278, 320, 481

preparatory attentional and memory processes (PAM) theory 371–2, 373
Price, Jill 232–3, 265, 310, 311, 482–3
primacy 48, 50
primacy model 47, 152, 153
primary memory 88
priming 15, 121–2, 211
proactive interference (PI) 86, 245–6, 334
procedural learning 122–4
procedural working memory (WM) 88
process dissociation procedure 221, 418
prosody 43
prosopagnosia 341
Prospective and Retrospective Memory Questionnaire (PRMQ) 363–4
prospective memory 17
    checking behavior 368–9
    conceptual model 364–5, 366
    effects of aging 419–20
    event-based and time-based 369–71
    in everyday life 365–9
    implementation intentions 373–4
    importance of 362
    improving 373–4
    multi-process theory 372–3
    obsessive compulsive disorder 368–9
    overview 361
    plane crashes 365–9
    preparatory attentional and memory processes (PAM) theory 371–2
    vs. retrospective memory 362–3
    self-report measures 363–4
psychogenic amnesia 268, 279–81, 318–20
psychogenic fugue 280
psychological theory 4–5
psychophysics 6

Q

Quintillian 127

R

random generation 80
rationalization 185
reading skills 73–4
reality orientation training (ROT) 456
reappearance hypothesis 317
recall delay 11
recall, over time 234
recency effect 11–12, 50–1, 59
recognition memory 156, 217–24, 234, 418–19
recognition tests 209, 217, 218
recollection 221
reconsolidation 131
reconstructive memory 215–17
recovered memory 287–92

reductionism 5
redundancy, of language 143–4
refreshing, of stimulus 97
rehabilitation, memory failure 456–60
rehearsal 44, 45, 51, 55, 147
relevance of cues 203–4
remember/know procedure 221
remembering and knowing 442
remembering names 475
reminiscence 283
reminiscence bump 304, 305–6, 317
reminiscence therapy 428, 456
repetition, and learning 115–16
repetition habits 141
repetition priming 211
repetition suppression 211
replication 53
reporting, forgetting during 10
repression 267–8, 275, 292, 396, 400
research, applied 15–17
resource sharing 88
resource-sharing hypothesis 88
response competition theory 251
retention 237–8 *see also* forgetting; memory failure; memory improvement
retention function 233–4
retention interval 364
retrieval 8, 52, 97
    attention to cues 202–3
    cognitive context-dependent memory 214–15
    context cues 207–8
    context-dependent memory 211–13
    cue-target associative strength 204
    direct tests 208–9, 210
    expanding 112–13
    failure 195–8
    incidental 200
    incidental context 211–17
    indirect tests 209–11
    intentional 200
    interference 241
    mood-congruent memory 213–14
    mood-dependent memory 214
    neuroimaging 256–7
    number of cues 204–5
    overview 195
    process 198–201
    recognition memory 217–23
    reconstructive memory 215–17
    relevance of cues 203–4
    repeated attempts 283–5
    repetition priming 211
    and retention 237–8
    retrieval mode 206–7
    selective 249
    signal detection theory 218
    source monitoring 223

specificity 254
state-dependent memory 213
strategy 206
strength of target memory 205–6
success factors 201, 202–7
tasks 208–11
tip-of-the-tongue state 195–7
retrieval cues 198–9
retrieval-induced forgetting (RIF) 248–51, 252, 253–4, 255, 257, 283, 292
retrieval inhibition hypothesis 272
retrieval practice paradigm 248, 459
retrieval structure 477
retrieval suppression 274–9
retroactive interference 127, 242–5, 252, 282, 334, 336
retrograde amnesia 166, 438, 444–8
retrospective memory 361–3
Ribot's law 445, 447
Rivermead Behavioural Memory Test 416

S

schemas 8, 139, 182–8, 332
schizophrenia 92
SCOLP (Speed and Capacity of Language Processing) 421
scripts 182, 183–4
second language learning 73
secondary memory 88
selection 95
selective rehearsal hypothesis 269–70
selective retrieval 249
self-awareness 308, 396–7
self-esteem 314
self-performed task effect 418
self-representation 300
semantic coding 71, 121–2, 144, 146, 148–50
semantic cues 121
semantic dementia 166–8, 175–6, 181, 182–3, 450, 454
semantic memory 14–15, 17, 137
    categorization 174–6, 177
    concept representations 176
    concepts within the brain 179–80
    cultural factors 175
    effects of aging 420–1
    vs. episodic memory 166–8
    errors and distortions 185–6
    hierarchical network model 169–72
    hub-and-spoke model 180–2
    as independent system 166–7
    as interdependent system 167–8
    naming objects 174–6
    organization of concepts 168
    overview 165–6
    schemas 182–8

scripts 183–4
    situated simulation theory 176–9
    spreading activation model 173–4
    usefulness of schematic knowledge 184–5
    using concepts 176–9
semantic relatedness 173
sensitivity 350
sensitization 34
sensory cues 306
sensory memory 9, 10–12
sensory preconditioning 386–7
sensory recruitment model 96
separation, of features 56
sequences, memory for 43
serial order 47–8
serial reaction time task 123
serial reaction times 96
serial recall 12, 141
seriation 152–4
shape, memory for 56–7
Shereshevskii 479
short-term memory (STM) 9, 12, 41
    deficits 70–1
    and long-term memory 68–9
    neuropsychological approaches 58
    use of term 41
    verbal 43–52
    verbal short-term memory deficits 58–9
    visual objects and spatial location 95
    visuo-spatial 52–60
    visuo-spatial short-term memory deficits 59–60
    and working memory 68–9
signal detection theory 218–20
Simon, Herbert 150
Simonides, 472
SIMPLE (Scale Invariant Memory, Perception, and Learning) model 49
single-cell recording 92
situated simulation theory 176–9
situation-specific amnesia 280
situationally accessible memory 315
skepticism 350–1
skills, effects of aging 415
sleep, and learning 127–9, 444
sleep deprivation, and learning 128
slips of attention 78–9
smell, as cue 306
snowball effect 108
SOB (Serial-Order-in-a- Box) model 49
social cultural theory 397–8
social pressure, and eyewitness testimony 335–6
source amnesia 440
source misattribution 335
source monitoring 223, 402
spacing effect 112–13
spatial coding 150–1
spatial manipulation tests 76–7

spatial memory 58, 93 *see also* visuo-spatial
short-term memory
spatial tapping 80
spatial working memory 94
specificity, of retrieval 254
speed-up principle 477
spontaneous recovery 281–3
sport, learning 110
spreading activation 173–4, 199
spreading activation semantic network 172
SQ3R 483–4
state-dependent memory 213
stem completion 121
stereotypes 185
Stewart, Patrick 411
stimulus array 11
stimulus refreshing 97
stimulus–response associationism 141
storage 8
story mnemonic 476–7
strength 48
strength-dependent competition 251–2
strength independence 254
strength values 218
stress 123, 255, 316
structural imaging 26–7
study skills 483–6
subjective organization 148–9
subsequent memory effect 205
subtraction method 32
suggestibility 400–1
supervisory attentional system (SAS) 78
suppression 267–8
suppression-induced forgetting 276–7
synaptic consolidation 236–7
synesthesia 479
systems consolidation 236, 447

T

Tantalus 197
target memory 198
target trace 198
task combination 415–16
task switching 74–5, 88
taxi drivers 158–9
teach back 125
telephone post analogy 51, 52
temporal lobes 222
terminology, motivated forgetting 267–8
testing, and learning 113–14
testing effect 484–6
the knowledge 158
theories of aging and memory 424–6
theories of autobiographical memory 306–18
calendrical autobiographical memory 309–12
flashbulb memories 312
social and emotional influences 313–15

theories of infant memory 383–4
theories of prospective memory 371–3
theories of working memory 84–8
think/no-think (TNT) paradigm 275, 276, 278, 292
Thinking About Life Experiences (TALE)
questionnaire 300
Thomson, Donald 344
thought substitution 278
time
and forgetting 233–5, 236
and incidental forgetting 238–9
and memory recovery 281–3
time-based prospective memory 361
time-based resource-sharing model 88
time-based trace decay interpretation 46
time windows 385
tip of the eye 284
tip-of-the-tongue state 195–7, 251
Titivillus 16
total time hypothesis 108, 145
trace decay 238
train task 384–5
transcranial magnetic stimulation (TMS) 28,
29, 181
transfer-appropriate processing 145–6
trauma 287–92
traumatic brain injury (TBI) 23–4, 448
traumatic events, childhood memory 400
Tulving, Endel 7, 14, 137, 303
Turvey, Michael 10
twin studies 34
two-stage theory 398
typicality effect 170, 171

U

unconscious transference 344
unlearning 252
unlearning hypothesis 252, 282
use-it-or-lose-it hypothesis 424
using concepts 176–9
utilization behavior 79

V

vagueness 172–3
vascular dementia 450
Velten technique 213
verbal learning 7
verbal memory, priming 121–2
verbal overshadowing 344–5
verbal short-term memory 43–52
competing theories 48–9
deficits 58–9
free recall 49–52
verbally accessible memory 315
verbatim learning 488–9
verbatim memory 391–2

violence-related amnesia 319
visual imagery 76, 142
    memory improvement 472–6
visual memory, priming 122
visual processing, nonhuman primates 94
visual span 57
visual working memory 455
visuo-spatial memory 93–4
visuo-spatial short-term memory 51–60
    active rehearsal 55
    deficits 59–60
    information uptake 55
    vs. long-term memory 53–5
    storage 55–7
    visuo-spatial distinction 57–8
visuo-spatial sketchpad 70, 76–8
vocabulary acquisition 73
vocabulary correlations 73
von Restorff effect 187, 470
Vygotsky, Lev 75

W

Watson, James 35
weapon focus 339–40
Wearing, Clive 3–4
Wechsler Adult Intelligence Scale (WAIS) 41
well-being 266
Wessex Head Injury Matrix Scale
    (WHIM) 448
word completion 121
word length effect 45–6
words, memory span 81–2
working memory capacity 390
working memory span 41, 84
working memory (WM) 12–13, 41, 70, 83
    as activated long-term memory 96–8
    aging 414–16

Alzheimer's disease 454–5
attention deficit hyperactivity disorder
    (ADHD) 91–2
attentional capacity 87–8
brain activity 90
central executive 70, 78–81
in childhood 387–91
declarative 88
educational applications 89–90
embedded processes model 85–6
episodic buffer 81–4
imagery 82
individual differences 84
inhibitory control model 86–7
long-term 151–2
and long-term memory 82–3
multicomponent model 69–76, 151
neuroimaging 93–6
neuroscience 92–6
phonological loop and action control
    74–6
procedural 88
resource-sharing hypothesis 88
and short-term memory 68–9
single-cell recording 92
spatial working memory 94
task-switching hypothesis 88
theories 84–8
time-based resource-sharing model 88
training 89–91, 478–9
use of term 41–2
visuo-spatial sketchpad 70, 76–8
working self 307

Y

yes/no recognition test 217, 218

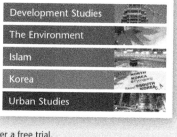